TESTIMONIALS

Well done! Your consultations with us these past several years have really opened our eyes to the "correct" way to price jobs, create budgets, and run our business efficiently. Your concepts, techniques and industry insights have been immeasurable. The audio CDs for *How to Price Landscape & Irrigation Projects* provide a clear cut overview to all you have taught us.

John Dellafiora
President
Pacific Lawn Sprinklers, Inc.

Jim Huston's book *How to Price Landscape & Irrigation Projects* is a **must have** for anyone who is serious about success in the landscape and irrigation business. Our business has benefited from utilizing many of Jim's principles of estimating since 1990. Each chapter of the book adds another layer of valuable information in an easy to understand format. The information is usable and allows you to take action *now.* It is a fantastic reference for developing an estimating system to be the hub of a wheel that you can drive to accomplish business success and create a prosperous future.

Dan Foley, CLP
President
D. Foley Landscape, Inc.
Walpole, Massachusetts

Whether you're new to the industry or are a seasoned veteran, Jim Huston's new book *How to Price Landscape & Irrigation Projects* will immediately be of benefit to you.

Jim has complied all of the necessary information for you to price landscape and irrigation work successfully and has done so in a manner that anyone can understand and apply. Using a combination of science and common sense, he presents methods and technology, which are proven and fool proof.

Jim gives step-by-step procedures for bidding from calculating direct costs to properly considering company overhead and adding profit. He gives insight on how to scope out your competition and figure your break-even point so you don't buy a job for the experience and end up losing money. These skills transcend the industry and can serve any construction enterprise or service industry.

With over 40 year's experience behind me, I've seen a lot of authors attempt to do what Jim has accomplished with this book. *If you are in business or are contemplating making that first step ... Jim's book is required reading.*

Rick Randall
President
Randall & Blake, Inc.
Littleton, Colorado

Jim Huston's new book expands on what was already the most comprehensive book available on landscape and irrigation estimating. Jim's in-depth knowledge of the landscape and irrigation business from the ground to the corporate board room makes his new book a **must have** reference for every landscape and irrigation contractor.

Bob Dobson
President
Middletown Sprinkler
Port Monmouth, New Jersey

Jim Huston's latest volume is a **must purchase** for landscape and irrigation contractors. Companies, no matter how large or small, can now find pertinent, easy-to-use information in one source. The business and pricing practices that Mr. Huston explains are the keys to working on your business instead of in your business. If you buy one business resource book this year, make this the one.

Jay Tripathi, CLP
President
Gardenworks, Inc.
Geyserville, California

Jim Huston has made a major difference in the success of Erickson Landscaping over many years. He has helped us implement values, principles, and systems that have contributed to that success. I look forward to spending time with Jim each year as he visits our company and reviews financials, budgets, and strategies for the upcoming year. I not only respect Jim for what he has done for our company but consider him to be a very good friend.

Ron Tatton
President
Erickson's Landscaping, Inc.
Salt Lake City, Utah

I thought your audio CDs for *How to Price Landscape & Irrigation Projects* were outstanding! The Q & A format was easy to follow and understand. You did a great job of highlighting the key points of your new book.

Dave Rykbost
President
Dave's Landscape, Inc.
Hudson, Massachusetts

How to Price Landscape & Irrigation Projects

James R. Huston, MBA, CPE

GreenBack Enterprises, LLC
P.O. Box 1244
Englewood, CO 80150-1244

DISCLAIMER

The recommendations and suggestions contained in this book have been successfully implemented by many construction and maintenance service contractors. However, they remain recommendations and suggestions. The author and J.R. Huston Enterprises, Inc. shall have neither liability nor responsibility to any person or entity with respect to any loss or damage caused, or alleged to be caused, directly or indirectly by the information contained in this book.

Avis is a trademark of the Avis Rent-a-Car System, Inc. Costco is a copyright of Costco Wholesale Corporation. *Dodge Reports* is a trademark of McGraw-Hill Companies. Equipment Watch is a trademark of the PRIMEDIA Business Magazines & Media, Inc. Microsoft Excel is a trademark of the Microsoft Corporation. The Gallup Organization is a trademark of the Gallup Organization Corporation. Hertz is a trademark of the Hertz Corporation. Home Depot is a registered trademark of Homer TLC, Inc. HomeBase is a trademark of Homebase Ltd. Lotus 1-2-3 is a trademark of the (IBM) Lotus Development Corporation. McDonald's Restaurants is a trademark of the McDonald's Corporation. *Money* magazine is a copyright of Time, Incorporated. Price Club is a trademark of the Price Corporation. Rain Bird is a trademark of the Rain Bird Corporation, Inc. Rediform is trademark of Rediform Inc. *Sesame Street* is a trademark of the Sesame Workshop. Toro is a trademark of the Toro Company. Hunter is a trademark of Hunter Industries.

Published in Denver, Colorado by GreenBack Enterprises, LLC

Printed in United States of America

Library of Congress Control Number: 2003100034

ISBN 0-9628521-4-7 $150.00 Hard cover

Library of Congress Cataloging in Publication Data

Huston, James Ray.
How to Price Landscape & Irrigation Projects / James Ray Huston
p. cm.
Includes index.
ISBN 0-9628521-4-7
1. Landscaping industry—Estimates. 2. Irrigation—Estimates.
I. Title. II. Title: How to Price Landscape & Irrigation Projects
SB472.565.H873 2003 635.9'068'1
QBI03-200041

Second Printing

GreenBack Enterprises, LLC
P.O. Box 1244
Englewood, CO 80150-1244
Phone: 800-451-5588
FAX: 800-451-5494
E-mail: jrhei@jrhuston.biz
Web site: www.jrhuston.biz

DEDICATION

These pages are either directly or indirectly about time. One way to view time is that we can waste it, trade it, or invest it. This is perhaps true. Another perspective is that time is simply a medium through which we sail. We cannot stop, accelerate, or even idle as we glide through it. However, we can attempt to make wise choices that contribute to the well-being of our families and friends and the success of our businesses. A legion of wise choices is the "stuff" that makes for great companies. Prudent entrepreneurs strive to surround themselves with adept counselors and lieutenants and market savvy ideas in order to make the best of the choices available to them. It is the accumulation of these choices that creates one's legacy.

One year has passed since I started this project. Much has happened during this period; some good, some not so good. Completing this book comprised a large portion of the "good" part. However, my grandson, Gabriel Pessoa Huston, entered this world and departed it as this text was being prepared. My son and illustrator for this project, Uriah, had a series of strokes that left him speechless and unable to write or draw. But, however difficult, we must all choose to move forward.

It is a great blessing then that there is yet another aspect regarding time that fuses it, our circumstances, and our choices to that which lies beyond the cosmos—that which is beyond items finite, quantifiable, and measurable. In some mysterious way, time can be redeemed. It can be changed for the better, reformed. No matter what our circumstance, our lot in life, our situation; we can improve.

Although I never met him in this world, I trust that I will in the next, Gabriel taught me about legacy—the need to create something beautiful and good to leave for future generations. Recovery for Uriah has been very slow and arduous. It is he who has been my inspiration for thirty-one years. No one on this earth has inspired me, motivated me, and driven me on as has Uri. It is to Gabriel and Uri that this work is fondly dedicated. May it in some way help us all to redeem our time.

JOEL 2:25

James R. Huston
May, 2003

CONTENTS

Do you remember "The Count" on Sesame Street? He loves to count. Numbers drive him wild.

Some people actually do love numbers. They love numbers so much so that they often think they can reduce the entire universe to laws of physics, figures, symbols, and numerals. Others are intimidated by anything involving math. Personally, I look at numbers as being something like cars: I want them to get me where I want to go without a whole lot of hassle.

Numbers are necessary for all of us; they can even be a friend. I'm amazed at how numbers can provide significant benefit and insight into a construction and maintenance company—if they're properly used.

Most contractors don't realize how important and beneficial the proper formatting and use of numbers can be to their company. I like what one large and very successful contractor advocates: he runs his entire company right from the bid sheet.

When I first published *Estimating for Landscape & Irrigation Contractors* in early 1994, I didn't realize how popular it would become. The principles outlined in it are still valid today. However, we've had many years of experience to supplement its basic methods, which have allowed us to fine tune and expound on its application. *How to Price Landscape & Irrigation Projects* builds on the foundation laid by *Estimating for Landscape & Irrigation Contractors.*

Audience

Students just starting their careers, professors and instructors teaching Green Industry management courses, those making a career change, start-up companies, and seasoned contractors should all find this text beneficial. The examples used are all real-life scenarios taken from actual Green Industry companies. While experience may be the best teacher, it's often better that it be someone else's experience from which we learn.

Pedagogical Features

To facilitate use by instructors, students, and contractors, several learning aids are available throughout the text.

Purpose Statements. Each section and chapter begins with a purpose statement that introduces the main points. The reader will gain an understanding of the content in this overview.

Introductory Paragraphs. A short introduction to each chapter covers preliminary ground while guiding the reader into the chapter material.

Summaries. Every chapter concludes with a brief summary. This assists the reader in reviewing the most important information covered in the chapter.

Key Terms. Chapters begin with a list of key terms to be introduced in the chapter. These key terms are bolded within the chapter, and their definitions can be found in the glossary on page 577.

Main Points. Pertinent information is called out in the margins. These points serve to reiterate vital content within the chapter.

How It Works. These elements feature real-life situations from the author's experiences that illustrate the concepts taught. This aid presents problems and provides solutions while offering understanding of what contractors deal with in their businesses. Occasionally this feature asks the reader to come up with the solution to a problem. Answers to these questions are provided on page 595.

Action Point. Every chapter ends with at least one action point. Instruction is provided on how to incorporate the knowledge learned into the business. These also can serve as practice problems for potential contractors.

Glossary. This feature provides definitions for key terms found in each chapter. This convenient aid helps the reader find any key term quickly and easily. The glossary is found on page 577 of the text.

New to This Edition

How to Price Landscape & Irrigation Projects contains more contractor stories and the related analyses of many of the diverse projects they've performed. Equipment utilization and costing have been updated to accommodate the numerous new pieces of equipment being used in the Green Industry today. Computer spreadsheet models have been updated and included throughout the text.

A Microsoft Excel spreadsheet CD-ROM containing all the figures, worksheets, and examples in the book is also available. It allows users to reproduce the material in the book and apply it directly to their companies. Users can prepare their budgets and bids using the worksheets on the CD-ROM. Professors and instructors can easily adapt the worksheets for classroom exercises.

An audio book CD series is also now available. It is comprised of six one-hour CDs. The question and answer format covers all of the material in the book in an informative and entertaining manner. It allows the listener to review the material in *How to Price Landscape & Irrigation Projects* while driving from job to job, exercising, or following along in the book. Professors and instructors can quickly review the material in the book. The CDs should also help them entertain creative ways to present the material in a classroom setting. Students should find the audio CDs invaluable for reviewing the material in *How to Price Landscape & Irrigation Projects*. Listening to the CDs allows contractors to put "windshield" time to better use. They should easily be able to listen to all six CDs (the entire book) in less than a week as they drive from job site to job site.

We've greatly amplified the Overhead and Profit Per Hour (OPPH) method of estimating and added many new tools to help you implement it. While the basics of the OPPH estimating method haven't changed, its implementation and application have.

These new tools are all designed and utilized to supplement our seminars, workshops, and consulting services. The combination of our products and services is designed to help you, the Green Industry professional, have a more successful career and/or operate your business more profitably.

Estimating (the science of determining the costs in a job) and bidding (the art of adding margins and markups to costs in order to determine a price for a job) are vital parts of any business. In fact, the way you price work is the foundation of your entire business—assuming, of course, that you're in a nation or culture that supports the free enterprise system.

If you can't price a job correctly, you don't want it. If you can't consistently put the right price on a job, you and your company either are in trouble or soon will be.

I've seen many landscape, irrigation, and tree service contractors around the country with fatal flaws in their estimating systems. For some, this has cost them their company. Others have identified the problem(s), made the necessary corrections, and moved ahead.

As I said earlier, estimating is the foundation of your entire company. Just about any problem you're experiencing, in one way or another, can be traced to the estimating process. Job costing/accounting, field production and scheduling, marketing, and strategic planning are all reflected in estimating.

We'll cover the six most common methods used in the market today to estimate costs and price work, outlining the pros and cons of each. You'll see the advantage of understanding these methods when pricing work at the bid table or when negotiating pricing with a prospective customer.

In this new edition, we've expanded our discussions to cover larger areas that affect your pricing. Market predisposition, Six Sigma quality control, marketing, company structure and growth patterns, evaluating your business, exit strategies, and the business life cycle are covered. All of these items either directly or indirectly affect how you price your work. In order to understand the "context" or market within which your company operates, it's necessary that you be aware of these larger issues.

A good estimating system doesn't operate in a vacuum. It should undergird and permeate your whole operation. That's why I say that an estimating system should provide you with a *plan* and a *process*, as well as with an accurate *price*.

These three items provide the skeleton of the "systems" in your company upon which all else hangs. And systems are the essential practical ingredient—the manifestation of the philosophies, methodologies, systems, and strategies which encompass the entire company. I refer to this as PMSS (Philosophies, Methodologies, Systems, and Strategies). You take care of the systems, and the systems will take care of you. You take care of the business, and the business will take care of you.

While you may not have firsthand experience in all of the areas discussed here, nor actual historic numbers to use in the examples provided, you can still achieve results as valid as those of any "seasoned" contractor by using estimated company start-up data.

Acknowledgments

The author has greatly benefited from discussion with and helpful comments from clients and associates throughout North America. Special recognition goes to Rick Randall, founder of the RBI Companies of Littleton, Colorado; Grant W. Reid, ASLA, Professor Landscape Design and Contracting program, Colorado State University, Fort Collins, Colorado; and Dan T. Stearns, Professor, Department of Horticulture, College of Agricultural Sciences, The Pennsylvania State University, University Park, Pennsylvania. The thorough reviews and comments provided by these individuals were invaluable in shaping the final text.

Purpose

The purposes of this book are to

1. Teach you the estimating process, step-by-step, so you can develop an accurate budget (a plan written in numbers) for your company and your jobs.

And to

2. Show you how to run your company with confidence right from the bid sheet, using the philosophy, methodologies, systems, and strategies explained in this book.

You don't have to love numbers (like "The Count") in order to succeed. You *must*, however, develop an appreciation for what they can do for you and for your business.

Let's get started.

James R. Huston
President
GreenBack Enterprises, LLC

The following individuals have contributed substantially to this work. Without their feedback and assistance its completion would have been impossible.

Sharon Green and Barb Swanson: Graphics West; production, design, project management, and cover design

Uriah Huston: illustrations

Bob Kelly: Wordcrafters, Inc.; editing

Cindy Mayhew: consultation

Gail Strickland: word processing, copyediting, and indexing

Cathy Waller: conceptual design, consultation, layout, and final editing

Contributing Contractors/Estimators/Educators/Vendors

Craig Bauer, landscape maintenance contractor, Bauer Lawn Maintenance, Inc., Maumee OH

Paul Davidson, landscape construction contractor, Concept Development & Fabrication, Dallas TX

John, Peter and Stephen Dellafiora, irrigation contractors, Pacific Lawn Sprinklers, Inc., College Point NY

Robert Dobson, irrigation contractor, Middletown Sprinkler Company, Inc., Port Monmouth NJ

Marc Dutton, irrigation contractor, Marc Dutton Irrigation, Inc., Waterford MI

Jack Fetig, landscape construction and maintenance contractor, Alpine Gardens, Fort Collins CO

Dan Fix, landscape construction and maintenance contractor, Dan Fix Landscape Construction, Inc., San Rafael CA

S. Michael Flowers, landscape construction and sports fields, Championship Turf Services, Harwinton CT

Roger Knoop, arborist, Almstead Tree and Shrub Care Company, New Rochelle NY

Chris Maroun, landscape construction and maintenance contractor, Miracle Farms Landscaping, Moultonborough NH

Gregory Maroun, landscape construction and maintenance contractor, Stecks Nursery and Landscaping, Bethel CT

Mark Pendergast, nurseryman and construction contractor, Salmon Falls Nursery, Inc., Berwick ME

Chad Person, marketing director, Almstead Tree Co., Inc., New Rochelle NY

Dan Potkay, landscape construction and maintenance contractor, Potkay Landscaping, Absecon NJ

Rick Randall, founder of the RBI Companies, Littleton CO

Grant W. Reid ASLA, Professor, Landscape Design and Contracting program, Colorado State University, Fort Collins CO

Dave Rykbost, landscape construction and maintenance contractor, Dave's Landscape Company, Inc., Hudson MA

Don Sharp, sales manager, Finn Corporation, Fairfield OH

Dan T. Stearns, Professor, Department of Horticulture, College of Agricultural Sciences, The Pennsylvania State University, University Park PA

Jay Tripathi and Peter Estournes, landscape construction and maintenance contractors, Gardenworks, Inc., Healdsburg CA

John Witonis, wholesale and retail distributor, Sherwin Williams, Inc., N. Windham ME

Planning is essential for any business person. It's especially valuable and necessary for the landscape and irrigation contractor. In order to plan properly, it's essential that a contractor or manager understand the context or market within which their business operates.

I like what Philip Crosby says in his book, *Quality Is Free*:

> *Good things happen only when planned.*
> *Bad things happen on their own.*

Business is a controlled science. It's the process of establishing goals, directing many diverse events toward those goals, collecting data to measure what's happening, analyzing the data, and then adjusting the whole process as necessary to achieve the goals. To accomplish this, business people employ the same methodology used by scientists to conduct research and development (experiments).

Webster's Encyclopedic Unabridged Dictionary defines the scientific method as: "A method of research in which a problem is identified, relevant data are gathered, a hypothesis is formulated from these data, and the hypothesis is empirically tested."

When applying this definition to the Green Industry business process, the project to be bid is the "problem." The "relevant data gathered" are the plans and specifications for the project (or job). The estimate or budget for the job (containing objective measurable standards for materials, labor, labor burden, equipment, etc.) is the "hypothesis." The "empirical testing of the hypothesis" is then accomplished by job costing. This is the "test"; the comparison of your budget to actual performance in the field as you perform the project.

Great strides and advancements have been made in the area of medicine over the last 100 years because of the use of the analytical methodology of science in that field. Green Industry contractors can achieve similar results if a similar methodology is used. Unfortunately, the methods of most contractors resemble "witch doctor" medicine and "voodoo" economics more than they do modern scientific medicine and business.

It's this very process that allows you to control your business and to grow in the same way scientists *control* their environments and make progress. The business process provides services and products and produces wealth, while the scientific process creates products that lead to progress in the areas of medicine, business, agriculture, and so forth. The ends may be different, but both can and usually do supplement one another because they employ the same methodology to achieve the results desired.

Business and science control this process by using *objective, analytical data*. It's this data and this methodology that provide the foundation upon which to build your business.

Budgets and Goals

Business needs two primary types of plans to be run effectively. The first is the **Strategic Business Plan**. Basically, this is a plan put into words; it is the subject of my first book, *Strategic Planning for Landscape & Irrigation Contractors*.

The second item you need is a *Budget*, which is a plan that's reduced to (rendered into) numbers. These numbers help you organize, control, and direct the company. They also provide the vital feedback necessary for analyzing the results and effectiveness of your organizational ability.

These two documents, the budget and the strategic business plan, are what you need to *drive*, *direct*, *change*, and *control* your company.

The budgeting process produces key standards (or targets) that will help you to run jobs, as well as the overall business. Figure 2-1 (see Chapter 2) provides a model for estimating. Figure I-1 provides such a model for your entire company.

As you can see, estimating is one portion of the four main functional areas in your business. I would say, however, that it's the most important, because everything else, including **total quality management (TQM)**, is built on it.

The budgeting process produces cost standards and targets for:

- Sales (by division)
- Direct costs (by division)
- Gross profit margin (by division)
- General and administrative (G&A) overhead (not necessarily by division)
- Net profit margin (not necessarily by division)
- Labor burden for office and field personnel (by division)
- Field-labor hours (by division)
- Equipment (by division)
- Average wage calculations (by division)

These cost standards are combined with other job-related information to determine the cost of the project. Once we identify direct costs on an individual job, we add margins and markups (net profit, G&A overhead, labor burden, sales tax, etc.). The **break-even point (BEP)** for the project is identified once G&A overhead has been added to the direct costs identified in Phases I and II of the bid. A contingency factor (if desired) and net profit are added to the BEP in order to arrive at the *Final Price* for the project.

It's these two numbers, the *BEP* and the *Final Price*, that you're constantly attempting to identify during the bidding process. They answer two critical questions and identify a bidding "envelope" or range within which you need to price your jobs. The BEP answers the question, "*How Low* can you go to get the job and still cover all costs?"

The BEP is a compilation of costs for a job and is therefore analytical in nature. However, the *Final Price* is subjective and addresses the question, "*How High* can you go and still get the job?" What pricing structure will the market bear? Can you add 40% gross profit margin (GPM) to the project and still get the job? Or will this market and this particular job realistically only allow you to add 15 to 18% GPM above direct costs in order to have a real chance of winning the bid?

We constantly want to identify and monitor the BEP and GPM on jobs being bid. We do so in order to measure, allocate, recover, and control (MARC) the G&A overhead dollars in our G&A overhead budget. Because G&A overhead costs are indirect costs, there is no right amount of G&A overhead costs to allocate to a job being bid. Nor is there a right way to allocate G&A overhead costs into a bid.

There simply is *no right way* to determine the amount of G&A overhead costs to put in a particular job being bid.

Consequently, the question to ask regarding G&A overhead and the six methods of pricing jobs we'll cover is not, "Which method is right?" There simply is *no right way* to determine the amount of G&A overhead costs to put in a particular job being bid. However, that doesn't mean there aren't wrong or inaccurate methods for allocating G&A costs into bids. We'll show mathematically in Chapters 37 and 38 that there are wrong ways to calculate the amount of G&A costs to put on a job.

The question to ask is not "How much G&A overhead should you add to a job and by which method?" Rather, it's "If you sell a particular job for a certain price and perform it on budget, will it help you achieve your budgeted gross and net profit dollar goals for the year?"

I. Management/Administration
(Directing the company)

1. Strategic planning
2. Marketing strategy
3. Estimating strategy
4. Training/safety
5. Networking/support groups
6. Finance
7. Quality control
8. Production control
9. Computer systems
10. Information management
11. Equipment planning
12. Budgeting/goal setting
13. Tax planning
14. Board of directors/advisors
15. ______________________
16. ______________________

II. Marketing: Sales/Estimating/ Contract Administration
(Getting the work)

1. Marketing strategy
2. Bidding strategy
3. Estimating budget
4. Field-labor hour budget
5. Bidding goals
6. Sales goals
7. Contract administration
8. Customer service
9. ______________________
10. ______________________
11. ______________________
12. ______________________
13. ______________________
14. ______________________

III. Field Production
(Producing the work)

1. Quality control
2. Pre-construction meetings
3. Job startup/coordination
4. Post-construction meetings
5. Daily field reports
6. Crew/job scheduling
7. Equipment scheduling
8. Training/safety
9. Computer systems
10. Customer service
11. Purchasing materials
12. Inventory control
13. ______________________
14. ______________________
15. ______________________
16. ______________________

IV. Finance/Accounting
(Keeping score)

1. Job costing
2. Purchase order control
3. Information management/systems
4. Accounts payable
5. Accounts receivable
6. Cash flow budget
7. Accounting system/software
8. Financial statements
9. Charts/graphs/reports
10. Bonus systems
11. ______________________
12. ______________________
13. ______________________
14. ______________________
15. ______________________

Figure I-1 Company Overview

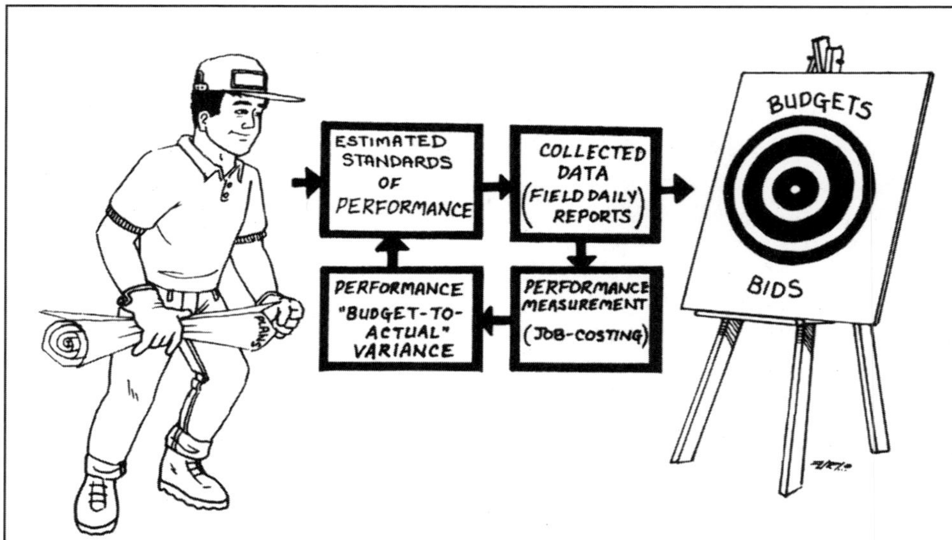

Budgets as targets

The question to ask is not "How much G&A overhead should you add to a job and by which method?" Rather, it's "If you sell a particular job for a certain price and perform it on budget, will it help you achieve your budgeted gross and net profit dollar goals for the year?"

The goal now is to measure, allocate, recover, and control (MARC) G&A overhead costs throughout the budget year, not to argue over which method is correct. There is none!

The process, however, doesn't stop at estimating. You need to constantly monitor the standards or targets identified above—for the company or division, as well as for individual jobs.

In order to run your jobs effectively, you job cost them. In order to run your company or division effectively, you monitor the **profit and loss (P&L) financial statement**, as well as the balance sheet. These are your report cards for the division or the company as a whole.

1. Individual jobs are monitored by job costing.
2. The entire company is monitored by the P&L statement as though it were one big job. What difference does it make that individual jobs are profitable if you don't have enough of them to support the G&A overhead structure and the costs for the company as a whole?

Major company items to monitor are as follows:

- Sales by division
- General and administrative overhead costs
- Field-labor hours and payroll costs
- Equipment costs
- Gross and net profit margins

These are two key items you need to be *checking constantly* in order to run your company effectively. These are in addition to job costing for individual jobs.

In a later section, we'll cover (in detail) the methods and reports used to monitor these two key areas of your business.

The budgeting and controlling process of a Green Industry contracting company involves a never-ending series of events that occur simultaneously. You're constantly setting goals (budgeting targets), taking action, monitoring progress, adjusting, and fine-tuning. The goal of this process is to have your company operate as smoothly as a Swiss watch amidst the constant tumult.

Proper budgeting and estimating won't solve *all* your problems, but it will address and provide the tools for solving the majority of them—certainly, the most important ones.

Fixing a tire on a moving car...

Three Kinds of Budgets

In a business, you need three types of budgets in order to plan and control the business effectively:

1. The *Estimating (or fair market value) Budget* is designed to help you bid your work and recover *all* costs accurately.
2. The *Accounting (or tax) Budget* is required in order to help you meet governmental tax requirements and regulations.
3. The Cash Flow Budget is designed to help you:
   - Predict your cash flow
   - Identify those periods where cash flow may be reduced so that you can take the necessary steps to compensate (e.g., by means of a loan or an increased line of credit).

In this book, we'll cover estimating budgets. You should consult with your accountant or certified public accountant (CPA) to develop the other two.

Budget Periods

We develop an estimating budget in twelve-month increments, not necessarily a fiscal or calendar year. It can be either, but we can also develop a budget for the immediate next twelve months, starting at any time during the year. It's easier to prepare an estimating budget parallel to a company's fiscal year (which may be the calendar year), but it's not necessary to do so.

It generally takes two to three seasons to implement all the tools outlined in this book and to get your operation under control. This may seem like a long time, but remember, what you're doing is like *trying to fix a flat tire on a moving car.* There will be lots of other things to do while you're implementing the philosophy, methodologies, systems, and strategies outlined in this book. Think long-term: the process takes time and persistence.

This may seem like a long time, but remember, what you're doing is like *trying to fix a flat tire on a moving car.*

Don't misunderstand. You can expect significant progress immediately. You'll see a real, initial impact on your business as a result of implementing these methodologies, systems, and strategies. However, there is *no magic wand* to wave nor any pixie dust to throw at your company. Plan on spending the next couple of years focusing and fine-tuning the entire process throughout your business.

We start by reviewing historical data: financial statements, balance sheets, insurance rates, etc. We build from there, based on assumptions tailored to your company.

How high? How low?

Historical Data: The Foundation

Hopefully, you have good historical data—data that are accurate, properly formatted, and consistent (categories that are consistently defined from one year to the next). Without good historical data, you cannot identify trends. If the data are inconsistent, inadequate, or not formatted correctly, you have what I call *Hysterical* (not historical) data; it makes no sense.

Start-Up Companies

We can easily budget for start-up situations. Even though we don't have historical data, we can put together a fairly accurate estimating budget by making estimates about our costs.

Incremental Goal Time Periods

Year One: The first year of this two- to three-year process is one of setting goals, making major changes in the estimating process, and collecting and monitoring data in specific formats.

Year Two: The second year is, generally, a period of reevaluation. We ask:

- Did we meet last year's goals?
- Did we budget and plan accurately and effectively?
- Did we make the appropriate adjustments when we repeated the budgeting process?

Year Three: The third year is more of the same: further evaluation and fine-tuning of the organization and the processes used to control and direct it.

Business Context

Pricing work doesn't happen in a vacuum. Neither does your business operate as an island. Economies are global, national, and regional. It's important to understand the environment and the market within which your business operates. I refer to this as business context. It is comprised of all of the external forces and market conditions that shape the environment surrounding your business.

We constantly use such terms as fair market value, industry benchmarks, and market predisposition in the bidding process. These terms all refer to context. When you compare your prices with those found throughout the industry, you're benchmarking your bidding process. In like manner, fair market value and market predisposition point beyond your company to the surrounding environment. Mathematics, or the science of numbers, by its very nature infers context and interrelationship with other numbers. Estimating and bidding are disciplines within this science.

We start with very analytical and methodical processes in cost estimating. The goal of cost estimating is to calculate costs accurately. We then evolve to the larger, more nebulous arena of the marketplace. To understand the market we utilize tools (gross profit margins, fair market value, market predisposition, industry benchmarks, etc.) that are more intuitive and less exact than the ones used for cost estimating. However, they're as valid as their more precise counterparts.

In order to understand the totality of a business and its setting we employ diverse tools, which may appear paradoxical at first glance. We balance the cold, hard analytical costs calculated in estimating with the trends and market patterns, which become evident as a result of educated market intuition.

Our goal is to be market driven and yet cost conscious. Think cost. Think market. Then consistently price and negotiate between the two.

We look at the jobs we're bidding from the bottom up (building cost upon cost) and the top down (predicting what the market will bear). It's the big picture of the marketplace being complemented with the little picture of cold, hard costs. Our goal is to be market driven and yet cost conscious. Think cost. Think market. Then consistently price and negotiate between the two. You'll be using both right and left brain functions; the logic of the left side of the cerebral cortex is complemented by the creativeness of the right.

Good analysis leads to trustworthy market intuition. Much like learning to drive a tractor (clutch in, engage gear, press on accelerator, let clutch out, etc.), the process is somewhat jerky and awkward at first. However, with practice it becomes second nature. So it is with market intuition.

Beware of the "paralysis of analysis." This is an action book. It's meant to lead you to action, not to endless and mindless analysis.

Mastering your business requires that you study and master both cost estimating and the market. If done properly, you should obtain plenty of repeat business and referrals. You should also develop a viable exit strategy as you do so. Beware of the "paralysis of analysis." This is an action book. It's meant to lead you to action, not to endless and mindless analysis.

As we teach you how to "fish" (not just give you a tuna), we'll stretch you with some new financial and operational terms you should find helpful. These aren't esoteric MBA (master of business administration) or banker terms. They're financial and operational terms you will find useful in understanding and running your business.

Quality Control: Six Sigma and Total Quality Management (TQM)

Once you develop your estimating budgets and begin to estimate properly (which you can begin to do after one or two days of training), you can then decide how to format and monitor key types of data throughout your business by using the objective, analytical scientific methodology described earlier.

Comparing objective, quantifiable (or measurable) plans (budgets, goals, targets, and standards) to actual performance is a measuring process that's at the heart of the Total Quality Control process for your company.

If you can't budget, estimate costs accurately, and produce an accurate price for a job, you can never achieve quality control, let alone total quality management of your company. Your estimating systems are the foundation on which you develop TQM throughout your entire organization.

TQM has evolved over the last ten years into what's now being referred to as Six Sigma. Six Sigma methods are being used to improve management processes and bottom lines in some of the most notable companies in the world. We'll discuss Six Sigma and some of its applications for the Green Industry in Chapter 47.

Summary

Even though your estimating system is only one segment of your business, it's the brain and nerve center (the command post) of the entire operation. It should not only provide you with a *Price*, but also with a communicable *Plan* and a quality control *Process* to facilitate total quality control throughout your company. This process is based on the objective, analytical, and quantifiable methods of science. It allows you and your staff to control the company and direct it to predetermined goals and profitability.

However, the process doesn't stop there. You have to consider the context or business environment within which your business operates. To do so, we use tools (fair market value, gross profit margins, industry benchmarks, market predisposition, etc.) that are more intuitive than the cold, analytical tools used in cost estimating. Just as you need both wings to fly an airplane, you need both the hard, cold cost data of estimating combined with an understanding of market patterns and trends.

Contracting Management

Facing the New Millennium

SECTION I

Contents

Purpose

The purpose of this section is to discuss general trends within the Green Industry and provide an overview of an estimating system

At the industry-wide or "macro" level, the Green Industry has been very dynamic the last ten years. Consolidations and a developing "turnkey" approach to business are quickly bringing our industry international recognition. These developments are also opening up new opportunities for capitalization as financial markets are beginning to take notice of an industry which, from their perspective, has finally come of age.

On a more micro level, too few contractors approach their estimating system from a holistic perspective. Some components of their estimating system may be fine; for example, they calculate costs accurately. Other components of their bidding may contain serious mathematical errors or faulty assumptions in arithmetic. Our estimating system overview is designed to help Green Industry contractors evaluate or "benchmark" their estimating system and to compare it to their current methods of bidding.

CHAPTER 1

Back to the Next Ten Years

Purpose

To explain some of the important trends in the Green Industry

Introduction

While the basic free enterprise philosophy may be the same, business methodologies, systems, and strategies continue to change at an amazingly accelerating rate. New and improved technological advances in the form of personal computers (PCs), personal data assistants (PDAs), voice recognition software, global positioning systems (GPS), holistic enterprise software for small business, and the Internet are being developed or improved on a daily basis. New technologies and field equipment are being developed so quickly that product and service obsolescence often occurs within months of their introduction to the marketplace.

Further compounding this problem for the landscape and irrigation industry is the fact that, as an industry, construction and maintenance service contracting trails the general business community in addressing and implementing these technological advances.

TRENDS

Two very important trends helped to shape the landscape and irrigation industry during the 1990s. They culminated in the roll-up and consolidation frenzy that began in the late 1990s and continues to this day. Round One of this consolidation pattern, which started in 1997, was characterized by a "gold rush" mentality that was poorly planned and just as poorly executed. However, we should expect that Round Two, which is currently underway, will build on the momentum developed in Round One and benefit from the mistakes made.

The Round One consolidators seemed drunk on the excitement of the "thrill of the deal." Little thought or planning was given to the long-term success of the newly created enterprise. Internal management controls and staffing were poorly thought out. Most of the initial consolidations didn't have any "legs." They made it out of the gate but didn't get far beyond it. The initial investors seemed focused on their individual exit strategies and financial portfolios, and on little else.

Round Two players, on the other hand, appear to be in the industry to stay. Having survived the feeding frenzy of the late 1990s, they appear to be thinking about long-term survival and profitability, focusing on the systems and related staffing necessary to make a business successful over the long haul. While still licking their wounds from the initial consolidations, they're regrouping and building on past mistakes. We should expect to see some very well run businesses by the end of the first decade of the new millenium.

Survival of the "Fattest"

It's easier to stay "king of the hill" than it is to get on top of that hill in the first place.

As noted in my first book, *Strategic Planning for Landscape & Irrigation Contractors*:

> *Landscape Management*, in an article entitled "Survival of the Fattest," hit on something very big when it noted an important, yet often overlooked, trend in construction today. It said, "Among those companies reporting gross sales above $3 million, the average increase in sales was $830,000. Smaller companies, on average, lost $55,000 in gross sales." Look at it this way: when you are playing "king of the hill," it is always easier to stay on top of the hill than it is to get there. Getting there the first time is the real battle.
>
> Construction contracting appears to be going through today what the farm industry went through years ago. At one time, there were hundreds of thousands of small farmers, each doing a relatively small amount of business. Today, there are far fewer farmers, but individually they are producing a far greater amount of gross sales.
>
> The *Landscape Management* article talked about the "staying power" of the big boys. I choose to call it "buying power," and the main commodity being purchased is strategic "people power." If you grow and are profitable in the process, you can afford to replace yourself in many key positions within the daily operation of your business. This allows you to research and develop key areas of the business (marketing, estimating, computers, standardizing field operations, finances, etc.) and to develop more effective systems and strategies for running it. As the saying goes, "It is impossible to drain the swamp when you are up to your (waist) in alligators." The big boys, if they are profitable and smart, buy themselves the opportunity to drain not only today's "swamp," but tomorrow's "swamp" as well.[2]

It's easier to stay king of the hill than it is to get on top of that hill in the first place.

The Turnkey (Franchise) Approach to Green Industry Contracting

While not entirely valid, this approach does have its applications. McDonald's Restaurants®, for example, developed and popularized the turnkey (franchise) approach to business. Essentially, it's the philosophy of placing proven methods, systems, and strategies in place before you unlock the front door and open for business. Success follows almost immediately, *if* you've done your homework and planned properly.

Although the turnkey approach has more validity in the landscape maintenance, tree service, and irrigation service businesses, the concept does have applications in the construction business as well.

How It Works

I've seen many young, aggressive contractors implement the right philosophies, methodologies, systems, and strategies and take off. Many have successfully weathered the inevitable storms of adversity and recession because they understand their businesses—and their methodologies, systems, and strategies—well enough to keep them on track.

On the other hand, I've seen some of the oldest and biggest landscaping contractors self-destruct because they ignored essential elements of their organization. They did not have a "holistic" approach to their business.

Keep in mind that if you only have three of the four tires necessary on a race car, you don't really have a race car. You just have an expensive piece of metal alloy, rubber, plastic, and steel. Similarly, if your landscape, irrigation, or tree service company

> Like the baby boomers rippling through our economy in one gigantic wave, these new $2 to $3 million companies are creating a new dynamic within the Green Industry and throughout the general economy.

lacks an essential component of the systems necessary to run it effectively, all you have is a disaster looking for a place to happen.

In the mid-1980s, Green Industry companies with gross annual sales over $1 million were fairly uncommon. However, many of these companies with sales under $1 million were developing the infrastructure for future growth. The recession of the late 1980s and early 1990s put many of these contractors through a refining fire of sorts. They emerged from this recession with proven systems that helped them survive a pretty tough downturn with a fresh appreciation of a good market.

The explosive growth that took place in the middle to late 1990s provided the fuel that allowed many of these companies to double or triple in size. Today there are hundreds of companies throughout the country with sales in the $2 to $3 million range that struggled for years to reach their first million dollars. Many of them simply didn't exist ten years ago. Like the baby boomers rippling through our economy in one gigantic wave, these new $2 to $3 million companies are creating a new dynamic within the Green Industry and throughout the general economy.

The landscape, irrigation, and tree service companies that will still be thriving in the year 2010 will be doing so because of proper planning. These firms will have met the tumult and pressures of the marketplace and will have learned to capitalize on and advance through adversity. They'll have done so because they implemented proven methodologies, systems, and strategies. Essentially, they will have heeded Tom Peters' challenge of "thriving on chaos" outlined in his book of the same name.

SUMMARY

There's a train that has left the station and is heading for the Green Industry future. During the last ten years it has picked up steam and gained momentum. This train is propelled by a revolution in Green Industry contracting management. Fortunately, there's plenty of room to board this train as it makes its stops along the way.

Exciting new software developments, technological advances, improved field equipment, management strategies, and financial markets are providing the tools for savvy entrepreneurs to build great companies that will stand the test of time. Smart contractors (large and small) are boarding this train in increasing numbers. The trip won't necessarily be an easy one, but it will be fun, and it should help many people make lots of money as they service their clients.

The choice, as always, is up to you. Will you board this train and join the growing number of savvy market- and business-wise contractors who are equipped for Round Two? Or will you be left standing at the station?

CHAPTER

2

Estimating System Overview

TERM

Estimating

Purpose

To provide an overview of an estimating system

Introduction

The primary objective of an estimating system is to calculate costs accurately. However, an estimating system should also provide the following:

- An accurate *Price* on a job for your company
- A communicable *Plan* the field can use to run the job
- An objective quality-control *Process* you can use to job cost the project, which will also help your estimators become more effective and can be used to train new estimators.

The most common complaint I hear from landscape and irrigation contractors is "I don't know if I'm making money on this project."

This process allows us to address the most common complaint I hear from landscape and irrigation contractors:

I don't know if I'm making money on this project.

Most estimating systems produce a questionable price for a job and little else. The system taught in this book will provide a *Price*, a *Plan* and a *Process*—a quality-control process for controlling the entire spectrum of events that occur within your company.

THE OVERVIEW

How It Works

I have talked with thousands of Green Industry contractors and have personally worked with hundreds of them. The vast majority of them had estimating systems which contained deficiencies. Some estimating systems did not account for all of the direct costs in a product. Others did not address general and administrative overhead costs effectively. I've seen some of these flaws cost contractors thousands of dollars. I have also seen more serious flaws cost contractors their companies. The basic problem was that these contractors did not have a clear and well-thought-out estimating system that addressed all of the contingencies that might arise.

We're going to cover a lot of ground in this book. In order to illustrate our points, we'll use two models or business paradigms. The first is The Company Overview shown in Figure I-1. The second is The Bidding Overview (The OPPH Method) shown in Figure 2-1. (Figure 2-2 on page 8, The Bidding Overview (The MORS Method), which will be discussed in detail in subsequent chapters, is included for comparison purposes.)

Keep referring back to these models, especially if you get confused. Once you put a bid together, use these models to help you to review the bid in order to check if you've forgotten anything.

Be on the constant alert for *Leaks*. For every check you write, you should ask, "Where is this expense included in the bid?"

Be on the constant alert for *Leaks*. For every check you write, you should ask, "Where is this expense included in the bid?" In other words, you should be able to find that check (or see where that check is recovered) in these estimating models. Also, you should look for areas where you may be *Double-Dipping*—that is, where you're charging twice for the same cost.

Let me guide you through the models and the three phases found in a bid.

I. Production of the Finished Product and/or Providing the Service

Materials	Labor	Equipment	Subcontractors
At rewholesale cost	Labor hours multiplied by crew average wage or specific labor rate	Equipment hours in job multiplied by a predetermined cost per hour	At cost

II. General Conditions

Materials	Labor	Equipment	Subcontractors
At rewholesale cost	Labor hours multiplied by crew average wage or specific labor rate	Equipment hours in job multiplied by a predetermined cost per hour	At cost

III. Margins and Markups

A. Tax on materials (if applicable)

B. Labor burden on labor

C. G&A overhead recovery (total number of field-labor hours in items I and II above multiplied by company G&A overhead cost per field-labor hour OPH).

_________ (No. hours) × _________ (OPH) = $_________

D. Contingency factor (if applicable)

E. Net profit margin (a straight percentage margin on the total of all costs for the job. Or, if desired, company/division average profit per hour (PPH) multiplied by total number of field-labor hours shown in items I and II above).

_________ (No. hours) × _________ (PPH) = $_________

FIGURE 2-1 Bidding Overview: The OPPH Method

I. Production of the Finished Product and/or Providing the Service

Materials	Labor	Equipment	Subcontractors
At rewholesale cost	Labor hours multiplied by crew average wage or specific labor rate	Equipment hours in job multiplied by a predetermined cost per hour	At cost

II. General Conditions

Materials	Labor	Equipment	Subcontractors
At rewholesale cost	Labor hours multiplied by crew average wage or specific labor rate	Equipment hours in job multiplied by a predetermined cost per hour	At cost

III. Markups

A. Sales tax on materials

B. Labor burden on labor

C. G&A overhead

Materials	Labor	Equipment	Subcontractors
10%	Variable %	25%	5%

D. Contingency factor (if applicable)

E. Net profit (a percentage markup applied to the total of all costs for the job)

FIGURE 2-2 Bidding Overview: The Traditional or MORS Method

Three Phases of a Bid

I. Producing the Finished Product or Providing the Service

This phase of the bidding process includes costs for materials physically included in the finished product or service provided plus the labor, equipment, and subcontractor costs associated with it. If it's part of the finished product or service provided, the cost is included here in Phase I.

- *Material* is included *At Cost.*
- *Labor* is calculated in *Field-Labor Hours* multiplied by either a crew average wage (CAW) or specific wage rates for differing classes of labor.
- *Equipment* is included in the calculation by multiplying hours used by the cost per hour (CPH) for each piece of equipment.
- *Subcontractors* are included *At Cost.*

II. General Conditions

Included here are costs for those items required to produce the finished product or provide the service (material, labor, equipment, and subcontractors, as above), but which are not directly required to produce the end product or service. For instance, portable fences, toilets, or traffic control may be required by or "tied to" a specific job being bid, but they're not directly required to produce (mow) the mown lawn, plant or trim the trees, fertilize the site, or mulch the planting areas. Off-site labor time (load and unload, drive, warranty, supervision, job administration, picking up materials time, etc.) is usually included in general conditions.

Although there's sometimes a fine line between Phase I and II items, the list and detailed discussion of general condition items in Chapter 12 should clarify any confusion concerning them. It should also be noted that deciding whether a particular item should be in Phase I or II is less critical than ensuring that it's accurately included in one of them.

General condition items include, but are not limited to, the following:

- Crew pickup trucks, crew drive time, load/unload time
- Supervision of labor and related vehicles
- Labor and equipment to mobilize equipment to and from the job site
- Material-hauling labor and equipment costs
- Portable toilets, portable fences, permits, licenses, soil tests, as-builts
- Warranty labor and equipment
- Dumpsters, dump fees, lock boxes, freight charges, storage containers
- Traffic control, security, "rent-a-cops"
- Plant watering labor, design fees, commissions, estimator time, etc.

III. Margins and Markups

Sales tax

Appropriate sales tax markups are applied to materials and other items as required by state and local laws. In some states tax is now applied to the final price of the job, not just to the materials.

Field labor burden

Labor is marked up by a predetermined percentage in order to recover FICA, FUTA, SUTA, general liability insurance, field-crew vacations, holidays, sick days, workers' compensation insurance, medical insurance, and so forth.

General and administrative overhead or indirect costs

A number of methods are commonly used by contractors to recover general and administrative (G&A) overhead. Quite often, a percentage markup is used on materials, labor (including labor burden), equipment, and subcontractors (or just one or two of these items). A G&A overhead cost per field-labor hour may also be used. We will use a G&A overhead cost per field-labor hour.

Net profit margin

When added together, the items just listed produce your break-even point (BEP). *net profit* is then added to your BEP.

The specific amount of net profit to be added to a particular job is determined by

1. How badly you need the job
2. The size of the job
3. The risk involved
4. What the market will bear
5. Your ability to negotiate and to win the confidence and trust of the client.

Contingency factor

Contractors will sometimes add a fifth category. I often refer to it as the "aggravation factor." Basically, this is additional money tacked on to the price of a job that will make it worth it to you to incur additional risk or to put up with certain situations or individuals (architects, engineers, owners, developers, homeowners, etc.) with whom you'd rather not deal.

Remember that except for the contingency factor, you're constantly attempting to determine and differentiate between two numbers in the bidding process: *total costs* (which include direct and general and administrative overhead costs) or the BEP, and the *maximum price* the market will bear.

Direct costs consist of all costs in Phases I and II, plus sales tax on material and labor burden added to field labor. Indirect or general and administrative overhead costs are all of the costs that cannot be directly identified and tied to a particular job.

Completing the Bid

We can now equate or define **estimating** as determining those costs involved with Phases I and II (Figures 2-1 and 2-2), plus sales tax and labor burden.

The *bidding process* is completed when we add G&A overhead, net profit, and a contingency factor (if used) to the first two phases (plus sales tax and labor burden) and you will arrive at the *final price* for a particular job.

Now you can determine the gross profit margin, which is comprised of the G&A overhead, contingency factor, and net profit margin.

One last note: direct costs consist of all costs in Phases I and II, plus sales tax on material and labor burden added to field labor. Indirect or general and administrative overhead costs are all of the costs that cannot be directly identified and tied to a particular job.

Rounding and Decimal Points

Whenever feasible, round up the numbers used in your bids. For instance, if a crew average wage (CAW) calculates to be $14.57, I'd round the CAW for bidding purposes to $15.00. Seldom, if ever, do I use less than whole numbers when calculating costs. The few extra cents added to costs for materials, labor, equipment, and so forth will not (in most cases) affect your competitiveness at the bid table. By simplifying your mathematics you'll make calculations much easier and eliminate mistakes.

However, you must use common sense when rounding decimals. For example, you wouldn't round hydroseeding, which has a cost of eight cents per square foot, to $1.00 per square foot.

SUMMARY

The primary objective of an estimating system is to calculate costs accurately. Don't lose sight of this. A good estimating system should provide much more than just accurate costs. It should also produce a *Price*, a *Plan*, and a *Process*.

Formatting your bids properly and making sure of the data contained in them are very important. We break the bidding process into three phases: (1) the production of the finished product or providing the service, (2) general conditions, and (3) margins and markups.

Direct costs are comprised of all the costs in Phases I and II, plus the sales tax on materials and the field labor burden applied in Phase III.

The break-even point (BEP) is calculated when we add indirect general and administrative overhead costs to the total of all the direct costs contained in the bid. A contingency factor (if desired) and net profit are then added to the BEP in order to arrive at the final price for the job.

The gross profit margin is comprised of the G&A overhead, contingency factor, and net profit margin.

! Reminder

Think costs (both direct and indirect); think market (what the market will bear); then (consistently) price and negotiate your work between these two.

Establishing Annual Budgets

Determining Costs and Costing Standards

SECTION II

Contents

Purpose

To teach you how to develop and determine cost data and costing standards for your company or division for the budget items listed below. This data can be used to help you bid your jobs.

- Sales projections
- Direct costs for materials and subcontractors
- Direct costs for labor (labor hours and average wage rates)
- Direct costs for equipment and rental equipment
- Field and office labor burden
- General and administrative (G&A) overhead costs
- Per-hour and ratio analysis standards

TERMS

Cost of Goods Sold (COGS)
Direct Costs
Fair Market Value (FMV)
Over/Under Billing

The budgeting process is actually an exercise in goal-setting. You are really establishing standards or targets to aim for throughout your business.

Budgets reduce the diverse aspects of the business into numbers. The only difference between budgeting goals and goals written in words is that numbers can physically interact with each other (you can add, subtract, multiply, and divide), while words cannot.

More than *any* other tool, the "numbers" of your business—if properly formatted and correctly symbolized—can help you and your people run your company more effectively. However, to do so, your P&L statement, balance sheet, job costing, and other reports need to be set up properly. Unfortunately, most contractors don't understand the budgeting and accounting process well enough to take full advantage of what's available to them.

TYPES OF BUDGETS

Top management needs to be sure the following three types of budgets are in place and used:

The Cash Flow Budget

This simple budget is designed to project cash flow into and out of the company. If a shortfall is projected, management needs to obtain the funding to cover it. The cash flow budget is basically determined by the amount of cash in your checkbook.

The Accounting (Tax) Budget

This more complicated budget is designed to help you plan for and meet the tax requirements established by law. It should be addressed with the direct assistance of your accountant or Certified Public Accountant (CPA). The accounting budget is determined by both state and federal tax law.

The Estimating Budget

This detailed budget is designed to establish and to project fair market values for

- G&A overhead to recover
- Sales goals
- Gross and net profit margins (GPM and NPM)
- Direct costs or cost of goods sold (COGS)
- Average wage rates
- Office and field labor burden
- Field-labor hours
- Various ratios and per-hour standards

Once the estimating budget is established it should be monitored regularly by means of reports, graphs, and various visual aids. The estimating budget can and should be one of the key operational tools for establishing standards/goals by which to monitor the daily functions of your business. Unfortunately, in a landscape, irrigation, or tree service company, this budget is monitored too infrequently.

These three budgets are indeed similar, but they differ in some important aspects. For example, let's say that next year you're going to produce a color brochure for your company. Because of a quantity discount you decide to print enough brochures for three years, which will cost you $6,000 for the artwork, printing, and so on. For cash flow purposes, you put the entire $6,000 expense in next year's *cash flow budget* because you intend to pay all of it then. Likewise, if you're on the accrual accounting basis—which is generally best for contractors—the entire $6,000 will be

However, what's real and what's reasonable aren't necessarily the same.

included in your *tax planning budget* for this year (when you incur the expense), whether you pay for it now or later.

Your estimating budget, however, will account for only one year's worth of brochures (or $2,000) in the G&A overhead portion because it is not reasonable to charge next year's clients for brochures to be used later on. We'll also place $2,000 for G&A overhead recovery in the estimating budgets for the two following years, which is reasonable. It's not necessarily what's real, which is the $6,000 outlay however, *what's real and what's reasonable aren't necessarily the same.*

I often refer to the estimating budget as a **fair market value** budget. By that, I mean the estimating budget is based on what's reasonable in the market. As stated earlier, this budget doesn't always contain what's real, but rather what is fair market value.

INCOME OR PROFIT AND LOSS (P&L) STATEMENT

Figure II-1 on page 14 is a sample P&L statement—a very important report you need to monitor in order to understand what is (or isn't) happening in your company. I think of it as a job-cost report for all your jobs thrown together. Used properly and in conjunction with other data and reports, it can provide considerable insight into many aspects of your business.

MULTIPLE DIVISIONS

If you have multiple divisions, each doing different types of work, I'd provide separate P&L statements for divisions that comprise more than 20% of the gross sales of the business. You may even want to break a division down into separate subdivisions, which may or may not do the same types of work.

For instance, I know of a landscape maintenance company with more than 24 crews in one division (each crew consisting of four laborers). That division is broken down into six subdivisions or departments, each with four crews and a foreman. Each subdivision is tracked and compared to the others for profitability and cost.

FORMATTING THE P&L STATEMENT

Formatting the P&L statement is crucial. We encourage you to use a format similar to the one in Figure II-1 for accounting purposes. It's a P&L format for one division of a corporation. Sole proprietorships and partnerships should use a similar format, except for the officers' salaries (owner's draw), which is equivalent to the net profit margin or bottom line.

The estimating budget format, as illustrated in Figure II-1, is for corporations, sole proprietorships, partnerships, and limited liability corporations (LLCs). We build a fair market value salary into G&A overhead for owners of sole proprietorships and for partners. This allows us to bid projects on a par with corporations. Without this adjustment, our margins and G&A overhead recovery on bids would be skewed and not in line with industry benchmarks.

Sales

The sales for the division are at the top of the report, broken down by month and year-to-date (YTD).

	MONTH	%	Y-T-D	%
1. SALES REVENUES	83,333	100.0%	1,000,000	100.0%
2. COST OF GOODS SOLD (Direct costs)				
Materials (with tax)	26,667	32.0%	320,000	32.0%
Labor (field)	16,708	20.0%	200,491	20.0%
Labor burden (field)	5,440	6.5%	65,283	6.5%
Subcontractors	4,167	5.0%	50,000	5.0%
Equipment	5,569	6.7%	66,830	6.7%
Equipment rentals	292	0.4%	3,500	0.4%
Miscellaneous direct job costs	500	0.6%	6,000	0.6%
TOTAL COST OF GOODS SOLD (Total direct costs)	59,342	71.2%	712,104	71.2%
3. GROSS PROFIT MARGIN (GPM)	23,991	28.8%	287,896	28.8%
4. GENERAL and ADMINISTRATIVE (G&A) OVERHEAD (Indirect costs)				
Advertising	667	0.8%	8,000	0.8%
Bad debts	417	0.5%	5,000	0.5%
Computers, software, digitizers, plenimiters, etc.	208	0.3%	2,500	0.3%
Donations	17	0.0%	200	0.0%
Downtime	232	0.3%	2,782	0.3%
Downtime labor burden	75	0.1%	906	0.1%
Dues and subscriptions	71	0.1%	850	0.1%
Insurance (office staff and office)	667	0.8%	8,000	0.8%
Interest and bank charges	275	0.3%	3,300	0.3%
Licenses and related bonds	25	0.0%	300	0.0%
Office equipment	100	0.1%	1,200	0.1%
Office supplies	146	0.2%	1,750	0.2%
Professional fees	292	0.4%	3,500	0.4%
Radios and mobile phones	388	0.5%	4,650	0.5%
Rent	1,200	1.4%	14,400	1.4%
Salaries, office	4,167	5.0%	50,000	5.0%
Salaries, officer(s)	3,333	4.0%	40,000	4.0%
Salaries labor burden	959	1.2%	11,502	1.2%
Small tools/supplies	125	0.2%	1,500	0.2%
Taxes, business	0	0.0%	0	0.0%
Telephone	275	0.3%	3,300	0.3%
Training and education	167	0.2%	2,000	0.2%
Travel and entertainment	100	0.1%	1,200	0.1%
Uniforms and safety equipment	46	0.1%	550	0.1%
Utilities	50	0.1%	600	0.1%
Vehicles, overhead	693	0.8%	8,320	0.8%
Yard expense and lease-hold improvements	83	0.1%	1,000	0.1%
Miscellaneous	21	0.0%	250	0.0%
	0	0.0%	0	0.0%
TOTAL G&A OVERHEAD	14,797	17.8%	177,560	17.8%
5. NET PROFIT MARGIN	9,194	11.0%	110,336	11.0%
6. OVER/UNDER BILLING	______	0.0%	______	0.0%
7. REVISED NET PROFIT MARGIN	______	0.0%	______	0.0%

FIGURE II-1 The Profit and Loss Statement

Cost of Goods Sold or Direct Costs

Cost of Goods Sold (COGS) or **direct costs** follow sales and include everything that can be tied directly to a specific job.

You want to include as many costs as possible in direct costs, including field-labor burden (i.e., FICA, FUTA, workers' compensation insurance, general liability insurance, unemployment insurance, field-labor medical insurance, field holiday and vacation pay, etc.) and sales tax on materials. Depreciation for your field equipment should be identified and included in direct costs. However, depreciation for office G&A overhead items such as office vehicles and office equipment should be included in G&A overhead.

Gross Profit Margin (GPM)

The GPM is determined by subtracting all direct costs, including field-labor burden and sales tax, from sales.

G&A Overhead

G&A overhead is often referred to as indirect or G&A (General and Administrative) costs. The point is that you cannot directly pin G&A overhead costs to a particular field operation or job; hence, the term indirect or general is used to describe them.

Net Profit Margin (NPM)

Net profit margin, before taxes and interest, follows G&A overhead. Ten percent NPM is a good benchmark to shoot for after all fair market value costs have been included in the expense categories. Net profit margin is calculated prior to payment of company bonuses and before income taxes.

I like to graph the NPM "budget vs. actual" on a monthly or quarterly basis. I prefer that a company be on the accrual basis for its financial statements because it provides a more consistent picture of accurate sales and expenses.

Net Profit Adjustments

Some companies include an **over/under billing** adjustment category at the top or bottom of their P&L statement to reflect net profits more accurately, if they are, in fact, overbilled or underbilled on their jobs for a given period. Otherwise, your NPM may show dramatic variations from month to month because billings don't match expenses for the period in question. If your company reaches a certain size or enters into projects that require bonding, over/under billing will probably be required by your bonding company.

It's important that we *clearly define* and *consistently track* the items on a P&L statement. It's also important to maintain consistency in the types of information included in the categories containing budget (or actual) cost data. Otherwise, we'll destroy not only the integrity of the information but also its usefulness. If direct costs and/or G&A overhead definitions change from year to year, we won't be able to identify and monitor trends.

HISTORICAL DATA AND ESTIMATING BUDGETS

Estimating budgets project revenues and expenses for the next 12 months (or the next budget period in question). This is easiest to do a few months prior to a new fiscal year, which may or may not be the calendar year (January 1st to December 31st).

You should review your accumulated historical data (if available) and make adjustments to reflect changes that will occur during the next 12-month period.

If historical data isn't available (or if you're in a start-up situation), simply make your best "guesstimate" of projected revenues and/or expenses.

CHAPTER

3

Sales and Revenue Budget Projections

TERMS

Company
Division

Purpose

To explain the **company** and **division** budget format, to see the reason for establishing divisions, and to establish sales and revenue budget projections

Introduction

You should review historical data when making sales and revenue budget projections. If unavailable or if you are in a start-up situation, you will have to make your best "guesstimate." Whether or not you divisionalize your budget depends primarily upon the size of your company.

THE SAMPLE BUDGET

In our sample budget in Figure 3-1 on page 18, we have sales projections for both construction and service divisions. Direct costs, overhead (indirect or General and Administrative costs), and net profit margin are all allocated or identified by division. It is not uncommon for a landscape, irrigation, or tree service company doing over $1 to $2 million in gross annual sales to have two to four or more divisions (e.g., construction, maintenance, nursery, tree service, irrigation, pest control, equipment, etc.) for accounting, budgeting, and management purposes.

How It Works

A large Green Industry company in the western United States has nine divisions. Many of the divisions sell services to other divisions within the parent company. Detailed financial statements are produced on a monthly basis for each of the nine divisions. This allows division managers to track their profitability and to compare budget-to-actual figures throughout the year. It also allows corporate officers to review corporate-wide trends for the entire company and to reallocate resources if needed.

Seldom do companies divisionalize their accounting reports if gross annual sales are under $250,000. It's usually impractical to do so. I'd also add that, as a general rule,

J.R. Huston Enterprises, Inc.	All Divisions		Division 1		Division 2		Division 3		Division 4		Division 5		Division 6	
	Totals		G&A Overhead		Lawn Maintenance		Installation		Irrigation Service		Tree work		Winter work	
	Annual	%	Annual	%	Annual	%	Annual	%	Annual	%	Annual	%	Annual	%
SALES	960,000	100.0	0	100.0	250,000	100.0	300,000	100.0	110,000	100.0	250,000	100.0	50,000	100.0
COST OF SALES (Direct Costs):														
Material (with tax)	137,750	14.3	0	0.0	17,500	7.0	90,000	30.0	22,000	20.0	6,250	2.5	2,000	4.0
Labor	275,612	28.7	1	0.0	87,498	35.0	67,874	22.6	33,041	30.0	74,597	29.8	12,601	25.2
Labor Burden	96,604	10.1	0	0.0	26,873	10.7	22,146	7.4	11,470	10.4	33,097	13.2	3,018	6.0
Subcontractors	8,000	0.8	0	0.0	2,000	0.8	3,000	1.0	0	0.0	3,000	1.2	0	0.0
Equipment	118,858	12.4	0	0.0	26,904	10.8	24,265	8.1	8,863	8.1	51,617	20.6	7,210	14.4
Equipment Rental	9,200	1.0	0	0.0	3,000	1.2	3,000	1.0	1,200	1.1	2,000	0.8	0	0.0
Misc. Direct Job Costs	3,000	0.3	0	0.0	1,000	0.4	1,000	0.3	250	0.2	500	0.2	250	0.5
TOTAL COST OF SALES	649,025	67.6	1	0.0	164,776	65.9	211,284	70.4	76,824	69.8	171,061	68.4	25,079	50.2
GROSS PROFIT MARGIN	310,975	32.4	(1)	0.0	85,224	34.1	88,716	29.6	33,176	30.2	78,939	31.6	24,921	49.8
OVERHEAD (GENERAL & ADMINISTRATIVE OR INDIRECT) COSTS:							0							
Advertising	6,000	0.6	6,000	0.0	0	0.0	0	0.0	0	0.0	0	0.0	0	0.0
Bad debts	5,000	0.5	5,000	0.0	0	0.0	0	0.0	0	0.0	0	0.0	0	0.0
Computers, software	3,000	0.3	3,000	0.0	0	0.0	0	0.0	0	0.0	0	0.0	0	0.0
Donations	500	0.1	500	0.0	0	0.0	0	0.0	0	0.0	0	0.0	0	0.0
Downtime labor	9,489	1.0	0	0.0	3,292	1.3	2,364	0.8	1,047	1.0	2,786	1.1	0	0.0
Downtime labor burden	3,382	0.4	0	0.0	1,011	0.4	771	0.3	364	0.3	1,236	0.5	0	0.0
Dues and subscriptions	1,200	0.1	1,200	0.0	0	0.0	0	0.0	0	0.0	0	0.0	0	0.0
Insurance (office)	12,000	1.3	12,000	0.0	0	0.0	0	0.0	0	0.0	0	0.0	0	0.0
Interest and bank charges	1,200	0.1	1,200	0.0	0	0.0	0	0.0	0	0.0	0	0.0	0	0.0
Licenses and surety bonds	300	0.0	300	0.0	0	0.0	0	0.0	0	0.0	0	0.0	0	0.0
Office equipment	1,200	0.1	1,200	0.0	0	0.0	0	0.0	0	0.0	0	0.0	0	0.0
Office supplies	3,000	0.3	3,000	0.0	0	0.0	0	0.0	0	0.0	0	0.0	0	0.0
Professional fees	5,000	0.5	5,000	0.0	0	0.0	0	0.0	0	0.0	0	0.0	0	0.0
Radio systems	4,800	0.5	4,800	0.0	0	0.0	0	0.0	0	0.0	0	0.0	0	0.0
Rent (office and yard)	16,000	1.7	16,000	0.0	0	0.0	0	0.0	0	0.0	0	0.0	0	0.0
Salaries - office	53,220	5.5	53,120	0.0	100	0.0	0	0.0	0	0.0	0	0.0	0	0.0
Salaries - officers	54,000	5.6	54,000	0.0	0	0.0	0	0.0	0	0.0	0	0.0	0	0.0
Labor burden office	6,723	0.7	6,723	0.0	0	0.0	0	0.0	0	0.0	0	0.0	0	0.0
Small tools and supplies	3,000	0.3	3,000	0.0	0	0.0	0	0.0	0	0.0	0	0.0	0	0.0
Taxes	0	0.0	0	0.0	0	0.0	0	0.0	0	0.0	0	0.0	0	0.0
Telephone	3,000	0.3	3,000	0.0	0	0.0	0	0.0	0	0.0	0	0.0	0	0.0
Training and education	2,000	0.2	2,000	0.0	0	0.0	0	0.0	0	0.0	0	0.0	0	0.0
Travel and entertainment	2,500	0.3	2,500	0.0	0	0.0	0	0.0	0	0.0	0	0.0	0	0.0
Uniforms and safety equip.	2,000	0.2	2,000	0.0	0	0.0	0	0.0	0	0.0	0	0.0	0	0.0
Utilities	750	0.1	750	0.0	0	0.0	0	0.0	0	0.0	0	0.0	0	0.0
Vehicles, overhead	18,720	2.0	18,720	0.0	0	0.0	0	0.0	0	0.0	0	0.0	0	0.0
Yard exp./Leashold Imp.	1,000	0.1	1,000	0.0	0	0.0	0	0.0	0	0.0	0	0.0	0	0.0
Miscellaneous	250	0.0	250	0.0	0	0.0	0	0.0	0	0.0	0	0.0	0	0.0
Dumpster	2,250	0.2	2,250	0.0	0	0.0	0	0.0	0	0.0	0	0.0	0	0.0
	0	0.0	0	0.0	0	0.0	0	0.0	0	0.0	0	0.0	0	0.0
	0	0.0	0	0.0	0	0.0	0	0.0	0	0.0	0	0.0	0	0.0
	0	0.0	0	0.0	0	0.0	0	0.0	0	0.0	0	0.0	0	0.0
	0	0.0	0	0.0	0	0.0	0	0.0	0	0.0	0	0.0	0	0.0
	0	0.0	0	0.0	0	0.0	0	0.0	0	0.0	0	0.0	0	0.0
	0	0.0	0	0.0	0	0.0	0	0.0	0	0.0	0	0.0	0	0.0
	0	0.0	0	0.0	0	0.0	0	0.0	0	0.0	0	0.0	0	0.0
	0	0.0	0	0.0	0	0.0	0	0.0	0	0.0	0	0.0	0	0.0
	0	0.0	0	0.0	0	0.0	0	0.0	0	0.0	0	0.0	0	0.0
	0	0.0	0	0.0	0	0.0	0	0.0	0	0.0	0	0.0	0	0.0
Overhead Transfer to Divisions	0	0.0	(208,600)	0.0	53,125	21.3	66,000	22.0	23,925	21.8	53,750	21.5	11,800	23.6
TOTAL OVERHEAD	221,484	23.1	(87)	0.0	57,527	23.0	69,136	23.0	25,336	23.0	57,772	23.1	11,800	23.6
NET PROFIT MARGIN - NPM	89,491	9.3	86	0.0	27,697	11.1	19,580	6.5	7,840	7.1	21,167	8.5	13,121	26.2
PROFIT ADJUSTMENTS (Add'l salaries, bonuses, etc.)	0	0.0	0	0.0	0	0.0	0	0.0	0	0.0	0	0.0	0	0.0
REVISED NET PROFIT MARGIN	89,491	9.3	86	0.0	27,697	11.1	19,580	6.5	7,840	7.1	21,167	8.5	13,121	26.2
Sales Per Hour - SPH	49.65		-		32.52		61.82		62.06		58.12		69.35	
Overhead Per Hour - OPH	11.45		(87.00)		7.48		14.25		14.29		13.43		16.37	
Net Profit Per Hour - PPH	4.63		85.88		3.60		4.03		4.42		4.92		18.20	
Total Division Field Labor Hours	19,336		1		7,687		4,853		1,773		4,301		721	
Multiple Overhead Recovery %														
Material %	13,775	10.0%	0	10.0%	1,750	10.0%	9,000	10.0%	2,200	10.0%	625	10.0%	200	10.0%
Labor & Burden %	175,295	47.1%	(87)	-7737%	48,201	42.1%	53,170	59.1%	20,620	46.3%	43,593	40.5%	9,798	62.7%
Equipment %	32,015	25.0%	0	25.0%	7,476	25.0%	6,816	25.0%	2,516	25.0%	13,404	25.0%	1,803	25.0%
Subcontractors %	400	5.0%	0	5.0%	100	5.0%	150	5.0%	0	5.0%	150	5.0%	0	5.0%
	221,484		(87)		57,527		69,136		25,336		57,772		11,800	

FIGURE 3-1 The Company Budget

Seldom do companies divisionalize their accounting reports if gross annual sales are under $250,000. It's usually impractical to do so.

it's not practical to establish a separate division in your accounting and budgeting system for any activity that accounts for less than 15 to 20% of gross annual sales.

You may be asking, "Why divisionalize in the first place? What difference does it make?" I encourage you to divisionalize your budgets and your P&L statements, at least for sales and direct costs (Phases I and II on Figures 2-1 and 2-2), for the following reasons:

- It can help identify where you are making money, thus showing where you may want to allocate more resources and therefore increase sales.
- It can help identify where you are losing money and the possible steps to take in order to stop the "leaks" in your company.
- Start-up divisions (especially nurseries) can be tracked and monitored, thus identifying trends and future profitability. Unless they are separated from other divisions, start-up divisions will dilute the profit and loss performance of those divisions.
- Division P&L statements can serve as a division manager's "report card," thus helping top management decentralize the company and allowing division managers to operate more autonomously with less interference from top management.
- Productivity trends can be identified by division, and either corrective or reinforcing actions can be taken. Otherwise, one division may be improving while another is declining. If they are lumped together, they may appear to be unchanged and a damaging trend may be left unnoticed.
- Bonuses and incentives can be established based partially on division performance.
- It can facilitate the preparation of a budget for the entire company.
- Feedback can be supplied to division personnel. It should be noted that timely and accurate feedback (TAF) can be *your best motivator.*
- It can provide vital division "budget vs. actual" performance information to estimators, who can then take corrective actions, if necessary, in the estimating process.
- It can help you compare equipment costs to revenues generated by that equipment. Thus it can help you monitor whether or not equipment is covering its costs (justifying its existence) and/or if you're estimating it accurately.
- Different types of divisions usually have different gross profit margins (GPMs). Therefore, divisions with similar sales but with a higher GPM will be more profitable to a company and contribute more to the bottom line: net profit margin (NPM). This is assuming that the general and administrative (G&A) overhead is similar for the two divisions. Such information can be invaluable when planning and budgeting for future growth, cash flow, and profitability of the business.

➤ NOTE Whenever the term "company" appears in the text, it refers to either a division or to the company as a whole.

SUMMARY

Breaking your company into divisions can be very useful if done properly. However, it's generally unnecessary to divisionalize a company with gross annual sales of less than $250,000. Sales revenue for the budget year in question should be projected using historical growth patterns. Adjustments should be made as deemed necessary. Use your best judgment if good historical data is unavailable or if you're in a start-up situation.

ACTION POINT

Use the Exhibit 1 worksheets at the back of the book (using one sheet for each division), and fill in the sales projections for each division for the budget period in question. Review last year's sales figures to gain a historical perspective. Increase or decrease sales and revenue projections from the last year as deemed necessary. If past performance figures aren't available, or if you're in a start-up situation, use your best judgment to make a sales projection for the budget period.

CHAPTER

4

Direct Costs: Materials, Subcontractors, Equipment, and Commissions

TERMS

Commissioned Salespeople
Commissions
Draw Against Commissions
Material-to-Labor (M/L) Ratio
Salary
Straight Commission

Purpose

To explain how to establish budgets for direct costs

Introduction

The direct costs covered in this section are relatively easy to budget. Although actual costs may vary dramatically from our budget projections as we proceed into the year, this doesn't (necessarily) pose a significant problem in the estimating process.

It is important to note that field-labor and the related-labor burden are also direct costs, but they are covered in other chapters. Let's start with materials and supplies.

MATERIALS AND SUPPLIES (including the related sales tax)

Using Historical Data

If you have good historical data by division, you can use—for budget purposes—the percent of materials from last year as a percent of the materials you are going to use for the next budgeting year.

In other words, if materials and supplies were 30% of your sales last year and you anticipate a substantial sales increase in the coming year, simply take 30% of your new sales projection and use that number for your materials budget.

Using Ratios

If you don't have good historical data broken down by division, the best way to budget materials and supplies is to use a **material-to-labor (M/L) ratio** to calculate dollar amounts for materials. Simply multiply the projected field-labor payroll budget for the year by the appropriate ratio.

If you're in a start-up situation and have no historical data on which to base your calculations, you can use these ratios as a good way of projecting your costs for materials and supplies within the next budget period.

Plant Material Only (3:1) Companies that just install plant materials are usually able to install $3.00 of material for every $1.00 of gross field payroll (excluding labor burden) paid. For a company with an average wage of $10.00 per field-labor hour (FLH), a 3:1 M/L ratio translates into $30.00 of material costs per hour (MPH).

Hardscape and Plant Material (2 to 2.5:1) Companies that install plant materials and hardscape (bender board, boulders, decks, patios, etc.) usually have a 2 to 2.5:1 M/L ratio. In other words, they install $2.00 to $2.50 in materials for every $1.00 spent on field labor. If the average wage is again $10.00, the MPH would run between $20.00 and $25.00.

Irrigation, Hardscape, and Plant Material (1.5 to 1.75:1) Companies that install plants, hardscape, and irrigation generally have a M/L ratio from 1.5 to 1.75:1. Again, using an average wage of $10.00 per hour, the MPH ranges from $15.00 to $17.50.

Irrigation Only (1.5 to 2.0:1 and 2.0 to 3.0:1) Residential irrigation companies usually have a 1.5 to 2.0:1 M/L ratio. For every $1.00 spent on field labor, $1.50 to $2.00 is spent on material costs. However, irrigation contractors who do large commercial and golf course work often realize M/L ratios of 2 to 3:1.

Maintenance (.05 to .15:1) Lawn maintenance or management companies generally have a M/L ratio ranging from .10 to .15:1. This translates into an MPH ranging from $.50 to $1.50.

Tree Service (.02 to .05:1 and .8 to 1.2:1) General tree service work usually requires minimal materials and therefore has a M/L ratio of .02 to .05:1. Tree fertilization normally ranges close to .9 to 1.1:1. Insect pest management normally ranges between .3 and .5:1.

SUBCONTRACTORS

We can project subcontractor costs pretty much the same way we did materials and supplies. If subcontractors have been running 15% of sales on our P&L statement and we're going to increase or decrease sales in the next year, then we can multiply projected sales by the historical 15% in order to calculate projected subcontractor costs. If our sales are going to change significantly from the previous budgeting period, this procedure will make the appropriate adjustments.

In many cases subcontractor costs as a percent of sales will vary dramatically from year to year, and there's no way to project these fluctuations. This is adequate because it's really not crucial to identity this number with absolute precision.

How It Works

A California landscape contractor and I put together a $1 million budget for his company. However, all of the ratios and per-hour figures were out of line. It was then I noticed that subcontractor costs were 40% of the sales figure. This contractor did not have a $1 million company. Rather, he had a $500,000 company that did a lot of subcontracted work. You have to be careful or subcontractor costs can skew the ratios and per-hour figures in your budget.

How can you compensate for these skewed ratios and figures when preparing a budget with a lot of subcontractor costs in it?

Things to Look Into:

1. teaching - Social Sciences
2. Business Psychology
3. Research in Social/Developmental Psychology
4. Business
5. start studying for GRE's

1. research different areas of study
2. look at different programs
3. determine cost
4. begin studying for test to get in
5. apply
6. work on Excel Knowledge

elementary school: writing stories, organizing, plays, listening to music, playing outside

high school: school (learning), playing sports, organizing, playing guitar, crafts

college: reading, studying, history, psychology, history

now: working out, reading, crafts, guitar

\$526.32

Available \$486.30

Ours is 75/hr per man for Production

Things to Get Done Before March 1st

1. Denver Permits
2. Broomfield Permits
3. Arvada Permits
4. NO Sod List Audit for Dec./Jan./Feb.
5. Survey Letter
6. Oakwood Customs Update
7. Lennar Schedules/Work Note Issues
8. Software
9. Agenda for Oakwood Meeting

RENTAL EQUIPMENT

Budgeting for rental equipment functions very much like subcontractors, materials, and supplies: Costs usually stay fairly consistent. The best thing to do is look at what you've done in the past and make a projection with which you feel comfortable.

If you lack workable historical data, you might put a couple of thousand dollars in the rental equipment category. Track it and make adjustments as you go. It's not that important to project it accurately, so giving it your best "guesstimate" should suffice.

MISCELLANEOUS ITEMS

This is where you account for any cost that can be directly connected to a job but really doesn't fit into one of the other categories. I normally include such items as permits, dump fees, storage containers, dumpsters, bags for grass clippings, blueprints, as-builts, photography expenses, and so on.

COMMISSIONS

You may or may not have **commissioned salespeople** in your company. If you do, you should have a category in "direct costs" where you account for their **commissions**.

Usually residential contractors and tree service companies, both residential and commercial, are the only ones who have commissioned salespeople. Commercial landscaping and irrigation contractors generally do not. This is primarily due to the slim profit margins and to the fact that a job bid this year may not be installed for eight, ten, twelve, or even sixteen months. It's usually not financially practical to have someone selling that kind of work, nor to have them on a commission structure.

The key regarding commissions is to plan out the process and to *identify sales goals* for each individual salesperson. Consider the following factors:

1. Amount
   Commissions paid to salespeople generally run 8 to 12% of the price of a project.

   For instance, if a project is priced at $10,000, the commission to the salesperson would be between $800 and $1,200. The commission percent would include car expense reimbursement, medical insurance, and all other related benefits.
2. Sales Goals
   Determine the sales goal for a salesperson by dividing the desired pay for the year (including all expenses and benefits) by the percent of commission (e.g., 10%).

   Using an average commission of 10%, a commissioned salesperson wanting to make $50,000 per year would have to sell $500,000 worth of work throughout the year to reach that goal.

   The key is to tie the commission to a sales goal and to an all-inclusive commission percentage. A good range to use is 8 to 12%.
3. Responsibilities
   The next item to address about commissioned salespeople is, "What will they do? Do they only sell?" In other words, is it the responsibility of the commissioned salesperson just to sell, or does the salesperson also supervise the work and make sure the client (the customer) is happy throughout the entire process?

A. You have to keep commissioned salespeople involved in the project and interested in keeping the customer happy until the end of that project and collection of the final payment.

The salesperson doesn't just sell jobs. Your sales representative must have a vested interest in ensuring that each job meets the expectations of the client.

B. The commissioned salesperson should also be responsible for collecting the final check from the customer. This establishes a vital checkpoint, ensuring that the salesperson remains involved in the process from beginning to end.

C. Multiple Job Responsibilities

(1) Structure

If the sales rep is to have other responsibilities (e.g., designing jobs and performing some administrative duties), keep this entirely separate from the commission. For instance, if the rep will be making 8 to 12% on a project, I assume that no design work will be involved. If there is, then pay an hourly rate for design time in addition to the commission (or according to some other predetermined agreement), but keep the two separate.

If you structure the commissions this way and find really good salespeople, you probably won't want them spending a lot of time designing. In all likelihood, you'll want them to sell more and design less.

This structure also facilitates subcontracting design work. The result is that your company becomes more flexible structurally. You can expand and increase sales, or you can downsize quickly and with minimal difficulty.

(2) Establish Goals for Salespersons

If the salesperson is going to design (or whatever), subtract the projected salary for designing or other duties from the projected sales goal income. Divide what remains by your commission percentage (e.g., 10%). The result is the amount the salesperson needs to sell for the year.

As an example, a salesperson wants to make $50,000 a year, including about $10,000 for design work. Take the difference ($40,000) and divide that by 10%. The salesperson will have to sell $400,000 in order to make the additional $40,000 in commissions. This number can easily be monitored in order to see if the person is bringing in enough work to cover his annual paycheck.

4. Payment of Commissioned Salespersons

"How is the commissioned salesperson going to be paid?" Basically, there are three different methods.

A. Straight Commission on Sales

A **straight commission** means the salesperson doesn't get paid until he or she sells a job and collects the final check when that job is completed.

B. Draw Against Commissions

With a **draw against commissions**, unlike a straight commission, sales reps are paid prior to collecting the final check for the project. This is considered a draw against any future commissions they're to earn.

Commissions are still a percentage of sales, but they are paid prior to all moneys being collected. It's a little different from the straight commission method, but overall it's the same concept. The timing of the commission payment is the only difference.

C. Salary

The salesperson on **salary** receives a consistent paycheck that's the same from month to month.

Although different from the previous two methods, you still must tie pay to sales. The key thing to remember is that if the salesperson doesn't generate a certain amount of sales, he or she doesn't have a job. The fact that a salesperson has to bring a certain amount of sales into the company in order to earn a certain amount of pay doesn't change. However, the method of payment does. The salesperson gets paid steady, consistent amounts.

You must continually ask yourself, "Does the salesperson have a clearly identified sales goal? Is he or she bringing that amount into the company?" If not, you have to make appropriate adjustments.

Comparison and Warnings

The straight commission method is simpler for the company because, if the salesperson doesn't make the sale and collect the money, no compensation is due. The draw against commissions is a little more complex, but the concept is the same.

The salaried concept is also the same; however, it's a little harder to monitor. Quite often this is where a company gets into trouble. It puts a person on salary and never ties that salary to a particular amount of sales the person needs to generate. Memories get short; there's no method for comparing salary to revenue generated. I've seen cases where people have been paid for a year or two, and (because of the bureaucracy and other complications within the organization) no one ever really compares their salaries to the sales they are generating.

Earlier, I mentioned an 8-to-12% range for commissions on sales. I've seen cases where the percentage was 20 to 25% after dividing actual commissions paid by actual sales generated. It's simply impossible to justify having someone in the organization earn such a high commission, because you must add it to your general and administrative overhead costs while factoring in a net profit for the company. The market will simply not allow it.

Once you determine the amount of commission a person is going to earn throughout the year based on sales projections, enter that amount into direct costs in the commissions category. Remember that the commission's category does not include money paid for design fees or costs of administrative tasks that are going to be included in general and administrative overhead.

SUMMARY

Budgeting direct costs for materials and supplies, subcontractors, rental equipment, miscellaneous direct costs, and commissions on sales is fairly straightforward. You can do this by referring to historical data or by using industry ratios. Remember, the direct costs covered in this chapter don't include the field-labor and related-labor burdens, which are also direct costs. They are covered in a later chapter.

ACTION POINT

Fill in the appropriate direct cost categories in Exhibit 1 in the back of the book for the next budget period in question.

CHAPTER

5

Field-Labor Payroll and Hourly Budgets

TERMS

Average Wage
Billable Hours
Company/Division Average Wage (AW)
Field-Labor Payroll and Hourly Budget
Overhead Per Hour (OPH)
Overtime Factor (OTF)
Overtime Hours
Revenue Per Hour (RPH)
Risk Factor (RF)
Sale Per Hour (SPH)

Purpose

To explain and to establish the field-labor budget

Introduction

The **field-labor payroll and hourly budget** is one of the primary tools you'll use for

- *Measuring* your company's and/or division's **performance** by means of ratios and per hour analysis
- *Controlling* and *directing* the company as a whole and by individual divisions, if you have them so identified
- Allocating general and administrative (G&A) overhead to bids

The labor hours we include in this budget should be **billable hours**. These are the labor hours that are estimated and bid into jobs, or they are charged to the client on a time and materials (T&M) basis. Labor hours included in vacation, holiday, and sick time, training, and downtime are not billable and should therefore not be included in this budget. You'll notice that we make no such distinction in Exhibit 2 because it's very cumbersome and difficult to do so without using a computer spreadsheet.

We'll use the field-labor-hour budget in conjunction with other key information to monitor trends and to track vital company statistics. We could use percentage of sales to do this, but the field-labor-hour method is more accurate. For instance, company or division sales can be divided by the respective field-labor hours to obtain a company-wide or division **sales per hour (SPH)** or **revenue per hour (RPH)** figure, which we'll discuss later.

Company and/or division general and administrative (G&A) overhead costs will be divided by the respective field-labor hours in order to obtain an **overhead per hour (OPH)** figure.

FORMAT

We'll use Exhibit 2 in the back of the book to develop your company and/or division field-labor-hour budget figures. Fill in the information using historical data, if available. If you do not have good historical data or you are in a start-up situation, use your best judgment when completing the crew member information in the exhibit. Start with the landscape crew information and fill in the appropriate data. If you don't plan to divide your company into divisions, lump all of your labor data into the landscape crew section. Make extra copies and change the crew titles on Exhibit 2 if necessary.

AVERAGE WAGE

To calculate **average wage (AW)** start with the foreman in "1 A (1)" on the exhibit and fill in the columns as follows:

(a) Quantity of foremen in the company (and/or division) at a specific projected hourly rate for the budget year. If the foremen's hourly rate varies more than one to two dollars per hour, use two categories or average the salary. Projected hourly rates should include any anticipated raises for that category.

(b) Enter the average hours per month worked (i.e., 4.33 weeks per month × 9 hours per day × 5 days per week = 195 hours per month). Adjust appropriately for each category.

(c) Enter the number of months per year each category will work. Make seasonal adjustments accordingly.

(d) Multiply columns (a) × (b) × (c) and enter the total in column (d).

(e) Enter the hourly rate or average rate for a category, as appropriate.

(f) Multiply columns (d) × (e) and enter total projected payroll in column (f).

(2–6) Fill in the other labor classifications for the division.

(7) Total the field-labor hours and payroll on row (7).

(8) Compute the **company/division average wage (AW)** on row (8) by dividing the total payroll by the total field-labor hours.

(9) Complete row (9) on the exhibit after you calculate the OTF for the company/division in section 2 of the worksheet.

OVERTIME FACTOR

A. Fill in the average total number of hours actually worked per man per week (by division) throughout the entire year.

B. To calculate the **overtime factor (OTF)**, fill in the average number of hours qualifying for overtime per man per week throughout the entire year.

C. Fill in the average number of **overtime hours** paid per man per week. This is usually the number in row B multiplied by 1.5 (time-and-a-half). However, this may differ from state to state.

D. Review the example.

E, F, and G. Fill in your company/division overtime factor information here.

RISK FACTOR

The **risk factor (RF)** is applied to your average wage or your crew average wage (including OTF) on a job-by-job basis and is not used in this budget. However, I want to briefly discuss it here because questions often arise about the risk factor during the budgeting process. It usually ranges from 10 to 20% but it could go higher. If you feel very confident about the number of labor hours bid into a project, a risk factor of 10% is normally applied to your average wage including OTF.

Some contractors reduce the risk factor to zero when re-bidding maintenance projects that their crews have performed and for which they have good job cost information.

If, on the other hand, you're doing unfamiliar work and/or don't feel confident about the accuracy of the labor hours bid into a job, increase the risk factor accordingly and multiply your average wage and OTF by it.

TOTALS

Total the projected hours and payroll for the year.

A. Total your field-labor hours for all divisions.

B. Total your payroll for the year.

C. Note and compare your results to last year's hours, if available.

D. Note and compare your results to last year's payroll, if available.

How It Works

An installation contractor in the Northwest seemed to have too many field-labor hours in his budget. His historical data was very questionable. When we divided his budgeted general and administrative overhead costs by the inflated field-labor hours, the G&A overhead per hour amount was about $8. It should have been around $12. This could result in too little G&A overhead being allocated to jobs being bid.

What "safety check" do we use in the bidding process to safeguard from allocating too little or too much G&A overhead to jobs being bid?

SUMMARY

The field-labor payroll budget is one of the most important components of your estimating budget. It lays the foundation for measuring your company and/or division's performance, controlling and directing the company and/or division, and allocating G&A overhead to your bids.

ACTION POINT

Fill in Exhibit 2 in the back of the book and calculate your company/division field-labor-hour budget, average wage, and overtime factor.

CHAPTER

6

Crew Average Wage

TERMS

Crew Average Wage (CAW)
True Average Wage

Purpose

To explain how to calculate the crew average wage for individual jobs bid

Introduction

In Chapter 5 we covered how to calculate the company/division average wage, which could be referred to as a **true average wage**. It is the total field-labor payroll for a company/division, divided by the total number of billable field-labor hours in that company/division.

To be completely accurate we should subtract holidays, vacations, sick time, downtime hours, and so forth for each respective labor rate. I actually do this when I prepare a budget for a company, with the aid of a computer spreadsheet program such as Lotus 1-2-3 or Microsoft Excel. As insightful as this exercise may be, it is not necessary for purposes of estimating because we'll build a more accurate **crew average wage (CAW)** when bidding a specific job.

CAW is used to estimate labor costs on specific jobs. It is very simple to calculate, but before we determine these rates for your jobs let's discuss *why* they're important. Here's a specific example. I use a crew average wage when the entire crew is going to be on the job at the same time. It's unrealistic and inaccurate to attempt to use specific labor rates for specific tasks when the entire crew is on the job site. However, you should use specific labor rates for foremen, drivers, operators, supervisors, and other workers when they're working alone or when specific individuals are estimated into general conditions.

How It Works

A few years ago, I helped a design/build landscape and irrigation installation contractor bid a residential project. Two other companies were also bidding this project, which my client had designed and which we felt gave us a competitive edge. However, we knew we still had to be competitive with our price.

Our initial estimate was $33,345. There were 585 field-labor hours included in the bid. Initially, my client was going to place a three-man crew on the job: a foreman at $16 per hour, a leadman at $12, and a laborer at $8 per hour.

The crew average wage worked out to be $12. After putting the bid together, we looked at some alternative options concerning the crew. My client thought he could do the project with a five-man crew: a foreman at $16, a leadman at $12, and three laborers at $8 per hour. The crew average wage was then recalculated as $10.40 per field-labor hour.

As you study Table 6-1 on page 30, note what this change did to his bid.

TABLE 6-1 Crew Average Wage Cost Savings

Old CAW		$ 12.00
New CAW		$ 10.40
Savings per FLH		$ 1.60
Total FLHs in bid		× 585
	Subtotal	$ 936.00
Plus labor burden (30%)		$ 281.00
	Subtotal	$1,217.00
Plus 10% OTF		$ 122.00
	Subtotal	$1,339.00
Plus 10% RF		$ 134.00
Total cost savings		$1,473.00
Plus 10% net profit margin		$ 164.00
	Total price adjustment	$1,637.00

Note: To achieve a true 10% net profit margin, divide $1,473 by 1.0 minus the desired net profit margin ($1,473 ÷ (1.0 – .1)) = $1,473 ÷ .9 = $1,636.67 or $1,637.

This contractor was able to reduce his price or increase his profit margin (should he so choose) by a minimum of $1,637, simply by adjusting his crew composition in the field and his crew average wage in the bid.

There was another savings on the job: general conditions costs would also decrease. The larger crew would complete the job in approximately 12 days, compared to 20 days for the smaller crew. This would translate into additional cost savings as shown in Table 6-2.

TABLE 6-2 Additional Cost Savings

Crew pickup truck (8 days at $48 per day)	$384.00
Supervisory time (8 days at 1 hr/day at $35)	$280.00
Total cost savings	$664.00
Plus 10% net profit margin	$ 74.00
Total price adjustment	$738.00

The total possible savings on this project could exceed $2,375, a little more than 7% of the initial bid. All it took was a single adjustment regarding the composition of the crew working on the job and the crew average wage used in the bidding process.

By the way, this contractor lowered his price, although not by the full $2,375, and the resulting adjustment helped him win the bid.

CALCULATING THE CAW

Table 6-3 displays a sample crew average wage worksheet that's filled out for a planting crew. Review the table, and then calculate your own crew average wage rates for your most often used crew combinations. (For a more complete explanation of the Risk Factor, refer to Chapter 5.)

TABLE 6-3 Crew Average Wage Sample

Date: 10/22/20____
Job: Jones Residence
Type of Crew: Planting

Type of Labor	Name	Labor Rate
Foreman	Ed	$18.00
Leadman	Bill	$12.00
Laborer	N/A	$ 9.00
Laborer	N/A	$ 0.00
Laborer	N/A	$ 0.00
	Total	**$39.00**

1. Divide labor total ($39) by number of crew members (3) = ($39 ÷ 3) =		$13.00
2. Add OTF (10%)		$ 1.30
	Subtotal	$14.30
3. Add RF (10-20% depending on difficulty)		$ 1.43
	Subtotal	$15.73
4. Round up as you deem appropriate		**$16.00**

How It Works

I've seen $1 to $2 million jobs that have had 20,000 to 40,000 labor hours in them be won (or lost) by just a few thousand dollars. A $.50 cost differential in the CAW can easily make the difference between winning and losing such a job. In these situations, I always ask my clients, "Have you calculated your CAW accurately and with the correct size crew?"

SUMMARY

The crew average wage (CAW) is used to estimate labor costs on individual jobs. It is far more accurate than just using the average wage for the entire company. I use a crew average wage when the entire crew is going to be on the job at the same time. It's unrealistic and inaccurate to attempt to use specific labor rates for specific tasks when the entire crew is on the job site. However, you should use specific labor rates for foremen, drivers, operators, supervisors, and other workers when they're working alone or when specific individuals are estimated into general conditions. A risk factor and overtime factor are added to the crew average wage or specific labor rate as deemed necessary.

I always add net profit as a margin, not a markup, when calculating net profit onto a job or labor rate. To obtain a net profit margin, divide your costs by 1.0 minus the desired net profit margin.

ACTION POINT

Use Exhibit 3 in the back of the book. Calculate your crew average wage rates for your most common crew combinations.

CHAPTER 7

Labor Burden

TERMS

- FICA (Federal Insurance Contributions Act)
- FUTA (Federal Unemployment Tax Act)
- General Liability Insurance (GLI)
- Holidays
- Medical/Health Insurance
- SUTA (State Unemployment Tax Act)
- Sick Days
- Umbrella Policy
- Vacations
- Well Days
- Workers' Compensation Insurance (WCI)

Purpose

To explain how to calculate labor burden

Introduction

Labor burden consists of those items (FICA, FUTA, SUTA, Workers' Compensation Insurance (WCI), General Liability Insurance, etc.) that can be directly correlated to office and field payroll and that vary in direct proportion to it. The labor burden added to field labor is a direct cost. The labor burden added to G&A overhead payroll is an indirect G&A cost. It is calculated as a percentage that is then applied to field and office (or G&A administrative) payroll.

When calculating the labor burden to be applied to prevailing wage or rated government jobs, you should review the bid documents and specifications to ensure that you are using the correct labor rates with the appropriate fringe benefits. In some cases you may be duplicating items included in the fringe benefits when calculating your company labor burden amount in the bid. You may want to adjust your company labor burden accordingly. Check your bid documents and specifications or contact your contract administrator to ensure that the figures you are using are correct.

SET PERCENTAGES

Most labor burden items (FICA, FUTA, SUTA, WCI, GLI) are assigned to you as a fixed percentage that will vary little when calculated into your labor burden. For instance, FICA is currently 7.65%. This doesn't change whether you are calculating labor burden for prevailing wage projects or for non-rated ones.

ACCUMULATED WORK TIME

Other labor burden items, such as sick pay, paid holidays, and/or vacation time, are based on accumulated paid non-work time (usually days or man-hours) and need to be calculated differently when bidding rated or non-rated jobs.

The usual range for labor burden in the United States is between 12 and 15% for office personnel and from 20 to 35% for field personnel. Tree crews will usually have a much higher labor-burden rate, primarily due to their high workers' compensation insurance rate.

The labor burden in Canada generally runs 10 to 20% (plus or minus 2 or 3%) for both office and field personnel. This is primarily due to the method by which Canada handles its health insurance, workers' compensation insurance, and FICA and FUTA equivalents.

REVIEWING LABOR BURDEN "BUDGET-TO-ACTUAL"

Labor burden calculations should be reviewed every four to six months and adjusted whenever your insurance rates or experience modification changes. You should also review and adjust your labor burden if you are bidding rated jobs and haven't done so in the recent past.

Some companies actually have accounting software, which allows them to produce financial statements that display labor burden "budgeted" for actual field and office payroll compared to "actual" accumulated expenses for labor burden items. For example, if labor burden is calculated to be 32% for field-labor payroll, the accounting software will make the calculations and then compare the result (in dollars and as a percentage) to the actual amount spent for FICA, FUTA, WCI, GLI, holiday pay, vacation pay, and so on. This is an excellent method for ensuring that your calculated labor-burden percentages are correct.

Another method for accomplishing the same thing is to establish a labor-burden checking account into which you deposit and accumulate labor-burden funds. The amount is determined simply by multiplying your payroll (e.g., $3,000) by your labor-burden percent (e.g., 32%). That amount ($960) is then deposited into the labor-burden checking account. These funds are then accumulated, and all labor-burden items (including holidays, vacations, etc.) are paid from that account.

If your labor-burden percentages are correct, you should be able to pay all labor-burden expenses from that account. If you can't cover labor-burden expenses, your calculations are probably wrong.

Use of Funds

Don't be too hasty to assume that the excess funds accumulated in this account can be withdrawn and spent for non-labor-burden expense purposes.

How It Works

One contractor in the Southwest thought he had extra money to spend in the last month of his fiscal year, which was also the last month of the calendar year. He proceeded to spend it (not all of it wisely, I might add) on nonessentials. A few months later, he received two bills—a combined total of over $40,000—for workers' compensation insurance and general liability insurance premiums that were due for the previous year.

Although he had charged the correct amount for labor burden on his jobs, he didn't collect and accumulate it throughout the year. When his insurance company did its annual audit, it determined that his business and his payroll had almost doubled in the previous 12 months. Because his insurance premiums were based on a much lower projected payroll amount for the year, he had paid only half of what he should have paid. Although he included the correct amount of labor burden in his bids and collected the correct amount of dollars from his customers to cover it, he spent the money on non-labor-burden items, assuming the extra money was additional net profit.

Don't just charge the correct amount for labor burden. Save and accumulate this amount in order to ensure that it's used to pay labor-burden expenses.

VIEW LABOR BURDEN AS AN INCENTIVE

Labor burden items (such as vacation pay, holiday pay, medical and/or dental insurance, sick pay, etc.) *must be earned.* I've had contractors ask me if they should provide various types of benefits and whether these benefits would serve as an incentive to productivity. Let me use some examples to explain my answer.

How It Works

One contractor provided virtually everyone in his field crew with a minimum of two weeks vacation, six paid holidays, and three sick days per year. Medical and dental benefits were also provided. Labor burden ran at well over 40% for the company. This company was very profitable, yet competitive with its pricing.

The key was that this company's field crew *earned* all these benefits. All had been with the company for at least eight years. They were budget- and production-oriented and they produced. An extremely high quality standard had been established and achieved throughout the company. Things were done right the first time, and mistakes were not tolerated. This company is still going strong today, and the owner still rewards his people for their results.

Another company provided similar benefits, but the field was not run properly. Project budgets and standards weren't clearly identified in the bidding process, nor were they (nor could they be) communicated clearly to the field. The owner thought he could increase productivity if he provided increased benefits (that is, labor burden). In reality, he actually rewarded his crew for poor results. This company self-destructed and is no longer in existence. Ultimately, it was the owner's fault because he failed to run his company effectively.

My point is this: vacation pay, holiday pay, health insurance plans, and so forth, don't significantly increase productivity. Not in and of themselves. They should be viewed as rewards for work well done. You can't just "throw" money and benefits at people and expect increased productivity.

If you want to *increase productivity* (any productivity), provide your people with

- Well-defined, reasonable *goals* and *budgets*
- Timely and accurate *feedback*
- Fair-market *wages*
- Results-oriented *incentives*

You won't necessarily increase productivity by increasing your labor-burden items.

CALCULATING LABOR BURDEN

Figure 7-1 on page 36 displays the labor-burden calculations for a company with multiple divisions. Office labor calculations are also included.

Perhaps your entire company consists of only construction, maintenance, irrigation, or tree service. Perhaps you choose to lump your entire labor force into one labor division. This is fine; but once a division accounts for more than 20% of your gross annual sales, I would encourage you to separate it in your financial statements and calculate its individual labor burden.

Notice that office labor burden has no labor-burden percentage figure for general liability insurance, vacation pay, holiday pay, sick pay, or medical and health insurance. These items, except for general liability insurance, are included in general and administrative (G&A) overhead totals for these people.

J.R. Huston Enterprises, Inc.

Labor Burden % Calculations by Division

	Division 1 G&A Overhead	Division 2 Lawn Maintenance	Division 3 Installation	Division 4 Irrigation Service	Division 5 Tree work	Division 6 Winter work
F.I.C.A. Rate (Company Portion)	7.65%	7.65%	7.65%	7.65%	7.65%	7.65%
F.U.T.A. Rate (Federal Unemployment)	0.80%	0.80%	0.80%	0.80%	0.80%	0.80%
S.U.T.A. Rate (State Unemployment)	3.50%	3.50%	3.50%	3.50%	3.50%	3.50%
Workers' Compensation Insurance Rate with Experience Modification	0.50%	9.00%	9.00%	9.00%	21.00%	9.00%
General Liability Insurance Rate (1)	Not Applicable	2.50%	2.50%	2.50%	2.50%	2.50%
Vacations (2)	Not Applicable	1.04%	2.47%	2.26%	2.79%	0.00%
Holidays (2)	Not Applicable	2.91%	2.47%	4.51%	2.23%	0.00%
Sick Days (2)	Not Applicable	0.00%	0.00%	0.00%	0.00%	0.00%
Medical / Health Insurance (3)	In Admin Budget	2.81%	3.73%	4.00%	3.40%	0.00%
Other	0.00%	0.00%	0.00%	0.00%	0.00%	0.00%
Other	0.00%	0.00%	0.00%	0.00%	0.00%	0.00%
Totals	**12.45%**	**30.21%**	**32.13%**	**34.22%**	**43.87%**	**23.45%**

1) General Liability Insurance: Use policy rate per hundred dollars of field payroll.

Or Annual Premium divided by	$ 6,875		
Annual Field Payroll per Policy	$ 275,000	=	2.50%

2) Percentages by Division from Worksheet #3, Field Labor Hrs & Payroll.

3) Medical / Health Insurance: Enter Total Premium by Division in this row.	$ 2,400.00	$ 2,400.00	$ 1,200.00	$ 2,400.00	$ -

FIGURE 7-1 Labor Burden Calculation

In the event an individual's payroll amount (whether based on salary or on an hourly wage) is partly in G&A overhead and partly in field payroll, split the burden amounts accordingly. For instance, if 50% of an owner's time is spent working in the field and the other 50% on administrative tasks, you should put half of the vacation time, holiday pay, sick pay, and medical insurance premiums in G&A overhead and the other half in the respective field division labor-burden category.

Please note that labor burden includes only the portion that's paid by the company for that item. The portion for FICA, FUTA, and SUTA that is taken out of an individual's gross pay is not included in our labor-burden calculations.

EXAMPLE

Calculating Labor Burden

In our calculations, we'll display decimals for percentages. For example: .27 is 27% and .008 is .8%. Some labor-burden items will have "caps." This means the rate only applies to a certain amount of payroll on each individual. For instance, a state's SUTA rate may be capped at $15,000 for any given year. This means the SUTA amount is only paid on the first $15,000 of payroll per individual per year. Accumulated payroll amounts above the $15,000 cap are exempt from the rate.

We won't apply these caps in our examples, as they are generally insignificant and very difficult to calculate accurately. However, when I prepare a budget using our budget software, it takes these caps into consideration. Use either Exhibit 4 for the United States or Exhibit 5 for Canada to calculate your labor burden.

- **Federal Insurance Contributions Act (FICA)** The present **FICA** rate is .0765 (or 7.65%). Enter .0765 into the respective columns.
- **Federal Unemployment Tax Act (FUTA)** The present **FUTA** rate is .008 (or .8%). Enter .008 into the respective columns.
- **State Unemployment Tax Act (SUTA)** Enter the appropriate **SUTA** rate for your respective state and/or county, if applicable.

If there is a ceiling (or cap) on what you have to pay for an individual (e.g., SUTA is paid on only the first $7,000 of an individual's gross annual payroll), you could use the method below to calculate the correct percentage that will be entered into labor burden. Please note that I include this example for instructional purposes only.

You have eight people on payroll. The SUTA rate is 3.5%. The SUTA ceiling is $7,000. Therefore, you pay 3.5% on the first $7,000 of payroll for a specific individual. Once payroll for the year exceeds $7,000 for that individual, you are exempt from further SUTA taxes (in this example only).

Three employees earn more than $7,000 per year, for a total of $45,000. The remaining five people earn under $7,000, for a total of $25,000. You calculate your labor burden SUTA rate as follows:

A. For the three employees earning more than the cap:

3 (# of people) × $7,000 (the cap) = $21,000

Multiply the $21,000 × .035 = $735

B. For the remaining five employees earning less than the cap:

$25,000 (combined payroll) × .035 = $875

Total projected SUTA payment: $735 + $875 = $1,610

C. Divide the total projected SUTA payment by the total projected payroll for the company (or the respective division).

$1,610 ÷ ($45,000 + $25,000) = $ 1,610 ÷ $70,000 = .023 = 2.3%

You'd use 2.3% (not 3.5%) for your SUTA labor-burden percentage.

Workers' Compensation Insurance

Enter the respective **Workers' Compensation Insurance (WCI)** percentage in the appropriate division column. Factor in your experience modification, if applicable. A WCI rate of 7% would be adjusted to 6.3% if your experience modification rate was .9, or 90%.

General Liability Insurance and Umbrella Insurance Policies

These labor-burden items are calculated for field company or division payroll only and are indicated as such on your policy.

General Liability Insurance (GLI) and **umbrella policy** rates are sometimes difficult to translate into labor-burden percentages. However, with a little effort or a phone call to your insurance agent you should be able to obtain the necessary information.

We'll combine these two types of insurance into one labor-burden percent category.

A. General Liability Insurance (GLI)
Your policy will usually display GLI insurance rates in one of two ways

1. *Rate per thousand.* This method indicates your rate as a dollar amount of premium for each $1,000 of field payroll. For instance, a rate of $29 per thousand will translate into a GLI rate of .029, or 2.9%. You divide $29 by $1,000 to obtain the rate. If you have no umbrella premium, you'd use 2.9% as your GLI labor-burden percent.
2. *Premium per total payroll.* This method simply states that your premium is based on a certain amount of payroll. If your company/division payroll is $50,000 per year and your premium is $1,450 per year, divide the annual premium by the projected payroll amount (i.e., $1,450 ÷ $50,000 = .029, or 2.9%). If you have no umbrella policy, you will again use 2.9% as your GLI labor-burden percent.

B. Umbrella Policy
If your policy includes an umbrella feature, simply divide the premium amount by the projected payroll amount on the policy. For an annual premium of $600, divide $600 by $50,000 or .012 (which is 1.2%). Add the .012 to your GLI portion (which we determined to be .029) in your GLI labor-burden percent. In this case, it would equal .041, or 4.1%. If your policy doesn't provide a projected annual payroll amount, or if you can't find the information you need to calculate your general liability insurance labor-burden percent, contact your insurance agent.

C. Average National Rates
Rates for the GLI portion of the labor-burden factor usually range from 1.5 to 3.5% nationally.

If your GLI labor-burden percent is 3.5% or higher, it's time to shop around for insurance coverage. Contact several insurance agents three to four months before your present policy expires. Be sure to provide exactly the same information to each agent for quotes. Otherwise, when you compare the quotes, you won't be comparing apples to apples.

Inform your current agent of what you're doing (if you'd like, mention that I told you to do so). You may be surprised at how creative and competitive your current carrier can be when faced with some competition.

Vacations

To obtain the labor-burden **vacation** percent, determine the total weeks of paid vacation for the field-labor force, for the company as a whole, or for a particular division. Divide that number by the total number of actual weeks worked by the company. Don't include downtime (see Chapter 8 for a detailed explanation), equipment repair time, paid holidays, paid vacations, paid sick days, and so forth in the actual weeks worked.

How It Works

To illustrate, ABC Landscaping and Irrigation Company has three field laborers who each work 40 weeks a year. The average work week per man is 45 man-hours (five days a week times nine man-hours per day). Everyone receives four paid holidays. One individual receives two weeks paid vacation during the season, another receives one week, and the third does not qualify for a paid vacation.

From reviewing past payroll records (time cards and memory), the owner determines that he'll budget 40 man-hours per season per field-crew member for downtime. Equipment repairs will total 20 man-hours per field-crew member per season.

Actual work weeks are computed as follows:

A. Dividing weeks by weeks

Total paid vacation weeks	3
Approximate total man-hours paid per year: 45 (hrs/wk) × 40 (wks/yr) × 3 (men)	5,400
Minus paid holiday man-hours: 3 (men) × 4 (days) × 8 (hrs/day)	–96
Minus paid vacation man-hours: 3 (wks) × 40 (hrs/wk)	–120
Minus projected downtime: 3 (men) × 40 (hrs/yr)	–120
Minus equipment repair time: 3 (men) × 20 (hrs/yr)	–60
Actual field worked	5,004
Convert to actual weeks worked: 5,004 man-hours ÷ 45 average man-hours/week	111
Convert to vacation labor-burden decimal: Divide vacation weeks by actual weeks worked 3 paid vacation weeks ÷ 111 work weeks = .027 or 2.7%	.027

B. Dividing man-hours by man-hours (a more accurate method)

Total vacation man-hours: 3 paid vacation weeks × 40 hrs/wk	120
Total actual man-hours worked	5,004
Vacation labor burden percent: 120 man-hours ÷ 5,004 man-hours worked = .024 or 2.4%	

Comparison

Notice that if we hadn't deducted downtime man-hours, holidays, and so on from our actual weeks worked, our vacation labor-burden decimal would have been higher in both cases.

Method "A"

5,400 man-hours ÷ 45 man-hours/week = 120 actual weeks worked

3 paid vacation weeks ÷ 120 = .025 or 2.5%

Method "B"

Paid vacation man-hours = 120 ÷ 5,400 (approximate total man-hours paid) = .0222 or 2.2%

It's not a lot of difference, but the higher decimals (.024 and .027) are more accurate calculations.

Holidays

Because we've already done most of the work determining the vacation labor-burden decimal, calculating **holiday** labor burden will be much easier. Let's continue to use the above example.

A. **Dividing days by days**
Total paid holidays: 3 (men) × 4 (paid holidays) = 12 total paid holidays
Total man-days worked per year:

5,004 actual man-hours worked per year ÷ 9 man-hours per day per man = 5,00 ÷ 9 = 556 man-days per year

Holiday labor burden decimal: = 12 ÷ 556 = .0216 or 2.16%

B. **Dividing man-hours by man-hours**
Total paid holiday man-hours:

(12 days × 8 man-hours/day) = 96

Total man-hours worked per year = 5,004

Holiday labor burden decimal: = 96 ÷ 5,004 = .0192 or 1.92%

Of the two methods, "B" is the more accurate, although a little more complex. However, either is accurate enough for our purposes.

! Reminder

Consider only the field-labor holidays, vacation time, and so forth when calculating the GLI, vacation, holiday, sick days, and medical/health insurance portions of labor burden. Put a portion (e.g., 50%) of a person's paid vacations, premiums, etc., in the labor-burden totals if that person is actually working in the field for a portion of his or her total work time.

Sick Days (sometimes referred to as "well" days)

If you provide paid time off to your field employees when they're sick, compute **sick days** or **well days** into the appropriate company/division labor-burden decimal just as you did for the holiday labor-burden calculations.

Use this method for any other similar type of benefit provided by the company.

Medical/Health Insurance

Divide total annual **medical/health insurance** premiums paid by the company, which are not reimbursed by the employees, by the company/division projected total annual field payroll.

Total premiums paid by company \$3,300 ÷ total projected field payroll \$75,000 = \$3,300 ÷ \$75,000 = .044 or 4.4%

When I compile a budget for a company, I actually deduct holiday, vacation, and sick pay, as well as pay for downtime and equipment repairs, from the total projected field payroll. However, I use a personal computer and a somewhat sophisticated spreadsheet program to do so. The above method will suffice for our purposes.

In the United States your labor burden percent for field divisions will normally fall between 20 and 35%. In Canada (and elsewhere outside the United States) it normally runs from the high teens to the mid-twenties.

Companies outside the United States can use the same methods shown in our examples, making the appropriate category adjustments.

SUMMARY

Labor burden is primarily comprised of payroll taxes, unemployment taxes, and various forms of insurance. Field-labor burden also includes general liability insurance, paid holidays, sick days, vacation time, and medical insurance benefits. Other items such as employer 401K and retirement contributions could also be included.

Both field-labor burden and office-labor burden are calculated as percentages and added to payroll costs in our budget. The field-labor burden is also directly used in the estimating process.

Field-labor burden is a direct cost, while office-labor burden is an indirect G&A cost.

Labor-burden items should be viewed as incentives that have to be earned by everyone as a result of productivity in the office and the field.

Future labor-burden costs are often overlooked. They should be monitored and the funds accumulated in a savings account. Otherwise, they may be forgotten and the funds spent.

ACTION POINT

Use Exhibit 4 in the back of the book to determine your company/division labor-burden percentages for companies in the United States.

Use Exhibit 5 in the back of the book to determine your company/division labor-burden percentages for companies in Canada.

CHAPTER

8

General and Administrative Overhead

TERMS

Asset Tax
Bad Debts
Corporate Overhead Per Hour (COPH)
Divisions Overhead Per Hour (DOPH)
Downtime Labor
Fair Market Value (FMV)
General and Administrative (G&A) Overhead
Indirect Costs
Leasehold Improvements
Licenses
Mill Tax
Opportunity Cost
Professional Fees
Small Tools
Surety Bonds
Total Overhead Per Hour (TOPH)
Yard Expense

Purpose

To define the categories contained in the general and administrative overhead budget

Introduction

We will now turn our attention to the estimating budget for **general and administrative (G&A) overhead** budget costs. It is significant that we combine the terms *general and administrative* and *overhead.* We want to define our terms precisely and clearly throughout the estimating process. The term *overhead* is probably abused most often within estimating circles. Sometimes labor burden, as we define it, is called labor overhead. General conditions are sometimes referred to as indirect job overhead. For our purposes, "overhead" will appear only in reference to general and administrative overhead.

Quite often contractors either overlook or have no systematic way to allocate G&A overhead costs to their jobs, and it gets them into big trouble. Our objective is to define G&A overhead costs, allocate them to our divisions if appropriate, and ensure that they are bid into our jobs.

GENERAL AND ADMINISTRATIVE OVERHEAD PARAMETERS

This budget is for the next 12 months, which may or may not be the same as your fiscal year or for the period designated for tax purposes. For instance, if your tax year is the same as the calendar year and it is the middle of July, you can still prepare a G&A overhead budget for the next 12 months and use that for estimating purposes. This is perfectly legitimate. You don't have to be at the very beginning of your fiscal year, or your tax year, to prepare a G&A overhead budget.

Remember, this is a **fair market value** budget. Not all categories in your estimating G&A overhead budget will reflect actual cash flow expenses, nor will they be the same as the expenses expressed on your profit and loss (P&L) statement. The P&L statement is designed to meet legal tax accounting requirements and standards. Consequently, those categories (as defined by tax law) are not necessarily the ones we'll use for estimating purposes.

We will use *historical data* as we prepare our G&A overhead estimating budget, but only as a point of reference. Just because there is a specific amount in last year's P&L statement doesn't mean we're going to use that same amount for our projected budget. We'll look at each category and ask ourselves: Will that amount *increase* or *decrease* over the next 12-month period? We'll then make the appropriate adjustments for purposes of budget projections.

If you are in a *start-up situation*, you can still prepare an estimating G&A overhead budget—but without the use of historical data. You'll simply approximate your expenses and make your projections as accurately as possible.

It is very important that we don't include anything in G&A overhead categories that can be directly tied to a job. Job-related expenses on specific bids should be included in direct costs and not in G&A overhead. We refer to G&A overhead costs as **indirect costs.** As such, they can't be broken down and bid into jobs as specific costs incurred on a job. For instance, how much of your monthly office electricity bill should you allocate to a half-day job of removing a tree from Mrs. Jones' backyard? There's simply no practical way to make this G&A overhead cost a direct cost.

Although we'll break down G&A overhead into 28 different categories, keep in mind that it is not as important in which category we place an expense item as it is to ensure that the item is included somewhere in G&A overhead.

If necessary, we'll divisionalize our G&A overhead. If you have more than one division and you wish to have separate budgets for each, we can take each expense category and attempt to place the appropriate amount of G&A overhead expense in the respective division. This can get somewhat complicated. In some cases you'll have to make calculated guesses to arrive at what you think is a fairly accurate number.

How It Works

If you have three divisions with equal sales and a $12,000 annual expense budgeted for telephone costs, you can put $4,000 into each division's annual budget for these costs. However, what do you do if one division has budgeted sales of $1.2 million and the other two divisions have budgeted sales of $300,000 each?

Because some G&A overhead costs are impossible to separate and accurately allocate to specific divisions (how much of your office electric bill should be put in your landscape installation division as compared to in your maintenance division?), I simply allocate an amount of G&A overhead costs to each division. Often I take the total company G&A overhead as a percent of the total annual sales and allocate that percentage to each division.

EXAMPLE

G&A Allocation

If total G&A overhead costs are 20% of the total company sales, I multiply the division sales by 20% to calculate the G&A overhead for that division. Or I might allocate G&A overhead costs to a division based on a G&A overhead per hour (OPH) basis. For instance, a construction division usually has an OPH of about $12 per field-labor hour. To obtain the G&A overhead for that division, I will multiply the total billable budgeted field-labor hours for the division by the $12 OPH. That gives you the G&A overhead for the division.

You can also use a combination of the two methods. However, the important thing is to ensure that all your budgeted G&A overhead costs are allocated to and recovered in your divisions.

Large corporations, generally those with over $10 million in gross annual sales (or over 7 or 8 divisions), may desire to have corporate as well as division G&A

overhead budgets. The corporate budget would include the same categories as the division ones but would be specifically for costs for the corporate G&A overhead staff and related expenses. Corporate G&A overhead would then be allocated to divisions and jobs being bid within those divisions as an addition to the division G&A overhead per hour (OPH) cost.

Corporate general and administrative (G&A) overhead should then be allocated to divisions in one of two ways.

1. Total corporate G&A overhead could be allocated to divisions as a lump-sum dollar amount, which individual divisions would add to their G&A overhead budget as an additional line item.
2. Total corporate G&A overhead could be divided by the sum total of all field-labor hours contained in all divisions. This calculation would produce a **corporate overhead per hour (COPH)**, which would then be added to the **divisions overhead per hour (DOPH)** for each division to produce a **total overhead per hour (TOPH)**. The TOPH (which would be different for each division) would be used by divisions for estimating purposes.

Corporate G&A overhead could also be allocated to divisions a third way, as a percentage of sales, but the above two methods are much more accurate and manageable. Of the two methods described above, I personally prefer the latter.

G&A overhead is frequently 20% ± 8% as a percent of sales. Large companies with sales over $10 million will usually have a G&A overhead cost in the mid-teen range. Smaller companies under $1 million in sales will usually have a G&A overhead cost ranging from 20 to 28%.

For this chapter, you will need the following items:

- Your previous year-end P&L statement
- Your latest P&L statement
- A calculator
- Pencils (and an eraser)
- Scratch pads
- A copy of the budget format. See Exhibit 1 in the back of the book.
- Insurance policies for office contents, medical, dental, and keyman insurance
- Applicable budget spreadsheets

Let's now examine, in detail, the estimating budget categories:

GENERAL AND ADMINISTRATIVE OVERHEAD CATEGORIES

1. Advertising Advertising, or promotion, would include the following items:

"Yellow Page" Advertisements You'll usually find this expense included in your monthly telephone bill. Make sure you include only that portion pertaining to the advertising section listing.

Company Brochure *(printing costs, artwork, design, etc.)* Be sure to prorate these costs; that is, spread them out over a period of time in order to reflect the periods of actual use, not the period in which the entire expenditure is incurred. For instance, if you purchase a three-year supply of a company brochure and the cost is $6,000, don't place the entire expenditure in this year's estimating G&A overhead budget. That isn't fair to this year's clients.

For estimating purposes, place only one-third of that expense (or $2,000) in this year's budget.

Newspaper Advertisements

Help-Wanted Advertisements

Magazine Advertisements

Billboards

Door Hangers, Flyers, Business Cards, etc.

Bulk and Direct Mail Expenses

Garden, Trade or Home Shows *(expenses for materials, labor, booth/space fees, etc.)*

Company Resumes *(graphics and printing costs, etc.)*

Website Development You should enter the cost for your company to develop a Web site. I'd prorate these costs over a three-year period. If it cost $4,500 to have someone design a Web site for you, I'd enter $1,500 in the G&A overhead estimating budget.

Website Maintenance Fees Expenses for maintaining and updating your Web site should be included in this category, along with the telephone line or high-speed Internet access line.

Garden or Home Shows *(where you have a display and/or booth)*

All Other Advertising I usually limit advertising to no more than 1% of a company or division's gross annual sales.

2. Bad Debts **Bad debts** are money owed to you by customers; money that you don't expect to collect. I usually limit bad debts to .5 to 1% of gross annual sales.

If you do a lot of government work, small jobs, or maintenance work, limit bad debts to ½ of 1% of your gross sales. If you do a lot of commercial work or large jobs for clients you don't know well, I'd raise this to 1%.

Again, base this on historical data. However, if you have a rather large, substantial bad debt ($30,000 to $50,000 from the past year or past few years), you can't put the entire amount in your G&A overhead budget. You have to "cap" the figure. Otherwise, your bids won't be competitive. You can't charge future clients for the "sins of the past" in G&A overhead. Some of it will have to be taken out of net profit.

3. Computers, Software, Hardware, and Digitizers Included in this category are the purchase of computers, software, hardware, and digitizers, and training for the use of same (if not included in Item 22, Training and Education).

I generally depreciate these amounts over a three- to five-year period. If you purchase a rather expensive accounting system, which for software alone can easily cost $10,000 to $25,000, spread that expense over a five- to ten-year period, depending on the anticipated useful life of the software. Include any anticipated upgrade expenses. Spread the cost of computer hardware over a three-year period. I generally like to recoup expenses for hardware within three years. Because of technological advances, plan to replace that computer at the end of the three-year period. Included in this category would be training costs, consultants for in-house training of your staff, and any maintenance contracts and repairs on subject equipment (unless these costs are in Item 22, Training and Education).

Digitizers come in three types: table models, electronic arms, and sonic measuring devices. These machines usually last a long time. Depending on what you think is reasonable, spread the expense over a five- to seven-year period.

If the costs for computer-aided design (CAD) hardware and software exceed $10,000, spread this cost over a seven- to ten-year period. Otherwise, depreciate them over a three- to five-year period.

4. Donations Donations are comprised of cash donations, labor, and/or equipment costs incurred for charitable work your company performs in your community. For instance, if you donate cash to the YMCA, a civic project, or a charity, include that in this category. If you donate a crew to work a half-day at a local church or community park, include the labor and equipment costs in this category as well.

Another donation might be the sponsorship of a Little League team. If your name is on the uniforms, you can underwrite that cost in this category. I think it best to put the cost in "advertising," but the important thing is to include it somewhere in G&A overhead.

I would not include donations that are driven by tax accounting purposes in this category. If at the end of the tax year, your accountant says you have accumulated excess profits (I can never understand that term, *excess profits*) and recommends some donations, don't include them in G&A overhead and attempt to charge them to next year's clients. Consider this a donation from net profit.

For the purposes of estimating G&A overhead, I like to cap the total amount of donations at between $500 and $1,000. Anything more than that should be deducted from net profit. If you put too much into this G&A overhead category, it's really your clients who are making the donations. You are merely the one taking the tax deduction.

5. Downtime Labor These are the man-hours that field crews are being paid when they're not working in the field (or producing billable man-hours). Tabulate **downtime labor** in man-hours, then multiply the man-hours by your average wage.

This can include paid labor man-hours for the following:

Bad Weather During bad weather field crews may work in the office, nursery, yard, or elsewhere. It also includes lost man-hours when crews are non-productive in the field due to weather conditions, but are still being paid.

Equipment Breakdown Time *(to and from jobs)* For instance, if a crew pickup truck breaks down en route to a job resulting in a two to three man-hour wait for repairs or replacement transportation, include this in downtime man-hours.

Busywork Busywork includes fixing small tools, cleaning or repairing the office or yard area, and other nonspecific work.

Field-Crew Meetings, Tailgate Meetings, Safety Meetings, and Seminars Total this time and include it in downtime. As an example: If you consistently have 10 people in the field and if you hold a 30-minute safety meeting once a week, this totals 5.0 man-hours per week of downtime (10 people × .5 man-hours = 5.0 man-hours per week).

Nursery Watering Time If your nursery isn't a separate division on your financial statement, watering time for nursery stock by your crew should be included in downtime. However, if your nursery is a separate division, the labor expended on it should be included in direct labor costs for that division.

Two important notes:

- The time spent on equipment repair is not included in downtime; it is incorporated as a portion of equipment costs.
- Drive time for the crew, mobilization of equipment to and from job sites, material acquisition and hauling, and so forth are excluded from this category. These expenses are included under "general conditions" in a specific bidding situation.

EXAMPLE

Calculating Downtime Annual Cost

Total downtime man-hours for the year and multiply by your company/division average wage.

Downtime man-hours normally average one to one-and-one-half man-hours per week per full-time field employee. If you have 10 people in the field 40 weeks a year, downtime man-hours will probably total between 400 to 600 man-hours per year.

40 weeks per year × 10 men × 1 man-hour per week = 40 × 10 × 1 = 400 man-hours per year

40 weeks per year × 10 men × 1.5 man-hours per week = 40 × 10 × 1.5 = 600 man-hours per year

6. Downtime Labor Burden Multiply your company/division field-labor burden by the dollar amount in Item 5 (downtime labor). Enter this amount in your budget for downtime labor burden.

7. Dues and Subscriptions This includes dues, fees, subscriptions, and membership charges for the following:

Various State and National Associations or Organizations

Chamber of Commerce

Better Business Bureau

Professional Magazines

Dodge Reports

Plan Rooms

Green Sheets

Business-Related Publications

Discount Outlets and Warehouse Store Dues/Memberships

8. Insurance This includes insurance for

Office Contents

Dental and Medical Insurance for G&A Overhead Personnel This includes benefits for owners, secretaries, receptionists, administrative help, accountants, bookkeepers, estimators, field supervisors, and anyone else whose hours you cannot directly account for within specific bid calculations.

Keyman Insurance for Corporate Officers This is included when the company or corporation is the beneficiary.

Notice that we're not including within this section any policy premiums for vehicle and equipment coverage, general liability or umbrella insurance, or insurance on buildings.

9. Interest and Bank Charges

Interest on Credit Cards

Interest on Your Line of Credit

Start-Up Fees for Establishing Your Line of Credit

Interest on Outstanding Debts to Your Suppliers

Bank Fees *(service charges, penalties, bounced check fees, etc.)*

Credit Card Processing Fees

If you have no line of credit, then you're using the company's retained earnings to finance your business and provide working capital. This amount is normally equal to four or five weeks of payroll.

Since this amount is usually tied up and being used by the company throughout the year, you should multiply this amount by the current savings interest rate (as though it were deposited in a savings or money market account and drawing interest) and include the interest portion here as a cost of money expense.

This is a legitimate expense item to include within G&A overhead. If you did have a line of credit you'd be paying interest on it, and we'd put that interest payment in G&A overhead. Because the company is providing its own line of credit, you can't place these funds into a savings account. Therefore, you're losing the interest you'd normally collect from placing that money in the bank. In financial terms this is called an **opportunity cost**. Although there's no actual cash transaction involved, it's reasonable or *fair market value* to include this cost here.

Note that this category does not include interest on past-due receivables (money owed to you), interest on equipment loans, or interest on your mortgage for your office building (or space).

10. Licenses and Surety Bonds This includes the fees for your state contractor and city business **licenses** (if applicable) and the cost of the **surety bond** (not a performance bond) on your license. However, in many cases city licenses for specific jobs should be included in general conditions for that job, not in G&A overhead.

11. Office Equipment This includes new purchases, repairs, and service contracts for office equipment. It does not include any item of (or related to) field equipment, G&A overhead vehicles, computers, telephones, radios, beepers, pagers, or digitizers. For new equipment that you expect to purchase during the budget period, divide the cost by its useful life expectancy and include the cost for one year in this category.

For office equipment presently on hand, list the items using their replacement cost at new fair market value (FMV) prices. Then divide the FMV replacement cost by the useful life expectancy. Enter that amount in this category.

File Cabinets and Durable Furniture *(desks, tables, sofas and chairs)* These items usually last at least ten years. Although some items may last longer, you want to recoup their costs within ten years.

Copy Machines The cost of a copy machine can be spread over three to five years, depending on its estimated useful life. Supplies and toner are included in office supplies costs.

Blueprint Machines These can be depreciated over a 10-year period.

Calculators *(1 to 2 years)*

Plan Racks and Drafting Tables *(10 years)*

Typewriters *(manual—10 years)*

Typewriters *(electric—10 years)*

Refrigerators, Microwave Ovens, etc. *(5 to 7 years)*

Plants, Pictures, Artwork, Paintings, etc.

Many high-end residential construction companies bring their clients to their offices. Considerable expense is often incurred in order to make a favorable impression. This cost should be included in G&A overhead as a legitimate cost of doing business. Depreciate artwork, pictures, etc., over a 10-year period. Plant costs should be spread over just 1 year.

12. Office Supplies Office supplies are consumable items that are used on a regular basis. They include

Pens, Pencils, Paper, Paper Clips, and Miscellaneous Items

Paper and Toner or Cartridges for Copiers, Computers, Fax Machines

Printing Costs *(letterhead, forms, artwork, etc.)*

Stationery

Postage

13. Professional Fees **Professional fees** include the following:

CPA or Bookkeeper *(one not on your regular payroll)*

End-of-Year Tax Preparation

Legal Fees A reasonable legal fee amount is between $500 and $1,000 per year. This covers having an attorney scrutinize your policy manuals, write a few routine letters, the costs for your annual corporate meeting, and so forth.

This fee does not cover costs for litigation. It is unreasonable to put this expense into G&A overhead; consequently, it must come out of profits. The premise is that it's not reasonable to charge next year's clients for the "sins of the past."

Outside Payroll Services

Consultants This item includes consultants other than those for your computer, which are in the computer G&A overhead category.

Incorporation Costs These costs can be spread over a three- to five-year period.

14. Radio Systems, Beepers/Pagers, and Car/Mobile Telephones

Two-Way Radio Systems Depreciate the purchase price over a 10-year useful lifetime period. Include monthly repeater and/or line charges.

Beepers and Pagers Include monthly service charges.

Cellular Telephone Depreciate the purchase price over a two-year period. Also include monthly toll and usage charges.

Maintenance, Maintenance Contracts, Repairs for Radios, Pagers and Cellular Telephones

15. Rent (Office and Yard) Use fair market value, especially if you own the facilities. For instance, if you had to rent a similar facility on the open market, what would you have to pay? Quite often, your monthly mortgage payment may be much lower than fair market value. Even if your facility is paid for, it's reasonable to include a fair market value rent in your G&A overhead.

Remember, don't confuse your estimating G&A overhead budget with your tax accounting budget (or financial statement) where you account for your actual or "real" payment. You need to place a reasonable fair market value amount of expense for rent within your G&A overhead budget. You also need to account for your property (and/or asset) taxes on the facilities and fire insurance on the building. If you rent your office and yard space, enter that amount in this category.

16. Salaries for Office Personnel These are individuals who are not corporate officers, partners, or owners. Included are the following:

Bookkeepers

Office Manager

Secretaries

Receptionists

Estimators

Designers *(administrative portion of salary only, if applicable)*

Field Supervisor Attempt to allocate as much of a supervisor's time as possible to specific jobs in the field. If a supervisor generally spends half of the day in the field supervising and working on jobs and the other half doing administrative work, then put 50% of his or her salary in G&A overhead. The other 50% will be bid into jobs. Prorate supervisor salaries (50/50, 60/40, 25/75) to coincide as closely as possible with where they actually spend their time.

Anyone in the Office *(other than salespeople)* Sales commissions are usually included in direct costs. See Chapter 4 for an extensive discussion on commissions and sales personnel.

17. Salaries for Corporate Officers, Owners, and Partners Calculate officers' salaries according to fair market value. If a corporate officer were working for another company, what salary could that person expect to be paid? If you were to hire another person to run your company in place of the owner, what should that person expect as adequate, reasonable compensation?

It's important to realize that this amount may not equal actual ("real") pay. However, for estimating purposes we must place in G&A overhead what's *reasonable*—that is, the fair market value amount for that individual.

The total for combined office and officer salaries should be between 8 and 12% of gross annual sales.

For example, some of my clients who are owners prefer to draw less than a fair market value salary (only $400 to $500 per week) and keep the extra money working within the company. Other clients choose to take far more than a fair market value salary; but it's not reasonable to put all this amount into G&A overhead for estimating purposes. It would make bids too high. Even though officers' "real" pay may be more or less, we still estimate G&A overhead costs using a fair market value amount in G&A overhead. (The total for combined office and officer salaries should be between 8 and 12% of gross annual sales.)

If your company is a large commercial operation doing over $10 million in annual sales, the total of these two categories will probably be below 8%. Extremely large companies, well over $10 million in annual sales, will be even lower. Smaller commercial and high-end residential companies will run about 12%. You should not exceed these percentages in G&A overhead. If actual pay for office staff and officer(s) combined exceeds target percentages, don't put the excess in G&A overhead. Rather, make a net profit adjustment at the bottom of your budget (after net profit margin) for additional excess salaries or bonuses. Then work on increasing sales. This will bring your percentages in line.

18. Salary Labor Burden This amount is determined by multiplying the office labor-burden percentage by the total salaries for office personnel and corporate officers. It covers FICA, FUTA, SUTA, WCI, and so on. This percentage is discussed in detail in Chapter 7, Labor Burden.

19. Small Tools and Supplies This includes any **small** (non-motorized) **tools** or supplies you purchase throughout the year for general use and not for particular jobs. For example

Wheelbarrows

Hand Tools

Rakes, Shovels, Hoes, Tarps

Paint, Nails, Wire

Miscellaneous Hardware

Bags for Grass Clippings

This doesn't include purchase or repair costs for lawnmowers, chainsaws, weedeaters, blowers, edgers, trimmers, etc. These are a direct cost expense and are included in direct equipment costs.

20. Taxes (Equipment/Asset Tax or Mill Tax on Business) Some cities or counties will charge an **asset tax**, which is a percentage of the total value of your equipment and assets. Asset taxes on field equipment and facilities (office space and/or yards) are not included in this category. Only asset tax on office equipment (furniture, computers, etc.) is included. Asset taxes on facilities are accounted for within "rent." Asset taxes on field equipment should be included in hourly rates for the same.

Mill taxes are rare, although they do exist. A mill tax is a general tax based on sales. It usually runs no more than $200 to $300 per year.

This category does not include company or corporate state and/or federal income taxes. These taxes are paid out of net profit.

21. Telephones

Monthly Line Charges

Long-Distance Charges

Telephone Rental *(if applicable)*

Answering or Voice Mail Services

Telephone Systems This includes the purchase and/or installation price depreciated over a 5- to 10-year period.

Repairs and/or Maintenance Contracts for Telephone Equipment

Answering Machines and/or Fax Machines

DSL Line or Internet Cable Fees

22. Training and Education

Books, Audio Tapes, Videos, etc.

Workshops and Seminar Registration Fees

Community College/Continuing Education Classes

Convention Entrance and Registration Fees *(garden and home shows, etc.)*

Video and Digital Cameras

There is no pat answer as to how much should be spent on training and education. The key is to determine whether your people are being trained and educated properly to run the systems that are needed in your company. If you are spending your money wisely and getting results, you can invest almost any reasonable amount in training and education.

23. Travel and Entertainment

Travel Costs to Seminars, Workshops, Conventions

Hotel Bills *(directly associated with the above)*

Lunches and Dinners *(including those for clients)*

Gifts for Clients and Employees This includes the company Christmas party, company season tickets to sporting events, and so on.

24. Uniforms and Safety Equipment

T-Shirts and Ball Caps for Crews

Uniform Rental/Cleaning Services

Safety Equipment Includes items not included in small tools and supplies such as goggles, gloves, ear protectors, hard hats, etc.

Cold Weather Gear

25. Utilities

Monthly Water, Electric, and Sewer Bill for Office/Yard

Heating Gas (or oil) for the Office/Yard

Trash Service or a Dumpster that's Not Job-Related

Office Janitorial Service

Security Service

Trash Dumpster for the Yard

➤ **NOTE** Be careful not to include expenses for nurseries, which are a separate division and incur large wintertime expenses for heating, in another division's G&A overhead expense.

26. Vehicles, G&A Overhead (Vehicles used by G&A overhead personnel)

Automobiles and Pickup Trucks This category does not include crew pickup trucks.

Mileage Reimbursement for Private Vehicles

➤ **NOTE** For personnel whose salaries are accounted for in both field labor and office categories, prorate vehicle expenses between the categories as you do salaries for individuals using the vehicles.

27. Yard Expense (Leasehold Improvements)

Yard Expenses This includes costs associated with maintaining a nursery area, installing mulch beds or drip irrigation, spreading gravel over a driveway, putting up a fence, etc.

Leasehold Improvements to Your Office The following are depreciated over the life of the improvements:

- Carpeting
- Painting Costs
- Partitions
- Various Tenant Improvements, etc.

For instance, if you install carpeting and padding for $2,500 and its projected useful life is 10 years, divide the $2,500 by 10. This amounts to $250 per year and should be included in leasehold improvements.

Building an entire building on your property is not a leasehold improvement to be included here. This cost should be accounted for by a fair market value increase in monthly rent.

Costs for storage yard or nursery area improvements might involve

- Fences
- Gravel Spread over Driveways
- Nursery Mulch Beds
- Drip Irrigation for Nursery Areas

Again, these costs should be depreciated over the useful life expectancy of the improvement involved.

Generally, labor expended for leasehold improvements is included in downtime labor.

28. Miscellaneous Listings under this category should be kept to a minimum, preferably under $500 ($1,000 at most). All, or most, of your expenses should be in the categories previously listed.

I once had dealings with a company that had a miscellaneous category of over $57,000. I told that company it needed a little better idea of where the money was being spent. Miscellaneous is not a catchall category. You can't just lump everything together here. You need to define G&A overhead expenses in order to have effective control of them.

SUMMARY

Bidding G&A overhead costs into jobs is often overlooked by contractors. Fair market values for G&A overhead items are calculated based on historical data, if available. If good historical data isn't available or if a contractor is in a start-up situation, costs are estimated for the upcoming budget year.

Some G&A overhead categories tend to overlap (for instance, advertising and donations). This doesn't matter. The key is to be consistent with your definitions and to continue to put the same item in the same category year after year.

Because there is no accurate or practical way to put G&A overhead costs into a bid as a specific cost for doing the job, they are referred to as indirect costs as compared to direct costs. Often G&A overhead costs are divisionalized and allocated to separate divisions within the company. Each division will then allocate its portion of G&A overhead costs to jobs being bid throughout the year.

The format we're using is a profit and loss (P&L) statement for a corporation. Even though you may be a sole proprietorship, for estimating budget and bidding purposes you should still use this format and enter a salary for yourself into your G&A overhead budget.

You should keep in mind that the items and amounts on your CPA/accountant's P&L statement are going to look a little different from the ones described in this chapter. The format used here is for estimating purposes and is somewhat different than a tax accounting P&L statement.

ACTION POINTS

Use Exhibit 1 in the back of the book and fill in the different categories for your G&A overhead budget. Use Exhibit 6, which is a recap of the different categories, to help you in this exercise.

CHAPTER

9

Equipment Costs

TERMS

Acquisition Cost Per Hour
Cost Per Hour (CPH)
Fuel Cost Per Hour
Lifetime Hours
Maintenance Cost Per Hour
Meter Time
Mileage Rates
Useful Life

Purpose

To calculate both field and general and administrative (G&A) overhead equipment and vehicle costs for budgeting purposes

To differentiate between direct field equipment, trucks, and G&A overhead vehicle costs

To calculate equipment cost per hour amounts for the various types of equipment and vehicles in your company/division

Introduction

The best method for budgeting equipment (or any item) is to review historical data as a point of reference and then make the appropriate adjustments for the budget period being developed. However, this isn't always possible. If you're in a start-up situation or if your historical data is unavailable, inaccurate, or not properly formatted, you must make educated calculations (guesstimates).

It is important to understand the reasoning behind differentiating direct field equipment and truck costs, which are bid into jobs based on **costs per hour (CPH)** and the number of hours to be used on a specific job, and indirect (or G&A overhead) vehicle costs. The latter is bid into individual jobs as a part of G&A overhead costs.

Some estimating systems place all equipment costs (tractors, pickups, dump trucks, G&A overhead vehicles, etc.) into G&A overhead and allocate them to specific jobs in their G&A overhead markup. This is usually shown as an overall percentage markup or as a specific dollar amount multiplied by estimated field-labor hours on a particular job. This method is inaccurate. Whether you're in a construction or a maintenance bidding situation, it invariably understates or overstates the actual equipment costs for the job being bid.

Our goal is (1) to identity correctly specific equipment costs on a per hour basis, and (2) to multiply that specific hourly cost by the estimated number of hours a particular piece of equipment is to be used on a particular job. We do this in order to determine the total amount of equipment cost we'll bid into each individual job.

If the job requires only pickup trucks and wheelbarrows, then we want to include only those costs in the bid. If, on the other hand, the job requires dozers, large dump trucks, and tractors, we want to include those costs in the bid. Including all equipment costs in G&A overhead and indiscriminately spreading them evenly like peanut butter over all your jobs precludes accurate and competitive bidding. Refer to Chapters 11 and 12 for a more detailed discussion of bidding equipment on your projects.

BUDGETING FOR EQUIPMENT COSTS

If you are in a start-up situation or lack accurate historical data on equipment costs, use either the percent of sales or the equipment-to-labor ratio method outlined in Chapter 10 to calculate your projected annual equipment cost budget.

If you have accurate company/division historical data for both direct equipment and G&A overhead vehicle cost, make appropriate adjustments to your projected equipment budget by using one (or a combination) of the following methods:

1. Increase or decrease direct equipment costs (including repairs and maintenance costs at market rates, in-house mechanics, fuel, and depreciation) by the same percentage of projected increase or decrease in sales. For example, if gross annual sales are projected to increase by 15%, increase direct equipment costs by the same amount.
2. Increase or decrease budget projections for direct equipment costs by multiplying the historical percentage (the percent of previous gross annual sales allotted to direct equipment) by the projected amount of gross annual sales. For example, if direct equipment costs have historically been 8% of gross annual sales, multiply (for budget purposes) next year's projected gross annual sales by 8% to obtain projected direct equipment costs for next year's budget.
3. This third method is possible only if you've established a formal equipment division with its own P&L statement and have accumulated accurate maintenance and repair costs for each piece of equipment. If you are adding, replacing, or deleting field equipment, they increase or decrease your projected budget costs as follows:

   A. Cost out the piece of equipment that's being added or deleted by using the costing section of this chapter (to determine its CPH) and the cost data accumulated in your accounting software. Divide real costs accumulated by actual meter hours on the piece of equipment.

   B. Multiply the CPH by the projected increase or decrease in hours used.

   C. Adjust your projected costs accordingly.

   If you are replacing a piece of equipment with one that has the same CPH, there's no need to adjust your projected costs unless the projected hours of use will increase or decrease significantly (that is, by 15 to 20%). In that case, you'd adjust the projected cost to reflect the change in hours used.

   If the replacement equipment CPH differs from the original (and the projected use hours are roughly the same), multiply the difference in CPH by the projected hours used and adjust projected costs accordingly. For example:

   $15 (new CPH) minus $12 (old CPH) = $3

   $3 (CPH difference) × 1,000 (projected use hours) = $3,000 to be added to projected costs

   If hours of use are also projected to change, calculate that change in your adjusted cost.

Once you've calculated total costs for the budget year for each piece of equipment in your company, combine all the totals to determine your total equipment cost budget for the year. Add G&A overhead vehicle costs to the field equipment total. Your new total is now your equipment division's sales or income budget for the year. You'll achieve this sales goal as you "rent" equipment at cost to the other divisions throughout the year.

As you accumulate sales, you'll also accumulate costs on your equipment division P&L statement. Repair parts cost, in-house mechanics, mechanics' tools and vehicles, and repair work done outside the company are entered as direct costs: as materials, labor, equipment, and subcontractor costs, respectively. G&A overhead for the equipment division is calculated just as in Chapter 8.

The goal of the equipment division is to break even. Sales to other divisions are calculated at the predetermined CPH multiplied by the hours used by that division. This amount is then charged to the respective divisions as an equipment direct cost.

The goal of the equipment division is to break even.

If you've accurately projected your usage hours and your CPH for each piece of equipment, sales in the equipment division should equal the sum of all costs, both direct and G&A overhead. If your equipment division doesn't break even, review your costs and meter hours for each piece of equipment to determine where you went wrong.

G&A Overhead Vehicle Costs

Even if you have accurate historical cost data for G&A overhead vehicles and associated costs, these costs don't necessarily increase or decrease in direct proportion to sales.

You could easily increase sales by 15 to 25% without adding another G&A overhead vehicle. Consequently, costs remain the same. You only adjust your G&A overhead vehicle costs if the number of G&A overhead vehicles varies.

To determine G&A overhead vehicle cost:

1. Identify the specific vehicles to be included in G&A overhead. These will be the company-owned vehicles used by persons listed in the "G&A overhead salary" category. (If a person's salary is only partially included in G&A overhead, then a corresponding percentage of any related vehicle cost will be included in G&A overhead.)
2. Determine the CPH for the G&A overhead vehicle (e.g., $6 per hour).
3. Multiply the CPH for the respective vehicles by the projected hours of use. For example:

   $6 CPH × 2,080 (52 weeks × 40 hours per week) hours for full-time G&A overhead vehicle use

   $6 CPH × 1,040 hours for 50% part-time G&A overhead vehicle use

4. Add projected mileage reimbursed to G&A overhead personnel for use of their personal vehicles (and any other G&A overhead vehicle expense) to the totals for company-owned vehicles. Place this amount into your projected G&A overhead budget.

For tax purposes, you may have a number of G&A overhead vehicles that appear on your P&L statement. Unless realistically these vehicles are used in direct support of G&A overhead personnel, you can't include all their costs in your estimating budget. Your bids will not be competitive. Again, what's real isn't always what's reasonable to put in your estimating G&A overhead budget. Ask yourself if all these vehicles really reflect fair market value expenses. For instance, if you have only two people in G&A overhead, you can't list four vehicles (at 2,080 hours each) in your estimating G&A overhead budget. It's just not realistic or reasonable to do so.

If you don't have reliable company/division historical data to use for budget projections or if you're in a start-up situation for a company or division, use a percentage of labor as outlined in Appendix E to project direct equipment costs. To calculate G&A overhead vehicle costs, use the procedures described earlier in this chapter.

CALCULATING EQUIPMENT COST PER HOUR

There are two reasons for calculating the cost per hour (CPH) for a piece of equipment. You need to know

1. Budget projections for direct equipment and G&A overhead vehicle costs
2. The amount of direct equipment costs to include in a job in the bidding process.

Our goal is to recover all of our company/division equipment costs for the year in the jobs we complete and bill in that year. In order to do so, we must

- Accurately determine costs
- Allocate the correct amount of these costs to each job
- Complete and bill enough work/jobs in the field to cover all our equipment costs for the year.

It may help to think of yourself as an equipment rental company or a car rental firm (such as Hertz or Avis). They, just like you, need to know vehicle/equipment costs (purchase price, interest rates, repair and maintenance, etc.) in order to determine appropriate customer rental rates.

These rates are based on an hourly, daily, or weekly cost figure that's marked up to cover corporate G&A overhead and net profit. If vehicle/equipment costs aren't identified accurately, subsequent rental rates will be either too high (prompting customers to shop elsewhere) or too low (causing the company to lose money).

I know of construction and maintenance companies, both large and small, that lost customers and hundreds of thousands of dollars because they didn't bid their equipment costs accurately. Nor did they track their equipment costs (and the revenues generated) in order to cover these costs in jobs completed. They didn't ensure that they'd at least break even for such costs. We'll discuss this in greater detail in Chapter 45.

How It Works

A contractor in New England with whom I was consulting questioned whether he even needed to use my pricing methods. He did not have to competitively bid his work. He did the work and then gave his clients a bill. They always paid whatever he charged them because the contractor did good work, and the customers trusted him. As it turned out, his invoices were *more* than reasonable.

During the course of the day of consulting, the contractor kept complaining about how he thought that his sales revenue for the year was nearly $75,000 short of what it should have been. Sales revenue should have been about $575,000, not the $500,000 that he had charged. Finally, I asked him to explain to me how he had priced his work for the previous year.

His 20% markup on material costs was fine. The $35 charge per labor hour, including general condition time, was accurate. There was nothing wrong with the 15 to 20% markup that he put on subcontractor costs. However, when I asked him how he charged for his equipment, he looked stunned. He replied that he did not think that he should charge for equipment as it was *just a cost of doing business.*

I responded by acknowledging that he was correct in stating that it was a cost of doing business. However, I wanted to know how he passed this $60,000 cost of doing business for equipment on to his customers. He had not. With a proper markup for net profit and G&A overhead, this $60,000 would have accounted for the missing $75,000.

Think of it! Had this contractor written out invoices totaling $575,000 for the year, his clients would have paid it without question. He simply shorted himself $75,000. And it was all profit.

How would you have corrected this flaw in this contractor's estimating system? Do you have similar flaws in your estimating system?

We need to make the following distinctions (or assumptions) concerning our method of equipment costing:

Useful Life and Meter Time

- For cars and trucks under one ton in size and below, useful life will be 8,320 hours (2,080 hours per year × 4 years).

  We want to recover our costs for these "light" vehicles in either four years at 2,080 hours per year (8 hrs/day × 5 days/wk × 52 wks/yr) or (for seasonal companies), in five years (8 hrs/day × 5 days/wk × 42 wks/yr). Incidentally, in this case, the 8 hours per day is not necessarily meter (or engine running) time.

  After four or five seasons these vehicles are usually worn out. If they last longer, great! However, we want to be conservative in recovering our costs. We prefer to recoup our costs sooner than later, in no more than four to five years.
- The **useful life** of heavy-duty trucks (larger than one ton), tractors, dozers, trenchers, mowers, and so forth consists of projected actual **meter time**/hours prior to that piece of equipment needing a major overhaul.

  We'll use 10,000 engine running or meter hours for heavy-duty trucks before needing such an overhaul. However, the 10,000 hours may be spread over 10 to 15 years, not just four or five like light-duty trucks.

  Useful life and meter time/hours for tractors, dozers, trenchers, or mowers will generally be considerably fewer than those for heavy-duty trucks. They can, however, also last 10 to 15 years before needing a major overhaul. This equipment is built to last and to withstand the wear and tear. If you don't use it, it won't wear out (for the most part) in four or five years as do the lighter trucks and vehicles.

As a general rule, I like to project **lifetime hours** for gas engines at 100 hours of life per horsepower. Diesel engines I project at 125 hours of life per horsepower. However, I cap lifetime hours for equipment as indicated in Table 9-1.

TABLE 9-1 Lifetime Hours for Engines

Engine Horsepower	Gas Engine	Diesel Engine
20 to 25	2,000 to 2,500	2,500 to 3,000
25 to 30	2,500 to 3,000	3,000 to 3,500
30 to 40	3,000 to 4,000	3,500 to 4,500
40 to 50	4,000 to 5,000	4,500 to 5,000
50 to 100	Cap at 5,000	Cap at 7,500
Over 100	Cap at 7,500	Cap at 10,000

Seasonality

Light-duty trucks (one ton and below) that aren't used in winter have the same useful life in hours (8,320) as ones that are; but useful life is spread out over five years rather than four. This is because seasonal use is shortened to approximately 1,600 hours (40 weeks × 40 hours per week) per year, sometimes less. However, it generally evens out at a total useful life of 8,320 hours.

Costs for New vs. Used Equipment

Even if you plan to buy used equipment, you should cost it out by using the "new" purchase price. The CPH will generally be the same for new and used equipment. Another reason for using the new price is because useful life and repair and maintenance costs are easier to determine for new equipment. Using the new purchase price also automatically adjusts equipment rates for inflation and price increases.

In essence, purchasing new versus old equipment is not a question of operating savings; it's a question of capital. Can you afford to buy new equipment? Used equipment may be cheaper to purchase, but it is usually more expensive to maintain. Therefore, the CPH will tend to remain the same.

Renting vs. Owning Equipment

As a general rule, unless you use and bill for a piece of equipment at least 50% of the time (20 hours/week), it's not financially practical to own it.

If a piece of equipment is either not readily available or would be impractical to rent, it usually pays to purchase it. However, before purchasing, you should assess the financial feasibility of owning it by comparing projected revenues and operating savings generated to projected costs incurred.

Leasing vs. Buying Equipment/Vehicles

Leasing equipment and/or vehicles may or may not provide cost benefits to your company or division. Often, the leasing-versus-buying option is driven by tax benefits (check with your CPA or accountant) rather than savings for operational costs.

To determine the costs and benefits of leasing, cost out the leased equipment/vehicles as you would those you might purchase. Be sure you adjust the "Purchase Price Column" so it reflects all lease payments and other appropriate items (i.e., periodic maintenance included in lease agreements, extended warranties). Other costs, such as fuel costs and life expectancy, should remain the same.

If the lease-life for the equipment/vehicle is significantly shorter than the normal expected life (should you purchase), adjust the life expectancy to the shorter term. Adjust maintenance and fuel costs to account for the shorter period as well.

For example, a leased vehicle that's to be replaced every two years by a "new" leased vehicle should have an adjusted life expectancy of 4,160 hours (2 years × 2,080 hours per year) versus 8,320 lifetime hours. Anticipated maintenance, insurance, and fuel costs should cover only the two-year period. Theoretically, there should be little or no anticipated repair or maintenance costs, especially if periodic routine maintenance (replacing worn belts; lube, oil, and filters, etc.) is included in the lease.

Finally, compare the lease CPH to the purchase CPH in order to determine any savings. If there are, adjust your estimating budgets accordingly and weigh the option of using the higher or lower CPH in your bids. While the lower is realistic, the higher would provide a "contingency" (or "fudge") factor that should translate into a slightly increased net profit margin. You should be able to detect this increased margin in your job-costing reports for individual projects.

Small Tools/Non-Motorized Items

Small tools and non-motorized items such as shovels, rakes, hoes, and wheelbarrows are reflected in general and administrative (G&A) overhead and are not discussed in this chapter.

In-House Labor on Equipment/Vehicles

Unless you have a separate equipment company/division with separate financial statements, calculate your projected maintenance costs by utilizing the prices and rates obtained from outside equipment repair shops. These prices will include materials, labor, labor burden, G&A overhead, net profit, and so on at fair market value.

If you attempt to calculate your cost per hour figures using in-house labor (including labor burden), you'll greatly complicate the costing process. In addition, your rates will probably be higher than those on the open market. If so, you should save the money and have the work done outside. If, on the other hand, you can do it cheaper, use the open market rates (which are a fair market value rate) in your equipment costing and put the extra money in your pocket.

MILEAGE RATES

Using established **mileage rates** to reimburse your employees for the use of their own vehicles as G&A overhead transportation is fine on a limited basis. These costs are included in G&A overhead. Reimbursing field employees in a similar manner for using their own vehicles on the job is also fine. However, we don't bid costs into a job based on mileage rates for company-owned vehicles/equipment. Rather, we use hourly rates. Let me use an example to explain why.

How It Works

You have two similar-sized jobs. One is 50 miles from your office; the other is only five miles away. If you want to bid a half-ton pickup truck into the jobs, you should calculate (using sample rates) as follows:

1. *Mileage rate method*: Lifetime costs $49,920 ÷ Lifetime mileage 100,000 miles = .4992 = $.50
2. *CPH method*: Lifetime costs $49,920 ÷ Lifetime hours 8,320 = $6

Job A (50 miles away)

Method 1: 100 (miles/day) × $.50 (per mile) = $50

Method 2: $6 CPH × 8 hours/day = $48

Job B (5 miles away)

Method 1: 10 (miles/day) × $.50 (per mile) = $5

Method 2: $6 CPH × 8 (hours/day) = $48

G&A overhead and net profit will be added to both jobs in order to determine the price to charge the customer.

The mileage method breaks down for the following reasons:

1. Most of the wear and tear (broken mirrors, lights, windows, flat tires, etc.) on the truck will probably occur traveling around the job site. The highway is probably the safest place for the truck. Costing the vehicle based on miles driven to and from the site doesn't take this into account.
2. Although both methods are comparable for Job A, you have to drive a vehicle 50 miles (one way) in order to gain equity. If all your jobs are this far away, this method might have some merit. However, this probably would rarely be the case.
3. Hours are easier to job cost than mileage. For example, four hours per day, eight hours per day, 40 hours per week are easier to job cost than so many miles per day actually driven. Also, how do you figure job costs if the vehicle stays at the job site overnight? What if this one particular vehicle is used on

three jobs in any one day? It is extremely difficult to prorate each job and to job cost the individual projects accurately.

WORKSHEET EXERCISES

Let's turn to the "Equipment Costing per Hour Calculation Worksheet" in Exhibit 7 and cost out some sample equipment and vehicles.

Mini Pickup Truck

Used by owner for administrative purposes and for transportation to and from job sites. Will last four years and have approximately 100,000 miles on it when traded in.

Acquisition Cost Per Hour In order to calculate the acquisition cost per hour, add the purchase price (including tax, registration, racks, tool boxes, special paint, etc.) to total lifetime interest to be paid. If this total interest is not on the contract, use the following formula and subtract the anticipated salvage value when you replace the vehicle.

(Purchase price × number of years of payments × interest rate) ÷ 2

($13,500 × 4 × .12) ÷ 2 = 6,480 ÷ 2 = $3,240

Purchase Price		$13,500
Interest		3,240
	Subtotal	$16,740
Salvage Value		– 4,500
	Total	$12,240

Divide by lifetime hours (8,320): $12,240 ÷ 8,320 = $1.47

Enter $1.47 in the worksheet column (1).

Maintenance Cost Per Hour (total projected costs)

1. Insurance: 4 years at $1,000/per yr. (average)	$4,000
2. License fees: 4 years at $150 per yr. (average)	600
3. Lube, oil, and filters every 3,000 miles: 33 × $25	825
4. Brake jobs: 2 at $350 each	700
5. Clutch jobs: 2 at $430 each	860
6. Tune-ups: 3 at $155 each	465
7. Smog certification: 3 at $50 each	150
8. Tires: 2 sets at $300 each	600
9. Miscellaneous (batteries, mirrors, belts, windshields)	3,000
10. 1 blown engine for every 3 vehicles (average): $2,400 ÷ 3	800
Total	$12,000

Divide total by lifetime hours: $12,000 ÷ 8,320 = $1.44

Enter $1.44 in the worksheet column (2).

Fuel Cost Per Hour Determine the fuel CPH for automobiles and trucks under one ton by using one of the methods below. Then enter the amount in worksheet column (3).

Method: Total Miles Used Per Useful Life or Per Year

1. Total miles driven per year = 20,000.
2. Divide by miles per gallon: 15.

   20,000 ÷ 15 = 1,333 gallons/year

3. Convert gallons to dollars at: $1.50/gallon.

   1,333 × $1.50 = $2,000 per year

4. Divide $2,000 by hours per year.

   $2,000 ÷ 2,080 = $0.96 per hour

Suggestions:

- You can use useful life hours and respective miles for the preceding method, as well.
- If vehicle is used only part of the season, reduce hours accordingly but increase number of lifetime years for vehicle.

Method: Number of Fill-Ups Per Month (or week)

1. Determine number of fill-ups per month: 5.
2. Multiply tank size by approximate number of gallons per fill-up: 20.

   5 fill-ups × 20 gallons = 100 gallons per month

3. Multiply by average price per gallon.

   100 × $1.50 = $150

4. Divide total costs by hours per month or week.

   40 hours/week × 4.33 weeks/month = $150 ÷ 173 = $.87

Total CPH Add columns (1), (2), and (3). This will give you your total costs per hour (CPH) for a mini pickup.

$1.47 + $1.44 + $0.96 = $3.87 (round up to $4)

Mini pickups generally cost $4 to $5 per hour to operate, depending upon the type of options added to the vehicle purchase price (four-wheel drive, air conditioning, AM/FM radio, deluxe interior package, etc.).

➤ **NOTE** The CPH is only your projected cost for the vehicle. It is *not* the price charged to the customer because it hasn't yet been marked up for G&A overhead and net profit. ■

Now let's cost out a piece of field equipment.

21″ Rotary Mower

Purchase Price	$1,100
Use	Approximately 2.5 hours/day, 5 days/week, 30 weeks/year
Life Expectancy	Two seasons (then replaced or rebuilt)
Interest	None (if paid for in cash)
Salvage Value	None

Acquisition CPH

Divide purchase price by projected lifetime hours:

$1,100 ÷ (2.5 × 5 × 30 × 2) = $1,100 ÷ 750 hours = $1.47

Enter $1.47 in worksheet column (1).

Estimate Lifetime Maintenance Costs (repair parts, labor, blades, spark plugs, oil changes, filters, etc.) Check with your equipment dealer who will often have such data available. We'll estimate costs at $600.

Divide lifetime maintenance costs by lifetime hours: $600 ÷ 750 hours = $0.80

Enter $.80 in worksheet column (2).

Fuel CPH Determine running time (meter time) fuel consumption by one of the following methods:

Ask

How long does one gallon of gas last for this piece of equipment? If all day (for two and a half hours used per day), divide the price of a gallon of gas by 2.5 hours. Add oil additive costs for two-cycle engines.

$1.50 per gallon ÷ 2.5 hours = $0.60

Ask

If I used this piece of equipment during a typical day (two hours meter time), how many times would I have to stop and refill the tank (e.g., one time)? Multiply the number of fill-ups by the size of tank (e.g., one gallon).

1.0 gallon × 1 fill-up = 1 gallon

Multiply result by price for a gallon of gas and divide by 2.5 hours.

1 gallon × $1.50 = $1.50

$1.50 ÷ 2.5 hours = $0.60

Enter $.60 in worksheet column (3).

Total CPH Add columns (1), (2), and (3). This will give you a CPH for a 21″ rotary mower.

$1.47 + $0.80 + $.60 = $2.87 (round to $3)

➤ **NOTE** These figures will vary depending on the type of preventive maintenance (PM) program you have and the original purchase price of the equipment.

The best method for determining CPH amounts is to use company historical data. However, most companies don't have such information readily available.

Small Tractor

Purchase Price	$23,000
Life expectancy: 300 hours per year for 10 years	
Interest ($23,000 × 4 × .12) ÷ 2	$ 5,520
Salvage Value	$ 8,000

Acquisition CPH

Divide purchase price + interest – salvage value by projected lifetime hours.

($23,000 + 5,520 – 8,000) ÷ 3,000 hours = $20,520 ÷ 3,000 = $6.84

Enter $6.84 in column (1).

Estimate Lifetime Maintenance Costs (repair parts, labor, engine costs, tires, filters, oil changes, etc.) Check with your equipment dealer, who'll sometimes have such data available.

Divide lifetime maintenance costs by lifetime hours:
$18,000 ÷ 3,000 = $6

Enter $6 in column (2).

Fuel CPH Determine running time (meter time) fuel consumption. For the sake of brevity, let's say the cost of fuel and oil consumption is $2.25 per hour.

1.5 gallons per hour at $1.50 per gallon

Enter $2.25 in column (3).

Total CPH Add columns (1), (2), and (3). This will give you a CPH for a small tractor.

$6.84 + $6.00 + $2.25 = $15.09

Again, these figures will vary depending upon the type of tractor and other variables.

Rototiller, Walk-Behind

Purchase Price	$2,500 (including interest and any salvage value)
Lifetime Hours	750

Acquisition CPH

Divide purchase price by projected lifetime hours:
$2,500 ÷ 750 = $3.33

Enter $3.33 in column (1).

Estimate Lifetime Maintenance Costs (repair parts, labor, spark plugs, oil changes, filters, etc.)

Divide lifetime maintenance by lifetime hours:
$1,000 ÷ 750 = $1.33

Enter $1.33 in column (2).

Fuel CPH Determine running time (meter time) fuel consumption. In this instance, let's say the fuel is consumed at the rate of one gallon per hour at $1.50 per gallon.

Total CPH Add columns (1), (2), and (3). This will give you a CPH for a rototiller.

$3.33 + $1.33 + $1.50 = $6.16

I would round this up to $6.50.

VERIFICATION

To verify your calculated CPH figures, consider the following:

- Contact your local equipment dealer. Check your owner's manual to verify maintenance costs, production rates, fuel consumption, lifetime hours, etc.
- Compare your hourly, daily, weekly or monthly rates to those of your local equipment rental company. Reduce rental rates by 40 to 50% (to remove G&A overhead and net profit) in order to determine the CPH for that piece of equipment. Your CPH rates should be reasonably close to theirs.
- Contact the offices of your state/local Department of Transportation (DOT). They have manuals that contain CPH data for both maintenance and construction equipment. These offices are usually very helpful, and you can use their CPH figures for comparison purposes.
- Obtain a copy of the *Labor & Equipment Production Times for Landscape Construction* noted in the reference section in the back of this book.
- Equipment Watch (a division of PRIMEDIA Business Magazines & Media, Inc.) offers a *Contractors Equipment Cost Guide* that can be used for comparison purposes. It's expensive, over $500, but thorough. Call 1-800-669-3282 to order a copy, or access them on the Internet at www.ironmax.com.

You can easily use a personal computer spreadsheet program (such as Lotus 1-2-3® or Microsoft Excel®) to cost out your equipment. This can simplify the process, and the program will make the necessary adjustments quickly and accurately.

SUMMARY

Some estimating systems put all equipment costs, for both field and office related equipment, in G&A overhead. This is a big mistake that can cause you to charge too much for labor intensive jobs and too little for equipment intensive ones. We calculate a cost per hour (CPH) for each piece of field equipment. This CPH is then multiplied by the amount of hours the piece of equipment is going to be used to do the job. Costs for vehicles used by G&A overhead personnel are included in the G&A overhead budget.

The CPH for a given piece of field equipment is comprised of three items: the acquisition cost, the maintenance cost, and the fuel cost. In order to maintain fair market value for equipment, the acquisition cost is calculated using the current replacement price for a given truck or piece of field equipment.

In order to ensure that equipment is paying for itself, many companies will create a separate equipment checking account from which all expenses for equipment are paid. Jobs are charged an intracompany rental rate for using the equipment, and these charges are recorded in the equipment checkbook. Larger companies often form a separate equipment division or company, which pays all equipment expenses. These divisions or companies charge a rental rate to the users of the equipment and bill them accordingly.

ACTION POINTS

1. Compute your projected field equipment and general and administrative (G&A) overhead vehicle budget amounts and enter them in Exhibit 1.
2. Using Exhibit 7 in the back of the book, calculate the CPH amounts for your equipment and vehicles and compare to those in Appendix C.
3. Review the section in Chapter 52 regarding mechanics for equipment and equipment hours.

CHAPTER

10

Budget Recap and Ratio Analysis

TERMS

Direct Costs Per Hour (DCPH)
Equipment Per Hour (EQPH)
Equipment-to-Labor (EQ/L) Ratio
Gross Profit Margin Per Hour (GPMPH)
Gross Annual Sales (GAS)
Material Per Hour (MPH)
Material-to-Labor (M/L) Ratio
Profit Per Hour (PPH)

Purpose

- To provide a quick-reference spreadsheet for recapping vital data and ratios in order to evaluate and monitor budget-to-actual information
- To outline a format that you can utilize for customizing reports in your accounting software

Introduction

Ratios, percentages and per-hour calculations can provide some significant insight into your budget-to-actual performance if they're formatted and used properly. Review Tables 3-1 and 10-1 and Figure 44-2 as we cover the ratios and the budget recap analysis below. After you fill in the recap report, compare your ratios and percentages to the industry benchmarks set forth in Chapter 46 and Appendix E.

It is *important to note* that all percentages and ratios provided in Chapter 46 and Appendix E are generalizations and approximations. They should only be used for comparison purposes. Actual figures for your company/division will vary.

BUDGET RECAP ANALYSIS

The purpose of the budget recap analysis spreadsheet is to provide you with a format that allows you to easily compare your budget-to-actual data.

1. Gross Annual Sales (GAS) or "Sales"
   The **Gross Annual Sales (GAS)** or sales is the revenue for the company or division for the given period.
2. Direct Costs
   A. Materials and Supplies
      This figure includes sales tax if it's paid on materials.
   B. Field Labor
      Supervisors may be included in this category. However, unless they spend at least 50% of their time actually working on jobs doing production work, they are normally included in G&A overhead.

C. Field-Labor Burden

This category contains all items included in field-labor burden: FICA, FUTA, SUTA, GLI, WCI; holiday, vacation and sick time pay; medical benefits, etc.

D. Equipment

Depreciation cost figures may be difficult to obtain for a given month. You may want to use an average depreciation figure for the period in your actual costs. All costs for field equipment and field trucks should be

TABLE 10-1 Budget-to-Actual Recap Report

	June Budget	June Actual	June Variance	June Actual %	Y-T-D Budget	Y-T-D Actual	Y-T-D Variance	Y-T-D Actual %
1. SALES	115,905	130,688	14,783	100.0%	695,430	723,089	27,659	100.0%
2. COST OF GOODS SOLD:								
MATERIAL	18,708	32,345	(13,637)	24.7%	112,250	137,752	(25,502)	19.1%
FIELD LABOR	13,274	12,898	376	9.9%	79,644	94,227	(14,583)	13.0%
FIELD LABOR BURDEN	4,580	2,656	1,924	2.0%	27,480	27,589	(109)	3.8%
* EQUIPMENT	2,967	698	2,269	0.5%	17,800	6,016	11,784	0.8%
EQUIPMENT RENTALS	1,225	888	337	0.7%	7,350	12,705	(5,355)	1.8%
SUBCONTRACTORS	26,400	25,769	631	19.7%	158,400	141,408	16,992	19.6%
MISCELLANEOUS	347	1,222	(875)	0.9%	2,083	2,500	(418)	0.3%
TOTAL	67,501	76,476	(8,975)	58.5%	405,007	422,197	(17,191)	58.4%
3. GROSS PROFIT MARGIN	48,404	54,212	5,808	41.5%	290,424	300,892	10,469	41.6%
4. G&A OVERHEAD:	29,167	29,219	(52)	22.4%	175,000	206,338	(31,338)	28.5%
A. OFFICE SALARIES	3,000	3,300	(300)	2.5%	18,000	18,900	(900)	2.6%
B. OFFICERS' SALARIES	5,000	5,000	0	3.8%	30,000	30,000	0	4.1%
5. NET PROFIT	19,237	24,993	5,756	19.1%	115,424	94,554	(20,870)	13.1%
6. NET PROFIT ADJUSTMENT	0	0	0	0.0%		0		0.0%
7. REVISED NET PROFIT	19,237	24,993	5,756	19.1%	115,424	94,554	(20,870)	13.1%

8. RATIOS/PER HR INFO:	June Budget	June Actual	June Variance	Y-T-D Budget	Y-T-D Actual	Y-T-D Variance
A. SALES PER HOUR	$59.99	$63.72	$3.73	$59.99	$64.97	$4.98
B. DIRECT COSTS PER HOUR	$34.94	$42.04	$7.10	$34.94	$37.93	$3.00
C. GPM PER HOUR	$25.05	$21.68	($3.38)	$25.05	$27.03	$1.98
D. G&A OVERHEAD PER HOUR	$15.10	$16.06	$0.97	$15.10	$18.54	$3.44
E. NET PROFIT PER HOUR	$9.96	$13.74	$3.78	$9.96	$8.50	($1.46)
F. MAT'L/LAB RATIO	1.41	2.51	1.10	1.41	1.46	0.05
G. MATERIAL PER HOUR	$9.68	$17.78	$8.10	$9.68	$12.38	$2.69
* H. EQUIP/LABOR RATIO	22.3%	5.4%	16.9%	22.3%	6.4%	16.0%
* I. EQUIPMENT PER HOUR	$1.54	$0.38	$1.15	$1.54	$0.54	$0.99
J. AVERAGE WAGE	$6.87	$7.09	($0.22)	$6.87	$8.47	($1.60)
K. BILLABLE FIELD HOURS	1,932	1,819	113	11,593	11,130	463

* ACTUAL FIGURES MAY NOT INCLUDE DEPRECIATION.

included here (depreciation, interest expense, fuel, repairs, mechanics' pay, insurance, etc.).

E. Rental Equipment

Include costs for all field equipment rentals.

F. Subcontractors (can vary dramatically)

Due to distortions to ratios and percentages caused by subcontractor costs, I often make a separate division for subcontractor costs and revenue.

G. Miscellaneous

This is a catchall category into which I often put commissions paid to salespeople, dumpsters, portable toilets, as-builts, and so forth.

3. Gross Profit Margin (GPM)
   This is one of the most important calculations on the Budget Recap Report (see Table 10-1). Try to calculate it as accurately as possible.
4. General and Administrative (G&A) Overhead Costs
   Ensure that you adjust officers' salaries to reflect fair market value.
5. Net Profit Margins
   Net profit margin (NPM) is calculated with a fair market value salary for owners and before bonuses and corporate taxes are paid.
6. Net Profit Adjustments
   This category includes the portion of G&A overhead salaries in excess of the 8 to 12% cap imposed in our estimating G&A overhead budget (including anticipated bonuses). There is no specified percentage or range for this category.
7. Revised Net Profit Margin
   This category is simply the result of subtracting Item 6 from Item 5. Therefore, there's no prescribed target percentage or range.
8. Ratio and Per-Hour Calculations
   The following per-hour items are calculated by dividing period amounts by the respective period's total billable field-labor hours. Ratios are obtained by dividing the cost of the first item by the second. For instance, the material-to-labor ratio is obtained by dividing material costs by labor costs.

A. Sales per Hour (SPH)

I also refer to this as Revenue per Hour (RPH).

B. Direct Costs per Hour

While not commonly used, the **Direct Costs per Hour (DCPH)** can be helpful for comparison purposes.

C. Gross Profit Margin per Hour

Gross Profit Margin per Hour (GPMPH) is also a calculation unfamiliar to many contractors, but it can be very valuable when analyzing your production performance.

D. G&A Overhead per Hour (OPH)

Your actual division or company OPH may vary significantly due to fluctuations in a given period's costs or field-labor hours. Monitor it in conjunction with the G&A overhead percentage.

E. Profit per Hour or Net Profit Margin per Hour

Your budgeted **Profit per Hour (PPH)** is determined by multiplying your company/division projected net profit margin percentage by your projected SPH.

For example: If your projected Net Profit Margin (NPM) was 10% and your projected sales per hour (SPH) was \$55 (for construction), or \$22 (for maintenance), you'd have a projected PPH of $5.50 and $2.20, respectively.

Actual figures will vary dramatically, depending on type of work (construction or maintenance) and geographical location. My figures are generalizations. Your figures will be accurate for your business.

F. Material-to-Labor Ratio

Material costs and the related **Material-to-Labor (M/L) Ratio** are seldom analyzed by Green Industry contractors. *Remember*: material costs include sales tax on materials, and direct labor costs do not include labor burden.

G. Material per Hour

To calculate **Material per Hour (MPH)**, we simply divide materials costs for the period by the respective billable field-labor hours.

H. Equipment-to-Labor Ratio

The **Equipment-to-Labor (EQ/L) Ratio** is another category that's seldom analyzed. Include rental equipment costs in equipment and exclude labor burden from labor costs.

I. Equipment per Hour

Similar to the equipment-to-labor ratio, divide the same equipment costs by the field-labor hours for the given period to calculate **Equipment per Hour (EQPH)**.

J. Company/Division Average Wage (AW) or Direct Field-Labor per Hour

Divide the field payroll for the given period by the respective billable field-labor hours.

K. Billable Field-Labor Hours

Here we compare the budgeted billable field-labor hours to the actual ones for the period.

How It Works

About nine months into the year, a contractor in the Northeast thought his sales were on track for the season. However, upon further analysis, we discovered that his subcontractor costs were almost double their budgeted amounts. The margins on his subcontracted work were about half of those for the work done by his own crews. Consequently, while overall sales were on target for the year, gross and net profit margins were not. They were down considerably.

What should this contractor have done to catch and correct this problem earlier in the year?

SUMMARY

If formatted properly, budget-to-actual comparisons can provide significant insight into your operations. However, you must first format your data properly.

ACTION POINT

Calculate the various ratios and per-hour calculations described in this chapter for your individual company or divisions, and then monitor those figures throughout the year in order to identify particular trends that apply specifically to you. Compare your calculations to the industry benchmarks outlined in Appendix E and discussed in Chapter 46.

Estimating Projects

Costs, Bids, and Strategies

SECTION III

Contents

Purpose

To explain in detail how to arrive at a final price for a job

Now that you have your budgets in place, let's refresh our memories as to how we use them in the estimating process by reviewing the models in Figures 2-1 and 2-2.

First, we calculate the material, labor, equipment, and subcontractor costs for the production and general conditions phases of the bid. Then, we can begin to add markups and margins. After we add sales tax and labor burden, we'll have determined the total of direct costs for the job being bid. This is, of course, prior to adding the general and administrative (G&A) overhead, net profit, and a contingency factor (if used).

We then determine how much G&A overhead cost to add to a specific job. Our estimated break-even point (BEP) is identified once we add the G&A overhead to recover on the job to our previously determined total direct costs, which include sales tax and labor burden.

The break-even point (BEP) is the estimated dollar amount equal to all costs incurred on that particular job. Net profit and a contingency factor, if desired, are then added to the BEP to arrive at the final price for the job. It's at this point—determining the break-even point—that most estimating systems fail. All systems have their strengths and weaknesses, whether the system is based on

What will the market bear? How much net profit margin can you add on top of your BEP? Basically, you're asking, "*How high* can I go and still get the job?"

- Material-times-two (factoring)
- Total direct costs marked up by a predetermined gross profit margin (GPM) percent. This method is sometimes referred to as the single overhead recovery system (SORS).
- Market-driven unit pricing (MDUP)
- The dual overhead recovery system (DORS)
- The multiple overhead recovery system (MORS)
- The overhead and profit per hour (OPPH) method

Keep in mind that throughout the bidding process you're attempting to determine two numbers in order to answer the following two questions:

1. *How low* can you go and still cover all your costs (your BEP)?
2. What will the market bear? How much net profit margin can you add on top of your BEP? Basically, you're asking, "*How high* can I go and still get the job?"

Remember that a good estimating system not only projects your BEP consistently and accurately, but also does so in such a way that your net profit *floats* on top of all costs (the BEP) incurred on a job.

Now, let's turn our attention to determining production costs, general conditions costs, and completing the bid.

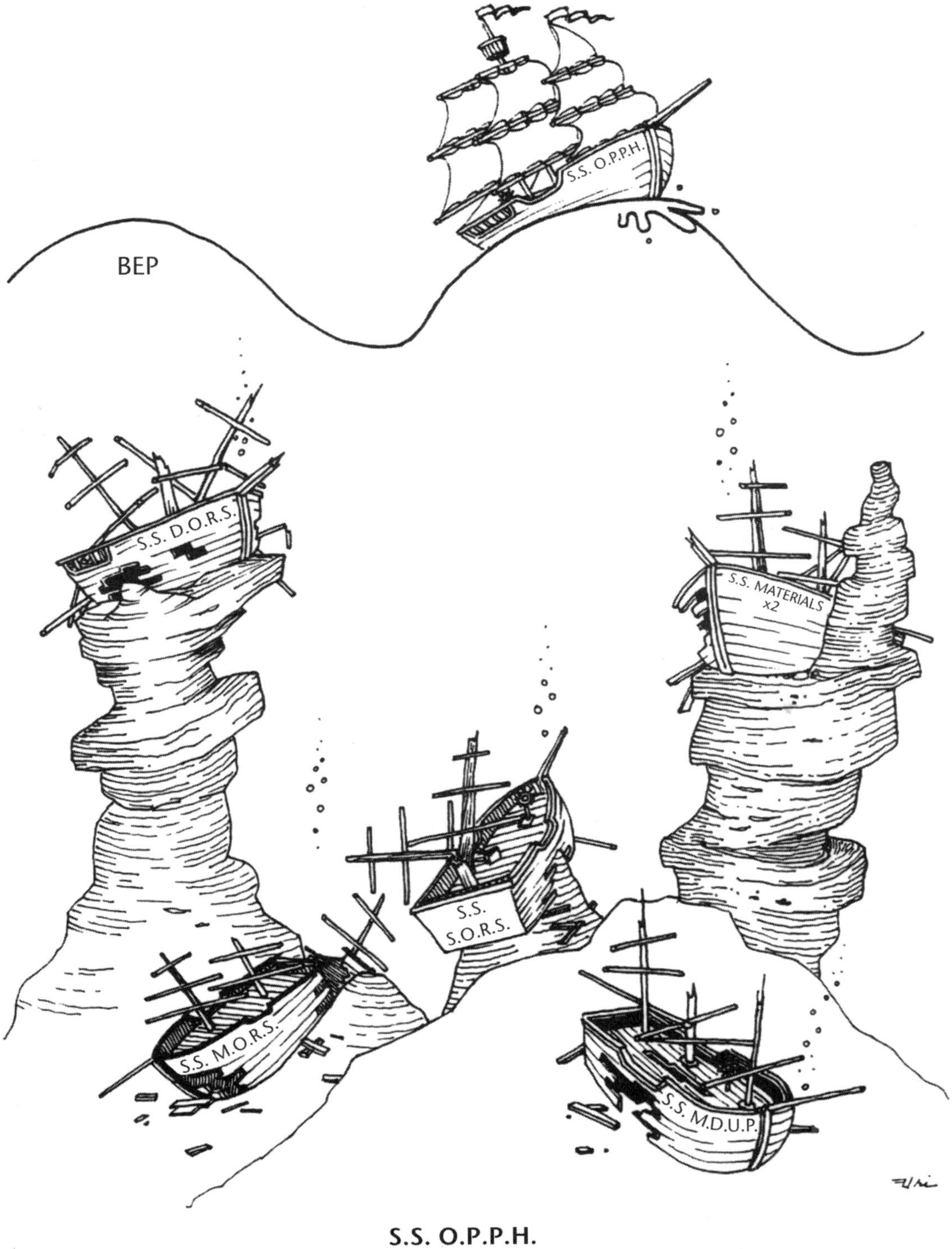

S.S. O.P.P.H.

CHAPTER 11

Phase I: Production Costs

TERMS

Equipment Mobilization
Lifetime Guarantee
Loaded CAW
Rewholesale
Risk Management
Time and Motion Study
Warranty of Materials
Wholesale

Purpose

To identify and define production costs and to explain how to include them in the bidding process

Introduction

We begin a lump-sum bid by identifying takeoff quantities and estimating the direct costs—material, labor, equipment, and subcontractors (M/L/E/S)—used in the production of the finished product. This is identified as Phase I on Figures 2-1 and 2-2.

Finished product/service production costs differ from general condition costs (Phase II) in that they're the actual material, labor, equipment, and subcontractor costs used to produce the finished product or provide the service (i.e., trees, shrubs, irrigation, patio, mulching, lawn mowing). While general condition material, labor, equipment, and subcontractors costs are required to do the job, they are not part of the finished product or service. For instance, portable toilets, temporary fences, permits, dumpsters, bags for grass clippings, and so on may be required by the job as the related M/L/E/S costs, but these items are not part of the finished product. This will become clearer when we discuss general conditions in Chapter 12.

ESTIMATING PHASE I PRODUCTION COSTS

If you are preparing your bid manually, make copies of Exhibit 8 for each phase/type of work to be performed (i.e., irrigation, planting, hardscape, maintenance, spring and fall clean ups, mulching). Otherwise, use computer worksheets similar to the ones in our examples. For purposes of illustration, I will complete some of our examples on both a manual and a computer worksheet. Prepare one manual worksheet marked "Recap" and one marked "General Conditions." Enter the phase/type of work in the "Type of Work" block on the worksheets. Number the pages (1 of 8, 2 of 8, 3 of 8, etc.) in the top right corner of each worksheet. Staple them together, with the recap worksheet first and general condition worksheet second, on top of the others.

Build the job in your mind and on paper (your bid worksheets) in the same sequence you'd build it in the field. Keep this principle in mind as the bid progresses. If questions arise about the job, or if a phase being bid becomes cloudy or overlaps with another phase, picture the production steps and the sequences involved as they would be performed in the field.

Put these steps on paper the way you visualize them. Although not perfect, this method can be very helpful. Even though some bid items (or phases) will occur simultaneously in the field, you cannot and need not show that parallel sequence in the bidding process or on the bid worksheets.

Fill in the recap sheet as shown in Figure 11-1. Start with the first phase of work, proceed to the second, third, and so forth. Skip a couple of lines after the last phase of work (in case you have to add bid items or phases to the project), and then enter general conditions on the bottom portion of the recap bid worksheet.

Before you begin, take a moment to collect all the tools you'll need during the bidding process—bid worksheets, plans, specifications, pencils, scales, calculator, scratch pads, and so forth. Tell your staff to hold all calls and that you don't want to be interrupted, or let your voice mail or answering service take all your calls. Interruptions that cause you to lose your train of thought during the bidding process can cost you lost time now and lost dollars later.

Enter the first bid item for the first phase of the project on the top line in the description column of the bid worksheet pertaining to that phase (see the sample formats in Figures 11-2A and 11-2B on pages 78 and 79). Enter:

- Quantity
- Unit (EA, SF, LF, CY, LS, etc., as appropriate)
- Unit cost or rate
- Materials
- Labor
- Equipment
- Subcontractors

Materials

Wholesale and Rewholesale Costs

Enter material costs in column (5) at the **rewholesale** price to a contractor.

Contractors who buy materials and resell them to other contractors should enter into their bid the rewholesale cost at which they would resell the materials to other contractors. If feasible, include freight and delivery charges in the price of the materials; otherwise, put them into general conditions at the end of the bidding process.

Companies that grow some of their own nursery stock should also use the rewholesale price in column (5). This is the price at which you'd resell these items to other landscape contractors or the price you, as a contractor, would have to pay if you bought the materials on the open market.

As a general rule, we'll almost always use the rewholesale cost of materials for bidding purposes for the following reasons:

1. The **wholesale** price paid for materials bought by a nursery for resale to a landscape contractor is usually marked up 30 to 60% above cost and then sold to the contractor. This is to cover handling, stocking, G&A overhead costs, and net profit.

   The marked-up price (above a nursery's wholesale purchase price) is called the rewholesale price and is charged to the landscape contractor.

BID WORKSHEET

PROJECT: JONES RESIDENCE PAGE (1) OF (6)

LOCATION: 123 MAIN ST. ANAHEIM DATE PREPARED: 12 / 15 / 20__

P.O.C./G.C.: JERRY JONES OTF = 10% ESTIMATOR: I. M. DUNN

DUE: 1 / 15 / 20__ PH.: 714-941-7442 FAX: RF = 10% CREW SIZE: 3 < 16·10·10 >

TYPE WORK: RECAP HOURS/DAY: 10 CAW: $ 15.00

REMARKS:

① DESCRIPTION	② QTY	③ UNIT	④ U/C	⑤ MAT'L	⑥ LABOR	⑦ EQUIP	⑧ SUBS
I. PRODUCE THE PRODUCT							
- SOIL PREP							
- PLANTING							
- SOD							
- MULCH							
II. GENERAL CONDITIONS							

FIGURE 11-1 Bid Recap Worksheet

BID WORKSHEET

PROJECT: JONES RESIDENCE — PAGE (3) OF (6)

LOCATION: ______ — DATE PREPARED: ___/___/___

P.O.C./G.C.: ______ OTF = 10% — ESTIMATOR: ______

DUE: ___/___/___ PH.: ______ FAX: ______ RF = 10% — CREW SIZE: 3

TYPE WORK: PLANTING — HOURS/DAY: 10 — CAW: $ 15.00

REMARKS:

① DESCRIPTION	② QTY	③ UNIT	④ U/C	⑤ MAT'L	⑥ LABOR	⑦ EQUIP	⑧ SUBS
- RED MAPLE 24" BOX/2" CAL	4	EA	185-	740-			
- LABOR <2 MHR/TREE>	8	HR	15-		120-		
- AMENDMENTS <3CF/TREE>	.5	CY	20-	10-			
- PLANT TABS <8/TREE>	32	EA	.10	3-			
- STAKE KITS	4	KIT	10-	40-			
- LABOR <2/MHR>	2	HR	15-		30-		
- CRAPE MYRTLE 15 GAL	10	EA	45-	450-			
- LABOR <1/MHR>	10	HR	15-		150-		
- AMENDMENTS <1.5CF/EA>	.5	CY	20-	10-			
- PLANT TABS <5/TREE>	50	EA	.10	5-			
- STAKE KITS	10	KIT	10-	100-			
- LABOR <4/MHR>	2.5	HR	15-		38-		
- SHRUBS 5 GAL	30	EA	15-	450-			
- LABOR <5/MHR>	6	HR	15-		90-		
- AMENDMENTS <1CF/EA>	1	CY	20-	20-			
- PLANT TABS <2/EA>	60	EA	.10	6-			
- SHRUBS 1 GAL	55	EA	5-	275-			
- LABOR <15/MHR>	4	HR	15-		60-		
- AMENDMENTS <100/CY	.5	CY	20	10-			
- PLANT TABS <1/EA>	55	EA	.10	6-			
				2125-	488-	-0-	-0-

FIGURE 11-2A Production (Manual) Worksheet

Project:	Jones Residence	Date:	12/15/20___
Location:	123 Main St. Anaheim	Estimator:	I.M. Dunn
P.O.C./G.C.:	Jerry Jones	Crew Size:	3
Phone / Fax:	714-941-7442	Hours/Day:	10
Due Date:	1/15/20___	CAW:	$ 12.50
Type Work:	Planting	Risk Factor	10%
		OT Factor	10%

CAW Loaded	$ 15.00

Phase 1	Quantity	Unit
Total Labor Hrs	32.5	Hrs L

# Description	Column Calculations			#VALUE!	#VALUE!	#VALUE!	#VALUE!
	Quantity	Unit	Unit Cost	Material	Labor	Equip	Subs
TOTALS				2,125	488	-	-
Red Maple 24" box / 2" Cal.	4.0	EA	185.00	740			
Labor (2 MHR/Tree)	8.0	Hrs L	15.00		120		
Amendments (3 CF/EA)	0.5	CY	20.00	10			
Plant tabs (8/EA)	32.0	EA	0.10	3			
Stake kits (1/Tree)	4.0	KIT	10.00	40			
Labor to stake tree (2/MHR)	2.0	Hrs L	15.00		30		
Crape Myrtle, 15 GL	10.0	EA	45.00	450			
Labor (1 /MHR)	10.0	Hrs L	15.00		150		
Amendments (1.5 CF /EA)	0.5	CY	20.00	10			
Plant tabs (5/EA)	50.0	EA	0.10	5			
Stake kits (1/Tree)	10.0	KIT	10.00	100			
Labor (4/MHR)	2.5	Hrs L	15.00		38		
Shrubs, 5 GL	30.0	EA	15.00	450			
Labor (5/MHR)	6.0	Hrs L	15.00		90		
Amendments (1 CF/EA)	1.0	CY	20.00	20			
Plant tabs (2/EA)	60.0	EA	0.10	6			
Shrubs, 1 GL	55.0	EA	5.00	275			
Labor (15/MHR)	4.0	Hrs L	15.00		60		
Amendments (100/CY)	0.5	CY	20.00	10			
Plant tabs (1/EA)	55.0	EA	0.10	6			

FIGURE 11-2B Production (Computer) Worksheet

The rewholesale price is what the contractor should use in column (5), even if that contractor has a nursery division/operation and sells materials to other landscapers. The original lower wholesale price should not be used in column (5) because it may not include all incurred costs (storage, handling, freight/delivery, etc.).

Unless you have a written quote for materials to be purchased for a specific job and have incorporated into the bid *all* additional costs to be incurred (handling, re-delivery, etc.) for processing the materials, stick with the rewholesale cost for bidding purposes in column (5).

2. To arrive at a price for retail customers, nursery retail outlets usually mark up their wholesale costs by 100 to 200%. The landscape contractor can buy the same material with only a 30 to 60% markup added to it (see *Note* in Table 11-1).

   Retail (residential) customers are accustomed to paying 50% (and more) above the rewholesale price a landscape contractor pays for the same material (nursery stock in particular). The bid should reflect this pricing differential in the net profit margin markup, not in the cost of material used on the bid worksheet.

   Therefore, you'd still enter the rewholesale cost on the bid worksheet, not the retail or list price paid by the retail customer. Otherwise, you'll distort sales tax, G&A overhead, and net profit margins because you're compounding an already inflated cost.

   By using a retail or list price versus the more accurate rewholesale cost on the bid worksheet, you're marking up the materials almost an extra 15% above your true costs. The true net profit markup is actually close to 30%, not the 15% indicated in the example. Table 11-1 demonstrates this problem.

   Use true costs on the bid worksheet; otherwise, you're lying to yourself and building inaccuracies into your bids and into the bidding process.

3. I know of large landscape companies that have five to ten divisions (commercial construction, residential design/build, reclamation, maintenance, golf course construction, irrigation service, nursery, equipment, etc.). Many

TABLE 11-1 Rewholesale vs. Retail Pricing Differential

	Contractor's Rewholesale Price	Retail Customer's Price	Variance
Base cost/price	$1.00	$1.50	$ .50
6% Sales tax markup	.06	.09	.03
Subtotal	1.06	1.59	.53
10% G&A overhead markup	.106	.159	.053
Subtotal	1.166	1.749	.583
15% Net profit markup	.1749	.2624	.0875
Subtotal	1.3409	2.0114	.6705
Markup passed on to customer	.3409	.5114	.1705*
Total price with markups	$1.3409	$2.0114	$0.6705
Markup variance (*) % of price	12.72%	8.48%	N/A

Note: Due to the advent of warehouse chains (e.g., Costco, Home Depot, etc.), the historical gap between retail, wholesale, and rewholesale is narrowing.

of these divisions sell services and/or materials to one another. To keep intracompany pricing honest, it's best to use fair market value (FMV) prices obtained from the open, competitive market as a transfer price between divisions. This will also allow estimators to use open market prices in their bidding.

How It Works

One of my client's estimators is encouraged (not required) to use rewholesale prices from the company's nursery division. However, if he can beat that price by obtaining quotes from outside nurseries, he is to do so. The same rule holds true when buying materials. Purchasing agents are allowed to purchase materials from sources/vendors outside the company, but only if quality standards are maintained and if their own nursery can't match the price.

Warranty of Materials

1. Calculating **Warranty of Materials** in Bid Costs is done as follows:
   Labor and equipment costs for product warranties will be included in general conditions; however, we'll include the material replacement costs in the purchase cost of the material itself.

How It Works

When bidding a particular size and type of tree, build in your warranty factor as follows:

1. Ask yourself, "How many of this particular tree can I expect to lose if I plant one hundred of them on this particular job site, under the existing conditions?" Take into account the time of year, location, weather conditions, site conditions, and so on. If you think you'll lose two, that's 2%; five would be 5%; six would be 6%.
2. Increase the unit cost for the tree by the estimated loss percentage.

A tree that costs you $95—with an anticipated loss of five trees per 100 planted (5%)—would be multiplied by 105% or 1.05.

$95.00	Unit cost
× 1.05	1 plus loss percent
$99.75	**Total** (unit cost with material warranty cost)

Another method would be:

$95.00	Unit cost
× .05	5% (decimal format)
$ 4.75	Material warranty cost
+ 95.00	Unit cost
$99.75	**Total** (unit cost with material warranty cost).

Some contractors simply add an across-the-board percentage markup to their entire bid (i.e., 1 to 2% of the total price), or they increase only the planting portion of the bid by a certain percentage (e.g., 5 to 6%). Other contractors even have a historical basis for markup. They track their actual warranty material, labor, and equipment costs, and then arrive at a warranty percent by dividing total actual costs by either the gross sales or the planting costs (costs for material, labor, and equipment).

The problem with this method, even if it's based on accurate historical data, is that it's too general. Although a company-wide aggregate warranty percent may have a certain overall accuracy, jobs usually vary a great deal from one to another. We need to be more analytical and job-specific, especially in competitive markets and in times of economic downturns.

! Reminder

There are no "good surprises" in business.

There are other methods for guaranteeing plants, products, and/or services. Basically, you're providing a form of insurance for your client and, therefore, managing future exposure or risk. I call this "surprise" control. You're attempting to ensure predictability, consistency, and certainty for your client by ruling out surprises—both good and bad.

2. The Lifetime Guarantee

   One method of offering your clients "risk control" is to extend a **lifetime guarantee** (except for acts of God and vandalism) on plant materials installed.

   This option is offered only on condition that the installer perform the maintenance on the project according to predetermined specifications. If the client breaks the maintenance contract or doesn't have the prescribed maintenance performed, the lifetime warranty is voided, much as a car warranty would be broken if servicing requirements weren't met.

   The reasoning behind the lifetime warranty is threefold.

   A. The risk to the customer is minimized.

   B. The customer never has to worry about future landscape problems.

   C. The budget for the customer's landscape requirements is predetermined.

   In turn, the landscape contractor increases maintenance sales with minimal exposure to risk. If the contractor installed the project and maintains the property properly, there should be a minimal loss of plant materials. It can be a win-win situation for all concerned.

How It Works

Theoretically, you actually could take out an insurance policy on plant materials (or other products) similar to crop insurance in the agricultural industry (with your customer as the beneficiary) in the event the materials don't perform as warranted. A client and I briefly considered pursuing this type of "warranty" option in the following situation.

One of his residential customers wanted a 120″ box tree installed. The rewholesale cost of the tree to my client (with delivery and crane charges) was $12,000. A four-man crew with a backhoe could install the tree in half of an eight-hour day. My client had $13,000 in costs (M/L/E/S) in the project.

The installed price to the customer was a little under $24,000. Net profit margin would be a little over $10,000—not bad for a day's work. There are times when pricing your work by factoring, or "material-times-two," is appropriate.

When my client described all this to me, I said it sounded like an excellent return for his efforts—as long as he managed and minimized his risk if something happened to the tree. I asked him, "What happens if the tree dies?" and, "Are you going to guarantee the tree?"

His response was that this was why he was paying me to tell him what to do.

Think about it. Using a traditional one-year warranty method, you can either win big ($10,000), or you can lose big by spending $13,000 to replace the tree. When you're only dealing with one very expensive tree, there's not much room for error.

My initial thought was to recommend a one-year warranty, except for vandalism and "acts of God." (Jokingly, I suggested that if something happened to the tree and it appeared it was going to die, the contractor could pay someone $100 to chainsaw the tree down on a dark, moonless night. That's vandalism!) After we discussed it further, we decided to ask the nursery if it would be willing to guarantee the tree.

My client had an excellent reputation with the nursery. His customer was motivated to buy the tree. The nursery was *very* motivated to sell a $12,000 tree. My client was *extremely* motivated to install said $12,000 tree for $13,000 and be paid almost $24,000 to do so. I was motivated to solve the problem for my client, earn my pay, and maintain a client as a future customer.

However, *all* of us wanted to minimize our downside risk, just in case the future didn't turn out as we hoped. That is, what would happen if this very beautiful, very expensive, *very profitable* tree died?

Warranties are simply a form of risk management. They're an insurance policy that should apply as much to you (the contractor) as to your customer.

The nursery had confidence in my client's ability to optimize the chances for the tree's survival and agreed to replace the tree at no cost if it died. If, however, the tree did die, they could only replace it with two 60″ box trees because they had no other 120″ box tree available. My client presented this to his customer, who agreed. Everyone was satisfied, and everyone's risk was minimized.

Warranties are simply a form of **risk management**. They're an insurance policy that should apply as much to you (the contractor) as to your customer. As such, warranties can take many forms. Be creative.

Include warranties as part of the written contract with your client, but be sure your legal bases are covered. Have your attorney review the warranty clause in your contracts.

ACTION POINT (1)

Review Figures 11-1, 11-2A, and 11-2B, and complete portions A and B of Exercise 11-1 in Appendix A.

Field or Direct Labor

Multiply labor hours for each function by your crew average wage (CAW) or specific labor rate for non-crew members and/or non-crew functions (ones performed not as part of a crew).

! Reminder

Be aware that the rates provided in these books are averages *and often tend to be conservative. Adjust these rates to reflect specific site conditions and your crews' productivity.*

Production Rates

Ideally, it's best to use crew production rates based on past performance (historical data); however, this may not always be possible. There are production rate reference books available. Titles and addresses for ordering these books are listed in the back of this book in the "For Further Reading/Reference Materials" section.

If you have neither past performance data nor a reference manual, ask an experienced foreman or another contractor for input.

Another option would be to do a miniature **time and motion study**. If feasible, have a crew perform part of, or a limited quantity of, a certain function. Otherwise, you'll have to use your best "guesstimate." In this case, clearly visualize the steps involved. Be conservative with the amount of time you allot to a function (owners and managers generally tend to be too optimistic when estimating production rates).

If you bid using unproven production rates, it is best (if practical) that the individual running the crew perform the task. This helps to determine the rate used in the bid.

Also, *before* starting that particular task (or any task, for that matter) be *sure* the foreman:

- Knows the hours budgeted for it, and
- Clearly understands the production process/sequence to be used.

Bid worksheet procedure: Review Figures 11-2A and 11-2B and enter information on the bid worksheet as follows:

- The word "LABOR" (or project) in "Description" column
- "3/MH" (three per man-hour) as the production rate beside description
- Quantity of hours for the function in column (2)
- "HR" or "MHR" in unit column (3) for hour
- Labor rate or CAW in column (4)
- Multiply hours in column (2) by labor rate in column (4) and enter the product (total) in column (6).

Crew Average Wage

First, determine your crew size and then the crew average wage (CAW) by dividing the total sum of the crew labor rates by the number of people in the crew. For example:

1 at \$14 + 1 at \$12 + 1 at \$10 = \$36 for 3 men.

Divide \$36 by 3. Your CAW is \$12 per hour.

Use a CAW (including OTF and RF) for bid items when the whole crew is on the site and when the item being bid is performed by a member of that crew.

Use specific rates when an individual is not a member of the crew (e.g., drivers, non-crew member operators, etc.) or for specific individuals in general conditions (e.g., foremen's supervisory time, superintendents, designers, estimators, etc.).

Overtime Factor

If the crew works more than a 40-hour week and overtime is paid, add the overtime factor (OTF) to your labor rates. If you know the job being bid will require 50-hour weeks, bid it accordingly. Otherwise, use yearly/seasonal averages (e.g., 45 or 50 hours per week throughout the season).

Divide the number of overtime hours paid by the number of straight-time hours paid. For example, for a 50-hour week it would be:

5.0 OT hours paid ÷ 50 straight time hours paid = .10 = 10% OTF

Increase the CAW by adding the OTF.

CAW	\$12.00
OTF (\$12 × 10%)	+ 1.20
Total (CAW + OTF)	\$13.20

Do the same for specific labor rates, if they're used and if such individuals are paid overtime.

Risk Factor

See the Chapter 5 worksheet for an explanation of the Risk Factor.

Add your RF to the CAW and OTF.

CAW + OTF	\$13.20
RF (10%)	+ 1.32
CAW + OTF + RF	\$14.52

I would round this to $14.50 or even $15.

Enter $15 in column (4) for your labor rate. I refer to this rate as the "**loaded**" **CAW** (i.e., it includes the OTF and RF).

ACTION POINT (2)

Complete section C of Exercise 11-1 in Appendix A.

Field or Direct Equipment

Bid field equipment (bucket trucks, tractors, skid steers, mowers, etc.) into the job on an item-by-item basis. This is more accurate than either lumping it all together in general conditions or accounting for it in G&A overhead.

Use the actual meter (or running) time that the piece of equipment will be used for each bid item. Enter equipment information on the bid worksheet as follows:

- Enter the description of the piece of equipment in column (1).
- Beside the description, enter the production rate for this piece of equipment (100′/HR).
- Enter the number of meter hours in column (2).
- Enter "HR" in column (3).
- Enter the CPH in column (4).
- Multiply the number of meter hours in column (2) by the CPH in column (4). Enter the total in the "Equipment" column (7).

Rental Equipment

If a piece of rental equipment is to be used for only one bid item, enter its entire rental cost (plus fuel expense and delivery, if applicable) in that item.

However, if a piece of rental equipment will be used on more than one bid item—for example, a trencher rented for $130 a day (including fuel and delivery) that's to be used on both main line and lateral line trenching—you could put it into general conditions or calculate its cost per hour (CPH) and allocate its cost to individual bid items accordingly. To do so, first determine its CPH.

To determine your rental cost per hour (rental CPH), divide the rental rate plus fuel costs plus delivery (if applicable) by the anticipated number of actual hours used per day. For example:

$85 (rental/day) + $35 (delivery) + $10 (fuel) = $130

$130 ÷ 7 hours/day (meter time) = $18.57 CPH

I'd round this up to a $19 or even $20 CPH.

The CPH will be the same on each bid item (if it's used on more than one). Be sure the total in column (7) for the two bid items equals at least the total cost ($130) for the rental equipment.

Crew Pickup Trucks, Company Delivery Trucks, and Driver Time

Crew pickup trucks, company delivery trucks, and drivers are normally included in general conditions. You can also include these costs in a specific bid item, if you so choose. For instance, you can include delivery time with materials in a bid item. Or **equipment mobilization** time (e.g., delivery time for a trencher) can be included with the main or lateral line irrigation bid items. However, it's usually simpler just to put these items in general conditions.

Include equipment operator time on the line directly below the piece of equipment. If the operator's rate is calculated in with the CAW, use the loaded CAW (with overtime and risk factors) in column (4). If the operator isn't part of the crew, enter the operator's rate in column (4).

ACTION POINT (3)

Complete section D of Exercise 11-1 in Appendix A.

Subcontractors

Subcontractors are added onto the bid sheet at cost. The following list shows a simplified procedure for keeping accurate records of subcontractor costs:

- Enter the description in column (1).
- Enter "1" and "LS" (lump sum) as the quantity and unit for subcontractors for which no other quantity and unit apply.
  - If desired—and if possible—enter actual production units and quantities—e.g., 22,000 SF of hydroseed.
- Enter unit cost in column (4).
- Multiply the quantity in column (2) by the unit cost in column (4) and enter the product (total) in column (8).
- Once all bid items and their components are entered on a bid worksheet, put a double line under the last items in columns (5) through (8).
- Total each column and enter the total for each column under the double lines.
- Proceed to fill out the bid sheets for the other phases of work to be done.

SUMMARY

Phase I production costs are those costs required to produce the finished product or provide the service. While general condition material, labor, equipment, and subcontractor costs are required to do the job, they're not part of the finished product or service. We separate the two in the bidding process. This differentiation allows us to analyze them more precisely once the bid is completed.

ACTION POINT (4)

Complete Exercise 11-2 in Appendix A.

CHAPTER 12

Phase II: General Condition Costs

TERMS

Crew Days
Job Duration

Purpose

To identify and define general condition items and explain how to include them in the bidding process

Introduction

General conditions costs represent some of the most misunderstood aspects of estimating. Quite often in a bid they are either calculated incorrectly or not at all. Contractors have lost thousands of dollars because they do not have a simple, yet effective means of calculating general condition costs.

How It Works

A commercial landscape company in the West was billing about $1 million in annual sales revenue. Net profit on this type of work should have been at least 10%, or $100,000. However, the two owners were barely breaking even when they called me in to consult with them for a day.

I knew there had to be a pretty big "leak" in the operation and was trying to find it. I asked the two owners to describe a typical production day. They related that they had ten people in the field who arrived in the morning and punched in on the time clock. They'd then go next door to a donut shop and buy coffee and donuts. (Can't imagine why they punched in on the clock first!)

With coffee and donuts in hand, they'd load the trucks. Then, crews would drive to the job sites a minimum of 30 to 45 minutes away. At the end of the day, they'd drive back to the yard, unload the trucks, and punch out.

Coffee, donut, load/unload, and drive time totaled a minimum of 1.5 man-hours per day. For a season lasting 200 days, that totals 3,000 man-hours per year (200 days × 10 men × 1.5 man-hours per day). At a crew average wage of $10 plus 30% for labor burden, that's $39,000 per year.

I asked the owners who were paying the $39,000 if they were putting the 3,000 man-hours in their bids in general conditions and passing them on to the client to pay? Or were they paying the $39,000 out of their pockets—out of profits?

I'll never forget the expressions on their faces. They looked at me, turned and looked at each other, and then turned back to me. Right there, it hit them. You could see the sinking expression on their faces.

We found a $39,000 leak, or about 40% of the missing $100,000 net profit. That's a pretty big leak!

BIDDING GENERAL CONDITION COSTS

General conditions (GC) constitute Phase II of a bid as outlined in Figures 2-1 and 2-2. The costs for general condition items are bid the same as Phase I production costs. Materials are bid at cost. Field labor is bid as man-hours multiplied by a loaded (including the OTF and RF) crew average wage (CAW) or labor rate. Equipment is bid as hours multiplied by a predetermined cost per hour (CPH). Subcontractors are bid at cost.

DETERMINING CATEGORIES

Enter general condition items on the general conditions bid worksheet. Costs for items such as dumpsters, dump fees, soil tests, trailers, toilets, permits, and so on, can be entered in the "Materials" column. Design fees can be entered as "Subcontractors" or, in the case of in-house designers, as actual labor hours multiplied by a labor rate. Lodging and per diem costs should be placed in the "Materials" column although, technically, you could also put them in the "Subcontractors" column. Figure 12-1A displays the general conditions bid worksheet for the Jones residence project. Figure 12-1B on page 90 is a computerized version of Figure 12-1A.

Let's now turn our attention to, and review in detail, the most common general condition items and how to bid them.

CALCULATING JOB DURATION

The amount of certain general condition items (supervisory time, crew pickup truck time, foreman administrative time, drive time, cleanup time, etc.) can be directly tied to the number of visits or hits a maintenance crew makes at a particular site or to the number of days a construction crew is on a job site.

The number of visits a maintenance or service crew makes to a given site is usually predetermined by the duration of the season and/or the type of service desired by the client. Therefore, determining the number of visits is generally somewhat easier than doing so for a construction project. Construction crews can determine **job duration** or **crew days** in two steps, using one of two methods.

- First, calculate the number of man-hours the crew is on the job in the Phase I portion of the bid. Do so by simply counting the number of such man-hours or by dividing Phase I payroll by the CAW for the bid.
- Second, divide the number of Phase I man-hours by the number of man-hours worked by the crew per day. Refer to the upper right-hand portion of Figure 12-1A where we've done such a calculation for the Jones project.

How It Works

52.5 man-hours ÷ 30 (man-hours per day) = 1.75 job or crew days

or

$788 (Phase I payroll) ÷ $15.00 (CAW) = 52.5 man-hours

52.5 ÷ 30 = 1.75 job or crew days

[See Figure 11-2A on page 78 and Figure 14-6 on page 106 to obtain total production man-hours.]

52.5 MHRS / 30.0 CREW MHRS/DAY = 1.75 CREW DAYS

BID WORKSHEET

PROJECT: JONES RESIDENCE

PAGE (6) OF (6)

LOCATION: ____

DATE PREPARED: ___/___/___

P.O.C./G.C.: ____ OTF = 10%

ESTIMATOR: ____

DUE: ___/___/___ PH.: ____ FAX: ____ RF = 10%

CREW SIZE: 3

TYPE WORK: GENERAL CONDITIONS

HOURS/DAY: 10 CAW: $ 15.00

REMARKS:

DESCRIPTION	QTY	UNIT	U/C	MAT'L	LABOR	EQUIP	SUBS
-SUPERVISOR <1MHR/DAY>	2	HR	25-		50-		
-SUPERVISOR'S TRUCK	2	HR	6-			12-	
-FOREMAN ADMIN <.5MHR/DAY>	1	HR	20-		20-		
-CREW TRUCK <8HR/DAY>	16	HR	8-			128-	
-LOAD/UNLOAD <.33MHR/DAY/MAN>	2	HR	15-		30-		
-DRIVE TIME <.5MHR/DAY/MAN>	3	HR	15-		45-		
-CLEAN UP <.33MHR/DAY/MAN>	2	HR	15-		30-		
-WARRANTY LABOR	4	HR	15-		60-		
-WARRANTY TRUCK	4	HR	8-			32-	
				0	235-	172-	0

FIGURE 12-1A General Conditions Bid (Manual) Worksheet

Project:	**Jones residence**	**Date:**	**Dec. 15, 20___**	
Location:	**123 Main St. Anaheim**	**Estimator:**	**I.M. Dunn**	**CAW Loaded $ 14.40**
P.O.C./G.C.:	**Mr. Jones**	**Crew Size:**	**3**	
Phone / Fax:	**714-941-7442**	**Hours/Day:**	**10**	
Due Date:	**Jan. 15, 20___**	**CAW:**	**$ 12.00**	
Type Work:	**General Conditions**	**Risk Factor**	**10%**	
		OT Factor	**10%**	

Phase 2	**Quantity**	**Unit**
Total Labor Hr:	**14**	**Hrs L**

# Description	**Column Calcualtions**			#VALUE!	#VALUE!	#VALUE!	#VALUE!
	Quantity	**Unit**	**Unit Cost**	**Material**	**Labor**	**Equip**	**Subs**
TOTALS				**-**	**235.00**	**172.00**	**-**
Superintendent (1 hour per day)	2.0	Hrs L	25.00		50.00		
Superintendent Truck	2.0	Hrs	6.00			12.00	
Foreman (.5 MHR/Day)	1.0	Hrs L	20.00		20		
Crew truck (8 HR/Day)	16.0	HR	8.00			128	
Load / unload time (.33 hr/day/man)	2.0	Hrs L	15.00		30		
Drive time (.5 hr/day / man)	3.0	Hrs L	15.00		45		
Clean up time (.33 hr/day/man)	2.0	Hrs L	15.00		30		
Warrantee labor	4.0	Hrs L	15.00		60		
Warrantee equipment / truck	4.0	HR	8.00			32	

FIGURE 12-1B General Conditions Bid (Computer) Worksheet

A more accurate (but more complicated) method is to subtract the average daily crew general condition man-hours from the total man-hours worked per day.

30.0	Man-hours per day
– .5	Foreman administration time
– 1.0	Cleanup time
– 1.0	Load/unload time
– 1.5	Drive time
26.0	Phase I man-hours per day

52.5 ÷ 26.0 = 2.0 job or crew days

The .25 crew days (2.0 – 1.75) is not a lot of difference for the Jones residence job. However, for larger projects it would be. Use the second method for jobs lasting more than one week.

MOST COMMON GENERAL CONDITION ITEMS

When bidding general condition items, enter the item nomenclature in the description portion of the bid worksheet, with the production rate (1 HOUR/DAY) beside it. The "HOUR/LABOR" and "LS/MATERIALS" on the right indicate the unit and category (materials, labor, equipment, or subcontractors) in which to total your costs for that particular line item.

➤ **NOTE** Crew average wage and other labor rates, when used in this chapter and throughout the remainder of the book, refer to a "loaded" rate that includes an overtime and risk factor, if applicable. The hours used in our examples are for instructional purposes only. Your hours will probably vary from those used here.

Superintendent (1 Hr/Day) Hr/Labor

Superintendent time is the time an owner or supervisor spends on the job site. Put the number of hours (1 hour/day) an owner or field superintendent will actually be on the job site beside the description. You may also include drive time to and from the site.

Usually, a portion of this person's salary is in G&A overhead and a portion in general conditions. Reduce the total amount of the salary that's in G&A overhead accordingly. For instance, if a superintendent can be bid into jobs 50% of the time (4 hours a day), only enter 50% of the salary into G&A overhead. If you put the full salary into G&A, and four hours per day are also included in your bids, you're "double-dipping," or charging twice for that particular cost.

Superintendent's Truck (1 Hr/Day) Hr/Equipment

This is the time to cover the cost of the superintendent's truck. Enter the number of hours (1 hour/day) that an owner or field superintendent will be using his or her truck to supervise jobs.

Foreman Administration Time* (1 Hr/Day) Hr/Labor

This is the time a foreman spends on nonproduction tasks—tasks not included in Phase I on Figures 2-1 and 2-2. It includes time to

- Fill out daily field reports
- Lay out the job

- Order and receive materials
- Coordinate with subcontractors or the general contractor/owner
- Coordinate with the home office, etc.

Ask yourself, "On average, how much time does the foreman (or do you) spend on items not directly involved with the end product or service?" The answer is usually about one to two hours each day.

Multiply the number of hours per day by the projected number of days for that particular job and enter the resulting total in the quantity column. Multiply the total number of foreman's administrative hours by the labor rate in the "Unit Cost" column and enter that foreman's hours in the "Quantity" column on the bid worksheet.

Crew Pickup Truck (8 Hr/Day) Hr/Equipment

This is the vehicle the crew uses on the job site. Multiply the number of days projected for the particular job by eight hours per day regardless of actual meter/running time hours. Use ten hours per day if you're on the job site that long and only work four days per week.

If you use a truck larger than a one-ton on the job site, use four hours per day or actual running time per day, whichever is greater. If you're on a job less than a full day, reduce your hours accordingly.

Crew Load/Unload Time (.5 Hr/Mday) Hr/Labor

This is the time the crew (or foreman) spends loading/unloading the trucks at the job site and at the yard in the morning and/or evening.

Multiply the number of crew members by the time each member loads/unloads per day. Multiply this figure by the projected number of days for the job. For example: On average, each member of a three-man crew spends 15 minutes in the morning and evening on this task.

3 (men) × .5 (hr/mday) = 1.5 hrs/mday × 10 (# of days) = 15 man-hours

For the above example, we'd use the crew average wage for "Unit Cost." If the foreman is the only one doing the loading/unloading, then you'd use that labor rate.

Drive Time To/From Job (1 Hr/Day) Hr/Labor

If you pay drive time, enter it into general conditions in this category. Use your crew average wage if the entire crew is paid drive time; if your foreman is the only one paid drive time, use that labor rate.

Whether you should or shouldn't pay drive time isn't the issue here. The issue is whether (1) the customer is paying for the drive time, or (2) the company is paying for it out of net profit because you're not charging the customer by including it in your bid.

Some companies pay drive time only to individuals who are driving company vehicles to and from the job. Others pay all crew members to and from the job. Still others only pay crews one way. My concern is that you bid your work so that it accurately reflects your company's practice. If you don't, you have a *leak* in your estimating system. That is, you have a cost that's not included in your bids.

Begin by accurately identifying and measuring your drive time. You should then weigh the pros and cons as to what your company policy should be. Make sure you're aware of the legal ramifications involved and that you're in compliance with any requirements that may exist in your state.

Depending on the particular job (or competitive situation), it's sometimes best to have a variable policy regarding drive time. In some cases, the amount of drive time can be the determining factor between winning a bid or losing it. In other cases, landscape and irrigation contractors have realized it is cheaper (on certain jobs) to eliminate drive time by accommodating crews in a motel near the job site.

Mobilization Of Equipment (Labor) Hr/Labor

Labor time required to transport equipment (tractors, trenchers, backhoes, dozers, etc.) to and from jobs—time that's not included in crew drive time—should be separately identified and bid into jobs under general conditions. You could include this item in the particular phase of work requiring it. For example, trencher mobilization time could be bid into the irrigation phase of the bid. However, I prefer to identify and include this item in general conditions.

Include labor time to load and unload the equipment onto a trailer (if applicable) and the drive time to and from the job site. Remember, in most cases you'll make two separate trips to and from the job for each piece of equipment—one to deliver it to the job and another to remove it.

If there are a number of pieces of equipment to be mobilized on/off jobs, there's the tendency to think you can reduce mobilization (by half) by removing one piece on the same trip that you deliver another piece to the site. Good luck! If you genuinely think you can do it that way, then bid it so. Frankly, I think you're probably being overly optimistic.

Enter the driver's labor rate or an average wage (if more than one person is involved in mobilization), include an overtime factor (OTF) and risk factor (RF) as necessary in the "U/C" (unit cost) column, and extend the costs accordingly on the bid worksheet.

Mobilization Of Equipment (Equipment) Hr/Equipment

The second component of mobilization is the equipment required to mobilize to and from the job site.

Use the cost per hour (CPH) for the vehicle hauling the equipment in the "U/C" column. Include actual meter/idle time. Don't make the mistake one contractor made of adding extra "meter time" in his bids for a tractor while it was being hauled to the job site on a trailer. I don't know about your operation, but most tractors aren't running when being hauled on a trailer.

Remember to include two round trips in your bid—one to transport the equipment to the job site and one to remove it later.

Freight/Delivery Charges LS/Materials

Freight or deliver charges that aren't included in the materials cost portion of the bid for planting, irrigation, hardscape, and so on, should be identified and included within general conditions. On the bid worksheet, use a quantity of "1" (one) and "LS" (lump sum) for the unit.

Hauling Materials (Labor) Hr/Labor

Hauling materials comprises driver and truck time used to obtain materials from nurseries and other suppliers or for employees who deliver materials throughout the day as their primary function.

Enter the driver's labor rate (or an average wage if more than one person is involved in deliveries) in the "U/C" column.

Remember to include both load and unload time, as well as drive time to and from the job site. Beware of duplication if you've already listed these times under (1) crew load and unload time, or (2) drive time to and from the job site.

Hauling Materials (Equipment) Hr/Equipment

Calculate the hours for vehicles and equipment used to load and haul materials to the job site. Include time for skid steers and other pieces of equipment used in the process.

Construction Trailers, Portable Toilets, Storage Containers Mo/Wk/Materials

Place these items in the materials column (5). However, you could technically call them equipment and enter them into column (7). Use the appropriate unit (Wk, Mo, LS) and unit cost in their respective columns.

Permits, Licenses, and Fees Ea/LS/Materials

As in item 11 above, enter these items also in the "Materials" column. Use "Ea" or "LS" as the unit and enter the unit cost in column (5).

Soil Tests Ea/LS/Materials

Same as item 12.

Dump Fees Ld/LS/Materials

Same as item 12. Use "Ld" (load) or "LS" (lump sum) as the unit.

Dumpsters Ea/LS/Materials

Same as item 12.

Traffic Control LS/Subcontractors or Hr/Labor

If handled by a subcontractor, enter as such. If company employees are used, enter in the "Labor" column. Enter unit and unit costs and extend/multiply out as appropriate.

Plant Watering Time (Labor) Hr/Labor

Watering plants immediately after they're planted is usually included with the planting phase of the bidding process, much as is the staking of trees. You can also place watering under general conditions. In either case, you'll probably have additional hand-watering labor after the planting takes place. Enter that time in general conditions.

Plant Watering Time (Equipment) Hr/Equipment

Include any equipment required for watering purposes (trucks, water buffaloes, etc.).

Cleanup at End of Day (.25 Hr/Mday) Hr/Labor

This is the time the crew uses at the end of the day to put tools away, sweep the site, store materials, and lock and secure the site. This usually takes about 15 minutes for each man per day. Use the crew average wage unit cost as appropriate.

Haul Debris (Labor) (2 Mhr/Trip) Hr/Labor

Calculate the amount of time required to load, haul to a dumpsite, and unload debris (remember to include time for the return trip). Multiply the time required for one trip by the projected number of trips in order to determine total labor hours.

Use the crew average wage for regular crew labor or a specific rate for noncrew drivers and/or operators.

Haul Debris (Equipment) Hr/Equipment

Include trucks and equipment (loaders, skid steers, etc.) used to load and unload and haul debris to dump sites, and the time used on the return trip.

Lodging ($35/Day)** Day/Wk/Mo/Material

If applicable, include costs for crew quarters. Use the appropriate unit and unit cost (e.g., $35/day, $245/wk, $1,050/mo, etc.) and enter beside "Lodging" in the "Description" column.

Per Diem ($15/Day) and/or Food Allowance** Day/Wk/Mo/Material

Same as Lodging.

Warranty (Labor) Hr/Labor

Once the production phases of the bid are completed, ask yourself: "How many trips (or how much time) will be spent on this job to repair the irrigation system, replace dead plant material, and so on?"

View the job in its entirety. Compare it to other jobs you've done where the warranty time and conditions were similar. Think in terms of half or full days and the number of people who'll be needed. Bid replacement labor just as you would any other labor item. For instance, you may anticipate that one job will require two men for two full days during the warranty period. That would be

2 men × 2 man-days × 8 man-hours/day = 32 man-hours

Another job may only require one person for half a day. That would be

1 man × 4 man-hours = 4 man-hours

If you have limited experience regarding warranties on a particular type of work, seek out some advice from your suppliers, foremen, or other contractors. Remember, replacement will generally take longer than the initial installation. You must remove existing materials, replace them, and then dispose of the debris.

Material replacement costs are included in the costs bid into Phase I (the production phase) of the project. In Phase I we simply increased plant materials cost by an anticipated replacement percentage. The attempt, however, to use such a percentage (or method) for replacement labor and equipment is too narrow a procedure. I feel it's much better (and more realistic) to calculate warranty hours for labor and equipment within general conditions.

Average the labor rates for those who are most likely to perform the warranty work. This rate is usually higher than your crew average wage because it's usually your foreman (or leadman) who'll do the replacement work, either alone or with the help of a laborer.

Warranty (Equipment) Hr/Equipment

After you've determined labor hours for warranty work, estimate the hours for vehicles and/or equipment. If you estimate two men for two full days, or 32 man-hours, remember that you'll need a truck for the same number of days, but for only eight hours a day.

Include all equipment that may be needed for replacement purposes (tractors, mowers, trenchers, etc.). Be sure to factor in disposal time (for both labor and equipment) and disposal fees for debris, if necessary.

Design Fees** Hr/Labor or LS/Subcontractor

Design fees can be entered into a bid either in general conditions or in Phase I (production). In-house landscape architects and/or designers can be bid as you would other labor, or considered "Subcontractors" and entered into that column as a lump sum expense. "Legitimate" subcontracted landscape architects and/or designers should be bid as such, using a lump sum price.

Too often contractors don't charge for design fees. I prefer to charge for designs with a contract totally separate from the contract for the actual installation of the project. I encourage my clients to give their prospects a free hour of consultation and perhaps a very simple conceptual pencil sketch during this free hour. However, if the prospect desires a design, I recommend you give them a ballpark fee (for instance, $500) and your hourly rate. You should be paid 50% of the fee right then and there. The balance should be calculated and collected when the completed design is presented to the prospect.

Commissions* LS/Subcontractors

As a general rule, commissions should only be paid on residential projects. Commercial bidding situations don't lend themselves to a commission-type payment structure because of the thin profit margins and the lag time between bidding, signing, and receiving payment for them. In-house estimators should handle such bidding and, in most cases, be put on salaries.

There are at least two options when including commissions in a bid. The first is to enter commissions in general conditions as a subcontractor cost. However, before you do so, ensure that all payroll taxes, insurance (FICA, FUTA, SUTA, and WCI), and expense reimbursements (auto, mileage, etc.) are taken into consideration and included in the figure entered as a commission. This figure will subsequently be marked up with a net profit margin.

If you don't want to mark up commissions in this manner, use the second option. This method simply adds the commission amount (including all taxes,

---

* Convert salaried payroll to an hourly labor rate by dividing the weekly, monthly, or annual salary by the actual amount of man-hours worked, not the amount of man-hours paid. For example, a foreman works 45 man-hours per week and is paid a weekly salary of $500. Determine the hourly rate to be used in bids as follows: $600 ÷ (40 + 5) = $600 ÷ 45 = $13.33. I would round up to $13.50 or $14 and use that number in your bids. Add a risk factor, if necessary. An overtime factor is unnecessary, as the $14 already includes the OTF.

** In extremely competitive bidding situations, these items are often included in general conditions, but are not marked up for net profit. I call this "washing through" or "passing on" an item in a bid. To eliminate these increases (assuming a 10% net profit margin is being used on the bid), divide such costs by 1.0 + the net profit margin, as follows: 1.0 + .1 = 1.1. For example, your net profit is 10% on a particular job you're bidding. Lodging and per diem costs total $1,000, but you don't want to add net profit to these two items. How do you include these in your bid without increasing them? Divide the lodging and per diem costs ($1,000) by 1 plus 10 percent (the net profit margin): $1,000.00 ÷ 1.1 = $909. Enter this amount into general conditions for lodging and per diem costs. The actual calculation will be a little more than the $1,000 cost, but is acceptable in most cases. Later, when you add the 10% net profit margin, the final price in the bid for lodging and per diem will calculate out to be $1,010. This is very close to the actual cost "washed through" the bid: $909.00 ÷ (1.0 – .1) = $909 ÷ .9 = $1,010. Due to the mathematical methods and the rounding you may have used, you actually add a few dollars above the original $1,000. This is insignificant. Of course, it goes without saying that if you can add net profit to these items and still get the job, by all means, do so.

insurance, and expense reimbursements) to the calculated price for the job, which already includes G&A overhead and net profit.

If commission, including all taxes, insurance, and expense reimbursements, is calculated to be 8% and your normal residential net profit margin is 15%, add the two together and increase your bid by 23%. If the market won't allow such a high margin, you may have to reduce it to a more realistic one. Consequently, some of the 15% net profit margin will have to be used to cover the 8% commission paid to the salesperson.

Job Detail Time Hr/Labor

This is time, normally at the end of the job, for the crew to inspect the job site and ensure that everything is up to specification and ready for a walk-through inspection.

The items we've outlined are the most common items entered into general conditions. You may want to include others. The estimator's time to bid the job is an example of one item you may want to add to our list.

> **NOTE** The above list of common items usually included within general conditions is certainly not all-inclusive. Other items, such as temporary fences, road signs, traffic barriers, security, rent-a-cops, etc., could be added. Include such items in your bids as required and follow the methods illustrated in this chapter.

SUMMARY

General conditions constitute the second phase of the bidding process. General condition costs usually equate to 6 to 10% of the price of a construction job and up to 15% of the price of a service or maintenance job. Labor hours in general conditions usually comprise 15 to 25% of all of the hours in a bid. *Leaks* in a contractor's estimating system can often be traced back to general conditions missed in the bidding process. Study the list of general condition items provided and accurately include in your bids the ones that apply to a particular job.

Figure 12-2 on page 98 contains a list of the common general condition items that I check for on every bid that I do.

ACTION POINT

Complete Exercises 12-1 and 12-2 in Appendix A.

Project:	List of possible general conditions	Date:	
Location:		Estimator:	
P.O.C./G.C.:		Crew Size:	3
Phone / Fax:		Hours/Day:	10
Due Date:		CAW:	$ 12.00
Type Work:	General conditions	Risk Factor:	10%
		OT Factor:	10%

CAW Loaded	$ 14.40
Crew days	1.20

Phase 2	Quantity	Unit
Total Labor Hrs	46.5	Hrs L

# Description	Column Calculations			#VALUE!	#VALUE!	#VALUE!	#VALUE!
	Quantity	Unit	Unit Cost	Material	Labor	Equip	Subs
TOTALS				1,800	706	222	-
Superintendent (1 hour per day)	1.0	Hrs L	20.00		20.00		
Superintendent Truck	1.0	Hrs	6.00			6.00	
Foreman (.5 MHR/Day)	1.0	Hrs L	17.00		17		
Crew truck (8 HR/Day)	8.0	HR	8.00			64	
Load / unload time (.33 hr/day/man)	1.0	Hrs L	14.40		14		
Drive time (.5 hr/day / man)	1.5	Hrs L	14.40		22		
Clean up time (.33 hr/day/man)	1.0	Hrs L	14.40		14		
Warrantee labor	8.0	Hrs L	14.40		115		
Warrantee truck	4.0	HR	8.00			32	
Mobilization/demobilization labor	4.0	Hrs L	17.00		68		
Mobilization/demobilization truck	4.0	HR	10.00			40	
Haul/pickup materials, labor	4.0	Hrs L	14.40		58		
Haul/pickup materials, truck	4.0	HR	10.00			40	
Trailers, toilets, fences	1.0	LS	100.00	100.00			
Permits, licenses, fees	1.0	LS	100.00	100.00			
Dump fees	1.0	LS	100.00	100.00			
Dumpsters	1.0	LS	250.00	250.00			
Storage containers	1.0	LS	100.00	100.00			
Haul debris, labor	4.0	Hrs L	14.40		58		
Haul debris, truck	4.0	HR	10.00			40	
Freight/delivery fees	1.0	LS	100.00	100.00			
Soil tests	1.0	LS	100.00	100.00			
Detailing of job	8.0	Hrs L	14.40		115		
Crew watering time	8.0	Hrs L	14.40		115		
Commissions	1.0	LS	300.00	300.00			
Design fees	1.0	LS	500.00	500.00			
As-builts	1.0	LS	150.00	150.00			
Estimator time	5.0	Hrs L	18.00		90		

FIGURE 12-2 General Conditions List (Computer) Worksheet

CHAPTER 13

Phase III: Completing the Bid

TERMS

Aggravation Factor
Bidding Process
Contingency Factor
Estimating Process
Sales Tax
Total Direct Costs

Purpose

To explain how to add markups and margins to the Phase I and II costs and to arrive at the final price for a bid

Introduction

Once we calculate all the direct costs contained in Phases I and II, we then add the markups and margins contained in Phase III. The sales tax and field-labor burden are the final two direct costs estimated even though they're included in Phase III. When these two items are added to the direct costs in Phases I and II, the total direct costs (TDC) for the job have been calculated.

The break-even point (BEP) is calculated once we add G&A overhead costs to the TDC.

The bid is completed once net profit and a **contingency factor**, if desired, are added to the BEP. Some estimators like to add the contingency factor into the bid in general conditions. Others prefer to add it either before or after net profit. Personally, I like to add the contingency factor after I add net profit to the bid and have had a chance to review the gross profit margin. Wherever you put the contingency factor, it is important that you understand what it is and why it is used in the bidding process.

The break-even point (BEP) is calculated once we add G&A overhead costs to the TDC.

COMPLETING THE BID

The **estimating process** (the science of determining the costs in a job) is completed when we calculate the total direct costs in a project. The **bidding process** is completed when we add G&A overhead to the total direct costs, net profit to the break-even point, and a contingency factor, if used. You could argue whether the G&A overhead costs of the bid should be included in the cost estimating or the bidding portion of this process. I choose to put G&A overhead costs in the final bidding portion of the bidding process.

The estimating process (the science of determining the costs in a job) is completed when we calculate the total direct costs in a project.

How It Works

An irrigation client in the Midwest was losing too many commercial installation jobs to a competitor. When we analyzed the competitor's bids, we concluded that he was bidding his jobs by multiplying his material costs by a factor of 2.05. We then began to compare our bids to the competitor's with the material factor in mind. By lowering our net profit by a few points, we were able to price our jobs with a slightly lower material factor. This more than evened the odds as my client began to win his share of the jobs.

Sales Tax

Appropriate **sales tax** markups are applied to materials and other items as required by state and local laws. In some states, tax is now applied to the final price of the job, not just to the materials.

Field-Labor Burden

Field-labor costs are marked up by a predetermined percentage in order to recover FICA, FUTA, SUTA, general liability insurance, field-crew vacations, holidays, sick days, workers' compensation insurance, medical insurance, and so forth.

General and Administrative (G&A) Overhead or Indirect Costs

A number of methods are commonly used by contractors to recover G&A overhead costs. Quite often a percentage markup is applied to materials, labor (including labor burden), equipment, and subcontractor costs (or to just one or two of these items). Sometimes a G&A overhead cost per field-labor hour is used. Chapter 38 covers these various pricing models in great detail. I use the G&A overhead cost per field-labor hour method to calculate the amount of G&A overhead to add to a job because I believe it's the best way to measure, allocate, recover, and control (MARC) G&A overhead costs.

However, I always check the gross profit margin on bids to ensure that it is neither too high nor too low. This is of particular importance when bidding projects that have disproportionate amounts of equipment, subcontractor, or material costs in them. In these cases, you have to be careful when using the G&A overhead cost per field-labor hour method as you may understate your gross profit margin and leave money at the bid table.

Break-Even Point

Our estimated break-even point (BEP) for a job is identified once we add the G&A overhead dollar amount to the direct costs, including sales tax (if applicable) and field-labor burden.

The BEP is the estimated dollar amount equal to all costs incurred on a particular job. Net profit and a contingency factor, if desired, are then added to the BEP to arrive at the final price for the job.

It's at this point, determining the break-even point, that most estimating systems fail. All systems have their strengths and weaknesses, whether the system is:

- Material-times-two (factoring)
- Market-driven unit pricing (MDUP)
- Total direct costs marked up by a predetermined gross profit margin (GPM) percent. This method is sometimes referred to as the single overhead recovery system (SORS).

- The dual overhead recovery system (DORS)
- The traditional multiple overhead recovery system (MORS)
- The G&A overhead and profit per hour (OPPH) method

Keep in mind that throughout the bidding process you're attempting to determine two numbers in order to answer two questions:

- *How low* can you go and still cover all your costs (your BEP)? and
- What will the market bear? How much net profit margin can you add on top of your BEP? Basically, you're asking, "*How high* can I go and still get the job?"

Remember, a good estimating system not only estimates your BEP consistently and accurately, but it also does so in such a way that your net profit "floats" on top of all costs (the BEP) incurred on a job.

Net Profit

When added together, the items identified up to now produce your break-even point. Net profit is then added to the BEP. The specific amount of net profit to add on to a particular job is determined by

- How badly you need the job
- The size of the job
- The risk involved
- What the market will bear
- Your ability to negotiate and to win the confidence and trust of the client.

When considering the net profit margin for a job

- Set a net profit percentage range appropriate for the respective market in which the job falls (e.g., 15-25% for residential installation or 10-15% for commercial maintenance).
- Determine a percentage within that range for each of the five categories listed.
- Total the five categories and divide by five.

The result should reflect an accurate net profit percent to put on a project.

The five categories are

Need Gravitate toward the low end of your range if

- This job is likely to be installed during a slow time of year.
- This is a period when you have no work and it's not likely you'll get any more.
- You need the work immediately.

Otherwise, use a percentage toward the higher end of your range.

Size Projects that are smaller than your typical job should be bid with more net profit. Conversely, ones larger than your norm call for a smaller amount of profit. For instance, many of my clients won't do a residential installation project for less than 20% net profit if it's under $5,000. On the other hand, they'll often reduce the net profit margin to 15 to 18% for residential installation projects over $100,000.

Risk Projects that are familiar to you and to your crews, those that pose a very small risk factor (that is, they should come in *on budget*), generally warrant a little less net profit than those that are more uncertain.

The less familiar you are with the work, the greater the risk. Think of it as an insurance policy of sorts. As unfamiliarity and risk increase, add more net profit margin.

Market (What the market will bear) Scale down your net profit if you're in a situation where

- "Low bidder takes all"
- There's no hope of negotiating the job
- You think your pricing is in the general ballpark with the other contractors. Otherwise, why waste time bidding the project?

Keep in mind your two numbers (especially the second)

- How low can you go and still cover all costs? What's your BEP?
- How high can you go and still get the job?

Don't be afraid to push the high end of the scale.

Negotiating Ability If, on the other hand, you're able to negotiate into the project (you're the contractor of choice for the project), gravitate toward the higher end of the range. It's understood, of course, that when someone else is the contractor of choice, the reverse is true.

Your ability to negotiate should be reflected in your net profit percentage. You should know from past experience what the market will bear and how well you're able to win the trust and confidence of the client and negotiate into the project.

Contingency Factor

The contingency factor is a totally subjective number. Add it to the job if the owner, architect, general contractor, or other authority figure rubs you the wrong way.

Contractors will sometimes add additional net profit to a job to cover what I often refer to as the **aggravation factor**. Basically, it's additional money tacked on to the price of a job that will make it worthwhile to incur additional risk, put up with certain situations, or tolerate certain individuals (architects, owners, developers, homeowners, subcontractors, etc.) with whom you'd rather not deal.

Although difficult to analyze, add a lump sum dollar amount of additional net profit margin to a job as an added risk contingency factor. Add it to your net profit after you've determined an amount for net profit using the five categories above.

The contingency factor is a totally subjective number. Add it to the job if the owner, architect, general contractor, or other authority figure rubs you the wrong way. Add it if you just feel uneasy about the project. Call it "bribing" yourself. What additional dollar amount would it take to make this project worth it to you to put up with the potential hassles and frustrations that might go along with it?

Remember, except for the contingency factor, you're constantly attempting to differentiate between and to determine two numbers in the estimating process: total costs (which include direct and G&A overhead costs) or the BEP, and the maximum price the market will bear.

The bidding process is completed when we add G&A overhead to the total direct costs, net profit to the break-even point, and a contingency factor, if used.

The gross profit margin (GPM) for the project is calculated when you total the G&A overhead, contingency factor, and net profit.

We can now define estimating as determining those costs involved with Phases I and II in Figures 2-1 and 2-2, plus sales tax and labor burden.

The bidding process is completed when we add margins and markups in Phase III to the first two phases and arrive at the final price for a particular job.

SUMMARY

Once we calculate all the direct costs contained in Phases I and II, we then add the markups and margins contained in Phase III. The TDC (**total direct costs**) is calculated when we add sales tax and labor burden to the direct costs contained in Phases I and II. The BEP (break-even point) is calculated when we add G&A overhead costs to the TDC. The estimating portion of the process is completed once we calculate the TDC. The final price for the project is determined when we add net profit on top of the BEP and a contingency factor, if desired. It's at this point that the cost estimate becomes a finished bid.

The gross profit margin (GPM) for the job can be calculated after net profit and a contingency factor are added to the break-even point. To calculate the GPM dollar amount on the bid, add your G&A overhead in the bid to your net profit and contingency factor. To calculate the GPM percentage for the bid, simply divide the GPM dollar amount by the final price for the project.

ACTION POINT

Compare your current bidding process to the one described here. Adjust it accordingly in order to calculate your total direct costs (TDC), break-even point, and gross profit margin.

Complete Exercises 13-1 through 13-6 in Appendix E.

CHAPTER

14

Unit Price Bids

TERMS

Double-Check
Unit Price Bids
Unit Prices

Purpose

To explain how to calculate accurate unit prices that include all costs and net profit

Introduction

Calculating **unit prices** and **unit price bids** manually, without the aid of a computer, is one of the most difficult aspects of estimating. It involves more arithmetic and more diverse steps (see Figures 14-1 and 14-2 on pages 105 and 106) than just about anything else you'll do when estimating.

Calculating unit prices and unit price bids manually, without the aid of a computer, is one of the most difficult aspects of estimating.

Once you understand, though, how to accurately reflect your company/division G&A overhead, general conditions, and net profit in your unit prices, you'll be well armed to negotiate your work with much more confidence.

Because unit prices are so essential and powerful, *if calculated accurately* (a rather large "if"), on virtually every job I bid I use a personal computer (PC) estimating software program that simultaneously produces both lump sum and unit prices. Using unit prices generated from an accurate estimating system allows you to compare your unit prices to those found in your market. This comparison can provide invaluable insight and confidence as you compare your unit prices to those commonly seen in your market.

Although I now use a computer for virtually all of the bidding that I do, I consider it essential that the novice estimator learn how to bid manually by using a calculator, pencil and paper, and an eraser.

Although I now use a computer for virtually all of the bidding that I do, I consider it essential that the novice estimator learn how to bid manually by using a calculator, pencil and paper, and an eraser.

Changes in net profit margins, crew average wage, general conditions, and so forth can be made and recalculated in seconds by using a computer. Diverse "what if" scenarios can be run and evaluated, providing more intelligent options as you analyze your company/division estimates. Changes customers want to incorporate into bids can be accommodated, accomplished right there in front of them, and communicated to them in terms of unit prices.

Even though calculating unit prices manually is more complex and time-consuming than doing so on a PC, it's still a powerful tool for the effective running of your company or division.

Before we calculate unit prices, however, we must first complete a company/division G&A overhead budget for estimating purposes. With that in place, we can then determine our Phase I material/labor/equipment production costs for each bid item requiring a unit price.

JONES RESIDENCE

FOR SOIL PREP:
1. 507 <IN COL 8> ÷ .61 = 831 <ENTER IN COL 9>
2. 831 <IN COL 9> ÷ 2000 SF <IN COL 1> = .416 <ENTER IN COL 10>
3. ROUND .416 <IN COL 10> TO .45 <ENTER IN COL 11>
4. .45 <IN COL 11> x 2000 <IN COL 1> = 900 <ENTER IN COL 12>

UNIT PRICE WORKSHEET — SMITH HUSTON, INC.-16-A

ITEM NO.	DESCRIPTION	QUANTITY (1)	UNIT (2)	MATERIALS + SALES TAX (3)	(4)	LABOR + BURDEN (5)	(6)	EQUIPMENT (7)	TOTALS (8)	MARKUP .61 (9)	UNIT PRICE (10)	UNIT PRICE ROUNDED (11)	TOTAL PRICES (12)
I.	PRODUCE PRODUCT / SERVICE												
1	SOIL PREP	2000	SF	277-		160-		70-	507-	831-	— .416	— .45	900-
2	RED MAPLES 24" BOX	4	EA	841-		200-		—	1041-	1707-	426.75	430. —	1720-
3	CRAPE MYRTLE 15 GL	10	EA	599-		250-		—	849-	1392-	139.20	140. —	1400-
4	SHRUBS 5 GL	30	EA	505-		120-		—	625-	1025-	34.17	35. —	1050-
5	SHRUBS 1 GL	55	EA	308-		80-		—	388-	636-	11.56	12. —	660-
6	SOD	1000	SF	320-		100-		—	420-	689-	— .689	— .70	700-
7	MULCH	6	CY	127-		140-		20-	287-	470-	78.33	80. —	480-
	SUBTOTAL <#1>			2977-		1050-		90-	4117-	<DOUBLE CHECK #1>			6910-
II.	GENERAL CONDITIONS					306-		172-	478-				
	SUBTOTAL <#2>			2977-		1356-		262-	4595-	<DOUBLE CHECK #2>			
III.	MARGINS & MARKUPS <OPH 12.00>	67-	HR						804-	<DOUBLE CHECK #3>			
	SUBTOTAL <#3>								5399-				
	CONTINGENCY FACTOR								Ø-				
									5399-				
	NET PROFIT MARGIN	20-	%		6749	- 5399	= 1350	= →	1350-				
	FINAL PRICE				5399	÷ <1.0-.2>	= 5399 ÷ .8	= →	6749-	→			161-
											DIFFERENCE DUE TO ROUNDING DECIMAL		
	CALCULATING MARKUP %/ DECIMAL												
1.	Col 8 FINAL PRICE - COL 8 <SUBTOTAL #1>			6749 - 4117 =		2632							
2.	#1 TOTAL ÷ FINAL PRICE			2632 ÷ 6749 =		.3899							
3.	ROUND UP			.3899 → .39									
4.	SUBTRACT ROUNDED DECIMAL IN #3 FROM 1.0 TO DETERMINE MARKUP DECIMAL/%. ENTER AT TOP OF COL 9.			1.0 - .39 =		.61	= 61%						
								ADD SUBCONTRACTORS <W/ALL MARKUPS> HERE					Ø
													$ 6910

FIGURE 14-1 Jones Residence Unit Price Worksheet

BID WORKSHEET

PROJECT: JONES RESIDENCE <UNIT PRICES> PAGE ( ) OF ( )

LOCATION: ____ DATE PREPARED: ___/___/___

P.O.C./G.C.: ____ ESTIMATOR: ____

DUE: ___/___/___ PH.: ____ FAX: ____ CREW SIZE: 3 <$15.00 x 1.32> =

TYPE WORK: ____ HOURS/DAY: 10 CAW: $ 20.00

REMARKS:

DESCRIPTION	QTY	UNIT	U/C	MAT'L (W/TAX)	LABOR (W/LB)	EQUIP	SUBS
① SOIL PREP	2000	SF					
-AMENDMENTS	10	CY	21.20	212–			
-SOIL CONDITIONER	2	BAG	8.48	17–			
-FERTILIZER	3	BAG	15.90	48–			
-LABOR	1	HR	20–		20–		
-TRACTOR	2	HR	20–			40–	
-OPERATOR	2	HR	20–		40–		
-ROTOTILLER	3	HR	10–			30–	
-OPERATOR	3	HR	20–		60–		
-FINE GRADE	2	HR	20–		40–		
				277	160–	70–	Ø
⑥ SOD	1000	SF	.32	320–			
-LABOR TO INSTALL	4	HR	20–		80–		
-LABOR TO ROLL	1	HR	20–		20–		
				320–	100–	Ø	Ø
⑦ MULCH 2" DEEP	6	CY					
-REDWOOD BARK	6	CY	21.20	127–			
-LABOR	6	HR	20–		120–		
-TRACTOR	1	HR	20–			20–	
-OPERATOR	1	HR	20–		20–		
				127–	140–	20–	Ø

FIGURE 14-2 Sample Unit Price Bid Worksheet

How It Works

A landscape contractor in New England was asked to provide a bid for a small installation project. His client wanted the bid broken down into unit prices for the 15 items on the bid. The client, a retired engineer, obtained similar proposals from two other landscape contractors in the local area. The totals for the three bids were very close but the unit prices differed somewhat. The retired engineer then began negotiating with all three contractors. His objective was to have one contractor incorporate the lowest unit prices from all three bids into one proposal. My client nearly went crazy but eventually won the bid.

Unit price bids are a two-edged sword. In the hands of the wrong people, they can cause lots of headaches. Unless handled properly, some clients think that unit price bids offer an open-ended smorgasbord.

How would you handle the situation with the retired engineer?

CALCULATING UNIT PRICES

Calculate Phase I subcontractor unit prices on a separate bid worksheet by adding a GPM markup percentage for G&A overhead and net profit to the prices quoted by the subcontractor. Add the unit and lump sum prices for subcontractors to columns (11) and (12) of the unit price worksheet under the third double-check (see Figure 14-1).

General conditions are then determined for the entire project and calculated into a markup percentage that includes G&A overhead and net profit. This is then added to Phase I production material/labor/equipment (M/L/E) costs for each bid item.

We begin a unit price bid by first identifying the individual bid items for which we want to calculate unit prices, using a 12-column accounting pad as displayed in Figure 14-1.

Production of Finished Product/Service

- Enter the bid items in the "Description" column.
- Enter the quantity and unit in columns (1) and (2), respectively.
- Skip a few lines after the last bid item and enter "Subtotal" lines for the columns as indicated in Figure 14-1.
- Label columns (1) through (12) accordingly. Note that materials in column (3) include taxes and that labor in column (5) includes labor burden.
- Next, take several blank bid worksheets and enter the Material/Labor/Equipment information for two to three bid items per page as shown in Figure 14-2.
- Number each bid item on the bid worksheet with the same number it has in Figure 14-1.
- Line through the "Subs" column and write "Total" over it.
- Enter, step by step, the production line items for each bid item in the bid worksheets. Remember to include taxes with materials, and labor burden with labor, in their respective columns.
- Place a dash (–) in the M/L/E columns that have no numbers to enter in them.
- Enter a circle (in pencil) where you don't yet have, but will obtain later, the quantity or price. This is done to help ensure that you don't forget to enter these items.
- Total each M/L/E column after placing a double or solid line after the last M/L/E production line item for each bid item.

- Add the three M/L/E column totals. Enter this total into the "Total" column (formerly the "Subs" column) on the right-hand side of the worksheet.
- Enter the M/L/E column totals onto the 12-column pad on the respective bid item line.
- Add columns (3) through (7) across and enter the M/L/E bid item total onto column (8) of the pad.
- Repeat the above steps for the remaining bid items.
- Subtotal columns (3) through (8) for the Phase I M/L/E items.
- Perform the *first double-check* of your work by totaling columns (3) through (7) across. Compare your total to the total of column (8) for all bid items. The two totals should be the same. If not, check your arithmetic for errors.

You're now ready to calculate the general condition costs for the project.

General Conditions

- Fill out a bid worksheet for the general conditions as shown in Figure 14-3.
- Enter the Phase II M/L/E individual line items. Include general condition subcontractor costs (if any) with your material costs.
- Total these costs as you did for the Phase I production bid items.
- Next, enter your general condition column totals onto the appropriate line on your 12-column pad directly under the Phase I M/L/E items.
- Place a line under general conditions, and subtotal columns (3) through (8) as appropriate.
- Do a *second double-check* of your totals. Compare the total of the subtotal line for columns (3) through (7) to the subtotal of column (8).

These two numbers should be the same. If not, check your arithmetic; you've made an error somewhere.

Markups and Margins

Calculate your G&A overhead on the line directly under your Phases I and II subtotal line. Write "G&A overhead" in brackets on the line followed by your OPH. You then

- Determine your total field-labor hours included in the bid. Divide the total labor in Phases I and II in column (5) by your CAW rate plus labor burden, or simply total all hours in Phases I and II.
- Multiply the total field-labor hours in the job by your OPH.
- 67 × $12 = $804
- Enter the total G&A overhead amount in column (8) of your 12-column pad.
- Add the G&A overhead amount to your Phases I and II subtotal.
- Enter that total on the subtotal line directly below "G&A overhead."

Next, write "Net profit & contingency" on the line directly under the "Subtotal #3" line (if desired, enter your PPH), and calculate your net profit and contingency markup. You can either

- Multiply your total field-labor hours for the job by your projected budget profit per hour (PPH); or
- Use the percentage margin method (i.e., 10, 15, or 20%).

BID WORKSHEET

PROJECT: JONES RESIDENCE <CONT'D> PAGE ( ) OF ( )

LOCATION: DATE PREPARED: / /

P.O.C./G.C.: ESTIMATOR:

DUE: / / PH.: FAX: CREW SIZE: 3 <15.00 x 1.32> = 2

TYPE WORK: GENERAL CONDITIONS HOURS/DAY: 10 CAW: $ 20.00

REMARKS: W/TAX W/LB

DESCRIPTION	QTY	UNIT	U/C	MAT'L	LABOR	EQUIP	SUBS
- GEN CONDS	1	LS					
- SUPERVISOR	2	HR	33-		66-		
- SUPERVISOR'S TRUCK	2	HR	6-			12-	
- FOREMAN ADMIN	1	HR	20-		20		
- CREW TRUCK	16	HR	8-			128-	
- LOAD / UNLOAD	2	HR	20-		40		
- DRIVE TIME	3	HR	20-		60		
- CLEAN UP	2	HR	20-		40		
- WARRANTY LABOR	4	HR	20-		80		
- WARRANTY TRUCK	4	HR	8-			32-	
				Ø	306-	172-	Ø

FIGURE 14-3 General Conditions (Manual) Worksheet

To do so, subtract your desired net profit margin from 1.0 (e.g., 1 – .2 = .8) and divide your subtotal line above it (#3) by the results. This will provide a true 20% net profit for the following example:

$5,399 ÷ .8 = $6,749

$6,749 is the price for the job with a net profit and G&A overhead added to the Phase I and II costs.

In order to determine unit prices for the job, we must first determine a markup percentage for general conditions, G&A overhead, and net profit to add to the individual bid item totals in column (8). To do so, proceed with the three steps at the bottom left portion of Figure 14-1 as follows:

1. Subtract the subtotal (#1) of the Phase I bid items in column (8) from the total price for the job.

   $6,749 – $4,117 = $2,632

2. Divide the result obtained in Step 1 by the total price for the job. Round up the decimal to two decimal places.

   $2,632 ÷ $6,749 = .39

3. Subtract the rounded decimal in Step 2 from 1.0. We've now calculated the markup percentage.

   1.0 – .39 = .61 = 61%

Enter your percentage (in our example, 61%) at the top of column (9). We'll now calculate the column (9) "Markup" totals for the individual Phase I bid items.

- Divide the column (8) total for the first bid item by the markup decimal point.
- Soil prep: $507 ÷ .61 = $831.15
- Round to whole dollars ($831).
- Enter this amount in column (9).

Calculate the column (10) "Unit Price" by

- Dividing the column (9) total by the quantity in column (1).
- $831 ÷ 2,000 = $.416
- Enter this amount in the column (10) "Unit Price" column.

Display your unit prices to three decimal points for items with low unit price amounts, usually under $1 or $2 (i.e., soil prep, sod, grading, etc.)

- Round up your calculated unit prices to the amount at which you'll sell to your customers (i.e., soil prep: $.416 to $.45)
- Enter that amount in column (11).

Determine your final "Total Prices" in column (12) by

- Multiplying the unit price in column (11) by the quantity in column (1).
- $2,000 × .45 = $900
- Enter the total in column (12).
- Repeat this process for the remaining Phase I bid items.
- Subtotal the column (12) Phase I bid items (see Figure 14-1).

The total of the prices in column (12) should be the same as, or greater than, the total price calculated in column (8).

- Conduct a *third double-check* of your work by subtracting the total price in column (8) from the total price in column (12).
- \$6,910 – \$6,749 = \$161

> **NOTE** Due to rounding your unit prices in column (11), the product of the unit prices multiplied by the quantities in column (1) is greater than the total in column (8).

Figure 14-4 on page 112 is a computer spreadsheet for our example outlined in Figure 14-1. Notice that I was able to add a few extra columns in order to separately calculate and display Phase I individual bid items unit costs, as well as showing these items marked up for general conditions, G&A overhead, a contingency factor, and net profit. The spreadsheet price is a little bit less than the manual worksheet price due to not rounding the hours in the G&A overhead calculation.

Note also the *fourth double-check* I've built into the lower-right portion of the spreadsheet.

When bidding irrigation or maintenance, follow the steps and procedures formats we've just used. The service or product may change, but the process is exactly the same.

To make sure you don't make and include a mathematical error in your calculations, remember to include the three double-checks in your work.

Compare your calculated unit prices to ones commonly used on the open market (that is, Market-Driven Unit Prices), knowing that yours include all your costs plus net profit and that they accurately reflect your company's G&A overhead structure, projected net profit, and production rates.

With a little extra arithmetic you can easily calculate your GPM, G&A overhead, and net profit percentages for your unit priced jobs. This information will allow you to compare these calculations to similar ones, using the GPM/SORS, DORS, MORS, or the OPPH estimating methods.

SUMMARY

Unit pricing your jobs manually is, perhaps, the most difficult aspect of estimating. However, by following the right procedures and by formatting your data properly, you can make the process much easier.

Unit prices that are calculated accurately can provide significant insight into your bidding as you compare your unit prices to those commonly seen in your market.

Remember to **double-check** your work. This will ensure that you don't make and include errors in your mathematical calculations.

ACTION POINT

Complete Exercises 14-1, 2, and 3 in Appendix A.

SALES TAX:	6.0%	PRICE:	$6,910	G&A OVHD:	11.84%
CAW:	$12.50	SPH:	$103.91	NET PROFIT:	20.00%
OTF:	10.0%			GPM:	31.84%
RF:	10.0%				
CAW (w/OTF & RF):	$15.00				
OPH:	$12.00	HRS:	66.5	PPH:	$20.27
DESIRED MINIMUM PPH:	$5.00	CREW:	4	GPM:	31.84%
LABOR BURDEN:	32.00%	HRS/DAY:	8	GC:	7.09%
NET PROFIT AS A %	20.00%				

#	DESCRIPTION	QTY	UNIT	MATL+TAX	LABOR+LB	EQUIP	TOTALS	U/C	+ G.C.	+OH (BEP)	+ Net Profit	U/P	ROUNDED	TOTAL BID	VARIANCE
									10.40%	14.80%	20.00%				
								SET------>	10.40%	14.80%	20.00%				
		1	2	3	5	7	8	CALCS	10.40%	14.80%	20.00%	10	11	12	
1	Soil prep	2000	SF	277	160	70	507	0.25	566	664	830	0.42	0.450	900.00	69.83
2	Red Maple 2"/24" box	4	EA	841	200		1,041	260.25	1,162	1,364	1,705	426.14	430.000	1,720.00	15.45
3	Crape Myrtle 15 GL	10	EA	599	250		849	84.90	948	1,112	1,390	139.02	140.000	1,400.00	9.83
4	Shrubs 5 GL	30	EA	505	120		625	20.83	698	819	1,023	34.11	35.000	1,050.00	26.61
5	Shrubs 1 GL	55	EA	308	80		388	7.05	433	508	635	11.55	12.000	660.00	24.68
6	Sod	1000	SF	320	100		420	0.42	469	550	688	0.69	0.700	700.00	12.28
7	Mulch	6	CY	127	140	20	287	47.83	320	376	470	78.32	80.000	480.00	10.06
8		1	EA				0	0.00	0	0	0	0.00	0.00	0.00	0.00
9		1	EA				0	0.00	0	0	0	0.00	0.00	0.00	0.00
10		1	EA				0	0.00	0	0	0	0.00	0.00	0.00	0.00
11		1	EA				0	0.00	0	0	0	0.00	0.00	0.00	0.00
12		1	EA				0	0.00	0	0	0	0.00	0.00	0.00	0.00
13		1	EA				0	0.00	0	0	0	0.00	0.00	0.00	0.00
14		1	EA				0	0.00	0	0	0	0.00	0.00	0.00	0.00
15		1	EA				0	0.00	0	0	0	0.00	0.00	0.00	0.00
16		1	EA				0	0.00	0	0	0	0.00	0.00	0.00	0.00
17		1	EA				0	0.00	0	0	0	0.00	0.00	0.00	0.00
18		1	EA				0	0.00	0	0	0	0.00	0.00	0.00	0.00
19		1	EA				0	0.00	0	0	0	0.00	0.00	0.00	0.00
20		1	EA				0	0.00	0	0	0	0.00	0.00	0.00	0.00
21		1	EA				0	0.00	0	0	0	0.00	0.00	0.00	0.00
22		1	EA				0	0.00	0	0	0	0.00	0.00	0.00	0.00
	SUBTOTAL:			2,977	1,050	90	4,117	61.1%	4,595	5,393	6,741	XXXXXXX	XXXXXXX	6,910	169
	General conditions			0	306	172	478	10.40%	V						
	SUBTOTALS:			2,977	1,356	262	4,595	68.16%	$0.00 0.00%						
	G&A overhead	66.5	Hours x OPH		$12.00		798	14.80%	(DBL CK-1)	V					
	SUBTOTALS:						5,393	------->	------->	$0.00					
	Net protig margin	20.00%					1,348	20.00%		0.00%				V	
										(DBL CK-2)	V			VARIANCE	
							6,741	100.00%	------->	------->	$0.00	------->	------->	$168.75	
											0.00%			2.50%	
											(DBL CK-3)			(DBL CK-4)	

FIGURE 14-4 Unit Price Computer Spreadsheet

CHAPTER

15

Reviewing Completed Bids

TERM

Checks and Balances

Purpose

To explain the need for and the process of reviewing a bid after it's completed

Introduction

I review a lot of bids for clients. Some are faxed but most are sent to me via e-mail. I also review a lot of bids with clients by telephone. I use a copy of the Bid Analysis/ Review (BAR) Worksheet in Exhibit 9, or a computerized version of it called Quick Bid. Quite often, the client and I discover the need to change the bid in order to make it more accurately reflect actual costs. We often make the bid more competitive in doing so.

Even though I may not have all the plans, specifications, and bid documents in front of me when I review a bid, there are usually plenty of areas where I can make a difference.

Having a "*second set of eyes*" review the bid usually allows us to catch those mistakes that may cost you a lot of money. Also, it can help you identify those areas (and/or methods) where you can decrease costs and improve productivity.

Many owners have their field foreman or superintendent review and "sign off" on bids before finalizing the price. In this way, field personnel become involved in the bidding process (brought into the information loop, so to speak), as they observe, recommend, and are given the opportunity to improve the bidding process.

Some companies have very formal bid review procedures; others have none at all. Some companies have found checklists to be useful. The *key* is to have a set of procedures that will ensure that oversights (errors in math, forgotten items, misplaced decimal points, etc.) don't occur. Most oversights can be prevented by some simple forethought and planning.

The *key* is to have a set of procedures that will ensure that oversights (errors in math, forgotten items, misplaced decimal points, etc.) don't occur. Most oversights can be prevented by some simple forethought and planning.

How It Works

I know of one large company that insists a bid be completely finalized and ready for submission at least 24 hours before it's due; otherwise, it's not submitted. Evidently, someone in that company learned the hard way the necessity of controlling the bidding process through checks and balances.

REVIEWING A BID

Read and Review Documents

Thoroughly *read* and *review all* bid documents, specifications, plans, and so on. Don't rely on memory or make assumptions. Ensure that irrigation materials are bid correctly (e.g., brass vs. plastic fittings, type heads, controllers, etc.) and that other materials are bid as specified (e.g., number of cubic yards of soil amendments per thousand square feet, correct thickness of mulch, quantity and types of tree stakes, etc.).

Also, *verify* that *all phases* of the project that are supposed to be bid *are* included in the bid.

Residential projects often don't involve bid documents and blueprints. In this case, the estimator should not be the salesperson (especially one on commission), unless it's the owner of the company. Otherwise, there's the temptation to underprice jobs and make them unprofitable just to get a commission. Owners and managers should compare the finished bid to the desires of the client by talking to the salesperson. Review the estimate and all items in it with them. Have the salesperson review his or her notes of discussions with the client and ensure (as much as is possible) that the client's desires are addressed in the bid.

Government/Municipal Contracts Much information about government work is public record. Check these records in order to obtain the dollar amounts for existing maintenance contracts that are out for bid. Quite often you can use the Internet to do so.

Review the "invitation to bid" documents carefully. Be sure you adhere to all *deadlines* and *formats* and that you obtain all necessary *signatures* and *certifications* (and if necessary, the services of a notary public).

How It Works

A company once flew me in to review a $7 million multi-phase landscape and irrigation project. I was told that all the necessary preliminary work had been done. During the review process, I discovered that the required bid format had not been followed. Sure, all the information was there, but it took us two days to unscramble it and format it correctly.

Review Line Item by Line Item

Review the bid, line item by line item. Check material costs and production rates for labor and equipment. Verify your production rates by comparing them to standards provided in the reference manuals listed in the back of this book.

Rethink your equipment use. Consider how you might make more effective use of your own equipment or how you might increase productivity by renting additional specialty equipment. Verify subcontractor prices in writing.

One of the benefits of our estimating software program is that it allows you to verify a unit price that includes material, labor, equipment, and subcontractor costs—as well as G&A overhead recovery, general conditions, a contingency factor and net profit.

These unit prices provide a fast and accurate means of confirming your bid prices by comparing unit prices from previous bids and those found in the open market. You have, at your fingertips, ready reference to such items as

- Prices per square foot for such things as seeding, soil prep, sod, ground cover, concrete, and flatwork

- Unit prices for specific sizes and species of plants, irrigation heads, etc.
- Linear-foot prices for wiring, irrigation main and lateral line, and header board.

General Conditions

General conditions usually constitute 5 to 10% of the price of an installation job and 12 to 15% of a service or maintenance project. There are, however, several ways you can possibly reduce them, if you ask the right questions.

Foreman Supervision Hours This can be bid at the average wage for the crew (not the actual foreman rate) for those hours the foreman is supervising and the entire crew is on the job site. This may lower your labor rate $3 to $4 per labor hour (not including labor burden).

Drive Time To/From the Job Site It's very common for installation crews to be paid for drive time only when they're on the job. This is especially true if crews are working at a particular job site for lengthy periods of time—more than two weeks. Otherwise, drive time (ride and sleep time for nondrivers) is normally paid only one way, rather than both to and from the job site.

If drive time costs on a particular job are too high, consider putting your crew into a motel overnight or in a house that's rented on a month-to-month basis. Some contractors even pay drive time at minimum wage, not the normal hourly employee rate.

If drive time is significant enough that it may mean the difference between winning the bid or not, total it up (add labor burden, G&A overhead, and net profit) and show it to your crew. Ask them if they're willing to give it up for the sake of getting additional work. Quite often, crews will work with you, especially if you're running out of work or are looking at a job that takes place toward the end of the season.

What to Wash Through If necessary, motels, delivery charges, permits, and contingency factors can be "washed through" the bid without adding G&A overhead or net profit to them. However, if the market will bear it, add G&A overhead and net profit to these items.

Prevailing Wage Rates Labor hours for off-site fabrication of irrigation assemblies and pumps, drive time, hauling material, mobilization of equipment, and so on, don't necessarily have to be paid at the prevailing wage rate. Check your bid documents, labor tables, or labor board to be sure.

Crew Size If you can effectively double the size of your crew, you should see a doubling of your production, thereby cutting in half the number of days on a job. This, of course, isn't always possible, but it will illustrate my point. As a result, your crew pickup truck hours, supervisor hours, dumpsters, and anything where cost is tied to the length of a project may decrease as well.

Analyze Your Bid Price

After you put your bid together, analyze your price according to the six most common ways of pricing projects in use today. These six methods are discussed in greater detail in Chapter 38. They are

1. Factoring
2. Market-Driven Unit Pricing (MDUP)

3. The Single Overhead Recovery System (SORS)/GPM Method
4. The Dual Overhead Recovery System (DORS) Method
5. The Multiple Overhead Recovery System (MORS) Method
6. The G&A Overhead and Profit Per Hour (OPPH) Method

Factoring To determine the "Factor" for a job, divide the total price of the project by total material costs.

Installation projects will normally have a ratio of 3 or 4:1. This means material will comprise 25 to 33% of the price of a project. Maintenance projects usually have a ratio of 10 to 20:1, or 5 to 10% of the price.

If your "Factor" for an installation project is 2:1 or less (meaning that materials comprise over 50% of the price of the job), you'd better look at it very carefully. Either you're installing very expensive materials, or using very aggressive production rates, or both. Just be sure you feel confident of your production rates for labor and for equipment.

Market-Driven Unit Pricing (MDUP) Unless your estimating is computerized and your software is programmed correctly, deriving unit prices is one of the most difficult aspects of estimating. Compare unit prices for your bid to those for previous jobs and to those commonly seen in your market. If your unit prices are too low, adjust them up individually by adding a little more net profit margin. If they seem high, check your production rates and material costs, and adjust them downward if warranted. You can do this by either increasing production rates or decreasing net profit margins.

Gross Profit Margin (GPM) The GPM on a bid can be a very reliable "truth teller" in many markets. It can be one of your most important tools for evaluating a bid.

Once you've tracked your GPM on a number of jobs for a particular market (commercial or residential construction or maintenance, irrigation for golf courses, commercial or residential installation, etc.), you'll have a better understanding of both your market and how your bids relate to it. Review and compare the GPM on a job being bid to historical ones in that market.

The Dual Overhead Recovery System (DORS) Method If you've used the DORS method, you might want to reprice the bid using your DORS markup percentages on material and labor costs. A comparison may be very insightful.

The Multiple Overhead Recovery System (MORS) Method Although the MORS method is cumbersome and overly complex, if you've used it in the past (and have a feel for how the market responds to prices produced by it), I'd encourage you to review your G&A overhead recovery by "backing" into your G&A overhead recovery percentages on labor and labor burden.

This is accomplished by following these steps:

1. Determine the total G&A overhead to be recovered in your bid.

   $4,800

2. Multiply materials (including tax) by 10%.

   $10,000 × .10 = $1,000

3. Multiply equipment costs by 25%.

   $1,424 × .25 = $356

4. Multiply total subcontractor costs by 5%. There are none in our example.
5. Subtract G&A overhead recovered from material, equipment, and subcontractors from total G&A overhead to be recovered on the bid.

   $4,800
   – 1,000
   – 356
   $3,444

6. The result is the remaining G&A overhead to be recovered from labor and labor burden.

   To determine the markup percentage on labor and labor burden, simply divide the amount to be recovered (e.g., $3,444) by the total cost of labor plus labor burden (e.g., $6,490).

   $3,444 ÷ $6,490 = .531 or 53%

   Compare the percentage markup on labor and labor burden for this job to those that were established by the MORS budget for the year (if you have one and if you've used this method in the past).

The G&A Overhead and Net Profit Per Hour (OPPH) Method The OPPH method is the preferred pricing method, which you should have used to bid your job in the first place. Consequently, you've already analyzed your bid using this method. However, after reviewing your bid by using some or all of the other methods of pricing, if your PPH (Net Profit per Hour) is higher or lower than your budgeted PPH for the year, you might want to increase or decrease your net profit margin on the bid to bring it more in line with your budgeted PPH.

A safe, minimum amount of net profit to put on your jobs is your budgeted PPH for the year. You should not go much below it unless you're in a time and materials billing (T&M) situation.

Your PPH on material-intensive jobs, however, may be significantly higher than your budgeted one. An example may help.

EXAMPLE

Calculating GPM

Materials at wholesale cost (including tax) for the Johnson's landscape and irrigation renovation for her home total $10,000. Labor and labor burden total another $6,490. Equipment costs are $1,424. No subcontractors are used on the job. The bid analysis appears in Figures 15-1 and 15-2 on pages 118 and 119.

G&A overhead, net profit margin (NPM), and the GPM percent on this project are calculated as follows:

1. G&A overhead % = G&A overhead ($4,800) ÷ Total price ($28,392) = 16.9%
2. Material (minus tax) as a percent of the job = $9,524 ÷ $28,392 = 33.6%
3. NPM % = Net profit ($5,678) ÷ Total Price ($28,392) = 20.0%
4. GPM = G&A overhead ($4,800) + Net profit ($5,678) ÷ Total price ($28,392)
   = $10,478 ÷ $28,392 = 36.9%

A GPM of 36.9% is about right for most residential markets. The PPH for this bid is $17.77 ($5,678 ÷ 320 man-hours), which is high but okay because this is a high-production and somewhat material-intensive job.

Scenario cost data	$ or %	Remarks
Crew size (# people)	3.0	Crew leader and 2 laborers
Crew average wage (CAW)	$ 13.00	
Overtime factor (OTF)	10.0%	50 hours per week
Risk factor (RF)	10.0%	
Crew average wage w/OTF & RF	$ 15.60	
Labor burden	30.0%	
Sales tax	5.0%	
G&A overhead per hour (OPH)	$ 15.00	
Net profit margin	20.0%	
Van	$ 8.00	
Curb-time man-hours per day	250.0	
Number of units	1.0	Lump sum

Scenario	Materials	Labor		Equipment	CPH	Hours	Item
I. Production (curb-time) costs							
	$ 9,524.00	250.0	Man-hours	$ 880.00	$ 20.00	44.0	Skid steer
	$ -			$ -	$ -	0.0	
	$ -	$ 15.60		$ -	$ -	0.0	
	$ 9,524.00	$ 3,900.00		$ 880.00			
II. General conditions (off-site or non-curb-time) costs							
		70.0	Man-hours	$ 544.00	$ 8.00	68.0	One ton truck
		0.0		$ -	$ -	0.0	
	$ -	$ 15.60		$ -	$ -	0.0	
	$ -	$ 1,092.00		$ 544.00			
Subtotals	**$ 9,524**	**$ 4,992**		**$ 1,424**			
III. Margins & markups							
A. Sales tax	$ 476						
B. Labor burden		$ 1,498					
Subtotals	**$ 10,000**	**$ 6,490**		**$ 1,424**			

Total direct costs (TDC)		**$ 17,914**	**TDC**
C. G&A overhead costs 320 (Total number of man-hours x OPH)	$ 15.00 =	$ 4,800	
BEP (TDC + G&A overhead)		**$ 22,714**	**BEP**
D. Contingency factor (if desired)		$ -	
E. Net profit margin 20.00%		$ 5,678	
F. Total price		**$ 28,392**	

IV. Scenario analysis

A. Sales or revenue per hour (Total price ÷ total hours)

$ 28,392	divided by	320.0 =	**$ 88.73**	**SPH**

B. Material-to-labor ratio (Total price ÷ total materials)

$ 28,392	divided by	$ 9,524 =	**2.98 : 1**	**M/L ratio**

C. Gross profit margin ((G&A overhead + Net profit) ÷ Total price)

$ 10,478	÷	$ 28,392 =	**36.9%**	**GPM**

FIGURE 15-1 Johnson Residence (Computer) Worksheet

Date: 2 / 25 / 20___ **Job:** Johnson Residence

I. PRODUCTION OF FINISHED PRODUCT/SERVICE:

Materials	Labor	Equipment	Subcontractors
(A) $ 9,524	(B) $ 3,900	(C) $ 880	(D) $ Ø

II. GENERAL CONDITIONS:

	Materials	Labor	Equipment	Subcontractors
	(A) $ Ø	(B) $ 1,092	(C) $ 544	(D) $ Ø
(Subtotal 1)	$ 9,524	$ 4,992	$ 1,424	$ Ø

III. MARGINS and MARKUPS:

A. $ 476 (Sales tax 5.0 % on materials)

B. (Labor burden % 30.0) $ 1,498

(Subtotal 2)	$ 10,000	$ 6,490	$ 1424	$ Ø

(Subtotal 3) Total direct costs or **TDC** (Sum of all items in subtotal 2 above)	$ 17,914
C. G&A overhead recovery (Total hours in I & II multiplied by OPH)	$ 4,800
D. **BEP**: (Total direct costs plus G&A overhead)	$ 22,714
E. Contingency factor if applicable	$ Ø
F. Net profit margin	$ 5,678
G. Total price for the job (D+E+F)	$ 28,392

IV. RATIO / PER HOUR ANALYSIS:

A. SPH / RPH:	$ 88.73		J. MAT/LAB:	1.91 : 1
B. DCPH:	$ ___.___		K. MPH:	$ ___.___
C. OPH:	$ 15.—		L. EQ/LAB:	___ : 1
D. PPH:	$ ___.___		M. EQPH:	$ ___.___
E. BEP:	$ 22714.—	80.0 %	N. GC:	$ 1636.—
F. G&A ovhd.:	$ 4,800.—	16.9 %	O. GCPH:	$ ___.___
G. NPM:	$ 5,678.—	20.0 %	P. GCH/TH:	___.___ %
H. GPM:	$ 10,478.—	36.9 %	Q. FACTOR:	2.98
I. GPMPH:	$ 32.74	36.9 %	R. UNIT PRICE:	$ ___.___

FIGURE 15-2 Bid Analysis/Review (BAR) Worksheet

Other Considerations

Ratio Analysis Once a bid is complete, you should compare ratios for your bid to those in your budget. If they vary significantly, analyze your bid in order to ascertain why. In most cases, there's usually a simple explanation (e.g., expensive plant materials in the bid, large amount of equipment, no equipment needed for the job, etc.).

Let's examine our most common ratios and per hour calculations that come from your annual budget projections for your company or division.

1. Sales or revenue per hour (SPH or RPH): The result of dividing annual sales per division by total annual projected field-labor hours.
2. G&A overhead cost per hour (OPH): Arrived at by dividing total G&A overhead by total annual projected field-labor hours.
3. Net profit margin per hour (NPMPH or PPH): Obtained by dividing net profit margin plus the contingency factor, if used, by total annual projected field-labor hours.
4. Gross profit margin per hour (GPMPH): Obtained by adding OPH to NPMPH.
5. Material-to-labor ratio (M/L): The total projected material costs divided by the total projected field-labor dollar costs.
6. Material per hour (MPH): Infrequently used, this figure is obtained by dividing total projected material costs by total projected field-labor hours.
7. Equipment per hour (EQPH): Obtained by dividing total projected equipment costs (plus rentals) by total projected labor hours.
8. Equipment-to-labor ratio (EQ/L): The ratio obtained by dividing total projected equipment costs (plus rentals) by total projected field-labor costs.
9. G&A overhead recovery (the Traditional or MORS method): This calculates the dollar amount and the average markup percentage that needs to be added to labor and burden in order to recover G&A overhead on the job using the MORS method.

Material, equipment, and subcontractor markup percentages are set at 10%, 25%, and 5%, respectively. The balance is obtained from labor and burden. Note that the four percentages don't have to add up to 100%.

Reviewing Net Profit Margin (NPM) If you've calculated your net profit margin as we outlined in Chapter 13, the answer should be close to where you want it to be. However, it is worth reviewing the procedure and your calculations when analyzing a completed bid. I recommend that you recalculate your net profit margin to ensure that it is neither too high nor too low.

Prevailing Wage Projects *Do your homework.* This is a law that must govern all bidding situations and is especially true of those using prevailing wage rates.

1. *Verify* your labor rates. Because CAW (crew average wages) on rated jobs can be double (even triple) those of nonrated ones, it's imperative that you use the correct CAW in the bid. An erroneously high CAW can render your bid

noncompetitive. Erroneously low ones can cause significant underbidding and losses on the project.

Obtain the labor rates *in writing.*

- They're included in the bid documents and federal and state labor tables.
- If necessary, call your state or federal labor board, or consult a labor attorney who specializes in this area.

➤ NOTE Quite often, you're allowed to have varying types of labor with diverse rates in your prevailing wage crews.

---

2. Verify your labor burden. Required benefits aren't always easily calculated for rated projects. Company ESOPs, pension plans, medical benefits, etc., may legitimately substitute for those identified in the bid documents and/or labor specifications. When calculating labor burden onto labor, ensure that you're neither double-dipping (charging twice) nor excluding required benefits.
3. Review general conditions. Look for those labor functions that may not require prevailing wage rates. For example, off-site fabrication, drive time, warranty work, owner's on-site labor, etc., may or may not be excluded from prevailing wage rates. Check the wage determination table in the bid documents/job specifications or call the state labor board or U.S. Department of Labor.

"Double-Dipping" the Owner's Salary This is a means of dropping your CAW considerably. The scenario is realistic and can be used in extremely competitive situations.

If all of an owner's salary is in G&A overhead and if he or she is going to work in the field and be part of production hours on a certain project, you could (theoretically) compute your CAW with one member's wage (the owner's) being zero.

More often than not, however, you'd probably underprice the project and leave money on the table. To prevent this, enter a "fair market value" (realistic labor rate) for the owner when calculating your CAW.

When in doubt, leave it out. Risk management is the name of the game.

Exclusions and Deletions *"When in doubt, leave it out." Risk management* is the name of the game. If there are portions of a job where you feel the risk is too great and/or your experience level with that type of work isn't up to the challenge, don't be afraid to submit a bid excluding that portion of the work. You could also subcontract that portion of the job to reduce your risk.

The Old "*Gut*" Check After you've done your homework (reviewed, analyzed, and scrutinized a bid), sit back and take note of how you *feel* about it. Your "gut" can tell you a lot.

Once a bid is completed, I wouldn't recommend shaving more than a couple of points of net profit from it. However, I'd never be afraid of pushing it higher—embarrassingly high, in some cases. It's always smart to occasionally explore the high limit of a market with an unjustifiably high net profit margin.

Of course, remember to take into consideration how accurate your "gut" has been in the past and make adjustments as appropriate.

SUMMARY

Reviewing completed bids can be a very quick and informal event, or it can be a lengthy, formal process.

Reviewing completed bids can be a very quick and informal event, or it can be a lengthy, formal process. The key is to prevent tunnel vision and oversights by using a system of **checks and balances**. That "extra set of eyes" can prove invaluable, saving you lost dollars and lost opportunities.

ACTION POINT

Review three or four jobs you've already bid and completed. This exercise should prove invaluable as you compare your estimated costs and margins to those actually achieved.

If you'd like to discuss this process, review a specific bid, or obtain a copy of the computerized version of the worksheets, please contact our offices.

CHAPTER

16

Estimating Strategies

TERMS

Add Value
Business Strategies
Constant Improvement
Estimating Strategy
Hidden Agendas
Manage the Expectations
Meaningful Managerial Terms (MMT)
Objective Reference Points
Overdeliver
Referrals
Repeat Business
Underpromise
Value Engineering

Purpose

To outline some key strategies to use at the bid table

Introduction

Estimating, or bidding your work, and **business strategies** must go hand in hand. What's good at the bid table usually has a positive effect on the business as a whole, and good business strategy will impact your estimating. If your business strategy isn't accurately reflected at the bid table and in your bids, you're asking for trouble down the line.

Business sales may take off, but if work is priced wrong, the more work you get, the more money you may lose. Forgetting to connect estimating with business strategy is like the stagecoach driver who forgets to hitch the horses to the coach. You can bet he won't be short on excitement (or bumps).

As we discuss strategy, I want to stress again that the foundational principle on which we'll build comes from a statement by Philip Crosby in his book, *Quality Is Free.*

> *Good things happen only when planned. Bad things happen on their own.*[3]

Good, sound planning is a process. It's a skill that requires constant learning and adjustment. The more skilled we are at it, the better the results.

We'll discuss **estimating strategy** by breaking it into four sections.

- Your *Bids*
- Your *Customers*
- Your *Business*
- Your *Jobs*

Good things happen only when planned. Bad things happen on their own.

This should help you compartmentalize and relate to the process more effectively. We need not go into great detail, as most of the strategies are actually rather simple. Let's get started.

YOUR BIDS

Be Organized and Methodical

- Remember PATT = Plan the Place, the Activity, the Time, and the Tools.
- *Block out* the time on a schedule and ask not to be disturbed. Have your voice mail or secretary record calls that can be returned later.
- *Be sure* you have all the tools you need *before* you start (plans, pencils, pads, counter, etc.).

Pre-Bid Site Review

- Visit the proposed construction site (if possible).
- *Insist* on clear, detailed specifications, bid documents, plans and/or designs, and addenda. Do not hesitate to ask for clarification.

Bid the Job

Bid it *step-by-step* in your mind and on paper, just as you'll build it in the field.

Use Objective Reference Points

- *Verify* your production rates by checking past job-cost data or outside reference books/manuals. See the reference list in the back of the book for further details.
- *Obtain* quotes, in writing, from suppliers and subcontractors.

Delegate

If possible, *delegate* tedious work (takeoffs, costing materials, etc.).

Be Selective

- *Know* your strengths *and* your weaknesses.
- *Study* your company (division), and do an honest appraisal of what you do best (residential, design/build, commercial construction and/or maintenance, athletic fields, etc.).
- Pursue these markets (what you do best) *aggressively.*

Crystallize Your Thinking

Don't deal in generalities. Think *specifics* and be *exact.* Don't just SWAG (scientific wild anti-analytical guess) it or use some sort of mystical factors (ones you hope will save you). Ask

- What size crew will effectively get the job done?
- What's the desired GPM on the job being bid?
- How many 1-, 5-, 15-gallon shrubs can your crew plant per hour?
- Consider as many questions as you can. Ad infinitum.

Make Money Everywhere

- Don't think "loss leader."
- Don't think the amount of net profit you're willing to give up on a job is your advertising budget for the year.
- Accurately identify time and materials (T&M) rates by including labor burden and an overtime factor, if applicable.

Think Risk Management

Labor production rates and conditions can vary dramatically from job to job. *Remember, variables increase risk.*

- When bidding work, think in terms of best-case and worst-case scenarios. Ask yourself, "What's the worst set of circumstances that could happen on this job? What's the best?"
- Determine the most likely set of circumstances and plan accordingly.
- Bid according to the scenario chosen by adjusting your risk factor on labor.
- Subcontract work to another contractor who's more familiar with that type of work if you consider the risk too great.

Variables increase risk.

Have Someone Check Your Bid

Guard against tunnel vision. Think "extra set of eyes," be it a foreman, field superintendent, or whoever. I personally review a lot of bids for contractors over the telephone. By asking certain questions, I can sometimes dramatically change the pricing.

Check Your Gut

- Do you "have" to get this job?
- Are you being too pessimistic or too optimistic about the risk factors involved?
- Is a developer or general contractor trying to manipulate you or back you into a corner?
- Are you rushing or "forcing" the bidding process and overlooking key items?
- Are you impatient, stressed out, and/or overwhelmed?
- Do you often feel remorse (bidder's remorse) after you get a job?

Your emotions before, during, and after the bidding process can tell you a lot. Be aware of your emotions and take the necessary steps that will make the bidding process a positive, rather than a negative, event.

Let Your Price Do Your Talking

Don't get caught up in long, undesirable discussions—especially when you don't really want the job (at any price).

If the job is too small, inconvenient, or not worth the hassle with an owner, architect, etc., add 20 to 30% (or more) net profit to your bid.

Give the client your price, step back, and watch. Don't attempt to justify it. Just say this is what you need to cover your costs on the job, realizing that 20 to 30% of the price is the emotional cost to you.

Let your price do your talking.

YOUR CUSTOMERS

See the Job Through the Customers' Eyes

- *Take notes.*
- *Ask* dozens of *questions.*
- Realize that most residential clients don't entirely understand what they're getting into. Get on their "wavelength" by asking insightful questions, and by using the next step.
- *Be observant*—Stop, look, and listen!

Uncover and Identify Hidden Agendas

Most of us have already met "the customer from hell." Some people have **hidden agendas**. The earlier we identify them, the better our chance of managing the situation, the customer's expectations, and the job (should we decide to take it).

Clients may be asking for your bid merely as a part of their process of shopping around with leads from the "Yellow Pages" and other such directories. Be aware that they're usually looking for the lowest price. Some people will attempt to grind you to get your prices down. Others will nickel-and-dime you to death.

How It Works

One of my clients did work for an attorney. Halfway through the job, my client noticed the attorney's license plate. It read, "SUE EM." This is what I call a hidden agenda. Identify them (the client and the agenda) early, before you sign a contract if you can.

Manage the Expectations of Your Customers

Customers (people) want "certainty." In business, certainty is achieved when the performance standard achieved is equal to the one that was desired and planned. Many expectations (or standards) are *nonnegotiable* ones concerning ethical treatment, courtesy, safety, legalities, and so on. Other expectations *are negotiable*, such as pricing, schedules, and the production process.

Remember, in business, there is no such thing as a good surprise.

There's usually a lot of room for negotiation and flexibility. However, once expectations are set and communicated to the client, you should *meet* or *exceed* them. Learn how to identify, direct, and control: in essence, **manage the expectations** of your clients and meet or exceed them.

Meeting your customers' expectations will build credibility, trust, referrals, and/or repeat business: **underpromise** and **overdeliver**.

Surprises do just the opposite. Remember, in business, there is *no such thing as a good surprise*.

Educate Your Customer

Whenever possible, educate your client about the product and/or service provided. Explain irrigation timing, maintenance and fertilization requirements, plant material, etc. Nurture and cultivate your leads and customers, and make them more *informed customers*.

Solve Your Clients' Problems

Teach everyone in your business to see themselves as problem solvers. Train them to look for, identify, and solve customers' problems.

Add Value in Your Client's Eyes

- Be aware of the studies and statistics that will help your client be confident of the value of his or her investment. If appropriate, share this information with your client.

How It Works

According to brochures published by the Associated Landscape Contractors of America (ALCA), the American Nursery & Landscape Association (ANLA), and the Professional Plant Growers' Association (PPGA):

- *MONEY Magazine* reports that landscaping can have a recovery value of 100-200 percent.

! Reminder

If customers could (had the time, talent, tools, and/or desire) solve their own problems, they wouldn't need you.

- The Gallup Organization reports that, overall, new home buyers and buyers of previously-owned homes estimate that landscaping, on the average, adds 14.8 percent to the value or selling price of their home.[4]

Brochures with this information and other similar literature are available through ALCA, ANLA, and PPGA. See the List of Associations in the back of this book to obtain contact information for these and other associations.

Use this type of information to your and your clients' advantage.

- Think **value engineering**. By this, I mean that you should attempt to improve the project from the client's perspective. Large and small things can add value to a product or service by making a client's life simpler and less encumbered. Some large items are
  - Cost savings
  - Automatic controllers
  - Full-service maintenance
  - Lifetime warranties of plant materials

  Smaller items may be
  - Conveniently placed stepping stones
  - Strategically located annual plants that enhance the grounds and make the site "pop" out at you

  All of these (and more) can add value in the eyes of the client. Some items may have direct monetary value, others may not.

Negotiate from a Position of Strength

Information is power. If you know your "numbers" concerning a bid, this will translate into a sense of confidence, and confidence engenders trust. *Trust* wins the negotiating battle. As George Schultz (former United States Secretary of State) said, "Trust *is* the coin of the realm."

Listen, Listen, Listen

Trust wins the negotiating battle. As George Schultz (former United States Secretary of State) said, "Trust *is* the coin of the realm."

Most problems and disputes boil down to improper communication. If you analyze the disagreements, arguments, and surprises you've experienced, you'll probably find that 99% of them were caused because somebody didn't listen. Listen intently and carefully.

- Play back (repeat) to the other party what you think you heard.
- Ask him or her if "such-and-such" is what was meant.
- Stop and ask questions such as: "Does this make sense to you?" or "Do you mean ...?"
- Listen and *take notes.*
- Observe *body language.*

Add Credibility to Your Information

Use references to bolster your position.

- A newspaper or magazine article can help build the trust factor between you and your clients.

- Use association produced materials wisely. They can build trust.
- Computer printouts can, if used properly, add immense credibility to your position.

I'm amazed at the number of my clients who've told me they won jobs, in large part, because prospective customers were so impressed by the spreadsheets and the information generated by our estimating software. Properly formatted, accurate information builds credibility.

Know that Your Customers Can Pay

Ensure that your potential customers have the ability to pay.

- Do a credit check.
- Check bank references.
- Check credit cards.
- Talk to other contractors doing work for the potential client. Ask them how the client pays and what they are like to work with.
- If the job is important or big enough, have your bank or bonding company review the potential client's credit history.

YOUR BUSINESS

Management

- Develop and pursue *written goals* and *budgets*. Remember what Tom Peters says in his book, *Thriving on Chaos*: "What gets measured gets done ..."[5]

  If you can't measure it, you can't direct and control it. Management by mysticism does not get results.
- Think and communicate in **meaningful managerial terms** (MMTs).

  If you want to excite and motivate your people, you must
  - Be *specific.*
  - Use *solid* (concrete) *terminology.*
  - Speak in terms of *objective measurable standards.*

  If you can't measure it, you can't direct and control it. Management by mysticism does not get results.

  Vague terms, nebulous goals, and an almost mystical sense of direction will never provide the direction or drive necessary for a successful business. Explorers make charts and maps of their discoveries so others can follow in their tracks. Doctors, researchers, and scientists employ the scientific method (with all its shared documentation) in order to unravel the unknown. So too, business people must use MMTs as they strive to communicate and improve the process of providing excellent products and services.
- Encourage *creativity.* Adapt and develop new markets, products, and services.
- Link TQM (Total Quality Management) to measurable standards, goals, and results. Implement TQM and measurable standards throughout the company, not just in the field.
- Think **constant improvement**. Every process, product, and service can be improved. Nothing ever "arrives" and remains at a point of stasis forever. Refine, refine, and refine should be your constant theme.
- See the *big picture.* Legitimate business is the process of accumulating wealth while providing worthy products and services that assist others in the pursuit of worthwhile goals.

Business, good business, is really the people-growing business. While sound estimating and business strategy can help you make money, there's more. See yourself as a coach who develops (nurtures) his or her team (the people) and strives for constant improvement everywhere. Every person, place and/or thing, in all aspects of your life, should be better when you leave than when you arrived.

Marketing

- *Know* your market.
  - Know where you fit in.
  - Be selective.
  - Understand what you do best and be aware of your weaknesses. Be very cautious when you approach work that has been trouble for you in the past.
  - Pursue your strong suit with a vengeance.
- See the *long-term* cash flow consequences of **repeat business** and **referrals**.

How It Works

Due to poor quality control, a commercial landscape and irrigation maintenance company lost a municipal contract—one that had brought in $500,000 a year for a number of years. Not only did it lose a half million dollars of revenue for that year, but for ____ years in the future. You fill in the blank.

Your customers are your best advertisement. Whereas a satisfied customer may tell two or three other potential clients about you, statistics show that a dissatisfied customer will tell nine or ten.[6] It's up to you to determine if these "ads" are going to be good or bad ones for your business.

For example, a gas company was putting in a seven-mile-long, four-inch gas main through a town where one of my clients lived. The company had to trench and install the line across lawns and backyards. The areas had to be resodded and/or hydroseeded. When asked for suggestions as to who should perform the work, the homeowners insisted that my client receive the contract. When my client was invited to bid the work, he didn't even know the job was up for bid. He asked the gas company who he'd be bidding against. When told, he informed the company representative that his (my client's) prices were always higher than the other two bidders. My client was told that as long as his price was reasonable, he'd get the work. Thanks to customer referrals, my client got the job and did similar work for the gas company all over that part of the country.

Imagine it. This contractor had the job before he even knew there was a job to be had. He got the referral, which will probably lead to even more "repeat" business.

Do you understand the long-term implications of how you conduct your business?

- Don't fall into the trap of having to be "low bidder."

  A commercial landscape and irrigation contractor once told me that if he wasn't the low bidder, he didn't get the job. He rarely, if ever, negotiated work. After seeing him and his operation in action, I knew why: No one in their right minds would want to repeat the experience they'd had with this guy.

  If you have to be low bidder to get a job, you're probably doing something wrong. See it as a symptom of a larger problem.

- Don't wrestle with a pig. He likes it; you get dirty.

  Smart generals choose their battles wisely. The battles not fought—the ones you'd probably lose—are the most important ones of all.

- Selectively *experiment* with *marketing.*

  There are many, many marketing ideas and methods you could pursue. I know contractors who've lost thousands of dollars, hundreds of hours invested, and even their companies due to poorly-thought-out marketing methods.

  - Conduct small experiments that cost you only a few dollars.
  - Monitor the results and then throw gasoline where the fire is.

  In other words, see success before you commit large amounts of money or time to a new, unproven approach.

- *Target* your markets. I encourage landscape and irrigation contractors to identity

  - Landscape architects
  - Developers
  - Designers
  - General contractors
  - Purchasing agents
  - Base purchasing offices and officers
  - City parks and recreation departments
  - Condominium associations
  - Property managers

  Enter their names, addresses, telephone and FAX numbers, Web site and e-mail addresses into a computer database. Begin to develop and groom relationships with these potential clients (and sources of projects) by sending them a cover letter and some basic information about your company and its capabilities.

  - Keep it simple.
  - Follow up the letter with a phone call.
  - Ask about opportunities to bid work on any future projects.
  - Identify specific projects coming up for bid and refer to them in future telephone conversations.
  - Take notes.
  - Use a computer database.
  - Don't give up!

  Constantly *groom this list* as you develop relationships with the individuals on it. Calculate the approximate number of clients you'll need to serve in order to meet your short-term and long-term goals. Visualize the process of solving their problems, which is why you're in business. Store vital information about them in your database. Use this approach in conjunction with the Bid Board that is discussed in Chapter 19.

Your Finances

- Train your company bureaucrats to support the field operation, and insist that they do so. Help them understand that's their job. Put them to work out in the field one or two days a month (or quarter).

  Set a goal to have your office staff prepare and provide *daily* job-cost reports for the field. This is an excellent goal that will focus their attention and their energies on supporting the people in the trenches with timely, accurate feedback.

- Train your field personnel to support the bureaucrats.
  - Purchase orders should be used throughout the company. Insist that field personnel use them.
  - Insist that field daily reports (FDRs), delivery tickets, and related paperwork be delivered to the office each and every day.

YOUR JOBS

Daily Job-Cost Reports

Timely, accurate feedback (TAF) can be the number one motivator for the whole company, if used properly. At a minimum, provide the field and key staff with daily job-cost reports for labor hours, comparing labor hours bid to actual performance.

"Re-" Bid the Job

Once you've won the job, go through it again from beginning to end. Look for mistakes and for hidden opportunities to make money.

How It Works

I once reviewed a $170,000 bid for a client. The contractor had misplaced a decimal point, costing him $6,000 in labor costs that should have been included in the bid. This contractor had neglected to account for the labor involved in the placement of a granite pathway. His unit cost was calculated to be $2.93 a square foot. It should have been $4.50.

The owner of the project was already leaning toward the installation of a concrete-type walkway. My client could subcontract this out for $2.50 a square foot. He got on the phone and persuaded the owner to "tilt his lean" into a change order. Rebidding turned a potential $6,000 loss into a nice gain.

Rebid your jobs after they're won. It pays!

Plan, Plan, Plan!

Murphy's law tends to prevail in this industry: If something can go wrong, it will—and at the worst possible time.

Murphy's law tends to prevail in this industry: If something can go wrong, it will—and at the worst possible time.

It's up to you to impose corporate willpower on circumstances that will naturally tend to disintegrate and self-destruct. Planning is the neverending process of focusing the corporate will on chaos and confusion.

Manage Your Risk by Using Subcontractors.

When in doubt, sub it out.

"When in doubt, sub it out." If the situation warrants, don't be afraid to pass the risk along, or at least to "share" it.

SUMMARY

We've only touched on some of the key strategies you might use. Of course, the possible strategies are endless. Study your industry and your business. Become a student of both.

Use a systematic, objective planning process as you implement your estimating strategy. When doing so, consider the following four areas:

- Your bids
- Your customers
- Your business
- Your jobs

This will help you compartmentalize and relate to the process more effectively.

ACTION POINT

Review the list of reference materials located in the back of this book. It will help you locate more sources of sound business and estimating strategy.

CHAPTER 17

Common Mistakes

Who's Through in Landscape & Irrigation Contracting?

TERM

Fatal Flaw

Purpose

To identify common bidding mistakes

Introduction

Businesses usually become dysfunctional for at least one of the following three reasons:

1. There's a serious (perhaps even fatal) flaw in the estimating system regarding
   - *General and administrative (G&A) overhead* recovery
   - Estimating and tracking *equipment* use
   - Estimating and handling of *field labor*

In this chapter we'll only address equipment and field labor, as we've already covered G&A overhead in previous chapters.

2. *Personal pride* (ego) interferes with the daily implementation of sound business principles and practices.
3. Owners are simply *not prepared* to be in business for themselves. They are overwhelmed because
   - They don't have the know-how (at this stage of their life) and training; and/or ...
   - They lack the emotional stamina required to meet and address the challenges of running a business.

NINE SCENARIOS

The following nine scenarios will help illustrate the most common mistakes made by contractors. I've labeled them as follows:

1. "Iron Man" Mike
2. The Sugar Daddy High
3. Too Much Caffeine (or Testosterone)

4. The Vampire Syndrome
5. Egomania
6. Looking for "Foxes" in All the Wrong Places ...
7. In God We Trust (All Others Use Purchase Orders)
8. The Psychology of Going Broke
9. Monopoly Money

"Iron Man" Mike (Mike Isn't His Real Name)

A construction company intended to employ enough field labor to total approximately 50,000 field-labor hours for the year. That's about 25 people full time, year round. Total equipment costs were estimated at about $450,000 for the year. Indirect general and administrative (G&A) overhead was estimated at another $300,000.

For bidding purposes, direct costs (material, labor, labor burden, and subcontractors) were included in the bid at cost. Equipment costs were combined with G&A overhead and added to the bid at $15 per estimated field-labor hour ($450,000 equipment costs plus $300,000 G&A overhead, both divided by the 50,000 projected field-labor hours).

Sounds simple enough, but there was a **fatal flaw** in the process. Equipment costs were not bid based on what would be needed for a particular job. All equipment costs were averaged and bid into all jobs the same, regardless of how much or how little equipment was required on each. Jobs requiring nothing more than pickup trucks and wheelbarrows were charged the same ($15 per hour) as those needing skid steers, trenchers, and backhoes.

"Iron Man" Mike

It is not uncommon for contractors to estimate their jobs in this manner. The consequences are subtle and eventually can be disastrous.

- Labor-intensive jobs (requiring only pickup trucks and wheelbarrows) are estimated far too high with inflated equipment costs. Consequently, you don't get these jobs in a competitive market because your price is too high.
- Jobs that are extremely equipment-intensive are estimated too low for equipment costs. Because the bids are underpriced, you get these jobs—and you keep getting them. The result is that you're using all your equipment but charging your customers for only a fraction of its actual cost.

Two things need to happen in order to correct this scenario.

1. Equipment bid into every job should be bid the same as you'd bid labor. Equipment should be included in bids only as the job requires. *Actual usage*, in hours, should be multiplied by a predetermined cost per hour (CPH) figure.
2. Equipment usage must be monitored through job costing on a job-by-job basis. This will ensure that equipment costs bid into specific jobs are compared to equipment costs actually incurred on the job.

The Sugar Daddy High

A commercial landscape and irrigation contractor and a large homebuilder developed a close relationship. The homebuilder provided the contractor with over $1 million of work a year.

This contractor was the envy of other landscape and irrigation contractors in his market. The pricing of the work was reasonable; the builder paid the contractor within ten days of being invoiced. Yet the contractor managed to go broke. Why? For a couple of reasons.

1. There were no *internal controls*.
   Jobs were bid accurately and competitively, but they weren't job costed. There was no effective planning or quality control in the field. The crews weren't directed properly, and the client's problems weren't addressed and solved quickly and effectively. As a result, jobs would drag on because the crews didn't develop a "sense of urgency" to complete them.

   The company kept digging itself into a larger and larger hole as it scrambled to *rob Peter* (bill new work) to *pay Paul* (pay off old bills for jobs completed 6 to 12 months earlier).

Don't get intoxicated on a "sugar daddy high." It's not a question of *if* you'll lose your sugar daddy, but *when*.

2. The landscape and irrigation firm became a *captive* subcontractor.
   It was subtle at first, but in the end the consequences were inevitable. Eventually, the contractor relinquished control of his company to the builder.

   The builder began to dictate schedules that precluded the landscaper from working for other clients. The homebuilder began to ask the contractor to do a few free "favors" (i.e., landscape his home, his secretary's home, his purchasing agent's home, a local church, etc.). The homebuilder also didn't expect to be charged for legitimate extras.

   When the economy in that area began to go into recession (in 1990), the homebuilder had no work to give the landscaper. The landscaper, who hadn't pursued other clients, had nowhere to turn. His cash flow stopped, but past-due payables and payroll taxes didn't. Because of his entrenched bad habits, he was unable to turn his business around. He skipped town owing over $145,000 to suppliers, the IRS, and former friends.

My point is this: Don't get intoxicated on a "sugar daddy high." It's not a question of *if* you'll lose your sugar daddy, but *when*.

Too Much Caffeine (or Testosterone)

A few years back, a hard-charging, concrete contractor in the Southwest was feeling pretty good. He'd just had a year with over $1.5 million in gross sales and a net profit of well over 15%. He decided to "put the pedal to the metal," so to speak, and grow even more. He had office help, but decided he needed a full-time estimator. So he hired one—one who had very little experience.

Over the next 12 months, his sales increased to $2.5 million. Unfortunately, his bottom line went from a 15% net profit for the year to a 10% loss, even with the increased sales.

What went wrong? I boiled it down to three main items.

1. Bids weren't reviewed.
   The new (and unproven) estimator was allowed to bid work without the owner or someone else reviewing his work. This cost the company about $150,000.
2. Field communication and audit trails were not in place.
   People in the field made decisions and changed the product without proper approval or documentation from inspectors or the owner. One retaining wall had to be replaced, which cost the contractor over $50,000. Other similar mistakes cost another $40,000 to $50,000.
3. Proven systems and office staff weren't in place prior to growth.
   This company could just about handle the pace of $1.5 million in gross annual sales. There were problems (the flow of paperwork would become congested, job costing would be late or not done at all, change orders wouldn't be adequately documented), but these problems were not insurmountable.

   Unfortunately, the owner didn't try to resolve these problems in his systems before he decided to increase sales. Management was soon overwhelmed. Lack of documentation, litigation, and disorganization cost

You take care of the business, and the business will take care of you. If you don't, it won't.

another $150,000 to $200,000. The owner (and the company) never did recover.

Simply put, the owner managed neither himself nor his company. He thought he could run his company on adrenaline (of which, by the way, he had plenty).

The moral of the story is: "You take care of the systems, and the systems will take care of you," or "You take care of the business, and the business will take care of you." If you don't, it won't.

Some contractors are so ego-driven they eventually deceive themselves.

The Vampire Syndrome

It would be so easy if all you had to do was to put bureaucracy in place (systems and procedures) and then watch things take off. There is, however, one added ingredient—people.

I'm convinced that some people, given the chance, could destroy a McDonald's fast food restaurant. They'd change the menu, eliminate the hamburgers, and fire the help. They'd find or invent some way to make it fail. Show them a hundred times how to do it right, and they'd change it and do it wrong.

Vampires are like that. They love to live in the dark. If you show them the light of day, they immediately run back into the dark and back to their habitual coffins. And a coffin is simply a rut with ends installed.

Some contractors are so ego-driven they eventually deceive themselves. They live in a "coffin" of sorts. The very thought of implementing good procedures and sound systems (the "light of day") makes them run for cover (the dark). No amount of coaching can draw them out of their cavernous lifestyles, and, unlike bats, they can't see in the dark.

Egomania

A rather large landscape management and construction company self-destructed. At its height this firm employed upwards of 400 to 500 people. In a well-publicized merger, the company almost doubled in size overnight and showed up in markets everywhere.

In their eyes, top management of this company could do no wrong. Marketing, advertising, and obtaining market share became paramount. Size went to their heads, and they began to believe they deserved all the attention being paid to them (attention that was primarily the result of their own marketing efforts). Three years later, they disintegrated. Why?

Image and marketing (a three-piece-suit-and-tie mentality) became the focal point of the company; but the systems necessary for daily direction and control weren't in place, nor were they developed. Estimating wasn't well developed; job-costing reports for specific jobs and crucial financial reports were never available. Some employees went for almost a year without knowing who they worked for or to whom they should report.

In essence, top management didn't understand that tried-and-proven systems, combined with a bureaucracy forced to focus upon supporting field operations, are the *heart* of any good landscape and irrigation construction or services operation.

Forget "image" and the marketing of that image if you don't have good systems. Without the proper systems, you'll only dig a deeper hole in which to bury yourself.

Looking for "Foxes" in All the Wrong Places

A large landscape construction and services company ($4 to $5 million in gross annual sales) spent nearly four years trying to get an accounting and job-costing

Fixin' the Right Problem

system into place. It went through a couple of software programs and as many comptrollers and bookkeepers. Management just couldn't get it together, and the recommendations of competent consultants always fell on deaf ears. The delay cost hundreds of thousands of dollars—most noticeably in the field. The estimator could produce good bids, so that wasn't the problem. Unfortunately, the field was incapable of bringing a job in on budget or on schedule.

Everyone knew there were multiple problems, but no one would listen to or implement any viable solutions. Everyone "hop-scotched" around the real problem. Activity, not results, became the focus.

Field production turned into a "Three Stooges" scene because there was no well-thought-out game plan. Things never improved because there was no job costing to identify specific problems. Labor-hour budgets weren't clearly spelled out to field personnel, nor was there any timely, accurate feedback to management or field crews. There was no scoreboard.

Because of all the confusion and lack of controls that would indicate if jobs were coming in on budget or not, the field superintendent was able to take advantage of the situation. He "ghosted" the company (put fictitious people on the field payroll) to the tune of about $50,000.

Things went from bad to worse. Wrong solution followed wrong solution in an attempt to fix the problems. It was like the chicken farmer who had a fox in his chicken coop. The farmer's solution was to throw more chickens into the coop. When that didn't work, he decided that what he needed was a larger chicken coop ("Let's see ... if we move this wall out to here ... add another down there ... buy some more chickens ...".)

As the saying goes, "Some days, chicken; other days, feathers."

In God We Trust (All Others Use Purchase Orders)

A landscape contractor was grossing approximately $500,000 to $600,000 a year in the residential and commercial installation market. Purchase orders (the paper trail

! Reminder

"A lock isn't meant to keep a thief out. It's meant to keep an honest man honest."

that identified who was ordering what for which job) weren't used. There was no system in place for job costing in order to compare bid-to-actual material costs. Invoices from suppliers were paid without proper documentation.

"Blind faith" replaced the control that a sound system of checks and balances (purchase orders) would have provided. Abuse was almost inevitable. Key (previously good) employees ran materials for "side" jobs through the company and embezzled approximately $40,000. I'm convinced that, had purchase orders been used properly, this problem could have been prevented. The temptation was just too much for employees to resist.

The Psychology of Going Broke

A landscape contractor, who was doing about $1 million in annual sales and losing money, had me bid a project for a general contractor (GC). This guy was desperate for cash; cash flow was his constant headache. This contractor had underpriced jobs for so long he could never catch up and pay off his suppliers. He desperately needed the cash flow from new jobs to pay off vendors for jobs up to 12 months old.

I came up with a price of $96,000 for the bid. The gross profit (net profit and G&A overhead) on the project was about $25,000. Direct costs were nearly $71,000.

The contractor called me from the GC's office to get the price for the job. I told him it was $96,000, with 10% ($9,600) net profit and 26% ($25,000) gross profit built into it. He asked me if I thought we could do it for $76,000. I explained to him that direct costs were $71,000. He asked me again if I thought we could do it for $76,000. The landscaper went on to tell me the GC had a check written out for $76,000, and if he agreed to do the job for that price, he'd get the job and the check that day.

Here's the rest of the story. This landscaper desperately needed the $76,000. The general contractor knew it. Suppliers were constantly calling and screaming at the landscaper for their money. His wife was constantly screaming at him for "her" money.

What would you do? Of course, the landscaper would dig a deeper hole for himself if he took the job at $76,000. However, it would almost be worth it for him to get everyone off his back, especially his wife.

I was totally baffled by the mentality of the landscaper until I realized this was the psychology behind going broke. It's a neverending downward spiral. It's like the alcoholic who, in order to stop the "shakes," has another drink. A short-term "false" solution creates a long-term "real" problem, one which many people won't survive. An intervention is needed to stop the downward spiral.

The landscaper took the $76,000 check and is still having cash flow problems.

Monopoly Money

During the height of the consolidation frenzy a few years ago, a number of my clients were approached by members of the consolidators' acquisition teams. I helped by coaching my clients through the acquisition process. A couple of them ended up selling their companies. Most decided not to go through with the deal.

A year after one client sold his company the buyer still hadn't inventoried the equipment involved in the deal. Another client, who refused to sell, was convinced the buyer (a corporate raider) was more interested in his dozen or so experienced account managers than in helping his existing business grow and serve his clients better. The account managers, he thought, would be sent to other recently purchased companies that were shorthanded. They were shorthanded because their managers all bailed out and left the newly acquired company.

A former client who did sell his business went to work for one of the big consolidators. He was appalled at the lack of planning, budgeting, systems, and

To the timeless adage, "Experience is the best teacher," we should add, "... preferably, someone else's."

forethought, given the number of companies that were bought. He thought he was joining a professionally run team. As it turned out, the atmosphere was more that of a Monopoly game where managers were playing with Monopoly money (and with people's lives and careers). Once again, shortsighted gains overrode long-term stability and profitability.

SUMMARY

It is my hope that these common-mistake scenarios will provide you with added insight about the management quagmires into which some people place themselves. To the timeless adage, "Experience is the best teacher," we should add, "... preferably, someone else's."

ACTION POINTS

1. For those of you who've committed these mistakes, cry.
2. For those of you who've avoided these mistakes, laugh.
3. For those of you who are currently making these mistakes, call or e-mail me.

Special Bidding Situations

Flat Rate, Specialty, and Maintenance Pricing

SECTION IV

Contents

Purpose

To provide some basic illustrations of the process and techniques for calculating prices of the more common products and services within the Green Industry

The costs used in our scenarios are for illustration purposes only. Your costs will vary from the ones used in these examples. The key is for you to build a typical one-day scenario for the crew, materials, and equipment mixes you use. Round up these rates as appropriate. If your costing structure is accurate, the rates you calculate should be very close to your current ones and to those generally seen in your market.

The scenarios chosen for this section do not, nor are they intended to, cover all possible scenarios or field techniques. You should adapt these illustrations to accommodate your specific production methods and market.

CHAPTER 18

Flat-Rate Pricing

TERMS

Curb Time
Enhancements
Flat Rate
Flat-Rate Pricing
Hurdle Amount
Maintenance Extras
Rate Card
Show-Up Fee
Standards
Trip Charge

Purpose

To introduce you to the concept of flat-rate pricing and to explain how flat-rate prices are calculated

Introduction

Flat-rate pricing is most commonly used in the plumbing and auto repair industries. Basically, it's a form of pricing that attempts to simplify the pricing process by charging an all-inclusive **flat rate** for a particular product or service. The flat rate includes labor, materials, and any equipment needed to perform the task. Essentially, you're providing the client with a grocery list of sorts from which to choose services and products.

How It Works

Last fall I had my furnace repaired. The technician arrived and identified the problem. He then pulled out a list that contained virtually all the potential repair services and products he might have to perform in the field. It took him no time at all to calculate a price for the needed work. Because the bill exceeded a minimum **hurdle amount**, the **trip charge** was waived. Otherwise, I would have had to pay a $65 show-up fee.

The auto repair industry does something very similar. Once the problem is diagnosed, a service representative pulls out a list of services and products and quotes a fee for each respective item. What you don't see is a comprehensive manual produced by each automobile manufacturer, listing all repairs and services by model year. This manual contains **standards** or benchmark labor hours and the materials required to perform the task in question. Service providers then attach their labor rates and material prices to these standards in order to calculate the price for each task or service.

The producers of these standards and manuals are wise enough to provide only labor hours and material lists. They realize that G&A overhead, labor costs, and burden all vary from one repair shop to the next. Therefore, they don't provide labor rates and material pricing.

Means Site Work & Cost Data Manual and *Kerr's Cost Data Manual for Landscape Construction* attempt to provide similar tools for the landscape industry. Unlike the manuals provided for the auto industry, these landscape manuals provide prices for labor and materials that include G&A overhead and labor burden.

The flat rate includes labor, materials, and any equipment needed to perform the task. Essentially, you're providing the client with a grocery list of sorts from which to choose services and products.

CALCULATING FLAT RATES

Calculating flat rates is a rather simple process. Basically, flat rates are unit prices similar to those calculated in other chapters. However, two items tend to complicate the pricing process. The first is the need to have a "trip" charge or **show-up fee**, where the non-site time for the day is covered and paid for by the client. Under normal circumstances, a typical service requires a minimum of one half-hour of non-site time to load/unload the truck and to drive to the client's site.

The second item that complicates the flat-rate pricing process is labor-only work. Irrigation service technicians often have to troubleshoot problems, or adjust heads and/or track valves. In this case, a predetermined labor rate is required to cover labor-only costs.

We'll cover three scenarios involving flat-rate pricing for the Green Industry. With some slight variations to our models, you should be able to calculate flat-rate prices for your products and services, and I'd encourage you to consider publishing a **rate card** listing them. This rate card can be for internal company purposes only. The important thing is to have your flat rates written down so that you can remember them.

Flat Rates for Maintenance Extras and Enhancements

Calculating flat rates for **maintenance extras** or **enhancements** is probably the easiest of our scenarios, whether it be for the commercial or residential market. The process is greatly simplified because the crews performing the work are usually on site on a regular basis. Or a full-time enhancement crew may perform all this work. Let's calculate a flat-rate price for installed flats of annual color. See Figure 18-1 as we discuss our scenario.

Scenario

We want to calculate a scenario for either a half or a whole day of producing the product in question. In this case, we'll use a whole day. Our two-person crew is working an 8-hour day and a 40-hour week. The crew average wage, risk factor, labor burden, and so on are as outlined in Figure 1-18 on page 147. Note that the crew will be installing color for seven of the eight hours per day, at a production rate of two flats per man-hour.

Our price per flat calculates to be a little over $33. I'd probably round this up to $35.

Flat Rate for Irrigation Spray Heads

Scenario

In this case, we'll calculate a scenario for a half day of installing spray heads. Our service technician is working a 10-hour day and a 50-hour week. The crew average wage, risk factor, labor burden, and so on are as outlined in Figure 18-2 on page 148. I used a production rate of four heads per hour. This may be conservative, but I'd rather understate than overstate our production rate. Note that ancillary materials (the funny pipe and elbow) are also included. I even included warranty call-back time and materials.

Our price per head calculates to be almost $39. Again, I'd round this up to $40 or higher, if at all possible.

However, we have problems. What if you only need to replace one head and it takes you an hour to get to and from the site? What if you get to the site and the head is only clogged? You have no materials to charge to the customer.

Scenario cost data	$ or %	Remarks
Crew size (# people)	2.0	Crew leader and laborer
Crew average wage (CAW)	$ 10.00	
Overtime factor (OTF)	0.0%	40 hours per week
Risk factor (RF)	10.0%	
Crew average wage w/OTF & RF	$ 11.00	
Labor burden	30.0%	
Sales tax	6.0%	
G&A overhead per hour (OPH)	$ 8.00	
Net profit margin	20.0%	
Crew truck	$ 6.00	
Curb-time man-hours per day	N/A	
Number of units	28.0	Flats of annual color

Scenario	Materials	Labor		Equipment	CPH	Hours	Item
I. Production (on-site or curb-time costs)							
28 Flats	$ 280.00	14.0	Man-hours	$ -	$ -	0.0	
5% Warranty	$ 14.00			$ -	$ -	0.0	
	$ -	$ 11.00		$ -	$ -	0.0	
	$ 294.00	$ 154.00		$ -			
II. General conditions (off-site or non-curb-time costs)							
		2.0	Man-hours	$ 48.00	$ 6.00	8.0	Crew truck
		1.0	Warranty	$ 6.00	$ 6.00	1.0	Warranty truck
	$ -	$ 11.00		$ -	$ -	0.0	
	$ -	$ 33.00		$ 54.00			
Subtotals	**$ 294**	**$ 187**		**$ 54**			
III. Margins & markups							
A. Sales tax	$ 18						
B. Labor burden		$ 56					
Subtotals	**$ 312**	**$ 243**		**$ 54**			

Total direct costs (TDC)		**$ 609**	**TDC**
C. G&A overhead costs 17.0 (Number of man-hours x OPH)	$ 8.00 =	$ 136	
BEP (subtotal of TDC + G&A overhead)		**$ 745**	**BEP**
D. Contingency factor (if desired)		$ -	
E. Net profit margin 20.00%		$ 186	
F. Total price		**$ 931**	**Total price**

IV. Scenario analysis

A. Unit flat rate (Total price ÷ units)			
$ 931 divided by	28.0 =	**$ 33.25**	**Unit price**
B. Sales or revenue per hour (Total price ÷ all man-hours)			
$ 931 divided by	17.0 =	**$ 54.76**	**SPH or RPH**
C. Gross profit margin ((G&A overhead + Net profit) ÷ Total price)			
$ 322 divided by	$ 931 =	**34.6%**	**GPM**

FIGURE 18-1 Flat Rate for Flats of Annual Color

Scenario cost data

	$ or %	Remarks
Crew size (# people)	1.0	Service technician
Crew average wage (CAW)	$ 15.00	
Overtime factor (OTF)	10.0%	50 hours per week
Risk factor (RF)	10.0%	
Crew average wage w/OTF & RF	$ 18.00	
Labor burden	35.0%	
Sales tax	6.0%	
G&A overhead per hour (OPH)	$ 12.00	
Net profit margin	20.0%	
Crew truck or van	$ 8.00	
Curb time man-hours per day	N/A	
Number of units	12.0	Spray heads with 18" funny pipe and elbow

Scenario	Materials	Labor		Equipment	CPH	Hours	Item
I. Production or "Curb" time costs							
12 Spray heads	$ 120.00	3.0	Man-hours	$ -	$ -	0.0	
5% Warranty	$ 6.00			$ -	$ -	0.0	
	$ -	$ 18.00		$ -	$ -	0.0	
	$ 126.00	$ 54.00		$ -			
II. General conditions (off-site or non-curb-time costs)							
		2.0	Man-hours	$ 32.00	$ 8.00	4.0	Crew truck
		0.5	Warranty	$ 4.00	$ 8.00	0.5	Warranty truck
	$ -	$ 18.00		$ -	$ -	0.0	
	$ -	$ 45.00		$ 36.00			
Subtotals	**$ 126**	**$ 99**		**$ 36**			
III. Margins & markups							
A.Sales tax	$ 8						
B.Labor burden		$ 35					
Subtotals	**$ 134**	**$ 134**		**$ 36**			

Total direct costs (TDC)		**$ 303**	**TDC**
C. G&A overhead costs			
5.5 (Number of man-hours x OPH)	$ 12.00 =	$ 66	
"BEP" (subtotal of total direct costs + G&A overhead)		**$ 369**	**BEP**
D. Contingency factor (if desired)		$ -	
E. Net profit margin 20.00%		$ 92	
F. Total price		**$ 462**	**Total price**

IV. Scenario analysis:

A. Unit flat rate (Total price ÷ units)

$ 462 divided by 12.0 = **$ 38.46** **Flat rate**

B. Sales or revenue per hour (Total price ÷ all man-hours)

$ 462 divided by 5.5 = **$ 83.91** **SPH or RPH**

C. Gross profit margin ((G&A overhead + Net profit) ÷ Total price)

$ 158 ÷ $ 462 = **34.3%** **GPM**

FIGURE 18-2 Flat Rate for Irrigation Spray Heads

This is where I think you need to include a trip charge and an hourly rate. You can always waive the trip fee if, like the plumber, the bill exceeds a predetermined "hurdle" amount. We'll discuss the trip charge in more detail in Chapter 24.

Flat Rate for Stump Grinding

Scenario

Here, our arborist is working a 9-hour day and a 45-hour week. The crew average wage, risk factor, labor burden, and so on are as outlined in Figure 18-3 on page 150. I used a production rate of 20 12″ stumps per day on three different sites. Again, this may be conservative, but I'd rather understate than overstate our production time.

Our price per 12″ stump calculates to be a little over $33. Again, I'd round this up to $35 or higher, if at all possible. The per-inch price is almost $3.

Again, we have a potential problem. What if there's only one small stump to grind? Here a minimum could apply, which you could waive if the bill exceeds a predetermined hurdle amount.

SUMMARY

Calculating flat rates for the automobile repair and plumbing industries is much simpler than for the Green Industry. The variables within an auto repair shop or for a plumber are far fewer than those for an irrigation service technician, arborist, or landscaper. They don't have to dig through 12 inches of mud and muck to get to the problem. Nor do they have to work in the freezing rain.

A published rate card can also help, even if it's only used for internal company purposes.

While determining flat rates for the Green Industry is more difficult, it can be done. However, you must think through the possible scenarios as thoroughly as possible and account for labor-only situations. To do so, a trip charge is often used. A published rate card can also help, even if it's only used for internal company purposes.

ACTION POINT

If you perform these types of services, you might want to evaluate and explore the possibility of providing your customers with flat-rate pricing. Use the methods outlined here but be sure to cover any contingency that you might face.

➤ NOTE The costs used in our scenarios are for illustration purposes only. Your costs will vary from the ones used in these examples. The key is for you to build a typical one-day scenario for the crew, materials, and equipment you use. Round up these rates as appropriate. If your costing structure is accurate, the rates you calculate should be very close to your current ones and to those generally seen in your market.

Scenario cost data	$ or %	Remarks
Crew size (# people)	1.0	One man crew
Crew average wage (CAW)	$ 16.00	
Overtime factor (OTF)	6.0%	45 hours per week, rounded up
Risk factor (RF)	10.0%	
Crew average wage w/OTF & RF	$ 18.56	
Labor burden	45.0%	
Sales tax	6.0%	
G&A overhead per hour (OPH)	$ 15.00	
Net profit margin	20.0%	
One ton truck	$ 12.00	
Curb-time man-hours per day	7.0	
Number of units	20.0	Number of 12" stumps per day on three sites

Scenario	Materials	Labor	Equipment	CPH	Hours	Item
I. Production (on-site or curb-time costs)						
	$ -	7.0 Man-hours	$ 90.00	$ 15.00	6.0	Medium 25 HP stump grinder
	$ -		$ -	$ -	0.0	
	$ -	$ 18.56	$ -	$ -	0.0	
	$ -	$ 129.92	$ 90.00			
II. General conditions (off-site or non-curb-time costs)						
		2.0 Man-hours	$ 64.00	$ 8.00	8.0	One ton truck
			$ -	$ -	0.0	
	$ -	$ 18.56	$ -	$ -	0.0	
	$ -	$ 37.12	$ 64.00			
Subtotals	**$ -**	**$ 167**	**$ 154**			
III. Margins & markups						
A.Sales tax	$ -					
B.Labor burden		$ 75				
Subtotals	**$ -**	**$ 242**	**$ 154**			
Total direct costs (TDC)					**$ 396**	**TDC**
C. G&A overhead costs 9 (Number of man-hours x OPH)			$ 15.00	=	$ 135	
BEP (subtotal of TDC + G&A overhead)					**$ 531**	**BEP**
D. Contingency factor (if desired)					$ -	
E. Net profit margin 20.00%					$ 133	
F. Total price					**$ 664**	**Total price**

IV. Scenario analysis

A. Stump grinding rate for a 12" stump (Total price ÷ # 12" stumps per day)

$ 664 divided by 20.0 = **$ 33.20** **Unit price per stump**

B. Stump grinding rate per inch (Total price ÷ total inches per day)

$ 664 divided by 240.0 = **$ 2.77** **Unit price per inch**

C. Gross profit margin ((G&A overhead + Net profit) ÷ Total price)

$ 268 ÷ $ 664 = **40.3%** **GPM**

FIGURE 18-3 Flat Rate for Tree Stump Grinding

CHAPTER

19

Time and Materials Pricing

TERMS

Curb-Time Rates
Portal-to-Portal Rates
Time and Materials (T&M)

Purpose

To explain the process of calculating time and materials prices

Introduction

"Measure once, cut twice. Measure twice, cut once." So it is with **time and materials** (T&M) pricing. Preparation in two areas is essential. First, you have to calculate your prices accurately for every contingency. I often spend many hours with clients calculating T&M prices. Second, you have to market and "sell" not only your prices but the process. You have to not only negotiate the prices, but you must also educate your client in the process. Otherwise, you're opening yourself up to a possible disaster. Calculating the prices is the easy part. Managing the customer's expectations is the tough one.

Measure once, cut twice. Measure twice, cut once. So it is with time and materials (T&M) pricing.

How It Works

A contractor in the Northeast had me help him develop T&M prices for a large multimillion-dollar residential installation project. Basic labor was priced at $25 per man-hour. All G&A overhead was calculated into this hourly rate. We also put together some basic unit prices. Sod installed was priced at $.65 per square foot. The sod cost $.20 per square foot, with $.45 for soil prep and installation. The project had a 5,000-square-foot courtyard my client was going to prep, grade, and install sod on. There was also a 16-acre horse corral on which the contractor was going to do some light prep work. He would then seed it.

The courtyard went from brown dirt one day to beautiful green crimson sod the next. The owners were so impressed they asked the contractor if he could sod the 16-acre horse corral. His reply was, "Yes, the cost will be $.65 per square foot plus $25 per man-hour."

"When can we start?"

This contractor was prepared. This job actually helped him to retire early and move with his family to another part of the country.

Another contractor was not so prepared. He called me in a panic one day and asked me to help him readjust some T&M pricing he'd been using for another very large residential project, which ended up well over $4 million.

The three-man crew was using some rather large pieces of equipment to move and place boulders. The initial billing rate was $125 per man-hour or $1,250 per man per day, including the equipment. This was fine until the crew had to water plants and trees; $125 per man-hour was a bit excessive for holding a hose and spraying water over the countryside.

The owner and general contractor were withholding a $500,000 progress billing from my client until he went back and recalculated his T&M rates and applied them retroactively to the whole job. Needless to say, my client was anxious to get paid, keep the job, and make everybody happy.

My client had excellent records for the whole project. I recalculated all the T&M rates—with and without the large equipment. My client and I then went back and readjusted all previous billings. He then had to "sell" the new pricing to both the owner and the general contractor. Fortunately, the old total was not very different from the new one. My client got paid and went on to finish a very beautiful project.

Another contractor, who called me one day, wasn't so lucky. He'd done close to $10 million of T&M installation work for a very wealthy residential client over an 8-year period. Apparently, one of his competitors was jealous of his relationship with this client. The other landscaper got the ear of the client and convinced him he'd been overcharged during the previous eight years. The client had his attorney send the landscaper a letter demanding a re-evaluation of all his previous charges and a refund. This is when I got the initial phone call.

I told the contractor I could help him calculate and validate T&M rates for the previous eight years of work. We could then make any adjustments as we deemed necessary. However, it was going to be a bureaucratic nightmare, as this project would take hundreds of hours and cost thousands of dollars. To top it off, what do you think the chances were of salvaging the relationship with this client who'd provided over $10 million of work?

MATERIALS PRICING

I recommend charging for repair materials, independent of labor rates. For commercial customers, you'd normally add a minimum margin of 20% to invoice cost. While not necessarily accurate, you could justify the 20% by calling it 10% for G&A overhead and 10% for net profit. Residential markets will usually allow you to charge retail prices for materials.

SUBCONTRACTOR PRICING

The going margin I see around the country applied to subcontractor costs ranges from 10% to 20%. Rarely is it higher or lower, and 15% is a pretty good benchmark. You could market the 15% by saying 5% was for G&A overhead and 10% for net profit. However, you have to think about your market when adding a margin to subcontractors.

How It Works

A client in Pennsylvania called me a number of years ago. He was bidding a large commercial project with a $100,000 soil prep and jute netting subcontractor on it. The landscaping part of the job was only about $36,000. My client asked me what I thought he should add on to the subcontractor cost. He said he was thinking of adding 15%. His rationale was that 5% was for G&A overhead and 10% was for net profit.

I asked him if the subcontractor was reputable and if he'd need much supervision on this job. My client said he'd done lots of work with him and that he needed little or no supervision. He added that when it came time for the subcontractor to do his work, all my client would have to do was make a telephone call and then send an invoice to the general contractor when the work was completed. I told my client it appeared he wanted to charge $15,000 ($100,000 × .15) to make a phone call and send an invoice. He chuckled and said, "I guess so." I asked him if he thought he could charge $15,000 to do that and, if so, I'd make the call and split the $15,000 with him. We both laughed.

Of course, if you can charge $15,000 for the call and invoice, by all means do so. However, this contractor realized that, in this case, $5,000 would probably be sufficient.

Think cost, but also think market!

EQUIPMENT PRICING

Chapters 9 and 45 cover equipment costing and pricing very well. You should allow the market to help you out in a T&M situation as it often "predisposes" various pricing levels. If at all possible, you should attempt to charge equipment rental rates for the equipment you own. Treat rented equipment as you would a materials or subcontractor cost and mark it up accordingly.

You should provide prices for every piece of motorized equipment that will show up on the job site. Often my clients will use daily, weekly, or even monthly rates for trucks, tractors, skid steers, and other motorized equipment. I'd treat portable toilets, dumpsters, storage containers, and so on the same as general rental equipment.

Don't forget to charge for the crew truck. I often build the cost for the crew truck into the labor rate. You should also charge for delivery trucks and trucks making dump runs. For these, I like to charge a minimum of four hours per day or engine-running time, whichever is greater.

I think it's usually best to include the charge for the supervisor's truck in the rate for the supervisor.

LABOR (CURB-TIME AND PORTAL-TO-PORTAL RATES)

Every hour you pay for should be passed on to the client in a T&M situation. This is why crew day-rates can be very helpful when doing T&M work. **Curb-time rates** are applied to on-site time. **Portal-to-portal rates** apply to every hour of the payroll day.

For instance, if you are charging $400 per crew member for a 10-hour day and the crew is on site for eight hours of curb time, the curb-time rate would be $50 per man-hour ($400 ÷ 8 curb man-hours = $50). However, the portal-to-portal rate would be $40 ($400 ÷ 10 total man-hours = $40).

Drive time or non-site time can be handled in one of the following three ways:

- It can be included in the hourly rate charged to the client. The client is, therefore, charged an hourly rate based on curb time.
- The client is charged for actual drive time to the job site. Essentially, the clock begins to run once the crew clocks in or leaves the yard and stops when the job is completed. This method has some inherent problems if the driver starts from a location other than the yard, gets stuck in traffic, or has to make other stops along the way.

  Instead, an average time can be allocated to the job, but this puts you into the third method.

- You can charge a show-up fee that includes drive time plus a certain amount of time on the job (i.e., the first 15 to 30 minutes). Time after that is charged at a set hourly rate.

When negotiating T&M labor rates, use the terms portal-to-portal and curb time. No one knows what they mean and you'll appear much smarter than you actually are.

It's usually wise to have multiple rates. For instance, you might have labor rates as follows:

Category	*Labor Rate*
Basic laborer	\$30 per hour portal-to-portal
Leadman	\$35 per hour portal-to-portal
Foreman or Crew Leader	\$45 per hour portal-to-portal
Supervisor	\$55 per hour portal-to-portal with truck

Don't forget yourself. If you step on the job site, you should be charging for your time. Get your clients in the habit of reaching for their wallets or checkbooks whenever they see you. Your attorney does it this way. Why should it be different for you and your clients?

RATE CARDS

I encourage my clients to print a rate card with all their rates on it. This card may be for internal use only, or you might give it to clients. In either case, it will save you time and the embarrassment of not knowing what you charge. You can attach your rate card to contracts or hand it out as needed. In any case, it will make you look more professional.

A SIMPLE ILLUSTRATION

Figure 19-1 illustrates how I cost out the T&M rate for a three-man crew with a crew truck for a 10-hour day. The crew average wage, labor burden, overtime factors, etc. are as indicated in the figure.

This crew needs to bill out \$1,200 per day. This includes the crew truck, all G&A overhead and net profit. The curb-time rate calculates out at a little under \$44 and the portal-to-portal rate at just over \$39. I'd round these to \$45 and \$40, respectively.

SUMMARY

Time and materials (T&M) or cost plus billings can be an excellent way to perform work. However, you must do your homework. You need to know your rates cold. Once you've calculated your rates, the job's not over. You must communicate effectively with your client and manage client expectations. You're constantly negotiating on a T&M project. Develop and keep a rate card with you at all times. It will save you a lot of aggravation.

Don't hesitate to get help or a second opinion when calculating your T&M rates. Remember, "Measure once, cut twice. Measure twice, cut once."

Scenario cost data	$ or %	Remarks
Crew size (# people)	3.0	Crew leader, leadman and laborer
Crew average wage (CAW)	$ 11.00	
Overtime factor (OTF)	10.0%	50 hours per week
Risk factor (RF)	10.0%	
Crew average wage w/OTF & RF	$ 13.20	
Labor burden	30.0%	
Sales tax	6.0%	
G&A overhead per hour (OPH)	$ 12.00	
Net profit margin	20.0%	
Crew truck	$ 8.00	
Curb-time man-hours per day	27.0	
Number of units	27.0	Curb-time man-hours

Scenario	Materials	Labor		Equipment	CPH	Hours	Item
I. Production (on-site or curb-time costs)							
	$ -	27.0	Man-hours	$ -	$ -	0.0	
	$ -			$ -	$ -	0.0	
	$ -	$ 13.20		$ -	$ -	0.0	
	$ -	$ 356.40		$ -			
II. General conditions (off-site or non-curb-time costs)							
		3.0	Man-hours	$ 64.00	$ 8.00	8.0	Crew truck
		0.0		$ -	$ -	0.0	
	$ -	$ 13.20		$ -	$ -	0.0	
	$ -	$ 39.60		$ 64.00			
Subtotals	**$ -**	**$ 396**		**$ 64**			
III. Margins & markups							
A. Sales tax	$ -						
B. Labor burden		$ 119					
Subtotals	**$ -**	**$ 515**		**$ 64**			
Total direct costs (TDC)						**$ 579**	TDC
C. G&A overhead costs							
30.0 (Number of man-hours x OPH)				$ 12.00	=	$ 360	
BEP (subtotal of TDC + G&A overhead)						**$ 939**	BEP
D. Contingency factor (if desired)						$ -	
E. Net profit margin 20.00%						$ 235	
F. Total price						**$ 1,174**	**Total price**

IV. Scenario analysis

A. Curb-time rate (total price ÷ curb-time hours)

$ 1,174 divided by 27.0 = **$ 43.46** **Curb-time rate**

B. Portal-to-portal rate (total price ÷ all man-hours)

$ 1,174 divided by 30.0 = **$ 39.12** **Portal-to-portal rate**

C. Gross profit margin ((G&A overhead + Net profit) ÷ Total price)

$ 595 ÷ $ 1,174 = **50.7%** **GPM**

FIGURE 19-1 Crew Time and Materials Rate

ACTION POINT

Calculate your T&M rates, both curb-time and portal-to-portal, for your various field personnel using the techniques mentioned here. Be sure to include the cost for the crew truck or van. Establish daily revenue goals not including materials. Compare the revenue goals that you calculate to ones actually achieved by your crews.

➤ NOTE The costs used in our scenarios are for illustration purposes only. Your costs will vary from the ones used in these examples. The key is for you to build a typical one-day scenario for the crew, materials, and equipment you use. Round up these rates as appropriate. If your costing structure is accurate, the rates you calculate should be very close to your current ones and to those generally seen in your market.

CHAPTER

20

Bark Blowing

Purpose

To explain how to calculate bark-blowing prices

Introduction

Bark blowing has changed considerably in recent years. The introduction of economical tow-behind units as well as the large tractor and trailer ones, customized specifically for spreading huge quantities of bark, has changed this service completely. It has also changed the pricing and related costs for providing this type of service. The contractor who knows his or her production rates and the related costs and who sets both daily and annual production goals will be miles ahead of the competition.

How It Works

A contractor in New England bought a new tow-behind bark blower for just under $40,000. He wants to blow bark for his own maintenance clients and to subcontract out bark blowing to other contractors in the area. He needs to price out the various Scenarios 1 through 5 as follows:

Scenario 1

How much should he charge per day when he subcontracts his bark blower, a one-ton truck, and himself?

Scenario 2

How much should he charge per day when he subcontracts his bark blower, a one-ton truck, himself, and a helper?

Scenario 3

How much should he charge per day when he subcontracts his bark blower, a one-ton truck, himself, and two helpers?

Scenario 4

How much should he charge per cubic yard for installing 50 CY of bark per day with his bark blower, a one-ton truck, himself, and two helpers? Bark mulch costs him $20 per cubic yard.

Scenario 5

How much should he charge per cubic yard for installing 100 CY of bark per day with his bark blower, a one-ton truck, himself, and two helpers? Bark mulch costs him $20 per cubic yard.

Additional Scenario Information

- The bark blower cost per hour is $20, and it will be used for 8.5 hours per day.
- The labor rate for additional laborers is $10.
- Crews will work and get paid for 10 hours per day, 50 hours per week.
- The overtime factor, risk factor, sales tax, etc., are as indicated on the figures in this chapter.
- The owner desires to obtain a minimum of 20% net profit margin for bark blowing.

Scenario 6

A contractor in Florida wants to investigate the purchase of a large tractor and trailer unit especially made for bark blowing. The contractor wants to know how many cubic yards of mulch he has to install per season to cover all his costs and make a profit. He also wants to know the price per cubic yard he needs to charge to make a 10% net profit and his break-even point per cubic yard when installing 50 and 100 cubic yards of bark per day.

Additional Scenario Information

- The tractor and trailer unit cost per hour is $50, and it will be used for eight hours per day.
- The crews will install bark mulch a minimum of 200 days per year.
- Crews will work and get paid for 10 hours per day, 50 hours per week.
- The overtime factor, risk factor, sales tax, etc. are as indicated on the figures in this chapter.
- The owner desires to obtain a minimum of 10% net profit margin for bark blowing.
- The re-wholesale price for bark mulch is $15 per cubic yard.

PRICING BARK BLOWING

Subcontracting Bark Blowing (Scenarios 1, 2, and 3)

Figures 20-1 on page 159, 20-2 on page 160, and 20-3 on page 161 outline the pricing for Scenarios 1, 2, and 3, respectively. The daily price for the crews and all equipment plays out as follows:

Owner alone	$ 781 (round up to $800)
Owner with one helper	$1,101 (round to $1,100)
Owner with two helpers	$1,421 (round up to $1,450)

Scenario cost data

	$ or %	Remarks
Crew size (# people)	1.0	Owner alone
Crew average wage (CAW)	$ 18.00	
Overtime factor (OTF)	10.0%	50 hours per week, 10 hours per day per man
Risk factor (RF)	10.0%	
Crew average wage w/OTF & RF	$ 21.60	
Labor burden	30.0%	
Sales tax	6.0%	
G&A overhead per hour (OPH)	$ 10.00	
Net profit margin	20.0%	
One ton truck	$ 8.00	
Curb-time man-hours per day	9.0	
Number of units	9.0	Curb-time man-hours

Scenario	Materials	Labor		Equipment	CPH	Hours	Item
I. Production (on-site or curb-time costs)							
	$ -	9.0	Man-hours	$ 170.00	$ 20.00	8.5	Finn 302 Bark Blower
	$ -			$ 10.00	$ 5.00	2.0	Back pack blower
	$ -	$ 21.60		$ -	$ -	0.0	
	$ -	$ 194.40		$ 180.00			
II. General conditions (off-site or non-curb-time costs)							
		1.0	Man-hours	$ 64.00	$ 8.00	8.0	One ton truck
				$ -	$ -	0.0	
	$ -	$ 21.60		$ -	$ -	0.0	
	$ -	$ 21.60		$ 64.00			
Subtotals	**$ -**	**$ 216**		**$ 244**			
III. Margins & markups							
A. Sales tax	$ -						
B. Labor burden		$ 65					
Subtotals	**$ -**	**$ 281**		**$ 244**			

Total direct costs (TDC)			**$ 525**	**TDC**
C. G&A overhead costs 10 (Number of man-hours x OPH)	$ 10.00	=	$ 100	
BEP (subtotal of TDC + G&A overhead)			**$ 625**	**BEP**
D. Contingency factor (if desired)			$ -	
E. Net profit margin 20.00%			$ 156	
F. Total price			**$ 781**	**Total price**

IV. Scenario analysis

A. Curb-time rate (Total price ÷ curb-time man-hours)

$ 781 divided by 9.0 = **$ 86.78** **Curb-time rate**

B. Portal-to-portal rate (Total price ÷ all man-hours)

$ 781 divided by 10.0 = **$ 78.10** **Portal-to-portal rate**

C. Gross profit margin ((G&A overhead + Net profit) ÷ Total price)

$ 256 ÷ $ 781 = **32.8%** **GPM**

FIGURE 20-1 Bark Blowing, 1-Man Crew

Scenario cost data	$ or %	Remarks
Crew size (# people)	2.0	Owner with one laborer
Crew average wage (CAW)	$ 14.00	
Overtime factor (OTF)	10.0%	50 hours per week, 10 hours per day per man
Risk factor (RF)	10.0%	
Crew average wage w/OTF & RF	$ 16.80	
Labor burden	30.0%	
Sales tax	6.0%	
G&A overhead per hour (OPH)	$ 10.00	
Net profit margin	20.0%	
One ton truck	$ 8.00	
Curb-time man-hours per day	18.0	
Number of units	18.0	Curb-time man-hours

Scenario	Materials	Labor		Equipment	CPH	Hours	Item
I. Production (on-site or curb-time costs)							
	$ -	18.0	Man-hours	$ 170.00	$ 20.00	8.5	Finn 302 Bark Blower
	$ -			$ 10.00	$ 5.00	2.0	Back pack blower
	$ -	$ 16.80		$ -	$ -	0.0	
	$ -	$ 302.40		$ 180.00			
II. General conditions (off-site or non-curb-time costs)							
		2.0	Man-hours	$ 64.00	$ 8.00	8.0	One ton truck
				$ -	$ -	0.0	
	$ -	$ 16.80		$ -	$ -	0.0	
	$ -	$ 33.60		$ 64.00			
Subtotals	**$ -**	**$ 336**		**$ 244**			
III. Margins & markups							
A. Sales tax	$ -						
B. Labor burden		$ 101					
Subtotals	**$ -**	**$ 437**		**$ 244**			

Total direct costs (TDC)		**$ 681**	**TDC**
C. G&A overhead costs			
20 (Number of man-hours x OPH)	$ 10.00 =	$ 200	
BEP (TDC + G&A overhead)		**$ 881**	**BEP**
D. Contingency factor (if desired)		$ -	
E. Net profit margin 20.00%		$ 220	
F. Total price		**$ 1,101**	**Total price**

IV. Scenario analysis

A. Curb-time rate (Total price ÷ curb-time man-hours)

$ 1,101 divided by 18.0 = **$ 61.17** **Curb-time rate**

B. Portal-to-portal rate (Total price ÷ all man-hours)

$ 1,101 divided by 20.0 = **$ 55.05** **Portal-to-portal rate**

C. Gross profit margin ((G&A overhead + Net profit) ÷ Total price)

$ 420 ÷ $ 1,101 = **38.2%** **GPM**

FIGURE 20-2 Bark Blowing, 2-Man Crew

Scenario cost data	**$ or %**	**Remarks**
Crew size (# people)	3.0	Owner with two people
Crew average wage (CAW)	$ 12.67	
Overtime factor (OTF)	10.0%	50 hours per week, 10 hours per day per man
Risk factor (RF)	10.0%	
Crew average wage w/OTF & RF	$ 15.20	
Labor burden	30.0%	
Sales tax	6.0%	
G&A overhead per hour (OPH)	$ 10.00	
Net profit margin	20.0%	
One ton truck	$ 8.00	
Curb-time man-hours per day	27.0	
Number of units	27.0	Curb-time man-hours

Scenario	**Materials**	**Labor**		**Equipment**	**CPH**	**Hours**	**Item**
I. Production (on-site or curb-time costs)							
	$ -	27.0	Man-hours	$ 170.00	$ 20.00	8.5	Finn 302 Bark Blower
	$ -			$ 10.00	$ 5.00	2.0	Back pack blower
	$ -	$ 15.20		$ -	$ -	0.0	
	$ -	$ 410.40		$ 180.00			
II. General conditions (off-site or non-curb-time costs)							
		3.0	Man-hours	$ 64.00	$ 8.00	8.0	One ton truck
				$ -	$ -	0.0	
	$ -	$ 15.20		$ -	$ -	0.0	
	$ -	$ 45.60		$ 64.00			
Subtotals	**$ -**	**$ 456**		**$ 244**			
III. Margins & markups							
A. Sales tax	$ -						
B. Labor burden		$ 137					
Subtotals	**$ -**	**$ 593**		**$ 244**			

Total direct costs (TDC)		**$ 837**	**TDC**
C. G&A overhead costs			
30 (Number of man-hours x OPH)	$ 10.00 =	$ 300	
BEP (TDC + G&A overhead)		**$ 1,137**	**BEP**
D. Contingency factor (if desired)		$ -	
E. Net profit margin 20.00%		$ 284	
F. Total price		**$ 1,421**	**Total price**

IV. Scenario analysis

A. Curb-time rate (Total price ÷ curb-time man-hours)

$ 1,421 divided by 27.0 = **$ 52.63** **Curb-time rate**

B. Portal-to-portal rate (Total price ÷ all man-hours)

$ 1,421 divided by 30.0 = **$ 47.37** **Portal-to-portal rate**

C. Gross profit margin ((G&A overhead + Net profit) ÷ Total price)

$ 584 ÷ $ 1,421 = **41.1%** **GPM**

FIGURE 20-3 Bark Blowing, 3-Man Crew

The contractor in Figure 20-3 could also have half-day and hourly rates to charge for bark blowing. However, he wanted to keep things simple. If clients didn't want to use him for a whole day, he wasn't interested. If you decide to charge for half days, I'd recommend establishing a half-day minimum and then charging an hourly rate for anything above four hours on the job. This scenario is shown in Figure 20-4 for a three-person crew for half a day.

Scenarios 1, 2, and 3

Looking at Figure 20-4, we see that we reduced on-site time from nine to four hours per man. However, the general condition time for the labor remained the same. The half-day minimum charge calculates out to $702, which I'd round to $700. I'd probably charge $150 per crew hour for time over four hours on site. This would provide revenue of $1,450 ($700 minimum + 5 crew hours at $150 each) for a nine-hour day, which is very close to your day rate for a three person crew. You should adjust your rates as the market dictates.

Scenarios 4 and 5

Owner installing bark mulch for his own clients with a three-person crew

50 CY installed per day	$54.92 per CY (round up to $55 per CY)
100 CY installed per day	$40.71 per CY (round up to $41 per CY)

Figures 20-5 on page 164 and 20-6 on page 165 display the price for the installed bark mulch, including the 20% net profit the contractor desires. However, the contractor should increase or decrease these prices to take into account market conditions. The prices calculated here should be considered minimum prices to shoot for.

It's important to note how the number of cubic yards of mulch installed per day affects the price to the customer. The unit cost per cubic yard decreases significantly for labor, labor burden, equipment, G&A overhead, and so on, as the number of units per day increases. However, the material cost per unit remains constant.

Scenario 6

Tractor and Trailer Bark Blowing Unit

This scenario changes dramatically due to daily production of either 100 or 50 cubic yards. See Figures 20-7 on page 166 and 20-8 on page 167, respectively. The crew and equipment costs remain the same per day, but the number of units installed and the related material costs vary. Pricing elasticity is directly tied to the economies of scale created by installing the larger number of cubic yards of bark per day.

Crew Installing 100 CY of Bark Mulch per Day

Unit price with 10% net profit	$31.76 per CY
Break-even point unit cost	$28.58 per CY
Gross profit margin (this is very low)	17.6%

Crew Installing 50 CY of Bark Mulch per Day

Unit price with 10% net profit	$45.85 per CY
Break-even point unit cost	$41.27 per CY
Gross profit margin (this is still low)	20.5%

Scenario cost data	$ or %	Remarks
Crew size (# people)	3.0	Owner with two people
Crew average wage (CAW)	$ 12.67	
Overtime factor (OTF)	10.0%	50 hours per week, 10 hours per day per man
Risk factor (RF)	10.0%	
Crew average wage w/OTF & RF	$ 15.20	
Labor burden	30.0%	
Sales tax	6.0%	
G&A overhead per hour (OPH)	$ 10.00	
Net profit margin	20.0%	
One ton truck	$ 8.00	
Curb-time man-hours per day	12.0	
Number of units	12.0	Curb-time man-hours

Scenario	Materials	Labor		Equipment	CPH	Hours	Item
I. Production (on-site or curb-time costs)							
	$ -	12.0	Man-hours	$ 70.00	$ 20.00	3.5	Finn 302 Bark Blower
	$ -			$ 5.00	$ 5.00	1.0	Back pack blower
	$ -	$ 15.20		$ -	$ -	0.0	
	$ -	$ 182.40		$ 75.00			
II. General conditions (off-site or non-curb-time costs)							
		3.0	Man-hours	$ 40.00	$ 8.00	5.0	One ton truck
				$ -	$ -	0.0	
	$ -	$ 15.20		$ -	$ -	0.0	
	$ -	$ 45.60		$ 40.00			
Subtotals	**$ -**	**$ 228**		**$ 115**			
III. Margins & markups							
A. Sales tax	$ -						
B. Labor burden		$ 68					
Subtotals	**$ -**	**$ 296**		**$ 115**			

Total direct costs (TDC)			**$ 411**	**TDC**
C. G&A overhead costs				
15 (Number of man-hours x OPH)	$ 10.00	=	$ 150	
BEP (TDC + G&A overhead)			**$ 561**	**BEP**
D. Contingency factor (if desired)			$ -	
E. Net profit margin 20.00%			$ 140	
F. Total price			**$ 702**	**Total price**

IV. Scenario analysis

A. Curb-time rate (Total price ÷ curb-time man-hours)

$ 702 divided by 12.0 = **$ 58.48** **Curb-time rate**

B. Portal-to-portal rate (Total price ÷ all man-hours)

$ 702 divided by 15.0 = **$ 46.78** **Portal-to-portal rate**

C. Gross profit margin ((G&A overhead + Net profit) ÷ Total price)

$ 290 ÷ $ 702 = **41.4%** **GPM**

FIGURE 20-4 Bark Blowing, 3-Man Crew for One-Half Day

Scenario cost data	$ or %	Remarks
Crew size (# people)	3.0	Owner with two people
Crew average wage (CAW)	$ 12.67	
Overtime factor (OTF)	10.0%	50 hours per week, 10 hours per day per man
Risk factor (RF)	10.0%	
Crew average wage w/OTF & RF	$ 15.20	
Labor burden	30.0%	
Sales tax	6.0%	
G&A overhead per hour (OPH)	$ 10.00	
Net profit margin	20.0%	
One ton truck	$ 8.00	
Curb-time man-hours per day	27.0	
Number of units	50.0	CY per day, Bark costs $20 per CY

Scenario	Materials	Labor		Equipment	CPH	Hours	Item
I. Production (on-site or curb-time costs)							
50.0 CY of Mulch	$ 1,000.00	27.0	Man-hours	$ 170.00	$ 20.00	8.5	Finn 302 Bark Blower
$ 20 per CY	$ -			$ 10.00	$ 5.00	2.0	Back pack blower
	$ -	$ 15.20		$ -	$ -	0.0	
	$ 1,000.00	$ 410.40		$ 180.00			
II. General conditions (off-site or non-curb-time costs)							
		3.0	Man-hours	$ 64.00	$ 8.00	8.0	One ton truck
				$ -	$ -	0.0	
	$ -	$ 15.20		$ -	$ -	0.0	
	$ -	$ 45.60		$ 64.00			
Subtotals	**$ 1,000**	**$ 456**		**$ 244**			
III. Margins & markups							
A. Sales tax	$ 60						
B. Labor burden		$ 137					
Subtotals	**$ 1,060**	**$ 593**		**$ 244**			

Total direct costs (TDC)			**$ 1,897**	**TDC**
C. G&A overhead costs				
30 (Number of man-hours x OPH)	$ 10.00	=	$ 300	
BEP (TDC + G&A overhead)			**$ 2,197**	**BEP**
D. Contingency factor (if desired)			$ -	
E. Net profit margin 20.00%			$ 549	
F. Total price			**$ 2,746**	**Total price**

IV. Scenario analysis

A. Cubic yard unit price (Total price ÷ number of units)

$ 2,746 divided by 50.0 = **$ 54.92** **CY price**

B. Cubic yard break-even unit cost (Break-even total ÷ number of units):

$ 2,197 divided by 50.0 = **$ 43.94** **CY BEP**

C. Gross profit margin ((G&A overhead + Net profit) ÷ Total price)

$ 849 ÷ $ 2,746 = **30.9%** **GPM**

FIGURE 20-5 Bark Blowing, 3-Man Crew 50 CY per Day

Scenario cost data	$ or %	Remarks
Crew size (# people)	3.0	Owner with two people
Crew average wage (CAW)	$ 12.67	
Overtime factor (OTF)	10.0%	50 hours per week, 10 hours per day per man
Risk factor (RF)	10.0%	
Crew average wage w/OTF & RF	$ 15.20	
Labor burden	30.0%	
Sales tax	6.0%	
G&A overhead per hour (OPH)	$ 10.00	
Net profit margin	20.0%	
One ton truck	$ 8.00	
Curb-time man-hours per day	27.0	
Number of units	100.0	CY per day, Bark costs $20 per CY

Scenario		Materials	Labor		Equipment	CPH	Hours	Item
I. Production (on-site or curb-time costs)								
100.0	CY of Mulch	$ 2,000.00	27.0	Man-hours	$ 170.00	$ 20.00	8.5	Finn 302 Bark Blower
$ 20	per CY	$ -			$ 10.00	$ 5.00	2.0	Back pack blower
		$ -	$ 15.20		$ -	$ -	0.0	
		$ 2,000.00	$ 410.40		$ 180.00			
II. General conditions (off-site or non-curb-time costs)								
			3.0	Man-hours	$ 64.00	$ 8.00	8.0	One ton truck
					$ -	$ -	0.0	
		$ -	$ 15.20		$ -	$ -	0.0	
		$ -	$ 45.60		$ 64.00			
Subtotals		**$ 2,000**	**$ 456**		**$ 244**			
III. Margins & markups								
A. Sales tax		$ 120						
B. Labor burden			$ 137					
Subtotals		**$ 2,120**	**$ 593**		**$ 244**			

Total direct costs (TDC)		**$ 2,957**	**TDC**
C. G&A overhead costs 30 (Number of man-hours x OPH)	$ 10.00 =	$ 300	
BEP (TDC + G&A overhead)		**$ 3,257**	**BEP**
D. Contingency factor (if desired)		$ -	
E. Net profit margin 20.00%		$ 814	
F. Total price		**$ 4,071**	**Total price**

IV. Scenario analysis

A. Cubic yard unit price (Total price ÷ number of units)

$ 4,071 divided by	100.0 =	**$ 40.71**	**CY price**

B. Cubic yard break-even unit cost (Break-even total ÷ number of units):

$ 3,257 divided by	100.0 =	**$ 32.57**	**CY BEP**

C. Gross profit margin ((G&A overhead + Net profit) ÷ Total price)

$ 1,114 ÷	$ 4,071 =	**27.4%**	**GPM**

FIGURE 20-6 Bark Blowing, 3-Man Crew 100 CY per Day

Scenario cost data	$ or %	Remarks
Crew size (# people)	3.0	Owner with two people
Crew average wage (CAW)	$ 13.00	
Overtime factor (OTF)	10.0%	
Risk factor (RF)	10.0%	50 hours per week, 10 hours per day per man
Crew average wage w/OTF & RF	$ 15.60	
Labor burden	30.0%	
Sales tax	6.0%	
G&A overhead per hour (OPH)	$ 8.00	
Net profit margin	10.0%	
Tractor & trailer	$ 50.00	
Curb-time man-hours per day	24.0	
Number of units	100.0	CY per day, Bark costs $15 per CY

Scenario	Materials	Labor		Equipment	CPH	Hours	Item
I. Production (on-site or curb-time costs)							
100.0 CY of Mulch	$ 1,500.00	24.0	Man-hours	$ 400.00	$ 50.00	8.0	Tractor & trailer
$ 15 per CY	$ -			$ 20.00	$ 5.00	4.0	Back pack blower
	$ -	$ 15.60		$ -	$ -	0.0	
	$ 1,500.00	$ 374.40		$ 420.00			
II. General conditions (off-site or non-curb-time costs)							
		6.0	Man-hours	$ -	$ -	0.0	
				$ -	$ -	0.0	
	$ -	$ 15.60		$ -	$ -	0.0	
	$ -	$ 93.60		$ -			
Subtotals	**$ 1,500**	**$ 468**		**$ 420**			
III. Margins & markups							
A. Sales tax	$ 90						
B. Labor burden		$ 140					
Subtotals	**$ 1,590**	**$ 608**		**$ 420**			

Total direct costs (TDC)		**$ 2,618**	**TDC**
C. G&A overhead costs			
30 (Number of man-hours x OPH)	$ 8.00 =	$ 240	
BEP (TDC + G&A overhead)		**$ 2,858**	**BEP**
D. Contingency factor (if desired)		$ -	
E. Net profit margin 10.00%		$ 318	
F. Total price		**$ 3,176**	**Total price**

IV. Scenario analysis

A. Cubic yard unit price (Total price ÷ number of units)

$ 3,176 divided by 100.0 = **$ 31.76** **CY price**

B. Cubic yard break-even unit cost (Break-even total ÷ number of units)

$ 2,858 divided by 100.0 = **$ 28.58** **CY BEP**

C. Gross profit margin ((G&A overhead + Net profit) ÷ Total price)

$ 558 ÷ $ 3,176 = **17.6%** **GPM**

FIGURE 20-7 Bark Blowing, 3 Men, Tractor and Trailer Unit, 100 CY per Day

Scenario cost data	$ or %	Remarks
Crew size (# people)	3.0	Owner with two people
Crew average wage (CAW)	$ 13.00	
Overtime factor (OTF)	10.0%	50 hours per week, 10 hours per day per man
Risk factor (RF)	10.0%	
Crew average wage w/OTF & RF	$ 15.60	
Labor burden	30.0%	
Sales tax	6.0%	
G&A overhead per hour (OPH)	$ 8.00	
Net profit margin	10.0%	
Tractor & trailer	$ 50.00	
Curb-time man-hours per day	24.0	
Number of units	50.0	CY per day, Bark costs $15 per CY

Scenario		Materials	Labor		Equipment	CPH	Hours	Item
I. Production (on-site or curb-time costs)								
50.0	CY of Mulch	$ 750.00	24.0	Man-hours	$ 400.00	$ 50.00	8.0	Tractor & trailer
$ 15	per CY	$ -			$ 20.00	$ 5.00	4.0	Back pack blower
		$ -	$ 15.60		$ -	$ -	0.0	
		$ 750.00	$ 374.40		$ 420.00			
II. General conditions (off-site or non-curb-time costs)								
			6.0	Man-hours	$ -	$ 50.00	0.0	
					$ -	$ -	0.0	
		$ -	$ 15.60		$ -	$ -	0.0	
		$ -	$ 93.60		$ -			
Subtotals		**$ 750**	**$ 468**		**$ 420**			
III. Margins & markups								
A. Sales tax		$ 45						
B. Labor burden			$ 140					
Subtotals		**$ 795**	**$ 608**		**$ 420**			

Total direct costs (TDC)		**$ 1,823**	**TDC**
C. G&A overhead costs			
30 (Number of man-hours x OPH)	$ 8.00 =	$ 240	
BEP (TDC + G&A overhead)		**$ 2,063**	**BEP**
D. Contingency factor (if desired)		$ -	
E. Net profit margin 10.00%		$ 229	
F. Total price		**$ 2,293**	**Total price**

IV. Scenario analysis

A. Cubic yard unit price (Total price ÷ number of units)

$ 2,293 divided by 50.0 = **$ 45.85** **CY price**

B. Cubic yard break-even unit cost (Break-even total ÷ number of units)

$ 2,063 divided by 50.0 = **$ 41.27** **CY BEP**

C. Gross profit margin ((G&A overhead + Net profit) ÷ Total price)

$ 469 ÷ $ 2,293 = **20.5%** **GPM**

FIGURE 20-8 Bark Blowing, 3 Men, Tractor and Trailer Unit, 50 CY per Day

Calculating the number of cubic yards this contractor needs to install per season is not as easy as determining the cubic-yard price and break-even point. Without creating an elaborate scenario analysis, we can approximate the number of cubic yards per year this crew has to install. The crew can make money installing a minimum of 50 cubic yards per day for 200 days a year. This translates into 10,000 cubic yards per season (200 days × 50 CY per day = 10,000 CY per season). Naturally, the crew will be more profitable installing more than this amount.

SUMMARY

If you don't know your costs and maintain an efficient operation with clearly established goals, it won't just be bark that you are blowing.

Bark blowing can be very profitable if you know your costs and establish minimum daily production rates and charges. The scenarios are endless, but keep it simple. Remember, production and economies of scale are the name of the bark-blowing game. If you don't know your costs and maintain an efficient operation with clearly established daily (and in some cases annual) goals, it won't just be bark that you are blowing.

ACTION POINT

If you provide bark blowing services, calculate your unit prices as we have outlined. If you do not provide these services, you might want to explore doing so. Remember to set daily revenue and production goals for your crews.

➤ **NOTE**

The costs used in our scenarios are for illustration purposes only. Your costs will vary from the ones used in these examples. The key is for you to build a typical one-day scenario for the crew, materials, and equipment you use. Round up these rates as appropriate. If your costing structure is accurate, the rates you calculate should be very close to your current ones and to those generally seen in your market.

CHAPTER

21

Christmas Decorations

Purpose

To explain how to price Christmas decoration work

Introduction

Because this service is seasonal and the market is in its infant stages, margins for Christmas decoration work are still very high as compared to those for landscape or irrigation installation.

A number of my clients have been installing Christmas decorations for many years. One arborist in New England uses his bucket truck to install lights on some rather large trees. With the advent of Christmas decoration franchises, this revenue source has gained popularity in recent years.

Because this service is seasonal and the market is in its infant stages, margins for Christmas decoration work are still very high as compared to those for landscape or irrigation installation. Gross profit margins of 40 to 50% are not uncommon.

How It Works

A contractor in the Southwest wants to start a Christmas decorating division. He wants to know

1. How much he should charge per man-hour and per day for his two-person crew
2. His gross profit margin for a typical day of installing lights, wire, and the related hardware.

Additional Scenario Information

- Crews will work and get paid for 10 hours per day, 50 hours per week for eight weeks.
- The overtime factor, risk factor, sales tax, and so on are as indicated on Figures 21-1 on page 170 and 21-2 on page 171.
- The owner desires to obtain a minimum of 25% net profit margin for Christmas decoration work.
- The crew should be able to install between $700 and $1,000 of materials at the contractor's cost per day.

Scenario cost data	$ or %	Remarks
Crew size (# people)	2.0	
Crew average wage (CAW)	$ 13.00	
Overtime factor (OTF)	10.0%	50 hours per week, 10 hours per day
Risk factor (RF)	10.0%	
Crew average wage w/OTF & RF	$ 15.60	
Labor burden	30.0%	
Sales tax	6.0%	
G&A overhead per hour (OPH)	$ 10.00	
Net profit margin	25.0%	
Crew truck or van	$ 8.00	
Curb-time man-hours per day	16.0	
Number of units	16.0	Curb-time man-hours

Scenario	Materials	Labor		Equipment	CPH	Hours	Item
I. Production (on-site or curb-time costs)							
	$ -	16.0	Man-hours	$ -	$ -	0.0	
	$ -			$ -	$ -	0.0	
	$ -	$ 15.60		$ -	$ -	0.0	
	$ -	$ 249.60		$ -			
II. General conditions (off-site or non-curb-time costs)							
		4.0	Man-hours	$ 64.00	$ 8.00	8.0	Crew truck or van
		0.0		$ -	$ -	0.0	
	$ -	$ 15.60		$ -	$ -	0.0	
	$ -	$ 62.40		$ 64.00			
Subtotals	**$ -**	**$ 312**		**$ 64**			
III. Margins & markups							
A. Sales tax	$ -						
B. Labor burden		$ 94					
Subtotals	**$ -**	**$ 406**		**$ 64**			

Total direct costs (TDC)		**$ 470**	**TDC**
C. G&A overhead costs			
20.0 (Number of man-hours x OPH)	$ 10.00 =	$ 200	
BEP (TDC + G&A overhead)		**$ 670**	**BEP**
D. Contingency factor (if desired)		$ -	
E. Net profit margin 25.00%		$ 223	
F. Total price		**$ 893**	**Total price**

IV. Scenario analysis

A. Curb-time rate (Total price ÷ curb-time man-hours)		
$ 893 divided by 16.0 =	**$ 55.80**	**Curb-time rate**
B. Portal-to-portal rate (Total price ÷ all man-hours)		
$ 893 divided by 20.0 =	**$ 44.64**	**Portal-to-portal rate**
C. Gross profit margin ((G&A overhead + Net profit) ÷ Total price)		
$ 423 ÷ $ 893 =	**47.4%**	**GPM**

FIGURE 21-1 Christmas Decorations, 2-Man Crew for One Day

Scenario cost data	$ or %	Remarks
Crew size (# people)	2.0	
Crew average wage (CAW)	$ 13.00	
Overtime factor (OTF)	10.0%	50 hours per week, 10 hours per day
Risk factor (RF)	10.0%	
Crew average wage w/OTF & RF	$ 15.60	
Labor burden	30.0%	
Sales tax	6.0%	
G&A overhead per hour (OPH)	$ 10.00	
Net profit margin	25.0%	
Crew truck or van	$ 8.00	
Curb-time man-hours per day	16.0	
Number of units	16.0	Curb-time man-hours

Scenario	Materials	Labor		Equipment	CPH	Hours	Item
I. Production (on-site or curb-time costs)							
Lights	$ 600.00	16.0	Man-hours	$ -	$ -	0.0	
Wiring	$ 75.00			$ -	$ -	0.0	
Hardware, misc.	$ 100.00	$ 15.60		$ -	$ -	0.0	
	$ 775.00	$ 249.60		$ -			
II. General conditions (off-site or non-curb-time costs)							
		4.0	Man-hours	$ 64.00	$ 8.00	8.0	Crew truck or van
		0.0		$ -	$ -	0.0	
	$ -	$ 15.60		$ -	$ -	0.0	
	$ -	$ 62.40		$ 64.00			
Subtotals	**$ 775**	**$ 312**		**$ 64**			
III. Margins & markups							
A. Sales tax	$ 47						
B. Labor burden		$ 94					
Subtotals	**$ 822**	**$ 406**		**$ 64**			

Total direct costs (TDC)			**$ 1,291**	**TDC**
C. G&A overhead costs				
20.0 (Number of man-hours x OPH)	$ 10.00	=	$ 200	
BEP (TDC + G&A overhead)			**$ 1,491**	**BEP**
D. Contingency factor (if desired)			$ -	
E. Net profit margin 25.00%			$ 497	
F. Total price			**$ 1,988**	**Total price**

IV. Scenario analysis

A. Revenue per person per day (Total price ÷ # people in crew)

$ 1,988	divided by	2.0 =	**$ 994.07**	**Revenue per person** per day

B. Sales or revenue per hour (Total price ÷ all man-hours)

$ 1,988	divided by	20.0 =	**$ 99.41**	**SPH or RPH**

C. Gross profit margin ((G&A overhead + Net profit) ÷ Total price)

$ 697	÷	$ 1,988 =	**35.1%**	**GPM**

FIGURE 21-2 Christmas Decorations, 2-Man Crew for One Day with Materials

THE CREW MAN-HOUR AND DAY RATES

Figure 21-1 illustrates the pricing for the crew labor only for a typical day of work. The curb-time rate calculates to be just under $56 per man-hour. The portal-to-portal man-hour rate calculates to be just under $45. I would round these up to a minimum of $56 and $45, respectively. The crew should bill $900 for a full day of work. This does not include any materials. Note that the gross profit margin is near the 50% mark.

THE CREW WITH MATERIALS FOR A TYPICAL DAY

Figure 21-2 illustrates the same crew installing lights, wiring, and miscellaneous hardware for a typical day. The daily revenue per person is almost $1,000. The sales or revenue per man-hour is almost $100. While these figures are high compared to landscape and irrigation work, I'd monitor the gross profit margin (under 40% in this case) and try to keep it in the 40 to 50% range. In this scenario, I'd seriously consider adding another 5 to 10% net profit.

SUMMARY

Christmas decoration work can be very lucrative. Margins for this type of work are still very high, as this market is somewhat new and expanding. Your labor rates for Christmas decorations will, in all likelihood, be higher than labor rates for your normal seasonal work. Set daily revenue goals for your crews, with and without materials.

ACTION POINT

If you perform Christmas decoration services, evaluate and calculate your net profit and gross profit margins. Also, remember to set hourly and daily revenue goals for your crews. If you do not provide these services, you might want to explore the possibility of doing so.

➤ NOTE The costs used in our scenarios are for illustration purposes only. Your costs will vary from the ones used in these examples. The key is for you to build a typical one-day scenario for the crew, materials, and equipment you use. Round up these rates as appropriate. If your costing structure is accurate, the rates you calculate should be very close to your current ones and to those generally seen in your market.

CHAPTER

22

Hydroseeding

Purpose

To explain the process of pricing both large and small commercial hydroseed jobs as well as residential ones

Introduction

Hydroseeding offers excellent margins for the contractor who achieves economies of scale and operational efficiency. With the advent of smaller, economical hydroseeding units, it can also be an excellent way to provide additional services to your smaller residential clients while contributing to the bottom line.

How It Works

A contractor in the Northeast installs and maintains athletic fields, primarily for private schools, colleges, and municipalities. He has two hydroseeders, a large 1,500-gallon, truck-mounted unit that costs in the vicinity of $37,000 new, and a small 500-gallon, tow-behind unit that costs about $17,000 new. He'd like to keep these two units as busy as possible by bidding on some commercial jobs. However, because of the competitiveness of the commercial hydroseeding market, he needs to calculate his costs and break-even points more accurately on a couple of different scenarios so he can know how far he can drop his prices without hurting himself.

1. How much should he target to bill per day and per square foot for large commercial jobs using the truck-mounted unit?
2. What is his break-even point for this scenario?
3. How much should he target to bill per day and per square foot for smaller commercial jobs and touch-up work using the smaller tow-behind unit?
4. What is his break-even point for this scenario?
5. How much should he target to bill per day and per square foot for residential jobs using the tow-behind unit?
6. What is his break-even point for this scenario?

Additional Scenario Information

- Crews will work and get paid for 10 hours per day, 50 hours per week.
- The equipment cost per hour is shown on the figures in this chapter.

- The overtime factor, risk factor, sales tax, etc. are as indicated on the figures in this chapter.
- The owner desires to obtain a minimum of 20% net profit margin (NPM) for this work. He also wants to compare his minimum 20% NPM prices with the going square-foot-rate in his market and adjust them accordingly.
- The crews should be able to shoot an average of 110,000 square feet of commercial work per day using the large truck-mounted unit.
- The crews should be able to shoot an average of 35,000 square feet of residential or 45,000 square feet of small commercial work or touch-ups per day using the tow-behind unit.

PRICING HYDROSEEDING WORK

Commercial Applications Using the Truck-Mounted Unit

Figures 22-1 and 22-2 outline this scenario. Note that each member of the crew works eight hours on site per day. Two hours per day are allotted to general condition drive time, load time, and so forth. The truck-mounted unit, which combined has a cost per hour of $25, is running approximately eight hours per day, but we will cost it in our scenario for 10 hours. We will also include some time for call-backs.

To achieve the desired 20% net profit margin, this two-man crew has to bill over $5,500 per day. This will cover all costs, both direct and indirect. The price per square foot calculates out to be $0.0508. The daily break-even point is $4,471 or $0.0406 per square foot.

Project:	Commercial hydroseeding
Location:	
P.O.C./G.C.:	
Phone / Fax:	
Due Date:	
Type Work:	Large commercial jobs

Date:	5/30/20__
Estimator:	I.M. Dunn
Crew Size:	2
Hours/Day:	10
CAW:	$ 16.00
Risk Factor	10%
OT Factor	10%

CAW Loaded	$ 19.20

Phase 1	Quantity	Unit
Total Labor Hrs	22	Hrs L

# Description			Column Calculations			#VALUE!	#VALUE!	#VALUE!	#VALUE!
			Quantity	Unit	Unit Cost	Material	Labor	Equip	Subs
TOTALS		Tanks/day				3,005	422	275	-
Materials	Seed (175 # per 1,500 GL tank)	5	875.0	LB	2.00	1,750			
	Tacifier (20 # per tank)	5	100.0	LB	3.25	325			
	Fibre mulch (15 bales per tank)	5	75.0	BL	10.00	750			
	Fertilizer (150 # per tank)	5	15.0	BG	12.00	180			
	Water	5	7,500.0	GL	-	-			
						-			
						-			
Labor	2 men, 20 man-hours per day		20.0	Hrs L	19.20		384		
	Call back time		2.0	Hrs L	19.20		38		
			-				-		
Equipment	Truck with mid-size hydroseed unit		10.0	HR	25.00			250	
			-					-	
	Truck with mid-size hydroseed unit		1.0	HR	25.00			25	
	(Call back time)							-	

FIGURE 22-1 Hydroseeding Large Commercial Jobs Materials List

Scenario cost data	$ or %	Remarks
Crew size (# people)	2.0	Crew leader and laborer
Crew average wage (CAW)	$ 16.00	
Man-hours per man per day	10.0	
Overtime factor (OTF)	10.0%	50 hours per week
Risk factor (RF)	10.0%	
Crew average wage w/OTF & RF	$ 19.20	
Labor burden	35.0%	
Sales tax	6.0%	
G&A overhead per hour (OPH)	$ 20.00	
Net profit margin	20.0%	
One ton crew truck	$ 25.00	
Curb-time man-hours	NA	
Number of units	110,000	Square feet

Scenario	Materials	Labor	Equipment	Subcontractors	Subtotals
I. Production (on-site or curb-time costs)					
	$ 3,005.00	$ 422.40	$ 275.00	$ -	
	$ 3,005.00	$ 422.40	$ 275.00	$ -	**$ 3,702**
II. General conditions (off-site or non-curb-time costs)					
	$ -	$ -	$ -	$ -	
	$ -	$ -	$ -	$ -	**$ -**
Subtotals	**$ 3,005**	**$ 422**	**$ 275**	**$ -**	**$ 3,702**
III. Margins & markups					
A.Sales tax	$ 180				
B.Labor burden		$ 148			
Subtotals	**$ 3,185**	**$ 570**	**$ 275**	**$ -**	
Total direct costs (TDC)				**$ 4,031**	**TDC**
C. G&A overhead costs					
22.0 (Number of man-hours x OPH)			$ 20.00 =	$ 440	
BEP (TDC + G&A overhead)				**$ 4,471**	**BEP**
D. Contingency factor (if desired)				$ -	
E. Net profit margin 20.00%				$ 1,118	
F. Total price				**$ 5,588**	**Total price**

IV. Scenario analysis

A. Square foot price (Total price ÷ units)

$ 5,588 divided by 110,000.0 = **$ 0.0508** **SF price**

B. Square foot break-even cost (BEP ÷ units)

$ 4,471 divided by 110,000.0 = **$ 0.0406** **SF BEP**

C. Gross profit margin ((G&A overhead + Net profit) ÷ Total price)

$ 1,558 ÷ $ 5,588 = **27.9%** **GPM**

FIGURE 22-2 Hydroseeding Large Commercial Jobs Recap

Commercial Touch-Up Applications Using the Tow-Behind Unit

Figures 22-3 and 22-4 outline this scenario. Again, each member of the crew works eight hours on site per day and two hours per day are allotted to general condition drive time, load time, and so forth. The tow-behind unit combined with a one-ton truck has a cost per hour of $25. It is running approximately eight hours per day, but we will still cost it in our scenario for 10 hours.

To achieve the desired 20% net profit margin, this two-man crew has to bill over $3,000 per day. This will cover all costs, both direct and indirect. The price per square foot calculates out to be $0.0672. The daily break-even point is $2,419 or $0.0538 per square foot.

Residential Applications Using the Tow-Behind Unit

Figures 22-5 on page 178 and 22-6 on page 179 outline this scenario. The labor and equipment hours remain the same as in the commercial scenarios.

To achieve the desired 20% net profit margin, this two-man crew has to bill $2,800 per day. This will cover all costs, both direct and indirect. The price per square foot calculates out to be $0.0796. The break-even point is $0.0637 per square foot and $2,230 per day.

Project:	Commercial hydroseeding	Date:	5/30/20__
Location:		Estimator:	I.M. Dunn
P.O.C./G.C.:		Crew Size:	2
Phone / Fax:		Hours/Day:	10
Due Date:		CAW:	$ 16.00
Type Work:	Small jobs & touch up work	Risk Factor	10%
		OT Factor	10%

CAW Loaded	$ 19.20

Phase 1	Quantity	Unit
Total Labor Hrs	22	Hrs L

# Description		Tanks/day	Quantity	Unit	Unit Cost	Material	Labor	Equip	Subs
			Column Calcualtions			#VALUE!	#VALUE!	#VALUE!	#VALUE!
TOTALS						1,070	422	275	-
Materials	Seed (50 # per 500 GL tank)	6	300.0	LB	2.00	600			
	Tacifier (5 # per tank)	6	30.0	LB	3.25	98			
	Fibre mulch (5 bales per tank)	6	30.0	BL	10.00	300			
	Fertilizer (50 # per tank)	6	6.0	BG	12.00	72			
	Water	6	500.0	GL	-	-			
						-			
						-			
Labor	2 men, 20 man-hours per day		20.0	Hrs L	19.20		384		
	Call back time		2.0	Hrs L	19.20		38		
			-				-		
Equipment	Truck with tow-behind hydroseed unit		10.0	HR	25.00			250	
			-					-	
	Truck with tow-behind hydroseed unit		1.0	HR	25.00			25	
	(Call back time)							-	
								-	

FIGURE 22-3 Hydroseeding Small Commercial Jobs Materials List

SUMMARY

This contractor now has the information he needs to competitively price his hydroseeding work. Armed with this information, he can adjust his profit margins as he deems necessary.

Scenario cost data	**\$ or %**	**Remarks**
Crew size (# people)	2.0	Crew leader and laborer
Crew average wage (CAW)	\$ 16.00	
Man-hours per man per day	10.0	
Overtime factor (OTF)	10.0%	50 hours per week
Risk factor (RF)	10.0%	
Crew average wage w/OTF & RF	\$ 19.20	
Labor burden	35.0%	
Sales tax	6.0%	
G&A overhead per hour (OPH)	\$ 20.00	
Net profit margin	20.0%	
One ton crew truck	\$ 25.00	
Curb time man-hours	NA	
Number of units	45,000	Square feet

Scenario	**Materials**	**Labor**	**Equipment**	**Subcontractors**	**Subtotals**
I. Production (on-site or curb-time costs)					
	\$ 1,069.50	\$ 422.40	\$ 275.00	\$ -	
	\$ 1,069.50	\$ 422.40	\$ 275.00	\$ -	\$ 1,767
II. General conditions (off-site or non-curb-time costs)					
	\$ -	\$ -	\$ -	\$ -	
	\$ -	\$ -	\$ -	\$ -	\$ -
Subtotals	**\$ 1,070**	**\$ 422**	**\$ 275**	**\$ -**	**\$ 1,767**
III. Margins & markups					
A.Sales ta	\$ 64				
B.Labor burden		\$ 148			
Subtotals	**\$ 1,134**	**\$ 570**	**\$ 275**	**\$ -**	
Total direct costs (TDC)				**\$ 1,979**	**TDC**
C. G&A overhead costs					
22.0 (Number of man-hours x OPH)			\$ 20.00 =	\$ 440	
BEP (TDC + G&A overhead)				**\$ 2,419**	**BEP**
D. Contingency factor (if desired)				\$ -	
E. Net profit margin 20.00%				\$ 605	
F. Total price				**\$ 3,024**	**Total price**

IV. Scenario analysis

A. Square foot price (Total price ÷ units)

\$ 3,024 divided by	45,000.0 =	**\$ 0.0672**	**SF price**

B. Square foot break-even cost (BEP ÷ units)

\$ 2,419 divided by	45,000.0 =	**\$ 0.0538**	**BEP SF price**

C. Gross profit margin ((G&A overhead + Net profit) ÷ Total price)

\$ 1,045	÷ \$ 3,024 =	**34.6%**	**GPM**

FIGURE 22-4 Hydroseeding Small Commercial Jobs Recap

Project:	Residential hydroseeding	Date:	5/30/20___	
Location:		Estimator:	I.M. Dunn	CAW Loaded $ 19.20
P.O.C./G.C.:		Crew Size:	2	
Phone / Fax:		Hours/Day:	10	
Due Date:		CAW:	$ 16.00	Phase 1 — Quantity — Unit
Type Work:	Small residential jobs	Risk Factor	10%	Total Labor Hrs — 22 — Hrs L
		OT Factor	10%	

# Description		Tanks/day	Column Calcualtions Quantity	Unit	Unit Cost	#VALUE! Material	#VALUE! Labor	#VALUE! Equip	#VALUE! Subs
TOTALS						891	422	275	-
Materials	Seed (50 # per 500 GL tank)	5	250.0	LB	2.00	500			
	Tacifier (5 # per tank)	5	25.0	LB	3.25	81			
	Fibre mulch (5 bales per tank)	5	25.0	BL	10.00	250			
	Fertilizer (50 # per tank)	5	5.0	BG	12.00	60			
	Water	5	500.0	GL	-	-			
						-			
						-			
Labor	2 men, 20 man-hours per day		20.0	Hrs L	19.20		384		
	Call back time		2.0	Hrs L	19.20		38		
			-				-		
Equipment	Truck with tow-behind hydroseed unit		10.0	HR	25.00			250	
			-					-	
	Truck with tow-behind hydroseed unit		1.0	HR	25.00			25	
	(Call back time)							-	
								-	

FIGURE 22-5 Hydroseeding Residential Jobs Materials List

The hydroseeding market has changed in the last 10 to 15 years. Normally, whenever you combine labor with expensive materials, large (or lots of) equipment, specialty services or products, new services or products, or chemicals and fertilizers, you should think "market opportunity."

> As the supply of qualified hydroseed applicators increased, prices decreased.

Net and gross profit margins on this type of work are extremely high. This was true when hydroseeding was first introduced into the market in the early 1980s. Few contractors had hydroseeders, and the first units were large and expensive. These two factors created a market opportunity for owners of these units. Prices and margins were high. However, as more and more operators bought hydroseeders and as the smaller units became available, prices on seeding dropped. As the supply of qualified hydroseed applicators increased, prices decreased.

ACTION POINT

If you provide hydroseeding services for your clients, calculate your net profit and gross profit margins. Run various scenarios through these models in order to identify your break-even point for them. Compare the unit prices that you calculate with your current ones. And be sure to set hourly and daily revenue goals for your crews.

➤ NOTE The costs used in our scenarios are for illustration purposes only. Your costs will vary from the ones used in our examples. The key is to build a typical one-day scenario for the crew, materials, and equipment mixes you use. Round up these rates as appropriate. If your costing structure is accurate, the rates you calculate should be very close to your current ones and to those generally seen in your market.

Scenario cost data	$ or %	Remarks
Crew size (# people)	2.0	Crew leader and laborer
Crew average wage (CAW)	$ 16.00	
Man-hours per man per day	10.0	
Overtime factor (OTF)	10.0%	50 hours per week
Risk factor (RF)	10.0%	
Crew average wage w/OTF & RF	$ 19.20	
Labor burden	35.0%	
Sales tax	6.0%	
G&A overhead per hour (OPH)	$ 20.00	
Net profit margin	20.0%	
One ton crew truck	$ 25.00	
Curb-time man-hours	NA	
Number of units	35,000	Square feet

Scenario	Materials	Labor	Equipment	Subcontractors	Subtotals
I. Production (on-site or curb-time costs)					
	$ 891.25	$ 422.40	$ 275.00	$ -	
	$ 891.25	$ 422.40	$ 275.00	$ -	$ 1,589
II. General conditions (off-site or non-curb-time costs)					
	$ -	$ -	$ -	$ -	
	$ -	$ -	$ -	$ -	$ -
Subtotals	**$ 891**	**$ 422**	**$ 275**	**$ -**	**$ 1,589**
III. Margins & markups					
A.Sales ta	$ 53				
B.Labor burden		$ 148			
Subtotals	**$ 945**	**$ 570**	**$ 275**	**$ -**	
Total direct costs (TDC)				**$ 1,790**	**TDC**
C. G&A overhead costs					
22.0 (Number of man-hours x OPH)			$ 20.00 =	$ 440	
BEP (TDC + G&A overhead)				**$ 2,230**	**BEP**
D. Contingency factor (if desired)				$ -	
E. Net profit margin 20.00%				$ 557	
F. Total price				**$ 2,787**	**Total price**

IV. Scenario analysis

A. Square foot price (Total price ÷ units)

$ 2,787	divided by	35,000.0 =	**$ 0.0796**	**SF price**

B. Square foot break-even cost (BEP ÷ units)

$ 2,230	divided by	35,000.0 =	**$ 0.0637**	**BEP SF price**

C. Gross profit margin ((G&A overhead + Net profit) ÷ Total price)

$ 997	÷	$ 2,787 =	**35.8%**	**GPM**

FIGURE 22-6 Hydroseeding Residential Jobs Recap

CHAPTER

23

Interior Landscape Pricing

TERMS

Interior Landscape Services
Interiorscaping

Purpose

To explain how to price interior landscape projects

Introduction

Interior landscaping, or **interiorscaping**, is becoming more and more popular. Banks, office complexes, model homes, and upscale residences are just some of the market segments taking advantage of this relatively new service.

Plants used for this service are often sold to the clients but may be rented or leased to them. One benefit of the interior landscape business is that it's not seasonal. This fact alone has caught the attention of a number of landscape contractors in the colder climates.

How It Works

An exterior landscape contractor in southern California has been approached by numerous clients and asked to provide **interior landscape services** to complement her outdoor services. She wants to know what her curb-time, portal-to-portal, and daily-billable rates should be. She also wants to know what she should charge for installing a plant that costs her $150.

Labor rates for interiorscaping are rather easy to calculate. Figure 23-1 illustrates a typical day for a one-person crew.

Additional Scenario Information

- The labor rate is $10.
- The technician will work and get paid for eight hours per day, 40 hours per week.
- Curb time will be approximately six of the eight hours per day.
- The overtime factor, risk factor, sales tax, and so on are as indicated on Figure 23-1 on page 181 and Figure 23-2 on page 182.
- A minimum 10% net profit margin is desired.

Scenario cost data

	$ or %	Remarks
Crew size (# people)	1.0	Technician
Crew average wage (CAW)	$ 10.00	
Overtime factor (OTF)	0.0%	40 hours per week
Risk factor (RF)	10.0%	
Crew average wage w/OTF & RF	$ 11.00	
Labor burden	25.0%	
Sales tax	6.0%	
G&A overhead per hour (OPH)	$ 8.00	
Net profit margin	10.0%	
Van	$ 5.00	
Curb-time man-hours per day	6.0	
Number of units	6.0	Curb-time man-hours

Scenario	Materials	Labor		Equipment	CPH	Hours	Item
I. Production (on-site or curb-time costs)							
	$ -	6.0	Man-hours	$ -	$ -	0.0	
	$ -			$ -	$ -	0.0	
	$ -	$ 11.00		$ -	$ -	0.0	
	$ -	$ 66.00		$ -			
II. General conditions (off-site or non-curb-time costs)							
		2.0	Man-hours	$ 40.00	$ 5.00	8.0	Van
		0.0		$ -	$ -	0.0	
	$ -	$ 11.00		$ -	$ -	0.0	
	$ -	$ 22.00		$ 40.00			
Subtotals	**$ -**	**$ 88**		**$ 40**			
III. Margins & markups							
A. Sales tax	$ -						
B. Labor burden		$ 22					
Subtotals	**$ -**	**$ 110**		**$ 40**			

Total direct costs (TDC)			**$ 150**	**TDC**
C. G&A overhead costs				
8 (Number of man-hours x OPH)	$ 8.00	=	$ 64	
BEP (TDC + G&A overhead)			**$ 214**	**BEP**
D. Contingency factor (if desired)			$ -	
E. Net profit margin 10.00%			$ 24	
F. Total price			**$ 238**	**Total price**

IV. Scenario analysis

A. Curb-time rate (Total price ÷ curb-time hours)

$ 238 divided by 6.0 = **$ 39.63** **Curb-time rate**

B. Portal-to-portal rate (Total price ÷ all hours)

$ 238 divided by 8.0 = **$ 29.72** **Portal-to-portal rate**

C. Gross profit margin ((G&A overhead + Net profit) ÷ Total price)

$ 88 ÷ $ 238 = **36.9%** **GPM**

FIGURE 23-1 Interior Landscaping, 1-Man Crew

Scenario cost data	$ or %	Remarks
Crew size (# people)	1.0	Technician
Crew average wage (CAW)	$ 10.00	
Overtime factor (OTF)	0.0%	40 hours per week
Risk factor (RF)	10.0%	
Crew average wage w/OTF & RF	$ 11.00	
Labor burden	25.0%	
Sales tax	6.0%	
G&A overhead per hour (OPH)	$ 8.00	
Net profit margin	10.0%	
Van	$ 5.00	
Curb time man-hours per day	0.5	
Number of units	1.0	Potted plant

Scenario	Materials	Labor		Equipment	CPH	Hours	Item
I. Production (on-site or curb-time costs)							
	$ 150.00	0.5	Man-hours	$ -	$ -	0.0	
	$ -			$ -	$ -	0.0	
	$ -	$ 11.00		$ -	$ -	0.0	
	$ 150.00	$ 5.50		$ -			
II. General conditions (off-site or non-curb-time costs)							
		1.5	Man-hours	$ 10.00	$ 5.00	2.0	Van
		0.25	Warranty	$ 1.25	$ 5.00	0.25	Van warranty
10% Warranty	$ 15.00	$ 11.00		$ -	$ -	0.0	
	$ 15.00	$ 19.25		$ 11.25			
Subtotals	**$ 165**	**$ 25**		**$ 11**			
III. Margins & markups							
A. Sales tax	$ 10						
B. Labor burden		$ 6					
Subtotals	**$ 175**	**$ 31**		**$ 11**			

Total direct costs (TDC)			**$ 217**	**TDC**
C. G&A overhead costs				
2.25 (Number of man-hours x OPH)	$ 8.00	=	$ 18	
BEP (TDC + G&A overhead)			**$ 235**	**BEP**
D. Contingency factor (if desired)			$ -	
E. Net profit margin 10.00%			$ 26	
F. Total price			**$ 261**	**Total price**

IV. Scenario analysis

A. Unit price (Total price ÷ # units)

$ 261	divided by	1.0 =	**$ 261.21**	**Unit price**

B. Sales or revenue per hour (Total price ÷ total hours)

$ 261	divided by	2.25 =	**$ 116.09**	**SPH or RPH**

C. Gross profit margin ((G&A overhead + Net profit) ÷ Total price)

$ 44	÷	$ 261 =	**16.9%**	**GPM**

FIGURE 23-2 Interior Landscaping, Potted Plant Pricing

LABOR RATES

The calculated labor rates are as follows:

Curb-time labor rate	$ 39.63
Portal-to-portal labor rate	$ 29.72
Day rate or daily billable goal	$238.00

I'd round these to $40, $30, and $240, respectively.

MATERIAL PRICING

Materials provided to interiorscaping clients will normally have a 25 to 35% margin on them. A warranty factor in the range of 5 to 10% is normally applied to all materials provided. Depending on the particular plant provided, the warranty percent is sometimes below 5%. Occasionally, it's also above 10%. Adjust the warranty percentage as plant loss experience dictates.

Figure 23-2 illustrates a pricing scenario for a potted plant that costs the contractor $150. Note that the time to place the plant at the client's office is minimal compared to the time to obtain the plant and travel to and from the client's office. I also added 15 minutes of warranty labor time. While it would take longer than 15 minutes to replace this plant if it became necessary, we predict chances are 1 in 10 of that happening. Fifteen minutes should more than cover this contingency.

SUMMARY

While the product and service of interiorscaping is somewhat new and unique, the process for pricing it is not.

While the product and service of interiorscaping is somewhat new and unique, the process for pricing it is not. Interiorscaping can add an excellent revenue source for your business, while expanding your current service base. It can also provide year-round revenue, which is very appealing to the contractor looking for winter work opportunities.

ACTION POINT

If you provide interior landscaping services, calculate your net profit and gross profit margins. Also, determine what your daily billing rates should be and check to see if your crews are achieving them on a regular basis.

➤ NOTE

The costs used in our scenarios are for illustration purposes only. Your costs will vary from the ones used in these examples. The key is for you to build a typical one-day scenario for the crew, materials, and equipment you use. Round up these rates as appropriate. If your costing structure is accurate, the rates you calculate should be very close to your current ones and to those generally seen in your market.

CHAPTER

24

Pricing Irrigation Service Work

TERM

Global Positioning System (GPS)

Purpose

To explain the process of pricing irrigation service work

Introduction

Irrigation service work for small jobs lasting less than a day or two can be some of the most lucrative work you perform—if you price it correctly. However, there are potential pitfalls to be aware of when it comes to pricing your irrigation service work. They are (1) covering drive-time labor (and other non-site time labor such as loading the trucks at the yard, picking up materials, etc.) and the service truck, and (2) establishing daily billable goals for individuals and/or crews performing the work.

There are potential pitfalls to be aware of when it comes to pricing your irrigation service work.

You can also use the methods outlined here to calculate time and material (T&M) rates for other types of work. Substituting *your* costs for materials, labor, labor burden, G&A overhead, and so on, in place of the ones used in the examples, will allow you to develop accurate labor rates to use in T&M situations. Your pricing will probably be close to that established in the examples. However, you should take the time to complete these exercises, using *your* costs in order to ensure that *your* rates are accurate.

How It Works

A few winters ago, I met with an irrigation contractor in New England. He wanted to calculate his rates for his service work. At the time, he was charging $40 per hour for service repairs. After a fairly thorough analysis of costs and the market, we determined that he needed to charge $50 per man-hour. This was a 25% increase, which he thought was a pretty hefty increase. However, he implemented it.

Six months later I revisited him and asked if he'd lost any customers as a result. He told me not only had he not lost any customers, but that only two of them had even mentioned the increase.

This contractor provided excellent service to his customers but was underpricing his work. As a result of the analysis I did for his company, which I'm going to share with you, he put an extra $23,000 in his pocket in the first six months of his season.

PRICING IRRIGATION REPAIR/SERVICE WORK

Before you start developing your labor rates, you need to address how to handle the pricing of the materials used for repairs and non-site time (e.g., drive time, load time, picking-up-materials time, etc.). I recommend charging for repair materials independent of labor rates.

Most contractors charge clients the manufacturer's list price for irrigation materials used in T&M service work. Sometimes, list prices will be lowered for commercial customers. However, I recommend marking up materials a minimum of 20 to 25% above actual invoice cost. Residential irrigation markets will usually allow you to mark up materials 40 to 50% above invoice cost, which should bring your pricing for materials very close to the "list" or retail price residential customers would have to pay on the open market.

Off-site labor time (drive, load, and picking-up-materials time, etc.) can be handled in one of three ways.

1. It can be included in the hourly "curb-time" rate charged to the client. Curb time is the actual time a technician or crew is on the job site. It starts when they arrive at the site (curb) and ends when they leave. Hence, the term "curb time" is used. You calculate the curb-time rate by dividing the total price (including all costs except for materials and net profit) for an average day of service work by the average amount of on-site (curb-time) labor hours. In our example in Figure 24-1 on page 186, the price of $534 is divided by eight hours of curb time. The resultant curb-time rate is $66.72 per curb-time man-hour, which I'd round up to at least $67. I'd charge $67 per curb-time man-hour if that was the way I charged for irrigation service work.
2. The client is charged for actual off-site time (primarily drive time to the job site). This is often referred to as "portal-to-portal" billing. Essentially, the clock begins to run once the driver leaves the yard and stops when the job is completed, or in some cases when the driver returns to the yard. This method has some inherent problems, especially if the driver starts from a location other than the yard, gets stuck in traffic, or has to make other stops along the way. In our example, the portal-to-portal price is $53.38 per man-hour, which I'd round up to at least $54 if not $55 or $60.

   An average amount of off-site time could be allocated to the job instead, but this puts you into the third method.
3. You can charge a show-up or "trip charge" fee that includes drive time and other non-site time plus a certain amount of time on the job (e.g., the first 30 minutes on site). Time after that is normally charged at a predetermined rate and in 15-minute increments or part thereof.

   In our example, I'd charge $55 to show up, knowing the average job was 20 minutes from your office/yard and required approximately 10 minutes of additional off-site time for loading the truck, etc. The trip-charge rate would include these 30 minutes, plus the first 30 minutes of time on the job. Additional time on the job would be charged out at $13.75 per 15-minute increment or part thereof.

Let's look at Figure 24-1 and the scenario that follows to see how we determined these rates:

- Our sprinkler technician works alone and gets paid for 10 hours a day, 50 hours per week, which means the overtime factor (OTF) is 10% (five hours of overtime divided by 50 hours of straight time equals a 10% OTF).

Scenario cost data	$ or %	Remarks
Crew size (# people)	1.0	Irrigation technician
Crew average wage (CAW)	$ 15.00	
Overtime factor (OTF)	10.0%	50 hours per week
Risk factor (RF)	10.0%	
Crew average wage w/OTF & RF	$ 18.00	
Labor burden	35.0%	
Sales tax	6.0%	
G&A overhead per hour (OPH)	$ 12.00	
Net profit margin	20.0%	
Service van	$ 8.00	
Curb-time man-hours per day	8.0	
Number of units	8.0	Curb-time man-hours

Scenario	Materials	Labor		Equipment	CPH	Hours	Item
I. Production (on-site or curb-time costs)							
	$ -	8.0	Man-hours	$ -	$ -	0.0	
	$ -			$ -	$ -	0.0	
	$ -	$ 18.00		$ -	$ -	0.0	
	$ -	$ 144.00		$ -			
II. General conditions (off-site or non-curb-time costs)							
		2.0	Man-hours	$ 64.00	$ 8.00	8.0	Crew truck
		0.0		$ -	$ -	0.0	
	$ -	$ 18.00		$ -	$ -	0.0	
	$ -	$ 36.00		$ 64.00			
Subtotals	**$ -**	**$ 180**		**$ 64**			
III. Margins & markups							
A. Sales tax	$ -						
B. Labor burden		$ 63					
Subtotals	**$ -**	**$ 243**		**$ 64**			

Total direct costs (TDC)			**$ 307**	**TDC**
C. G&A overhead costs				
10 (Number of man-hours x OPH)	$ 12.00	=	$ 120	
BEP (TDC + G&A overhead)			**$ 427**	**BEP**
D. Contingency factor (if desired)			$ -	
E. Net profit margin 20.00%			$ 107	
F. Total price			**$ 534**	**Total price**

IV. Scenario analysis

A. Curb-time rate (Total price ÷ curb-time man-hours)

$ 534	divided by	8.0 =	**$ 66.72**	**Curb-time rate**

B. Portal-to-portal rate (Total price ÷ all hours)

$ 534	divided by	10.0 =	**$ 53.38**	**Portal-to-portal rate**

C. Show-up fee or "Trip" charge rate (Total price ÷ all hours)

$ 534	divided by	$ 10 =	**$ 53.38**	**Trip charge**

FIGURE 24-1 Irrigation Service Work

- Although all work is performed on a "T&M" basis with a theoretical risk factor of zero, I'd still calculate a 10% risk factor into this scenario to cover contingencies.
- The technician's hourly rate is $15.
- Labor burden is 35%.
- The technician drives a van that calculates out to $8 cost per hour (CPH).
- An average job is 20 minutes from the office.
- An additional 40 to 60 minutes per day are required to load the truck, pick up materials, do administrative work, etc.
- You plan to perform and bill a minimum of four jobs per day.
- Materials are charged to the customer at current list prices.
- Approximately $100 of materials (at cost) is to be installed per day.
- The G&A overhead cost per labor hour (OPH) amount has previously been calculated to be $12.
- A combined net profit margin and contingency factor of 20% is to be included in the work.

Turning to Figure 24-1

- We've put eight man-hours in our Phase I curb-time production costs.
- Phase II general conditions contain the remaining two man-hours of estimated daily load, drive, administration, and materials-pick-up time.
- The service van is also included in Phase II general conditions at eight hours for the day. We use eight hours because the cost per hour is calculated using an eight-hour day. You can use ten hours in your daily costs if desired.
- The total price, including all costs and 20% net profit, for an average day of sprinkler repair work is $534 (which is indicated at the bottom of the Phase III calculations).

Total revenue that must be generated per day to cover all costs (including G&A overhead and providing a 20% net profit margin) is $534. In other words, we must bill $534 per day, excluding materials, to cover all costs and show a 20% net profit.

Let's break this down into more meaningful scenarios using the trip-charge method.

Scenario 1

You bill four jobs per day and keep the service technician busy (billable) all day. Generated revenues are as follows:

4 (jobs) × $55 (show-up charge)	$220
6 hours billed at $55/hour	$330
Total	$550

You've exceeded your goal of $534 by $16.

Scenario 2

You bill five jobs per day and keep the repairman billable all day.

5 (jobs) × $55 (show-up charge)	$275
5 hours billed at $55/hour	$275
Total	$550

You've exceeded your goal of $534 by $16.

Scenario 3

You bill six jobs per day and keep the repairman billable all day.

6 (jobs) × \$55 (show-up charge)	\$330
4 hours billed at \$55/hour	\$220
Total	\$550

You've exceeded your goal of \$534 by \$16.

Each of the three scenarios produces an extra \$16 of net profit in addition to the \$107 net profit built into the day rate. And remember, this net profit is also supplemented by the net profit on the materials each day. The difference between your cost and what you charge the customer is pure net profit.

The key is to keep your technician busy and billable all day, and to bill a minimum of \$534 per day excluding any materials. If that occurs, you're making money and any revenue billed above the \$534 is extra net profit.

You should track your irrigation service work on a daily basis. Many of my clients use **global positioning system (GPS)** software to track their service vans. At a minimum, the items that should be monitored are

- Sales or total billable dollar amounts per day per technician.
- Labor hours and job tasks (e.g., Drive to Jones' residence, 15 minutes; repair two heads, 35 minutes; return to shop, 15 minutes; pick up irrigation materials, 20 minutes; etc.).
- Materials used and billed per job

Once you have historical data from which to work, go back and adjust your hourly rates and trip-charge rate, if desired.

SUMMARY

Irrigation service work and time and materials (T&M) work can and should be some of your most profitable work—if you calculate your pricing correctly. Be sure to include off-site labor time and vehicles in your prices and to set daily goals for billable production hours and revenue. Use the example to calculate your labor rates. Add a service helper if desired.

You can be confident that you're going to make money every time a service truck leaves your yard.

Remember, the net profit on materials is pure profit. Also remember that these pricing methods are to be used for jobs of short duration and that are fairly typical of your work. If a T&M job requires lots of extra drive time or includes difficult job-site conditions, adjust your pricing accordingly.

If, after you calculate your T&M prices, they look too good to be true, they probably are. Go back and check your arithmetic and don't be afraid to add some extra net profit if they appear too low. Your rates should be reasonably close to market rates. The main difference is that now you have confidence in knowing how you arrived at your rates and how to adjust them if conditions change. You can also set well-defined daily production and revenue goals using them.

You can price your irrigation service with confidence, knowing all your costs are covered by your rates. You can also be confident that you're going to make money every time a service truck leaves your yard. And pricing with confidence is what the irrigation service business is all about.

ACTION POINT

Validate your irrigation service T&M unit prices and ensure that you set hourly and daily revenue goals for your technicians.

➤ NOTE The costs used in our scenarios are for illustration purposes only. Your costs will vary from the ones used in these examples. The key is for you to build a typical one-day scenario for the crew, materials, and equipment mixes you use. Round up these rates as appropriate. If your costing structure is accurate, the rates you calculate should be very close to your current ones and to those generally seen in your market.

CHAPTER

25

Lawn Maintenance Packages

TERMS

Daily Billable Goals
Day Rate
Generic Day
Lawn Maintenance Package
Minute Rate

Purpose

To explain how to price lawn maintenance packages

Introduction

Pricing landscape maintenance crew and equipment packages poses some unique challenges. The **lawn maintenance package** approach is normally used to price residential jobs of short duration. We'll basically average our costs for the day and then calculate an hourly, daily, and per minute price. This is valid as long as the crew is working on a project that falls within our average job scenario. Once the crew starts to work outside this "normal" job scenario, cost accuracy suffers.

The **day rate** for the crew is a critical number for everyone to keep in mind. This is the amount this crew has to bill every day in order to cover all costs and be profitable. The day rate is a goal the crew, managers, and owners should strive to meet every day of the season. If it's achieved, you can virtually guarantee you're making money with this crew.

The **minute rate** is also important, because it allows you to quickly verify that your jobs are priced correctly. Multiply the number of minutes the crew is on the job site by the minute rate. Compare this calculated amount to what you're charging the customer. If they're not equal, make adjustments if at all possible.

The lawn maintenance package approach is normally used to price residential jobs of short duration.

LANDSCAPE MANAGEMENT OR MAINTENANCE ESTIMATING

We'll follow our usual three-phase format but, instead of using it for one specific job, we'll enter the costs for one **generic day** of work.

- Calculate Phase I production costs.
- Calculate Phase II general condition costs.
- Add markups and margins in Phase III in order to arrive at the final price, either in lump-sum or unit-price formats.

This three-phase format is excellent for bidding specific large residential and commercial projects—those billing over $500 per month (or which include more than 15 to 20 man-hours per month). However it's impractical and too time-consuming for pricing smaller jobs. Using the maintenance package bidding approach for smaller jobs greatly speeds up the estimating process without sacrificing accuracy.

How It Works

A residential lawn maintenance contractor in New England wanted to calculate the rate to charge his customers. He also wanted to verify that the total price on his contracts for these customers was correct. He had good job tracking for each of his clients and knew how long it took his crews to perform the contracted work.

To address our contractor's concerns, we first determine our maintenance package crew and equipment requirements for a typical day. For purposes of our example, we'll use the following two-person crew:

Labor	*$/%*
Leadman/driver	$12/hr
Laborer	$ 8/hr
Labor burden	30%
OTF (50 hours/week, 10 hours/day)	10%
RF (risk factor)	10%
OPH	$ 8/hr

Equipment	*CPH*
Crew truck with trailer	$8
Mower, 36″ walk-behind	$5
Mower, 21″ (1)	$3
Blower (1)	$3
Edger (1)	$3
Stick trimmer (1)	$3

Now, we determine the average amount of drive time per day for this crew if they only work on the smaller types of jobs for which the maintenance package would be used.

As you'll see, this is a crucial consideration. If the crew completes eight to ten job sites per day, with an average drive time of 10 minutes between jobs, the drive time for each day would be as follows:

30 minutes load/unload time per day	30 minutes
8 jobs at 10 minutes drive time each	80 minutes
Plus 10 to return to yard	10 minutes
Total at end of day	120 minutes

This translates to two man-hours per day per man, for a total of four man-hours.

We're now ready to cost out our maintenance package. Remember to round up to the nearest whole dollar whenever practical. See Figure 25-1 on page 192.

We first calculate our Phase I production costs. To obtain our Phase I production labor hours, we must subtract our drive-time hours from the total paid labor hours for the day. In our example, there are 20 total paid labor hours for the day; after we subtract the four off-site man-hours, the result is 16 production labor hours.

We then calculate the *average* number of hours the mowers, blower, and edger will be used during production hours.

Subtotal your Phase I costs, as shown on Figure 25-1.

Scenario cost data	**$ or %**	**Remarks**
Crew size (# people)	2.0	Crew leader with a laborer
Crew average wage (CAW)	$ 10.00	
Overtime factor (OTF)	10.0%	50 hours per week
Risk factor (RF)	10.0%	
Crew average wage w/OTF & RF	$ 12.00	
Labor burden	30.0%	
Sales tax	6.0%	
G&A overhead per hour (OPH)	$ 8.00	
Net profit margin	10.0%	
Crew truck & trailer	$ 8.00	
Curb-time man-hours per day	16.0	
Number of units	16.0	Curb-time man-hours

Scenario	**Materials**	**Labor**		**Equipment**	**CPH**	**Hours**	**Item**
I. Production (on-site or curb-time costs)							
	$ -	16.0	Man-hours	$ 30.00	$ 5.00	6.0	36" WB mower
	$ -			$ 6.00	$ 3.00	2.0	21" mower
	$ -	$ 12.00		$ 12.00	$ 3.00	4.0	Edger & stick trimmer
	$ -	$ 192.00		$ 48.00			
II. General conditions (off-site or non-curb-time costs)							
		4.0	Man-hours	$ 64.00	$ 8.00	8.0	Crew truck & trailer
				$ -	$ -	0.0	
	$ -	$ 12.00		$ -	$ -	0.0	
	$ -	$ 48.00		$ 64.00			
Subtotals	$ -	$ 240		$ 112			
III. Margins & markups							
A. Sales tax	$ -						
B. Labor burden		$ 72					
Subtotals	$ -	$ 312		$ 112			

Total direct costs (TDC)		$ 424	**TDC**
C. G&A overhead costs			
20 (Number of man-hours x OPH)	$ 8.00 =	$ 160	
BEP (TDC + G&A overhead)		$ 584	**BEP**
D. Contingency factor (if desired)		$ -	
E. Net profit margin 10.00%		$ 65	
F. Total price		$ 649	**Total price**

IV. Scenario analysis

A. Curb-time man-hour rate (Total price ÷ curb-time man-hours)

$ 649 divided by 16.0 = **$ 40.56** **Curb-time rate**

B. Portal-to-portal rate (Total price ÷ all man-hours)

$ 649 divided by 20.0 = **$ 32.44** **Portal-to-portal rate**

C. Gross profit margin ((G&A overhead + Net profit) ÷ Total price)

$ 225 ÷ $ 649 = **34.7%** **GPM**

FIGURE 25-1 Lawn Maintenance Package with 16 Hours of Curb Time

Phase II general conditions are calculated next. Load/unload and drive time (non-site time) and the crew truck at eight hours per day are included here.

In this example, it's assumed that lunch and break times are not paid and are not, therefore, included in the production or general condition labor hours. If, for example, a 15-minute break in the morning is part of the paid eight labor hours per day per man, include it in general condition labor hours.

2 men × .25 hrs/day = .5 hrs/day

Subtotal Phase II general condition costs. Subtotal both the Phases I and II costs. You're now ready to add Phase III markups and margins to the bid. Check the following bulleted items to be sure everything is accounted for:

- There are no materials involved on these jobs and therefore there is no markup for sales tax.
- The 30% labor burden is then applied to the total labor for the job.
- Subtotal your bid once again.
- Add equipment to your labor and labor burden totals.
- Subtotal again.
- Calculate your general and administrative overhead and add it to the bid.
- Subtotal again (this is your break-even point).
- Add a net profit margin and a contingency factor (if desired) to the break-even point.

You've now arrived at your final price for a *generic* day for your maintenance package. Round up this number as you deem appropriate. I'd round the $649 to $650.

To calculate the curb-time rate used for estimating smaller jobs:

- Divide the total daily price by the production hours. (I'd round this to $41.)

  $650 ÷ 16 on-site man-hours = $40.63 curb-time man-hour rate

- Multiply this rate by the number of people on the crew to obtain your crew curb-time rate. This translates into

  $41 × 2 = $82 per curb crew hour

You can now easily bid smaller jobs by first estimating your crew's curb time at a particular job.

- For a job site that requires 30 minutes of curb time

  30 minutes of curb time × $82 = .5 × $82 = $41 per visit to the job site

Remember, curb time starts when your crew pulls up to the curb (at the site being bid) and ends when they drive away (going to the next job or back to the yard). Note the impact that estimated drive time makes on your curb man-hour rate of $41 if it increases to three hours per day per man or drops to one hour per man per day.

Drive Time Decreases

Drive time drops from two hours to one hour per day per man. See Figure 25-2 on page 194.

Step (1): Total price for a day ÷ Total production man-hours = $650 = 18 man-hours = $650 ÷ 18 = $36.11. (I'd probably round this to $36.)

Step (2): Multiply $36 by number of crew members. $36 × 2 = $72 curb crew hour rate.

Scenario cost data	$ or %	Remarks
Crew size (# people)	2.0	Crew leader with a laborer
Crew average wage (CAW)	$ 10.00	
Overtime factor (OTF)	10.0%	50 hours per week
Risk factor (RF)	10.0%	
Crew average wage w/OTF & RF	$ 12.00	
Labor burden	30.0%	
Sales tax	6.0%	
G&A overhead per hour (OPH)	$ 8.00	
Net profit margin	10.0%	
Crew truck	$ 8.00	
Curb-time man-hours per day	18.0	
Number of units	18.0	Curb-time man-hours

Scenario	Materials	Labor		Equipment	CPH	Hours	Item
I. Production (on-site or curb-time costs)							
	$ -	18.0	Man-hours	$ 30.00	$ 5.00	6.0	36" WB mower
	$ -			$ 6.00	$ 3.00	2.0	21" mower
	$ -	$ 12.00		$ 12.00	$ 3.00	4.0	Edger, stick trimmer, & blower
	$ -	$ 216.00		$ 48.00			
II. General conditions (off-site or non-curb-time costs)							
		2.0	Man-hours	$ 64.00	$ 8.00	8.0	Crew truck
				$ -	$ -	0.0	
	$ -	$ 12.00		$ -	$ -	0.0	
	$ -	$ 24.00		$ 64.00			
Subtotals	**$ -**	**$ 240**		**$ 112**			
III. Margins & markups							
A. Sales tax	$ -						
B. Labor burden		$ 72					
Subtotals	**$ -**	**$ 312**		**$ 112**			

Total direct costs (TDC)			**$ 424**	**TDC**
C. G&A overhead costs				
20 (Number of man-hours x OPH)	$ 8.00	=	$ 160	
BEP (TDC + G&A overhead)			**$ 584**	**BEP**
D. Contingency factor (if desired)			$ -	
E. Net profit margin 10.00%			$ 65	
F. Total price			**$ 649**	**Total price**

IV. Scenario analysis

A. Curb-time man-hour rate (Total price ÷ curb-time man-hours)

$ 649 divided by 18.0 = **$ 36.05** **Curb-time rate**

B. Portal-to-portal rate (Total price ÷ all man-hours)

$ 649 divided by 20.0 = **$ 32.44** **Portal-to-portal rate**

C. Gross profit margin ((G&A overhead + Net profit) ÷ Total price)

$ 225 ÷ $ 649 = **34.7%** **GPM**

FIGURE 25-2 Lawn Maintenance Package with 18 Hours of Curb Time

Drive Time Increases

Drive time increases from two to three hours per man per day. See Figure 25-3 on page 196.

Step (l): Total price for a day ÷ Total production man-hours = $650 = 14 man-hours = $650 ÷ 14 = $46.43 (I'd round this to $46.50.)

Step (2): Multiply $46.50 by number of crew members. $46.50 × 2 = $93 curb crew hour rate.

As you can see, drive time has a considerable impact on the curb price you should charge in a maintenance package bidding situation.

The maintenance package bidding approach can easily accommodate any number of formats. For instance, one contractor in southern California charges clients $325 per month for a three-person crew being on the site for one crew hour per week. If his crews spend more than one hour per week on a site, he knows he's in trouble on that job. The arithmetic works out as follows:

Curb-time rate per man-hour	$ 25.00
Crew size	× 3.00
	$ 75.00
Average # of weeks per month	× 4.33
Total	$324.75
Round up to	$325.00

The Day Rate

The day rate for this generic day of lawn maintenance is $649, which I'd round up to $650. Owners, managers, and crews should religiously track this number on a daily or weekly basis. You're making money and being profitable every day you hit this number.

The Minute Rate

The curb-time minute rate for the crew calculates out as follows:

- First, determine the daily billable goal for the crew. I'd set it at $650.

  $650 ÷ (crew curb-time minutes per day) = $650 ÷ (8 hours × 60 minutes) = $650 ÷ 480 = $1.35

- If the crew is on a job site for 45 crew minutes (i.e., from 8:00 to 8:45 am), you should be charging $61

  45 crew minutes × $1.35 = $60.75

- To verify the crew minute rate, multiply the total crew curb-time minutes for the day by the minute rate. For the whole day this calculates to be $648, which is close enough to our goal of $650.

  480 (8 hours × 60 minutes) curb-time crew minutes × $1.35 = $648

SUMMARY

When calculating your curb-time rates, adjust your crew size, equipment mix, and drive time as appropriate. If the rates you calculate look too good to be true, they probably are. Go back, review, and recalculate your work. Don't include materials or subcontractors in your curb-time rates, as they'll greatly confuse the matter.

Scenario cost data	$ or %	Remarks
Crew size (# people)	2.0	Crew leader with a laborer
Crew average wage (CAW)	$ 10.00	
Overtime factor (OTF)	10.0%	50 hours per week
Risk factor (RF)	10.0%	
Crew average wage w/OTF & RF	$ 12.00	
Labor burden	30.0%	
Sales tax	6.0%	
G&A overhead per hour (OPH)	$ 8.00	
Net profit margin	10.0%	
Crew truck	$ 8.00	
Curb-time man-hours per day	14.0	
Number of units	14.0	Curb-time man-hours

Scenario	Materials	Labor		Equipment	CPH	Hours	Item
I. Production (on-site or curb-time costs)							
0.0	$ -	14.0	Man-hours	$ 30.00	$ 5.00	6.0	36" WB mower
$-	$ -			$ 6.00	$ 3.00	2.0	21" mower
	$ -	$ 12.00		$ 12.00	$ 3.00	4.0	Edger, stick trimmer, & blower
	$ -	$ 168.00		$ 48.00			
II. General conditions (off-site or non-curb-time costs)							
		6.0	Man-hours	$ 64.00	$ 8.00	8.0	Crew truck
				$ -	$ -	0.0	
	$ -	$ 12.00		$ -	$ -	0.0	
	$ -	$ 72.00		$ 64.00			
Subtotals	**$ -**	**$ 240**		**$ 112**			
III. Margins & markups							
A. Sales tax	$ -						
B. Labor burden		$ 72					
Subtotals	**$ -**	**$ 312**		**$ 112**			

Total direct costs (TDC)		**$ 424**	**TDC**
C. G&A overhead costs			
20 (Number of man-hours x OPH)	$ 8.00 =	$ 160	
BEP (TDC + G&A overhead)		**$ 584**	**BEP**
D. Contingency factor (if desired)		$ -	
E. Net profit margin 10.00%		$ 65	
F. Total price		**$ 649**	**Total price**

IV. Scenario analysis

A. Curb-time man-hour rate (Total price ÷ curb-time man-hours)

$ 649 divided by 14.0 = **$ 46.35** **Curb-time rate**

B. Portal-to-portal rate (Total price ÷ all man-hours)

$ 649 divided by 20.0 = **$ 32.44** **Portal-to-portal rate**

C. Gross profit margin ((G&A overhead + Net profit) ÷ Total price)

$ 225 ÷ $ 649 = **34.7%** **GPM**

FIGURE 25-3 Lawn Maintenance Package with 14 Hours of Curb Time

Your primary objective is to bill your day rate amount. Variances in curb rates are fine as long as you're hitting your daily billable target.

I'd encourage you to mark up materials a minimum of 25%. In most cases, you should be able to charge retail prices for materials used on residential accounts. Mark up any costs for subcontractors used on the sites from 10 to 25%. This is the normal and acceptable range for marking up subcontractor costs.

Remember to set **daily billable goals** for the crews. Track your actual daily billable amount and compare it to your daily target. Ensure that everyone is aware of this information.

Track your actual on-site time and off-site time. Adjust your per hour and minute curb rates accordingly. Use your calculated minute curb rate to verify your pricing for specific jobs.

While changes in actual on/off-site time will affect your curb rates, your daily billable goal shouldn't change if the total amount of paid hours per day remains the same. Your primary objective is to bill your day rate amount. Variances in curb rates are fine as long as you're hitting your daily billable target.

ACTION POINT

If you need to create lawn maintenance package pricing, use the models provided here to do so. Validate the unit prices that you calculate and compare them to your current prices. Be sure to set hourly and daily revenue goals for your crews.

➤ **NOTE** The costs used in our scenarios are for illustration purposes only. Your costs will vary from the ones used in these examples. The key is for you to build a typical one-day scenario for the crew, materials, and equipment mixes you use. Round up these rates as appropriate. If your costing structure is accurate, the rates you calculate should be very close to your current ones and to those generally seen in your market.

CHAPTER

26

Large Maintenance Jobs and On-Site Maintenance Projects

TERM

On-Site Maintenance

Purpose

To explain the process of pricing large maintenance and on-site maintenance projects

Too often, contractors use formulas and methods that are archaic and inflexible, which cost the contractor using them jobs and money.

Introduction

Knowing your costs and using accurate cost estimating methods is critical for successfully bidding large commercial maintenance projects. Too often, contractors use formulas and methods that are archaic and inflexible. These methods often contain false mathematical assumptions, which cost the contractor using them jobs and money. Today's competitive market requires estimating methods that calculate costs accurately and that can adapt to new market strategies.

How It Works

George and his partner Bill had a thriving full-service maintenance business, which specialized in the municipal market. Multi-year contract options were common. Many projects reached annual amounts of $500,000 plus. Crews were on the same site five days a week. When bidding a job, George and Bill would get into one of their pickup trucks together and drive the site.

The rule was that neither would say a word, unless they had a question about the site, until each was ready to make a "guesstimate." They'd then go back and forth trying to decide how many full-time laborers they'd need on the job. It was all very subjective, but their combined 40 years of experience usually got them close. Once the number of full-time laborers was decided, equipment, materials, subcontractor costs, margins, and markups were then applied to the bid. George and Bill wanted to break into the commercial maintenance market and knew they needed a more accurate and flexible method to calculate their costs and price their jobs.

Bob, on the other hand, had started his company in the mid-1980s while going to college. He specialized in residential lawn maintenance work. His sales in 1990 were a little over $200,000. He also wanted to break into the commercial, full-service maintenance market. His method of estimating was similar to what George and Bill used, but on a smaller scale. Bob would look at a site and "guesstimate" the amount of time his crew would be at the residence. He would then multiply the amount of time by his hourly rate. For instance, a two-man crew on site for 30 minutes would bill out at $25 (.5 crew hours × $50/crew hour). Bob was smart enough to realize he needed more accurate methods for bidding the larger commercial work.

THE CHALLENGE AND THE OPPORTUNITY

Large maintenance jobs, which bill at a minimum of 40 hours per week, pose particular challenges (and opportunities) for the seasoned estimator who knows his or her numbers. The 40-hour-per-week minimum is significant because it opens the possibility to **on-site maintenance**, where a designated one-man crew can be on site five days a week. Substantial savings in drive-time labor and the crew pickup truck costs may be possible, along with increased productivity. On-site maintenance also offers some significant marketing advantages through increased customer satisfaction. Many customers like the idea of a full-time, designated "gardener" on their site.

Small residential jobs (where the crew visits 10 to 15 sites per day) and even some small commercial maintenance projects can be effectively bid using a crew-hour maintenance package approach (i.e., $90/crew hour for a three-man crew). However, jobs billing $500 to $1,000 per month and more require more accurate bidding methods.

THE METHOD

When bidding large maintenance projects, you should first decide if the site can possibly qualify for a designated full time on-site crew throughout the season. To do so, the customer must agree with the concept, but there are important logistical hurdles to cover. Where will equipment and materials be stored? Will the crew have a secure office? How will the crew communicate with the main office? Will a pickup truck be needed on site 40 hours per week or will a less costly utility cart be sufficient? Each of these questions and their answers can affect the costs involved on such a project and, consequently, the final price to the customer.

Production Costs

Once the on-site maintenance question is effectively addressed, the project should be broken down into its phases (i.e., spring cleanup, mulching, fertilizations, pesticide applications, mowing, fall cleanup, shrub and tree pruning, etc.). These phases are then broken down into their on-site production cost components: materials, labor with burden, equipment, and subcontractor costs. Review Exhibit 10 as we discuss bidding large maintenance projects

Mowing areas should be measured and the hours for each mower used on the job should be calculated based on its hourly production rate. Hours of use for trimmers, edgers, blowers, and so on should likewise be calculated. These hours and the accompanying labor hours should then be multiplied by their respective cost per hour and crew average wage rates.

General Condition Costs

Your general conditions, which contain the same four cost components identified in production costs, are then added either to each phase or as a lump-sum item on the bid. Estimated material costs are included at cost. Estimated labor hours are multiplied by the crew average wage or by a specific rate for supervisors, crew leaders, and other categories. Equipment hours are multiplied by the predetermined cost per hour for the respective pieces of equipment. Subcontractor costs are included at cost.

Your general conditions should contain such things as drive time, load/unload time, the crew pickup or utility cart, supervisory time, administration time for the crew leader, dump fees, time to pick up materials, etc. I define general conditions in great detail. As a benchmark, general condition costs usually comprise eight to 15 percent of the final price of a maintenance project. Labor hours in general conditions usually comprise 15 to 25 percent of the total labor in the bid.

Breaking out general conditions this way provides the estimator with a checklist of ratios and percentages that can be used to compare to industry benchmark standards. However, the key issue is not whether an item is in production costs or general condition costs but whether it's included in the bid at all.

On-site maintenance impacts general condition costs in at least two important areas. First, drive time is usually significantly reduced. Drive time usually comprises 10 to 15% of the total paid hours per day for a normal maintenance route. On-site projects, where the crew reports to the site, can reduce drive time significantly. Overtime is often eliminated and/or the crew can spend more time on site. Replacing a crew pickup truck with a utility cart or reducing the time it spends on site can also reduce costs. These savings can then be passed on to the customer, thus making your bid more competitive. Or, you can maintain your price and increase your net profit margin on the job.

Margins and Markups

Margins and markups are added to the production and general condition costs. Sales tax is added to materials (in some states, it's added to all costs). Labor burden (e.g., FICA, FUTA, SUTA, workers' compensation, general liability and medical insurance for field labor, field labor vacations, sick pay and holidays) is added to labor.

G&A overhead is then applied to the bid using the G&A overhead per hour (OPH) method. Your G&A OPH will usually range from under $4 per billable field-labor hour to over $12. Extremely large commercial and municipal maintenance companies that operate in the field 12 months a year realize a very low OPH. Smaller companies that operate in the field 8 to 10 months a year have a much higher OPH. To calculate the amount of G&A overhead to allocate to a job, simply multiply the number of labor hours in a bid by the OPH for your company or division.

Remember two important caveats regarding your G&A OPH

- First, for your OPH to be accurate, your projected G&A overhead costs and billable field-labor hours need to be within 15% of what they actually are or will be at the end of the year. This is why you should monitor these costs and hours throughout the year to ensure their accuracy.
- Second, indirect G&A overhead costs should not include field equipment or field labor burden costs. Otherwise, you'll overstate your OPH. You'll also run into other more significant field cost problems down the line.

Once you allocate indirect G&A overhead costs to the bid, you've calculated the break-even point (BEP) for the job. This is the dollar amount that equals all your costs (both field and office) for the job. Next you add a contingency factor to your BEP, if desired. The contingency factor is a subjective amount you may or may not add to a bid to absorb some risks about which you're uncertain.

Your net profit margin is then added to the bid. This amount usually ranges from 8 to 15%. However, it's the sum total of net profit, G&A overhead recovery, and the contingency factor that provides the estimator with a very useful tool or benchmark standard. The sum of these three numbers determines the gross profit margin (GPM) on the bid. Put another way, GPM = Price – total direct costs.

The GPM on large commercial and residential maintenance projects usually falls in the 30 to 40% range. However, I've seen it drop to the low 20s in extremely competitive markets. On occasion I've also seen it climb to the high 30s or low 40s in some markets.

Negotiated work usually has a GPM that's 5 to 10% higher than competitively bid jobs. Estimators need to keep this in mind when bidding. Otherwise, they might leave money on the bid table. Because negotiated work has the highest profit margins and usually comprises the least amount of risk for the contractor, it should be a contractor's goal to obtain as much negotiated work as possible, especially multi-year contracts.

COMMON MISTAKES

The previous method for bidding large maintenance projects is detailed and requires that the estimator know production rates, equipment costs, and more. In essence, it requires the estimator to do his or her homework. Some consider it too complex and detailed. I'd agree, if the contractor could bid work faster and make plenty of money on the bottom line without going to all this trouble. However, as markets tighten and/or as bottom lines erode, more thorough cost analysis and bidding methods are required.

Many contractors use quick, simplistic methods, which contain erroneous mathematical assumptions and fatal flaws. One mistake is including field equipment costs in indirect general and administrative overhead. These costs are then allocated to bids on a percentage basis, or they're put onto jobs using a per-hour method similar to the OPH method described earlier.

The market isn't stupid. If you're willing to underprice work, the market will give you plenty of it. Anyone can get plenty of work by underpricing it.

Both are inaccurate, because field equipment costs are evenly spread on jobs. Jobs requiring very little equipment are bid with the same amount of equipment costs as jobs that are very equipment intensive. Consequently, labor intensive jobs are bid too high and equipment intensive ones too low. The contractor can't be competitive on labor intensive jobs, while he wins the equipment intensive ones because he's underpriced them.

A second common mistake occurs when the contractor bids jobs using a flat rate (i.e., $25, $30, or $35 per man-hour). Essentially this method makes a mistake similar to the one above. Labor intensive work is overpriced while equipment intensive work is underpriced. Why charge the same $35 per hour for an $8-an-hour laborer pulling weeds as you would for your $14-an-hour crew leader mowing grass with a 72″ ride-on mower that costs you $9 per hour to operate? It's not mathematically accurate. Your costs and prices for a bid should accurately reflect true costs and reality.

Remember, "The market isn't stupid." If you're willing to underprice work, the market will give you plenty of it. Anyone can get plenty of work by underpricing it.

BACK TO THE FUTURE (Where Are They Now?)

How It Works

George and Bill never made the adjustments in their estimating methods. Consequently, they weren't successful entering the commercial maintenance market. They're still battling it out in the extremely competitive municipal maintenance market. They've consistently lost market share because they failed to develop the tools and methods to accurately adjust their bidding according to new production methods and costs.

Bob, on the other hand, made the adjustments and has made a complete shift from residential to full-service commercial maintenance work. His company is very profitable and his annual revenue is well over $2 million (and climbing). On-site maintenance comprises much of his work, while the balance consists of a mix of regular weekly visits and installation extras for his existing client base. The future is very bright for Bob, even though he's in a very competitive market. This contractor has developed flexible estimating tools and methods, which allow him to accurately calculate a job's true costs in any situation.

SUMMARY

Bidding large maintenance projects requires special estimating skills, methods, and tools. The contractor bidding such work often uses inflexible, antiquated methods that simply do not calculate job costs accurately. These methods contain faulty mathematical assumptions, which can do a contractor much harm. Many a "good old boy" contractor has been done in by "bad old boy" arithmetic in his estimating system.

Many a "good old boy" contractor has been done in by "bad old boy" arithmetic in his estimating system.

On the other hand, many aggressive young contractors, armed with flexible yet accurate estimating methods, are grabbing market share. They're very profitable because they have the tools to bid jobs and to adapt to virtually any production method or market. They know their costs and they know their markets. And that's a recipe for success.

ACTION POINT

Review the large commercial maintenance bid in Exhibit 10 in the back of the book.

➤ NOTE The costs used in our scenarios are for illustration purposes only. Your costs will vary from the ones used in these examples. The key is for you to build a typical one-day scenario for the crew, materials, and equipment mixes you use. Round up these rates as appropriate. If your costing structure is accurate, the rates you calculate should be very close to your current ones and to those generally seen in your market.

CHAPTER 27

Lawn Fertilization

Purpose

To explain how to price lawn fertilization

Introduction

A large number of contractors apply chemicals in the form of lawn fertilization. This work can be very lucrative. However, many applicators do not know how profitable it is or what their break-even point is regarding specific products or applications. The following scenarios will help address these issues.

How It Works

Scenario 1 A high-end residential installation and maintenance contractor on the East Coast does work in a very upscale area. He'd like to know his costs and break-even point for applying a fertilizer on his clients' lawns. The average lawn is approximately .75 acres. This contractor believes his crew can do an average of 10 to 12 lawns per day. He'd like to know the following:

A. How much should he bill per day per 1,000 SF, per 10,000 SF, and per acre for this type of work?

B. What is his BEP per day per 1,000 SF, per 10,000 SF, and per acre for this type of work?

Additional Scenario Information

- Crews will work and get paid for 10 hours per day, 50 hours per week.
- The equipment cost per hour is indicated on the figures in this chapter.
- The overtime factor, risk factor, sales tax, etc. are also as indicated on the figures in this chapter.
- The owner desires to obtain a minimum of 25% net profit margin for this work.

Scenario 2 A commercial maintenance contractor in the western states is bidding on a large 40-acre site. He needs to know his costs and break-even point for applying fertilizer on this site. The specifications call for three pounds of fertilizer per 1,000 square feet. A 50-pound bag of fertilizer will cost him $13. He believes his two-man crew can apply five bags of fertilizer per man-hour using a utility cart with a spreader. The second man on the crew will help load the bags of fertilizer and blow off sidewalks with a backpack blower. The contractor would like to know the following:

A. How much should he charge per acre for this type of work?

B. What's his break-even point per acre for this type of work?

Additional Scenario Information

- Crews will work and get paid for 10 hours per day, 50 hours per week.
- The equipment cost per hour is indicated on the figures in this chapter.
- The overtime factor, risk factor, sales tax, etc. are also as indicated on the figures in this chapter.
- The owner desires to obtain a minimum of 15% net profit margin for this work.

Scenario 3 A residential lawn maintenance contractor in the mid-Atlantic states does work in middle- to upper-middle-class neighborhoods. He'd like to know his costs and break-even point for applying a fertilizer on his clients' lawns. The average lawn is from 5,000 to 10,000 square feet. This contractor believes his one-man crew can average 100,000 square feet of lawns per day. He'd like to know the following:

A. What should his minimum charge be for a lawn up to 5,000 square feet?

B. How and what should he charge for lawns over 5,000 square feet?

Additional Scenario Information

- The technician will work and get paid for 10 hours per day, 50 hours per week.
- The equipment cost per hour is indicated on the figures in this chapter.
- The overtime factor, risk factor, sales tax, etc. are also as indicated on the figures in this chapter.
- The owner desires to obtain a minimum of 25% net profit margin for this work.

PRICING LAWN FERTILIZATION

Large Residential Estate Lawn Fertilization with a Two-Man Crew

Figure 27-1 on page 205 outlines this scenario. Note that each member of the crew works eight hours on site per day. Two hours per day are allotted to general condition drive time, load time, etc. An extra two labor hours, one crew truck hour, and one utility cart hour are included for call-backs. The cart, which costs $10 per hour, is running approximately six hours per day.

To achieve the desired 25% net profit margin, this two-man crew has to bill over $1,700 per day. This will cover all costs, both direct and indirect. The price per 1,000 square feet is $5.46 and the price per 10,000 square feet is $54.55. The per acre price calculates out to be $237.63.

The prices calculated with a 25% net profit margin are a little light. This contractor thinks he can charge up to a 45% NPM and still get plenty of work.

Large Commercial Lawn Fertilization with a Two-Man Crew

Figure 27-2 on page 206 outlines our commercial scenario. The crew works eight hours on site per day. Two hours per day are allotted to general condition drive time, load time, etc. An extra four labor hours, two crew truck hours, and two utility cart

Scenario cost data	**$ or %**	**Remarks**
Crew size (# people)	2.0	Crew leader with a laborer
Crew average wage (CAW)	$ 14.00	
Overtime factor (OTF)	10.0%	50 hours per week
Risk factor (RF)	10.0%	
Crew average wage w/OTF & RF	$ 16.80	
Labor burden	30.0%	
Sales tax	6.0%	
G&A overhead per hour (OPH)	$ 12.00	
Net profit margin	25.0%	
One ton truck	$ 8.00	
Curb-time man-hours per day	16.0	
Number of units	326,700	Square feet per day or
Number of units	7.5	Acres per day

Scenario	**Materials**	**Labor**		**Equipment**	**CPH**	**Hours**	**Item**
I. Production (on-site or curb-time costs)							
$ 13 per 50# bag	$ 424.71	16.0	Man-hours	$ 60.00	$ 10.00	6.0	Utility cart with spreader
5.0 Lbs / 1000 SF	$ -			$ -	$ -	0.0	
	$ -	$ 16.80		$ -	$ -	0.0	
	$ 424.71	$ 268.80		$ 60.00			
II. General conditions (off-site or non-curb-time costs)							
		4.0	Man-hours	$ 64.00	$ 8.00	8.0	Crew truck
		2.0	Call backs	$ 8.00	$ 8.00	1.0	Crew truck for call backs
	$ -	$ 16.80		$ 10.00	$ 8.00	1.0	Utility cart for call backs
	$ -	$ 100.80		$ 82.00			
Subtotals	**$ 425**	**$ 370**		**$ 142**			
III. Margins & markups							
A. Sales tax	$ 25						
B. Labor burden		$ 111					
Subtotals	**$ 450**	**$ 480**		**$ 142**			

Total direct costs (TDC)			**$ 1,073**	TDC
C. G&A overhead costs				
22 (Number of man-hours x OPH)	$ 12.00	=	$ 264	
BEP (TDC + G&A overhead)			**$ 1,337**	**BEP**
D. Contingency factor (if desired)			$ -	
E. Net profit margin 25.00%			$ 446	
F. Total price			**$ 1,782**	**Total price**

IV. Scenario analysis

A. Unit price per square foot (Total price ÷ square feet):

				Unit Price	Unit BEP
$ 1,782 divided by 326,700 =	**$ 0.0055**	Per 1,000 SF is		$ 5.46	$ 4.09
		Per 10,000 SF is		$ 54.55	$ 40.91
		Per acre is		$ 237.63	$ 178.22

B. Daily revenue goal (Total price ÷ 1 day)

$ 1,782 divided by 1.0 = **$ 1,782** **SPH or RPH**

C. Gross profit margin ((G&A overhead + Net profit) ÷ Total price)

$ 710 ÷ $ 1,782 = **39.8%** **GPM**

FIGURE 27-1 Lawn Fertilization for Residential Applications

Scenario cost data	**$ or %**	**Remarks**
Crew size (# people)	2.0	Crew leader with a laborer
Crew average wage (CAW)	$ 14.00	
Overtime factor (OTF)	10.0%	50 hours per week
Risk factor (RF)	10.0%	
Crew average wage w/OTF & RF	$ 16.80	
Labor burden	30.0%	
Sales tax	6.0%	
G&A overhead per hour (OPH)	$ 12.00	
Net profit margin	15.0%	
One ton truck	$ 8.00	
Curb-time man-hours per day	21.0	
Number of units	1,742,400	Square feet
Number of units	40.0	Acres

Scenario		**Materials**	**Labor**		**Equipment**	**CPH**	**Hours**	**Item**
I. Production (on-site or curb-time costs)								
$ 13	per 50# bag	$ 1,359.07	21.0	Man-hours	$ 90.00	$ 10.00	9.0	Utility cart with spreader
3.0	Lbs / 1000 SF	$ -			$ -	$ -	0.0	
		$ -	$ 16.80		$ -	$ -	0.0	
		$ 1,359.07	$ 352.80		$ 90.00			
II. General conditions (off-site or non-curb-time costs)								
			8.0	Man-hours	$ 96.00	$ 8.00	12.0	Crew truck
			4.0	Call backs	$ 16.00	$ 8.00	2.0	Crew truck for call backs
		$ -	$ 16.80		$ 20.00	$ 10.00	2.0	Utility cart for call backs
		$ -	$ 201.60		$ 132.00			
Subtotals		**$ 1,359**	**$ 554**		**$ 222**			
III. Margins & markups								
A. Sales tax		$ 82						
B. Labor burden			$ 166					
Subtotals		**$ 1,441**	**$ 721**		**$ 222**			
Total direct costs (TDC)							**$ 2,383**	**TDC**
C. G&A overhead costs								
33.0 (Number of man-hours x OPH)					$ 12.00	=	$ 396	
BEP (TDC + G&A overhead)							**$ 2,779**	**BEP**
D. Contingency factor (if desired)							$ -	
E. Net profit margin 15.00%							$ 490	
F. Total price							**$ 3,270**	**Total price**

IV. Scenario analysis

A. Unit price per square foot (Total price ÷ square feet):

					Unit Price	**Unit BEP**
$ 3,270	divided by	1,742,400 =	**$ 0.0019**	Per 1,000 SF is	$ 1.88	$ 1.60
				Per 10,000 SF is	$ 18.77	$ 15.95
				Per acre is	$ 81.75	$ 69.48

B. Sales or revenue per hour (Total price ÷ all hours)

$ 3,270 divided by 33.0 = **$ 99.09** **SPH or RPH**

C. Gross profit margin ((G&A overhead + Net profit) ÷ Total price)

$ 886 ÷ $ 3,270 = **27.1%** **GPM**

FIGURE 27-2 Lawn Fertilization for Large Commercial Applications

hours are included for call-backs. The cart, which costs $10 per hour, is running approximately six hours per day.

To achieve the desired 15% net profit margin, the crew has to bill almost $82 per acre. This will cover all costs, both direct and indirect. The break-even point per acre calculates out to be just over $69.

Small to Mid-Sized Residential Lawn Fertilization with a One-Man Crew

Figure 27-3 on page 208 outlines this scenario. Note that the technician works seven hours on site per day. Three hours per day are allotted to general condition drive time, load time, etc. An extra labor hour, crew truck hour, and spreader hour are included for call-backs. The spreader, which costs $3 per hour, is used approximately six hours per day.

To achieve the desired 25% net profit margin, the technician has to bill $850 per day. This will cover all costs, both direct and indirect. The price per 5,000 square feet works out to be just over $42. However, after considering the small size of the job and market conditions, the contractor decides to charge $55 for a 5,000 square foot job and $8.50 per additional 1,000 square feet up to 10,000 square feet. Lawns with at least 10,000 square feet of turf are charged a minimum of $85 and $7.50 per additional 1,000 square feet over 10,000.

SUMMARY

They were aware that this type of work was very profitable, but they now know exactly what their costs and break-even points are.

These contractors now have the basic information they need to price lawn fertilization work. They were aware that this type of work was very profitable, but they now know exactly what their costs and break-even points are. They can adjust their margins and prices according to market expectations.

ACTION POINT

Evaluate your lawn fertilization work and determine break-even points, gross profit margins, and daily revenue goals.

➤ **NOTE** The costs used in our scenarios are for illustration purposes only. Your costs will vary from the ones used in these examples. The key is for you to build a typical one-day scenario for the crew, materials, and equipment mixes you use. Round up these rates as appropriate. If your costing structure is accurate, the rates you calculate should be very close to your current ones and to those generally seen in your market.

Scenario cost data	$ or %	Remarks
Crew size (# people)	1.0	Crew leader with a laborer
Crew average wage (CAW)	$ 16.00	
Overtime factor (OTF)	10.0%	50 hours per week
Risk factor (RF)	10.0%	
Crew average wage w/OTF & RF	$ 19.20	
Labor burden	30.0%	
Sales tax	6.0%	
G&A overhead per hour (OPH)	$ 12.00	
Net profit margin	25.0%	
One ton truck	$ 8.00	
Curb-time man-hours per day	7.0	
Number of units	100,000	Square feet per day
Number of units	2.3	Acres per day

Scenario		Materials	Labor		Equipment	CPH	Hours	Item
I. Production (on-site or curb-time costs)								
$ 13	per 50# bag	$ 130.00	7.0	Man-hours	$ 18.00	$ 3.00	6.0	Spreader
5.0	Lbs / 1000 SF	$ -			$ -	$ -	0.0	
		$ -	$ 19.20		$ -	$ -	0.0	
		$ 130.00	$ 134.40		$ 18.00			
II. General conditions (off-site or non-curb-time costs)								
			3.0	Man-hours	$ 64.00	$ 8.00	8.0	Crew truck
			1.0	Call backs	$ 8.00	$ 8.00	1.0	Crew truck for call backs
		$ -	$ 19.20		$ 3.00	$ 3.00	1.0	Spreader
		$ -	$ 76.80		$ 75.00			
Subtotals		**$ 130**	**$ 211**		**$ 93**			

III. Margins & markups	Materials	Labor	Equipment		Amount	Remarks
A. Sales tax	$ 8					
B. Labor burden		$ 63				
Subtotals	**$ 138**	**$ 275**	**$ 93**			
Total direct costs (TDC)					**$ 505**	TDC
C. G&A overhead costs						
11 (Number of man-hours x OPH)			$ 12.00	=	$ 132	
BEP (TDC + G&A overhead)					**$ 637**	BEP
D. Contingency factor (if desired)					$ -	
E. Net profit margin 25.00%					$ 212	
F. Total price					**$ 850**	**Total price**

IV. Scenario analysis

A. Unit price per square foot (Total price ÷ square feet):

$ 850 divided by 100,000 = **$ 0.0085**

	Unit Price	Unit BEP
Per 1,000 SF is	$ 8.50	$ 6.37
Per 5,000 SF is	$ 42.49	$ 31.87
Per 10,000 SF is	$ 84.98	$ 63.74

B. Sales or revenue per man-hour (Total price ÷ total man-hours)

$ 850 divided by 11.0 = **$ 77.26** **SPH or RPH**

C. Gross profit margin ((G&A overhead + Net profit) ÷ Total price)

$ 344 ÷ $ 850 = **40.5%** **GPM**

FIGURE 27-3 Lawn Fertilization for Small Residential Applications

CHAPTER

28

Outdoor Lighting

TERM

Bidding Template

Purpose

To explain the process of pricing lighting work

Introduction

Outdoor lighting is becoming more and more popular for security as well as for decorative purposes. Many contractors are taking advantage of this growing market. However, you have to ensure that you follow local licensing laws and employ competent people. Knowing your costs and setting specific revenue goals can add to the bottom line.

How It Works

A contractor in the Southeast wanted to increase his outdoor lighting sales. To do so, he wanted a **bidding template** that would speed up the estimating process. He also wanted the capability to adjust labor hours and costs, material costs, material upgrade costs, and the equipment used on the job. Here's a template similar to what we came up with for this contractor.

Additional Scenario Information

- Crew members will work and get paid for 10 hours per day, 50 hours per week.
- The equipment use and cost per hour are indicated on the figures in this chapter.
- The overtime factor, risk factor, sales tax, etc. are also as indicated on the figures in this chapter.
- The owner desires to obtain a minimum of 20% net profit margin for this work.

OUTDOOR LIGHTING

A Typical Lighting Job (as if one exists)

Figure 28-1 on page 210 lists the materials used in this scenario. Figure 28-2 on page 211 outlines the overview of this scenario including the labor hours and equipment.

Each member of the crew works nine hours on the site per day, except the supervisor, who is on the site for one hour per day. One hour per day per crew member is allotted to general condition drive time, load time, etc. Four hours of warranty labor is included in the general condition costs, as well as two hours to adjust the lights at night once the job is completed. For simplicity sake, I included both production and general condition costs on the same worksheet.

To achieve the desired 20% net profit margin, which translates into a 32+% gross profit margin, this contractor has to charge almost $2,700 for the installation of this standard 10-light system. This will cover all costs, both direct and indirect. The contractor thinks this price is a little low and that he could sell this system with close to a 40% GPM by increasing the net profit margin to 29.5%. Figure 28-3 on page 212 shows this same scenario with a 40% gross profit margin.

Project:	**Outdoor lights**	**Date:**	**12/20/20___**
Location:		**Estimator:**	**Ben Hadd**
P.O.C./G.C.:		**Crew Size:**	**2**
Phone / Fax:		**Hours/Day:**	**10**
Due Date:		**CAW:**	**$ 15.00**
Type Work:		**Risk Factor**	**10%**
		OT Factor	**10%**

CAW Loaded	**$ 18.00**

Phase 1	**Quantity**	**Unit**
Total Labor Hrs	**27**	**Hrs L**

# Description		**Column Calculations** Quantity	**Unit**	**Unit Cost**	#VALUE! **Material**	#VALUE! **Labor**	#VALUE! **Equip**	#VALUE! **Subs**
TOTALS					**1,000**	**488**	**120**	**-**
Lights	Light kits	10.0	EA	85.00	850			
	Wire	500.0	LF	0.15	75			
	Wire nuts	100.0	EA	0.50	50			
	Misc. hardware	1.0	LS	25.00	25			
					-			
					-			
Labor	2 men, 20 man-hours per day	20.0	Hrs L	18.00		360		
	Adjust lights at night (1 person)	2.0	Hrs L	18.00		36		
	Call back /warranty time (1 person)	4.0	Hrs L	18.00		72		
	Supervisor	1.0	Hrs L	20.00		20		
		-					-	
Equipment	Crew truck	8.0	HR	8.00			64	
	Adjust lights at night	2.0	HR	8.00			16	
	Call back /warranty time	4.0	HR	8.00			32	
	Supervisor	1.0	HR	8.00			8	

FIGURE 28-1 Outdoor Lighting Job Materials List

SUMMARY

Installing outdoor lighting can be very profitable, if you know your costs and set reasonable production goals.

Installing outdoor lighting can be a very profitable part of your business if you know your costs and set reasonable production goals for your crews. Bidding lighting installations can be simplified by using a spreadsheet program that allows you to take into account all your costs and the variables that go into the various lights and accessories available on the market today.

Scenario cost data	$ or %	Remarks
Crew size (# people)	2.0	
Crew average wage (CAW)	$ 15.00	
Man-hours per man per day	10.0	
Overtime factor (OTF)	10.0%	50 hours per week
Risk factor (RF)	10.0%	
Crew average wage w/OTF & RF	$ 18.00	
Labor burden	30.0%	
Sales tax	6.0%	
G&A overhead per hour (OPH)	$ 12.00	
Net profit margin	20.0%	
One ton crew truck	$ 8.00	
Curb-time man-hours	NA	
Number of units	10	Each

Scenario	Materials	Labor	Equipment	Subcontractors	Subtotals
I. Production (on-site or curb-time costs)					
	$ 1,000.00	$ 488.00	$ 120.00	$ -	
	$ 1,000.00	$ 488.00	$ 120.00	$ -	**$ 1,608**
II. General conditions (off-site or non-curb-time costs)					
	$ -	$ -	$ -	$ -	
	$ -	$ -	$ -	$ -	**$ -**
Subtotals	**$ 1,000**	**$ 488**	**$ 120**	**$ -**	**$ 1,608**
III. Margins & markups					
A. Sales tax	$ 60				
B. Labor burden		$ 146			
Subtotals	**$ 1,060**	**$ 634**	**$ 120**	**$ -**	
Total direct costs (TDC)				**$ 1,814**	**TDC**
C. G&A overhead costs					
27.0 (Number of man-hours x OPH)			$ 12.00 =	$ 324	
BEP (TDC + G&A overhead)				**$ 2,138**	**BEP**
D. Contingency factor (if desired)				$ -	
E. Net profit margin					
20.00%				$ 535	
F. Total price				**$ 2,673**	**Total price**

IV. Scenario analysis

A. Unit price (Total price ÷ units)

$ 2,673 divided by	10.0 =	**$ 267.30**	**Unit price**

B. Sales or revenue per hour (Total price ÷ all hours)

$ 2,673 divided by	27.0 =	**$ 99.00**	**SPH or RPH**

C. Gross profit margin ((G&A overhead + Net profit) ÷ Total price)

$ 859 ÷	$ 2,673 =	**32.1%**	**GPM**

FIGURE 28-2 Outdoor Lighting Job Recap

Scenario cost data	$ or %	Remarks
Crew size (# people)	2.0	
Crew average wage (CAW)	$ 15.00	
Man-hours per man per day	10.0	
Overtime factor (OTF)	10.0%	50 hours per week
Risk factor (RF)	10.0%	
Crew average wage w/OTF & RF	$ 18.00	
Labor burden	30.0%	
Sales tax	6.0%	
G&A overhead per hour (OPH)	$ 12.00	
Net profit margin	29.5%	
One ton crew truck	$ 8.00	
Curb time man-hours	NA	
Number of units	10	Each

Scenario	Materials	Labor	Equipment	Subcontractors	Subtotals
I. Production (on-site or curb-time costs)					
	$ 1,000.00	$ 488.00	$ 120.00	$ -	
	$ 1,000.00	$ 488.00	$ 120.00	$ -	**$ 1,608**
II. General conditions (off-site or non-curb-time costs)					
	$ -	$ -	$ -	$ -	
	$ -	$ -	$ -	$ -	**$ -**
Subtotals	**$ 1,000**	**$ 488**	**$ 120**	**$ -**	**$ 1,608**
III. Margins & markups					
A.Sales tax	$ 60				
B.Labor burden		$ 146			
Subtotals	**$ 1,060**	**$ 634**	**$ 120**	**$ -**	
Total direct costs (TDC)				**$ 1,814**	**TDC**
C. G&A overhead costs					
27.0 (Number of man-hours x OPH)			$ 12.00 =	$ 324	
BEP (TDC + G&A overhead)				**$ 2,138**	**BEP**
D. Contingency factor (if desired)				$ -	
E. Net profit margin 29.50%				$ 895	
F. Total price				**$ 3,033**	**Total price**

IV. Scenario analysis

A. Unit price (Total price ÷ units)

$ 3,033 divided by	10.0 =	**$ 303.32**	**Unit price**

B. Sales or revenue per hour (Total price ÷ all hours)

$ 3,033 divided by	27.0 =	**$ 112.34**	**SPH or RPH**

C. Gross profit margin ((G&A overhead + Net profit) ÷ Total price)

$ 1,219 ÷	$ 3,033 =	**40.2%**	**GPM**

FIGURE 28-3 Outdoor Lighting Job Recap with 40% GPM

ACTION POINT

Use the template in our example, or one similar to it, to calculate your outdoor lighting jobs. You can easily adjust material costs or upgrades, labor rates, and the equipment used on the job.

➤ **NOTE** The costs used in our scenarios are for illustration purposes only. Your costs will vary from the ones used in these examples. The key is for you to build a typical one-day scenario for the crew, materials, and equipment mixes you use. Round up these rates as appropriate. If your costing structure is accurate, the rates you calculate should be very close to your current ones and to those generally seen in your market.

CHAPTER

29 Outdoor Ponds

Purpose

To explain and illustrate the process for pricing outdoor pond work

Outdoor ponds are popping up everywhere. New technology, marketing, and manufacturing techniques have made them attractive, affordable, and easy to maintain.

Introduction

Outdoor ponds are popping up everywhere. New technology, marketing, and manufacturing techniques have made them attractive, affordable, and easy to maintain. Like outdoor lighting, many contractors are taking advantage of this growing market. You can too if you know your costs and set specific revenue goals for your crews. The smart contractors are making sure that their personnel are well trained in the most current production methods before jumping in (the pond).

How It Works

A contractor in the Northwest wanted to increase his outdoor pond sales. To do so, he wanted a bidding template similar to the one that we used for outdoor lighting, which would speed up the estimating process and allow him to quickly change costing information, if necessary.

Additional Scenario Information

- Crews comprised of three people will work and get paid for 10 hours per day, 50 hours per week.
- The equipment use and cost per hour are indicated on the figures in this chapter.
- The overtime factor, risk factor, sales tax, etc. are as indicated on the figures in this chapter.
- The owner desires to obtain a minimum of 20% net profit margin for this work.

Project:	Outdoor Pond	Date:	07/15/20__					
Location:		Estimator:	I.M. Dunn		CAW Loaded	$ 16.80		
P.O.C./G.C.:		Crew Size:	3					
Phone / Fax:		Hours/Day:	10					
Due Date:		CAW:	$ 14.00		Phase 1	Quantity	Unit	
Type Work:		Risk Factor	10%		Total Labor Hrs	66	Hrs L	
		OT Factor	10%					
		Column Calcualtions			#VALUE!	#VALUE!	#VALUE!	#VALUE!
# Description		Quantity	Unit	Unit Cost	Material	Labor	Equip	Subs
TOTALS					1,931	1,115	436	-
Pond kit	11' x 16' kit, standard	1.0	LS	1,500.00	1,500			
	Pump, upgrade (4PU)	-	EA	450.00	-			
	Liner, stream 25' x 6'	150.0	SF	0.75	113			
	Sand	1.0	Ton	23.00	23			
	Top soil	3.0	CY	15.00	45			
	2" PVC flex pipe	25.0	LF	2.50	63			
	Seam tape	6.0	LF	2.00	12			
	Water fall foam	2.0	CAN	32.48	65			
	Pump & basket kit	1.0	EA	75.00	75			
	Water fill valve	1.0	EA	35.71	36			
						-		
						-		
							-	
							-	
							-	
							-	
							-	
Labor	3 men, 30 man-hours per day	60.0	Hrs L	16.80		1,008.00		
	Waranty hours	4.0	Hrs L	16.80		67.20		
	Supervisor	2.0	Hrs L	20.00		40.00		
Equipment	BC-773	12.0	HR	20.00			240.00	
	Crew truck (Chevy 3500, 8 hr/day)	16.0	HR	10.00			160.00	
	Supervisor's truck	2.0	HR	8.00			16.00	
	Waranty truck hours	2.0	HR	10.00			20.00	

FIGURE 29-1 Outdoor Pond Materials List

OUTDOOR PONDS

A Standard 11′ × 16′ Pond

Figure 29-1 lists the materials used in this scenario. Figure 29-2 on page 216 outlines the overview of this scenario with the labor hours and equipment. I've combined production and general condition costs onto one worksheet. Each member of the crew works nine hours on the site per day, except the supervisor, who is on the site for one hour per day. One hour per day per crew member is allotted to general condition drive time, load time, etc. Four hours of warranty labor is included in the general condition costs.

To achieve the desired 20% net profit margin, which translates into over a 33% gross profit margin, this contractor has to charge almost $6,000 for this standard 11′ × 16′ pond kit installed. This will cover all costs, both direct and indirect. This price appears a little low to the contractor who thinks that he could get a 40% GPM for this pond. To do so, he increases the net profit margin to 28%. Figure 29-3 on page 217 shows this same scenario with a 40% gross profit margin.

Scenario cost data	$ or %	Remarks
Crew size (# people)	3.0	Crew leader and two laborers
Crew average wage (CAW)	$ 14.00	
Man-hours per man per day	10.0	
Overtime factor (OTF)	10.0%	50 hours per week
Risk factor (RF)	10.0%	
Crew average wage w/OTF & RF	$ 16.80	
Labor burden	30.0%	
Sales tax	6.0%	
G&A overhead per hour (OPH)	$ 12.00	
Net profit margin	20.0%	
One ton crew truck	$ 10.00	
Curb-time man-hours	N/A	
Number of units	1	Each

Scenario	Materials	Labor	Equipment	Subcontractors	Subtotals
I. Production (on-site or curb-time costs)					
	$ 1,930.67	$ 1,115.20	$ 436.00	$ -	
	$ 1,930.67	$ 1,115.20	$ 436.00	$ -	$ 3,482
II. General conditions (off-site or non-curb-time costs)					
	$ -	$ -	$ -	$ -	
	$ -	$ -	$ -	$ -	$ -
Subtotals	$ 1,931	$ 1,115	$ 436	$ -	$ 3,482
III. Margins & markups					
A. Sales tax	$ 116				
B. Labor burden		$ 335			
Subtotals	$ 2,047	$ 1,450	$ 436	$ -	
Total direct costs (TDC)				$ 3,932	TDC
C. G&A overhead costs					
66.0 (Number of man-hours x OPH)			$ 12.00 =	$ 792	
BEP (TDC + G&A overhead)				$ 4,724	BEP
D. Contingency factor (if desired)				$ -	
E. Net profit margin 20.00%				$ 1,181	
F. Total price				$ 5,905	Total price

IV. Scenario analysis

A. Unit price (Total price ÷ units)

$ 5,905 divided by 1.0 = **$ 5,905.34** **Unit price**

B. Sales or revenue per hour (Total price ÷ all hours)

$ 5,905 divided by 66.0 = **$ 89.47** **SPH or RPH**

C. Gross profit margin ((G&A overhead + Net profit) ÷ Total price)

$ 1,973 ÷ $ 5,905 = **33.4%** **GPM**

FIGURE 29-2 Oudoor Pond Recap

Scenario cost data	**$ or %**	**Remarks**
Crew size (# people)	3.0	Crew leader and two laborers
Crew average wage (CAW)	$ 14.00	
Man-hours per man per day	10.0	
Overtime factor (OTF)	10.0%	50 hours per week
Risk factor (RF)	10.0%	
Crew average wage w/OTF & RF	$ 16.80	
Labor burden	30.0%	
Sales tax	6.0%	
G&A overhead per hour (OPH)	$ 12.00	
Net profit margin	28.0%	
One ton crew truck	$ 10.00	
Curb-time man-hours	N/A	
Number of units	1	Each

Scenario	**Materials**	**Labor**	**Equipment**	**Subcontractors**	**Subtotals**
I. Production (on-site or curb-time costs)					
	$ 1,930.67	$ 1,115.20	$ 436.00	$ -	
	$ 1,930.67	$ 1,115.20	$ 436.00	$ -	$ 3,482
II. General conditions (off-site or non-curb-time costs)					
	$ -	$ -	$ -	$ -	
	$ -	$ -	$ -	$ -	$ -
Subtotals	**$ 1,931**	**$ 1,115**	**$ 436**	**$ -**	**$ 3,482**
III. Margins & markups					
A.Sales tax	$ 116				
B.Labor burden		$ 335			
Subtotals	**$ 2,047**	**$ 1,450**	**$ 436**	**$ -**	
Total direct costs (TDC)				**$ 3,932**	**TDC**
C. G&A overhead costs					
66.0 (Number of man-hours x OPH)			$ 12.00 =	$ 792	
BEP (TDC + G&A overhead)				**$ 4,724**	**BEP**
D. Contingency factor (if desired)				$ -	
E. Net profit margin 28.00%				$ 1,837	
F. Total price				**$ 6,561**	**Total price**

IV. Scenario analysis

A. Unit price (Total price ÷ units)				
$ 6,561 divided by	1.0 =		**$ 6,561.49**	**Unit price**
B. Sales or revenue per hour (Total price ÷ all hours)				
$ 6,561 divided by	66.0 =		**$ 99.42**	**SPH or RPH**
C. Gross profit margin ((G&A overhead + Net profit) ÷ Total price)				
$ 2,629	÷	$ 6,561 =	**40.1%**	**GPM**

FIGURE 29-3 Outdoor Pond Recap with 40% GPM

SUMMARY

Installing outdoor ponds can be a very profitable part of your business if you know your costs and set reasonable production goals for your crews. Bidding pond installations can be simplified by using a spreadsheet program that allows you to take into account all your costs and the variables that go into the diverse number of pond kits and accessories on the market today.

ACTION POINT

Use the template in our example, or one similar to it, to calculate your outdoor pond projects. You can easily adjust material costs or upgrades, labor rates, and the equipment used on the job.

➤ **NOTE**

The costs used in our scenarios are for illustration purposes only. Your costs will vary from the ones used in these examples. The key is for you to build a typical one-day scenario for the crew, materials, and equipment mixes you use. Round up these rates as appropriate. If your costing structure is accurate, the rates you calculate should be very close to your current ones and to those generally seen in your market.

CHAPTER 30

Pricing Pavers

Purpose

To explain the process of pricing pavers

Introduction

Paver or brick installations for patios, walkways, and driveways can supplement the existing palate of services and products offered by any contractor. Crew productivity is critical to the success and profitability of such a product line.

How It Works

A contractor in New England installed pavers in both the residential and commercial markets. However, as competition intensified, a price war of sorts broke out. Competitors were selling paver installation jobs at what appeared to be ridiculously low prices. My client wanted to maintain his market share and grow. Therefore, he needed to know how low he could go with his unit prices and not hurt himself.

The solution was to identify both his square foot price and break-even point on a job by job basis. Armed with that information, he could lower his prices and compete effectively. However, if the competition priced a job too low, he also had the information that would tell him to walk away from the job.

JOE'S "DESIGNER" PATIOS

I met Joe while flying from Denver to Los Angeles. I was on my way to Palm Springs to see my client and good friend, Jay Tripathi of Gardenworks, Inc., installed as president of the California Landscape Contractors Association.

Joe was a retired corporate accountant and an admitted anal-retentive perfectionist. He was on his way to Katmandu, Nepal, to climb mountains for five weeks. After retiring, he had the opportunity to install a brick patio for himself. He did a great job and soon was doing patios for his neighbors. Shortly after that, he was no longer retired: he was installing custom residential "designer" patios all over the south side of Denver.

Joe was on his way to Katmandu, Nepal, to climb mountains for five weeks.

Joe is very good at what he does. He's the highest priced brick paver installer in Denver, and worth every penny. He knows he's good and worth his price. He does everything by hand, and his patios are simply the best. Joe won't tolerate prospects who don't appreciate him or his quality of workmanship, and it's not uncommon for him to encourage prospects to call someone else if they don't seem to be the type of client with whom he wants to work.

I often wanted to sit down and pencil out Joe's pricing.

Additional Scenario Information

- Joe can complete a 300-square-foot patio by himself in one 40-hour week.
- The overtime factor, risk factor, sales tax, etc. are indicated on the figures in this chapter.
- I guessed at and selected a minimum of 25% net profit margin.
- I also guessed at Joe's wage rate and used $25 per hour.
- Re-wholesale prices for materials are as indicated on the figures in this chapter.

Rick's "Vanilla" Brick Road

Rick's crew installs pavers in the New England residential market. Their work is good but it does not match the high quality achieved by Joe. Occasionally, Rick's crew installs a commercial job. He wants to know the range for pricing pavers in his mid- to upper-middle-class residential market.

Additional Scenario Information

- Crews will work and get paid for 10 hours per day, 50 hours per week.
- Crews install roughly 10 square feet of pavers per man-hour during production time.
- The overtime factor, risk factor, sales tax, etc. are indicated on the figures in this chapter.
- The owner desires to obtain a minimum of 20% net profit margin.
- Re-wholesale prices for materials are as indicated on the figures in this chapter.

Scenario 1 for Joe's Patios

No wonder Joe takes the winters off and climbs mountains.

Putting Joe's wage rate at $25 per hour and adding a 25% net profit margin to his work still prices his brick pavers under the $20 per square foot he demands and gets. Using these figures, his paver square-foot price is still only $16.49 (see Figures 30-1 and 30-2 on pages 221 and 222). His gross profit calculates out to be 35%.

In order to match Joe's $20 per-square-foot price, we have to add an additional 12% net profit to his margin. This brings the unit price to $20 and the gross profit margin to over 45% (see Figure 30-3 on page 223). No wonder Joe takes the winters off and climbs mountains.

Scenario 2 for Rick's Three-Man Crew

Interestingly, Joe's production rate just about matches that for Rick's three-man crew. However, the crew gets the job done in just over one day.

Incorporating Rick's cost structure and a 20% net profit margin, his unit price for brick pavers calculates to be just over $14 (see Figure 30-4 on page 224 and Figure 30-5 on page 225). The gross profit for this scenario is just over 32%. Rick might be able to add another 5% net profit to some jobs. Others will require him to lower his net a bit. The unit price range for pavers installed in Rick's residential market will probably be from $12 to $15. He'll probably have to drop his unit price $2 to $4 per square foot to be competitive in the commercial market.

Project:	Joe's "Designer" Patio	Date:	8/14/20___
Location:		Estimator:	Joe
P.O.C./G.C.:		Crew Size:	1
Phone / Fax:		Hours/Day:	8
Due Date:		CAW:	$ 25.00
Type Work:		Risk Factor	10%
		OT Factor	0%

CAW Loaded	$	27.50

Phase 1	Quantity	Unit
Total Labor Hrs	42	Hrs L

# Description		Quantity	Unit	Unit Cost	Material	Labor	Equip	Subs
		Column Calcualtions			#VALUE!	#VALUE!	#VALUE!	#VALUE!
TOTALS					1,345	1,155	336	-
Materials	Brick pavers	750.0	EA	1.50	1,125			
	Sub base	5.0	CY	20.00	100			
	Sand	1.0	CY	20.00	20			
	Edgers	66.7	EA	1.50	100			
		-		-	-			
					-			
					-			
Labor	Joe	40.0	Hrs L	27.50		1,100		
	Call back time	2.0	Hrs L	27.50		55		
		-				-		
Equipment	3/4 ton pickup	40.0	HR	8.00			320	
		-					-	
	3/4 ton pickup (for call backs)	2.0	HR	8.00			16	
							-	

FIGURE 30-1 Joe's Patio Job Materials List

SUMMARY

Installing pavers can be very lucrative if you know your numbers and if your crew's productivity is up to par. Unit prices can vary significantly, even within the residential market. Prices normally drop drastically in the commercial market as there tends to be more competition. Jobs are often much larger in that market, and prices drop due to some economies of scale.

ACTION POINT

Use the template in our example or one of your own to calculate your paver unit prices. Incorporate your costs, both direct and indirect, and your crew's production rates. Vary the net profit margin until you achieve your current unit price. Calculate your gross profit margin to see if it exceeds 30%.

➤ NOTE The costs used in our scenarios are for illustration purposes only. Your costs will vary from the ones used in these examples. The key is for you to build a typical one-day scenario for the crew, materials, and equipment you use. Round up these rates as appropriate. If your costing structure is accurate, the rates you calculate should be very close to your current ones and to those generally seen in your market.

Scenario cost data	$ or %	Remarks
Crew size (# people)	1.0	Joe
Crew average wage (CAW)	$ 25.00	
Man-hours per man per day	8.0	
Overtime factor (OTF)	0.0%	40 hours per week
Risk factor (RF)	10.0%	
Crew average wage w/OTF & RF	$ 27.50	
Labor burden	30.0%	
Sales tax	6.0%	
G&A overhead per hour (OPH)	$ 12.00	
Net profit margin	25.0%	
One ton crew truck	$ 8.00	
Curb time man-hours	N/A	
Number of units	300	Square feet

Scenario	Materials	Labor	Equipment	Subcontractors	Subtotals
I. Production (on-site or curb-time costs)					
	$ 1,345.00	$ 1,155.00	$ 336.00	$ -	
	$ 1,345.00	$ 1,155.00	$ 336.00	$ -	$ 2,836
II. General conditions (off-site or non-curb-time costs)					
	$ -	$ -	$ -	$ -	
	$ -	$ -	$ -	$ -	$ -
Subtotals	**$ 1,345**	**$ 1,155**	**$ 336**	**$ -**	**$ 2,836**
III. Margins & markups					
A.Sales tax	$ 81				
B.Labor burden		$ 347			
Subtotals	**$ 1,426**	**$ 1,502**	**$ 336**	**$ -**	
Total direct costs (TDC)				**$ 3,263**	**TDC**
C. G&A overhead costs					
42.0 (Number of man-hours x OPH)			$ 12.00 =	$ 504	
BEP (TDC + G&A overhead)				**$ 3,767**	**BEP**
D. Contingency factor (if desired)				$ -	
E. Net profit margin 25.00%				$ 1,256	
F. Total price				**$ 5,023**	**Total price**

IV. Scenario analysis

A. Unit price (Total price ÷ units)

$ 5,023 divided by 300.0 = **$ 16.7431** **Unit price**

B. Sales or revenue per hour (Total price ÷ all hours)

$ 5,023 divided by 42.0 = **$ 119.59** **SPH or RPH**

C. Gross profit margin ((G&A overhead + Net profit) ÷ Total price)

$ 1,760 ÷ $ 5,023 = **35.0%** **GPM**

FIGURE 30-2 Joe's Patio Job

Scenario cost data	$ or %	Remarks
Crew size (# people)	1.0	Joe
Crew average wage (CAW)	$ 25.00	
Man-hours per man per day	8.0	
Overtime factor (OTF)	0.0%	40 hours per week
Risk factor (RF)	10.0%	
Crew average wage w/OTF & RF	$ 27.50	
Labor burden	30.0%	
Sales tax	6.0%	
G&A overhead per hour (OPH)	$ 12.00	
Net profit margin	37.2%	
One ton crew truck	$ 8.00	
Curb-time man-hours	N/A	
Number of units	300	Square feet

Scenario	Materials	Labor	Equipment	Subcontractors	Subtotals
I. Production (on-site or curb-time costs)					
	$ 1,345.00	$ 1,155.00	$ 336.00	$ -	
	$ 1,345.00	$ 1,155.00	$ 336.00	$ -	$ 2,836
II. General conditions (off-site or non-curb-time costs)					
	$ -	$ -	$ -	$ -	
	$ -	$ -	$ -	$ -	$ -
Subtotals	**$ 1,345**	**$ 1,155**	**$ 336**	**$ -**	**$ 2,836**
III. Margins & markups					
A. Sales tax	$ 81				
B. Labor burden		$ 347			
Subtotals	**$ 1,426**	**$ 1,502**	**$ 336**	**$ -**	
Total direct costs (TDC)				**$ 3,263**	**TDC**
C. G&A overhead costs					
42.0 (Number of man-hours x OPH)			$ 12.00 =	$ 504	
BEP (TDC + G&A overhead)				**$ 3,767**	**BEP**
D. Contingency factor (if desired)				$ -	
E. Net profit margin 37.21%				$ 2,232	
F. Total price				**$ 6,000**	**Total price**

IV. Scenario analysis

A. Unit price (Total price ÷ units)

$ 6,000 divided by	300.0 =	**$ 20.00**	**Unit price**

B. Sales or revenue per hour (Total price ÷ all hours)

$ 6,000 divided by	42.0 =	**$ 142.85**	**SPH or RPH**

C. Gross profit margin ((G&A overhead + Net profit) ÷ Total price)

$ 2,736 ÷	$ 6,000 =	**45.6%**	**GPM**

FIGURE 30-3 Joe's Patio Job Recap at $20 per Square Foot

Scenario cost data

	$ or %	Remarks
Crew size (# people)	3.0	Crew leader with two laborers
Crew average wage (CAW)	$ 13.00	
Man-hours per man per day	10.0	
Overtime factor (OTF)	10.0%	50 hours per week
Risk factor (RF)	10.0%	
Crew average wage w/OTF & RF	$ 15.60	
Labor burden	35.0%	
Sales tax	6.0%	
G&A overhead per hour (OPH)	$ 12.00	
Net profit margin	20.0%	
One ton crew truck	$ 8.00	
Curb-time man-hours	N/A	
Number of units	300	Square feet

Scenario	Materials	Labor	Equipment	Subcontractors	Subtotals
I. Production (on-site or curb-time costs)					
	$ 1,345.00	$ 686.40	$ 496.00	$ -	
	$ 1,345.00	$ 686.40	$ 496.00	$ -	$ 2,527
II. General conditions (off-site or non-curb-time costs)					
	$ -	$ -	$ -	$ -	
	$ -	$ -	$ -	$ -	$ -
Subtotals	$ 1,345	$ 686	$ 496	$ -	$ 2,527
III. Margins & markups					
A.Sales tax	$ 81				
B.Labor burden		$ 240			
Subtotals	$ 1,426	$ 927	$ 496	$ -	
Total direct costs (TDC)				$ 2,848	TDC
C. G&A overhead costs					
44.0 (Number of man-hours x OPH)			$ 12.00 =	$ 528	
BEP (TDC + G&A overhead)				$ 3,376	BEP
D. Contingency factor (if desired)				$ -	
E. Net profit margin 20.00%				$ 844	
F. Total price				$ 4,220	Total price

IV. Scenario analysis

A. Unit price (Total price ÷ units)

$ 4,220 divided by 300.0 = **$ 14.07** **Unit price**

B. Sales or revenue per hour (Total price ÷ all hours)

$ 4,220 divided by 44.0 = **$ 95.92** **SPH or RPH**

C. Gross profit margin ((G&A overhead + Net profit) ÷ Total price)

$ 1,372 ÷ $ 4,220 = **32.5%** **GPM**

FIGURE 30-4 Rick's Patio Job

Project:	**Rick's "Vanilla" Brick Road**	**Date:**	**8/14/20___**
Location:		**Estimator:**	**Rick**
P.O.C./G.C.:		**Crew Size:**	**3**
Phone / Fax:		**Hours/Day:**	**10**
Due Date:		**CAW:**	**$ 13.00**
Type Work:		**Risk Factor**	**10%**
		OT Factor	**10%**

CAW Loaded $ 15.60

Phase 1	**Quantity**	**Unit**
Total Labor Hrs	**44**	**Hrs L**

Column Calcualtions

# Description		Quantity	Unit	Unit Cost	Material	Labor	Equip	Subs
					#VALUE!	#VALUE!	#VALUE!	#VALUE!
TOTALS					**1,345**	**686**	**496**	**-**
Materials	Brick pavers	750.0	EA	1.50	1,125			
	Sub base	5.0	CY	20.00	100			
	Sand	1.0	CY	20.00	20			
	Edger bricks	66.7	EA	1.50	100			
		-		-	-			
					-			
					-			
Labor	3 men, 50 hours per week	40.0	Hrs L	15.60		624		
	Call back time	4.0	Hrs L	15.60		62		
		-				-		
Equipment	3/4 ton pickup	40.0	HR	8.00			320	
	Skid steer	8.0	HR	20.00			160	
	3/4 ton pickup (Call back time)	2.0	HR	8.00			16	
							-	
							-	

FIGURE 30-5 Rick's Patio Job Materials List

CHAPTER 31

Shrub Fertilization and Insect Control

TERM

Economies of Scale

Purpose

To explain the process for pricing shrub fertilization and insect and weed control

Contractors need to know their costs and their margins because they have to compete with some very large competitors who enjoy significant economies of scale due to their size.

Introduction

Specialty products and services are generally very profitable. Numerous contractors are reaping the benefits of providing shrub fertilization and insect and weed control applications for their clients. However, contractors need to know their costs and their margins because they have to compete with some very large competitors who enjoy significant **economies of scale** due to their size.

How It Works

A maintenance contractor in New England wanted to seize a market opportunity to provide shrub fertilization and insect control services to his existing client base as well as to new customers. One of his technicians would perform these services, which would supplement the work that he was already doing. The contractor wanted to calculate unit prices for shrub soil injections for insect control for two- to three-foot shrubs. He also wanted to calculate unit prices for granular fertilization for the same size shrubs. Consequently, he needed to determine a daily revenue goal for his technician for each service. I used the Quick Bid templates shown in the figures in this chapter and calculated prices for my client.

PRICING SHRUB FERTILIZATION AND INSECT CONTROL WORK

Shrub Insect Control

Additional Scenario Information

- A technician will work and get paid for 10 hours per day, 50 hours per week.
- One hour per day is included to cover any call-backs that may be necessary.
- The overtime factor, risk factor, sales tax, etc. are indicated on the figures in this chapter.

- The owner desires to obtain a minimum of 25% net profit margin for this work.
- The powdered insecticide comes in 2-ounce bottles costing $42 per bottle. One bottle will produce 64 ounces of product. A 2- to 3-foot shrub requires 3 ounces of product.
- The technician can inject approximately 150 shrubs per man-hour.

Figure 31-1 on page 228 outlines this scenario. Note that the technician is on site six hours a day. Four hours are devoted to prep and cleanup time, and travel.

To achieve the desired 25% net profit margin, the technician has to bill over $3,100 per day. This will cover all costs, both direct and indirect. The unit price per shrub calculates to be almost $3.50. However, look at the net profit per man-hour. It is over $70 per man-hour. Now look at the gross profit margin. It is *only* 28.5%.

Shrub Granular Fertilization

Additional Scenario Information

- The technician will work and get paid for 10 hours per day, 50 hours per week.
- One hour per day is included to cover any call-backs that may be necessary.
- The overtime factor, risk factor, sales tax, etc. are indicated on the figures in this chapter.
- The owner desires to obtain a minimum of 25% net profit margin for this work.
- The granular fertilizer comes in 50-pound bags. A 2- to 3-foot shrub requires approximately 1 pound of fertilizer.
- The technician can fertilize approximately 150 shrubs per man-hour.

Figure 31-2 on page 229 outlines this scenario. The technician works six hours on site per day. Four hours per day are allotted to general condition drive time, load time, cleanup time, etc.

To achieve the desired 25% net profit margin, the technician has to bill almost $950 per day. This will cover all costs, both direct and indirect. The unit price per shrub calculates to be a little over $1 at $1.06. The gross profit margin is over 36% but the net profit per man-hour is a little less than $22 per man-hour. This is not bad but it is not close to the net profit per man-hour realized on insect control, which is primarily due to the high cost of the materials being used.

SUMMARY

Shrub insect-control injections and fertilizations can be a profitable part of your business. Knowing and calculating your production rates accurately and establishing daily revenue targets can make this type of work easy to manage and very profitable.

ACTION POINT

Evaluate your shrub chemical applications and calculate your net profit margins, net profit per man-hour, and gross profit margins.

Scenario cost data	**$ or %**	**Remarks**
Crew size (# people)	1.0	Technician
Crew average wage (CAW)	$ 14.00	
Overtime factor (OTF)	10.0%	50 hours per week
Risk factor (RF)	10.0%	
Crew average wage w/OTF & RF	$ 16.80	
Labor burden	35.0%	
Sales tax	6.0%	
G&A overhead per hour (OPH)	$ 10.00	
Net profit margin	25.0%	
One ton truck	$ 8.00	
Curb-time man-hours per day	6.0	
Number of units	900.0	2-3 foot shrubs, 120 to 180 per man-hour 21 2-3 foot shrubs per 2 OZ bottle

Scenario	**Materials**	**Labor**		**Equipment**	**CPH**	**Hours**	**Item**
I. Production (on-site or curb-time costs)							
43 Preventative	$ 1,800.00	6.0	Man-hours	$ -	$ -	0.0	
insecticide	$ -			$ -	$ -	0.0	
2 OZ bottle,	$ -	$ 16.80		$ -	$ -	0.0	
$42 @	$ 1,800.00	$ 100.80		$ -			
II. General conditions (off-site or non-curb-time costs)							
		4.0	Man-hours	$ 64.00	$ 8.00	8.0	One ton truck
		1.0	Call backs	$ 8.00	$ 8.00	1.0	One ton truck (call backs)
	$ -	$ 16.80		$ -	$ -	0.0	
	$ -	$ 84.00		$ 72.00			
Subtotals	**$ 1,800**	**$ 185**		**$ 72**			
III. Margins & markups							
A.Sales tax	$ 108						
B.Labor burden		$ 65					
Subtotals	**$ 1,908**	**$ 249**		**$ 72**			

Total direct costs (TDC)		**$ 2,229**	**TDC**
C. G&A overhead costs 11.0 (Number of man-hours x OPH)	$ 10.00 =	$ 110	
BEP (TDC + G&A overhead)		**$ 2,339**	**BEP**
D. Contingency factor (if desired)		$ -	
E. Net profit margin 25.00%		$ 780	
F. Total price		**$ 3,119**	**Total price**

IV. Scenario analysis

A. Unit price (Total price ÷ total units)

$ 3,119 divided by 900.0 =	**$ 3.47**	**Unit price**

B. Net profit per hour (Net profit margin ÷ all hours)

$ 780 divided by 11.0 =	**$ 70.89**	**PPH**

C. Gross profit margin ((G&A overhead + Net profit) ÷ Total price)

$ 890 ÷ $ 3,119 =	**28.5%**	**GPM**

FIGURE 31-1 Shrub Insect Control

Scenario cost data

	$ or %	Remarks
Crew size (# people)	1.0	Technician
Crew average wage (CAW)	$ 14.00	
Overtime factor (OTF)	10.0%	50 hours per week
Risk factor (RF)	10.0%	
Crew average wage w/OTF & RF	$ 16.80	
Labor burden	35.0%	
Sales tax	6.0%	
G&A overhead per hour (OPH)	$ 10.00	
Net profit margin	25.0%	
One ton truck	$ 8.00	
Curb-time man-hours per day	6.0	
Number of units	900	2-3 foot shrubs, 120 to180 per man-hour 50 2 to 3 foot shrubs per 50# bag

Scenario		Materials	Labor		Equipment	CPH	Hours	Item
I. Production (on-site or curb-time costs)								
18.0	Granular	$ 270.00	6.0	Man-hours	$ -	$ -	0.0	Spray unit
bags	fertilizer	$ -			$ -	$ -	0.0	
	50# bag	$ -	$ 16.80		$ -	$ -	0.0	
	$15 @	$ 270.00	$ 100.80		$ -			
II. General conditions (off-site or non-curb-time costs)								
			4.0	Man-hours	$ 64.00	$ 8.00	8.0	One ton truck
			1.0	Call backs	$ 8.00	$ 8.00	1.0	One ton truck (call backs)
		$ -	$ 16.80		$ -	$ -	0.0	
		$ -	$ 84.00		$ 72.00			
Subtotals		**$ 270**	**$ 185**		**$ 72**			
III. Margins & markups								
A.Sales tax		$ 16						
B.Labor burden			$ 65					
Subtotals		**$ 286**	**$ 249**		**$ 72**			

Total direct costs (TDC)			**$ 608**	**TDC**
C. G&A overhead costs				
11.0 (Number of man-hours x OPH)	$ 10.00	=	$ 110	
BEP (TDC + G&A overhead)			**$ 718**	**BEP**
D. Contingency factor (if desired)			$ -	
E. Net profit margin				
25.00%			$ 239	
F. Total price			**$ 957**	**Total price**

IV. Scenario analysis

A. Unit price (Total price ÷ total units)

$ 957 divided by 900.0 = **$ 1.06** **Unit price**

B. Net profit per hour (Net profit margin ÷ all hours)

$ 239 divided by 11.0 = **$ 21.75** **PPH**

C. Gross profit margin ((G&A overhead + Net profit) ÷ Total price)

$ 349 ÷ $ 957 = **36.5%** **GPM**

FIGURE 31-2 Shrub Fertilization

➤ **NOTE** The costs used in our scenarios are for illustration purposes only. Your costs will vary from the ones used in these examples. The key is for you to build a typical one-day scenario for the crew, materials, and equipment you use. Round up these rates as appropriate. If your costing structure is accurate, the rates you calculate should be very close to your current ones and to those generally seen in your market. ■

CHAPTER

32

Snow Plowing, Salting, and Sanding

TERMS

Fixed/Variable Contract
Flex Contract
Per-Push Contract

The biggest snow job you may face is a diluted profit and loss (P&L) statement that gives you a false sense of security.

Purpose

To explain the process for pricing winter snow and sanding work

Introduction

Snow removal, sanding, and/or salting work (some parts of the country spread pure salt) can be some of your most profitable work as long as you don't depend on the weather. Too many contractors rely on Mother Nature, rather than a well-thought-out business plan and accurate pricing that minimizes risk while optimizing chances for increased profitability. Otherwise, the biggest snow job you may face is a diluted profit and loss (P&L) statement that gives you a false sense of security.

How It Works

John owns a full-service landscape company. He wants to reevaluate his pricing structure for his winter snow removal and sanding work. The market for winter work is competitive. The going rate for sanding is $100 per cubic yard and $75 per hour for snow plowing with a one-ton truck. However, John isn't sure the $75 per hour rate covers his crew's drive time and 30 minutes of prep time before and after each storm. John has five drivers who plow snow. Three of the drivers also spread sand.

John's crews will be paid an average of 10 hours per storm. Eight hours will be spent on site, plowing or sanding. The other two hours will include drive time from job to job and a minimal amount of prep time at the yard before and after each storm. The typical winter will have 10 storms and three drivers will spend approximately five hours sanding per storm.

The average driver will be paid $15 per hour and will put in approximately 100 hours sanding and/or plowing. Sand mixed with salt costs $25 per cubic yard. Sales tax is 6% on materials. A driver can spread roughly two cubic yards of sand mix per hour, including load time, using a one-ton truck. Labor burden (e.g., FICA, FUTA, SUTA, workers' compensation insurance, general liability insurance, etc.) is 25%. The overtime factor is zero.

The owner wants a risk factor of 20% included in the labor rate to offset any error in the average drive time estimated for the two scenarios and a minimum net profit of 20% on all winter work. G&A overhead costs for the year are $100,000. Billable field-labor hours during the regular season total 10,000. Dividing the G&A overhead amount by the billable hours produces an overhead per hour (OPH) cost of $10. Even though all G&A overhead for the year is theoretically covered during the regular season, John wants to add $10 OPH to each hour of winter work.

He also wants to calculate a minimum curb-time rate for snow plowing and a per-cubic-yard rate for sanding to take into account the above criteria and cover all costs. He wants to know if he can make any money at current market rates, and how much winter work contributes toward his G&A overhead costs.

To price his snow removal, sanding, and/or salting work, John prepares a bid scenario for a typical storm for both types of work. Once he completes these pricing scenarios, he can then address his questions.

PRICING SNOW REMOVAL WORK

John breaks the bidding process for snow removal work into three phases on a legal-size yellow pad. (We'll put this scenario into a spreadsheet as in Figure 32-1, with some slight differences in our numbers due to rounding.) The first phase contains the labor and equipment costs when the driver is on site plowing. The second phase contains the hookup and drive time for the truck and driver when both are not on site plowing. The total of these two numbers should equal the total of paid hours for a driver for the day. The third phase includes the margins and markups for the bid (e.g., labor burden, G&A overhead, net profit, and a contingency factor, if desired).

Phase 1. Providing the Service

John increases the driver's labor rate of $15 by the 20% risk factor to obtain a "loaded" rate of $18. He then multiplies the eight hours of Phase 1 plowing time by this figure and enters the product on his bid worksheet.

John knows his one-ton trucks cost him $7 per hour to operate. He doubles this amount to cover the extra wear and tear he thinks winter work will cause. John then calculates his plow cost per hour (CPH) by dividing the purchase and lifetime maintenance costs ($4,000 + 1,000 = $5,000) by the projected lifetime billable hours for a plow (8 seasons × 80 billable hours per season = 640 hours). He rounds the 640 to 650 lifetime billable hours and divides projected lifetime costs by the 650 hours ($5,000 ÷ 650 hours = $7.69), which he rounds up to an $8 CPH. John then adds the doubled truck CPH to the plow CPH and multiplies this total by the Phase 1 equipment hours (8 hours × $22 = $176). He enters the total on the bid worksheet.

Phase 2. General Conditions

John calculates general conditions just as he did Phase 1 costs, but with one important difference. He doesn't include the cost of the plow in the equipment calculations because it's not being used or incurring wear and tear during general condition time.

Phase 3. Margins and Markups

John multiplies his labor cost in Phases 1 and 2 by the 25% labor burden amount and enters it onto the bid worksheet. He multiplies the 10 labor hours in Phases 1 and 2 by the OPH of $10 to determine how much G&A overhead to add to the bid worksheet. He then totals all of these figures to determine the break-even point (BEP) for the scenario. Finally, John adds his desired 20% net profit margin to the BEP.

Scenario cost data	$ or %	Remarks
Crew size (# people)	1.0	Driver
Crew average wage (CAW)	$ 15.00	
Overtime factor (OTF)	0.0%	None
Risk factor (RF)	20.0%	
Crew average wage w/OTF & RF	$ 18.00	
Labor burden	25.0%	
Sales tax	6.0%	
G&A overhead per hour (OPH)	$ 10.00	
Net profit margin	20.0%	
One ton truck	$ 14.00	
Curb-time man-hours per day	8.0	
Number of units	1.0	Typical day of plowing

Scenario	Materials	Labor		Equipment	CPH	Hours	Item
I. Production (on-site or curb-time costs)							
	$ -	8.0	Man-hours	$ 176.00	$ 22.00	8.0	One ton truck with plow
	$ -			$ -	$ -	0.0	
	$ -	$ 18.00		$ -	$ -	0.0	
	$ -	$ 144.00		$ 176.00			
II. General conditions (off-site or non-curb-time costs)							
		2.0	Man-hours	$ 28.00	$ 14.00	2.0	One ton truck without plow
		0.0		$ -	$ -	0.0	
	$ -	$ 18.00		$ -	$ -	0.0	
	$ -	$ 36.00		$ 28.00			
Subtotals	**$ -**	**$ 180**		**$ 204**			
III. Margins & markups							
A. Sales tax	$ -						
B. Labor burden		$ 45					
Subtotals	**$ -**	**$ 225**		**$ 204**			

Total direct costs (TDC)		**$ 429**	**TDC**
C. G&A overhead costs			
10 (Number of man-hours x OPH)	$ 10.00 =	$ 100	
BEP (TDC + G&A overhead)		**$ 529**	**BEP**
D. Contingency factor (if desired)		$ -	
E. Net profit margin			
20.00%		$ 132	
F. Total price		**$ 661**	**Revenue goal per storm**

IV. Scenario analysis

A. Unit price (Total price ÷ # units)

$ 661 divided by 1 = **$ 661.25** **Revenue goal per storm**

B. Sales or revenue per hour (Total price ÷ total hours)

$ 661 divided by 10.0 = **$ 66.13** **SPH or RPH**

C. Gross profit margin ((G&A overhead + Net profit) ÷ Total price)

$ 232 ÷ $ 661 = **35.1%** **GPM**

FIGURE 32-1 Snow Plowing

Analysis

On average, John must bill $661 in a 10-hour period of snow removal in order to cover all costs and make a 20% net profit margin. G&A overhead recovery accounts for 15.1% of the total. By adding these two together, we arrive at our gross profit margin of 35.1%. To determine the hourly curb-time rate, John simply divides the desired total billable amount per day by the projected number of curb-time hours ($661 ÷ 8 curb-time hours = $82.63).

Dividing total direct costs of $429 per day by the 8 curb-time hours produces the direct costs per hour amount ($429 ÷ 8 curb-time hours = $53.63). The BEP per hour is calculated by dividing the BEP total of $529 by the 8 curb-time hours ($529 ÷ 8 = $66.13). In other words, for John to cover all his direct costs (labor, burden, equipment, sales tax), he must bill at least $53.63 per curb-time hour. Seen another way, any amount billed above this $53.63 amount goes toward gross profit.

Conclusion on Snow Removal Work

John can't match the market rate of $75 per curb hour while maintaining both a 20% net profit margin and two hours of non-billable general condition labor time per day. However, reducing general condition labor time to one hour (if possible) per day drops John's rate to $73.44 ($661 ÷ 9 on-site or curb-time hours) while maintaining his goal of a 20% net profit margin.

Reducing net profit to 10% produces a rate of $73.50 ($588 ÷ 8 = $73.50) without reducing general condition time. Reducing both net profit margin and general condition time to 10% and one hour, respectively, would allow John to drop his price to $65.33 ($588 ÷ 9 = $65.33) if market conditions dictated. Note that John will experience his best GPM if he can somehow schedule his crews to incur only one hour of general condition time per day.

John has one other option. He could possibly reduce his non-billable drive time to one hour if he could add 5 to 10 minutes of drive time to the bills for each of his customers, if he's billing on an hourly basis. Of course, customers should be aware of this practice prior to receiving their bills.

There are two important things for John to note from this exercise. The first is the impact non-billable time has on hourly curb-time rates. The second is that any billable amounts above direct costs contribute directly to the bottom line of the company at the end of the year. Therefore, it's important for John to focus on his direct costs per day and per billable hour. These two numbers will provide him with easily targeted minimum billable amounts, ensuring that he covers all of his direct costs, no matter what the scenario.

PRICING SANDING/SALTING WORK

John prices out his sanding work as outlined on Figure 32-2. The sander cost per hour is $13. With a 20% net profit margin on top of all his costs, John must bill a minimum of $621 per driver per storm. This translates into a unit price of a little over $77.58 per cubic yard, which is well within the market price of $100 per cubic yard.

A more accurate GPM for sanding work at the market rate of $100 per cubic yard is 44.1% ([$800 – $447 TDC] ÷ $800 = 44.1%). John could improve his GPM by increasing his production above his benchmark of two cubic yards per curb-time hour. Decreasing the general condition hours through better scheduling and/or more efficient loading of sand would also increase the overall GPM on sanding work.

Scenario cost data	**$ or %**	**Remarks**
Crew size (# people)	1.0	Driver
Crew average wage (CAW)	$ 15.00	
Overtime factor (OTF)	0.0%	None
Risk factor (RF)	20.0%	
Crew average wage w/OTF & RF	$ 18.00	
Labor burden	25.0%	
Sales tax	6.0%	
G&A overhead per hour (OPH)	$ 10.00	
Net profit margin	20.0%	
One ton truck	$ 14.00	
Curb-time man-hours per day	4.0	
Number of units	8.0	Cubic yards

Scenario		**Materials**	**Labor**		**Equipment**	**CPH**	**Hours**	**Item**	
I. Production (on-site or curb-time costs)									
8.0	Sand mix CY	$ 200.00		4.0 Man-hours	$ 108.00	$ 27.00	4.0	One ton truck with sander	
$ 25	per CY	$ -			$ -	$ -	0.0		
		$ -	$ 18.00		$ -	$ -	0.0		
		$ 200.00	$ 72.00		$ 108.00				
II. General conditions (off-site or non-curb-time costs)									
				1.0 Man-hours	$ 14.00	$ 14.00	1.0	One ton truck without sander	
				0.0	$ -	$ -	0.0		
		$ -	$ 18.00		$ -	$ -	0.0		
		$ -	$ 18.00		$ 14.00				
Subtotals		**$ 200**	**$ 90**		**$ 122**				
III. Margins & markups									
A. Sales tax		$ 12							
B. Labor burden			$ 23						
Subtotals		**$ 212**	**$ 113**		**$ 122**				
Total direct costs (TDC)							**$ 447**	**TDC**	
C. G&A overhead costs									
5 (Number of man-hours x OPH)					$ 10.00	=	$ 50		
BEP (TDC + G&A overhead)							**$ 497**	**BEP**	
D. Contingency factor (if desired)							$ -		
E. Net profit margin 20.00%							$ 124		
F. Total price							**$ 621**	**Revenue goal per storm**	

IV. Scenario analysis:

A. Curb-time rate (Total price ÷ Curb-time hours)

$ 621 divided by 4.0 = **$ 155.16** **Curb-time rate**

B. Unit price per cubic yard (Total price ÷ units)

$ 621 ÷ 8.0 = **$ 77.58** **TDC rate /CY** **$ 55.81**

C. Gross profit margin ((G&A overhead + Net profit) ÷ Total price)

$ 174 ÷ $ 621 = **28.1%** **GPM**

FIGURE 32-2 Sanding or Salting

John could also increase his GPM by charging a minimum one-cubic-yard amount (e.g., $100) for sanding on smaller jobs requiring less than one CY of sand. By doing so and by "stacking" these jobs back to back, John could easily bill up to $200 to $300 per curb-time hour. The GPM on this type of work could easily surpass the 44.1% figure by another 10 to 20%.

Conclusion on Sanding/Salting Work

The key is for John to bill a minimum amount per storm. He and his drivers should focus on billing a minimum of $200 per curb-time hour (when drivers are on site sanding) and a minimum of $800 per storm per driver. If they meet these criteria, they'll be making money.

Scenario Summary

To answer John's initial questions, there's no doubt his winter work is profitable and probably could be more so. Scheduling, establishing minimum prices for sanding/salting work, and setting targeted minimum hourly and daily billable dollar amounts will all contribute toward a healthier bottom line. Sanding is John's most profitable winter work, which is normal.

However, John must keep in mind that with winter work the market pretty much sets the prices. He has to be able to play the market's game and win. He must understand his numbers and how drive time and prep time can affect his profitability.

John's question regarding the winter work contribution to G&A overhead costs can be answered rather simply. Included in his winter prices is $10 for each labor hour drivers are paid. The total hours paid to drivers is 500 (5 drivers × 10 storms × 10 hours per storm). We obtain the amount of G&A overhead costs included in the winter billings by multiplying the 500 hours by the $10 OPH = $5,000. Winter work contributes $5,000 toward G&A overhead costs.

OTHER CONSIDERATIONS

The Profit and Loss (P&L) Statement

In order for John or any contractor to be able to monitor the profitability of snow and sanding work, the company profit and loss (P&L) financial statement should identify the sales and direct costs for both snow removal and sanding. Preferably, winter work should be a division of its own with its own P&L statement. This will help identify its GPM. Direct costs would include labor, labor burden, materials with sales tax, equipment, and any subcontractor costs. Once direct costs are subtracted from sales, the GPM for winter work will be identified.

Company P&L statements become diluted if winter work isn't separated from work performed during the regular season. Because winter work can often realize a GPM of 50 to 60%, it will distort figures and profit margins for other divisions. Once any type of work comprises more than 20% of total company sales, it's wise to separate it from other work by means of its own P&L statement.

Contractors who don't specifically measure and monitor winter work with a separate P&L that identifies GPM in terms of percentages and whole dollars often don't realize how much winter work contributes to their company's profitability. Unprofitable or marginally profitable divisions can be hidden, and the problem doesn't become apparent until an extremely mild winter occurs (with significantly lower winter revenue than normal). However, by then it's too late to address and fix the problem in the other division(s).

Contracts

Residential

Residential plowing is usually done on a **per-push basis**. The best way to ensure that you're pricing correctly and making money plowing residential accounts is to prepare a scenario analysis using your costs and production numbers. Be sure to include the net profit you desire. After each storm, you should enter your actual costs, hours and revenue into the scenario format to see how much money you made.

Commercial

How It Works

Commercial plowing and sanding is quite another story. Two clients come to mind. They were both in the same city on the East Coast. One contractor billed his commercial accounts strictly on a per-push basis. The other had a fixed monthly billing amount for the four months of December through March. The total of the monthly billings covered a five-year average for the amount of inches of snowfall for the winter. Anything over the average was billed out on a time and materials (T&M) basis at the end of the month of April. To make this type of contract more appealing, the contractor would plow up to 10 inches above the average at no charge. I call this a **fixed/variable** or **"flex" contract**.

In the mid-1990s, the East Coast went through a five-year period of record snowfall, followed by a year of almost no snow at all, and then another record year. The contractor with the flex contracts was happy. His revenue reflected the change in snowfall from year to year. Most importantly, he covered his costs during the year when there was almost no snow at all. His clients were also happy because they had set budget numbers to deal with. While they didn't like the extra billing in the record snowfall year, they did get a price break.

The contractor on a strictly per-push basis couldn't win. One year he'd have minimal revenue, which didn't even cover his costs to have the equipment and labor standing by. He wasn't happy, but his clients were. The following year he had record amounts of revenue. He was happy, but his clients weren't.

At the end of one of the record snowfall years he charged one of his "best" clients $80,000 for one storm at the end of March. The client had already been charged far more than its budget allowed. The $80,000 bill, while legitimate according to the per-push contract, was the straw that broke the camel's back. The client only paid $40,000 and told my client to sue if he wanted more. No one was happy at the end of that season.

THE SNOW AND ICE MANAGEMENT ASSOCIATION (SIMA)

I encourage my clients to join SIMA, the Snow and Ice Management Association. The cost is minimal and the benefits large. You can call SIMA at 814-835-3577 or visit its Web site at www.sima.org. Their address is in the List of Major Associations in the back of the book.

SUMMARY

Winter work can be some of your most profitable work. However, it can cause a lot of trouble if you don't manage both your own and your client's risk properly.

Setting revenue goals for snow events and job costing each storm immediately afterward will help ensure that you're not the one getting snowed.

Marketing winter work by means of realistic contracts is just as important as pricing your work properly. Because the market often determines what you'll charge for plowing, sanding/salting work, you have to know your costs and ensure that you can make money playing the market's game. Setting revenue goals for snow events and job costing each storm immediately afterward will help ensure that you're not the one getting snowed.

ACTION POINT

Evaluate your winter work and calculate your net profit and gross profit margins, validate your unit prices, and ensure that you set hourly and daily (or per storm) revenue goals for the various forms of services that you provide.

➤ NOTE The costs used in our scenarios are for illustration purposes only. Your costs will vary from the ones used in these examples. The key is for you to build a typical one-day scenario for the crew, materials, and equipment you use. Round up these rates as appropriate. If your costing structure is accurate, the rates you calculate should be very close to your current ones and to those generally seen in your market.

CHAPTER 33

General Tree Work

TERM

General Tree Work (GTW)

Purpose

To explain the process for bidding general tree work

Introduction

These market forces make it imperative that the tree service provider know the numbers cold and also the margins that they contain.

Tree service work provided by professionally run contractors is increasingly in demand. However, while the market opportunities are legion, the cost of capitalization, insurance rates, labor problems, and competition from large consolidators is putting more pressure on the small- to mid-sized tree service operation than ever before. These market forces make it imperative that the tree service provider knows the numbers cold and also the margins that they contain.

How It Works

An arborist on the East Coast wanted to verify his pricing for the upcoming season. He wanted to price out his **general tree work** with one-, two-, three-, and four-man crews. He also wanted to price out a one-man crew with both a large and a medium-sized stump grinder. The arborist wanted to know how much revenue each crew scenario had to bring in each day and what his hourly crew rates should be.

1. How much should he bill per day and charge per crew hour for general tree work with a one-man crew?
2. How much should he bill per day and charge per crew hour for general tree work with a two-man crew?
3. How much should he bill per day and charge per crew hour for general tree work with a three-man crew?
4. How much should he bill per day and charge per crew hour for general tree work with a four-man crew?
5. How much should he bill per day and charge per crew hour for a large stump grinder with a one-man crew?
6. How much should he bill per day and charge per crew hour for a medium stump grinder with a one-man crew?

Additional Scenario Information

- Crews will work and get paid for nine hours per day, 45 hours per week.
- The equipment cost per hour is indicated on the figures in this chapter.
- The overtime factor, risk factor, sales tax, etc. are indicated on the figures in this chapter.
- The owner desires to obtain a minimum of 20% net profit margin for tree work.

PRICING GENERAL TREE WORK

General Tree Work with a One-Man Crew

Figure 33-1 outlines this scenario. Note that each member of the crew works 7.5 hours on site per day. One-and-one-half hours per day are allotted to general condition drive time, load time, etc. The mid-sized chipper is running two hours per day, and our crew leader will be operating a chain saw approximately four hours per day.

This one-man crew has to bill approximately $700 per day to achieve the desired 20% net profit margin and to cover all costs, both direct and indirect. The curb-time hourly rate calculates to be $95 per crew hour. The portal-to-portal rate is $79 per crew hour, which I'd round up to $80.

General Tree Work with a Two-Man Crew

Figure 33-2 on page 242 outlines the two-man scenario. Again, each member of the crew works 7.5 hours on site per day. One-and-one-half hours per day are allotted to general condition drive time, load time, and so on per person. The mid-sized chipper is running two hours per day, and our crew will be operating chain saws approximately eight hours per day.

This two-man crew has to bill approximately $1,200 per day to achieve the desired 20% net profit margin and to cover all costs, both direct and indirect. The curb-time hourly rate calculates to be $80 per man-hour and $160 per crew-hour. The portal-to-portal rate is $67 per man-hour and $134 per crew-hour. I'd probably round these up to $70 and $140, respectively.

➤ **NOTE** The crew rates decrease when additional crew members are added. This is primarily due to the lower labor rates and the spreading of the truck costs over more man-hours.

General Tree Work with a Three-Man Crew

Figure 33-3 on page 243 outlines the three-man scenario. Again, each member of the crew works 7.5 hours on site per day. One-and-one-half hours per day are allotted to general condition drive time, load time, and so on per person. Note how the equipment in this scenario has changed. The mid-sized chipper is running three hours per day, and our crew will be operating chain saws approximately 10 hours per day. The owner has added a bucket truck with a cost per hour (CPH) of $30. The chipper has been upgraded in order to handle logs up to 12″ in diameter, which increases the CPH to $25. A large utility truck, an F-800 or equivalent, is also added to the scenario. Its CPH is $20. The two trucks are each operating approximately four hours per day, and we'll include their costs in this scenario.

Scenario cost data	$ or %	Remarks
Crew size (# people)	1.0	Driver
Crew average wage (CAW)	$ 18.00	
Overtime factor (OTF)	6.0%	45 hours per week, rounded up
Risk factor (RF)	10.0%	
Crew average wage w/OTF & RF	$ 20.88	
Labor burden	45.0%	
Sales tax	6.0%	
G&A overhead per hour (OPH)	$ 15.00	
Net profit margin	20.0%	
F-450 or equivalent	$ 12.00	
Curb-time man-hours per day	7.5	
Number of units	7.5	Man-hours

Scenario	Materials	Labor		Equipment	CPH	Hours	Item
I. Production (on-site or curb-time costs)							
	$ -	7.5	Man-hours	$ 40.00	$ 20.00	2.0	Chipper, mid-size
	$ -			$ -	$ -	0.0	
	$ -	$ 20.88		$ 24.00	$ 6.00	4.0	Chain saws
	$ -	$ 156.60		$ 64.00			
II. General conditions (off-site or non-curb-time costs)							
		1.5	Man-hours	$ 96.00	$ 12.00	8.0	F-450 or equivalent
		0.0		$ -	$ -	0.0	
	$ -	$ 20.88		$ -	$ -	0.0	
	$ -	$ 31.32		$ 96.00			
Subtotals	**$ -**	**$ 188**		**$ 160**			
III. Margins & markups							
A. Sales tax	$ -						
B. Labor burden		$ 85					
Subtotals	**$ -**	**$ 272**		**$ 160**			

			Amount	
Total direct costs (TDC)			**$ 432**	**TDC**
C. G&A overhead costs				
9 (Number of man-hours x OPH)	$ 15.00	=	$ 135	
BEP (TDC + G&A overhead)			**$ 567**	**BEP**
D. Contingency factor (if desired)			$ -	
E. Net profit margin 20.00%			$ 142	
F. Total price			**$ 709**	**Total price**

IV. Scenario analysis

A. Curb-time rate (Total price ÷ Curb-time hours)

$ 709 divided by 7.5 = **$ 94.58** **Curb-time rate**

B. Portal-to-portal rate (Total price ÷ all hours)

$ 709 divided by 9.0 = **$ 78.82** **Portal-to-portal rate**

C. Gross profit margin ((G&A overhead + Net profit) ÷ Total price)

$ 277 ÷ $ 709 = **39.0%** **GPM**

FIGURE 33-1 GTW: 1 Man with F-450 and Chipper

Scenario cost data	$ or %	Remarks
Crew size (# people)	2.0	Crew leader and laborer
Crew average wage (CAW)	$ 16.00	
Overtime factor (OTF)	6.0%	45 hours per week, rounded up
Risk factor (RF)	10.0%	
Crew average wage w/OTF & RF	$ 18.56	
Labor burden	45.0%	
Sales tax	6.0%	
G&A overhead per hour (OPH)	$ 15.00	
Net profit margin	20.0%	
F-450 or equivalent	$ 12.00	
Curb-time man-hours per day	15.0	
Number of units	15.0	Man-hours

Scenario	Materials	Labor		Equipment	CPH	Hours	Item
I. Production (on-site or curb-time costs)							
	$ -	15.0	Man-hours	$ 60.00	$ 20.00	3.0	Chipper, mid-size
	$ -			$ -	$ -	0.0	
	$ -	$ 18.56		$ 48.00	$ 6.00	8.0	Chain saws
	$ -	$ 278.40		$ 108.00			
II. General conditions (off-site or non-curb-time costs)							
		3.0	Man-hours	$ 96.00	$ 12.00	8.0	F-450 or equivalent
		0.0		$ -	$ -	0.0	
	$ -	$ 18.56		$ -	$ -	0.0	
	$ -	$ 55.68		$ 96.00			
Subtotals	**$ -**	**$ 334**		**$ 204**			
III. Margins & markups							
A. Sales tax	$ -						
B. Labor burden		$ 150					
Subtotals	**$ -**	**$ 484**		**$ 204**			

Total direct costs (TDC)		**$ 688**	**TDC**
C. G&A overhead costs			
18 (Number of man-hours x OPH)	$ 15.00 =	$ 270	
BEP (TDC + G&A overhead)		**$ 958**	**BEP**
D. Contingency factor (if desired)		$ -	
E. Net profit margin 20.00%		$ 240	
F. Total price		**$ 1,198**	**Total price**

IV. Scenario analysis

A. Curb-time rate (Total price ÷ Curb-time hours)

$ 1,198 divided by 15.0 = **$ 79.87** **Curb-time rate**

B. Portal-to-portal rate (Total price ÷ all hours)

$ 1,198 divided by 18.0 = **$ 66.56** **Portal-to-portal rate**

C. Gross profit margin ((G&A overhead + Net profit) ÷ Total price)

$ 510 ÷ $ 1,198 = **42.5%** **GPM**

FIGURE 33-2 GTW: 2 Men with F-450 and Chipper

Scenario cost data	$ or %	Remarks
Crew size (# people)	3.0	Crew leader and 2 laborers
Crew average wage (CAW)	$ 15.00	
Overtime factor (OTF)	6.0%	45 hours per week, rounded up
Risk factor (RF)	10.0%	
Crew average wage w/OTF & RF	$ 17.40	
Labor burden	45.0%	
Sales tax	6.0%	
G&A overhead per hour (OPH)	$ 15.00	
Net profit margin	20.0%	
F-800 or equivalent	$ 20.00	
Curb-time man-hours per day	22.5	
Number of units	22.5	Man-hours

Scenario	Materials	Labor		Equipment	CPH	Hours	Item
I. Production (on-site or curb-time costs)							
	$ -	22.5	Man-hours	$ 75.00	$ 25.00	3.0	Chipper, large
	$ -			$ 120.00	$ 30.00	4.0	Bucket truck (4 hours run time)
	$ -	$ 17.40		$ 60.00	$ 6.00	10.0	Chain saws
	$ -	$ 391.50		$ 255.00			
II. General conditions (off-site or non-curb-time costs)							
		4.5	Man-hours	$ 80.00	$ 20.00	4.0	F-800 or equivalent (minimum 4 hours)
		0.0		$ -	$ -	0.0	
	$ -	$ 17.40		$ -	$ -	0.0	
	$ -	$ 78.30		$ 80.00			
Subtotals	**$ -**	**$ 470**		**$ 335**			
III. Margins & markups							
A. Sales tax	$ -						
B. Labor burden		$ 211					
Subtotals	**$ -**	**$ 681**		**$ 335**			

Total direct costs (TDC)		**$1,016**	**TDC**
C. G&A overhead costs 27 (Number of man-hours x OPH)	$ 15.00 =	$ 405	
BEP (TDC + G&A overhead)		**$1,421**	**BEP**
D. Contingency factor (if desired)		$ -	
E. Net profit margin 20.00%		$ 355	
F. Total price		**$1,777**	**Total price**

IV. Scenario analysis

A. Curb-time rate (Total price ÷ Curb-time hours)

$ 1,777 divided by 22.5 = **$78.96** **Curb-time rate**

B. Portal-to-portal rate (Total price ÷ all hours)

$ 1,777 divided by 27.0 = **$65.80** **Portal-to-portal rate**

C. Gross profit margin ((G&A overhead + Net profit) ÷ Total price)

$ 760 ÷ $ 1,777 = **42.8%** **GPM**

FIGURE 33-3 GTW: 3 Men with Bucket Truck, F-800, and Chipper

This beefed-up crew has to bill almost $1,800 per day to achieve the desired 20% net profit margin and to cover all costs, both direct and indirect. The curb-time hourly rate calculates to be $79 per man-hour and $237 per crew-hour. The portal-to-portal rate is $66 per man-hour and $198 per crew-hour. I'd round up these rates to the nearest $5 increment.

> **NOTE** The crew rates continue to adjust as additional crew members are added.

General Tree Work with a Four-Man Crew

Figure 33-4 outlines the four-man scenario. Again, each member of the crew works 7.5 hours on site per day. One-and-one-half hours per day are allotted to general condition drive time, load time, and so on per person. The equipment in this scenario has changed very slightly from our last one. The mid-sized chipper is running three hours per day, and our crew will be operating chain saws approximately 14 hours per day.

This "super" crew has to bill approximately $2,200 per day to achieve the desired 20% net profit margin and to cover all costs, both direct and indirect. The curb-time hourly rate calculates to be $73 per man-hour and $292 per crew-hour. The portal-to-portal rate is $61 per man-hour and $244 per crew-hour. Again, I'd round up these rates to the nearest $5 increment.

> **NOTE** The crew rates continue to adjust as additional crew members are added.

Stump Grinding with a Large Stump Grinder and a One-Man Crew

Figure 33-5 on page 246 outlines our stump-grinding scenario. The one member of the crew works 7 hours on at least three sites per day. Two hours per day are allotted to general condition drive time, load time, etc. The equipment in this scenario includes a large tow-behind 85-horsepower stump grinder pulled by a mid-sized utility truck. Review Chapter 18 and Figure 18-3 to see how we calculate per-log and per-inch pricing for stump grinding.

This stump grinder has to bill almost $750 per day to achieve the desired 20% net profit margin and to cover all costs, both direct and indirect. The curb-time hourly rate calculates to be $106 per man-hour. The portal-to-portal rate is $83 per man-hour. Again, I'd probably round up these rates to the nearest $5 increment.

Stump Grinding with a Medium-Sized Stump Grinder and a One-Man Crew

Figure 33-6 on page 247 outlines the stump-grinding scenario with a mid-sized stump-grinding unit. Again, the one member of the crew works 7 hours on at least three sites per day. Two hours per day are allotted to general condition drive time, load time, etc. The equipment in this scenario includes a mid-sized self-propelled 25-horsepower stump grinder and a one-ton truck.

The stump grinder in this scenario has to bill over $660 per day to achieve the desired 20% net profit margin and to cover all costs, both direct and indirect. The curb-time hourly rate calculates to be $95 per man-hour. The portal-to-portal rate is $74 per man-hour. I'd probably round up the portal-to-portal rate to $75.

Scenario cost data	$ or %	Remarks
Crew size (# people)	4.0	Crew leader and 3 laborers
Crew average wage (CAW)	$ 14.00	
Overtime factor (OTF)	6.0%	45 hours per week, rounded up
Risk factor (RF)	10.0%	
Crew average wage w/OTF & RF	$ 16.24	
Labor burden	45.0%	
Sales tax	6.0%	
G&A overhead per hour (OPH)	$ 15.00	
Net profit margin	20.0%	
F-800 or equivalent	$ 20.00	
Curb-time man-hours per day	30.0	
Number of units	30.0	Man-hours

Scenario	Materials	Labor		Equipment	CPH	Hours	Item
I. Production (on-site or curb-time costs)							
	$ -	30.0	Man-hours	$ 75.00	$ 25.00	3.0	Chipper, large
	$ -			$ 120.00	$ 30.00	4.0	Bucket truck (4 hours run time)
	$ -	$ 16.24		$ 84.00	$ 6.00	14.0	Chain saws
	$ -	$ 487.20		$ 279.00			
II. General conditions (off-site or non-curb-time costs)							
		6.0	Man-hours	$ 80.00	$ 20.00	4.0	F-800 or equivalent (minimum 4 hours)
		0.0		$ -	$ -	0.0	
	$ -	$ 16.24		$ -	$ -	0.0	
	$ -	$ 97.44		$ 80.00			
Subtotals	$ -	$ **585**		$ **359**			
III. Margins & markups							
A.Sales tax	$ -						
B.Labor burden		$ 263					
Subtotals	$ -	$ **848**		$ **359**			

Total direct costs (TDC)		$ **1,207**	**TDC**
C. G&A overhead costs 36 (Number of man-hours x OPH)	$ 15.00 =	$ 540	
BEP (TDC + G&A overhead)		$ **1,747**	**BEP**
D. Contingency factor (if desired)		$ -	
E. Net profit margin 20.00%		$ 437	
F. Total price		$ **2,183**	**Total price**

IV. Scenario analysis

A. Curb-time rate (Total price ÷ Curb-time hours)

$ 2,183 divided by 30.0 = $ **72.78** **Curb-time rate**

B. Portal-to-portal rate (Total price ÷ all hours)

$ 2,183 divided by 36.0 = $ **60.65** **Portal-to-portal rate**

C. Gross profit margin ((G&A overhead + Net profit) ÷ Total price)

$ 977 ÷ $ 2,183 = **44.7%** **GPM**

FIGURE 33-4 GTW: 4 Men with Bucket Truck, F-800, and Chipper

Scenario cost data

	$ or %	Remarks
Crew size (# people)	1.0	Driver
Crew average wage (CAW)	$ 16.00	
Overtime factor (OTF)	6.0%	45 hours per week, rounded up
Risk factor (RF)	10.0%	
Crew average wage w/OTF & RF	$ 18.56	
Labor burden	45.0%	
Sales tax	6.0%	
G&A overhead per hour (OPH)	$ 15.00	
Net profit margin	20.0%	
F-450 or equivalent	$ 12.00	
Curb-time man-hours per day	7.0	
Number of units	7.0	Man-hours

Scenario	Materials	Labor		Equipment	CPH	Hours	Item
I. Production (on-site or curb-time costs)							
	$ -	7.0	Man-hours	$ 120.00	$ 20.00	6.0	Large 85 HP stump grinder
	$ -			$ -	$ -	0.0	
	$ -	$ 18.56		$ -	$ -	0.0	
	$ -	$ 129.92		$ 120.00			
II. General conditions (off-site or non-curb-time costs)							
		2.0	Man-hours	$ 96.00	$ 12.00	8.0	F-450 or equivalent (minimum)
		0.0		$ -	$ -	0.0	
	$ -	$ 18.56		$ -	$ -	0.0	
	$ -	$ 37.12		$ 96.00			
Subtotals	**$ -**	**$ 167**		**$ 216**			
III. Margins & markups							
A.Sales tax	$ -						
B.Labor burden		$ 75					
Subtotals	**$ -**	**$ 242**		**$ 216**			

Total direct costs (TDC)			**$ 458**	**TDC**
C. G&A overhead costs				
9 (Number of man-hours x OPH)	$ 15.00	=	$ 135	
BEP (TDC + G&A overhead)			**$ 593**	**BEP**
D. Contingency factor (if desired)			$ -	
E. Net profit margin 20.00%			$ 148	
F. Total price			**$ 742**	**Total price**

IV. Scenario analysis

A. Curb-time rate (Total price ÷ Curb-time hours)

$ 742 divided by 7.0 = **$ 105.93** **Curb-time rate**

B. Portal-to-portal rate (Total price ÷ all hours)

$ 742 divided by 9.0 = **$ 82.39** **Portal-to-portal rate**

C. Gross profit margin ((G&A overhead + Net profit) ÷ Total price)

$ 283 ÷ $ 742 = **38.2%** **GPM**

FIGURE 33-5 1 Man with Large Stump Grinder

Scenario cost data

	$ or %	Remarks
Crew size (# people)	1.0	Driver
Crew average wage (CAW)	$ 16.00	
Overtime factor (OTF)	6.0%	45 hours per week, rounded up
Risk factor (RF)	10.0%	
Crew average wage w/OTF & RF	$ 18.56	
Labor burden	45.0%	
Sales tax	6.0%	
G&A overhead per hour (OPH)	$ 15.00	
Net profit margin	20.0%	
One ton truck	$ 8.00	
Curb-time man-hours per day	7.0	
Number of units	7.0	Man-hours

Scenario	Materials	Labor		Equipment	CPH	Hours	Item
I. Production (on-site or curb-time costs)							
	$ -	7.0	Man-hours	$ 90.00	$ 15.00	6.0	Medium 25 HP stump grinder
	$ -			$ -	$ -	0.0	
	$ -	$ 18.56		$ -	$ -	0.0	
	$ -	$ 129.92		$ 90.00			
II. General conditions (off-site or non-curb-time costs)							
		2.0	Man-hours	$ 64.00	$ 8.00	8.0	One ton truck
		0.0		$ -	$ -	0.0	
	$ -	$ 18.56		$ -	$ -	0.0	
	$ -	$ 37.12		$ 64.00			
Subtotals	**$ -**	**$ 167**		**$ 154**			
III. Margins & markups							
A. Sales tax	$ -						
B. Labor burden		$ 75					
Subtotals	**$ -**	**$ 242**		**$ 154**			

Total direct costs (TDC)			**$ 396**	**TDC**
C. G&A overhead costs 9 (Number of man-hours x OPH)	$ 15.00	=	$ 135	
BEP (TDC + G&A overhead)			**$ 531**	**BEP**
D. Contingency factor (if desired)			$ -	
E. Net profit margin 20.00%			$ 133	
F. Total price			**$ 664**	**Total price**

IV. Scenario analysis

A. Curb-time rate (Total price ÷ Curb-time hours)

$ 664 divided by 7.0 = **$ 94.86** **Curb-time rate**

B. Portal-to-portal rate (Total price ÷ all hours)

$ 664 divided by 9.0 = **$ 73.78** **Portal-to-portal rate**

C. Gross profit margin ((G&A overhead + Net profit) ÷ Total price)

$ 268 ÷ $ 664 = **40.3%** **GPM**

FIGURE 33-6 1 Man with Medium Stump Grinder

SUMMARY

Our arborist now has the information he needs to price his tree work. The hourly rates provide him with the information he needs to price his work to his customers, either on a curb-time or a portal-to-portal basis. The method he uses depends on which one he feels most comfortable with. Although I wouldn't recommend it, he could use both, depending on the situation. The daily revenue goals for each scenario tell him exactly how much revenue each crew should bring in every day. Now this arborist has not only the ability to price his work accurately, but he can also ensure that every crew is making money every day.

ACTION POINT

Evaluate your tree service work as we did in our figures and calculate unit prices as well as your net profit and gross profit margins. Ensure that you set hourly and daily revenue goals for the various forms of services that you provide.

➤ **NOTE** The costs used in our scenarios are for illustration purposes only. Your costs will vary from the ones used in these examples. The key is for you to build a typical one-day scenario for the crew, materials, and equipment you use. Round up these rates as appropriate. If your costing structure is accurate, the rates you calculate should be very close to your current ones and to those generally seen in your market. ■

CHAPTER

34

Tree Fertilization and Insect Preventive Maintenance

Purpose

To explain and outline the process for pricing tree fertilization and insect preventive maintenance work

Introduction

Operational efficiency and daily revenue goals can make all the difference in achieving this lucrativeness.

Like lawn and shrub fertilization and insect control, the same services provided by a qualified arborist can be very lucrative. Operational efficiency and daily revenue goals can make all the difference in achieving this lucrativeness.

How It Works

Our arborist in the previous chapter now wants to price tree fertilization by the gallon and include an insect preventive maintenance (IPM) program. He'd like to know how much revenue each scenario should bring in each day, as well as the respective unit prices to charge his clients.

1. How much should he bill per day and per gallon for tree fertilization?
2. How much should he bill per day and charge for an "average" residential application for an insect preventive maintenance program (IPM)?

Additional Scenario Information

- Crews will work and get paid for nine hours per day, 45 hours per week.
- The equipment cost per hour is indicated on the figures in this chapter.
- The overtime factor, risk factor, sales tax, etc. are indicated on the figures in this chapter.
- The owner desires to obtain a minimum of 25% net profit margin for this tree work.

PRICING TREE FERTILIZATION AND INSECT CONTROL WORK

Fertilization Tree Work with a Two-Man Crew

Figure 34-1 outlines this scenario. Note that each member of the crew works seven hours on site per day. Two hours per day are allotted to general condition drive time, load time, etc. The spray rig, which has a cost per hour of $10, is running approximately six hours per day.

To achieve the desired 25% net profit margin, this two-man crew has to bill over $1,500 per day. This will cover all costs, both direct and indirect. The price per gallon calculates out to be $1.03. However, our arborist friend knows he can charge a minimum of $1.25 per gallon, and probably more.

Figure 34-2 on page 252 illustrates the adjusted daily revenue if this crew can spray 1,500 gallons of fertilizer per day and charge $1.25 per gallon. We know the daily revenue calculates to be 1,500 gallons × $1.25 = $1,875. We simply adjust our total price for the day by adding an extra $329 into our model in the contingency factor in Section III D. This adjustment increases our gross profit margin to over 52% or $986 per day. The net profit margin increases to almost 40%. Not bad for a day's work!

Insect Preventive Maintenance Work with a One-Man Crew

Figure 34-3 on page 253 outlines the IPM scenario. The technician works seven hours on site per day. Two hours per day are allotted to general condition drive time, load time, etc. The spray rig, which has a cost per hour of $10, is running approximately six hours per day.

Rather than using gallons as the unit of measure, the arborist desires to calculate an average price per application based on 10 of these "typical" applications per day. He'll then charge clients this average price, which will also be his minimum price, if their property falls close to this average. For larger properties, he'll charge more.

To achieve the desired 25% net profit margin the technician has to bill almost $700 per day. This will cover all costs, both direct and indirect. The price application calculates out to be $68 per application. The arborist knows he can charge a minimum of $100 per application, and maybe as much as $125.

Figure 34-4 on page 254 illustrates the adjusted daily revenue if this technician can spray a minimum of 10 properties, at a minimum price of $100 per application. We know the daily revenue calculates to be 10 applications × $100 = $1,000. Once again, we adjust our total price for the day by adding an extra $321 into our model in the contingency factor in Section III D. This adjustment increases our gross profit margin to over 62% or $626 per day. The net profit margin increases to a little over 49%. Again, not bad for a day's work!

SUMMARY

This arborist now has the information he needs to price his tree fertilization and insect preventive maintenance work. He always knew this type of work was very profitable, but now he knows exactly what his actual costs are. Just as important, he also knows the pricing per gallon and per application his market will bear. Armed with this information, he adjusts his daily revenue goals accordingly.

Whenever you combine labor with expensive materials, large (or lots of) equipment, specialty services or products, new services or products, or chemicals and fertilizers, you should think "market opportunity." Net and gross profit margins on this type of work are extremely high.

Scenario cost data	$ or %	Remarks
Crew size (# people)	2.0	Crew leader with laborer
Crew average wage (CAW)	$ 14.00	
Overtime factor (OTF)	6.0%	45 hours per week, rounded up
Risk factor (RF)	10.0%	
Crew average wage w/OTF & RF	$ 16.24	
Labor burden	35.0%	
Sales tax	6.0%	
G&A overhead per hour (OPH)	$ 15.00	
Net profit margin	25.0%	
One ton truck	$ 8.00	
Curb-time man-hours per day	14.0	
Number of units	1,500.0	Gallons of mixed fertilizer

Scenario		Materials	Labor		Equipment	CPH	Hours	Item
I. Production (on-site or curb-time costs)								
$ 5	Tanks, 300 GL	$ 350.00	14.0	Man-hours	$ 60.00	$ 10.00	6.0	Spray rig
70.0	per tank	$ -			$ -	$ -	0.0	
		$ -	$ 16.24		$ -	$ -	0.0	
		$ 350.00	$ 227.36		$ 60.00			
II. General conditions (off-site or non-curb-time costs)								
			4.0	Man-hours	$ 64.00	$ 8.00	8.0	One ton truck
			0.0		$ -	$ -	0.0	
		$ -	$ 16.24		$ -	$ -	0.0	
		$ -	$ 64.96		$ 64.00			
Subtotals		**$ 350**	**$ 292**		**$ 124**			
III. Margins & markups								
A. Sales tax		$ 21						
B. abor burden			$ 102					
Subtotals		**$ 371**	**$ 395**		**$ 124**			

Total direct costs (TDC)			**$ 890**	**TDC**
C. G&A overhead costs				
18 (Number of man-hours x OPH)	$ 15.00	=	$ 270	
BEP (TDC + G&A overhead)			**$ 1,160**	**BEP**
D. Contingency factor (if desired)			$ -	
E. Net profit margin 25.00%			$ 387	
F. Total price			**$ 1,546**	**Total price**

IV. Scenario analysis

A. Price per application (Total price ÷ # units)

$ 1,546 divided by	1,500.0 =	**$ 1.031**	**Unit price**

B. Daily revenue goal (Total price ÷ 1 day)

$ 1,546 divided by	1.0 =	**$ 1,546.18**	**Daily revenue goal**

C. Gross profit margin ((G&A overhead + Net profit) ÷ Total price)

$ 657 ÷	$ 1,546 =	**42.5%**	**GPM**

FIGURE 34-1 Tree Fertilization, 2-Man Crew

Scenario cost data	$ or %	Remarks
Crew size (# people)	2.0	Crew leader with laborer
Crew average wage (CAW)	$ 14.00	
Overtime factor (OTF)	6.0%	45 hours per week, rounded up
Risk factor (RF)	10.0%	
Crew average wage w/OTF & RF	$ 16.24	
Labor burden	35.0%	
Sales tax	6.0%	
G&A overhead per hour (OPH)	$ 15.00	
Net profit margin	25.0%	
One ton truck	$ 8.00	
Curb time man-hours per day	14.0	
Number of units	1,500.0	Gallons of mixed fertilizer

Scenario	Materials	Labor		Equipment	CPH	Hours	Item
I. Production (on-site or curb-time costs)							
$ 5 Tanks, 300 GL	$ 350.00	14.0	Man-hours	$ 60.00	$ 10.00	6.0	Spray rig
70.0 per tank	$ -			$ -	$ -	0.0	
	$ -	$ 16.24		$ -	$ -	0.0	
	$ 350.00	$ 227.36		$ 60.00			
II. General conditions (off-site or non-curb-time costs)							
		4.0	Man-hours	$ 64.00	$ 8.00	8.0	One ton truck
		0.0		$ -	$ -	0.0	
	$ -	$ 16.24		$ -	$ -	0.0	
	$ -	$ 64.96		$ 64.00			
Subtotals	**$ 350**	**$ 292**		**$ 124**			
III. Margins & markups							
A. Sales tax	$ 21						
B. Labor burden		$ 102					
Subtotals	**$ 371**	**$ 395**		**$ 124**			

Total direct costs (TDC)			**$ 890**	**TDC**
C. G&A overhead costs				
18 (Number of man-hours x OPH)	$ 15.00	=	$ 270	
BEP (TDC + G&A overhead)			**$ 1,160**	**BEP**
D. Contingency factor (if desired)			$ 329	Added net profit
E. Net profit margin 25.00%			$ 387	
F. Total price			**$ 1,875**	**Total price**

IV. Scenario analysis

A. Price per application (Total price ÷ # units)			
$ 1,875 divided by 1,500.0 =		**$ 1.250**	**Unit price**
B. Daily revenue goal (Total price ÷ 1 day)			
$ 1,875 divided by 1.0 =		**$ 1,875.18**	**Daily revenue goal**
C. Gross profit margin ((G&A overhead + Net profit) ÷ Total price)			
$ 986 ÷ $ 1,875 =		**52.6%**	**GPM**

FIGURE 34-2 Tree Fertilization with Increased Profit Margin

Scenario cost data	**$ or %**	**Remarks**
Crew size (# people)	1.0	Technician
Crew average wage (CAW)	$ 14.00	
Overtime factor (OTF)	6.0%	45 hours per week, rounded up
Risk factor (RF)	10.0%	
Crew average wage w/OTF & RF	$ 16.24	
Labor burden	35.0%	
Sales tax	6.0%	
G&A overhead per hour (OPH)	$ 15.00	
Net profit margin	25.0%	
One ton truck	$ 8.00	
Curb time man-hours per day	7.0	
Number of units	10.0	Average number of applications per day

Scenario		**Materials**	**Labor**		**Equipment**	**CPH**	**Hours**	**Item**
I. Production (on-site or curb-time costs)								
$ 10	Tanks, 300 GL	$ 50.00	7.0	Man-hours	$ 60.00	$ 10.00	6.0	Spray rig
5.0	per tank	$ -			$ -	$ -	0.0	
		$ -	$ 16.24		$ -	$ -	0.0	
		$ 50.00	$ 113.68		$ 60.00			
II. General conditions (off-site or non-curb-time costs)								
			2.0	Man-hours	$ 64.00	$ 8.00	8.0	One ton truck
			0.0		$ -	$ -	0.0	
		$ -	$ 16.24		$ -	$ -	0.0	
		$ -	$ 32.48		$ 64.00			
Subtotals		**$ 50**	**$ 146**		**$ 124**			
III. Margins & markups								
A. Sales tax		$ 3						
B. Labor burden			$ 51					
Subtotals		**$ 53**	**$ 197**		**$ 124**			

Total direct costs (TDC)		**$ 374**	**TDC**
C. G&A overhead costs			
9 (Number of man-hours x OPH)	$ 15.00 =	$ 135	
BEP (TDC + G&A overhead)		**$ 509**	**BEP**
D. Contingency factor (if desired)		$ -	
E. Net profit margin 25.00%		$ 170	
F. Total price		**$ 679**	**Total price**

IV. Scenario analysis

A. Price per application (Total price ÷ # units)

$ 679	divided by	10.0 =	**$ 67.91**	**Unit price**

B. Daily revenue goal (Total price ÷ 1 day)

$ 679	divided by	1.0 =	**$ 679.09**	**Daily revenue goal**

C. Gross profit margin ((G&A overhead + Net profit) ÷ Total price)

$ 305	÷	$ 679 =	**44.9%**	**GPM**

FIGURE 34-3 Tree Insect Preventive Maintenance, 1-Man Crew

Scenario cost data	$ or %	Remarks
Crew size (# people)	1.0	Technician
Crew average wage (CAW)	$ 14.00	
Overtime factor (OTF)	6.0%	45 hours per week, rounded up
Risk factor (RF)	10.0%	
Crew average wage w/OTF & RF	$ 16.24	
Labor burden	35.0%	
Sales tax	6.0%	
G&A overhead per hour (OPH)	$ 15.00	
Net profit margin	25.0%	
One ton truck	$ 8.00	
Curb-time man-hours per day	7.0	
Number of units	10.0	Average number of applications per day

Scenario		Materials	Labor		Equipment	CPH	Hours	Item
I. Production (on-site or curb-time costs)								
$ 10	Tanks, 300 GL	$ 50.00	7.0	Man-hours	$ 60.00	$ 10.00	6.0	Spray rig
5.0	per tank	$ -			$ -	$ -	0.0	
		$ -	$ 16.24		$ -	$ -	0.0	
		$ 50.00	$ 113.68		$ 60.00			
II. General conditions (off-site or non-curb-time costs)								
			2.0	Man-hours	$ 64.00	$ 8.00	8.0	One ton truck
			0.0		$ -	$ -	0.0	
		$ -	$ 16.24		$ -	$ -	0.0	
		$ -	$ 32.48		$ 64.00			
Subtotals		**$ 50**	**$ 146**		**$ 124**			

III. Margins & markups	Materials	Labor	Equipment		Total	
A. Sales tax	$ 3					
B. Labor burden		$ 51				
Subtotals	**$ 53**	**$ 197**	**$ 124**			
Total direct costs (TDC)					**$ 374**	**TDC**
C. G&A overhead costs 9 (Number of man-hours x OPH)			$ 15.00	=	$ 135	
BEP (TDC + G&A overhead)					**$ 509**	**BEP**
D. Contingency factor (if desired)					$ 321	Added net profit
E. Net profit margin 25.00%					$ 170	
F. Total price					**$ 1,000**	**Total price**

IV. Scenario analysis

A. Price per application (Total price ÷ # units)

$ 1,000	divided by	10.0 =	**$ 100.01**	**Unit price**

B. Daily revenue goal (Total price ÷ 1 day)

$ 1,000	divided by	1.0 =	**$ 1,000.09**	**Daily revenue goal**

C. Gross profit margin ((G&A overhead + Net profit) ÷ Total price)

$ 626	÷	$ 1,000 =	**62.6%**	**GPM**

FIGURE 34-4 Tree Insect Preventive Maintenance with Increased Profit Margin

ACTION POINT

If you perform these types of services, evaluate and calculate your net profit and gross profit margins. Also, validate your unit prices and ensure that you set hourly and daily revenue goals for your crews.

➤ **NOTE** The costs used in our scenarios are for illustration purposes only. Your costs will vary from the ones used in these examples. The key is for you to build a typical one-day scenario for the crew, materials, and equipment you use. Round up these rates as appropriate. If your costing structure is accurate, the rates you calculate should be very close to your current ones and to those generally seen in your market.

Understanding Market Predisposition

Contractor, Know Thy Market!

SECTION V

Contents

Purpose

The purpose of this section is to explain the concept of market predisposition and how an estimator can monitor it.

Market predisposition is a powerful concept that few people really understand. Fewer still are those who talk about it with any clarity. It is a concept that is primarily understood from an intuitive, rather than an analytical, perspective. Contractors sense from the "gut" more than they objectively know that there are parameters within which they must price their work. It is our objective to take the idea of market predisposition from the realm of the subjective to the realm of concrete structure, objectivity, and understanding.

CHAPTER

35

The Concept of Market Predisposition: Why Is It So Important?

TERM

Market Predisposition

Purpose

To explain the concept of market predisposition and how it applies in a bidding situation

Introduction

Brick pavers provide one of the best illustrations of **market predisposition**. The market rate around the country for brick pavers installed is $10 to $15 per square foot. Sometimes they're a little cheaper, but many times they are more expensive. As you'll recall from my opening story in Chapter 30, Joe, the accountant turned brick paver installer *par excellence*, was able to demand $20 per square foot in his market. Commercial pavers usually price out in the $7 to $9 range.

Market indicators can be product- or service-specific, or they can be more general in nature. Unit prices are specific. Here are a few examples; I'm sure you can add to the following list:

- Square-foot prices for installed pavers, sod, irrigation systems, lawn mowing, etc.
- Mowing priced by the acre, square foot, square yard, man-hour, crew hour, or cut
- Irrigation systems priced by the zone, head, or valve
- Bulk materials sold and installed by the cubic yard, ton, or bag
- Plants priced by the size of the tree or shrub
- Fertilizers and/or insecticides priced by the gallon, shrub, tree, square foot, or yard
- Apartment complex lawn maintenance priced per the "door knob"
- Annual color priced by the flat, pot, or plant
- Hourly rates for landscape architects, designers, supervisors, crew leaders, laborers, per irrigation repairs, etc.

The list is virtually endless.

Gross profit margin is a more general market indicator. Chapter 37 and Appendix E provide a more thorough list of GPM ranges for market segments throughout the United States. However, here are a few for normal (non-recessionary) markets.

Market Segment	*GPM Range*
Residential installation (all types)	30 to 40%
Commercial installation (all types)	20 to 30%
Maintenance, commercial and residential	30 to 40%
Tree work	30 to 40%
Fertilizations and insecticides	40 to 50%
Irrigation service	40 to 50%
Outdoor lighting	40 to 50%
Christmas decorations	40 to 50%

MARKET PREDISPOSITION DEFINED

The dictionary defines *predispose* as follows: "1. To incline or influence beforehand. 2. To make susceptible." Market predisposition means that prices in the market "lean" in a certain direction. There are certain market influences or forces that shape them. The trained eye can accurately observe market patterns or indicators in pricing.

How It Works

Tom was a landscape installation contractor on the East Coast. While driving another consultant and me to the airport, he mentioned that he was about to submit a bid for a commercial job that included about $6,000 in material costs. He told us that his price (including a reasonable net profit) was in the $11,000 range, and he felt very confident about it.

He went on to say that his competitors almost always priced their work by multiplying their materials by a factor of 2.0. Their price would be in the $12,000 range. He asked us what he should do. We told him to increase his net profit by pricing the job just under $12,000. He did, won the job, and put an extra thousand dollars in his pocket.

In the late 1990s, my company conducted 10 two-day estimating workshops throughout California over a two-month period. Starting in northern California, we worked our way southward and did the last workshops in San Diego County.

An interesting phenomenon came to light as we conducted the workshops. Landscape maintenance rates dropped as we headed south. Residential lawn maintenance rates in Marin County, just north of San Francisco, were roughly $32 per man-hour. Commercial rates were $26 to $28 per man-hour. Los Angeles rates were in the high teens to low twenties ($18 to $22) for both commercial and residential maintenance markets. San Diego rates plummeted to the low to mid teens ($13 to $17).

Two primary situations caused this trend. The first was the 12-month season in southern California, where G&A overhead costs could be spread over a full year, compared to the 9- or 10-month season in northern California. The second was the abundant supply of cheaper labor in southern California. The farther south we went, the more labor rates dropped.

An irrigation client in the Midwest was regularly losing golf course bids to a competitor. After some analysis, we stumbled onto the fact that the competitor was consistently multiplying his materials cost by a factor of 2.05 to arrive at his prices. We began to monitor this factor and lowered our prices to be just under the amount calculated by the 2.05 factor. After doing so, we began to win our share of the bids and to take work away from the competitor.

MARKETS ARE DYNAMIC

Markets are always changing due to the various forces that influence them. Contractors tend not to realize or be aware of the subtle and often not so subtle changing tides and currents that lie beneath the seemingly tranquil surface of the market in which they operate. The ebb and flow of market forces escapes them. Net profits and margins erode while market opportunities slip by. Navigating like a blind sailor on the ocean makes the chance of reaching port safely slim at best.

Sailors have tools to help them navigate the waters they sail. In like manner, there are objective, quantifiable reference points available for the contractor to help him or her along the way, if the contractor knows what to look for. Each one must be a trained observer.

Seasoned sea captains don't get that way by treading water. They spend a lot of time monitoring and studying the oceans. Before they become masters of the sea, they are students of the sea and the forces that influence it.

Contractors must do the same. They must know how to study their markets and the hidden signs contained therein. Fortunately, there are tools and training available to teach them, but these tools and methods must be studied and applied. As contractors study their markets and the jobs being bid, they need to continually ask, "Can I play this game and win? Does this job or market adaptation add to my company's bottom line?"

MARKET ADAPTATION ASSUMES PREREQUISITES

Before you can adapt to the marketplace, you first have to understand it. The first prerequisite is to have a clear vision of what to adapt to. You must have a definite "port" in mind, so to speak. This leads to the second prerequisite. The destination must be one worth going to for you and your company. There must be a "payoff" for taking the trip. It might be increased or maintained market share, or it might be realizing increased margins due to expansion into a new market. Third, you must have devices and tools to measure, quantify, and display information to help you stay on course and navigate the waters safely as you attempt to reach your destination.

THE COST-UP VERSUS MARKET-DOWN ANALYSIS

Market predisposition is a "top-down" concept. We start with what the market generally gives us and work down to the details of our cost structure. Throughout this book we've taken a "bottom-up" (not bottoms up) approach to pricing our services and products. We build cost upon cost for materials, labor, equipment, and subcontractors. We then add on our margins and markups to arrive at our final price.

With market predisposition, we start at the top by looking for market indicators. Both methods are valid. However, one without the other is dangerous. Cost-up is an analytical process while market-down is a much more intuitive one. Estimating costs accurately is a scientific process. Adding net profit margin to your costs to reach a market price is more like playing poker.

This doesn't mean you're gambling with your business. Rather, it means you don't know how your competitor is going to price his or her work. You have to make a calculated guess, if such a thing exists. The two methods may appear paradoxical, but they're actually complementary.

"MICRO" OR INTERNAL MARKET PREDISPOSITION

Micro market indicators are ones internal to your company. You'll uncover them as you analyze your bids. They're primarily made up of unit prices, gross profit margins, and material factors.

To obtain unit price indicators, you must first format your bids in unit prices. This doesn't mean you provide unit prices to your customers. Unit prices are a great tool to use for analyzing your bids, whether your client ever sees them or not. My clients primarily use unit prices for internal bidding quality control purposes.

If you've done an accurate takeoff and your unit prices look within reason, you probably have a pretty good bid. I believe unit pricing is one of your most valuable tools for analyzing your bids. For instance, if your price on a bid for installed pavers comes in at $75 per square foot, you'd better have some pretty good reasons or be the world's greatest salesperson.

Gross profit margin (GPM), on the other hand, is the best indicator of what's happening in your market. This may be a geographical or a specific industry-segment market within a given geographical market. GPM reflects the supply and demand curve. When times are good and work is plentiful, GPMs rise. When recessions hit and times are bad, GPMs fall.

Unit prices combined with GPMs provide the two most valuable tools for analyzing your bids. If your takeoff is accurate, your unit prices are in the ballpark, and your GPM looks good, you can be pretty sure you have a good bid. This doesn't guarantee that you'll get the job, but it does guarantee that 99.9% of the time you have a bid that accurately reflects your company's costs and desired margins.

The "Bid Board" outlined in Chapter 40 (a spreadsheet for tracking our bids) is our primary tool for tracking the GPM on individual jobs as well as the GPM average for the entire company.

Material factors are the third most common micro indicator. However, they're not nearly as useful as unit prices and GPM. Fortunately, they're being used less and less as a pricing indicator. "Materials times two" (or three or four or five or whatever the factor) just doesn't have much mathematical validity. Unfortunately, this method of pricing construction installation work is taught in some college courses. Even more unfortunate is the fact that some vendors, especially irrigation suppliers, encourage their customers to price their work by using factors.

It's a good practice to monitor your material factor and your material-to-labor ratio on individual bids. These two items can provide the estimator with some indicators that reflect the material intensity of the job. Taken into context with other ratios and indicators, material factors and ratios can be of some analytical use. However, by themselves they have very little relevance to our pricing.

"MACRO" OR EXTERNAL MARKET PREDISPOSITION

Macro market indicators are ones external to your company. They come in various shapes and sizes and are virtually limitless. Macro indicators may or may not affect your company's micro indicators. Just because your geographical or industry market is going through a recession doesn't mean you have to participate in it. I'll discuss only a few of the macro indicators.

Just because your geographical or industry market is going through a recession doesn't mean you have to participate in it.

Architects and Engineers

The landscape and irrigation construction industry is at the tail end of the construction process; this has its advantages and disadvantages. The good news is that you can sometimes see a slowdown coming. The bad news is trying to collect your money when the good news dries up. You can often obtain some significant insight into the job "pipeline" by monitoring the work flow in architectural and engineering firms. Simply ask the architects and engineers in your market what's in their pipeline and if they're bidding and/or negotiating a normal amount of work. This tactic applies to the commercial, municipal, and residential markets.

Plan Rooms, Green Sheets, Bidding Services, and Construction Newspapers

You can glean some excellent insight into the amount and types of work in your market by monitoring these publications and services.

Number of Bidders

As a market tightens up, you'll see the number of companies bidding on a job increase. This happens in both residential and commercial markets. Track this number, if at all possible.

Association Meetings and Golf Courses

Competitors who are members of the same association aren't always willing to share trade or market secrets. However, just by attending meetings and listening to the general tone of conversations you can tell a lot about how much work contractors have and how the pipeline looks. Spend three to four hours with a contractor on the golf course and you may learn more than you want to know.

Client Psychology

When the residential market is hot, the primary concern of the client is, "When can you start?" Once the market slows down and client tentativeness sets in, the main question is, "When can you get back with me and give me a price for all the changes and downsizing I've just done?" You could add, "For the fifth time."

Clients become very cautious when things slow down, the stock market takes a dive, or there's uncertainty in the air.

Geographical Regions

Atlanta to Washington, DC: Material factoring is prevalent in this part of the country. The factor is normally 3.0 for residential installation. I believe the primary proponent of this pricing method was, and in some cases still is, the landscape architecture departments in area universities. Contractors probably picked up these methods by osmosis. However, some contractors in this region didn't get the correct notes. They're pricing their work by multiplying their material costs by a factor of 3.0, but they are also adding labor on top of this.

Vendors

Vendors and suppliers also get in the pricing business by means of sharing "suggested" material factors and/or unit prices (head, zone, valve, and labor rate prices) with their customers. It's often the brand new contractor, desperate for any information at all, who falls prey to this advice.

Suppliers can also provide some valuable general information. By asking the right questions the attentive contractor can often find out how the competition is paying. Are their accounts receivables harder to collect? Is the supplier enforcing

C.O.D. payments more frequently? Who has recently filed for bankruptcy? Salespeople usually know this information and are often very willing to "traffic" it to inquisitive contractors.

Material Pricing

The prices being charged for materials by contractors can often provide some insight into what's happening in a market. However, first we need to review some pricing terminology.

Wholesale price is the price a supplier or nursery pays manufacturers and growers for their products.

The *retail price* is what a residential customer pays for materials. Retail garden centers and nurseries normally mark up the wholesale price by 200 to 300% to achieve a retail price. This material factor of 2.0 or 3.0 is calculated to cover shipping charges, inventory handling, G&A overhead, net profit, etc.

A *rewholesale price* is what a landscape contractor pays a "reseller" nursery for his or her materials. The rewholesale price is normally 25 to 35% below the retail price. Seen another way, the rewholesale price is roughly 50 to 75% above the wholesale price.

The *manufacturer's list price* is the suggested retail price for materials. Wholesale and rewholesale pricing margins are comparable to those for nursery materials.

Now that we understand the definitions of the basic materials pricing structure, let's look at how markups and margins are added to these material prices and passed on to a contractor's customer.

The commercial installation market throughout most of the United States and Canada was generally very competitive in the early 1990s. Some areas in the Midwest were still strong, but most of North America was recovering from a recession. Materials in bids usually had a 15 to 20% margin, as these costs were passed on to the commercial customer.

Materials in public works project bids had slightly higher margins. Material costs in residential bids carried an even higher margin, normally in the 20 to 30% range. Material costs in all types of maintenance jobs carried margins close to that experienced in the residential installation market. It wasn't until the mid to late 1990s that these margins began to change significantly.

In the mid-1990s, the North American economy began to become more bullish, and margins on materials in bids began to rise. By the end of the 1990s and early 2000s it was extremely common for materials in residential bids to be marked up to match full retail prices seen in retail nurseries. These materials, which were purchased by the contractor at the rewholesale price, had a 25 to 40% margin on them when passed on to the residential customer.

Materials in commercial installation work didn't have as hefty margins as did residential projects, but they had risen to the high teens or the high 20% range. Public works projects carried similar margins. The various maintenance markets maintained their margins of 20 to 30% and, in some cases, saw them increase slightly.

Subcontractor Pricing

The pricing of subcontractor work has always been interesting. Pricing within the subcontractor market is much more confusing than pricing within the market for materials. The lines of market delineation are much clearer in the materials market. Subcontractors often price their services without understanding the levels of pricing in the market for their work. However, there are pricing levels in the subcontractor market, in spite of the blurred lines separating them.

Theoretically (similar to materials) subcontractor costs should come in three levels depending on who's paying for the services.

- Subcontractors working directly for a residential client should charge that client a "retail" price. This translates into a 30 to 40% gross profit margin.
- Subcontractors working for general contractors, developers, or in the public works market would discount this retail price to a 20 to 30% gross profit margin. This allows the general contractor or developer to add a margin to the subcontractor's price and pass it on to the customer or end user.
- Subcontractors working for a landscape contractor (e.g., a mason subcontracting flat work to a landscape contractor on a residential project) should, theoretically, give the landscape contractor a rewholesale price that allows the landscaper to add a margin to it and charge the client a retail price.

In other words, the mason, if asked by the homeowner for a price for the flat work, should give the residential client a retail price for his work, while providing the landscape contractor a rewholesale price for the same work. Theoretically, this works almost the same as it does with materials. I say "theoretically" because most subcontractors don't understand these levels of pricing.

The reasoning behind these levels of pricing is simple. From a gross profit margin perspective, everyone in the construction and services food chain needs to make a gross profit and a net profit on work done. However, there's only so much margin you can add to a given service or product. Competitive forces hold these margins to a fair market value level in the respective retail, commercial, or public works market.

Looking at it from a cost perspective, the mason working for a general contractor or landscaper has less G&A overhead than a mason working directly for the homeowner. Commercial work simply requires much less managerial supervision than does residential work. Marketing and advertising costs are also much less because the general contractor and landscaper do all the marketing for the mason.

Gross margins added to subcontractor costs in a bid normally range from 10 to 20%. In other words, the price charged to the client for a mason working for a landscaper usually has a 10 to 20% margin on it. This range will vary slightly. Sometimes the landscaper can get up to a 25% gross margin, but it's rare. Occasionally, the landscaper will add a margin below 10% for large subcontractor projects. In some extremely competitive markets, it's not unheard of for the landscaper to pass along the subcontractor cost with little or no margin at all.

A commercial contractor in Utah was bidding on a golf course and was going to subcontract the irrigation portion. The irrigation subcontractor provided a price of over $500,000 to the landscaper, which was almost half of the project.

The landscaper knew the irrigation subcontractor very well and had done lots of other projects with him. He also knew he couldn't add a 10 to 20% margin on the irrigation subcontractor's price and still get the project. He settled for a margin in the 3 to 5% range, won the bid, and made a little money on the irrigation subcontractor in the process.

Of course, the landscaper would love to have made a 15% margin on the irrigation subcontractor, but because of market predisposition, he knew it was going to be 3 to 5% of something, or 10 to 20% of nothing.

Market predisposition for subcontractors working for you under normal conditions translates into a 10 to 20% gross margin. Occasionally, you'll realize a higher or lower margin, but contractors throughout North America generally report this range to me for the margin added to subcontractor costs.

Equipment Pricing

Equipment rental companies help to establish a pricing benchmark for equipment. I used to think companies renting equipment really knew the cost for operating individual pieces of equipment and their need for a gross profit on top of these costs. My theory was shattered after being introduced to the owner of such a company who really understood the rental equipment business. His daughter, the editor of a magazine to which I contributed articles, introduced me to him.

I asked him how he arrived at a price to charge for his equipment. He told me a major industry magazine surveyed all the equipment rental stores for their rates. This was done by geographical region throughout the country. The magazine compiled and published the rates for each region. Rental stores would then review the findings and adjust their rates accordingly. If this isn't circular reasoning, and throwing the anchor into the ship's hold, I don't know what is. So much for knowing your true costs and margins for each piece of equipment.

Equipment rental rates are normally 40 to 50% higher than your calculated cost per hour for a specific piece of equipment. In other words, the rental company will typically charge you, the renter, $16 to $18 per hour for an item that (if you owned it) would actually cost $10 per hour to operate. The difference includes the rental company's G&A overhead and net profit.

Because so few business people understand how to arrive at an actual cost to operate a piece of equipment and because there are still fewer sources for finding such costs, equipment rental rates tend to provide the most visible industry benchmarks for pricing equipment. If rental rates aren't used for pricing equipment in bids, the pricing varies with the estimating method used by the individual contractor.

Here are some of the most common trends.

EXAMPLE

Common Trends

Let's use a standard skid steer, which rents for $175 per day plus a $75 delivery fee. The actual cost to operate this skid steer, including all costs (purchase, interest, insurance, maintenance, fuel, etc.) and a trailer to haul it, will be about $18 per operating hour.

If the contractor actually rents this skid steer for the day, a 10 to 20% margin will usually be added to the $250 cost.

If the contractor owns the skid steer, it will usually be charged to the client in one of a variety of ways. None of the following costs include the cost of the operator:

- The contractor will charge the rental rate to the customer without any markup.
- The contractor will charge the rental rate to the customer plus a 10 to 20% margin.
- The contractor will charge $18 per operating hour plus a margin ranging from 15 to 35%.
- A four-hour minimum cost may be charged for the equipment plus a cost for each hour over the minimum.

The contractor may choose to charge a rate to include the operator. This rate normally has a four-hour minimum charge plus a specified rate for any hours above the minimum.

If you can charge equipment rental rates for your owned equipment, you'll realize a 40 to 50% gross margin on this equipment. Adding a 10 to 25% margin on top of the rental rate for equipment actually rented will more than adequately price rented equipment.

Labor Pricing

The primary market trend for pricing labor rates is very simplistic and has little or no basis in mathematical reality. Three times the labor rate paid to the laborer is the going pattern. Someone being paid $10 per hour would be billed out at $30 per labor hour. The $20 margin on the $10 gross payroll amount would theoretically cover labor burden, G&A overhead costs, and a net profit margin.

This method may be ample for highly paid individuals such as attorneys, CPAs, nurses, architects, and so on. However, it tends to break down when pricing individuals in the $10 to $20 range, because labor burden and G&A overhead costs are disproportionately higher for such individuals.

The other common pattern in the marketplace is to simply observe what other contractors are charging for their staff. The market will, in most cases, dictate the general pricing structure for these individuals. The following are some general pricing patterns I see around the country:

Labor Type	*Hourly Pricing Range*
Laborers, commercial construction	$20 to $30
Laborers, residential construction	$25 to $45
Laborers, all maintenance	$20 to $35
Crew leaders, commercial construction	$30 to $40
Crew leaders, residential construction	$35 to $55
Crew leaders, all maintenance	$30 to $45
Supervisors, commercial construction	$45 to $60
Supervisors, residential construction	$45 to $75
Designers	$25 to $75
Landscape architects	$50 to $100

Geographic Predisposition

Barry Goldwater is said to have asked this insightful question of an eager listener:

> *Question*: "Do you want to know where the best place to hunt ducks is?"
>
> *Answer*: "Where the ducks are."

The best place to make money in the construction business is where the money is. Where's the money? It's with the people who have it. Where are these people? They're generally in the cities throughout North America.

New York City and the surrounding areas within 50 to 100 miles (northern New Jersey, Pennsylvania, and Connecticut) have historically seen very high margins on all types of residential construction and service work. Toronto, Los Angeles, Detroit, San Francisco, Boston, Chicago, and many of the other major metropolitan areas of North America enjoy similar margins. The rise of the high-tech industry has created similar pockets of opportunity in the Silicon Valley in California, Washington State, and elsewhere.

> *Conclusion*: Follow the money! Go to the places where the rich and famous stay and play, and it will usually lead you to the areas where margins are the highest.

Government Trends

One very large contractor has hitched his wagon to the infrastructure market in the United States. This market, which primarily includes roads, underground utilities, related site work, bridges, and so forth, is robust and should remain so through 2015 or thereabouts.

OTHER MARKET PREDISPOSITION INDICATORS

While certainly not all-inclusive, here are some additional suggestions.

Monitor the golf market. For years the new golf course market was very robust. However, as courses are built out, this market is slowing. Contractors who build new courses are having to make significant adjustments; there's simply less new golf course work available. Not only is there less work, but there's much more competition. As these contractors adjust and enter other markets (golf course refurbishment, irrigation service, commercial and residential installation, etc.), it will cause a ripple effect that will influence those markets as well.

Ask questions. Do your own research. In any given day it's not uncommon for me to talk with 10 to 15 contractors. I always ask them how their market is doing. "How are the margins on your jobs? What's the labor market like? Are new leads plentiful? What are you hearing and seeing?" These are just a few of the questions I'm continually asking clients.

Monitor the unemployment and interest rates.

Read, read, read and listen, listen, listen! A friend once told me that "Leaders are readers." This is sound advice.

SUMMARY

Monitoring market predisposition is a neverending task. The market often provides clues as to how you should price your work. Often it's up to you whether you participate in an economic downturn or not. Do your homework and think through the pricing indicators we've covered here. And, certainly, you can come up with some of your own.

ACTION POINTS

1. Study these indicators and attempt to incorporate them into your bidding analysis.
2. Review the industry benchmarks outlined in Chapter 46 and Appendix E, and the discussion of gross profit margin in Chapter 37.
3. Review your bidding methods and format your bid information so you can identify the gross profit margin on your bids.
4. Conduct your own market research and add to the market indicators already mentioned.

CHAPTER

36

Margins and Markups: What's the Difference?

TERMS

Margins
Markups

Purpose

To explain the mathematical difference between a margin and a markup

Introduction

Misconceptions, faults, and outright mathematical errors exist in the minds of many contractors when it comes to using margins and markups in their estimating systems. Common or conventional wisdom can get the contractor into serious trouble if he doesn't understand the limitations of both as used in the bidding process.

However, when understood and used properly, margins and markups can provide the contractor with some very powerful tools. These tools can be used to not only analyze individual bids, but also to analyze trends in the marketplace. Increased bidding accuracy, more thorough ratio and margin analysis, and increased bidding flexibility are but a few of the tools that can be provided by properly applied margins and markups.

How It Works

During the break at an estimating workshop that I was conducting, a young contractor approached me to ask a question. He wanted to know why he was putting 25% net profit onto his bids but seeing about 15% net profit on his profit and loss statement. Somewhere, he thought, he was losing 10% net profit along the way. I asked him to explain how he was calculating the 25% net profit that he was putting onto his bids. As it turned out, he was putting the 25% net profit onto his bids as a markup, not as a margin. I explained to him that his arithmetic accounted for half of the missing 10%. The other 5% was probably lost in operational inefficiencies.

HISTORICAL DEFINITIONS

The dictionary defines **margins** and **markups** almost identically as, "the difference (amount or percentage) between the cost and the selling price." However, in common bidding usage, there's a slight variation when the two are applied to bidding jobs.

Example 1

A markup is commonly used in a bidding situation as a factor in the form of a percent or decimal multiplied by a direct cost or combination of direct costs. For instance, all direct costs (materials, sales tax, direct labor and labor burden, equipment, and subcontractors) might be increased by 25% to achieve the final selling price for a job. Mathematically it plays out as follows:

$10,000 (total direct costs (TDC)) × 1.25 (or 125%) = $12,500

The markup applied to all direct costs is 25%. Conventional wisdom says that if you desire a 25% gross profit margin (GPM) for your business at the end of the year, mark up all your direct bid costs in all your bids by 25%.

Example 2

A margin, on the other hand, is somewhat different. To achieve a 25% margin, the mathematical formula differs slightly from that used for the markup. We divide the total costs by one and subtract the desired margin to achieve it. It plays out as follows:

$10,000 (TDC) ÷ (1 – .25) = $10,000 ÷ .75 = $13,333

Notice the difference in the final price for the two examples. Example 2 has actually achieved a 25% margin on top of all costs. If you divide the margin amount by the price, you get .25 or 25%.

$3,333 ÷ 13,333 = .25 or 25%

However, if you divide the markup amount in Example 1 by the price, you lose 5%.

$2,500 ÷ 12,500 = .2 or 20%

A 25% markup translates into a true 20% margin. Let's look at what happens when 10% is used as the markup and margin.

1. $10,000 (TDC) × 1.1 (or 110%) = $11,000
2. $10,000 (TDC) ÷ (1 – .1) = $10,000 ÷ .9 = $11,111

Which method achieved the true 10% margin?

Example 1 has a true margin of $1,000 (the difference between TDC and price). However, this translates into .091 or 9.1%. Almost a whole percentage point was lost in the process.

Example 2 actually realizes a true 10% margin. The $1,111 difference between TDC and price, divided by the price, is .1 or 10%.

SO WHAT'S THE BIG DIFFERENCE?

Many contractors mark up costs by some factor or combination of factors without realizing that mathematically they're going to lose margin points along the way. If you're marking up your direct costs by 25% to achieve your final price, you automatically lose 5%. Even a 10% markup costs you 1% on your bids.

To achieve a true 25% margin using the markup method, you'd have to mark up the TDC by over 33%. Again, this may not seem like much, but if your sales are $500,000 per year over a career of 25 years, a 1% margin increase will get you an additional $125,000 of net profit.

$500,000 (sales per year) × 25 years = $12,500,000 career sales

$12,500,000 × .01 (or 1%) = $125,000

A 2% increase would get you an extra quarter of a million dollars over the course of your career. And that's all net profit that could go into your retirement account.

Many contractors don't understand this mathematical quirk and the difference between a markup and a margin. Once the math is understood, the foundation is laid for some important business concepts.

The first concept is gross profit margin (GPM). GPM is the margin, expressed in dollars or as a percent, or the difference between TDC and the selling price for a job. Put another way, GPM is the sum of indirect G&A overhead applied to a bid plus the net profit put on a job.

Net profit margin (NPM) is the amount on a bid that is in addition to all costs, both direct (TDC) and indirect (G&A). NPM is pure profit, so to speak.

The last concept is the break-even point (BEP). The BEP on a bid is the amount that covers all costs on a job, both direct and indirect. The mathematical formulas for the above are as follows:

GPM = Price − TDC	or	GPM = NPM + G&A overhead
BEP = TDC + G&A overhead	or	BEP = Price − NPM
NPM = Price − BEP	or	NPM = GPM − G&A overhead

COMMON MISCONCEPTIONS USING MARGINS AND MARKUPS

Let's get back to the basics. Applying sales tax to material costs, workers' compensation insurance rates to labor costs, and FICA, FUTA and SUTA rates to labor costs are all examples of markups properly applied to costs in the bidding process. For example, a materials sales tax rate of 6% is a markup. Every $100 of material costs is marked up $6 for sales tax. The mathematical formula is as follows:

Costs (materials) × .06 (sales tax markup) = sales tax dollars

or A × B = C

Factor A (material costs) multiplied by Factor B (sales tax) equals the Product C (sales tax dollars).

There is a direct mathematical correlation between Factor A, Factor B, and Product C. It's important to note that this formula is mathematically accurate because it accurately calculates the costs involved. Markups used in this manner in the bidding process are legitimate and accurate. Unfortunately, the use of markups is often stretched beyond their ability to accurately calculate bid costs.

The erroneous use of markups in the bidding process generally occurs in two areas. The first is in the recovery of indirect G&A overhead costs. The second involves achieving a desired GPM on the company profit and loss statement at the end of the year.

MARKUPS, MARGINS, AND G&A OVERHEAD COST RECOVERY

There are roughly four markup formulas used in the marketplace to recover indirect G&A overhead costs. Essentially, they all make the same erroneous mathematical assumption, but each has its own unique twist and attempted justification. As you can see, the formulas get more complex as they progress.

1. **Materials Times 2 (or 2.5 or 3.0 ...)**: Displayed mathematically, the formula is $M \times 2 = P$. Or, materials multiplied by a factor of two produces the desired price for the bid. The factor is supposed to cover indirect G&A overhead costs and net profit.
2. **The GPM Method**: Total direct costs are increased by a percent or factor to cover indirect G&A overhead costs and net profit. The mathematical formula is as follows:

   [(materials + tax) + (direct labor + labor burden) + (equipment costs) + (subcontractor costs)] × (1 + factor) = Price

3. **The Dual Overhead Recovery System (DORS)**: Material costs are increased by a predetermined percentage to recover indirect G&A overhead costs on materials. Direct labor costs are increased by another predetermined percentage to recover indirect G&A overhead costs on labor. Equipment costs, other than rental equipment, are usually included in the indirect G&A overhead markup percentages. Sales tax and labor burden are usually calculated in the respective markup percentages. Subcontractors are normally marked up independently of the other direct costs. Net profit may be included in the markup percentages, or it may be added at the end of the bid. The mathematical formula is as follows:

   (material costs × P1) + (direct labor costs × P2) = Price

4. **The Multiple Overhead Recovery System (MORS)**: To recover indirect G&A overhead costs, material costs (with tax) are usually marked up 10%, equipment costs are marked up 25%, subcontractors costs are marked up 5%, and direct labor (including labor burden) is marked up by a calculated percentage, usually ranging from 35 to 85%. Net profit margin is then added to the sum of these four items. The mathematical formula is as follows:

   [(material costs × 1.1) + (equipment costs × 1.25) + (subcontractor costs × 1.05) + (direct labor costs × 1 + 35 to 85%)] + net profit = Price

MARGINS AND THE YEAR-END FINANCIAL STATEMENT

Some accountants erroneously reason that to obtain a desired GPM (30% for example) at the end of the business year, a contractor should add a 30% gross profit margin to all jobs throughout the year. You could almost get away with this if every job you bid had exactly the same ratios of direct costs (materials, labor, equipment, subcontractors, etc.). However, 99 times out of 100 this isn't the case for landscape construction or maintenance jobs.

There is no arithmetical correlation between the amount of GPM you desire to achieve on your business at the end of the business year and the amount of GPM you should add to individual jobs being bid.

Without a detailed mathematical explanation, suffice it to say there is no arithmetical correlation between the amount of GPM you desire to achieve on your business at the end of the business year and the amount of GPM you should add to individual jobs being bid. Contractors can get into serious financial trouble using this pricing method.

SO WHAT'S THE PROBLEM?

Without getting into all the detailed explanations and arithmetic as to why the four markup formulas have mathematical faults, there's one overriding faulty mathematical assumption contained in all four.

> Markups and margins accurately reflect bid costs when applied to calculating direct costs such as sales tax, FICA, FUTA, SUTA, etc. The mathematical formula of $A \times B = C$ accurately calculates direct costs in such a situation. However, the four markup formulas noted attempt to go way beyond this. All four methods use factoring or a derivative thereof to calculate and recover indirect G&A overhead costs. Herein lies the problem in the arithmetic.
>
> Factoring or multiplication, by necessity, creates a direct correlation between the factors and the product (or price in our examples). If a factor (2 or 3) is changed in the equation $2 \times 3 = 6$, the product (6) is directly impacted. If the 2 is changed to an 8, the product increases in direct proportion to the change. It increases fourfold because the original factor of 2 was quadrupled.
>
> All the prices produced by the four markup formulas are supposed to contain indirect G&A overhead costs. Unfortunately, indirect G&A overhead costs don't act like direct costs (materials, direct labor equipment costs, etc.), which is why they're called "indirect" costs.
>
> There's no direct correlation between direct job costs and indirect G&A overhead costs. Indirect G&A overhead costs in a bid don't increase or decrease in direct proportion to an increase or decrease in material, labor, equipment costs, and so on. Office rent, office salaries, telephone bills, and advertising costs may increase or decrease as direct field costs fluctuate, but not in direct mathematical proportion to them.

Calculating and recovering indirect G&A overhead costs by using markups and margins in the bidding process, regardless of how complex the mathematical formula, assumes a direct mathematical relationship where there is none. These methods usually overstate or understate indirect G&A overhead costs in most common bidding situations. Consequently, bidding accuracy goes out the window.

WHEN TO USE MARKUPS AND MARGINS

Markups are very useful and necessary for calculating costs within a bid such as sales tax, FICA, FUTA, SUTA, etc. They're normally applied in a very narrow and well-defined mathematical context. Margins, on the other hand, can be very helpful as market analysis tools and are much wider in scope. The gross profit margin can be particularly beneficial if calculated on bids and monitored consistently.

For instance, around the country the GPM on a landscape residential installation job is usually 35% (plus or minus 5%). In other words, the indirect G&A overhead plus the net profit margin on such a job will normally fall between 30 and 40% of the total price of the job. If your GPM on jobs is lower, you should probably increase it. If it's higher, keep quiet. The GPM on commercial and residential maintenance work usually ranges from 25 to 35%. Commercial landscape installation work usually realizes a GPM of 25% (plus or minus 5%).

Competitively bid commercial landscape installation jobs will usually see GPMs at the low end of the range, while negotiated work should have GPMs at the middle to high end. Negotiated work should be your most profitable work and also the least risky work you do. Think about it! High margins, low risk—you should attempt to negotiate as much work as possible.

GPMs usually plummet as the economy enters a recession. They tend to increase as economies heat up. This makes sense from a supply-and-demand curve perspective. A constant number of contractors chasing a decreasing amount of work drives prices and margins down.

Surprisingly, margins don't always increase that much as the economy improves. Landscape contractors in some of the hottest spots in the country are bidding jobs at gross profit margins below 20%. Part of the problem is the sheer number of contractors chasing the work. There are many more landscape contractors in the market today than there were five or six years ago.

SUMMARY

Markups and margins, as commonly used in the construction and service industries, are different. Mathematical misconceptions ranging from simple quirks in arithmetic to faulty assumptions in complex indirect G&A overhead recovery cost formulas can cause the uninitiated estimator to overstate or understate important cost components in a bid.

Accurate cost estimating is the real issue here. Once properly understood and used, markups and margins can provide useful tools for the contractor to analyze not only individual bids, but also markets and market trends. These tools can not only help assure that today's jobs are bid accurately and competitively, they can help ensure that the contractor will be around to bid on tomorrow's jobs as well.

ACTION POINT

Evaluate your current estimating methods to determine if you are using margins and markups appropriately.

CHAPTER 37

Gross Profit Margin: An Estimator's Best Friend

Purpose

To explain how to

- Define GPM
- Calculate GPM
- Monitor market trends with GPM
- Evaluate a business with GPM

Introduction

Gross profit margin is one of the most valuable tools an estimator has. However, in today's market it's not being discussed in any real and meaningful way. Few estimators understand it, let alone track and use it in their bidding process. This is unfortunate.

How It Works

In the late 1980s a commercial landscape installation contractor in Maine consistently bid his work with a GPM in the mid-20% range. Jobs were plentiful and margins were good. However, in the fall of 1989 everything changed. The bottom fell out of the market, and for the next four to five years, gross profit margins on bids had to reflect recessionary market conditions.

During this period this contractor knew that if his GPM on a bid was over 18%, he might as well not waste his time bidding the job because he wouldn't be competitive enough to get it. Fortunately, from the mid-1990s on, this market changed, and today this contractor is again bidding his commercial installation work in the mid-20% range.

In the early 1990s, a high-end residential installation contractor in Los Angeles was bidding on Phase 2 of a large four-phase residential project. Four contractors, including the contractor who did Phase 1, were invited to bid on the project. The first phase was $350,000. Subsequent phases would be in the same price range.

The recession in southern California was in full swing at this time. Margins were tight and my client really wanted to get this job. He had me spend a day with him bidding this project. We were unsure why the owners were putting Phase 2 out for bid but thought they might be dissatisfied with the original contractor. Consequently, we felt that if we won Phase 2 we'd probably get Phases 3 and 4, which would mean the end of the recession for my client.

Prior to 1990, my client had bid large residential installation jobs with a GPM in the middle to high 30% range. Two years later, jobs were so scarce and the market so tight that we bid work in the very low 20% range. My client bid this $300,000+ job at 17% GPM.

Of the four bids provided, we were the second lowest. We'd beaten the original contractor's bid by $12,000 (he came in third). The fourth bid was much higher. The landscape architect and owners met and decided to throw out the low bid, which then made us the low bidder. My client was happy and so was I. I felt I'd done a good job for him.

However, the landscape architect called my client and informed him the owners decided that for $12,000 they didn't want to change horses in midstream. It was then we realized we'd been "shopped." The owners and landscape architect probably never intended to change contractors. Their intention, we believed, was to keep their guy honest—at the two other bidders' and our expense.

Imagine! We bid this project at 17% GPM and still didn't get the job. The lesson to be learned is that things get ugly in a recession, and all the rules change.

GPM DEFINED

Gross profit margin can be calculated one of two ways. The first is to subtract all of your cost of goods sold from sales (or job price). The formula is as follows:

Sales (or job price) – COGS = GPM

The second way to calculate GPM is to add the G&A overhead to the net profit. This formula is as follows:

G&A overhead + net profit = GPM

Both formulas provide you with the same answer, whether expressed in whole dollars or as a percentage.

GPM CALCULATED

To calculate the GPM on a bid you simply add the net profit to the G&A overhead allocated to the job. Or, you can subtract the COGS from the bid price. Let's look at the following bid illustration for a small residential installation job:

$ 3,000	Materials with sales tax
$ 2,000	Labor
$ 500	Labor burden of 25%
$ 1,000	Equipment costs
$ 6,500	Total direct costs
$ 2,000	G&A overhead allocated to the job
$ 8,500	Break-even point
$ 1,500	Net profit margin
$10,000	Price for the job

Use our two methods to calculate GPM.

1. GPM = Price – COGS or $10,000 – $6,500 = $3,500 or 35%
2. GPM = G&A overhead + net profit margin or $2,000 + $1,500 = $3,500 or 35%

GPM MARKET TRENDS

Gross profit margin is the best indicator of what's happening in your market.

Gross profit margin is the best indicator of what's happening in your market. This may be not only a geographical market, but also a market segment within a particular geographical market. For instance, high-end residential installation in the Greater San Francisco market may be slowing down considerably, while commercial maintenance in the same area is booming.

GPM reflects the supply-and-demand curve.

Basically, GPM reflects the supply-and-demand curve. In a "hot" economy there's more than enough work for qualified contractors to perform. A limited number of qualified contractors are pursuing a market with excessive amounts of work available. It's not uncommon for customers to be more concerned with getting on your schedule than they are with price.

This was generally the common theme for installation work around the country from the late 1990s through 2000. "When can you start?" was one of the main concerns, if not the top one, for potential clients. This hot market drove margins and prices up.

This all changed in 2001 when the stock market corrections hit many high-end residential markets in full force. Potential clients were much more timid and began to shop around more and more. Here, you had a limited amount of work being pursued by an excessive number of qualified contractors. This "soft" market drove prices and margins down.

During the mid-1990s, we began to see gross profit margins increase for almost all types of work throughout the country. Gross profit margins dropped to recessionary levels in many parts of the country almost overnight when the recession started (in the late 1980s and early 1990s). Some areas didn't even experience the recession. For areas hit by it, it took years to return to normal levels.

Around 1994 I had a discussion with Rick Randall, president of Randall & Blake, Inc. of Littleton, Colorado. RBI, now part of American Civil Constructors, is a large environmental contractor that does work throughout the western half of the United States. At that time, Rick told me there was plenty of work but that prices (margins) had not risen yet. As the economy continued to improve, margins and prices improved as well.

The following GPM ranges are for a "normal to hot" economy. Your GPM range may vary slightly.

Residential Installation	30 to 40%
Commercial Installation	
a. Normal to hot	20 to 30%
b. Negotiated work	25 to 35%
c. Competitive bid work	20 to 25%
Commercial and Residential Maintenance	30 to 40%
Irrigation Service	40 to 50%
General Tree Work (all)	30 to 40%
Chemical Applications (all)	40 to 50%
Lighting	40 to 50%
Christmas Decorations	40 to 50%

The following GPM ranges are for a "recessionary" economy. Again, your GPM may vary.

Residential Installation	20 to 30%
Commercial Installation	
d. Recessions	15 to 25%
e. Negotiated work	20 to 25%
f. Competitive bid work	15 to 20%
Commercial and Residential Maintenance	25 to 35%
Irrigation Service	30 to 40%
General Tree Work (all)	20 to 30%
Chemical Applications (all)	35 to 45%
Lighting	30 to 40%
Christmas Decorations	30 to 40%

EVALUATING A BUSINESS WITH GPM

How It Works

A large irrigation contractor in the Midwest was approached independently by the owners of two separate irrigation companies about buying them out. Sales for these two companies were in the $300,000 to $400,000 range. The mix of service and installation work for both companies was split about evenly.

After signing and exchanging the appropriate documents, the first thing my client, the prospective buyer, did was to determine the gross profit margin for these companies over a two- to three-year period. To do so, he took the profit and loss (P&L) statements from the two companies and reformatted them to clearly and accurately identify costs of goods sold, G&A overhead, and net profit. Upon completion of this exercise my client could compare the ratios for the information on the two sets of P&Ls to determine if they fell within normal standards for the industry. If they did, he could then confidently proceed to put a price on these companies.

There are a number of ways to evaluate a business and structure a buyout. Analyzing the GPM structure is one way to do so.

There are a number of ways to evaluate a business and structure a buyout. Analyzing the GPM structure is one way to do so. Market observations (helping a number of clients buy and sell businesses) indicate that the fair market value (FMV) for the "goodwill" or "blue sky" value of a service or maintenance business is approximately equal to its gross profit for one year. By goodwill or blue sky, I mean the value of the business apart from any of its assets.

Assets such as inventory, equipment, and real estate are evaluated separately and usually at fair market value. By fair market value I mean the value of an asset on the open market under current market conditions. For instance, when placing the value on a piece of equipment you could ask your local equipment dealer to provide you with its FMV. Because your dealer probably buys and/or sells used equipment, he'll probably have a pretty good idea what it sells for. This is fair market value. You could also determine the FMV for a piece of equipment by placing a for-sale sign on it and putting it in your front yard. The price you get for it is its FMV. Personally, I'd talk to the equipment dealer first.

Theories abound as to why one year of gross profit is the fair market value for goodwill for a service or maintenance business. Here are some reasons why I believe it's used.

- It's an easy, objective number to calculate.
- It's a number easily compared to industry standards.
- Buyers believe they can maintain the sales and gross profit margins and pay for the purchased company in one year (two to three years, at the very most).
- Buyers believe that their G&A overhead costs won't increase in proportion to the increased sales resulting from the purchase. Thus, the GPM on the increased sales for the purchased company will mostly be free and clear net profit that the buyer can apply to the purchase price, if desired.
- Two years of gross profit just seems like too much to pay for blue sky or goodwill.

How It Works

A large commercial maintenance contractor in New England was bidding on a $450,000+ contract in a recessionary market. He decided to bid it with a GPM near 28%. This was just above his break-even point (total direct costs plus G&A overhead costs). His theory was that if he won this job his G&A overhead for the company would not increase significantly.

Therefore, much of this 28% gross profit would actually be additional net profit for his company. Because he'd been monitoring the gross profit margins on his bids for some time, he knew a 28% GPM would be very competitive in his market and would probably win this contract for him. This strategy worked; he won the bid and it did help his bottom line.

For a number of years prior to the 2002 Winter Olympics, a mid-sized commercial installation company in Utah was realizing net profit margins in the vicinity of the high teens to low 20% range. A number of very large contractors came into the Utah market to pursue work related to the Olympics. However, the additional supply of qualified contractors doing commercial work didn't affect this contractor. There was plenty of work for everybody.

Most of the big boys left town after the Winter Olympics work was completed—all of them except one. As the amount of commercial installation work fell, this 800-pound gorilla began grabbing market share, thus driving margins down considerably. Until this company decides to leave town or increases the margins on their bids, or until the supply of work increases significantly, this market won't experience the margins it did in the 1990s.

SUMMARY

Gross profit margin is a critical concept for the serious estimator and contractor to understand. It's one of the most important tools an estimator has. It will provide the savvy business person with an "absolute" benchmark of sorts for measuring his or her bids against those of competitors.

GPM basically reflects the supply-and-demand curve. As the supply of work remains constant and the number of legitimate contractors increases, prices and margins will decrease. Conversely, as the supply of work increases and the number of legitimate contractors remains the same, prices and margins will increase. Essentially, gross profit margin is the best indicator of what's happening in your market because it reflects market conditions. On entering a recession, contractors often respond with knee-jerk reactions and start bidding jobs at their break-even point.

GPM is also a very helpful tool to use when evaluating the goodwill or blue-sky portion of a service or maintenance business. For whatever reason, one year of gross profit is the going rate or fair market value for the goodwill for such a business.

ACTION POINT

Review the GPM on bids that you have already completed. Do this for jobs that you have lost as well as for ones that you have won. Look for patterns and try to identify trends in the amount of GPM in your bids. You should also review the actual GPM achieved on the jobs that your crews have performed and completed in the field.

Compare the results of your analysis with the industry benchmarks discussed in this chapter, Chapter 46, and those contained in Appendix E.

CHAPTER

38

The Six Most Common Methods for Pricing Jobs

TERMS

Dual Overhead Recovery System (DORS)
Factoring Method
Hindsight Markup Factor
Market-Driven Unit Pricing (MDUP)
Multiple Overhead Recovery System (MORS)
Multiplier Method
Overhead and Profit Per Hour (OPPH)
Single Overhead Recovery System (SORS)

Purpose

To explain the six most commonly used methods in the market today for pricing Green Industry work

Introduction

Estimating is the science of determining what a project costs. Once we identify these costs, we then add margins and markups to arrive at a final price for the project. *Bidding* is the process of adding margins and markups to the identified costs of a project to arrive at a *final price.*

There are many methods used to price jobs. We'll cover six common ones used today in the marketplace. The important thing to keep in mind is to first correctly identify all costs, both direct and indirect. This determines the break-even point for a job. Then you add net profit and a contingency factor (if used) to the break-even point.

As we begin our analysis of these six methods we'll refer to the two jobs in Table 38-1 on page 282, which will serve as examples.

THE FACTORING OR "MULTIPLIER" METHOD

Using the **factoring method**, sometimes called the **multiplier method**, we simply multiply estimated material costs (or estimated material and labor costs) by a "factor." The factor may be based on past Profit & Loss statements or may be a number arrived at as a result of monitoring past competitive bidding situations.

The rationale is: If you ended a previous calendar or fiscal year with a sufficient net profit and if material costs were 33% of your gross sales for that year, then all you have to do is multiply material costs for the new year by a factor of 3.0. Supposedly, this will produce prices that will cover all costs and ensure sufficient net profit.

Sales taxes, field-labor burden, net profit, and G&A overhead are all included in the factor used. A contingency factor may be applied to the job if desired. However, that's not always the case.

TABLE 38-1 Information for Jobs A and B

	Job A	Job B	
Materials	$100,000	$40,000	
Labor with labor burden	15,000	60,000	
Equipment	5,000	20,000	
Subcontractors	0	0	
Total direct costs	$120,000	$120,000	
G&A OPH	$10.00	$10.00	
PPH (if used)	$ 5.00	$ 5.00	
Labor hours	1,000	4,000	
CAW w/33% labor burden	$15.00	$15.00	
Total company G&A overhead per calendar month			$10,000
Total company field payroll per calendar month with labor burden			$15,000
Job A duration			One calendar month
Job B duration			Four calendar months

The flaws in this method are almost too numerous to mention, but it's surprising how many landscape and irrigation contractors bid their work using this "material-times-two" approach.

The flaws in this method are almost too numerous to mention, but it's surprisng how many landscape and irrigation contractors bid their work using this "material-times-two" approach. The only variables that are addressed in this method are

- The amount of materials
- The factor

Unfortunately, it doesn't address many of the other variables that can, and usually do, apply to the jobs you bid. Some of the many items that may change from job to job and that need to be dealt with separately in the estimating process are

- General conditions
- Net profit markup
- Site conditions (soil conditions, access, time of year/weather, etc.)
- Expensive vs. inexpensive materials (with the same labor production rates)
- Size of crew
- Types of equipment
- Subcontractors
- Labor rates

The factoring method has its roots in the retail (as well as wholesale) supplier industry. To arrive at the price to charge customers, purchased goods are marked up by a "factor" or "multiplier." This method is commonly used by smaller, unsophisticated nurseries that must purchase the bulk of their nursery stock and irrigation supplies.

Because these smaller companies don't experience the wild fluctuations in types of materials, labor, equipment, subcontractors, site conditions, and so forth, this uncomplicated method can work in a very non-dynamic situation. However, once you leave this extremely controlled environment and enter the landscape and irrigation contracting arena where chaos tends to be the norm, the factoring method immediately breaks down.

Unfortunately, it's usually the owners of nurseries who fall victim to this mistake when, instead of just selling plants and supplies, they decide to install these plants for their customers. Factoring worked for them in the past in the nursery business. Why not use it for contracting?

Irrigation suppliers tend to reinforce the application of this pricing method in the landscape and irrigation industry. That is, in some parts of the country, irrigation vendors obtain sets of plans for work being bid in their area. They then do the takeoff and provide irrigation takeoff quantities and costs to the various contractors bidding on the job.

This is bad enough, but pricing advice (in the form of suggested factors) is often offered as well—saying, for instance, that residential irrigation systems may have a suggested factor of 2.0 to 2.2 while commercial work has one ranging from 1.8 to 2.0, or that the suggested factor for golf course materials may range as low as 1.65 to 1.8. Unfortunately, these factors have little to do with specific jobs. They only address general trends.

Even CPAs sometimes enter the factor-pricing picture (though, more often than not, their recommendations lean toward the GPM method).

My point is this: Pricing methods vary in their application. Some methods work well in one environment, but not in another. Factoring may be of limited use in a retail or supplier/vendor environment–but not in contracting. *Do not* use it to determine your prices.

There is, however, another tool called a **hindsight markup factor** we use to help evaluate our competition. We call it hindsight because we calculate it *after* we've priced the job correctly, having taken into account all costs and markups. In your next competitive bid situation

- Determine your Phases I and II direct costs
- Add the appropriate markups and margins to determine your price
- Divide the price by the material costs

This will give you your "hindsight" markup factor.

If your competitors are using the factoring method, track their bids and attempt to determine the factors they're using.

How It Works

A commercial irrigation client tracked a competitor's bids and discovered the competitor was consistently using a 2.05 multiplier. Once our client had identified the factor, he was able to adjust his own bids to beat it. He knew he could reduce his net profit margin only slightly to beat his competitor's 2.05 factor, and not hurt himself by doing so.

The decision to lower his price was based on sound analysis, accurate budgeting and estimating systems, and methodologies, not on some subjective factor. He knew he could play his competitor's game, beat him and survive. He cut his price, not his throat.

Another client, on the East Coast, was bidding a planting job. Plant materials on this job cost $6,000. With a 10 percent net profit margin (NPM), the estimate would total right at $10,000. It was a good bid, and he was confident of his production rates and price. However, he knew his competitors were using factoring for their pricing method (material-times-two). Their price would be around $12,000. Our client doubled his NPM, won the bid, and put an extra $1,000 in his pocket.

Let's return to Table 38-1 at the beginning of this chapter. If we use this "mythical" method of material times a factor of two, our price for jobs A and B are $200,000 and $80,000, respectively. Table 38-2 shows us how the arithmetic works out using the factoring method. As we build on these two bids and continue our analysis of the other five common methods of pricing work, the flaws of factoring will become quite apparent.

TABLE 38-2 Pricing Jobs A and B Using the Factoring Method

	Job A	Job B
Material Costs	$100,000	$40,000
Factor	× 2.0	× 2.0
Price	$200,000	$80,000

THE GROSS PROFIT MARGIN OR SINGLE G&A OVERHEAD RECOVERY SYSTEM METHOD

There are a number of popular derivatives of the GPM or **Single Overhead Recovery System (SORS)** approach to pricing, and there's often some historical basis for using these adaptations. Although this method has some merits and applications, virtually all these positives are only useful when they are incorporated into other more accurate and flexible estimating methods. Like factoring, the GPM/SORS method is useful for the purposes of "hindsight" analysis. Some of the popular applications of the GPM/SORS markup approach are discussed in the following paragraphs.

The 1/3, 1/3, 1/3 Rule

Although the specific fractions may change, their use is the same. The estimator, after reviewing past Profit & Loss statements (or recollecting from past experience—either his own or that of a trusted "source"), determines that material costs have comprised approximately 33% of gross sales (plus or minus 1 or 2%). Labor with burden and (possibly) equipment costs account for another 33% (+/–). The remaining 33% covers equipment costs (if not combined with labor), G&A overhead, and net profit.

Although we ***do not*** recommend this method, this is how to implement it.

1. First, determine material costs and assume that they "should" comprise one-third (or some other predetermined percentage) of the final price for the job.
2. Then add labor, labor burden, and possibly equipment costs (these "should" be roughly equal to material costs) to material costs. In this case, you double your material costs, and the result is roughly 66% of the price of the job.
3. Equipment costs (if not included with labor), G&A overhead, and net profit make up the remaining 34% of the total price for the job.

Using our two jobs as an example, the results would be as shown in Table 38-3.

➤ **NOTE** This specific example is not included in Table 38-9, Analysis of Jobs A and B, shown on page 302.

TABLE 38-3 Pricing Jobs A and B Using the GPM Method (A)

	Job A		Job B	
Material costs	$100,000	33.3%	$40,000	33.3%
Labor burden and equipment	100,000	33.3%	40,000	33.3%
Subtotal	$200,000	66.6%	$80,000	66.6%
G&A overhead and net profit	$100,000	33.3%	$ 40,000	33.3%
Total price	$300,000	100.0%	$120,000	100.0%

The GPM Markup Method

Although similar to the previous technique, the GPM markup method requires more homework. You must first accurately identify specific costs for material, labor, equipment (unless included in labor or in G&A overhead), and subcontractors. Sales taxes are then added to materials, and labor burden is added to field payroll. You then mark up the total according to a predetermined (or desired) gross net profit margin.

Using our examples, the process is shown in Table 38-4.

TABLE 38-4 Pricing Jobs A and B Using the GPM Method (B)

	Job A	Job B
Direct costs M/L/E/S	$120,000	$120,000
GPM markup (30%)	× 1.3	× 1.3
Total price	$156,000	$156,000

Another commonly used mathematical formula is as follows:

Jobs A and B

Divide the direct costs in M/L/E/S by 1.0 minus the GPM desired.

$120,000 ÷ (1.0 – .3) = $120,000 ÷ .7 = $171,429

Or, to adjust the formula to arrive at our original price of $156,000

a. Divide 1.0 by the sum of 1 plus the desired GPM (30%).

1.0 ÷ (1.0 + .3) = 1.0 ÷ 1.3 = .7692

b. Divide total direct costs by .7692.

$120,000 ÷ .7692 = $156,006

The pitfall of the GPM markup method is what happens to direct costs (M/L/E/S) once you calculate and identify them. Our two examples will help you understand the inherent error.

Jobs A and B both have the same direct costs. Assuming our company field payroll is $15,000 per month (including labor burden), Job A consists of one month of payroll while Job B consists of four months of payroll.

If net profit is 10% ($12,000) of the 30% GPM markup on both jobs, that leaves only $24,000 for G&A overhead—the remaining 20% of the GPM markup.

Both jobs would then have $24,000 included in the bid to cover G&A overhead costs. Utilizing the company's entire field-labor force, Job A will last one month. Accordingly, Job B will last four months—$60,000 job payroll (with burden) divided by the monthly payroll (with burden) of $15,000—but G&A overhead in the bid ($24,000) for a four-month job is the same as a one-month job. Job B should have four times more G&A overhead than Job A has, because it lasts four times longer.

The GPM/SORS markup method has a serious flaw (the duration of the job)–one that has proven fatal (or nearly so) to many contractors.

The GPM/SORS markup method has a serious flaw in this area—one that has proven fatal (or nearly so) to many contractors.

THE MARKET-DRIVEN UNIT PRICING METHOD

Don't make the mistake of assuming there's something inherently wrong with organizing and presenting an estimate in a unit-price format. The format is not the issue. The issue is the process (or lack of process) used to arrive at your unit price(s).

If correctly calculated, unit prices can provide considerable insight into an estimate and plenty of ammunition at the bid table when it's time to negotiate. For this reason, every time I bid a project on the computer the computer is programmed to simultaneously provide pricing in both a lump-sum and a unit-price format.

However, the prices are calculated after all costs for M/L/E/S, general conditions, and accurate markups are included in the estimate. These unit prices are then compared to ones normally found on the open market (e.g., so much for a 1-, 5-, or 15-gallon shrub or tree; $1 per square foot for sod, hydroseed at $.05 per square foot; $18 per man-hour for maintenance work; walls or fences at so much per linear foot; irrigation systems at $.60 or $.90 per square foot).

However, contractors who rely solely on the **market-driven unit pricing (MDUP)** method seriously shortcut the estimating and planning process. In turn, they short-circuit their business systems. Key information and data needed to direct and control individual jobs (as well as the entire company or division) are just not available. As a result, meaningful job costing isn't possible, and the company lurches forward in a fog.

It's hard to imagine an "estimating" method of less use in helping to run a company than factoring, but the market-driven unit pricing method is totally uselss.

It's hard to imagine an "estimating" method of less use in helping to run a company than factoring, but the market-driven unit pricing method is totally useless. Factoring, at least, requires that you build on the foundation of material costs. The MDUP system operates totally independent of any relevant data, budgets, costs, or strategic planning. Taxes, labor burden, G&A overhead, a contingency factor, and net profit are all "supposed" to be included in the market-driven unit price. Unfortunately, that's rarely the case.

How It Works

To illustrate the problem, let's suppose you've decided to enter the auto industry—GM, Ford, Chrysler, and Toyota move over. Your first model will be a half-ton pickup truck, of course! In order to cut G&A overhead, you decide to work from home and build the first production model in your garage. You have no idea (a) what your costs will be to build a truck, (b) how to determine your costs, or (c) how much you should charge for it. Your solution? Since you have to prove yourself first, you decide to sell it for a little less than comparable models already on the market.

No budgets! No planning! No cost data! No tracking system! No scoreboard! Just how long do you think you'll last?

The question isn't whether you can produce the truck (let's assume you can). It's not whether the other manufacturers can survive by selling trucks at the market-driven unit price for your type of production model. *The question is*: Can you organize and run your company in such a way that you can survive (and make money) by competing with the established market price?

Survival in the auto industry or any industry requires much more than a price (especially more than one arrived at by someone else). It requires

- An accurate *price*
- A well thought-out *plan*
- A self-correcting *process*

Don't be tricked or lulled into thinking a landscape and irrigation contractor can survive on anything less.

THE DUAL G&A OVERHEAD RECOVERY SYSTEM

Chapter 39 contains a thorough explanation of the **Dual Overhead Recovery System (DORS)** method. Some of the key points are discussed in brief in the following paragraphs.

The DORS method utilizes two elements of cost of goods sold—materials and labor with labor burden—and multiplies them by predetermined percentages. Costs for equipment owned by the company are included in indirect G&A overhead costs. Subcontractor costs are usually marked up separately. The markup percentages on the two cost-of-goods-sold items are calculated as follows:

$$\text{G\&A overhead markup on material costs} = \frac{\text{Total annual G\&A overhead}}{[(\text{OWF}) \times (\text{Labor \& burden})] + \text{Materials}}$$

$$\text{G\&A overhead markup on labor costs} = \frac{(\text{OWF}) \times (\text{Total annual G\&A overhead})}{[(\text{OWF}) \times (\text{Labor \& burden})] + \text{Materials}}$$

OWF is a G&A overhead weighting factor which is obtained from a chart.

The markups for the example company in Chapter 39 on page 316 work out as follows:

$$\text{G\&A overhead markup on material costs} = \frac{\$192{,}000}{[(2.56) \times (\$156{,}000)] + \$180{,}000}$$

$$= \frac{\$192{,}000}{\$579{,}360} = .33140$$

This is 33.14%. You'd round this up to .332 or 33.2%.

$$\text{G\&A overhead markup on labor costs} = \frac{(2.56) \times (\$192{,}000)}{[(2.56) \times (\$156{,}000)] + \$180{,}000}$$

$$= \frac{\$491{,}520}{\$579{,}360} = .848384$$

This is 84.84%. You'd round this to .85 or 85%.

Turning to our sample jobs, we can calculate a price for these jobs using the DORS method. These calculations are shown in Table 38-5 on page 288.

Advantages of the DORS Method

- It is mathematically based. Therefore, its mathematical assumptions can be tested and proved or disproved.
- It is based on company historical financial data.

- It acknowledges the errors in factoring, market-driven unit pricing, and the GPM/SORS methods and attempts to correct them.
- It attempts to allocate G&A overhead costs based on intangible job factors.
- Most costs are clearly identified in the estimating process.

TABLE 38-5 Pricing Jobs A and B Using the DORS Method

Job A

	Direct Costs		G&A Overhead %		G&A Markup
Materials (with sales tax)	$100,000	×	33.2%	=	$33,200
Labor with labor burden	15,000	×	85.0%	=	12,750
Equipment with rentals*	N/A	×	N/A	=	0
Subcontractors	0	×	N/A	=	0
Total	**$115,000**				**$45,950**

Total direct costs	$115,000
Total G&A overhead to recover on job	45,950
Break-even point (BEP)	$160,950
Net profit markup (10%)	16,095
Price for job	**$177,045**

Job B

	Direct Costs		G&A Overhead %		G&A Markup
Materials (with sales tax)	$ 40,000	×	33.2%	=	$13,280
Labor with labor burden	60,000	×	85.0%	=	51,000
Equipment with rentals*	N/A	×	N/A	=	0
Subcontractors	0	×	N/A	=	0
Total	**$100,000**				**$64,280**

Total direct costs	$100,000
Total G&A overhead to recover on job	64,280
Break-even point (BEP)	$164,280
Net profit markup (10%)	16,428
Price for job	**$180,708**

* Company owned equipment is included in the G&A overhead recovery percentages.

Disadvantages of the DORS Method

- It is extremely complex.
- The G&A overhead weighting factor (OWF) must be blindly accepted, without proof.
- Its basic assumptions in arithmetic can be disproved.
- Company-owned field equipment costs are included in G&A overhead and averaged into bids.
- Company-owned field equipment production rates are not identified in the bidding process.
- Estimating cost scenarios for varying company-owned field equipment production rates and their cost implications in individual bids isn't possible in the bidding process.
- Estimating cost scenarios considering the purchase of new field equipment and its implication on production rates and cost implications in individual bids isn't possible in the bidding process.
- While the DORS method addresses the M/L/E/S ratio problem (by using a multiple versus a single markup percent) that the SORS/GPM method does not, it treats *all* jobs throughout the year as if the mix of materials and labor were the same as your overall budget.

  Once you determine your labor and labor burden markup percent, it does not change until you recalculate your estimating G&A overhead budget. Consequently, you won't know until the end of the year if the amount of materials, labor and labor burden, equipment, and number of subcontractors used in your estimating budget were accurate. If they're not, your G&A overhead percent markup on labor and burden should have been higher or lower, depending upon the actual mix of direct costs.
- Prevailing wage projects present another problem. If you perform both prevailing wage and non-prevailing wage work, your labor and labor burden G&A overhead markup percentages for rated (prevailing wage) versus non-rated jobs should be different.
- Another shortcoming of the DORS method is that it's difficult to update and keep current. This is due in part to the fact that the G&A overhead recovered on jobs isn't easily accumulated, tracked, and compared to actual financial statements (that is, compared to the data generated by your accounting system). Additional calculations are required—calculations that are not inherent in the DORS estimating process.
- The DORS method is not easily and quickly adjusted. It is difficult to adapt to rapidly changing economies and/or special market situations with any degree of certainty. You can make adjustments to your G&A overhead markup percentages for materials and field labor, but due to the vast number of variables we've discussed, it's difficult to apply them accurately or with confidence.

The DORS method's basic assumptions in arithmetic can be disproved.

Table 38-9 shown on page 302 displays how the prices calculated according to the DORS method fall in line with the other estimating methods.

THE MULTIPLE G&A OVERHEAD RECOVERY SYSTEM OR "TRADITIONAL" METHOD

The **Multiple G&A Overhead Recovery System (MORS)** method of pricing projects has gained popularity in recent years and is being taught in estimating workshops throughout North America. In fact, I taught it in workshops in the late 1980s and early 1990s.

This method can have distinct advantages over the previous systems, but it also has definite disadvantages. It's overly complex, and it's difficult to make adjustments for varying market conditions. This becomes a particular liability in periods of rapid market change.

The MORS method can and should be firmly grounded on accurate historical data, current financial statements, well-thought-out estimating G&A overhead budgets, projected sales, and direct costs for the upcoming budget year.

Let's discuss how it works. Figure 2-2 shown in Chapter 2 provides an overview of the MORS method. M/L/E/S direct costs for both production items and general conditions are clearly identified in Phases I and II on the figure.

The MORS Method is overly complex, and it's difficult to make adjustments for varying market conditions. This becomes a particular liability in periods of rapid market change.

It must be understood, however, that if you do an inaccurate takeoff, miscalculate labor or equipment production rates, or miss other important site conditions or other bidding variables, then the most perfect of estimating systems will be of little help. You *must do your homework* and do it accurately!

Once you've calculated the costs for Phases I and II, you then add the following markups:

Sales Tax is added to materials.

➤ **NOTE** Some states now add sales tax not only to materials, but also to the entire job, just as though you were to add another 5 to 6% net profit to the whole job.

Labor Burden is then added to direct labor costs.

G&A Overhead is calculated (as described below).

Net Profit is added to the job based on a straight percentage markup on the total of all aforementioned costs.

Finally, a *Contingency Factor* is added, if desired.

Up to now, the MORS method is fairly straightforward. It's in G&A overhead recovery that the system begins to break down.

G&A Overhead

G&A overhead is recovered (added to a bid) by marking up the direct cost totals for Phases I and II by predetermined percentages.

- Material costs are usually marked up 10%.
- Field equipment costs are usually marked up 25%.
- Subcontractor costs are usually marked up 5%.

These percentages may vary in some applications, but normally remain as stated above.

The cornerstone of the MORS method is the percentage that labor (combined with labor burden) is marked up for G&A overhead recovery. Some of these percentages are as follows

- Large commercial companies (over $1.5 million in sales) usually range from 25% to 45%.
- Mid-sized companies ($750,000 to $1.5 million in sales) doing commercial and residential work usually range from 45% to 65%.
- Smaller (under $500,000) residential and commercial companies, or larger ($1 million plus) high-end residential companies, usually range from 65% to 100%.

Keep in mind that these percentage markups on labor will greatly vary from company to company, depending on the type of market served and the structure of the company. They should not be used without taking these other factors into consideration.

To determine the construction division labor and labor burden G&A overhead markup percentage, take the following steps:

- First, project a complete budget (sales, direct costs, and G&A overhead).
- Second, multiply direct costs (except for labor and labor burden) by their predetermined percentages (5, 10, and 25%).

Calculate and total projected G&A overhead recovered from materials, equipment, and subcontractors. For our example company on page 316 of Chapter 39, it works as follows:

	Budget Projection		MORS %		G&A Overhead to Recover
Material costs	$180,000	×	10%	=	$18,000
Equipment costs	72,000	×	25%	=	18,000
Subcontractor costs	12,000	×	5%	=	600
Subtotal					**$36,600**

Subtract the subtotal above from the total company or division G&A overhead to recover.

Total CO/DIV G&A overhead to recover for year	$120,000
Projected G&A overhead to recover from M/E/S	– 36,600
Remaining G&A overhead to recover from labor & burden	$ 83,400

Determine the labor and labor burden markup percentage to be used in estimating by dividing the remaining G&A overhead to recover by the projected company/division field-labor payroll plus labor burden.

$$\frac{\text{Remaining G\&A overhead to recover}}{\text{Projected annual labor and burden}} \qquad \frac{\$83,400}{\$156,000} = .5346 \text{ or } 54.0\%$$

The resulting percentage (in our example, 54%) provides the bidding G&A overhead markup percentage for the construction division labor and labor burden. Applying these percentages and the MORS method to our two examples in Table 38-1 will produce prices for the jobs as indicated in Table 38-6 on page 292.

As you can see, using a 54% versus a 30% G&A overhead markup on labor and labor burden would make a considerable difference on the final price. The 24% spread would be caused primarily by the economies of scale a larger company enjoys over a smaller one. The competitive advantage of the larger company is significant.

The company using the 54% markup is the one with combined gross sales under $1.0 million, while a larger company's markup will be below 54%.

Advantages of the MORS Method

The advantages of the MORS method are many, *if* it's based on accurate takeoff data and production rates, and a thorough job-site condition analysis.

- It can be based on historical data for your specific company.
- Direct COGS costs are clearly identified.

- Gross profit margin (GPM) is clearly identified.
- G&A overhead recovery is clearly identified.
- Net profit markup is clearly identified.
- It can be budget-driven. Progress can be measured against a predetermined budget/set of standards.

TABLE 38-6 Pricing Jobs A and B Using the MORS Method

Job A

	Direct Costs		G&A Overhead %		G&A Markup
Materials (with sales tax)	$100,000	×	10%	=	$10,000
Labor with labor burden	15,000	×	54%	=	8,100
Equipment with rentals	5,000	×	25%	=	1,250
Subcontractors	0	×	5%	=	0
Total	**$120,000**				**$19,350**

Total direct costs	$120,000
Total G&A overhead to recover on job	19,350
Break-even point (BEP)	$139,350
Net profit markup (10%)	13,935
Price for job	**$153,285**

Job B

	Direct Costs		G&A Overhead %		G&A Markup
Materials (with sales tax)	$40,000	×	10%	=	$ 4,000
Labor with labor burden	60,000	×	54%	=	32,400
Equipment with rentals*	20,000	×	25%	=	5,000
Subcontractors	0	×	5%	=	0
Total	**$120,000**				**$41,400**

Total direct costs	$120,000
Total G&A overhead to recover on job	41,400
Break-even point (BEP)	$161,400
Net profit markup (10%)	16,140
Price for job	**$177,540**

- It can help you plan and run the field during actual production. Since you're required to build the job step by step in your mind and on paper the way you'll build it in the field, the MORS method provides an excellent process for collecting the data needed to plan and to run the field during the project.
- It makes meaningful job costing possible. The MORS method provides M/L/E/S cost data, as well as hours for labor and equipment for budget-to-actual comparisons.

The advantages of the MORS method over factoring and the MDUP method should be obvious. The MORS method also has a distinct advantage over the SORS/GPM method, one that can be seen in Tables 38-3 and 38-4. The MORS method compensates for the M/L/E/S ratios within direct costs, while the SORS/GPM method generally does not.

In Figure 38-4, the price for both Jobs A and B was $156,000 because the direct costs for both were $120,000. The SORS/GPM method considers the M/L/E/S mix or ratios on a job equally. The MORS method varies the G&A overhead markup percent for each separate component of direct costs. It's more flexible and, therefore, more accurate.

Disadvantages of the MORS Method

Indeed, the MORS pricing method has its strengths, *but* it also has a considerable number of weaknesses that need to be considered, which make it an undesirable method for estimating.

- The main disadvantage is that it's very complex. Adjusting or adapting it to the various scenarios you may encounter (T&M, prevailing wage, rapidly changing markets, recessions, etc.) is tricky to say the least.
- While the MORS method addresses the M/L/E/S ratio problem by using a multiple-versus a single-markup percent (unlike the SORS/GPM method), it treats *all* jobs throughout the year as if the mix of materials, labor, equipment, and subcontractors were the same as your overall budget.

  Once you determine your labor and labor burden markup percent (for instance, 54% in our example), it doesn't change until you recalculate your estimating G&A overhead budget. Consequently, you won't know until the end of the year if the amount of materials, labor and labor burden, equipment, and subcontractors used in your estimating budget were accurate. If they were not, your G&A overhead percent markup on labor and burden should have been higher or lower, depending on the actual mix of direct costs.
- Another serious drawback of the MORS method is the "traditional" markups that are applied to materials, equipment, and subcontractors: traditionally 10%, 25%, and 5%, respectively. These percentages have no clear analytical basis. In and of themselves, they're (at best) "guesstimates." They're like factors and market-driven unit prices. Sometime in the past, for some job, they might have been accurate—but only for a specific company on a specific job within a particular year.

  How do you know you should mark up materials by 10% for G&A overhead recovery? Answers to that question range from "It's the customary market markup" to "It should cover your costs for ordering and processing materials." You'll even hear "It's what's taught" and "It's convenient."

  These percentages may be close to being accurate, but accurate percentages don't remain the same (10%, 25%, and 5%) from application to application and from job to job. Nor do they often come in such neat, rounded numbers as 10.0, 25.0, or 5.0. These numbers are just too "canned."

- Another disadvantage of the MORS method is that the M/L/E/S G&A overhead markup percentages used to bid jobs have little or no analytical justification when applied to T&M (time and material) job situations. For instance, if there are no materials involved in a T&M job, should you use the same G&A overhead markup percentage as determined on your yearly G&A overhead estimating budget (e.g., in our budget 54%)? Or should you increase it? If so, by how much?
- Prevailing wage projects present another problem. If you perform both prevailing wage and non-prevailing wage work, your labor and labor burden G&A overhead markup percentages for rated (prevailing wage) versus non-rated jobs should be different. For instance, if your G&A overhead markup percentage on labor and labor burden for non-rated jobs with a CAW of $10 is 36%, it would drop to 18% for rated jobs with a CAW of $20.

  This scenario is compounded if your original projected estimating budget contains a yearly field-labor payroll amount consisting of both prevailing and non-prevailing wage labor. If it does, your labor and labor burden G&A overhead markup percentages calculated on your estimating budget become an average percentage. Consequently, it's too high for prevailing wage jobs and too low for jobs performed at non-prevailing wage rates. You've sacrificed accuracy, competitiveness, or both. If, in your projected estimating budget, your ratio of non-prevailing wage and prevailing wage labor differs from the ratio of work you actually do for the year, your G&A overhead markup percentages on labor and labor burden would have been wrong, anyway.
- Another shortcoming of the MORS method is that it's difficult to update and keep current. This is due in part to the fact that the G&A overhead recovered on jobs isn't easily accumulated, tracked, and compared to actual financial statements (that is, compared to the data generated by your accounting system). Additional calculations are required—calculations that are not inherent in the MORS estimating process.
- The MORS method isn't easily and quickly adjusted. It's difficult to adapt to rapidly changing economies and/or special market situations with any degree of certainty. You can make adjustments to your G&A overhead markup percentages, but due to the vast number of variables we've discussed, it's difficult to apply them accurately or with confidence.

How It Works

The MORS method actually lost a client of mine $500,000 worth of work. He was using the MORS method before I introduced him to the OPPH method. After we prepared his budgets and had calculated the appropriate numbers/percentages, we re-bid some large jobs he'd lost the previous season. Using his numbers and the OPPH method, we found he could have won those jobs, covered all his costs, and made money. However, because the MORS method he was using was too inaccurate and complex, he didn't take his "best shot" at the bid table.

The Fallacy of Recovering G&A Overhead Utilizing Percentages

The MORS, DORS, and the SORS/GPM methods each contain a *fatal flaw*, which renders them ineffective. They contain a basic mathematical relational error. All three attempt to directly correlate the amount of G&A overhead dollars to add onto a job to the amount of direct costs in the job by means of one or a combination of percentages (or factor/multipliers). However, there's no such correlation (factor) between these two items. Let me explain by using two items that *do* directly correlate.

The amount of a workers' compensation insurance (WCI) premium is directly correlated (in direct proportion) to payroll by means of a rate per hundred dollars of payroll (e.g., $7 per hundred). This translates to a decimal of .07 or 7%. If annual payroll doubles from $50,000 to $100,000, the WCI premium doubles from $3,500 to $7,000. If payroll decreases, premiums decrease *in direct proportion* to the decrease. The percentage factor (or multiplier) remains constant but it *accurately links* premiums to payroll.

This is a *legitimate mathematical relationship* for calculating the cost of WCI. Premiums (actual real costs) are *always* in direct relation to payroll. Premiums and payroll are always linked by means of the same factor—the percentage. Sales tax on materials and GLI premiums are also examples of costs that are directly correlated to other costs by means of a multiplier.

Unfortunately, there's no such direct link (or multiplier) between the components involved in the MORS, DORS, and the SORS/GPM G&A overhead recovery methods. There is simply *no direct correlation* linking costs for G&A overhead and direct costs for a job in the field. Consequently, attempting to tie the two together by means of a single (SORS), dual (DORS), or multiple (MORS) multiplier—which never changes, because it's so complex and rigid—is automatically flawed, because there's no "multiplier" that accurately links the two. Attempting to link G&A overhead to direct costs by means of a percentage multiplier is simply too inflexible and inaccurate for the dynamic business of landscape and irrigation contracting.

The MORS, DORS, and the SORS/GPM methods are simply other versions of "materials-times-two," or factoring, dressed up in fancy terminology. The MORS method especially is just too complex and intrinsically inflexible. Fortunately, there's an easier method.

The MORS, DORS, and the SORS/GPM methods are simply other versions of "materials-times-two," or factoring, dressed up in fancy terminology. The MORS method especially is just too complex and intrinsically inflexible.

The alternative to the previous four methods discussed is to measure and allocate G&A overhead to jobs in terms of units of whole dollars—the OPH—in order to determine a break-even point (BEP). There is no need for percentage multipliers or factors. A GPM is calculated once a net profit margin is added to the BEP. This method is far more accurate than any of the other four; yet it is far simpler and easier to measure, monitor, manage, and control by means of per hour and ratio analysis calculated on the B.A.R. worksheet.

Let's get started!

THE G&A OVERHEAD AND NET PROFIT PER HOUR METHOD

Although not foolproof, the **Overhead and Profit per Hour (OPPH)** (or the Field-Labor Hour Recovery) pricing method provides considerable advantages over all the previous methods discussed.

Although not foolproof, the Overhead and Profit per Hour (OPPH) pricing method provides considerable advantages over all the previous methods discussed.

Advantages of the OPPH Method

- It begins by adding sales tax to materials and then adding labor burden to field payroll.
- It then becomes necessary to have a clearly identified G&A overhead amount on a company/division basis to recover for the year.
- The G&A overhead company/division amount is divided by the projected number of billable field-labor hours in the company/division to determine the G&A overhead per hour (OPH) dollar amount. The OPH for the budget example in Figure 3-1 is as follows on page 296:

Division	*OPH*
Lawn maintenance	$ 7.48
Installation	$14.25
Irrigation service	$14.29
Tree service	$13.43
Winter work	$16.37
Average for all divisions	$11.45

- G&A overhead is then allocated to projects on the basis of the number of field-labor hours estimated in each bid. For instance, a construction project that had 1,000 field-labor hours in Phases I and II of the bid would be marked up $14,250 for G&A overhead (1,000 hours × $14.25 OPH).

  There may be some slight variations, which we'll cover later, but this is essentially how it's done for G&A overhead recovery. The break-even point (BEP) is calculated once G&A overhead costs are added to the direct costs to include sales tax and labor burden.
- A net profit margin is then calculated and added onto the break-even point in one of two ways.

  1. To obtain a true net profit margin: Divide the BEP by 1.0 minus your desired net profit percent. A 10% net profit margin is calculated as follows:

     BEP ÷ (1.0 – .1) = BEP ÷ .9 = Price

     or
  2. You can determine your net profit margin by multiplying the number of field-labor hours in the bid by a predetermined net profit per hour (PPH) dollar amount. This PPH comes from your estimating budget. See Figure 3-1.

     The PPH method has some significant advantages over the conventional wisdom that exists behind the percentage markup. However, I always compare both when I bid a project.

     First, you establish a predetermined company/division net profit for every billable field-labor hour that is to occur in the field. Just as in G&A overhead, we've tied net profit to field-labor hours. The PPH for the budget example in Figure 3-1 is as follows:

Division	*PPH*	*Round up/set to*
Lawn maintenance	$ 3.60	$ 3.60
Installation	$ 4.03	$ 6.00 (approx. 10% of SPH of $61.82)
Irrigation service	$ 4.42	$ 6.00 (approx. 10% of SPH of $62.06)
Tree service	$ 4.92	$ 6.00 (approx. 10% of SPH of $58.12)
Winter work	$18.20	$20.00
Avg. for all divisions	$ 4.63	$ 5.00 (approx. 10% of SPH of $49.65)

Second, we can approach the bid table with our PPH in the back of our mind—based on a total dollar amount of net profit we want to bring into the company or division over a one-year period. In Figure 3-1, this amount is $89,491 for all divisions; rounded off it's $90,000. Our thinking is, "Who cares how we get the $90,000, as long as we get it."

Third, when we review our bid and finalize our numbers, we may find the PPH (calculated at an approximate 10% net profit margin) on material-intensive jobs is actually quite different from our budget average. For instance, it can easily be \$8 to \$10 per field-labor hour, or almost double your budget average. If you can win the job with this much net profit on it, by all means do so.

However, we have to realize that (in our example) we could drop our PPH to as low as \$6 and still be on target regarding our desired net profit for the year. In this particular instance, a \$6 PPH may be only a 5% net profit margin on the job, but we won't hurt ourselves by using the lower amount.

Conventional wisdom can't see the fallacies and/or shortcomings of the percentage markup method for either net profit or G&A overhead. The percentage markups that are used in factoring the SORS, DORS, and MORS methods are just too inflexible.

The OPPH method addresses these problems in a very simple, yet effective manner. If desired, a contingency factor may be added to the job. First, though, there are two critical requisites attached to the OPPH method.

1. Projected company/division field-labor hours must be reasonably accurate (within plus or minus 10% of actual hours for the year).
2. G&A overhead costs *must* be correctly defined (as we did in Chapter 8).

➤ NOTE If you include items such as field equipment costs and field-labor burden items in G&A overhead that should be in direct costs for the job being bid—payroll taxes, general liability, workers' compensation insurance, etc.—you'll seriously distort the effectiveness and accuracy of *any* estimating system, including the OPPH method.

If these two requisites are accomplished, the OPPH method can be quite simple, extremely accurate, and—we can't stress this important advantage enough—very adaptable at the bid table.

If these two requisites are accomplished, the OPPH method can be quite simple, extremely accurate, and—we can't stress this important advantage enough—very adaptable at the bid table.

Although it's easy to use, the OPPH method must be combined with accurate takeoff procedures along with field-labor and equipment production rates that accurately reflect the specific job and site conditions being bid.

If the job is built (planned) in your mind and on paper consistent with the way it will be produced in the field, the OPPH method facilitates and enhances production planning in much the same way as the MORS method. *All* data needed for effective job costing is a by-product of the OPPH method.

Other Strengths of the OPPH Method

It's budget-driven. The installation division OPH dollar amount (see Figure 3-1: \$14.25 per field-labor hour) is derived directly from your G&A overhead budget.

It applies to either prevailing wage or non-rated work. You don't have to adjust your OPH amount when bidding different types of work; and you don't have to worry about budget versus actual variations for one or the other, in comparison to your original budget.

It's easy to track. G&A overhead that's accumulated through bids won for the year is easy to track—because it's so easy to calculate.

The OPH is determined by only two numbers (billable field-labor hours and G&A overhead costs). Therefore, it's easy to compare your budgeted OPH to your actual OPH on a monthly and/or a year-to-date (YTD) basis.

The concept is easy to visualize. Tying your G&A overhead recovery method directly to billable field-labor hours creates another very important advantage: bureaucrats (owners, estimators, bookkeepers, etc.) begin to think of and measure G&A overhead in terms of field labor. Because the concept is so easy to visualize, field people and bureaucrats alike can better relate to it. For instance, if your OPH is $10, adding a full-time (2,080 hours per year) laborer in the field will allow you to increase your G&A overhead budget for the year by $20,800 (2,080 hrs/yr × $10 OPH) without increasing your OPH for estimating purposes.

You can become more competitive. If you add labor to your field crew and your yearly G&A overhead budget remains the same, your OPH will decrease accordingly. You can, therefore, drop your prices and become more competitive, or you can increase your net profit margin.

It is more manageable. By breaking down and thinking of G&A overhead in terms of OPH "units," it becomes more manageable and meaningful.

The OPPH method and its resulting data can easily be mathematically converted, reformatted, and compared to the factoring, SORS/GPM, or MORS methods. With the aid of a personal computer (PC) spreadsheet program (or a lot of manual work), the OPPH method can also be converted for comparison to the market-driven unit pricing method. Consequently, using the OPPH method encompasses the benefits of all five estimating pricing systems. By comparing one method against the other, you can adjust your bid to incorporate the strengths of each.

The OPPH system is easily adjusted in order to compensate for fast-changing markets. If sales are plummeting, so will billable field-labor hours. If you're tracking your OPH as faithfully as you should, you'll almost immediately see it rise and go through the roof. This says you need to address the issue (probably by cutting G&A overhead) and get your OPH back in line. If the economy or a particular market (meaning a specific division in your company) begins to accelerate and displays vigorous growth, you can quickly and easily adjust projected field-labor hours and your G&A overhead budget (thus changing your OPH accordingly) with no messy percentages or M/L/E/S ratios to worry about.

Gross and net profit margins are both easily identified. Accordingly, your break-even point (BEP) is also readily identified.

Caveats to Consider when Using the OPPH Method

With so many advantages, one would think the OPPH method would have few limitations or drawbacks. However, some necessary precautions need to be observed.

First, unless it's used in conjunction with and in comparison to the other pricing methods, you could become lazy, develop "tunnel vision," and/or "leave money on the table." If your competition is very unsophisticated and is using factors, the MDUP, or the SORS/GPM system, you should recalculate your bids using those methods in conjunction with the OPPH method. This can dramatically sharpen your skills at the bidding table.

When bidding jobs that have an inordinate amount of materials or equipment, you should pay particular attention to the ratios, per hour calculations, and the GPM to ensure that your profit margins are high enough. Otherwise, you might underprice jobs having a material-to-labor ratio above 5:1 and an equipment-to-labor ratio over .5:1.

You should also scrutinize jobs that have a high percentage of subcontractor costs (above 25%) in them. I would recommend removing the subcontractor costs from the main bid and pricing them independently. Pay particular attention to the GPM because high-intensity subcontractor costs will distort it.

By tracking bid results (if possible), you can begin to understand your competitors' bidding better than they do. Once you do you can begin to beat them at their own game as long as you can do so without hurting yourself.

It's also easy, while using the OPPH process, to leave money on the table when you encounter bidding situations with expensive materials, a high material-to-labor ratio, or a large number of subcontractors. These special situations make it necessary for you to monitor the GPM markup on your bids, as well as the MORS markup on labor and labor burden by backing out material, equipment, and subcontractor markups. To do so

A. Determine your OPPH method total G&A overhead on the bid.

B. Subtract from A: 10% of the material cost, 25% of the equipment cost, and 5% of the subcontractor cost. This is the respective MORS markup on these items.

C. Understand that the remaining amount is your G&A overhead markup dollar amount on labor and labor burden using the MORS method for this particular bid.

D. Divide this remaining amount by the total of field labor plus labor burden costs in the bid.

The result is your MORS G&A overhead markup percentage for labor and labor burden.

By first determining your total G&A overhead dollar amount to recover on a job using the OPPH method and then "backing into" your MORS labor and labor burden G&A overhead markup percentage as we did above, you'll be able to compare your OPPH bid method to the MORS method, if you so choose.

However, you'll see that the MORS G&A overhead markup percentage on labor and labor burden will fluctuate wildly due to the mixture of M/L/E/S on a particular job. It can fluctuate from 0% (at times) to the high 80 to 90% range.

By comparing the "backed into" MORS percentages to your overall estimating budget percentages (in conjunction with past bidding experience), you'll develop a feel for where the percentage markup on labor and labor burden ought to be. If it's too low (below 20%), perhaps you should add extra net profit to the job. If it appears inordinately high, you should investigate and check your gross profit margin on the bid.

Another drawback of the OPPH method is that it's not easy to manually convert (that is, without a computer) to unit prices. Remember, we covered this in greater detail in Chapter 14.

Finally, the OPPH method is only as good as the projections for your company's (or division's) G&A overhead budget and billable field-labor hours. If G&A overhead includes field equipment and/or labor burden, taxes, and insurance items, the OPPH method will be rendered inaccurate. Tables 38-7 and 38-8 on page 300 show pricing and a ratio/per hour analysis of the OPPH method.

Let's turn our attention back to Table 38-1 and complete the estimating process by utilizing the OPPH pricing method. The OPPH to be used is $10, which is taken from our sample company on page 316.

Our original examples in Tables 38-1 and 38-2 depict two extremes. Job A is material-intensive while Job B is labor-intensive. The material-to-labor ratio and the material per hour (MPH) identified in Tables 38-7 and 38-8 demonstrate these extremes. As you can see, there is ten times the amount of materials per field-labor hour in Job A as there are in Job B. Although I purposely chose these examples to drive home a number of points, you'll occasionally encounter such extremes (perhaps not quite so dramatic).

TABLE 38-7 Pricing Jobs A and B Using the OPPH Method

	Job A	%		Job B	%
Total direct costs	$120,000	83		$120,000	67
G&A overhead ($10 × 1,000)	10,000	7	($10 × 4,000)	40,000	23
Break-even point	$130,000	90		$160,000	90
Net profit margin (10%)	14,444	10	(10%)	17,778	10
	$144,444	100		$177,778	100
Contingency factor	0	0		0	0
Total price	$144,444	100		$177,778	100

The GPM in Table 38-8 is another key indicator. While 16.9% GPM on Job A is low, the 32.5% GPM on Job B may be excessive for the commercial market but not for the residential one. Once you've monitored your GPM on a number of bids in a particular market (e.g., commercial maintenance, commercial construction, high-end residential design/build, state or federal prevailing wage, etc.) you'll have gained considerable insight into what that particular market will bear. This information can be especially helpful and can bolster your confidence at the bid table.

In most markets you'd probably want your net profit percentage close to 10% for both jobs. However, although I'd probably not hesitate to increase the net profit on Job A 3 to 5 points, I'd be cautious about lowering the NPM on Job B too quickly unless I was certain that a 10% NPM was too unrealistic.

TABLE 38-8 Jobs A and B Ratio/per Hour Analysis of the OPPH Method

	Job A	Job B
SPH	$144.44	$44.45
DCPH	$120.00	$30.00
OPH	$ 10.00	$10.00
PPH	$ 14.44	$17.78
GPMPH	$ 24.44	$27.78
G&A overhead %	6.9%	22.5%
Net profit %	10.0%	10.0%
GPM %	16.9%	32.5%
BEP %	90.0%	90.0%
M/L ratio	8.9:1	.9:1
MPH	$100.00	$10.00
EQ/L	.44:1 (44%)	.44:1 (44%)
EQPH	$5.00	$5.00

ANALYSIS OF THE SIX METHODS

Table 38-9 on page 302 displays the various estimating methods as they apply to Jobs A and B. Only the GPM/SORS, MORS, and OPPH methods identify all direct costs in the estimating process. The DORS method identifies all direct costs except for company-owned equipment. Factoring only identifies the material costs, while the market-driven unit pricing method doesn't even identify that. Meaningful job costing is impossible unless you identify the direct costs used to job cost your jobs. Therefore, when you take shortcuts in the estimating process, you're really short-circuiting your ability to keep score on your jobs and control them.

G&A overhead (or indirect costs) is another area that deserves our analysis when comparing these six estimating methods. To do so, we first need to take note of two assumptions stated in Table 38-1. First, the total company field payroll with labor burden per calendar month is $15,000. Second, the total company G&A overhead per calendar month is $10,000.

The factoring, GPM/SORS, and market-driven unit pricing methods make no attempt to identify G&A overhead costs in the bidding process. At least the GPM/SORS method identifies the gross profit margin, but that's all. These methods make no attempt to identify or adjust their G&A overhead recovery from one job to the next. In large part, that's why these bidding methods are very inaccurate.

Let's turn our attention to the DORS, MORS, and the OPPH methods. We can now analyze and compare them as we keep in mind our two assumptions. We should also add that G&A overhead costs don't vary that much, if at all, from month to month. While there might be some variation, the vast majority of G&A overhead costs remain fairly constant. Rent, overhead salaries and related burden, telephone, advertising, overhead vehicle payments, and so forth don't change much. If they do, it's usually in the off-season. With this in mind, we take note that Job A is a one-month job and Job B is a four-month job. We next ask ourselves a simple series of questions.

For Job A

Question: If G&A overhead costs vary in insignificant amounts from month to month, how many months of G&A overhead cost do we allocate to a one-month job? (This is not a trick question.)

Answer: One month

Question: If G&A overhead is $10,000 per month, how much G&A overhead should be allocated to Job A?

Answer: $10,000

For Job B

Question: If G&A overhead costs vary in insignificant amounts from month to month, how many months of G&A overhead cost do we allocate to a four-month job? (Again, this is not a trick question.)

Answer: Four months

Question: If G&A overhead is $10,000 per month, how much G&A overhead should be allocated to Job B?

Answer: $40,000

Returning to Table 38-9, we see that the DORS method vastly overstated the G&A overhead allocated to Job A. Even after removing the $5,000 for equipment costs supposedly included in Job A G&A overhead, the DORS method adds four times as

	Total Direct Costs	G&A OH $	G&A OH %	BEP $	Net Profit $	Net Profit %	GPM %	Price $	$ Amount over low bid	Field labor hours	G&A OPH $	PPH $	GPMPH $	SPH $	Labor G&A OH % Markup
Job "A"															
Factoring	N/I	N/I	N/I	N/I	N/I	N/I	N/I	200,000	55,556	N/I	N/I	N/I	N/I	N/I	N/I
GPM/SORS	120,000	N/I	N/I	N/I	N/I	N/I	23.1%	156,000	11,556	1,000	N/I	N/I	N/I	$156.00	N/I
Market Driven Unit Pri	N/I	N/I	N/I	N/I	N/I	N/I	N/I	N/A	N/A	N/I	N/I	N/I	N/I	N/I	N/I
DORS	115,000 *	45,950	26.0%	160,950	16,095	9.1%	35.0% **	177,045	32,601	1,000	$45.95	$16.10	$62.05	$177.05	85.0%
MORS	120,000	19,350	12.6%	139,350	13,935	9.1%	21.7%	153,285	8,841	1,000	$19.35	$13.94	$33.29	$153.29	54.0%
OPPH	120,000	10,000	6.9%	130,000	14,444	10.0%	16.9%	144,444	0	1,000	$10.00	$14.44	$24.44	$144.44	-1.7%
Averages	**$118,750**	**$25,100**	**15.2%**	**$143,433**	**$14,825**	**9.4%**	**24.2%**	**$166,155**	**$27,138**	**1,000**	**$25.10**	**$14.82**	**$39.92**	**$157.69**	**45.8%**
Job "B"															
Factoring	N/I	N/I	N/I	N/I	N/I	N/I	N/I	80,000	0	N/I	N/I	N/I	N/I	N/I	N/I
GPM/SORS	120,000	N/I	N/I	N/I	N/I	N/I	23.1%	156,000	76,000	4,000	N/I	N/I	N/I	$39.00	N/I
Market Driven Unit Pri	N/I	N/I	N/I	N/I	N/I	N/I	N/I	N/A	N/A	N/I	N/I	N/I	N/I	N/I	N/I
DORS	100,000 *	64,280	35.6%	164,280	16,428	9.1%	44.7% **	180,708	100,708	4,000	$16.07	$4.11	$20.18	$45.18	85.0%
MORS	120,000	41,400	23.3%	161,400	16,140	9.1%	32.4%	177,540	97,540	4,000	$10.35	$4.04	$14.39	$44.39	54.0%
OPPH	120,000	40,000	22.5%	160,000	17,778	10.0%	32.5%	177,778	97,778	4,000	$10.00	$4.44	$14.44	$44.44	41.3%
Averages	**$115,000**	**$48,560**	**27.1%**	**$161,893**	**$16,782**	**9.4%**	**33.2%**	**$154,405**	**$93,006**	**4,000**	**$12.14**	**$4.20**	**$16.34**	**$43.25**	**60.1%**

Note(s): * Excludes field equipment costs
** Includes equipment costs

TABLE 38-9 Analysis of Jobs A and B Using All Six Methods

much G&A overhead costs as it should. It calculates the G&A overhead on Job B much more accurately.

The MORS method misses the mark less dramatically, but it is still not accurate. Job A G&A overhead allocation is almost double what it should be, while Job B G&A overhead is "almost" on target. However, it is overstated by almost $1,400.

The OPPH method allocates the G&A overhead costs for both jobs based on time. In our case, it's based on billable field man-hours. We should note that we could have allocated G&A overhead costs based on the crew hour, day, week, or month. We could even allocate G&A overhead costs on a man-minute basis, but even for me, this is a bit anal.

Since 85 to 95% of all G&A overhead costs are paid based on a time unit (per week, month, quarter, etc.), they're best allocated to jobs based on a similar type of time measuring unit.

My assertion is that the primary reason why the OPPH method more accurately allocates G&A overhead costs is that it ties these costs to a time unit. Since 85 to 95% of all G&A overhead costs are paid based on a time unit (per week, month, quarter, etc.), they're best allocated to jobs based on a similar type of time measuring unit.

Material, equipment, and subcontractor costs (I call these events) can vary dramatically from month to month and from job to job. Hitching G&A overhead costs to these direct costs, which vary so dramatically, makes no mathematical sense. Tying G&A overhead costs to gross sales makes even less mathematical sense.

Is the OPPH method goof-proof? Of course not! There are too many (of us) "goofs" (when) bidding work. Is it the best alternative? I think so, especially when you take into account the advantages of all six methods when you bid a job.

How It Works

Let's price another job, the Peterson residence (see Table 38-10), that's more the norm for a construction division. Materials total $9,540, including sales tax on materials which is 6%. CAW (including OTF and RF) is $16.80. Labor burden is 32%. The job is estimated to take 268 field-labor hours. Equipment costs total $1,184. The subcontractor mason will cost $2,000. OPH is $10. The contractor wants net profit at either his PPH of $5 or 10%, whichever is greater. There's no contingency factor on the job. The job prices out as indicated in Table 38-11 on page 304 and Figure 38-1 on page 305.

TABLE 38-10 Peterson Residence Bid Using the OPPH Method

Direct Costs	Totals	%
Materials	$ 9,000	37.9
Tax on materials (6%)	540	2.2
Labor (268 hours × $16.80 CAW)	4,502	19.0
Labor burden (32%)	1,441	6.0
Equipment	1,184	5.0
Subcontractors	2,000	8.4
Total direct costs	$18,667	78.7
Markups	**Totals**	**%**
G&A overhead ($10.00 OPH)	2,680	11.3
Break-even point (BEP)	21,347	90.0
Net profit margin 10.0%	2,372	10.0
Contingency factor	0	0.0
Total price	$23,719	100.0

TABLE 38-11 Peterson Residence Bid Ratio/per Hour Analysis

Item	Ratio	Cost	%
SPH		$88.50	100.0
G&A overhead OPH		$10.00	11.3
Net profit per hour		$8.85	10.0
GPM		$5,052.00	21.3
BEP		$21,347.00	90.0
Material/Labor ratio	2.0 to 1.0		
Materials per hour		$33.58	37.9
Equipment/Labor ratio	0.26		
Equipment per hour		$4.42	5.0

Table 38-11 contains the ratio/per hour analysis for this job. The only items that appear out of line are the equipment/labor ratio and the EQPH. Both are higher than would be expected for a typical landscape construction project. However, these indicators are driven up by the extra equipment needed for the site work.

Figure 38-1 is a printout of a Bid Analysis/Review (B.A.R.) Worksheet for the Peterson bid, using the OPPH method shown in Table 38-10.

SUMMARY

All six pricing methods have their strengths and weaknesses. At best, factoring and the MDUP methods are all but useless for determining accurate *costs* for your work; at worst, they can cause serious errors. While the SORS/GPM, DORS, and the MORS methods have some advantages, they should also be used with caution.

I recommend that you estimate your jobs using the OPPH method and compare your results to the other five methods, using the techniques mentioned earlier.

I recommend that you estimate your jobs using the OPPH method and compare your results to the other five methods, using the techniques mentioned earlier.

Direct costs for materials, labor, equipment, subcontractors, taxes, and labor burden are rather straightforward to determine for any given job—once you take into consideration all site conditions and production rates. Most estimating problems arise from G&A overhead. There's no "direct" or exact way to determine just how much G&A overhead to put on a particular job. By its very nature, it's vague. That's why it's referred to as a G&A (general and administrative) cost, or indirect cost, because it can't be directly costed to a job. If it could be directly tied to a job, it would then become a direct, not an indirect, cost.

During the estimating process, you're attempting to identify the following two numbers:

- *The total of your direct costs* (materials, sales tax, labor, labor burden, field equipment, and subcontractors) *plus the amount of G&A overhead* you need to recover on the job. These two combined determine your break-even point (BEP). Once you determine this first number, you can then address the second.
- *Net profit and a contingency factor,* if desired, combine to form the second number. How much net profit can you put on the job and still get it? And do you want to add a "cushion" (a contingency factor) into the net profit margin?

Scenario cost data	$ or %	Remarks
Crew size (# people)	3.0	Crew leader, leadman andone laborer
Crew average wage (CAW)	$ 14.00	
Man-hours per man per day	10.0	50 hours per week
Overtime factor (OTF)	10.0%	
Risk factor (RF)	10.0%	
Crew average wage w/OTF & RF	$ 16.80	
Labor burden	32.0%	
Sales tax	6.0%	
G&A overhead per hour (OPH)	$ 10.00	
Net profit margin	10.0%	
One ton crew truck	$ 8.00	
Curb-time man-hours	NA	
Number of units	1	LS

Scenario	Materials	Labor	Equipment	Subcontractors	Subtotals
I. Production (on-site or curb-time costs)					
	$ 9,000.00	$ 3,864.00	$ 640.00	$ 2,000.00	
	$ 9,000.00	$ 3,864.00	$ 640.00	$ 2,000.00	**$ 15,504**
II. General conditions (off-site or non-curb-time costs)					
	$ -	$ 638.40	$ 544.00	$ -	
	$ -	$ 638.40	$ 544.00	$ -	**$ 1,182**
Subtotals	**$ 9,000**	**$ 4,502**	**$ 1,184**	**$ 2,000**	**$ 16,686**
III. Margins & markups					
A. Sales tax	$ 540				
B. Labor burden		$ 1,441			
Subtotals	**$ 9,540**	**$ 5,943**	**$ 1,184**	**$ 2,000**	
Total direct costs (TDC)				**$ 18,667**	**TDC**
C. G&A overhead costs					
268.0 (Number of man-hours x OPH)			$ 10.00 =	$ 2,680	
BEP (TDC + G&A overhead)				**$ 21,347**	**BEP**
D. Contingency factor (if desired)				$ -	
E. Net profit margin 10.00%				$ 2,372	
F. Total price				**$ 23,719**	**Total price**

IV. Scenario analysis

A. Net profit per hour (Net profit ÷ all hours)

$ 2,372 divided by	268.0 =	**$ 8.85**	**Job price**

B. Sales or revenue per hour (Total price ÷ all hours)

$ 23,719 divided by	268.0 =	**$ 88.50**	**SPH or RPH**

C. Gross profit margin ((G&A overhead + Net profit) ÷ Total price)

$ 5,052 ÷	$ 23,719 =	**21.3%**	**GPM**

FIGURE 38-1 Peterson B.A.R. Worksheet Analysis

> *How high* can you go without losing the project? *How low* can you go to win the bid without hurting yourself (not covering all costs)? A good estimating system allows you to operate safely within this range.

Remember, a good estimating system produces more than just a *Price*. It also produces a *Plan* and a *Process* that will help you run your jobs and your company.

The key is to know your company and your game plan (or strategy) by means of an estimating budget and a solid estimating methodology. Then, and only then, can you play the estimating game and win.

Table 38-12 displays the same project estimated utilizing all six pricing methods.

G&A Overhead Recovery for the Peterson Residence Bid

A 54% markup on labor was utilized in the MORS method. This is a reasonable percentage to expect for a company using a $10 OPH. This percentage would have to drop to 22.4% in order to match the OPPH price calculated at $23,719. Such a drop in G&A overhead recovery, however, would be unrealistic for this company if you were using the MORS method to price your work.

Figure 38-2 on page 308 provides an encapsulation of the pros and cons of the various bidding methods. You can draw your own conclusions from the comparison.

The more often you conduct such an analysis of your bids, the more skilled you'll become in distinguishing the nuances of the various estimating methods. Had we used the PPH of $5 to price this project, our price would have been lowered by $1,032 to $22,687. It would have met our yearly budget projections for the company and made us more competitive had it been necessary.

Margins and Markups for the Jones Residence Bid

Figure 38-3 on page 309 displays the Manual Recap Bid Worksheet for the Jones residence discussed in Chapters 11, 12, and 14. Totals from the Phase I and II bid worksheets are transferred onto it. Phase III markups are then added at the bottom of the worksheet using a $10 OPH amount and a 10% net profit margin. Figure 38-4 on page 310 provides a B.A.R. worksheet for the Jones residence project.

ACTION POINT

Review three or four of your bids and compare them to the six methods outlined in this chapter.

	Total Direct Costs	G&A OH $	G&A OH %	BEP $	Net Profit $	Net Profit %	GPM %	Price $	$ Amount over low bid	Field labor hours	G&A OPH $	PPH $	GPMPH $	SPH $	Labor G&A OH % Markup
Factoring	N/I	N/I	N/I	N/I	N/I	N/I	N/I	19,080	(4,639)	N/I	N/I	N/I	N/I	N/I	N/I
GPM/SORS	18,667	N/I	N/I	N/I	N/I	N/I	23.1%	24,267	548	268	N/I	N/I	N/I	$90.55	N/I
Market Driven Unit Pr	N/I	N/I	N/I	N/I	N/I	N/I	N/I	N/A	N/A	N/I	N/I	N/I	N/I	N/I	N/I
DORS	17,483 *	8,219	29.1%	25,702	2,570	9.1%	38.2% **	28,272	4,553	268	$30.67	$9.59	$40.26	$105.49	85.0%
MORS	18,667	4,559	17.8%	23,226	2,323	9.1%	26.9%	25,549	1,830	268	$17.01	$8.67	$25.68	$95.33	54.0%
OPPH	18,667	2,680	11.3%	21,347	2,372	10.0%	21.3%	23,719	0	268	$10.00	$8.85	$18.85	$88.50	22.4%
Averages	**$18,371**	**$5,153**	**19.4%**	**$23,425**	**$2,422**	**9.4%**	**27.4%**	**$24,177**	**$573**	**268**	**$19.23**	**$9.04**	**$28.26**	**$94.97**	**53.8%**

Note(s): * Excludes field equipment costs
** Includes equipment costs

TABLE 38-12 Peterson Residence Bid Analysis Using All Six Methods

PROS	FAC	U/P	SORS	DORS	MORS	OPPH
1. Is fast	X	X				
2. Irrigation suppliers may provide	X					
3. Accurately identifies MLES costs			X		X	X
4. Identifies BEP				X	X	X
5. Identifies GPM markup			X	X	X	X
6. Identifies overhead markup				X	X	X
7. Identifies net profit markup				X	X	X
8. Provides sufficient data to job cost			X*	X	X	X
9. Builds on CO budget/historical data			X*	X	X*	X*
10. Net profit "floats" on BEP costs						X
11. Easily adjusted to rapid market changes						X
12. Easy to monitor and measure key data						X

CONS	FAC	U/P	SORS	DORS	MORS	OPPH
1. Ignores CO budget/historical data	X	X				
2. Does not ID labor/burden/equipment costs	X	X		X		
3. GPM not identified	X	X				
4. BEP not identified	X	X	X			
5. Ignores job-site variables	X	X				
6. Bid process does not pre-plan job	X	X				
7. Bid process provides no documentation	X	X				
8. Does not facilitate job costing	X	X				
9. Cannot job cost labor/equipment hours	X	X	X*	X		
10. Net rofit not identified on bid	X	X	X			
11. G&A overhead not identified on bid	X	X	X			
12. Factor not analytically based	X					
13. G&A overhead recovery inaccurately tied to direct costs		X	X	X		
14. Field equipment included in G&A overhead recovery		X*		X		
15. Net profit cannot "float" on BEP			X	X	X	
16. Extremely complex/inflexible				X	X	
17. PPH focus can miss extra profit						X

* Not always the case.

FIGURE 38-2 Bidding Methods Pros and Cons

BID WORKSHEET

PROJECT: JONES RESIDENCE — PAGE (1) OF (6)
LOCATION: 123 MAIN ST. ANAHEIM — DATE PREPARED: 12 / 15 / 20__
P.O.C./G.C.: JERRY JONES — OTF = 10% — ESTIMATOR: I. M. DUNN
DUE: 1 / 15 / 20__ PH.: 714-941-7442 FAX: — RF = 10% — CREW SIZE: 3 <16·10·10>
TYPE WORK: RECAP — HOURS/DAY: 10 — CAW: $ 15.00

REMARKS:

DESCRIPTION	QTY	UNIT	U/C	MAT'L	LABOR	EQUIP	SUBS
I. PRODUCE THE PRODUCT							
– SOIL PREP				261–	120–	70–	—
– PLANTING				2125–	488–	—	—
– SOD				300–	75–	—	—
– MULCH				120–	105–	20–	—
II. GENERAL CONDITIONS				—	235–	172–	—
				2806–	1023–	262–	—
III. MARGINS & MARKUPS							
– SALES TAX	6	%		168–		—	—
– LABOR BURDEN	32	%		—	327–	—	—
				2974–	1350–	262–	Ø
					2974–		
					262–		
			TDC		Ø–		
					4586–		
– G&A OVERHEAD	67	HR	#12–		804–		
					5390–	BEP	
– CONTINGENCY FACTOR					0–		
					5390–		
– NET PROFIT MARGIN	20	%			1348–		
– FINAL PRICE					6738		

FIGURE 38-3 Manual Bid Recap Worksheet for the Jones Residence Bid

Scenario cost data	**$ or %**	**Remarks**
Crew size (# people)	3.0	Crew leader and 2 laborers
Crew average wage (CAW)	$ 12.50	
Man-hours per man per day	10.0	
Overtime factor (OTF)	10.0%	50 hours per week
Risk factor (RF)	10.0%	
Crew average wage w/OTF & RF	$ 15.00	
Labor burden	32.0%	
Sales tax	6.0%	
G&A overhead per hour (OPH)	$ 12.00	
Net profit margin	20.0%	
One ton crew truck with trailer	$ 8.00	
Curb time man-hours	NA	
Number of units	1	LS

Scenario	**Materials**	**Labor**	**Equipment**	**Subcontractors**	**Subtotals**
I. Production or "Curb" time costs					
	$ 2,806	$ 788	$ 90	$ -	
	$ 2,806	$ 788	$ 90	$ -	**$ 3,683**
II. General conditions (off-site or non-curb-time costs)					
	$ -	$ 235	$ 172	$ -	
	$ -	$ 235	$ 172	$ -	**$ 407**
Subtotals	**$ 2,806**	**$ 1,023**	**$ 262**	**$ -**	**$ 4,090**
III. Margins & markups					
A.Sales tax	$ 168				
B.Labor burden		$ 327			
Subtotals	**$ 2,974**	**$ 1,350**	**$ 262**	**$ -**	
Total direct costs (TDC)				**$ 4,586**	**TDC**
C. G&A overhead costs					
66.5 (Number of man-hours x OPH)			$ 12.00 =	$ 798	
BEP (TDC + G&A overhead)				**$ 5,384**	**BEP**
D. Contingency factor (if desired)				$ -	
E. Net profit margin 20.00%				$ 1,346	
F. Total price				**$ 6,730**	**Total price**

IV. Scenario analysis

A. Unit price (Total price ÷ units)

$ 6,730 divided by 1.0 = **$ 6,730 Total price**

B. Sales or revenue per man-hour (Total price ÷ all man-hours)

$ 6,730 divided by 66.5 = **$ 101.20 SPH or RPH**

C. Gross profit margin ((G&A overhead + Net profit) ÷ Total price)

$ 2,144 ÷ $ 6,730 = **31.9% GPM**

FIGURE 38-4 Jones B.A.R. Worksheet Analysis

CHAPTER

39

The Mathematical Mistake of Using Percentages to Recover G&A Overhead Costs

TERM

Residual Capacity

Purpose

1. To explain the nature of general and administrative costs as an "indirect cost" versus direct costs, often called cost of goods sold
2. To illustrate with mathematical models how the two types of costs differ proportionally in various bidding situations

Introduction

There's much confusion when it comes to accounting for G&A overhead costs in bids. Unfortunately, not much has been added to this discussion in recent years to clarify the issues involved. Before we get started, we should identify a few guidelines that will aid in our discussions.

- There is no right way to estimate G&A overhead costs in a bid. By its very definition, G&A overhead costs are indirect costs. There is no directly proportional formula for adding these costs to your bids. Arguing over which G&A overhead recovery method is right misses the point of the discussion.
- While there may be no right method for estimating G&A overhead costs and including them in a bid, this doesn't imply there aren't "wrong" or mathematically inaccurate methods for identifying such costs and adding them into a bid.
- Let the arithmetic speak for itself. Don't attempt to force it to say something it doesn't mean.
- The real issue is how you MARC (Measure, Allocate, Recover, and Control) indirect G&A overhead costs. Illustrate your methods with mathematical models and let the market decide.
- The mathematical models we'll use illustrate faulty mathematical assumptions. As such, even though they fall outside the everyday norm in some cases, they're still valid. While not perfect (no mathematical model is), they more than adequately illustrate the issues in question.
- G&A overhead changes very little, if at all, from one time unit to the next. This is the case whether it be from week to week, month to month, or quarter to quarter. If it does change, it does not do so due to individual job-related

While there may be no right method for estimating G&A overhead costs and including them in a bid, this doesn't imply there aren't "wrong" or mathematically inaccurate methods for identifying such costs and adding them into a bid.

events (elements within COGS) but rather due to strategic long-term planning (i.e., a new office manager, receptionist, or division manager, new office location, overhead vehicles, computer system, etc.).

- By definition, general conditions are designed to cover short term G&A overhead increases (additional supervision, supervisor's truck, etc.) due to specific job requirements.

How It Works

Not too long ago, I received a frantic telephone call from a contractor who had just received his end-of-year financial statement from his CPA. Things did not turn out as he had expected. While cash flow was extremely tight during the year, he thought that everything would wash out in the end. Unfortunately, the financial statements showed that he had barely broken even for the year. He wanted me to help him figure out what had gone wrong.

This contractor had done a little over $1 million in landscape and irrigation construction sales the year before. G&A overhead was about $240,000. Direct field labor consisted of a full-time ten-person crew and totaled nearly $220,000. The crew average wage was $11.00 ($220,000 ÷ 20,000 man-hours). Net profit before taxes for the year was a little over 10%.

At the beginning of the current year, the year in question, a general contractor (GC) approached my caller and asked him to do a large development project on a time-and-materials basis. This development would keep half of the contractor's crews busy for the entire year. Billable hours would total about 10,000 (5 crew members × 2,000 man-hours per man per year). However, the GC wanted to pay the material and rental equipment invoices himself.

After discussing this opportunity and how to charge for it with his CPA, the contractor agreed to do the job as specified. There were no subcontractors on the job. Company owned equipment (a trencher, skid steer, and crew truck) would cost the contractor approximately $50,000 for the year. He would charge this to the GC with a 35% markup (25% for G&A overhead and 10% for net profit). Direct field labor was charged at a crew average wage rate, including 30% labor burden, of $14.30. Thirty-five percent was added to the $14.30 (25% for G&A overhead and 10% for net profit).

All things being equal, the contractor should have charged approximately half of his annual G&A overhead, roughly $120,000, to this project. He should also have charged the GC another 10% for net profit on top of the $120,000 for G&A overhead. However, as it turned out he charged barely over $40,000, plus 10% net profit, to the GC for G&A overhead. Here's how he shorted himself.

Approximate G&A overhead cost that he should have recovered	$120,000
G&A overhead included in the labor charged to the job:	
10,000 man-hours × 14.30 × 25% =	– 35,750
G&A overhead included in the equipment charged to the job:	
$50,000 × 25% =	– 12,500
G&A overhead shortfall	$ 71,750
10% net profit not added to shortfall and charged to GC	7,175
Total shortfall	**$ 78,925**

! Reminder

Using percentages to recover G&A overhead can get you into a lot of trouble.

DIRECT VERSUS INDIRECT COSTS

Figures 39-1 and 39-2 on page 314 illustrate how direct and indirect costs relate to increases in sales. Note how direct costs remain fairly consistent as a percentage of sales. The mathematical norm for direct costs varies slightly between 65 and 75%. That's not to say this is always the case. Golf course work often hovers around 80%, while irrigation service work may barely reach 50% in some markets.

This consistent proportionality to sales for direct costs is what this chapter is all about. The relationship between sales and direct costs is *almost* a direct one. I say almost because direct costs will vary somewhat as sales increase or decrease. However, for the most part they'll remain relatively proportional. For instance, as a contractor increases sales, the added buying power will often help the contractor realize price discounts for such things as materials, fuel, insurance, equipment purchases, and so forth. While direct costs may decrease due to economies of scale as compared to smaller competitors, the relationship between sales and direct costs within the company will remain relatively consistent.

Indirect G&A overhead costs, on the other hand, don't follow such a neat and predictable path. They're similar to teenagers or that crazy uncle you just can't quite figure out. Indirect costs are not as predictable as direct costs. They're certainly not random, but they don't follow in direct proportion as do direct costs. Let's review Figures 39-1 and 39-2.

Notice how indirect costs increase in steps while increases in direct costs, for the most part, follow a straight line. Think of it this way. A contractor just starting out has zero sales. He may have no direct costs, since he has no work. However, he does have indirect costs. There's the truck or automobile needed to make sales calls. Business cards, stationery, letterhead, computer, software, rent, his salary, pens, pencils, paper, telephone, yellow pages, bank checking account fees, and more are probably all incurred costs before making sales dollar number one. However, the contractor will probably not buy any plants, pavers, or lumber, hire on a full crew, or buy all the new equipment he wants until he's sold some work.

The first level of indirect costs will get the contractor to approximately $300,000 to $400,000 in annual sales. Up to this point the contractor is doing all the selling, marketing, supervising and working on jobs, administration, and accounting. To get to the next level the contractor will need to hire more office help. In many cases, a field supervisor or salesperson is brought into the company. This usually translates into more indirect costs. Because G&A overhead salaries comprise about 50% of all indirect costs, those costs will spike considerably. The goal for the contractor is to maximize sales as soon as possible.

Look at it this way. Your business is a car assembly line with the facilities, machinery, and labor to produce 100 cars per day. However, you're only producing 50 cars on a daily basis. You need to maximize your production to cover all your costs. You have what's called **residual capacity**. You *could* produce 50 more cars per day but, for whatever reason, you're not doing so.

Indirect costs increase in steps and provide you with a certain "capacity" of sales you can do in the field. You need to realize this and get to your optimal production level as soon as possible. Otherwise, you'll have residual unused capacity in your business, which will eat up profitability.

WHAT CAUSES DIRECT AND INDIRECT COSTS?

If sales cause direct costs or costs of goods sold (COGS), is there anything that causes indirect costs? Can we identify a mathematical relationship between indirect G&A costs and some other element or event in our bids? In other words, is there a formula

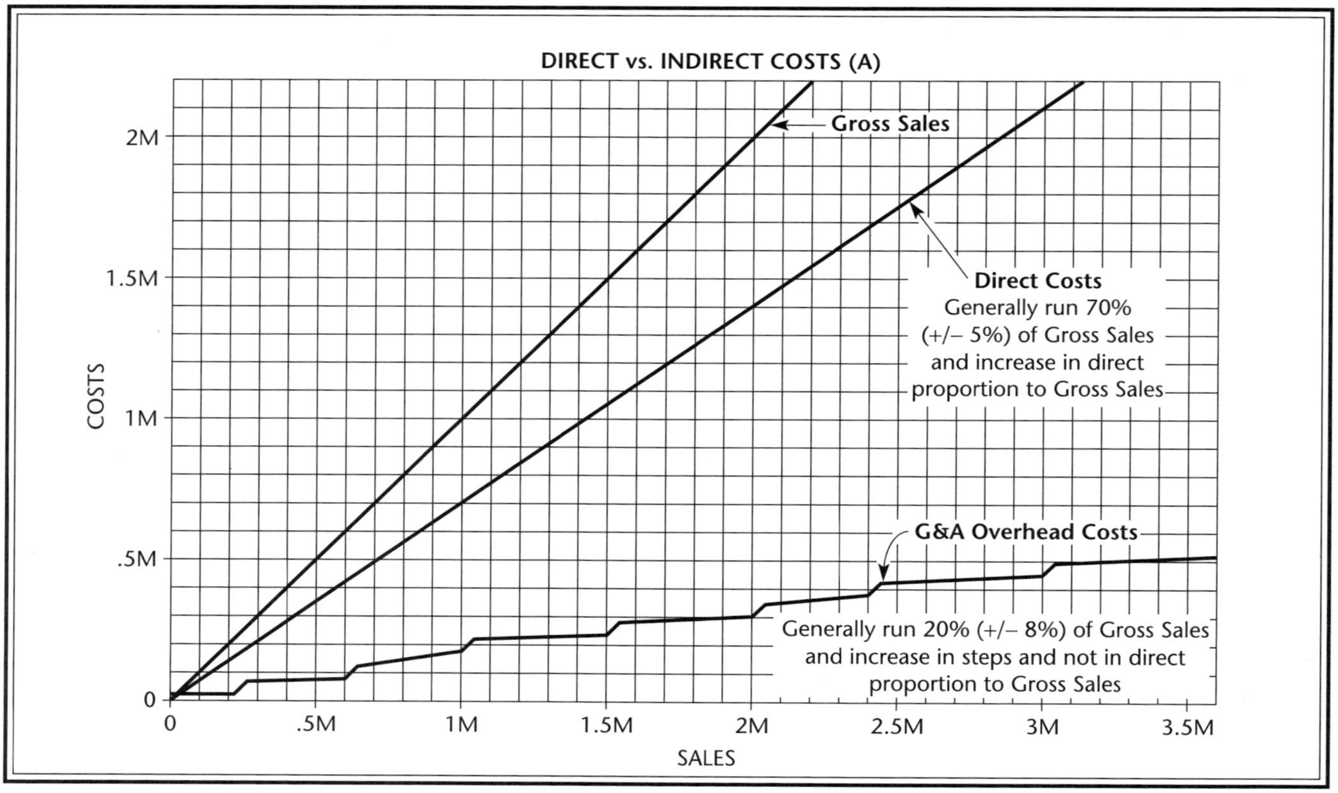

FIGURE 39-1 Direct vs. Indirect Costs in Relation to Sales

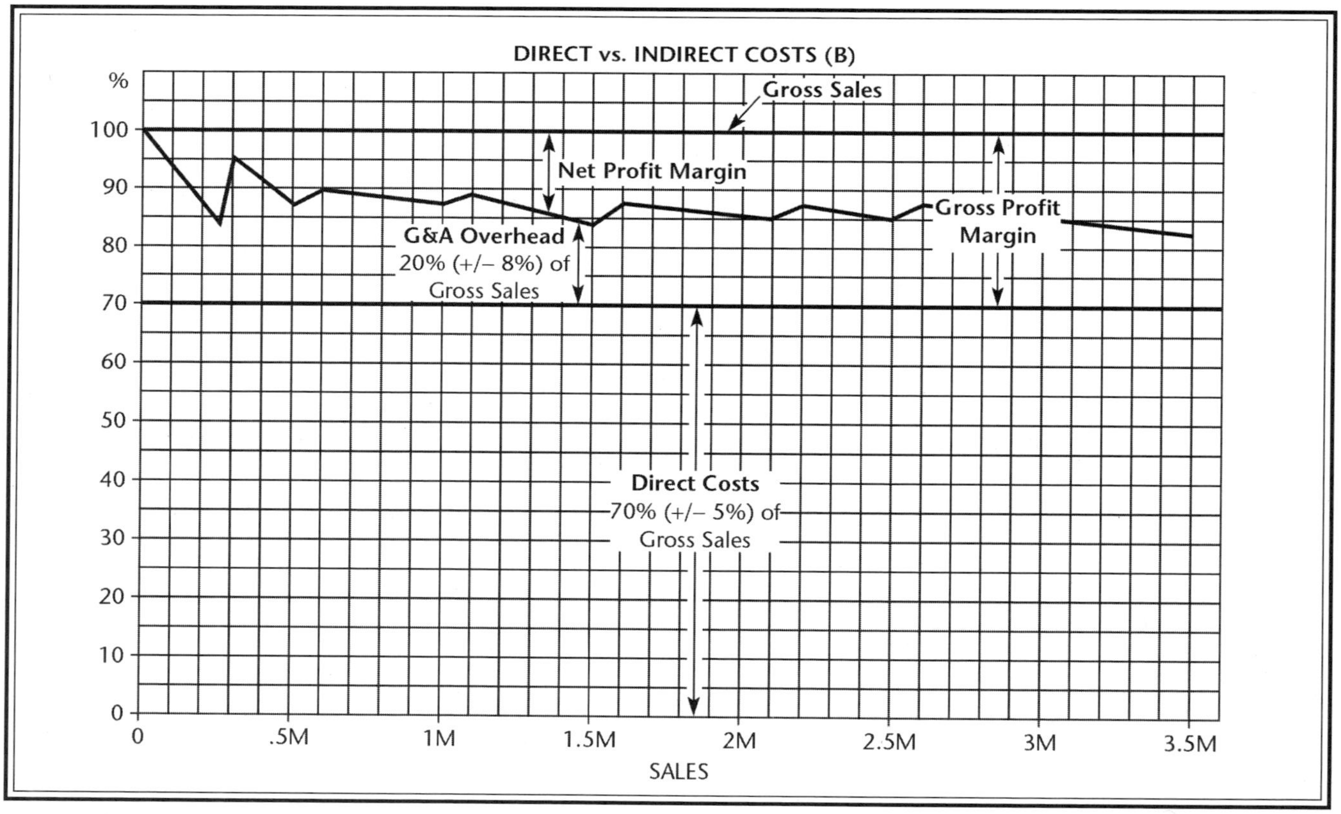

FIGURE 39-2 Direct vs. Indirect Costs in Relation to Net Profit

connecting sales and indirect costs, or a component of COGS and indirect G&A costs, or some other element or event in our bids?

Many estimating systems attempt to establish a firm mathematical relationship between revenue and indirect costs. Others try to establish such a formula between COGS and indirect costs. You could argue that such a relationship exists for revenue and indirect G&A overhead costs because G&A overhead costs normally comprise 20% +/– 8% of sales.

Generally, the smaller the revenue amount, the higher the percentage of G&A overhead costs for a company. Economies of scale cause this percentage to trend downward to single digits for larger companies. However, the range of 12 to 28% is adequate for our discussions. While a loose relationship exists between revenue and indirect costs, our mathematical models will illustrate why this loose relationship should not be used to calculate G&A overhead costs in a bidding situation.

The most common mistake made in estimating indirect costs is the attempt to establish a mathematical relationship between cost of goods sold and G&A overhead. While there are basically four elements that comprise COGS (costs for materials with sales tax, direct field labor and burden, field equipment, and subcontractors), there are three popular methods for mathematically linking COGS to indirect costs. They are the Single Overhead Recovery System (SORS), the Dual Overhead Recovery System (DORS), and the Multiple Overhead Recovery System (MORS). As their names connote, each focuses on different numbers of COGS components.

G&A Costs as They Relate to a Time Unit versus a COGS Element

When we analyze the components that make up general and administrative costs on our profit and loss statement, we notice that the majority of them are paid in relation to a time unit. For instance, G&A overhead salaries (roughly 50% of all G&A costs) are usually paid weekly, every other week, or semi-monthly. Rent, the telephone bill, bank charges, radios, cell phones, vehicles, and the like are normally paid on a monthly basis.

Clearly, 85 to 90% of all G&A overhead costs are paid in relation to time. That's one reason they don't vary much from month to month. If G&A overhead costs are incurred based on a time unit, it makes good mathematical sense to allocate them to jobs based on a time unit. This allows us to link "apples to apples," so to speak. The unit could be a year, quarter, month, week, man-day, crew-day, or man-hour. I choose to use the man-hour because I believe it's the common denominator for a service or construction company.

Other estimating methods, such as factoring, SORS, DORS, and MORS, calculate their G&A overhead allocation to jobs based on a component of cost of goods sold. In other words, they're event-related. For instance, if material costs increase on a job (an event), then the G&A overhead costs increase proportionately.

We should point out that the SORS, DORS, and MORS methods also use a time unit for totaling and measuring G&A overhead. This time unit is the budget year. However, once G&A overhead is calculated for the budget year, these methods make a false assumption or mistake in arithmetic when they then attempt to allocate and recover the totaled G&A overhead costs by means of linking them to elements within COGS. What if the material costs for a paver job remain the same but the labor almost doubles due to a complex pattern that requires a lot of customized work and cuts? These methods are too rigid and inflexible to accommodate the complexities of the modern construction and service market.

As the following illustrations will show, there's no consistent formula directly linking variations in indirect G&A costs to revenue and/or components of COGS.

The following information and cost data establish the parameters to be used in our illustrations.

Company Information

Annual construction sales	\$600,000 (approximately)
G&A overhead	\$10,000 per month
Field labor cost with 30% labor burden	\$13,000 per month
Field crew	5–6 people full time, year round
G&A overhead costs per labor hour	\$10
Field labor hours	1,000 per month, 12,000 per year

Assumptions

1. It makes no difference if sales revenue is level for 12 months or if it's achieved in an 8- to 10-month period.
2. Fluctuations in G&A overhead costs from month to month are minimal, if they vary at all.
3. We'll use jobs of one or multiple months duration for our examples.
4. We desire a 10% net profit margin on our illustration jobs.

The Single Overhead Recovery System (SORS) Method

The SORS method basically totals all elements of cost of goods sold and multiplies it by a predetermined factor. Subcontractor costs may be excluded from this factor and marked up separately. Certified public accountants (CPAs) and accountants often recommend this method for pricing work.

The mathematical assumption for using the SORS method is: If you desire a 30% gross profit margin at the end of the year, you should mark up each job and all your direct costs by a factor that will give you a 30% gross profit margin (GPM). Assuming a factor of 1.43, which gives us a 30.07% GPM, the formula is as follows:

[(materials + sales tax) + (field labor + labor burden) + (field equipment)] × 1.43 = Price

Expressed another way

Total Direct Costs (TDC) × 1.43 = Price

\$10,000 TDC × 1.43 = \$14,300

This formula achieves an approximate 30% gross profit margin.

(\$4,300 ÷ 14,300 = 30.07% GPM)

The SORS method breaks down with a few simple illustrations.

Annual Figures

Material with tax	Labor with burden	Equipment costs	Subs	Total direct costs
\$180,000	\$156,000	\$72,000	\$12,000	\$420,000

\$420,000 TDC × 1.43 = \$600,000 Annual sales (rounded)

Gross profit margin is \$180,000 ÷ 600,000 = .3 or 30%.

Job A

A labor-intensive job lasting 10 months or one where the owner provides the materials

Material with tax	Labor with burden	Equipment costs	Total direct costs
$13,000	$130,000	$12,000	$155,000

$155,000 TDC × 1.43 = $221,650 Price

Job B

A material-intensive job lasting one month

Material with tax	Labor with burden	Equipment costs	Total direct costs
$130,000	$13,000	$12,000	$155,000

$155,000 TDC × 1.43 = $221,650 Price

Analysis

Job A

Question: How many months of G&A cost should we put on a 10-month job?

Answer: Ten months, or 10 months × $10,000 = $100,000

$155,000 TDC + $100,000 G&A overhead = $255,000 BEP

$255,000 + $28,333 (10% net profit margin) = $283,333 Price

Summary: Using the SORS method, our price calculated out to be $221,650. However, our BEP was $255,000. To cover 10 months of G&A overhead costs and to achieve a 10% net profit margin, our price needed to be $283,333. The SORS method understated our price by almost $62,000.

Job B

Question: How many months of G&A cost should we put on a one-month job?

Answer: One month, or 1 month × $10,000 = $10,000

$155,000 TDC + $10,000 G&A overhead = $165,000 BEP

$165,000 + $18,333 (10% net profit margin) = $183,333 Price

Summary: Using the SORS method, our price calculated out to be $221,650. However, our BEP was only $165,000. To cover one month of G&A overhead cost and to achieve a 10% net profit margin, our price needs to be $183,333. The SORS method overstated our price by over $38,000.

If I'm pricing these jobs in a competitive market using the correct amount of G&A overhead costs, which job do I get? If you're my competitor using the SORS method, which job do you get? Why am I happy, for me, that you get this job?

The Dual Overhead Recovery System (DORS) Method

The DORS method utilizes two elements of cost of goods sold—materials and labor with labor burden—and multiplies them by predetermined percentages. Costs for equipment owned by the company are included in indirect G&A costs. Subcontractor costs are usually marked up separately.

The markup percentages on the two COGS items are calculated as follows:

$$\text{G\&A overhead markup on material costs} = \frac{\text{Total annual G\&A overhead}}{[(\text{OWF}) \times (\text{Labor \& burden})] + \text{Materials}}$$

$$\text{G\&A overhead markup on labor costs} = \frac{(\text{OWF}) \times (\text{Total annual G\&A overhead})}{[(\text{OWF}) \times (\text{Labor \& burden})] + \text{Materials}}$$

OWF is a G&A overhead weighting factor which is obtained from a chart.

The markups for our example company work out as follows:

$$\text{G\&A overhead markup on material costs} = \frac{\$192{,}000}{[(2.56) \times (\$156{,}000)] + \$180{,}000}$$

$$= \$192{,}000 \div \$579{,}360 = .33140$$

This is 33.14%. You'd round this up to .332 or 33.2%.

$$\text{G\&A overhead markup on labor costs} = \frac{(2.56) \times (\$192{,}000)}{[(2.56) \times (\$156{,}000)] + \$180{,}000}$$

$$= \$491{,}520 \div \$579{,}360 = .848384$$

This is 84.84%. You'd round this to .85 or 85%.

The DORS method breaks down with a few simple illustrations.

Annual Figures

Material with tax	Labor with burden	Equipment costs	Subs	Total direct costs
$180,000	$156,000	in G&A costs	$12,000	$348,000

$348,000 TDC + $192,000 G&A costs + $60,000 Net profit = $600,000 Annual sales

Gross profit margin is $180,000 ÷ 600,000 = .3 or 30%.

Job A

A labor-intensive job lasting 10 months, or one where the owner provides the materials

Material with tax	Labor with burden	Equipment costs	Total direct costs
$13,000	$130,000	in G&A costs	$143,000 TDC
× .332	× .85		
$ 4,316	$110,500		$114,816 G&A
Break-even point			$257,816
Net profit margin of 10%			$ 28,646
Total Price			**$286,462**

Job B

A material-intensive job lasting one month

Material with tax	Labor with burden	Equipment costs	Total direct costs
$130,000	$13,000	in G&A costs	$143,000 TDC
× .332	× .85		
$ 43,160	$11,050		$ 54,210 G&A
Break-even point			$197,210
Net profit margin of 10%			$ 21,912
Total Price			**$219,122**

Analysis

Job A

Question: How many months of G&A cost should we put on a 10-month job?

Answer: Ten months, or 10 months × $10,000 = $100,000

$155,000 TDC + $100,000 G&A overhead = $255,000 BEP

$255,000 + $28,333 (10% net profit margin) = $283,333 Price

Summary: Using the DORS method, our price calculated out to be $286,462. However, by using 10 months of G&A overhead and calculating equipment costs on an "as needed" basis plus a 10% net profit margin, our price was calculated to be $283,333. The DORS method overstated our price by a little over $3,000.

Job B

Question: How many months of G&A cost should we put on a one-month job?

Answer: One month, or 1 month × $10,000 = $10,000

$155,000 TDC + $10,000 G&A overhead = $165,000 BEP

$165,000 + $18,333 (10% net profit margin) = $183,333 Price

Summary: Using the DORS method, our price calculated out to be $219,122. However, by using one month of G&A overhead and calculating equipment costs on an "as needed" basis plus a 10% net profit margin, our price was calculated to be $183,333. The DORS method overstated our price by almost $36,000.

We can further demonstrate the inherent mathematical flaws in the DORS method by varying the material costs in a one-month job. Our illustrations play out in the following manner.

Job C

A normal material job lasting one month

Material with tax	Labor with burden	Equipment costs	Subs	Total direct costs
$15,000	$13,000	$6,000*	$1,000	$29,000
× .332	× .85			
$ 4,980	$11,050			$16,030
Break-even point				$45,030
Net profit margin of 10%				$ 5,003
Total Price				**$50,033**

* In G&A overhead and not included in totals

Gross profit margin on the job is $21,038 or 42.1% (as defined by the DORS method).

Job D

A material-intensive job lasting one month

Material with tax	Labor with burden	Equipment costs	Subs	Total direct costs
$30,000	$13,000	$6,000*	$1,000	$44,000
× .332	× .85			
$ 9,960	$11,050			$21,010
Break-even point				$65,010
Net profit margin of 10%				$ 7,223
Total Price				**$72,233**

* In G&A overhead and not included in totals

Gross profit margin on the job is $28,233 or 39.1% (as defined by the DORS method).

Job E

A job lasting one month but the owner provides the materials

Material with tax	Labor with burden	Equipment costs	Subs	Total direct costs
$ 0	$13,000	$6,000*	$1,000	$14,000
× .332	× .85			
$ 0	$11,050			$11,050
Break-even point				$25,050
Net profit margin of 10%				$ 2,783
Total Price				**$27,833**

* In G&A overhead and not included in totals

Gross profit margin on the job is $28,233 or 39.1% (as defined by the DORS method).

Here we see that the DORS method breaks down whenever we keep the duration of the job the same and the material costs for the job(s) vary. Changes in subcontractor costs would accomplish the same thing. If the material, labor, equipment, and subcontractor costs in a job are not in the same proportion as projected in our annual budget, the G&A overhead allocated to the job will be either too high or too low. Rarely is it allocated accurately.

Our one-month jobs, which require one month of G&A overhead ($10,000), have amounts of G&A overhead allocation ranging as follows:

Job C	$16,030	Minus job equipment costs of $6,000 = $10,030
Job D	$21,010	Minus job equipment costs of $6,000 = $15,010
Job E	$11,050	Minus job equipment costs of $6,000 = $ 5,050

That's a variance of almost $10,000. When we adjust our G&A overhead for the $6,000 of equipment costs that are supposed to be included in the DORS G&A overhead totals, our variance is still close to $10,000. We see that we're close to our actual $10,000 in monthly G&A overhead costs on Job C, but we've seriously overstated and understated our G&A overhead costs on Jobs D and E.

Job	Adjusted DORS G&A	1 month G&A	Variance
C	$10,030	–$10,000	+ $ 30
D	$15,010	–$10,000	+ $5,010
E	$ 5,050	–$10,000	– $4,950

Equipment utilization variances from job to job will create serious cost differences on these jobs. These differences are never accounted for in the DORS method of bidding.

The Multiple Overhead Recovery System (MORS) Method

The MORS method utilizes all four elements of cost of goods sold and multiplies them by predetermined percentages. The markup percentages on materials, including sales tax (10%); equipment, both owned and rental (25%); and subcontractor costs (5%) are almost always the same. The markup percentage on labor, including labor burden, is calculated by using the annual budget for the company.

The 10%, 25%, and 5% markups are multiplied by the projected annual budget totals for materials with tax, equipment to include rentals, and subcontractors, respectively. The total G&A overhead dollar amounts to be recovered from these three elements of COGS are then subtracted from the total G&A overhead budgeted for the year. The remaining G&A overhead amount is then divided by the projected labor and labor burden budgeted for the year. It calculates out for our example as follows:

Total G&A overhead costs projected for the year		$120,000
$180,000 materials with sales tax annual budget	× .10 = $18,000	
$72,000 equipment annual budget	× .25 = $18,000	
$12,000 subcontractor annual budget	× .05 = $ 600	
	$36,600	
Total G&A overhead projected to be recovered from the above		– $ 36,600
G&A overhead costs to be recovered from labor and labor burden		$ 83,400
$83,400 ÷ $156,000 labor with burden annual budget = .534615		54%

Net profit is then added to the sum of the direct costs plus G&A overhead.

The MORS method breaks down with a few simple illustrations.

Annual Figures

Material with tax	Labor with burden	Equipment costs	Subs	Total direct costs
$180,000	$156,000	$72,000	$12,000	$420,000
× .1	× .534615	× .25	× .05	
$ 18,000	$ 83,400	$18,000	$ 600	$120,000

Break-even point for the year	$540,000
10% net profit margin for the year	$ 60,000
Total projected sales for the year	**$600,000**

Gross profit margin is $180,000 ÷ 600,000 = .3 or 30%.

Job A

A labor-intensive job lasting 10 months, or one where the owner provides the materials

Material with tax	Labor with burden	Equipment costs	Subs	Total direct costs
$13,000	$130,000	$12,000	$ 0	$155,000
× .1	× .54	× .25	× .05	
$ 1,300	$ 70,200	$ 4,000	$ 0	$ 75,500

Break-even point for the year	$230,500
10% net profit margin for the year	$ 25,611
Total Price	**$256,111**

Gross profit margin on the job is $101,111 or 39.5%.

Job B

A material-intensive job lasting one month

Material with tax	Labor with burden	Equipment costs	Subs	Total direct costs
$130,000	$13,000	$12,000	$ 0	$155,000
× .1	× .54	× .25	× .05	
$ 13,000	$ 7,020	$ 4,000	$ 0	$ 24,020
Break-even point for the year				$179,020
10% net profit margin for the year				$ 19,891
Total Price				**$198,911**

Gross profit margin on the job is $43,911 or 22.1%.

Analysis

Job A

Question: How many months of G&A cost should we put on a 10-month job?

Answer: Ten months, or 10 months × $10,000 = $100,000

$155,000 TDC + $100,000 G&A overhead = $255,000 BEP

$255,000 + $28,333 (10% net profit margin) = $283,333 Price

Summary: Using the MORS method, our price calculated out to be $256,111. However, our BEP was $255,000. To cover ten months of G&A overhead costs and to achieve a 10% net profit margin, our price needed to be $283,333. The MORS method understated our price by over $27,000.

Job B

Question: How many months of G&A cost should we put on a one-month job?

Answer: One month, or 1 month × $10,000 = $10,000

$155,000 TDC + $10,000 G&A overhead = $165,000 BEP

$165,000 + $18,333 (10% net profit margin) = $183,333 Price

Summary: Using the MORS method, our price calculated out to be $198,911. However, our BEP was only $165,000. To cover one month of G&A overhead cost and to achieve a 10% net profit margin, our price needs to be $183,333. The MORS method overstated our price by more than $15,000.

If I'm pricing these jobs in a competitive market using the correct amount of G&A overhead costs, which job do I get? If you're my competitor, using the MORS method, which job do you get? Why am I happy, for me, that you get this job?

We can further demonstrate the inherent mathematical flaws in the MORS method by varying the material costs in a one-month job. Our illustrations play out in the following manner.

Job C

A normal material job lasting one month

Material with tax	Labor with burden	Equipment costs	Subs	Total direct costs
$15,000	$13,000	$6,000	$1,000	$35,000
× .1	× .54	× .25	× .05	
$ 1,500	$ 7,020	$1,500	$ 50	$10,070
Break-even point				$45,070
10% net profit margin				$ 5,008
Total Price				**$50,078**

Gross profit margin on the job is $15,078 or 30%.

Job D

A material-intensive job lasting one month

Material with tax	Labor with burden	Equipment costs	Subs	Total direct costs
$30,000	$13,000	$6,000	$1,000	$50,000
× .1	× .54	× .25	× .05	
$ 3,000	$ 7,020	$1,500	$ 50	$11,570
Break-even point				$61,570
10% net profit margin				$ 6,841
Total Price				**$68,411**

Gross profit margin on the job is $18,411 or 26.9%.

Job E

A job lasting one month but the owner provides the materials

Material with tax	Labor with burden	Equipment costs	Subs	Total direct costs
$ 0	$13,000	$6,000	$1,000	$ 20,000
× .1	× .54	× .25	× .05	
$ 0	$ 7,020	$1,500	$ 50	$ 8,570
Break-even point				$28,570
10% net profit margin				$ 3,174
Total Price				**$31,744**

Gross profit margin on the job is $11,744 or 37.0%.

Analysis

Here we see that the MORS method breaks down whenever we keep the duration of the job the same and the material costs for the job(s) vary. Changes in the equipment and subcontractor costs would accomplish the same thing. If the material, labor, equipment, and subcontractor costs in a job aren't in the same proportion as projected in our annual budget, the G&A overhead allocated to the job will be either too high or too low. Rarely is it allocated accurately.

The Overhead and Profit per Hour (OPPH) Method

Let's price our jobs using the OPPH method of estimating.

Job A

A labor-intensive job lasting 10 months, or one where the owner provides the materials

Material with tax	Labor with burden	Equipment costs	Subs	Total direct costs
$13,000	$130,000	$12,000	$ 0	$155,000

G&A overhead = 10,000 hours in the job × $10.00 OPPH	$100,000
Break-even point	$255,000
10% net profit margin	$ 28,333
Total Price	**$283,333**

Gross profit margin on the job is $128,333 or 45.3%.

Job B

A material-intensive job lasting one month

Material with tax	Labor with burden	Equipment costs	Subs	Total direct costs
$130,000	$13,000	$12,000	$ 0	$155,000

G&A overhead = 1,000 hours in the job × $10.00 OPPH	$ 10,000
Break-even point	$165,000
10% net profit margin	$ 18,333
Total Price	**$183,333**

Gross profit margin on the job is $28,333 or 15.5%.

Job C

A normal material job lasting one month

Material with tax	Labor with burden	Equipment costs	Subs	Total direct costs
$15,000	$13,000	$6,000	$1,000	$35,000

G&A overhead = 1,000 hours in the job × $10.00 OPPH	$10,000
Break-even point	$45,000
10% net profit margin	$ 5,000
Total Price	**$50,000**

Gross profit margin on the job is $15,000 or 30.0%.

Job D

A material-intensive job lasting one month

Material with tax	Labor with burden	Equipment costs	Subs	Total direct costs
$30,000	$13,000	$6,000	$1,000	$50,000

G&A overhead = 1,000 hours in the job × $10.00 OPPH	$10,000
Break-even point	$60,000
10% net profit margin	$ 6,667
Total Price	**$66,667**

Gross profit margin on the job is $16,667 or 25.0%.

Job E

A job lasting one month but the owner provides the materials

Material with tax	Labor with burden	Equipment costs	Subs	Total direct costs
$ 0	$13,000	$6,000	$1,000	$20,000

G&A overhead = 1,000 hours in the job × $10.00 OPPH	$10,000
Break-even point	$30,000
10% net profit margin	$ 3,333
Total Price	**$33,333**

Gross profit margin on the job is $13,333 or 40.0%.

SUMMARY

We need to be scientific in our analysis of the various estimating methods being promulgated in the marketplace today. The issue is: Do our estimating methods calculate both our direct and indirect G&A overhead costs accurately? If they do, fine. If not, we need to make a change.

Many individuals have advocated using percentages in the estimating process to allocate and recover G&A costs. I'm sure their intentions were good. However, I'm equally sure their arithmetic was not. The illustrations in this chapter have shown that the SORS, DORS, and MORS methods of estimating display serious mathematical flaws when used in specific bidding situations.

We need to take note of the fact that G&A overhead costs simply don't change that much, if at all, from month to month throughout the year. Most contractors realize this. While they may only work an 8- to 10-month season, their G&A overhead costs don't drop off considerably at the end of the working season.

We should also note how the gross profit margin changes from job to job using the DORS and MORS methods. These methods attempt to correct the faulty mathematical assumptions in the SORS method, but they create additional mathematical errors of their own in doing so.

It's also worthy of note that the gross profit margin varies from job to job when using the OPPH method. This variation between jobs is valid and refutes the popularly held notion that gross profit margins on individual jobs should be the same as the gross profit margin you desire to realize on your company profit and loss statement at the end of the year.

Categorically, we can state that there's no correlation between the amount of gross profit you desire to realize on your company profit and loss statement at the end of the year and the amount of gross profit you should put on individual jobs throughout the year.

> Categorically, we can state that there's no correlation between the amount of gross profit you desire to realize on your company profit and loss statement at the end of the year and the amount of gross profit you should put on individual jobs throughout the year.

Indirect G&A overhead costs are much more closely related to the duration of the job, whether it be for a year, month, week, man-day, crew-day, or man-hour, than to particular events (costs for materials, subcontractors, equipment, and labor) occurring within the job. Approximately 85 to 90% of the costs in G&A overhead are paid based on a time unit (rent per month, salaries per week, and so on).

The proponents of the SORS, DORS, and MORS methods in reality are doing something very similar when they prepare their company G&A overhead budget based on an entire year. The mistake they make is allocating these budgeted G&A overhead costs based on events, not a time unit.

All G&A overhead recovery systems use a basic time unit of one year to total and measure the G&A overhead to recover. They only disagree on what unit(s) to base their recovery system on. I use a time unit, primarily the man-hour. The other systems use events within COGS. This is where they make their mathematical mistake as they try to convert apples to oranges. It just does not work mathematically.

We could have included the factoring method in our discussion. Materials times 2.0 (or 3.0, or 4.0) uses a markup of 200%. However, I didn't include it in this section, as its flaws are somewhat self-evident.

> The proponents of the SORS, DORS, and MORS methods in reality are doing something very similar when they prepare their company G&A overhead budget based on an entire year. The mistake they make is allocating these budgeted G&A overhead costs based on events, not a time unit.

I can categorically state that my clients and I have never had a problem allocating G&A overhead to jobs based on linking it to a man-hour time unit. We have always been very competitive and able to win plenty of work.

My recommendation is that you calculate your bids using the Overhead and Profit per Hour method as your "default" estimating method. Then go back and price your work using your old method for pricing and/or the SORS, DORS, and MORS methods. You can easily do this with a software spreadsheet program.

The OPPH method will provide you with a "safety net" price. If your price is higher using your old method than the OPPH price and you can sell it to your client, by all means do so. However, if the OPPH price is higher than your old method, use it.

ACTION POINTS

1. Price your jobs using your current method of bidding and/or the SORS, DORS, and MORS methods.
2. Price your jobs using the Overhead and Profit per Hour method of bidding.
3. Compare the difference.

Keeping on Track

Running Your Company Right from the Bid Sheet

SECTION VI

Contents

Purpose

To provide some basic tools and illustrations that will help you control your company and your destiny

To help you understand how to build a legacy, not just a business

The topics covered in this section are not the "hard" analytical stuff of scientific cost estimating and bidding. Cost estimating and bidding affect sales, bonuses, strategies and so forth much more than you might suppose. And sometimes sales and strategies (along with the other topics listed) directly affect the estimating and bidding process.

My clients have found the coverage of the topics contained in this section to be very helpful and informative. At the risk of deviating too far from our primary topic of cost estimating and bidding, I've included them. I trust you'll find them useful.

CHAPTER

40

Sales: The Bid Board and the M.A.D. Report

Purpose

To explain various methods for monitoring sales performance

Introduction

Annual budgets establish your sales goals for the year. It's necessary, however, to *monitor* your "budget-to-actual" sales performance during the course of the year. We do so using a combination of tools that help us monitor the big picture.

The information displayed in the items that we will discuss in this section is very powerful. You and your staff should be very careful about who has access to this information both inside and outside of the company.

SALES CATEGORIES

Sales should be broken down into the following three categories:

- Contracts signed
- Work installed and billed
- Work installed but not billed

TOOLS FOR MONITORING YOUR SALES

The Bid Board

The Bid Board (shown in Figure 40-1 on page 332) displays and tracks much of the process of bringing business into the company. It helps you gain more control over and *accelerate* the bidding process. In turn, the bid board will motivate your people by providing effective feedback and a continuous flow of vital information. Without a doubt, it can be your most powerful tool. You'll obtain a grasp on what I call the "faucet," or the handle, that controls your company. Once you firmly grasp the handle, you can then turn it on or off in order to control the flow. Unfortunately, most contractors never find the handle.

The Bid Board is designed to *focus* your attention at crucial pressure points in the process of obtaining new work (jobs). It helps you quantify and measure the dynamic involved in this process, and it establishes goals relating to the sales process. Your management attention (your energy) can then be focused where it needs to be, when it needs to be.

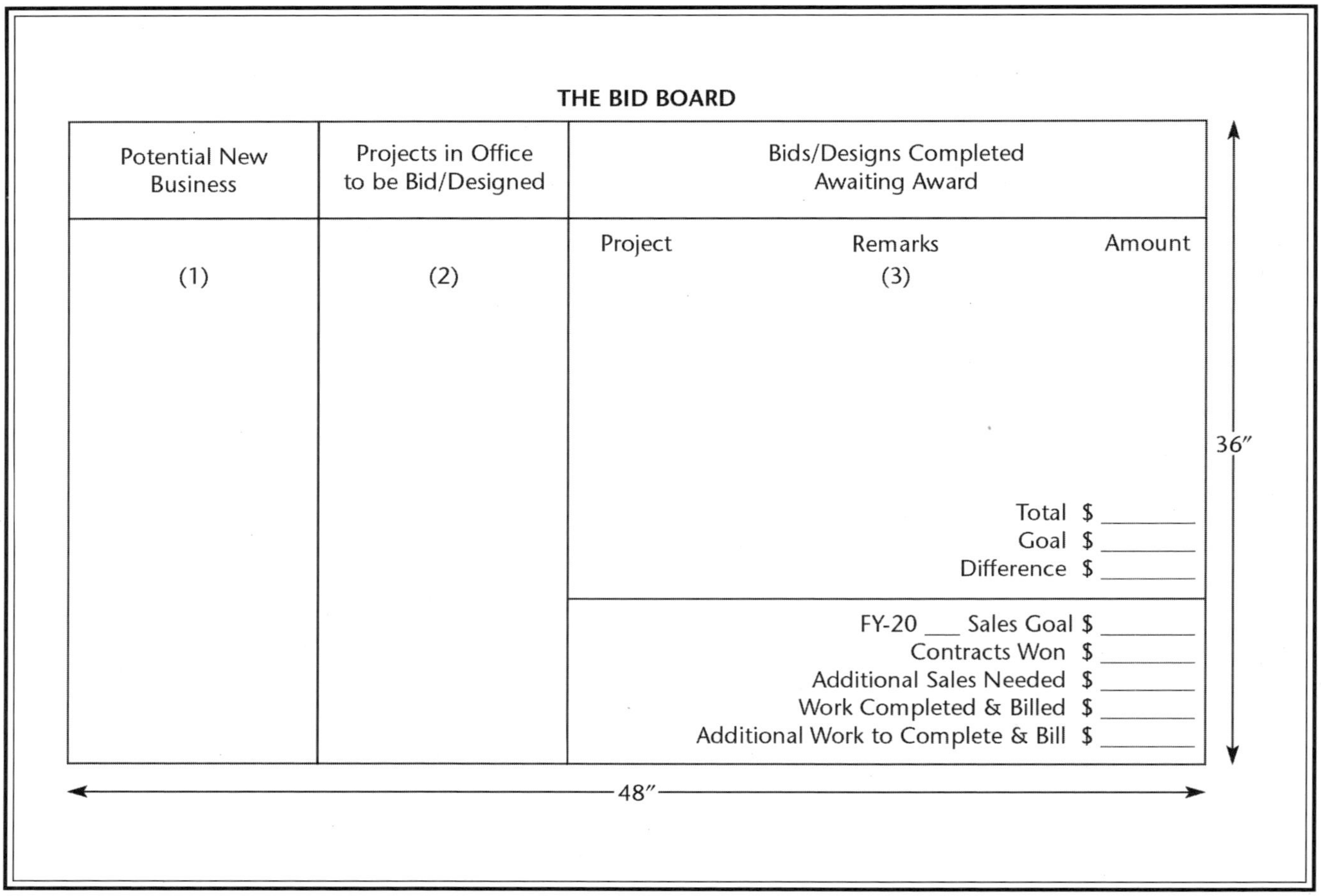

FIGURE 40-1 The Bid Board

How It Works

I created the Bid Board while working with a company in the Northwest. Two brothers were taking over a family business and their sales needed to increase from about $600,000 to over $1 million. Because so many things were happening at once, I sensed that the brothers needed some help keeping their focus on achieving their sales goal for the year.

They had a 3′ × 4′ erasable dry-ink, white board in their office that they were not using. I got to thinking and came up with the idea for the Bid Board. We placed it in a strategic position within the company where all the key staff could not help but see it. It was so effective that within five months this company blew right through their sales goal.

Construction of the Bid Board

- Start with a 3′ × 4′ erasable dry-ink, white board (available at an office supply store).
- Use a black dry-ink marker to fill in most of the board. Use red sparingly. If you clutter it up with other colors, it will lose its effect.
- Make entries in neat, one-inch high, block-style lettering.

Filling in the Bid Board

1 Potential New Business

In column 1 enter the names and telephone numbers of all possible leads and contacts, where you might obtain sets of plans for bidding, and so on. List as many of the following as are applicable:

- Developers
- Owners
- General Contractors
- Landscape Architects
- Homeowners' Associations
- Property Managers
- Government Agencies (city, state, federal, DOD, DOT, etc.)
- *Dodge Reports*, green sheets, plans rooms
- New projects coming up
- Geographical areas/markets to tap into, etc.

If it might lead to more work, it goes here.

The information is right there and at eye level. You know immediately where to look to get new ideas to find new work because the information's right in your face.

If an item is really *hot* and you want to pursue it aggressively, get out a red marker and put an asterisk (*) beside it. Mark only five or six items with red, or the effectiveness will be greatly diminished.

Rarely will you ever erase an item from column 1.

2 Projects in Office to be Bid/Designed

Column 2 is for sets of plans already in the office and ready for bidding, and for plans that need to be designed and then bid (usually residential ones). Enter the project or client name here.

Strive to keep 5 to 10 projects in this column at all times. If you need more work, increase this number to 12 to 15 (if possible). The important thing is that you begin to see the natural flow of how to bring business into your company and that you can often turn it on or off by taking some well-defined course of action.

Once you've designed and bid the project, erase it from column 2 and put it in column 3.

3 Bids/Designs Completed and Awaiting Award

Column 3 lists all projects for which you've submitted bids that have yet to be awarded. Include the project name, the dollar amount, and any remarks (dates, names, telephone numbers) that you feel necessary.

4 A Running Total of Bids Pending

I like to keep as many projects as possible in this column at all times. You might want to put these projects on a computer spreadsheet and tape it to this section of the Bid Board. I actually tape the Bid Status Report (see Figure 40-2) here and update it continually.

5 Your Goal

The Goal identifies the dollar amounts of bids that should be pending at any one time. This figure may be what you "feel" is necessary to keep enough work coming into the business, or it may be a more precise calculation.

EXAMPLE

Calculation of Bids Pending

If your sales goal is $500,000 for the year and you get roughly one out of 10 jobs you bid (10% or .10), divide $500,000 by .10. The result is $5,000,000. In other words, you need to bid about $5,000,000 of work that year in order to get your $500,000.

My residential clients get 50 to 80% of everything they bid. Therefore, they need to bid $625,000 to $1,000,000 in order to get their $500,000 for the year.

- Determine the turnaround time (TAT). Guesstimate how long it takes from the time you turn in a bid until you find out if you have the job. This may be only one week for residential work and up to four or five months, or longer, for commercial work.
- Divide the goal for the year by the number of TAT periods in a year.

Using a TAT of one month, there are 12 TAT periods in a year. When we divide $5,000,000 by 12, we get $416,667. We need to have $416,667 worth of bids pending at any one time to meet our sales goal for the year.

If our TAT is two weeks, we'll divide $5,000,000 by 26 TAT periods in one year. In this case we need $192,308 worth of bids pending at any one time.

A. Evaluate Seasonal Work

The above example assumes your work is spread evenly throughout the year, which is hardly ever the case. This is how you'd handle seasonal business:

- Determine the Sales Goal and then the amount you need to bid.
- Establish monthly sales and amount-pending goals for the upcoming season, starting with the month of September of the present season.

B. Target Specific Goals by Certain Dates

Initially, you won't necessarily know how much to shoot for, but it's not important. Just bid as much as you can, track it, and get a feel for how much work you have to bid in September in order to get a certain backlog by March 1of the following year. Strive to meet or exceed your goal. Adjust it as you acquire a feel for the process.

After you monitor this dynamic for 6 to 12 months these numbers will make a lot more sense to you, and you'll begin to wonder why you didn't track them sooner.

6 Difference

Subtract the Pending Total from the Goal. If you're below your goal, enter this sum on the Difference line in *red*. We want that red number to reach out and slap you in the face to motivate you to get more work.

Version 2003-1

		BUDGET	ACTUAL	VARIANCE		BUDGET	ACTUAL	VARIANCE		
1-PENDING	Sales budget for year——>	$900,000	$151,001	$748,999	Bids pending goal—>	$346,154	$214,677	$131,477	Percentage of bids won——>	20%
2-LOST	Field hour budget for year——>	16,000	2,334	13,666	Work billed——>	$900,000	$65,000	$835,000	Average bid turn-around-time——>	4.0
3-WON	Average sales per field labor hour——>	$56.25	$64.70	$8.45	Add'l work to complete & bill——>			$835,000	(in weeks)	

#	Bid #	SP	#	GC/Owner	Project	Date	Contact	Phone	Bid Hrs	Amount Bid	Pend-1	Lost-2	Won-3	Billed	Backlog	HRS YTD	SPH	G&A OH-%	Net Profit %	GPM-%	Remarks
	NO					Submitted		Totals——>	7,006	$412,680	$214,677	$47,001	$151,001	$65,000	$86,001	2,334	$64.70	AVE.	AVE.	AVE.	XXXXXXX
									43.8%	9.2%	52.0%	11.4%	36.6%	7.2%	9.6%	14.6%	XXXXX	16.4%	14.4%	30.8%	XXXXXXX
1	JCN	<—Enter job control number or name							1	1	0	0	0	0	0	0	1.00			0.0%	-
2	2003001	10	1	Douglas Const.	Corona H.S.				895	55,000	55,000	0	0	0	0	0	61.45	16.0%	12.0%	28.0%	-
3	2003002	10	2	P&P Builders	Little Park				479	25,000	0	25,000	0	0	0	0	52.19	14.0%	12.0%	26.0%	-
4	2003003	10	3	John Wyman	Wyman Res.				253	15,000	0	0	15,000	10,000	5,000	253	59.29	18.0%	20.0%	38.0%	-
5	2003004	10	1	Paul Butcher	Butcher Res.				327	18,000	18,000	0	0	0	0	0	55.05	16.0%	20.0%	36.0%	-
6	2003005	10	2	J&J Const.	Village Apts.				388	22,000	0	22,000	0	0	0	0	56.70	17.0%	12.0%	29.0%	-
7	2003006	10	3	ABC Const.	Motel 88				185	11,000	0	0	11,000	5,000	6,000	185	59.46	16.0%	12.0%	28.0%	-
8	2003007	10	1	J&J Const.	Stop & Go				1,296	75,000	75,000	0	0	0	0	0	57.87	16.0%	12.0%	28.0%	-
9	2003008	10	3	ABC Const.	NuCo				1,895	125,000	0	0	125,000	50,000	75,000	1,895	65.96	17.0%	12.0%	29.0%	-
10	2003009	10	1	Bill Robershaw	Robershaw Re				625	37,500	37,500	0	0	0	0	0	60.00	19.0%	20.0%	39.0%	-
11	2003010	10	1	RBK	Valley Crest				483	29,000	29,000	0	0	0	0	0	60.04	15.0%	12.0%	27.0%	-
12	2003011	10	2	CO.					1	1	0	1	0	0	0	0	1.00			0.0%	-
13	2003012	10	3	CO.					1	1	0	0	1	0	1	1	1.00			0.0%	-
14	2003013	10	1	CO.					1	1	1	0	0	0	0	0	1.00			0.0%	-
15	2003014	10	1	CO.					1	1	1	0	0	0	0	0	1.00			0.0%	-
16	2003015	10	1	CO.					1	1	1	0	0	0	0	0	1.00			0.0%	-
17	2003016	10	1	CO.					1	1	1	0	0	0	0	0	1.00			0.0%	-
18	2003017	10	1	CO.					1	1	1	0	0	0	0	0	1.00			0.0%	-
19	2003018	10	1	CO.					1	1	1	0	0	0	0	0	1.00			0.0%	-
20	2003019	10	1	CO.					1	1	1	0	0	0	0	0	1.00			0.0%	-
21	2003020	10	1	CO.					1	1	1	0	0	0	0	0	1.00			0.0%	-
22	2003021	10	1	CO.					1	1	1	0	0	0	0	0	1.00			0.0%	-
23	2003022	10	1	CO.					1	1	1	0	0	0	0	0	1.00			0.0%	-
24	2003023	10	1	CO.					1	1	1	0	0	0	0	0	1.00			0.0%	-
25	2003024	10	1	CO.					1	1	1	0	0	0	0	0	1.00			0.0%	-
26	2003025	10	1	CO.					1	1	1	0	0	0	0	0	1.00			0.0%	-
27	2003026	10	1	CO.					1	1	1	0	0	0	0	0	1.00			0.0%	-
28	2003027	10	1	CO.					1	1	1	0	0	0	0	0	1.00			0.0%	-
29	2003028	10	1	CO.					1	1	1	0	0	0	0	0	1.00			0.0%	-
30	2003029	10	1	CO.					1	1	1	0	0	0	0	0	1.00			0.0%	-
31	2003030	10	1	CO.					1	1	1	0	0	0	0	0	1.00			0.0%	-
32	2003031	10	1	CO.					1	1	1	0	0	0	0	0	1.00			0.0%	-
33	2003032	10	1	CO.					1	1	1	0	0	0	0	0	1.00			0.0%	-
34	2003033	10	1	CO.					1	1	1	0	0	0	0	0	1.00			0.0%	-
35	2003034	10	1	CO.					1	1	1	0	0	0	0	0	1.00			0.0%	-
36	2003035	10	1	CO.					1	1	1	0	0	0	0	0	1.00			0.0%	-
37	2003036	10	1	CO.					1	1	1	0	0	0	0	0	1.00			0.0%	-
38	2003037	10	1	CO.					1	1	1	0	0	0	0	0	1.00			0.0%	-
39	2003038	10	1	CO.					1	1	1	0	0	0	0	0	1.00			0.0%	-
40	2003039	10	1	CO.					1	1	1	0	0	0	0	0	1.00			0.0%	-
41	2003040	10	1	CO.					1	1	1	0	0	0	0	0	1.00			0.0%	-
42	2003041	10	1	CO.					1	1	1	0	0	0	0	0	1.00			0.0%	-
43	2003042	10	1	CO.					1	1	1	0	0	0	0	0	1.00			0.0%	-
44	2003043	10	1	CO.					1	1	1	0	0	0	0	0	1.00			0.0%	-
45	2003044	10	1	CO.					1	1	1	0	0	0	0	0	1.00			0.0%	-
46	2003045	10	1	CO.					1	1	1	0	0	0	0	0	1.00			0.0%	-
47	2003046	10	1	CO.					1	1	1	0	0	0	0	0	1.00			0.0%	-
48	2003047	10	1	CO.					1	1	1	0	0	0	0	0	1.00			0.0%	-
49	2003048	10	1	CO.					1	1	1	0	0	0	0	0	1.00			0.0%	-
50	2003049	10	1	CO.					1	1	1	0	0	0	0	0	1.00			0.0%	-

FIGURE 40-2 Bid Status Report

7 FY—Sales Goal

Enter the yearly sales goal in the FY—Sales Goal portion of column 3.

8 Contracts Won

Fill in the Contracts Won section and subtract it from the FY—Sales Goal in order to determine Additional Sales Needed. Again, use red if this number is below your goals.

9 Work Completed & Billed

Fill in the Work Completed & Billed section. Subtract it from the FY—Sales Goal. Enter the difference (in red, if necessary) in the Additional Work To Complete & Bill section.

Motivation

Used properly, the Bid Board can be one of your most powerful motivational tools. We recommend that you

- Have one per division, if appropriate
- Have one board for each sales person
- Fill in the board and keep it up to date *at all times*. This allows you to monitor the goals of your salespeople and provides a "report card" for a very crucial part of your business.

  It can greatly facilitate *communication* and *training*. You can help your staff set priorities and focus their energies as you review each board (and progress) throughout the year. You, the owner or manager, should be the only person allowed to mark the "hot" items with the red marker on the board. This technique can focus your staff on those items that *you* deem important.
- Place the Bid Board in a strategic location

  Out of sight leads to out of mind. Place the Bid Board in an area that's at eye level. Put it within a few feet of the desk where the person using it will be sitting and looking right at it during the course of the day. It can motivate the dickens out of your people. It will focus energy and enhance communication by sharing vital information and priorities with your staff.
- Be aware of who sees the Bid Board.

  The Bid Board contains vital company information your competitors would like to have. Be careful who has access to it and where you place it.

The Bid Status Report

The Bid Status Report (refer back to Figure 40-2) is a computerized spreadsheet version of the key elements on the Bid Board.

I developed the Bid Status Report because we were running out of room on the Bid Board for all projects awaiting award. We were weary from making all those continuous changes on the Bid Board and knew there had to be a better way to track the needed information. Hence, the Bid Status Report was born.

Many of our clients like the Bid Status Report because it displays so much useful information and analysis.

- It's a compact, orderly, and convenient record of every project you ever bid.
- If kept current and used properly, it's your most dependable means of tracking bids.
- It automatically adjusts to the flow of new information. It will accurately re-compute and fill in the appropriate columns (i.e., bids pending, lost, won).

It's a marvelous tool. If you're interested in purchasing a copy of the Bid Status Report on diskette, please contact our offices.

The Monthly Audit Data (M.A.D.) Report

The Monthly Audit Data (M.A.D.) Report (see Figures 40-3A and 40-3B on pages 338 and 339) is a monthly, systematic tracking report that charts the process of bringing sales into your business. This is solid statistical information. It is particularly useful for identifying key trends over a long period of time (6 to 18 months), and for analyzing information in more seasonal locations. This information can be used for identifying and comparing trends, backlogs, bids outstanding compared to sales, and so on. A blank M.A.D. Report can be found in Exhibit 11.

Many of our clients learn to appreciate its value more as they encounter periods of economic downturn because it provides solid numbers, versus anxious feelings, on which to base business decisions.

The M.A.D. Report form is also available on diskette through our offices.

The Sales "Budget vs. Actual" Graph

Figure 40-4 on page 340 depicts your gross sales budget compared to your actual sales and completed work that has been billed. You should update this graph weekly. The difference between actual sales and work completed and billed is your work backlog. Used in conjunction with the Work Backlog Graph, it can provide some excellent insight into the results of your sales efforts for the year.

The Work Backlog Graph

The Work Backlog Graph shown in Figure 40-5 on page 340 is a simple chart you can fill in weekly. It graphs both your backlog goal and actual performance.

SUMMARY

Establishing sales budgets (goals) and monitoring your progress toward achieving them are essential management tasks. Information properly formatted and collected in a timely manner can provide crucial diagnostic insight into the process of bringing sales into your company. It can also focus management energy and motivate staff to take corrective action if necessary. The Bid Board is an excellent tool for monitoring all of the jobs you've bid. The Monthly Audit Data (M.A.D.) Report and the other items presented here are excellent tools for monitoring crucial company information and market trends on a regular basis. However, be careful who has access to this information. It is very powerful and you do not want it to fall into the wrong hands.

Be careful who has access to this information. It is very powerful and you do not want it to fall into the wrong hands.

ACTION POINT

Review your methods of tracking your company's sales performance and incorporate the items discussed in this chapter as deemed appropriate.

Exhibit 11: The M.A.D. Report

From: John Date: 7 / 1 /20___

Subject: M.A.D. Report for the month of: June, 20___

1. Financial information:

A. Sales:

	(Month)	(Y-T-D)
Construction	$ 129,453	$ 379,185
Maintenance	$ 31,052	$ 108,760
Irrigation	$ 36,809	$ 111,226
Trees	$ 18,624	$ 48,035
______	$	$

B. Payables: $ 66,124 $ 13,281 $ 1,100 $ ⌀ $ 80,505

C. Receivables:

(Current)	(30)	(60)	(90)	(Total)
$ 187,062	$ 22,189	$ 10,928	$ 2,377	$ 222,556

D. Financial ratios:

(1). Total receivables ÷ total payables $ 222,556 ÷ $ 80,505 = 2.77

(2). Current receivables ÷ total payables $ 187,062 ÷ $ 80,505 = 2.32

(3). Quick ratio: Cash + Total Receivables / Current liabilities $ 68,218 + $ 222,556 / $ (66,124 + 8,800*) = 3.9

* Non-A/P payables

2. Production (Cost of Goods Sold):

A. Labor:

	Month $	Month Hours	Y-T-D $	Y-T-D Hours
(1). Construction	$ 27,090	2,465	$ 74,200	6,799
(2). Maintenance	$ 10,850	1,080	$ 36,720	3,602
(3). Irrigation	$ 8,099	675	$ 22,200	1,850
(4). Trees	$ 4,656	333	$ 12,008	865

B. Materials:

	Month $	Y-T-D $
(1). Construction	$ 41,280	$ 112,000
(2). Maintenance	$ 2,300	$ 9,810
(3). Irrigation	$ 9,210	$ 24,420
(4). Trees	$ 236	$ 728

C. Production ratios:

	Month SPH	Month CAW	Y-T-D SPH	Y-T-D CAW
(1). Construction	$ 52.52	$ 10.99	$ 55.77	$ 10.91
(2). Maintenance	$ 28.75	$ 10.05	$ 30.19	$ 10.19
(3). Irrigation	$ 54.53	$ 12.00	$ 60.12	$ 12.00
(4). Trees	$ 55.93	$ 13.98	$ 55.53	$ 13.88

D. Material / Labor ratios:

	Month	Y-T-D
(1). Construction	1.52 :1	1.51 :1
(2). Maintenance	0.21 :1	0.26 :1
(3). Irrigation	1.14 :1	1.10 :1
(4). Trees	0.05 :1	0.06 :1

FIGURE 40-3A M.A.D. Report

E. GPM per hour:

	Budget	Actual	Variance
(1). Construction	$ 18.00	$ 16.55	$ <1.45>
(2). Maintenance	$ 10.50	$ 10.75	$ 0.25
(3). Irrigation	$ 19.00	$ 20.40	$ 1.40
(4). Trees	$ 18.50	$ 19.25	$ 0.75

NOTES:
1. Get Budget GPMPH from Budget
2. Get Actual GPMPH by dividing P&L GPM by hours

F. G&A overhead per hour (OPH):

	Budget	Actual	Variance
(1). Construction	$ 12.00	$ N/A	$ N/A
(2). Maintenance	$ 7.50	$ N/A	$ N/A
(3). Irrigation	$ 12.00	$ N/A	$ N/A
(4). Trees	$ 12.00	$ N/A	$ N/A
(5) whole Company	# 11.10	# 12.18	# <1.08>

3. Estimating:

A. Sales:

	Construction	Maintenance	Irrigation	Trees
(1). Budget for the year	$ 1,000,000	$ 279,000	$ 325,000	$ 225,000
(2). Contracts signed Y-T-D	$ 729,144	$ 223,200	$ 191,000	$ 155,228
(3). Additional work needed	$ 270,856	$ 55,800	$ 134,000	$ 69,772
(4). Work installed and billed	$ 344,185	$ 108,760	$ 106,226	$ 48,035
(5). Work installed & to be billed	$ 35,000	$ Ø	$ 5,000	$ Ø
(6). Additional work to install & bill	$ 620,185	$ 170,240	$ 213,774	$ 176,965

B. Field-labor hours (Billable):

	Construction	Maintenance	Irrigation	Trees
(1). Budget for the year	16,650	9,425	5,900	4,100
(2). Actual Y-T-D	6,799	3,602	1,850	865
(3). Variance Y-T-D	9,851	5,823	4,050	3,235

C. Bidding (all categories as of the last day of the month):

	(const. only)
(1). # sets of plans in office to bid	10
(2). # projects in office to be designed	6
(3). # projects in office in process of being designed	2
(4). # jobs bid (pending) but not awarded yet	63
(5). $ amount of jobs bid (pending) but not awarded yet	$ 1,560,483
(6). Average $ amount of pending bids (5 ÷ 4)	$ 24,770

4. Management issues:

A. 5 Main challenges to be faced next month:

(1). TREE SERVICE SALES LOW
(2). DOCUMENTATION OF WEEKLY SAFETY/TAIL GATE MEETINGS
(3). CASH FLOW TIGHT
(4). JOB COST REPORTS NOT TIMELY
(5). FALL BACKLOG LOW

B. 5 Main goals for next month:

(1). START UP 2nd TREE SERVICE CREW AS PLANNED
(2). INCREASE LOC
(3). CREW LEADERS DOCUMENT ALL MEETINGS & PROVIDE BONUS
(4). " " PROVIDE ALL PAPERWORK TO OFFICE DAILY
(5). ESTIMATORS/OWNER CHECK GC'S RE: FALL WORK.

FIGURE 40-3B M.A.D. Report (continued)

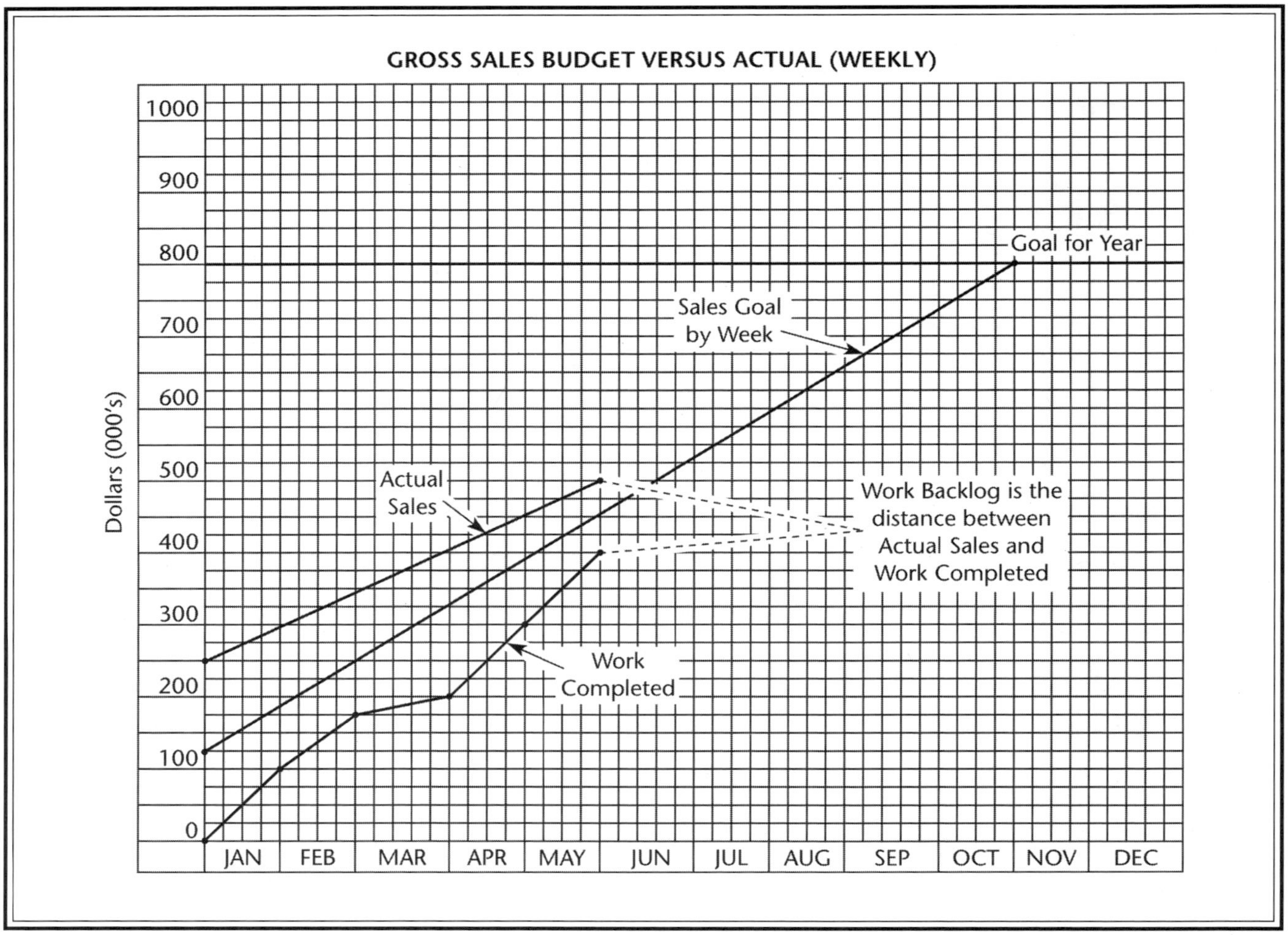

FIGURE 40-4 Sales "Budget vs. Actual" Graph

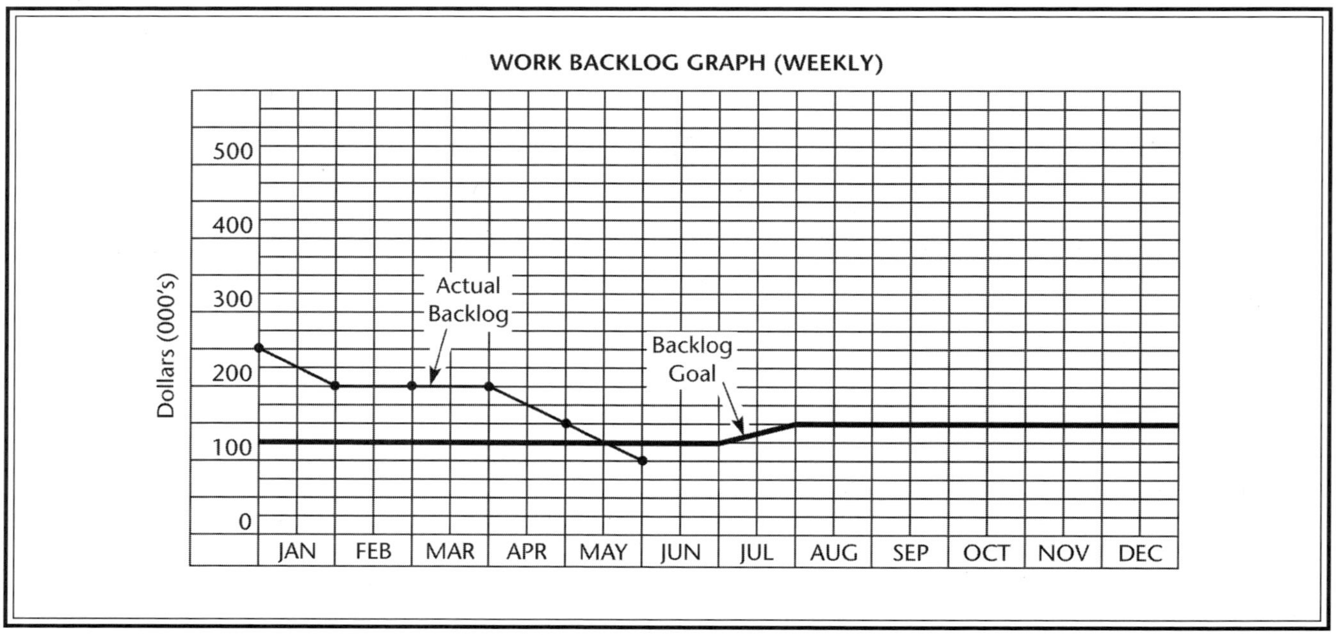

FIGURE 40-5 Work Backlog Graph

CHAPTER 41

Job Costing

Purpose

To explain the purpose and mechanics of a job-cost system and the steps necessary to start such a system

Introduction

The most common complaint I hear from contractors is "I just don't know if I'm making money on this job."

"I just don't know if I'm making money on this job." This is the most common complaint I hear from contractors. Their Profit and Loss Statement may tell them they're making money, but they usually don't know where. Worse yet, they don't even know where to start looking to find an adequate answer to their question.

The most important report for your bookkeeper to produce is a weekly (I prefer daily) job-cost report for each job in progress. Effective job costing (in combination with proper planning and scheduling) can turn losing jobs into winners. I've seen it happen time after time: *Proper Planning* and *Preparation Produce Profitable Projects*. Remember these six Ps.

I've seen it happen time after time: *Proper Planning* and *Preparation Produce Profitable Projects*. Remember these six Ps.

If bidding produces your pre-game strategy, it's job costing that keeps score during the game—it tells you where you are along the way. Think what measured events professional sports have become. Baseball's a game based on data collection, analysis, and comparison. Batting averages, ERAs, and RBIs are all results of "job costing," if you will. Professional football is an even more measured event. Goal lines, sidelines, hash marks, yard markers, goal posts, end zones, 1st, 2nd, 3rd and 4th downs, offense-defense, quarters, time-outs, two-minute warnings, and the 40-second clock make up just the playing field. Statistics are kept on everyone, including the coach. There are even guys on the field in "zebra" suits, throwing yellow hankies in the air and blowing whistles when someone's play is not up to the accepted standard.

My point is this. Professional sports teams use the same type of information management methodology as landscape and irrigation contractors should. Standards or performance targets are identified. Performance data is collected and compared to the standard. A variance is determined, and corrections are made to performance in an attempt to improve it. Coaches direct the game and adjust their playing strategy based on data that has been collected and analyzed.

If football coaches approached the game of football the way 99% of landscape and irrigation contractors run their companies, you'd see 22 guys beating each other's brains out on a 40-acre sea of green grass. No chalk lines, goal posts, boundaries, referees, or time clocks. No standards or data collected and analyzed. Not even a scoreboard—just 22 men going through a lot of pain and wondering which direction they should go.

Sound familiar?

Job costing is simply the process of measuring and comparing actual field performance to a predetermined standard or sets of standards included in your bid. Just like professional sports, it can be a very clear-cut, analytical process. If done properly, job costing can provide the objective foundation on which to build a total quality management (TQM) program for your company.

Profits, labor productivity, and management controls will all be maximized when job costing is properly put into place. For a contractor, job costing is the process of comparing direct costs (material costs, field-labor hours and dollars, equipment hours and dollars, and subcontractor costs bid into a specific project) to the actual hours and dollars expended on these same categories. Good job costing starts in the bidding process. Unless you establish appropriate, clearly defined standards in the bid, you have nothing against which to compare actual field performance.

There are four specific cost targets that need to be identified and quantified for each job in the bidding process. They are as follows:

1. Material costs to be used on the job (i.e., fertilizers, mulch, etc.)
2. Labor, identified in terms of hours estimated to be used on the job as well as the total payroll dollars to pay for those hours
3. Equipment hours for each piece of equipment to be used on the job (i.e., specific types of mowers, tractors, pickup trucks, string trimmers, etc.) and their corresponding cost per hour (CPH)
4. Subcontractor costs

A fifth "miscellaneous" category is sometimes used by contractors to collect and identify dumpsters, lock boxes, storage containers, permits, fees, commissions, and so forth.

The cost targets and/or standards identified in the bidding process are the specific amounts of materials, labor, equipment, and subcontractor costs required to *"safely"* meet the performance standards identified in the plans and specifications for the job being bid. Consequently, quality control and safety measurement become integrated with job costing. Because we've reduced our performance and safety standards and translated them into quantifiable, measurable cost standards, the job-costing process is now possible.

Job costing is best accomplished through a computerized construction and services accounting software program. Otherwise, the appropriate checks and balances and controls aren't in place to ensure that field-costing data is accurately allocated to the correct job. Job costing through your accounting system also eliminates duplication of work. I've seen contractors use a computer accounting system for their financial statements and a spreadsheet program for tracking their jobs. The two systems hardly ever agree, and at least twice the labor is required.

And all this effort obtains questionable results. Software programs that have adequate job costing are expensive ($5,000 to 15,000) and require a stable office staff to learn and run them. You'll probably pay as much for training on the software as for the software itself. However, any company doing over $1 million in annual sales should invest in such a system. The return will more than pay for itself if the software has the right capability, good support, and a strong and stable company behind it. I know of larger companies, ones doing over $20 million in annual sales, that have spent in excess of $200,000 on job-costing and accounting software.

Field payroll should be generated from the data you collect to produce job-cost reports. If you have two separate systems for collecting this data, payroll will be accurate and job costing will not. Combine these two systems, eliminate redundancy, and improve the accuracy of the data being collected.

TYPES OF DATA TO IDENTIFY

The types of information a job-costing system should provide and the format for this information are crucial. Whether your system is manual or computer-generated from an accounting program or a spreadsheet, you need the following direct cost information, at least weekly, for each of your jobs in progress:

1. *Material Costs.* Job-cost reports should identify all materials, sales taxes, and delivery fees used on a job. As much as is practical, vendor invoices should include materials used on one job only, and the name of the job should appear on the invoice to facilitate tracking purposes. Purchase orders or some sort of issue slip should be used for in-house inventory items used on projects. Otherwise, these items (i.e., bulk mulch, sprinkler repair parts, in-house grown and bulk purchase nursery materials) won't be charged to jobs accurately, and profit margins will appear erroneously high for the jobs in question.
2. *Field-Labor Costs.* It's important to identify labor hours and the actual monetary cost of those hours (if possible), and to compare them to your budget. If you don't track and compare both, you might bring the project in on-budget for hours but over-budget in dollars. This would happen if the crew actually performing the work on the job was comprised of higher-priced labor than that used to bid the project.

   Many maintenance contractors format their job-cost reports to identify labor-hour targets to be achieved for each crew visit to the site. For example, not more than 12 hours should be expended per visit, or 168 hours by the fourteenth visit of the season, for a particular site. Although not always possible at first, labor functions with budget-to-actual targets should eventually be identified on job-cost reports.

   For the job above using a three-person crew, your budget for each visit might include 45 minutes of drive time, 15 minutes to unload/load equipment, 4 hours for a 48″ mower, 4 hours for a 36″ mower, 1 hour for a 21″ mower, and 3 hours for trimming and edging. If done this way, you'll simultaneously capture equipment hours as well as labor hours.
3. *Equipment.* Identify equipment targets just as we did in the labor category above. Hours accounted for should only include equipment "meter" or running time. The only additional item to be accounted for is the truck used to transport the crew. However, track and combine its meter or running time (drive time) and its curb time (when it just sits at the site with its engine turned off). Convert equipment hours into dollars by multiplying the hours charged to a job by your cost per hour (CPH) for each piece of equipment.
4. *Subcontractors.* Just like materials, subcontractor costs should be identified and charged to jobs by means of specific invoices for each job.

Once the above four categories of information are converted to dollars in your job-cost system, you only need to add your field-labor burden percent (FICA, FUTA, SUTA, WCI, holiday and vacation pay, etc.) to your field labor to identify your actual gross profit margin (GPM). This assumes that sales tax has been included in material costs. Any good accounting job-cost software package will allow you to accomplish the above task and to compare it to these same categories in your original bid.

Although simple in concept, effective job costing is more a function of the technology (type of computer software) and training (skill levels of both office and field staff) needed to collect, assimilate, format, and distribute timely and accurate job-cost reports.

You won't be able to obtain timely and accurate reports with all of the information described above unless you have a rather sophisticated computerized construction and services management software program that includes job costing. Even if you have the software, without properly trained staff you'll be attempting to "push a rope," as far as job costing is concerned. Keep in mind that it takes 6 to 12 months to implement this type of sophisticated system (assuming you have the correct software). However, prior to implementing such a business solution, there are some interim alternatives.

A CONTRACTOR'S BIGGEST CHALLENGE

The biggest challenge faced in contracting, which threatens profitability more than any other factor, is field labor. Equipment follows at a distant second place. Tom Peters hits the nail on the head when he states in his book, *Thriving on Chaos*, that "What gets measured, gets done (controlled)."[7]

Contracting is labor. You win or lose depending on how you train and handle (control) people in the field. Materials and subcontractor costs present minimal risk in comparison. Consequently, I believe 70 to 80% of the benefit of job costing can be realized by obtaining timely and accurate feedback concentrating on field-labor and equipment hours only.

Don't get me wrong. I would like to have all the other information we've discussed. However, we're not always able to do so. As an interim measure (one any contractor can implement immediately), simply collect field-labor and equipment hours and compare them to your bid hours in the format that follows.

Preferably, use a computer spreadsheet program. If you can't, make a manual form, using the format shown in Figure 41-1 on page 345. Fill out or print the results daily, if possible, but at least once a week. Provide each foreman and/or crew leader with a copy of the report as soon as it's available. Get the information into the hands of the people who can make the biggest difference in the operation—the field crew leaders.

CONSTRUCTION JOB-COST REPORTS

Manual Job-Cost Report

Job costing need not be very complicated. You can start with your very next job if you can pull out labor and equipment hours, as well as your material and subcontractor costs, from your bid. Figure 41-1 is a format for normal job costing.

Column (1) is for budget amounts for direct costs (material, labor, labor burden, equipment, and subcontractors). Labor and equipment should be shown in hours; dollar amounts should be used for materials and subcontractors. I break down the material and labor into landscape, hardscape, irrigation, and general conditions.

Column (2) depicts the total dollars or hours expended to date. Column (3) is the percentage (%) of each category used. Simply divide column (2) by column (1) to obtain it. Subtract column (2) from column (1) to get column (4). Column (5) is your estimate percentage of the job completed. Column (6) is the projected amount of hours or dollars to complete the job, and is obtained by dividing column (2) by column (5). Column (7) shows you the projected amount you'll be over or under budget. You can make this form more detailed if you like, but don't make it too complex or you'll torpedo your job-costing efforts.

MANUAL CONSTRUCTION JOB-COSTING REPORT								
Job: Davis Residence							Date Prepared: 2-15-20__	
	(1)	(2)	(2÷1) (3)	(1–2) (4)	(5)*	(6)	(2÷6) (7)**	(1–7) (8)
Direct Costs	Budget Hours/$	Total Used	% Used	Balance	% Complete	Materials to Order	Total Projected Complete	Projected Over/ Under
1. Material Costs:								
A. Landscape	2000	1000	50%	1000	NA	950	1950	50
B. Hardscape	1500	1350	90%	150	NA	175	1525	−25
C. Irrigation	1450	1425	98%	25	NA	0	1425	25
D. General Conds.	200	80	40%	120	NA	80	160	40
E. ____________					NA			
Totals	5150	3855	75%	1295	NA	1205	5060	90
2. Labor Hours:						Projected Hrs. to go		
A. Landscape	100	60	60%	40	65%	35	95	5
B. Hardscape	40	30	75%	10	75%	10	40	–
C. Irrigation	110	100	91%	10	100%	0	100	10
D. General Conds.	25	20	80%	5	80%	5	25	–
E. ____________								
Totals	275	210	76%	65	80%	50	260	15
3. Equipment Hours								
A. Pick-up	96	80	83%	16	NA	16	96	0
B. 1 Ton	32	24	75%	8	NA	4	28	4
C. Dump Truck	30	24	80%	6	NA	4	28	2
D. Bobcat	24	26	108%	−2	NA	0	26	−2
E. Tractor	0	0	0%	0	NA	0	0	0
*** Totals	182	154	346%	28	NA	24	178	4
4. Subcontractors Costs								
A. L.R. Masonry	400	400	100%	0	100%	NA	400	0
B. ____________						NA		
C. ____________						NA		
D. ____________						NA		
Totals	400	400		0	100%	NA	400	0

* = Your estimate of % complete for that portion of project.

** = Projected amount of material costs or hours to complete project.

*** = Equipment totals are somewhat meaningless due to rate variances of equipment.

FIGURE 41-1 Manual Construction Job-Cost Report

Computerized Job-Cost Report

Figure 41-2 is a more complex computerized job-cost form. It can be very effective, if used properly.

How It Works

I developed the sample report format one day—out of frustration. It was designed in Lotus 1-2-3® and is only one of many formats that could be used. It's very basic, yet effective, if used properly. However, it's not intended to replace job costing that's integrated with an accounting software program.

I was trying to bring our company's accounting software job costing on line. It was taking far too long, and we had a million other things to do. We needed job costing desperately, because we had some rather large jobs ahead, and we felt it imperative that we track them closely. In desperation, I closed my office door, got out my laptop computer, and produced Figure 41-2. Let me explain what I was trying to accomplish.

The job was a medium-sized commercial landscape project. Bid information is located primarily on the left third of the form. Supplier information, in the middle of the page, is identified by vendor. I put labor hour information on the right side, by date. Company-owned equipment is entered under vendors.

We did well on the job since we beat the budget by quite a few dollars and 348 labor hours, some of which were later used to do warranty work. What really made a difference was that we gave the two foremen a copy of this report daily, usually within five minutes after they came into the office with their field report in the afternoon.

Not only did we have a plan (a bid), but we also provided constant feedback to the crews. They were excited because they wanted to beat the budget. We were excited because we wanted to stay in business. A few months earlier this company had tackled a $200,000 project only to lose $20,000, and we couldn't afford to repeat previous mistakes.

This job (and all future jobs) went more smoothly, and we didn't have to wait until the end of the job to see how it went. We could monitor our progress every day. Eventually, we were able to get the accounting job costing up and running, but I must admit I still like this format better, even with its limitations.

Figure 41-3 on page 348 shows a "labor only" job-cost report for the Henderson residence project.

MAINTENANCE JOB-COST REPORTS

Few maintenance contractors realize the impact job costing can have on their operation if the correct data is collected and formatted properly and provided to the right individuals in a timely and accurate manner. This is what TAF (timely-accurate feedback) is all about—empowering people.

A format similar to the one shown in Figure 41-4 on page 349 should be used for job costing, whether done manually or by your computer accounting system. Frankly, I'm amazed at how few contractors and managers implement simple, yet effective information feedback systems. Tom Peters, in his book, *Thriving on Chaos*, states that "The best leadership is that which insists on visible measures of what is going on in the trenches ... simple, visible systems are the [foundation] of success."[8]

	BID	%	ACTUAL	%	VARIANCE
Price	**230,412**	**100.0%**	**230,412**	**100.0%**	(0)
Materials	85,252	37.0%	86,282	37.4%	(1,030)
Direct labor	43,242	18.8%	40,511	17.6%	2,731
Labor burden	12,972	5.6%	12,153	5.3%	819
Equipment	11,359	4.9%	10,736	4.7%	623
Rental equip.	0	0.0%	1,131	0.5%	(1,131)
Subcontractors	5,100	2.2%	5,050	2.2%	50
Subtotal	157,925	68.5%	155,863	67.6%	2,062
General Conditions	0	0.0%	0	0.0%	0
Total direct costs	157,925	68.5%	155,863	67.6%	2,062
GPM	**72,487**	**31.5%**	**74,549**	**32.4%**	**2,062**
G&A overhead	40,204	17.4%	37,665	16.3%	2,539
NPM	**32,283**	**14.0%**	**36,884**	**16.0%**	**4,601**

	BID INFORMATION	
G&A OPH	$13.50	**(G&A overhead per hour)**
Labor burden	30.0%	
CAW	$14.52	**(With RF & OTF, no LB)**
SPH	$77.37	**(Sales per labor hour)**
PPH	$10.84	**(Net profit per labor hour)**
Mat / Lab	2.0	**(Material to labor ratio)**

Note: General condition costs in production totals

		BID		ACTUAL		VARIANCE
Materials (irrigation)	-->	24,528	-	24,972	=	(444)
Materials (landscape)	-->	60,724	-	61,310	=	(586)
Subcontractors	-->	5,100	-	5,050	=	50
Rental equipment	-->	0	-	1,131	=	(1,131)
Subtotal	-->	**90,352**	-	**92,463**	=	**(2,111)**

VENDORS	TOTAL	IRR	L/S	SUBS	RENTAL EQ.
ACTUAL TOTALS——>	**$92,463**	**24,972**	**61,310**	**5,050**	**1,131**
Artistic Nursery	2,682		2,682		
Burger Nursery	20,993		20,993		
Coastside Irrigation	530	368	162		
Haulaway Rentals	102				102
Hillsdale Nursery	638		638		
Hydrosystems Irrigation	24,897	24,604	293		
KDR Rock	273		273		
Mackey Construction Rentals	700				700
Muller Lumber	10		10		
ABC Road Service	329				329
Progressive Hardscapes	5,050			5,050	
San Diego Hydroseed	3,524		3,524		
Jennings Soil & Plant Labs	140		140		
Southville Sod Farms	5,843		5,843		
Sunburst Trees	2,975		2,975		
Valley Trees	23,779		23,779		
	0				
	0				

EQUIPMENT TOTALS——>	$10,736	CPH	BID HRS	USED	TO GO
Crew truck	4,960	$10.00	518	496	22
Supervisor Truck	744	$6.00	129	124	5
Skid steer	2,880	$20.00	156	144	12
Trencher, ride-on	1,540	$22.00	78	70	8
Auger, 2 man	612	$6.00	96	102	(6)
	0				0
	0				0
	0				0
	0				0

	BID	ACTUAL	TO GO		
TOTAL	**2,978**	**2,790**	**188**	**Crew days bid**	64.7
Irrigation	1,033	985	48	**Crew days used**	62.0
Landscape	1,945	1,805	140	**Crew days to go**	2.7

	IRR-NOV	L/S-NOV	IRR-DEC	L/S-DEC	IRR-JAN	L/S-JAN
	640	**0**	**345**	**1,027**	**0**	**778**
1	50 *		40		HOLIDAY	HOLIDAY
2	*OCT HRS		SAT	SAT	RAIN	RAIN
3			SUN	SUN		80
4			40			80
5			40			89
6			48			
7	6		56	8		
8			24	48		89
9	40		SAT	SAT		98
10			SUN	SUN		80
11	SAT	SAT		55		24
12	SUN	SUN	48	43		NA
13	48		16	80	SAT	6
14	48		16	72	SUN	
15	48		12	84		80
16	48		SAT	SAT		80
17	48		SUN	SUN		
18	SAT		4	54		
19	SUN			64		
20	40		1	71		
21	48			72		
22	48			72		
23	HOLIDAY		SAT	SAT		
24	40		SUN	SUN		
25	40	SAT	CMAS	CMAS		
26	40	SUN		72		32
27	48			72		40
28	NA			80		
29				80		
30				SAT		
31				SUN		

FIGURE 41-2 Computer Spreadsheet Construction Job-Cost Report

Date:	1/29, 20___			Crew size:			3									Crew days to go:		0.2
				Man-hours per day per man:			10									Man-hours to go:		14.0

	IRRIG Mhrs	SOILPREP Mhrs	GRADE Mhrs	TREES Mhrs	PALMS Mhrs	SHRUBS Mhrs	SOD Mhrs	GRND COV Mhrs	MULCH Mhrs	DRIVE Mhrs	WARRANTY Mhrs	FOREMAN Mhrs	SUPERV. Mhrs	______ Mhrs	GEN CON Mhrs	TOTAL Mhrs	DAYS	% COMP
TO GO	2.0	3.0	(1.0)	(0.5)	(1.0)	(1.0)	2.0	1.5	0.0	0.0	16.0	(3.0)	(5.0)	0.0	1.0	14.0	0.2	2.7%
BUDGET	**182.0**	**14.0**	**6.0**	**35.5**	**13.0**	**70.0**	**17.0**	**29.5**	**12.0**	**48.0**	**16.0**	**16.0**	**16.0**	**0.0**	**48.0**	**523.0**	**15.8**	**100.0%**
ACTUAL HRS	180.0	11.0	7.0	36.0	14.0	71.0	15.0	28.0	12.0	48.0	0.0	19.0	21.0	0.0	47.0	509.0	15.6	97.3%
JAN 1 (HOLIDAY)																0.0		0.0%
JAN 2																0.0		0.0%
JAN 3 (SUN)																0.0		0.0%
JAN 4	24.0									3.0		2.0	2.0		3.0	34.0		6.7%
JAN 5	24.0									3.0		2.0	2.0		3.0	34.0		13.4%
JAN 6	24.0									3.0		1.0	1.0		3.0	32.0		19.7%
JAN 7	24.0									3.0		1.0	1.0		3.0	32.0		26.0%
JAN 8	24.0									3.0		1.0	1.0		3.0	32.0		32.3%
JAN 9																0.0		32.3%
JAN 10 (SUN)																0.0		32.3%
JAN 11	24.0									3.0		1.0	1.0		3.0	32.0		38.7%
JAN 12	24.0									3.0		1.0	2.0		3.0	33.0		45.2%
JAN 13	12.0	11.0								3.0		1.0	1.0		3.0	31.0		51.3%
JAN 14			7.0	17.0						3.0		1.0	1.0		3.0	32.0		57.6%
JAN 15				16.0		8.0				3.0		1.0	2.0		3.0	33.0		64.1%
JAN 16																0.0		64.1%
JAN 17 (SUN)																0.0		64.1%
JAN 18				3.0	14.0	7.0				3.0		1.0	1.0		3.0	32.0		70.4%
JAN 19						24.0				3.0		1.0	2.0		3.0	33.0		76.9%
JAN 20						24.0				3.0		1.0	1.0		3.0	32.0		83.2%
JAN 21						8.0		16.0		3.0		1.0	1.0		3.0	32.0		89.5%
JAN 22								12.0	12.0	3.0		2.0	1.0		3.0	33.0		96.1%
JAN 23							15.0			3.0		1.0	1.0		2.0	22.0		100.4%
JAN 24 (SUN)																0.0		100.4%

FIGURE 41-3 Henderson Residence (labor only) Construction Job-Cost Report

Date:	5/30/20___						Valley View HOA							Visit #		3	
				Crew size:				2			Man-hours per day per man:			8			
	SPRING CLEAN-UP Mhrs	DRIVETIME LABOR Mhrs	LOAD/UN-LOAD Mhrs	21" MOW LABOR & EQ HRS	36" MOW LABOR & EQ HRS	52" MOW LABOR & EQ HRS	BLOW LABOR & EQ HRS	TRIM LABOR & EQ HRS	WEED & CLEAN-UP Mhrs	_____ LABOR Mhrs	_____ LABOR Mhrs	FALL CLEAN-UP Mhrs	SUPVSR. LABOR Mhrs	TOTALS Mhrs	BUDGET Mhrs TO-DATE	OVER/ UNDER Mhrs	OVER/ UNDER % COMP.
TO GO	0.0	7.3	7.5	25.3	25.7	0.0	6.4	12.8	11.8	0.0	0.0	14.0	5.5	116.1	N/A	N/A	0.6%
BUDGET	**14.0**	**9.0**	**9.0**	**28.0**	**28.0**	**0.0**	**7.0**	**14.0**	**14.0**	**0.0**	**0.0**	**14.0**	**7.0**	**144.0**	**144.0**	**0.0**	**20.0%**
ACTUAL MAN_HOURS	14.0	1.8	1.5	2.8	2.4	0.0	0.7	1.2	2.2	0.0	0.0	0.0	1.5	27.9	28.8	0.9	19.4%
SPRING CLN-UP (4/22)	14.00	1.00	1.00										1.00	17.0	17.0	0.0	11.8%
VISIT-1 (4/29)		0.25	0.20	1.50	1.25		0.20	0.40	0.20					4.0	3.9	(0.1)	14.5%
VISIT-2 (5/6) SITE VERY WET		0.25	0.10	0.00	0.00		0.20	0.20	2.00					2.8	3.9	1.2	17.3%
VISIT-3 (5/13)		0.25	0.20	1.25	1.10		0.25	0.60					0.50	4.2	3.9	(0.2)	20.0%
VISIT-4														0.0	3.9	3.9	22.7%
VISIT-5														0.0	3.9	3.9	25.4%
VISIT-6														0.0	3.9	3.9	28.2%
VISIT-7														0.0	3.9	3.9	30.9%
VISIT-8														0.0	3.9	3.9	33.6%
VISIT-9														0.0	3.9	3.9	36.4%
VISIT-10														0.0	3.9	3.9	39.1%
VISIT-11														0.0	3.9	3.9	41.8%
VISIT-12														0.0	3.9	3.9	44.5%
VISIT-13														0.0	3.9	3.9	47.3%
VISIT-14														0.0	3.9	3.9	50.0%
VISIT-15														0.0	3.9	3.9	52.7%
VISIT-16														0.0	3.9	3.9	55.5%
VISIT-17														0.0	3.9	3.9	58.2%
VISIT-18														0.0	3.9	3.9	60.9%
VISIT-19														0.0	3.9	3.9	63.6%
VISIT-20														0.0	3.9	3.9	66.4%
VISIT-21														0.0	3.9	3.9	69.1%
VISIT-22														0.0	3.9	3.9	71.8%
VISIT-23														0.0	3.9	3.9	74.6%
VISIT-24														0.0	3.9	3.9	77.3%
VISIT-25														0.0	3.9	3.9	80.0%
VISIT-26														0.0	3.9	3.9	82.7%
VISIT-27														0.0	3.9	3.9	85.5%
VISIT-28														0.0	3.9	3.9	88.2%
FALL CLEAN-UP														0.0	17.0	17.0	100.0%

FIGURE 41-4 Computer Maintenance Job-Cost Report)

BENEFITS OF JOB COSTING

The benefits of timely, accurate job-cost reports are numerous. Some are as follows:

- They can identify flaws in your estimating methodology.
- Weaknesses and strengths of your field operation will become apparent.
- Timely, accurate feedback will provide some of the best training your estimators will ever receive.
- Job-cost reports are the "scoreboard" for your operation, providing field crews and supervisors the feedback they need to make more timely operational decisions in the field.
- Field crews will be empowered to take corrective action. Operational problems will be solved faster and more creatively.
- The organization will become more "bottom-up" vs. "top-down" driven. The burden of field problem solving will shift from management (bureaucrats) to field people, where it belongs.
- Customer problems will be solved faster, improving customer relations.
- TQM will be simultaneously addressed and measured if TAF is established in the manner described.
- A bonus system can be integrated with this type of TAF system.
- The number-one motivator is timely, accurate feedback. Money and praise don't even come close. Simple job-cost reports in the hands of the right people will maximize motivation.
- Insisting that "bureaucrats" change their methods and schedules to provide TAF to the right people will focus all your bureaucracy. You will teach non-field (support) personnel what "good" bureaucracy (support) is all about. If this doesn't excite your bureaucrats, get new ones who do get excited.
- TAF/job costing applies to many facets of life. It will teach everyone in your company a valuable skill.
- Most important of all, good job costing will improve your bottom line.

MAINTENANCE ILLUSTRATION

To illustrate how TAF can improve your operation, let me address a common problem I see in the maintenance industry, one that applies to construction as well.

Too many maintenance contractors bid their work using a flat hourly rate for projects billing over $500 per month. I don't have a problem bidding smaller maintenance projects in this fashion by using the package approach covered in Chapter 25. However, if job costing were in place as outlined above, it would identify the following potential problems with this bidding method for larger projects, especially commercial ones.

First, drive time will be identified and charged to jobs. It might have to be charged to jobs as an average per day, achieved by dividing total drive time by the number of jobs visited for that day. This process more accurately identifies gross profit margins (GPM) for each job. By dividing the monthly customer invoice amount for the project by the number of labor hours actually charged to the job (including drive time), you will probably see a dramatic difference between your flat hourly rate "bid" versus the "actual" one realized in the field.

Second, actual equipment hours used on a job will be identified. Because you're charging the same flat rate for every hour you're on the job, it's a given that you're charging the same amount for each piece of equipment on the job. And unless each piece of equipment is used exactly the same amount of time as every other piece, your equipment cost portion of the bid is inaccurate. Therefore, your original bid was either overpriced or underpriced. This in turn leads to problem number three.

Third, string trimmers, edgers, and small push mowers cost less per hour to operate than large walk-behind or ride-on mowers. The *fatal flaw* occurs when, for instance, you bid a flat $25 man-hour rate. However, for your large ride-on mowers you should charge $28 per man-hour, $22 to $23 per man-hour for the smaller equipment functions, and $19 to $20 for labor only functions.

The market is not stupid. Over a period of time, it will start to give you more and more of the equipment-intensive work (because you've underpriced it), but it won't give you the labor-intensive jobs (which you've overpriced).

The market is not stupid. Over a period of time, it will start to give you more and more of the equipment-intensive work (because you've underpriced it), but it won't give you the labor-intensive jobs (which you've overpriced). Gradually, you'll see your bottom line deteriorate as your jobs shift towards the underpriced, less profitable equipment-intensive jobs. This problem becomes even more acute in periods of economic downturns.

Fourth, effective job costing will show that your estimating methods aren't flexible enough to accurately identify all your production costs during the bidding process. It should prompt you to ask questions and to seek a better method.

SUMMARY

Designing your management systems to provide timely accurate feedback (TAF) in the form of job-cost reports is one of the most important functions of top management. The process is relatively simple but, unfortunately, few contractors understand how to do it. Setting up timely, accurate job-cost reports is very much like turning on the "scoreboard" for your field and staff to see.

The benefits are numerous. Operating without your scoreboard keeps everybody in the dark, while turning it on can also "turn on" your field people and staff. Although job costing through your accounting software program is the best method, alternative methods, either manual or computerized, can achieve significant results for your operation.

Job costing provides a "reality check" for your bids. If you bid jobs at a 30% GPM, you should see a 30% GPM on your job-cost reports. If the two differ, job costing will give you the tools to research, identify, and correct this variance. Effective job costing can also provide you with a sound analytical process and the performance standards on which to build your total quality management (TQM) program.

A Caveat

Job costing has limitations, which top management needs to understand. It's designed to address only the variance between the gross profit margin (GPM) bid on a specific job versus the GPM actually achieved in the field. It's not meant to address office G&A overhead recovery or allocation, downtime costs for labor, or non-billable equipment costs.

Job costing only compares "budget-to-actual" performance for direct costs and for specific jobs. To track and monitor these other costs, you need an annual budget and "budget-to-actual" comparisons on your profit and loss (P&L) statements to identify targets for G&A overhead recovery, labor downtime, and equipment costs.

Basic Steps to Start a Job-Cost Report System

1. Make a master form similar to the sample job-cost report provided. It should contain the majority of the labor functions your crews perform. Leave a few blank spaces for add-on items. If possible, create it in a personal computer (PC) spreadsheet program. Designate the person in your office who is to fill it out, how often it's to be filled out for each job, and to whom the report is to be given.
2. Break down each job into its labor functions. Manually enter this budget data for each job onto a copy of your master job-cost report. Create a similar computer spreadsheet for each job, if possible.
3. Create a manual Field Daily Report (FDR) form, similar to the samples provided in Exhibits 12 and 13. It's to be used to collect field job site information on a daily basis.
4. Train your crew leader(s) and/or foremen on how to fill out the FDR. Notice that the sample FDR is very similar to the format for the job-cost report. This makes feedback to crews more familiar and therefore more meaningful.
5. Collect FDRs on a daily basis from your crew leaders and/or foremen. Emphasize the importance of obtaining them at the end of each day.
6. Complete the job-cost report and distribute it to crew leaders and/or foremen, supervisors, and managers on a weekly (preferably daily) basis. Require everyone to review the results (the scoreboard). Build focus and intensity into your company by holding supervisors, foremen, and other personnel accountable to budget goals.
7. *Make it fun.* Challenge your crews to bring their jobs in on-budget. Reward them with a monetary bonus, pizza, a special T-shirt, etc., if their crew labor hours are on-budget by a set date (e.g., mid-season, end of season). Share job-cost feedback with all crew members and discuss with them how to improve performance and beat the estimate.

ACTION POINT

Review your job-cost procedures and take steps to ensure that, at a minimum, key field personnel and management staff obtain "budget-to-actual" reports for field-labor hours.

CHAPTER

42

Billable Field-Labor Hour "Budget vs. Actual" Performance

Purpose

To explain how to focus the company bureaucracy and bureaucrats to support field operations, and how to measure company performance in relation to field operations

Introduction

Everything (G&A overhead, equipment, materials, net and gross profit, sales, etc.) should be tracked and compared to billable field-labor hours (FLH). Whenever field-labor hours are discussed in this chapter they refer to "billable" hours, unless otherwise noted.

RATIONALE

Billable field-labor hours should be the central item to which all others are compared. A contractor is really in the business of selling labor. First and foremost, a contractor is paid to field a team that can provide products and services to his or her clients. Certainly, there are materials, equipment, and subcontractors involved. However, without the field-labor component, a contractor is just a material supplier, rental equipment dealer, or general contractor. Let's define billable field-labor hours.

Definition: Billable field-labor hours are those hours included in a bid and for which a client is billed. Downtime hours, equipment repair hours, shop time, hours spent in the nursery caring for stock, and like time are not considered billable field-labor hours. However, time and materials (T&M) and general condition time are billable hours if the client pays for them and/or they are in the bid.

The following list clarifies why billable field-labor hours form the foundation of a contractor's success. Billable hours are

1. The *common denominator*
   Nothing really good is happening in the company unless your crews are working and billable in the field. The existence of the whole company finds

its justification (vindication for bureaucrats, if you will) by what happens in the field.

2. Easily *visualized* and graphed
   Sales or revenue per hour (SPH or RPH), net profit per hour (PPH), G&A overhead per hour (OPH), and so on are figures and ratios that are easily graphed and visualized. Everyone can relate to them quickly and easily.
3. Easily *monitored*
   Keeping track of these figures and ratios is a very simple process.
4. Connected to *job costing*
   Focusing and comparing everything to field-labor hours is the most effective way to monitor your field production. If you get into trouble on a job, it is probably because of field labor. Hence, you need to be able to focus on and monitor your field labor as much as possible.
5. Easily *related to*
   Virtually everyone can visualize field labor because labor and its results are a tangible commodity. Monitoring your sales, net and gross profit, and G&A overhead really doesn't mean much to very many people. However, monitoring these same areas as they relate to field labor will communicate vital information more effectively to everyone involved.
6. The *most influential* in your company
   Tracking and monitoring your company this way simply works better than anything else. It gets results.
7. Able to *focus bureaucrats*
   Bureaucrats tend to become aloof and build empires unto themselves. Having them focus on the field helps keep them in touch with reality (as everyone else knows it) and with the rest of the company. A company can survive for a long time without the office but will fail immediately without the field.

TRACKING FLH "BUDGET VS. ACTUAL" PERFORMANCE

It's crucial that you monitor your field-labor hour budget and compare it to actual labor hours used. If your actual field-labor hours consistently exceed your projections (and you expect this to hold true throughout the year), you can decrease your G&A overhead per hour (OPH) and increase your net profit margins. Or you can lower your prices and become more competitive.

On the other hand, if actual field-labor hours aren't going to meet budget projections, you should either increase your OPH (making you less competitive) or reduce G&A overhead expenses. This will either bring your OPH back in line with your budget, or it will lower your OPH and make your bids more competitive.

Field-labor hours must be monitored both on a job-by-job basis (by means of job costing), and for the overall company/division (by means of a chart similar to Figure 42-1). Individual jobs coming in on-budget don't do you much good if you're not meeting your yearly budget. Both are important. Both must be constantly tracked and attained or subsequently adjusted.

Figure 42-2 on page 356 illustrates a Weekly Field-Labor Hour Recap Sheet you should use. It identifies production time as compared to downtime, drive time, and so on. Add or delete categories as you desire. Figure 42-3 on page 357, the Yearly Field-Labor Hour Recap Sheet, is a yearly version of Figure 42-2. You can also use the "Bid Status Board" and the "MAD Report" covered in Chapter 40 to track field-labor hours.

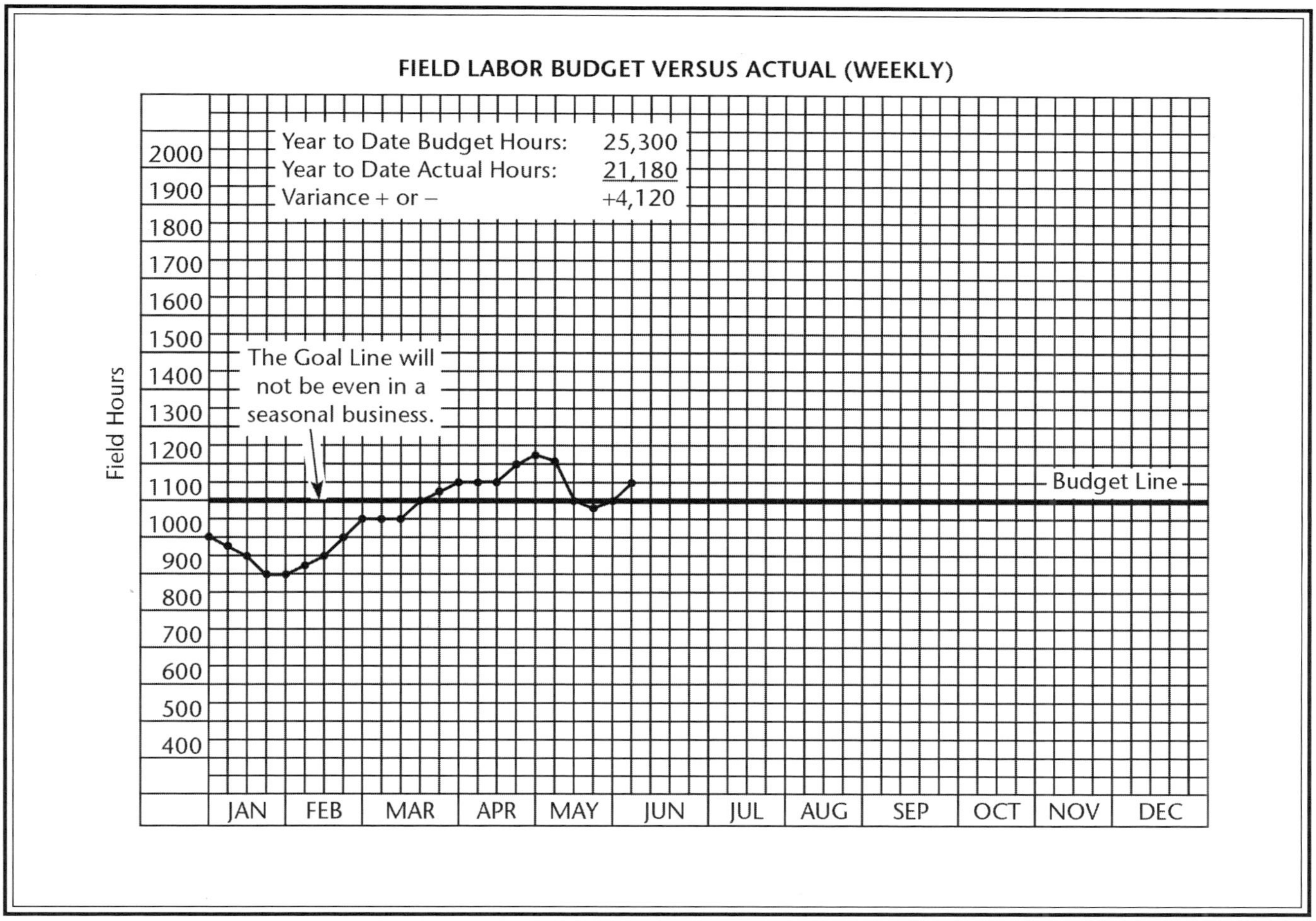

FIGURE 42-1 Field-Labor Hour "Budget vs. Actual" Graph

DOWNTIME

Field-labor hours paid for by the company but not bid into jobs can become subtle and critical leaks in your company if not monitored closely. Figures 42-2 and 42-3 are examples of how you might track them by using a computer spreadsheet program. Two specific examples come to mind.

How It Works

A commercial landscape and irrigation company in the Western United States, doing about $1 million in gross annual sales, was showing no net profit. When the two owners reviewed their field crew's daily routine, downtime was identified as one of the problem areas.

The field crew, which totaled 10 men, would show up at the yard at 6 A.M. and punch a time clock. Next to the yard was a donut shop, so guess where they went next? Crews stood around the yard eating donuts and drinking coffee (and occasionally loading trucks) for 15 to 30 minutes before driving to job sites. Driving time to job sites averaged 30 to 45 minutes one way. Crews would work all day, drive back 30 to 45 minutes to the yard, punch out, and go home.

I calculated that each man had 1.5 hours per day loading trucks in the morning and driving to job sites. The result: 10 men × 1.5 hours/day × 200 days/year or 3,000 hours/year. This came to $33,000 per year in labor dollars at an average wage

Date: 1/25/20___

	<—— BILLABLE HOURS								——>	<—— NON-BILLABLE HOURS								——>		
DIV / CREW	LOAD / UNLOAD	YARD AM / PM	EXTRAS	DRIVE TO/FM	MOBIL EQUIP	HAUL MATLS	PRO-DUCTION	MISC	SUBTOTAL	WARNTY	YARD	EQUIP MAINT	SAFETY / MEETINGS	NURSERY	MISC	MISC	SUBTOTAL	TOTALS	%
WEEK: 15-21 JAN	59.0 7.9%	10.0 1.3%	17.0 2.3%	97.0 13.0%	6.0 0.8%	20.0 2.7%	487.0 65.3%	11.0 1.5%	707.0 94.8%	7.0 0.9%	5.0 0.7%	12.0 1.6%	12.0 1.6%	2.0 0.3%	1.0 0.1%	0.0 0.0%	39.0 5.2%	746.0 100.0%	100.0%
PLANTING	5.0	5.0	0.0	15.0	6.0	8.0	122.0	6.0	167.0	4.0	3.0	2.0	2.0	2.0	0.0	0.0	13.0	180.0	24.1%
IRRIGATION	3.0	3.0	12.0	12.0	0.0	4.0	92.0	3.0	129.0	1.0	0.0	4.0	1.0	0.0	0.0	0.0	6.0	135.0	18.1%
HARDSCAPE	6.0	2.0	0.0	10.0	0.0	8.0	57.0	2.0	85.0	0.0	2.0	1.0	1.0	0.0	1.0	0.0	5.0	90.0	12.1%
MAINTENANCE	20.0	0.0	5.0	19.0	0.0	0.0	108.0	0.0	152.0	0.0	0.0	4.0	4.0	0.0	0.0	0.0	8.0	160.0	21.4%
IRR SERVICE	5.0	0.0	0.0	7.0	0.0	0.0	30.0	0.0	42.0	2.0	0.0	0.0	1.0	0.0	0.0	0.0	3.0	45.0	6.0%
FERTILIZATION	9.0	0.0	0.0	12.0	0.0	0.0	22.0	0.0	43.0	0.0	0.0	1.0	1.0	0.0	0.0	0.0	2.0	45.0	6.0%
TREE SERVICE	11.0	0.0	0.0	22.0	0.0	0.0	56.0	0.0	89.0	0.0	0.0	0.0	2.0	0.0	0.0	0.0	2.0	91.0	12.2%
________	0.0	0.0	0.0	0.0	0.0	0.0	0.0	0.0	0.0	0.0	0.0	0.0	0.0	0.0	0.0	0.0	0.0	0.0	0.0%
________	0.0	0.0	0.0	0.0	0.0	0.0	0.0	0.0	0.0	0.0	0.0	0.0	0.0	0.0	0.0	0.0	0.0	0.0	0.0%
________	0.0	0.0	0.0	0.0	0.0	0.0	0.0	0.0	0.0	0.0	0.0	0.0	0.0	0.0	0.0	0.0	0.0	0.0	0.0%
________	0.0	0.0	0.0	0.0	0.0	0.0	0.0	0.0	0.0	0.0	0.0	0.0	0.0	0.0	0.0	0.0	0.0	0.0	0.0%
________	0.0	0.0	0.0	0.0	0.0	0.0	0.0	0.0	0.0	0.0	0.0	0.0	0.0	0.0	0.0	0.0	0.0	0.0	0.0%
________	0.0	0.0	0.0	0.0	0.0	0.0	0.0	0.0	0.0	0.0	0.0	0.0	0.0	0.0	0.0	0.0	0.0	0.0	0.0%
________	0.0	0.0	0.0	0.0	0.0	0.0	0.0	0.0	0.0	0.0	0.0	0.0	0.0	0.0	0.0	0.0	0.0	0.0	0.0%
________	0.0	0.0	0.0	0.0	0.0	0.0	0.0	0.0	0.0	0.0	0.0	0.0	0.0	0.0	0.0	0.0	0.0	0.0	0.0%
________	0.0	0.0	0.0	0.0	0.0	0.0	0.0	0.0	0.0	0.0	0.0	0.0	0.0	0.0	0.0	0.0	0.0	0.0	0.0%
________	0.0	0.0	0.0	0.0	0.0	0.0	0.0	0.0	0.0	0.0	0.0	0.0	0.0	0.0	0.0	0.0	0.0	0.0	0.0%
________	0.0	0.0	0.0	0.0	0.0	0.0	0.0	0.0	0.0	0.0	0.0	0.0	0.0	0.0	0.0	0.0	0.0	0.0	0.0%
________	0.0	0.0	0.0	0.0	0.0	0.0	0.0	0.0	0.0	0.0	0.0	0.0	0.0	0.0	0.0	0.0	0.0	0.0	0.0%
________	0.0	0.0	0.0	0.0	0.0	0.0	0.0	0.0	0.0	0.0	0.0	0.0	0.0	0.0	0.0	0.0	0.0	0.0	0.0%
________	0.0	0.0	0.0	0.0	0.0	0.0	0.0	0.0	0.0	0.0	0.0	0.0	0.0	0.0	0.0	0.0	0.0	0.0	0.0%
________	0.0	0.0	0.0	0.0	0.0	0.0	0.0	0.0	0.0	0.0	0.0	0.0	0.0	0.0	0.0	0.0	0.0	0.0	0.0%
________	0.0	0.0	0.0	0.0	0.0	0.0	0.0	0.0	0.0	0.0	0.0	0.0	0.0	0.0	0.0	0.0	0.0	0.0	0.0%
________	0.0	0.0	0.0	0.0	0.0	0.0	0.0	0.0	0.0	0.0	0.0	0.0	0.0	0.0	0.0	0.0	0.0	0.0	0.0%
________	0.0	0.0	0.0	0.0	0.0	0.0	0.0	0.0	0.0	0.0	0.0	0.0	0.0	0.0	0.0	0.0	0.0	0.0	0.0%

FIGURE 42-2 Weekly Field-Labor Hour Recap Sheet

Date: 2/7/20___

	<--- BILLABLE HOURS								--->	<--- NON-BILLABLE HOURS							--->		
TYPE HOURS->	LOAD / UNLOAD	YARD AM / PM	EXTRAS	DRIVE TO/FM	MOBIL EQUIP	HAUL MATLS	PRO-DUCTION	MISC	SUBTOTAL	WARNTY	YARD	EQUIP MAINT	SAFETY / MEETINGS	NURSERY	MISC	MISC	SUBTOTAL	TOTALS	%
	281.0 8.1%	42.0 1.2%	76.0 2.2%	437.0 12.6%	34.0 1.0%	89.0 2.6%	2,262.0 65.4%	38.0 1.1%	3,259.0 94.2%	26.0 0.8%	28.0 0.8%	63.0 1.8%	49.0 1.4%	18.0 0.5%	13.0 0.4%	0.0 0.0%	202.0 5.8%	3,461.0 100.0%	100.0%
WEEK Jan 1-7	48.0	2.0	4.0	66.0	4.0	12.0	355.0	3.0	494.0	5.0	6.0	8.0	9.0	2.0 1	0.0	0.0	31.0	525.0	15.2%
Jan 8-14	57.0	11.0	15.0	88.0	8.0	22.0	466.0	7.0	674.0	2.0	6.0	14.0	10.0	5.0 1	0.0	0.0	38.0	712.0	20.6%
Jan 15-21	59.0	10.0	17.0	97.0	6.0	20.0	487.0	11.0	707.0	7.0	5.0	12.0	12.0	2.0 1	0.0	0.0	39.0	746.0	21.6%
Jan 22-28	62.0	11.0	15.0	101.0	7.0	17.0	472.0	6.0	691.0	3.0	7.0	14.0	8.0	6.0 1	6.0	0.0	45.0	736.0	21.3%
Jan 29 - Feb 4	55.0	8.0	25.0	85.0	9.0	18.0	482.0	11.0	693.0	9.0	4.0	15.0	10.0	3.0 1	7.0	0.0	49.0	742.0	21.4%
______	0.0	0.0	0.0	0.0	0.0	0.0	0.0	0.0	0.0	0.0	0.0	0.0	0.0	0.0	0.0	0.0	0.0	0.0	0.0%
______	0.0	0.0	0.0	0.0	0.0	0.0	0.0	0.0	0.0	0.0	0.0	0.0	0.0	0.0	0.0	0.0	0.0	0.0	0.0%
______	0.0	0.0	0.0	0.0	0.0	0.0	0.0	0.0	0.0	0.0	0.0	0.0	0.0	0.0	0.0	0.0	0.0	0.0	0.0%
______	0.0	0.0	0.0	0.0	0.0	0.0	0.0	0.0	0.0	0.0	0.0	0.0	0.0	0.0	0.0	0.0	0.0	0.0	0.0%
______	0.0	0.0	0.0	0.0	0.0	0.0	0.0	0.0	0.0	0.0	0.0	0.0	0.0	0.0	0.0	0.0	0.0	0.0	0.0%
______	0.0	0.0	0.0	0.0	0.0	0.0	0.0	0.0	0.0	0.0	0.0	0.0	0.0	0.0	0.0	0.0	0.0	0.0	0.0%
______	0.0	0.0	0.0	0.0	0.0	0.0	0.0	0.0	0.0	0.0	0.0	0.0	0.0	0.0	0.0	0.0	0.0	0.0	0.0%
______	0.0	0.0	0.0	0.0	0.0	0.0	0.0	0.0	0.0	0.0	0.0	0.0	0.0	0.0	0.0	0.0	0.0	0.0	0.0%
______	0.0	0.0	0.0	0.0	0.0	0.0	0.0	0.0	0.0	0.0	0.0	0.0	0.0	0.0	0.0	0.0	0.0	0.0	0.0%
______	0.0	0.0	0.0	0.0	0.0	0.0	0.0	0.0	0.0	0.0	0.0	0.0	0.0	0.0	0.0	0.0	0.0	0.0	0.0%
______	0.0	0.0	0.0	0.0	0.0	0.0	0.0	0.0	0.0	0.0	0.0	0.0	0.0	0.0	0.0	0.0	0.0	0.0	0.0%
______	0.0	0.0	0.0	0.0	0.0	0.0	0.0	0.0	0.0	0.0	0.0	0.0	0.0	0.0	0.0	0.0	0.0	0.0	0.0%
______	0.0	0.0	0.0	0.0	0.0	0.0	0.0	0.0	0.0	0.0	0.0	0.0	0.0	0.0	0.0	0.0	0.0	0.0	0.0%
______	0.0	0.0	0.0	0.0	0.0	0.0	0.0	0.0	0.0	0.0	0.0	0.0	0.0	0.0	0.0	0.0	0.0	0.0	0.0%
______	0.0	0.0	0.0	0.0	0.0	0.0	0.0	0.0	0.0	0.0	0.0	0.0	0.0	0.0	0.0	0.0	0.0	0.0	0.0%
______	0.0	0.0	0.0	0.0	0.0	0.0	0.0	0.0	0.0	0.0	0.0	0.0	0.0	0.0	0.0	0.0	0.0	0.0	0.0%
______	0.0	0.0	0.0	0.0	0.0	0.0	0.0	0.0	0.0	0.0	0.0	0.0	0.0	0.0	0.0	0.0	0.0	0.0	0.0%

FIGURE 42-3 Yearly Field-Labor Hour Recap Sheet

of $10 per hour. Adding 30% labor burden would increase the total to $39,000 per year.

I'm all for paying reasonable amounts for load and drive time for crews, but my question to the two owners was "Who was paying the $39,000? Was it included in general conditions in the bid?" If it was, the customer was paying for it. If it wasn't, the owners were paying, and it came out of net profit.

The two owners looked at each other. I saw lights go on in their heads, followed by facial expressions indicating a sinking feeling in their stomachs as they realized the problem. They had *not* passed the 3,000 labor hours on to their clients, and they'd "eaten" the $39,000 it had cost. That's what you call a rather *big leak* in a company. These costs were not recaptured in their bids.

An East Coast company identified a similar problem. When its sales dropped from $1.6 million to $800,000 due to the recession in 1989–90, net profits evaporated. The two partners liked equipment and had been equipment-heavy before the drop in sales. Fortunately, most of the equipment was paid for and didn't have as negative an impact on the company as you might expect. However, it caused another problem that surfaced when we looked at downtime.

Prior to my arrival, the bookkeeper had accounted for 8,000 labor hours that were not included in any of the bids. Approximately 4,000 hours were for two mechanics who were busy working on and repairing equipment. The good news was that the mechanics were busy. The bad news was that the equipment was not. This company could have kept four mechanics busy full-time because they owned so much equipment. Unfortunately, they couldn't even justify having one full-time mechanic, let alone two.

Approximately 2,500 of the remaining 4,000 hours of downtime hours should have been bid into jobs as drive time, load time, mobilization, and so forth. Yard time, busy work, and nursery time accounted for the balance.

SUMMARY

Downtime hours can eat up your profits faster than just about anything else. The one area where you'll make or lose the most money is in the way you handle field-labor hours. If you don't track them, you can't identify the problem. And you certainly can't fix a problem you can't see. The Weekly Field-Labor Hour Recap and the Yearly Field-Labor Hour Recap Reports are two tools you can use for tracking your field-labor hour "Budget to Actual" performance.

Downtime hours can eat up your profits faster than just about anything else.

ACTION POINT

Track and identify the billable versus non-billable (downtime) field-labor hours in your company and begin to measure company performance in relation to the field, where it can make the biggest impact and do the most good.

CHAPTER

43

The Company Break-Even Point (The *October Surprise*)

Purpose

To explain the importance of and how to monitor general and administrative costs

Introduction

It is essential that you monitor indirect costs, or general and administrative (G&A) overhead costs. Like field-labor downtime, G&A costs can get out of control and eat up your bottom line, while the individual job-cost reports look great.

I don't necessarily recommend allocating actual G&A overhead expenses to your jobs through job costing. Rather, I prefer to simply compare direct costs bid to actual performance by means of gross profit margin (GPM) on a job-by-job basis. If your GPM turns out better than estimated, great! If not, find the problem and fix it before the next time.

However, you do need to monitor G&A overhead on individual jobs. Figure 43-1 on page 360 is a sample profit and loss (P&L) financial statement format that compares monthly and year-to-date "budget vs. actual" categories. A good accounting software program should allow you to produce such a report. If you don't have that capability, you can produce it manually or enter the data into a computerized spreadsheet program.

THE BREAK-EVEN POINT (The October Surprise)

A company usually reaches its break-even point (BEP) in the ninth or tenth month of its fiscal year. You reach your BEP when your accumulated gross profit margin (G&A overhead costs plus net profit) equals your G&A overhead budget dollar amount for the year. If you hit your break-even point prior to the end of the fiscal year, any dollar amounts on bids above Phase I and II direct costs (plus sales tax and field-labor burden) will be net profit for that year. That's *if* the work is completed and billed prior to the end of the fiscal year.

Work bid after the BEP is met, which will be completed and billed before the fiscal year end, can be bid with the realization that any amount above direct costs in the bid goes to the net profit margin on the bottom line. If your net profit margin on a bid is 10% and your G&A overhead amounts to another 15%, your net profit margin is really 25%, since your G&A overhead is already covered for the year.

January to November, 20___

		NOV BUDGET	BUD %	NOV ACTUAL	ACT %	NOV VARIANCE	VAR %	Y-T-D BUDGET	BUD %	Y-T-D ACTUAL	ACT %	Y-T-D VARIANCE	BUD %
1. SALES (Revenues)		195,000	100.0%	188,500	100.0%	(6,500)	-3.3%	2,145,000	100.0%	2,080,000	100.0%	(65,000)	-3.0%
2. COST OF GOODS SOLD (Direct costs)													
MATERIAL (W/TAX)		58,500	30.0%	64,656	34.3%	(6,156)	-3.2%	643,500	30.0%	619,840	29.8%	23,660	1.1%
LABOR		35,100	18.0%	33,467	17.8%	1,633	0.8%	386,100	18.0%	389,126	18.7%	(3,026)	-0.1%
LABOR BURDEN	25.0%	8,775	4.5%	8,367	4.4%	408	0.2%	96,525	4.5%	120,629	5.8%	(24,104)	-1.1%
SUBCONTRACTORS		9,750	5.0%	8,500	4.5%	1,250	0.6%	107,250	5.0%	122,000	5.9%	(14,750)	-0.7%
EQUIPMENT		17,550	9.0%	16,525	8.8%	1,025	0.5%	193,050	9.0%	187,255	9.0%	5,795	0.3%
EQUIPMENT RENTAL		2,917	1.5%	500	0.3%	2,417	1.2%	32,087	1.5%	29,850	1.4%	2,237	0.1%
MISCELLANEOUS		1,250	0.6%	659	0.3%	591	0.3%	13,750	0.6%	14,525	0.7%	(775)	0.0%
TOTAL COST OF GOODS SOLD		133,842	68.6%	132,673	70.4%	1,169	0.6%	1,472,262	68.6%	1,483,225	71.3%	(10,963)	-0.5%
3. GROSS PROFIT MARGIN (GPM)		61,158	31.4%	55,827	29.6%	(5,331)	-2.7%	672,738	31.4%	596,775	28.7%	(75,963)	-3.5%
4. GENERAL & ADMINISTRATIVE OVERHEAD (G&A / Indirect costs)													
ADVERTISING		375	0.2%	425	0.2%	(50)	0.0%	4,125	0.2%	5,025	0.2%	(900)	0.0%
BAD DEBTS		2,500	1.3%	0	0.0%	2,500	1.3%	27,500	1.3%	32,000	1.5%	(4,500)	-0.2%
COMPUTERS, SOFTWARE		375	0.2%	375	0.2%	0	0.0%	4,125	0.2%	4,678	0.2%	(553)	0.0%
DONATIONS		42	0.0%	75	0.0%	(33)	0.0%	462	0.0%	600	0.0%	(138)	0.0%
DOWNTIME LABOR		6,000	3.1%	4,500	2.4%	1,500	0.8%	66,000	3.1%	67,025	3.2%	(1,025)	0.0%
DOWNTIME LABOR BURDEN	25.0%	1,500	0.8%	1,395	0.7%	105	0.1%	16,500	0.8%	20,778	1.0%	(4,278)	-0.2%
DUES AND SUBS		108	0.1%	0	0.0%	108	0.1%	1,188	0.1%	898	0.0%	290	0.0%
INSURANCE (OFFICE)		4,500	2.3%	4,500	2.4%	0	0.0%	49,500	2.3%	51,200	2.5%	(1,700)	-0.1%
INTEREST AND BANK CHARGES		600	0.3%	425	0.2%	175	0.1%	6,600	0.3%	5,535	0.3%	1,065	0.0%
LICENSES, BONDS		46	0.0%	0	0.0%	46	0.0%	506	0.0%	743	0.0%	(237)	0.0%
OFFICE EQUIPMENT		215	0.1%	215	0.1%	0	0.0%	2,365	0.1%	2,506	0.1%	(141)	0.0%
OFFICE SUPPLIES		500	0.3%	522	0.3%	(22)	0.0%	5,500	0.3%	5,800	0.3%	(300)	0.0%
PROFESSIONAL FEES		1,375	0.7%	1,049	0.6%	326	0.2%	15,125	0.7%	15,890	0.8%	(765)	0.0%
RADIO SYSTEMS		1,200	0.6%	1,189	0.6%	11	0.0%	13,200	0.6%	12,855	0.6%	345	0.0%
RENT		2,500	1.3%	2,500	1.3%	0	0.0%	27,500	1.3%	27,500	1.3%	0	0.0%
SALARIES-OFFICE		9,333	4.8%	9,500	5.0%	(167)	-0.1%	102,663	4.8%	105,555	5.1%	(2,892)	-0.1%
SALARIES-OFFICER(S)		6,667	3.4%	6,667	3.5%	0	0.0%	73,337	3.4%	73,337	3.5%	0	0.0%
SALARIES-LABOR BURDEN	11.5%	2,080	1.1%	1,859	1.0%	221	0.1%	22,880	1.1%	23,256	1.1%	(376)	0.0%
SMALL TOOLS / SUPPLIES		292	0.1%	256	0.1%	36	0.0%	3,212	0.1%	3,756	0.2%	(544)	0.0%
TAXES (BUSINESS)		67	0.0%	0	0.0%	67	0.0%	737	0.0%	1,024	0.0%	(287)	0.0%
TELEPHONE		400	0.2%	535	0.3%	(135)	-0.1%	4,400	0.2%	5,235	0.3%	(835)	0.0%
TRAINING / EDUCATION		250	0.1%	225	0.1%	25	0.0%	2,750	0.1%	3,465	0.2%	(715)	0.0%
TRAVEL / ENTERTAINMENT		200	0.1%	127	0.1%	73	0.0%	2,200	0.1%	1,604	0.1%	596	0.0%
UNIFORMS / SAFETY EQUIPMENT		250	0.1%	0	0.0%	250	0.1%	2,750	0.1%	3,000	0.1%	(250)	0.0%
UTILITIES		250	0.1%	265	0.1%	(15)	0.0%	2,750	0.1%	2,825	0.1%	(75)	0.0%
VEHICLES, OVERHEAD		1,563	0.8%	1,478	0.8%	85	0.0%	17,193	0.8%	18,027	0.9%	(834)	0.0%
YARD EXP. / LEASEHOLD IMPROVEMENTS		208	0.1%	35	0.0%	173	0.1%	2,288	0.1%	1,568	0.1%	720	0.0%
MISCELLANEOUS		42	0.0%	12	0.0%	30	0.0%	462	0.0%	864	0.0%	(402)	0.0%
		0	0.0%	0	0.0%	0	0.0%	0	0.0%	0	0.0%	0	0.0%
TOTAL G&A OVERHEAD		43,438	22.3%	38,129	20.2%	5,309	2.7%	477,818	22.3%	496,549	23.9%	(18,731)	-0.9%
5. NET PROFIT MARGIN (NPM)		17,720	9.1%	17,698	9.4%	(22)	0.0%	194,920	9.1%	100,226	4.8%	(94,694)	-4.4%
6. OVER / (UNDER) BILLING		0	0.0%	0	0.0%	0	0.0%	0	0.0%	0	0.0%	0	0.0%
7. REVISED NPM		17,720	9.1%	17,698	9.4%	(22)	0.0%	194,920	9.1%	100,226	4.8%	(94,694)	-4.4%

FIGURE 43-1 "Budget-to-Actual" P&L Report

Some contractors understand this concept and know that, after they meet their BEP, they can bid work cheaper than they normally would at the end of the year without really cutting net profit. I would not recommend this strategy unless you have a justifiable reason. Because of the inherent risk, especially in construction projects, you should always strive to work for profit.

Determining the BEP

Use the following formula to calculate a company/division's BEP:

BEP = Annual G&A overhead budget dollars ÷ Annual GPM%

For a company whose budget is as follows:

Sales	$1,000,000	100%
G&A overhead	$ 200,000	20%
Net profit	$ 100,000	10%
Gross profit	$ 300,000	30%

BEP = $200,000 ÷ 30% = $200,000 ÷ .3 = $666,667

The "projected" BEP is calculated to be $666,667.

In other words, once you hit $666,667 in sales for the year, theoretically you should have accumulated enough gross profit to cover all of your $200,000 G&A overhead costs. This is your break-even point. If your gross profit margin is approximately 30%, multiply $666,667 by .3 and you get $200,000.

Remember: This is the "projected" or budgeted BEP. Due to fluctuations in the GPM on individual jobs throughout the year and other variable factors, the "actual" BEP will in all likelihood be different from that shown on your profit and loss (P&L) statement. Therefore, it's necessary to monitor the "budgeted-to-actual" BEP by means of the P&L statement.

How It Works

A client in New England had wrapped up his landscaping season with a healthy bottom line. His fiscal year ended March 31. Late in the fall he was given the opportunity to bid on a winter pruning job that his crew would complete prior to the end of his fiscal year. He wanted the job because winter revenue, other than snow plowing and sanding, was hard to come by. This job would keep three people busy for a good part of the winter and the contractor could put his division manager on the crew. This would transfer the manager's winter hours and salary from a G&A overhead expense to billable hours. An additional benefit would be that the contractor would not have to lay off the other two crew members and risk losing them if they did not return in the spring. He knew that he had to be competitive to get the project.

With a 10% net profit and G&A overhead this job would normally go for about $42,000. My client turned in a bid for $28,000, which just covered his direct costs. And he still did not get the job.

SUMMARY

It's very important that you monitor your G&A overhead costs and break-even point by means of a P&L statement similar to the one in Figure 43-1. A company usually reaches its BEP in the ninth or tenth month of its fiscal year. You reach your BEP when your accumulated gross profit margin (G&A overhead costs plus net profit) equals your G&A overhead budget dollar amount for the year.

ACTION POINT

Calculate your company/division BEP and monitor it throughout the year as described above.

CHAPTER 44

The Profit and Loss Statement and the Recap Report

Purpose

To explain the profit and loss statement and the recap report

Introduction

The profit and loss (P&L) statement is a very important report that you need to monitor in order to understand what is (or isn't) happening in your company. I think of it as a job-cost report for all of your jobs thrown together. If used properly and in conjunction with other data and reports, it can provide considerable insight into many aspects of your business.

If you have multiple divisions, each doing different types of work, I'd recommend that you provide each division that generates over 15 to 20% of gross annual sales with its own P&L statement. You may even want to break a division down into separate subdivisions that may or may not do the same types of work.

For instance, I know of a landscape maintenance company with over 24 four-man crews in one division. That division is broken down into six subdivisions with four crews and a foreman in each one. Each subdivision is tracked and compared to the others for profitability and direct costs.

THE PROFIT AND LOSS STATEMENT

Formatting the profit and loss (P&L) statement is crucial. Figure II-1 in Section II displays a sample P&L statement for one division of a corporation (not a sole proprietorship), which I'd encourage you to use. The format will differ if your company is a sole proprietorship or partnership.

The sales for the division are at the top of the report and are broken down into monthly and year-to-date (YTD) categories. Cost of goods sold/sales or direct costs come next and include everything that can be tied directly to a specific job. Put as much as you possibly can into direct costs, including labor burden (i.e., FICA, FUTA, workers' compensation insurance, general liability insurance, unemployment insurance, field medical insurance, field holiday and vacation pay). Depreciation for your field equipment should be identified and included in direct costs. However, depreciation for office vehicles and office equipment should be included in G&A overhead.

G&A overhead is often referred to as indirect or general and administrative costs. The point to remember is that you can't pin G&A overhead costs to a particular field operation or job. Hence, the term indirect or general is used.

Net profit margin (NPM) before taxes and non-business-related interest follows G&A overhead. Ten percent (10%) NPM is a good target percentage to shoot for after all costs have been included in the expense categories. I like to track net profit margin "budget-to-actual" on a graph on a monthly or quarterly basis (see Figure 44-1). I also prefer that a company be on the accrual basis for its financial accounting. The accrual basis provides a more consistent and accurate sales-to-expense comparison because it enters the expenses for specific jobs in the same accounting period. The cash basis for accounting doesn't do this.

Some companies include an over-/under-billing category at the top or bottom of their P&L statement to reflect net profits more accurately. If they've over-billed or under-billed on their jobs for a given period, they subtract or add the same amount and adjust their P&L statement accordingly.

How It Works

One company in Colorado learned the hard way about the necessity of having an over-/under-billing category on their P&L statement. At the end of one year the owner paid out over $140,000 of what he thought was "net profit" in bonuses, vacations, cars, and so on only to find out later that he was spending money over-billed on an uncompleted project.

Ouch!

THE P&L RECAP REPORT

This report provides an encapsulated view of the P&L shown in Figure 44-2 on page 366 and compares "budget-to-actual" figures. Each division should have a separate recap sheet. G&A overhead is condensed into just three categories; I include payables and receivables in order to obtain some percentages at the bottom of the report.

These ratios are meaningless unless taken into consideration with the overall context of the business.

The ratios are very important, especially when you graph them over a 6- to 12-month period. Remember, however, that these ratios are meaningless unless taken into consideration with the overall context of the business. As an example, the material-to-labor ratio one month may be very high compared to another because the materials were bought one month and the labor to install it expended the next. Therefore, you need to view the monthly ratio in context with the yearly ratio.

SUMMARY

The profit and loss statement can provide invaluable insight into your business if it's formatted properly. It can be shortened or recapped to further help you identify key trends and to monitor "budget vs. actual" performance. The Recap report is an excellent tool that can help you monitor ratios and other important budget-to-actual data for your company.

ACTION POINT

Review the format of your P&L statement with your accountant or CPA and adjust the format in order to identify direct versus indirect costs more accurately and thoroughly.

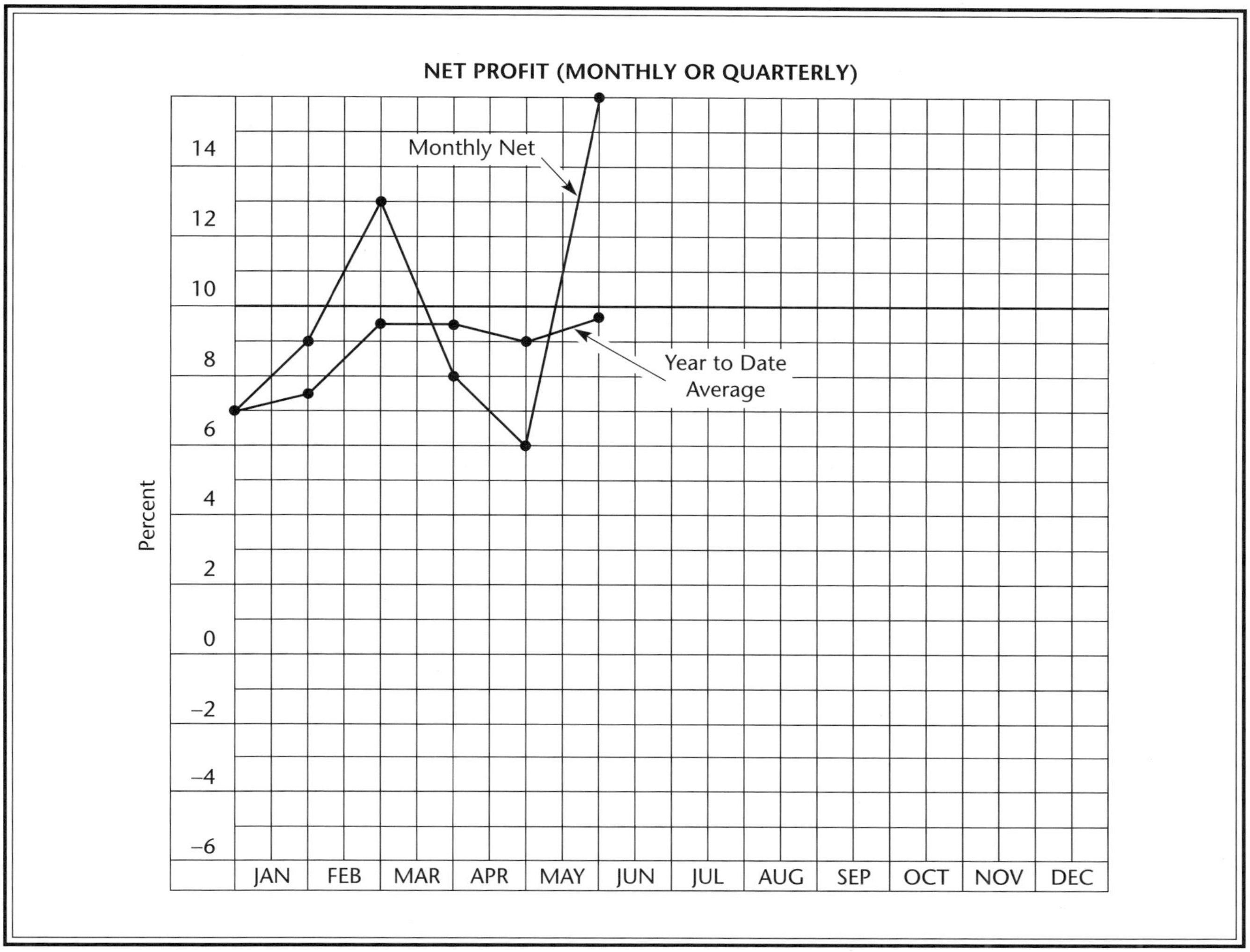

FIGURE 44-1 Net Profit Margin "Budget vs. Actual" Graph

	NOV BUDGET	BUD %	NOV ACTUAL	ACT %	NOV VARIANCE	VAR %	Y-T-D BUDGET	BUD %	Y-T-D ACTUAL	ACT %	Y-T-D VARIANCE	VAR %
1. SALES (Revenues)	195,000	100.0%	188,500	100.0%	(6,500)	-3.3%	2,145,000	100.0%	2,080,000	100.0%	(65,000)	-3.0%
2. COST OF GOODS SOLD (Direct Costs)												
MATERIALS	58,500	30.0%	64,656	34.3%	(6,156)	-3.2%	643,500	30.0%	619,840	29.8%	23,660	1.1%
DIRECT FIELD LABOR	35,100	18.0%	33,467	17.8%	1,633	0.8%	386,100	18.0%	389,126	18.7%	(3,026)	-0.1%
LABOR BURDEN	8,775	4.5%	8,367	4.4%	408	0.2%	96,525	4.5%	98,376	4.7%	(1,851)	-0.1%
EQUIPMENT	17,550	9.0%	16,525	8.8%	1,025	0.5%	193,050	9.0%	187,255	9.0%	5,795	0.3%
EQUIPMENT RENTALS	2,917	1.5%	500	0.3%	2,417	1.2%	32,087	1.5%	29,850	1.4%	2,237	0.1%
SUBCONTRACTORS	9,750	5.0%	8,500	4.5%	1,250	0.6%	107,250	5.0%	122,000	5.9%	(14,750)	-0.7%
MISCELLANEOUS	1,250	0.6%	659	0.3%	591	0.3%	13,750	0.6%	14,525	0.7%	(775)	0.0%
TOTAL COGS	133,842	68.6%	132,674	70.4%	1,168	0.6%	1,472,262	68.6%	1,460,972	70.2%	11,290	0.5%
3. GROSS PROFIT MARGIN (GPM)	61,158	31.4%	55,826	29.6%	(5,332)	-2.7%	672,738	31.4%	619,028	29.8%	(53,710)	-2.5%
4. G&A OVERHEAD TOTAL	43,438	22.3%	38,129	20.2%	5,309	2.7%	477,818	22.3%	496,549	23.9%	(18,731)	-0.9%
A. SALARY OFFICE	9,333	4.8%	9,500	5.0%	(167)	-0.1%	102,663	4.8%	105,555	5.1%	(2,892)	-0.1%
B. SALARY OFFICER	6,667	3.4%	6,667	3.5%	0	0.0%	73,337	3.4%	73,337	3.5%	0	0.0%
5. NET OPERATING INCOME	17,720	9.1%	17,697	9.4%	23	0.0%	194,920	9.1%	122,479	5.9%	(72,441)	-3.4%
OTHER INCOME / (EXPENSE)			0	0.0%					0	0.0%		
NET INCOME / (LOSS)			17,697	9.4%					122,479	5.9%		
6. TOTAL PAYABLES			135,000									
SUBTOTAL			135,000									
7. RECEIVABLES												
A. CURRENT			255,000									
SUBTOTAL			120,000									
B. OVER 30			78,000									
SUBTOTAL			198,000									
C. OVER 60			22,500									
SUBTOTAL			220,500									

8. RATIOS / PER HOUR ANALYSIS	BUDGET	ACTUAL	VARIANCE	BUDGET	ACTUAL	VARIANCE
A. MATERIAL / LABOR	1.67	1.93	0.27	1.67	1.59	-0.07
B. CURRENT RECV. / TOTAL PAYABLES		1.89			NA	
C. CURRENT RECV. / TOTAL RECV.		71.7%			NA	
D. OVER 30 / TOTAL RECEIVABLES		21.9%			NA	
E. OVER 60 / TOTAL RECEIVABLES		6.3%			NA	
F. EQUIPMENT / LABOR	58.3%	50.9%	-7.4%	58.3%	55.8%	-2.5%
G. SALES / LABOR	5.56	5.63	0.08	5.56	5.35	-0.21
H. G&A OVERHEAD / SALES	22.3%	20.2%	-2.0%	22.3%	23.9%	1.6%
I. G&A OVHD, SALARIES / SALES	8.2%	8.6%	0.4%	8.2%	8.6%	0.4%
J. SALES / LABOR HOUR (SPH or RPH)	$43.50	$41.11	($2.39)	$43.50	$37.74	($5.76)
K. FIELD LABOR BURDEN	25.0%	25.0%	0.0%	25.0%	25.3%	0.3%
L. AVERAGE WAGE	$7.83	$7.30	$0.53	$7.83	$7.06	$0.77
M. G&A OVHD. / FIELD-LABOR HOUR	$9.69	$8.32	$1.37	$9.69	$9.01	$0.68
N. BILLED FIELD-LABOR HOURS	4,483	4,585	(102)	49,310	55,117	(5,807)
O. NON-BILLED FIELD-LABOR HOURS	88	96	8	968	836	(132)
P. TOTAL FIELD-LABOR HOURS	4,571	4,681	(94)	50,278	55,953	(5,939)
Q. MATERIAL PER FIELD-LABOR HR	$13.05	$14.10	$1.05	$13.05	$11.25	($1.80)
S. SPH/AW (SAW)	5.56	5.63	0.08	5.56	5.35	(0.21)

FIGURE 44-2 P&L Statement Recap Report

CHAPTER 45

Field and G&A Overhead Equipment

Purpose

To explain how to monitor and control equipment costs

Introduction

It isn't enough to ensure that ample field equipment is available and maintained for use in the field. You must monitor equipment usage, and be sure equipment is paying for itself.

The key to effective equipment planning is to ensure that you're estimating your equipment accurately and to use your equipment enough to generate sales dollars to cover its costs. Construction and maintenance companies can get into serious trouble when the income generated by field equipment doesn't cover the cost of that equipment.

Often this problem gets buried in the operational maze. No one in the company is the wiser until the bottom line begins to deteriorate. Management has to divert valuable time and resources for an investigation of the problem, when it could have been avoided from the beginning, or at least identified much sooner.

It's important that you compare your "budget-to-actual" equipment costs for individual jobs as well as for your company as a whole.

FIELD EQUIPMENT COSTS BID INTO JOBS

Field equipment costs should be included in bids as the job requires. This equipment includes trucks used in the field, such as crew trucks, tractors, mowers, skid steers, and so on. Equipment is bid much the same as labor; actual usage in hours on a particular job should be multiplied by a predetermined cost per hour (CPH) figure.

Monitor equipment usage through job costing. Use the job-cost format in Figure 41-2 to track and compare "budget-to-actual" equipment costs for individual jobs. Track the use of equipment on each separate job to make sure that equipment bid into separate jobs is very close to the equipment actually used.

EQUIPMENT BUDGETS AND MONITORING COMPANY-OWNED EQUIPMENT

The primary function of accounting, as it relates to equipment and other than processing accounts payable invoices and loan payments for equipment, is to *keep score* by comparing your equipment budgets to the actual costs. One of three methods, or a combination of these methods, can be used to compare budgeted costs to actual costs for the entire company.

Establish an Equipment Checkbook

As you'd calculate payroll for labor (based on actual hours multiplied by a labor rate), do the same for equipment (hours used multiplied by the CPH for each piece of equipment). Total this amount for all equipment. Deposit the equipment "paycheck" into the equipment checkbook. All equipment expenses for fuel, repairs, monthly payments, insurance, and the like should be made from this account.

If this account always has too little money in it to cover all your equipment expenses, it's because

1. You have too much equipment, which can't be justified, or the equipment is being under utilized. This can and will kill you.
2. Your calculated cost per hour is too low.
3. A combination of both (1) and (2).

If you consistently have more money in this checking account than you need and your job costing shows that your equipment bid versus actually used is in line, accumulate this money for planned replacement of worn out equipment or for new equipment.

Establish an Equipment Division on Paper

To establish a division on paper you should create an equipment division profit and loss (P&L) statement in your accounting software. Remember the following facts:

- Direct costs consist of materials and labor expended on equipment and vehicle upkeep and repair, equipment insurance, lease payments, labor burden, fuel, equipment used for repairs and preventive maintenance, depreciation, subcontractor costs for repairs done outside the company, and any other expense directly related to equipment.
- General and administrative overhead costs for this division consist of indirect G&A expenses, or a portion of them that is used to support the equipment division.
- Sales are generated by charging field production divisions a rental fee (at the CPH rate) for equipment used. This fee is then charged to the respective division as a direct cost for equipment used.

The main purpose of the equipment division is to format a "scoreboard" for equipment costs in such a way as to indicate quickly and accurately whether equipment is paying for itself or not. The goal of the equipment division (at a minimum) is to break even. Division "profits" should be set aside in a separate bank account for future replacement costs of equipment.

You should seriously consider establishing an equipment division on paper, once your company reaches about $1.5 million in gross annual sales.

Form an "Actual" Division or Company

Many companies that establish a "paper" equipment division eventually formulate an actual division with a designated division equipment manager in charge. The manager's primary responsibility is to run this division and to service all of the corporate equipment needed, while keeping costs to a minimum. The equipment division's P&L statement serves as the manager's report card. For tax purposes, this division can eventually be split off as a separate company. If you desire to pursue this, consult with your CPA.

JUSTIFYING EQUIPMENT PURCHASES (the 50% Rule)

As a general rule, you need to be able to bill out a piece of equipment approximately 50% of the time in order to justify owning it.

For example, a tractor that has a cost per hour (CPH) of $20 should be included in bids, operated, and billed to jobs at least 20 hours each week. This would generate $400 per week in revenue (before net profit and G&A overhead markups) to cover its costs.

As a general rule, you need to be able to bill out a piece of equipment approximately 50% of the time in order to justify owning it.

If you can't bill out a piece of equipment 50% of the time, you probably won't generate enough revenue from it to cover its costs. Purchase of specialty pieces of equipment, and/or ones that are difficult to rent, may be justified if you believe the "convenience" of owning them offsets the lack of billable hours generated by them.

KEEPING SCORE

Keeping score means you're constantly verifying that the revenue generated from equipment bid in the jobs and installed in the field is sufficient to cover all your equipment expenses. By making a few variations to the job-cost format in Figure 41-2, as shown on Figure 45-1 on page 370, you can use it to combine all your costs and compare them to your equipment budget for the year.

It's best to have accounting software in order to compare equipment budget-to-actual costs. However, so few contractors have accounting software up and running (let alone providing budget-to-actual expense comparisons) that doing it manually, as described above, may be necessary as an interim measure.

Always ask yourself these all-important questions for each piece of equipment:

- Is this piece of equipment paying for itself?
- Is it justifying its existence and expense?

Let me attempt to make what I've said more real with an illustration of what I've observed in businesses ranging in size from $100,000 to $10,000,000 plus.

How It Works

A rather large landscape and irrigation company planned to employ enough labor in the field during the next year to total approximately 50,000 field-labor hours. Total equipment costs were estimated at about $450,000 for the year. Indirect costs (G&A overhead) were estimated at $300,000. For bidding purposes, direct costs (material, sales tax, labor, labor burden, and subcontractors) were included in the bid at cost. Equipment costs were combined with G&A overhead and added to the bid at $15 per estimated field-labor hour ($450,000 equipment costs plus $300,000 G&A overhead and both divided by the 50,000 projected field-labor hours).

It sounds simple enough, but there is a *fatal flaw* in the process. Equipment costs were not bid based on what was needed for particular jobs. Rather, all equipment was

Budget Recap

	BUDGET	%	ACTUAL	%	TO GO
Charged to jobs	**137,030**	**100.0%**	**68,089**	**49.7%**	**68,941**
Materials	40,000	29.2%	16,223	11.8%	23,777
Direct labor	35,280	25.7%	20,988	15.3%	14,292
Labor burden	12,348	9.0%	7,346	5.4%	5,002
Equipment payments	34,992	25.5%	19,089	13.9%	15,903
Rental equip.	500	0.4%	212	0.2%	288
Subcontractors	2,500	1.8%	755	0.6%	1,745
Subtotal	125,620	91.7%	64,613	47.2%	61,007
	0	0.0%	0	0.0%	0
Total direct costs	125,620	91.7%	64,613	47.2%	61,007
GPM	**11,410**	**8.3%**	**3,476**	**2.5%**	**(7,934)**
G&A overhead	9,800	7.2%	5,830	4.3%	3,970
NPM	**1,610**	**1.2%**	**(2,354)**	**-1.7%**	**(3,964)**

Month 7

BUDGET INFORMATION

G&A OPH	$5.00	**(G&A overhead per hour)**
Labor burden	35.0%	
CAW	$18.00	**(With RF & OTF, no LB)**
SPH	$69.91	**(Sales per labor hour)**
PPH	$0.82	**(Net profit per labor hour)**
Mat / Lab	1.1	**(Material to labor ratio)**

MONTHLY EQUIPMENT PAYMENTS / LEASE PAYMENTS

ITEM	PMT	PAID Y-T-D	(Month) 7
Totals	$2,916	$19,089	
Pickup # 1	$189	$1,323	
Pickup # 2	$205	$1,435	
Pickup # 3	$276	$1,932	
Pickup # 4	$354	$2,478	
1 Ton dump	$414	$2,898	
6 CY Dump truck	$486	$3,402	
Skid steer #1	$570	$3,990	
Skid steer #2	$422	$2,954	
Shop truck (paid off)	$0	$0	

Material, Equipment & Subcontractor Costs

		BUDGET	ACTUAL	TO GO	% TO GO
Materials (parts)	-->	18,000 -	6,201 =	11,799	65.6%
Fuel, oil, lubricants	-->	22,000 -	10,022 =	11,978	54.4%
Subcontractors	-->	2,500 -	755 =	1,745	69.8%
Rental equipment	-->	500 -	212 =	288	57.6%
Subtotal	-->	**43,000 -**	**17,190 =**	**25,810**	**60.0%**

VENDORS	TOTAL	Parts	Fuel / POL	SUBS	RENTAL EQ.
ACTUAL TOTALS------>	**$17,190**	**6,201**	**10,022**	**755**	**212**
AA Auto	3,853	3,853			
Spartan Auto Parts	525	525			
Hanover Oil Co.	5,766		5,766		
J & J Mufflers	255			255	
Daves Tire & Wheel	0				
Lube-N-Go	0				
RFI Equipment Rentals	212				212
Suburban Skid Steer	2,323	1,823		500	
Shell	1,854		1,854		
Texaco	2,233		2,233		
Mobil	126		126		
Conoco	43		43		
	0				
	0				
	0				
	0				
	0				
	0				

EQUIPMENT TOTALS---->	$68,089	CPH	BUD HRS	YTD HRS	TO GO
Pickup # 1	6,928	$8.00	2,080	866	1,214
Pickup # 2	6,928	$8.00	1,732	866	866
Pickup # 3	6,928	$8.00	1,732	866	866
Pickup # 4	6,928	$8.00	1,732	866	866
1 Ton dump	4,330	$10.00	866	433	433
6 CY Dump truck	7,361	$17.00	866	433	433
Skid steer #1	9,743	$20.00	866	487	379
Skid steer #2	10,284	$20.00	866	514	352
Shop truck	8,660	$10.00	2,080	866	1,214

Mechanic Labor Hours

	BUDGET	ACTUAL	%	TO GO	% TO GO
TOTAL	**1,960**	**1,166**	**59.5%**	**794**	**40.5%**
PM / Repairs	1,568	1,037	**66.1%**	**531**	**33.9%**
Admin	392	129	**32.9%**	**263**	**67.1%**

	Pay period		Hours- PM/repairs		Hours- Admin
	A= 1-15	B= 16-31		1,037.0	129.0
1	January	A		80.0	8.0
2	January	B		79.0	9.0
3	February	A		74.0	6.0
4	February	B		62.0	18.0
5	March	A		78.0	10.0
6	March	B		76.0	12.0
7	April	A		79.0	9.0
8	April	B		72.0	8.0
9	May	A		82.0	6.0
10	May	B		79.0	9.0
11	June	A		78.0	10.0
12	June	B		77.0	11.0
13	July	A		79.0	8.0
14	July	B	Vaca 1 wk.	42.0	5.0
15	August	A			
16	August	B			
17	September	A			
18	September	B			
19	October	A			
20	October	B			
21	November	A			
22	November	B			
23	December	A			
24	December	B			
25					
26					
27					
28					
29					
30					
31					

FIGURE 45-1 Equipment Job-Cost Report for Co./Div.

averaged on all jobs regardless of how much or how little equipment was required in the field for a specific job. Jobs requiring nothing more than pickup trucks and wheelbarrows were charged the same ($15 per field-labor hour) as ones needing bobcats, trenchers, and backhoes. You can get away with this only if every job requires the same amount of labor and equipment.

The consequences were subtle and eventually disastrous. Labor-intensive jobs (the ones requiring only pickup trucks and wheelbarrows) were estimated with too much cost included to cover equipment. Consequently, this company didn't get labor-intensive jobs because its prices for these jobs were too high.

Jobs that were extremely equipment-intensive were charged at too little for equipment costs but, because the bids were underpriced, this company loaded up on underpriced jobs. And it kept getting them. As a result, it was using all its equipment but charging customers for only a fraction of its actual cost. The problem was further compounded when the wrong solution was offered and implemented to remedy the problem: "Let's bid more jobs and increase sales volume." The bottom line evaporated, and this company lost more and more money until it finally went out of business.

It's like putting more chickens into a chicken coop with a fox in it. Until you get rid of the fox, you haven't dealt with the real problem.

Two things need to happen to correct this scenario.

1. Equipment should be included in bids as the job requires. Actual usage in hours should be multiplied by a predetermined cost per hour figure. In this manner, every job is bid with equipment much as it's bid with labor—estimated hours times cost per hour.
2. Equipment usage should be monitored through job costing on a job-by-job basis to ensure that equipment bid into specific jobs is very close to equipment actually used on the job.

SUMMARY

You must monitor equipment usage and ensure that equipment is paying for itself. Whether you simply have an equipment checking account, an equipment division/profit center with a manager, or an altogether separate equipment leasing company, remember: *Keeping score means you're constantly verifying that the revenue generated from your equipment bid into jobs is sufficient to cover all your equipment expenses.* Too few contractors track this data, even though it is actually fairly simple to do.

ACTION POINT

Review your company's ability to "keep score" of equipment costs. Ensure that all equipment usage is included in your bids and that all of your equipment costs are covered by revenue generated by your jobs in the field.

CHAPTER

46 Industry Benchmarks

Purpose

To provide industry benchmarks to be used for quick-reference comparisons to your company's financial statements and bids

Introduction

A benchmark is a standard of measurement or evaluation that's common in the Green Industry.

The dictionary defines a benchmark as "A standard of measurement or evaluation." For our purposes, a benchmark is a standard of measurement or evaluation that's common in the Green Industry. Many of the benchmarks we'll discuss are also applicable to other industries; however, we'll limit our discussion to the industry at hand.

How It Works

I've worked alongside of hundreds of estimators as I trained them to cost estimate on computers as well as on pads of yellow paper. Some of them have had twenty to thirty years of "experience" estimating. I was amazed at how little they knew about the benchmarks contained in the bids that they were compiling. Consequently, they would often miss opportunities to add extra net profit or make serious mistakes as they overlooked critical benchmark information.

On the other hand, I have seen "green" inexperienced estimators become very competent and shrewd at the bid table in less than twelve months, primarily because they consistently compared their bids to industry benchmarks.

IDENTIFYING INDUSTRY BENCHMARKS

In Appendix E, we identify and list Green Industry benchmarks as they're measured and observed by using three financial tools: the profit and loss (P&L) statement, the balance sheet, and individual bids. The final section of Appendix E covers general observations from the marketplace. Refer to Figure II-1 in Section II when reviewing the P&L statement and Figure 46-1 when reviewing the balance sheet.

We should note that when we talk about labor hours or years, we're talking about billable field-labor man-hours or man-years. These hours and years don't include

ASSETS			
CURRENT ASSETS			
Cash and marketable securities	15,000		
Accounts receivable	125,000		
Inventories	45,000		
Notes receivable	10,000		
Costs and estimated earnings in excess of billings	20,000		
Prepaid expenses	4,000		
Other current assets	2,000		
TOTAL CURRENT ASSETS		**221,000**	
FIXED ASSETS			
Total fixed assets	150,000		
Less: Accumulated depreciation	(50,000)		
NET FIXED ASSETS		**100,000**	
OTHER ASSETS	8,000		
		8,000	
TOTAL ASSETS			**329,000**
LIABILITIES			
Current liabilities			
Accounts payable	100,000		
Notes payable	10,000		
Billings in excess of costs and estimated earnings	15,000		
Accrued payables	10,000		
Other current liabilities	3,000		
Total current liabilities		**138,000**	
Long-term liabilities	110,000		
		110,000	
TOTAL LIABILITIES		**248,000**	
OWNERS EQUITY			
Capital stock	25,000		
Retained earnings	56,000		
TOTAL OWNERS' EQUITY		**81,000**	
TOTAL LIABILITIES AND OWNERS' EQUITY	-		**329,000**

FIGURE 46-1 Balance Sheet Format

vacation, holiday, sick or downtime hours. The benchmarks provided are for companies having up to $5 million in annual sales and apply to typical or normal conditions.

It's also worth noting that these benchmarks are fluid and in many cases evolving as product and service cycles mature. For instance, bark blowing is comparatively new to the market and production methods and techniques are still developing. Therefore, the benchmarks for this product are fluid—they're still evolving.

The annual benchmarks provided for the various market segments are determined by assuming an individual worked in that segment for the whole year. For instance, the 1,700 to 2,000 man-hours per man-year for pavers are for an individual who worked installing pavers all year. This isn't the case with many contractors; often crew members install many different types of products in a given year. If this is the case for your company, you should be able to arrive at a reasonable benchmark for your operation by averaging two or three different benchmarks.

The categories covered in Appendix E are as follows:

1. The Profit and Loss Statement (or Income Statement)
2. The Balance Sheet
3. Bidding Benchmarks
   A. Percent-won rate
   B. Risk factor
   C. Overtime factor (OTF)
   D. Field-labor rates and crew average wage (CAW)
   E. General conditions
   F. Net profit margin
   G. Commissions on bids
4. General industry benchmarks
   A. Goodwill or blue sky
   B. Material pricing
   C. Rental equipment pricing

SUMMARY

Industry benchmarks can be very useful tools as a quick-reference comparison guide for your company's financial statements and bids. However, you should use them with caution. They're averages, which may or may not be accurate for your operation. While the benchmarks discussed in this chapter are valid, variances in individual company production methods and costs must be taken into account when using them.

ACTION POINT

Compare the industry benchmarks contained in Appendix E to specific ones for your company or division. Remember, benchmarks will vary somewhat from company to company. They will also vary as new equipment and production methods are introduced into your company.

CHAPTER

47

Six Sigma: Total Quality Management (TQM) Reevaluated

TERMS

Magic Wand Management
Management by Mysticism
Rain-Dance Methods
Six Sigma
Total Quality Management (TQM)

Purpose

To evaluate the Total Quality Management movement and its successor, the Six Sigma Revolution

Introduction

Total Quality Management (TQM) was the buzzword echoing throughout the corporate world in the 1980s and early 1990s. National, state, and local trade associations picked up the rhetoric and added to the fervor. The TQM movement gained prominence throughout corporate America during this period. However, it was often misunderstood and treated more as a "social" improvement process than as a scientifically-based method for improving the processes within a business. Fortunately, TQM survived these distortions and evolved into the **Six Sigma** movement. Six Sigma has taken Total Quality Management to new levels of sophistication and effectiveness.

George Eckes states it best in his book, *The Six Sigma Revolution*. "Six Sigma is a quantitative approach that fuels improved effectiveness and efficiency in an organization. This approach was first created in the 1980s by Motorola. Then, in the 1990s, companies like AlliedSignal and General Electric contributed to making Six Sigma the most popular quality improvement methodology in history."

TQM EVALUATED

In the late 1980s the construction and maintenance services industry joined the TQM parade in no small way. The American Society for Quality Control (ASQC) addressed quality issues concerning the construction industry in its regional operations centers and conferences. The Association for Quality and Participation (AQP) formed a Construction Industry Division.

The Construction Industry Institute (CII) stated in August of 1989, "Companies which do not implement Total Quality Management in their firms will not be competitive in the national and international markets within the next 5–10 years!"[9] Ernst & Young's March/April 1992 issue of *Contractor Briefing* echoed CII when it stated, "To remain competitive, contractors must use (the) total quality management technique."[10]

Did the results justify the hundreds and thousands of dollars (and hours) expended on TQM? Was it just another fad that stressed-out and overworked contractors latched onto in desperation as they attempted to control the chaos surrounding them? Or was the TQM movement the panacea some claimed it was?

The answer to these questions was neither a resounding "yes" nor "no." Rather, the answer was probably best analogous to the advent of the personal computer (PC) and its arrival on the construction and maintenance services industry scene in the mid-1980s. After seven or eight years of horror stories and rave reviews, the dust began to settle. Some companies had made significant progress using PCs. Others improved neither their management methods nor their bottom line, even after spending thousands of dollars and hundreds of labor hours on personal computers.

The results obtained from TQM were not unlike those achieved with personal computers. Fortunately, there was hard data to help us ferret out the good from the bad.

There were basically two types of TQM programs. The first targeted incremental *results-driven* improvements by focusing on specific goals and the management processes involved to obtain them. The second was *activity-centered* and focused on employees doing the right types of activities. These activities would, in turn, improve performance as a natural by-product of the activity.

These two methods came under much scrutiny. Robert H. Schaffer and Harvey A. Thomson concluded in the January/February 1992 issue of the *Harvard Business Review* that, "Most corporate change programs mistake means for ends, process for outcome. The solution: focus on results, not on activities."

The performance efforts of many companies have as much impact on operational and financial results as a ceremonial rain dance has on the weather.

They further noted that, "The performance efforts of many companies have as much impact on operational and financial results as a ceremonial rain dance has on the weather. While (results-driven) companies constantly improve measurable performance, managers (in activity-centered ones) continue to dance round and round the campfire—exuding faith and dissipating energy. ... The 'rain dance' is the ardent pursuit of activities that sound good, look good, and allow managers to feel good—but which in fact contribute little or nothing to bottom line performance."

Schaffer and Thomson go on to cite a 1991 survey which covered over 300 electronics firms. Findings indicated that 73% of the companies had TQM programs, but 63% had improved quality defects by less than 10%. These were dismal results for efforts expended.[11]

The 'rain dance' is the ardent pursuit of activities that sound good, look good, and allow managers to feel good—but which in fact contribute little or nothing to bottom line performance.

Tracy E. Benson of *Industry Week* (IW) magazine stated in its October 5, 1992 issue that, "The large number of quality activities in U.S. firms 'that aren't making a difference' is alarming ... Remember 'The Emperor's New Clothes,' the fairy tale about the Emperor whose robes were made of fabric so opulent that it could not be seen by those who were unfit for their jobs or impossibly stupid? The Emperor paraded daily before the townspeople until one day a young boy could contain himself no longer. 'The Emperor has no clothes,' he cried. So it is with quality."[12]

In a May 3, 1993 *Industry Week* article, Benson wrote, "Employee-based programs that are designed to boost morale but are not tied directly to performance can actually frustrate and alienate workers instead." She goes on to quote the authors of *Quality on Trial* (West Publishing Co., 1992), Roger J. Howe, Dee Gaeddert and Maynard A. Howe. They state, "When the primary focus ... is measuring participation in activities (e.g., number of hours of training, number of team meetings, number of suggestions, and the like) rather than on the impact of those activities on business results, the corporation's time and money are wasted."[13]

How It Works

I visited a contractor on the East Coast shortly after he had returned from a seminar conducted by a major industry association. The association was making TQM the major theme for the year and it was also the topic of the seminar. I was interested to find out how the subject matter was taught. As it turned out, the contractor was given only theory at the seminar and little practical advice as to how to implement it. Future seminars and on-site visits to participating companies would certainly help him implement the desired improvements. He was determined to implement TQM throughout his company and make it work.

Nine months later, I revisited this contractor and his company. In frustration, he had given up on TQM, and he was disillusioned with the whole subject. Thanks to the sincere, yet misguided efforts of the association, this contractor threw out the TQM baby with the proverbial bath water.

VERDICT ON TQM

Change and quality improvement programs offered great hope to the contractor facing seemingly overwhelming problems and who was desperate for solutions. TQM had the potential not only to offer many real solutions while improving the bottom line, but also had the ability to revolutionize a company and the management structure within it.

However, buyer beware! TQM is not **magic wand management**. Like the dollars and labor hours spent on personal computers during the 1980s and 1990s, many contractors improved management performance and profits. Unfortunately, many other contractors wasted a lot of money and a lot of labor hours on PCs because precise expectations weren't established and compared to measurable, targeted results.

Contractors who made similar mistakes with TQM and who failed to target specific incremental results-driven improvements were very disappointed with the return on their investment and disheartened with the very concept of TQM. This was unfortunate, because many others obtained the results and saw the benefits of the tried and proven methods of TQM, when used properly.

TQM REEVALUATED

Philip B. Crosby, in his classic book *Quality is Free*, tackled two key myths regarding TQM and quality improvement. He stated, "The first erroneous assumption is that quality means goodness, or luxury, or shininess, or weight. The word 'quality' is used to signify the relative worth of things in such phrases as 'good quality,' 'bad quality,' and that brave new statement 'quality of life' ... It is a situation in which individuals talk dreamily about something without ever bothering to define it ... That is precisely the reason we must define quality as 'conformance to standards' if we are to manage it."[14]

In fact, quality is precisely measurable by the oldest and most respected of measurements—cold hard cash.

Crosby goes on to state, "In fact, quality is precisely measurable by the oldest and most respected of measurements—cold hard cash."[15]

Tom Peters builds on Crosby's basic premises when he challenges us to, "Measure what's important."[16] And to remember that in today's marketplace, "What gets measured gets done has never been so powerful a truth."[17]

TQM is simply the threefold process of (1) establishing a performance standard, (2) collecting actual performance data, and (3) comparing the two to obtain a variance (or deviation) between them. As pointed out in the introduction, this is a methodology similar to the one used by science. For the Green Industry, the first step is a budgeting or estimating process (which this book addresses) combined with quality standards for performance. The second and third steps are data collection and job-costing issues, which are really information management issues.

What gets measured gets done has never been so powerful a truth.

The typical contractor has problems with the very concept of TQM for the following reasons:

- He or she simply doesn't understand the methodology (or the very concept) of TQM as described above. The process remains too ethereal and non-quantifiable. The "rubber never meets the road," so to speak.
- Most contractors don't understand that you "de-mystify" TQM by means of the budgeting and estimating process, and therefore make it an integral part of a business.
- Typical contractors either don't have key staff trained to collect the right types of data and compare them to the original performance standards (budgets and estimates), or they lack a business management software system to do so in a cost-effective manner, or both.

Annual company/division budgets and individual job estimates provide the majority of the standards or targets required to run a landscape and irrigation company. It's the monthly Profit & Loss statement (for your company and/or division) and individual job-cost reports that provide the means of comparing "estimated" or budgeted standards to actual performance. It is this very process of identifying standards, collecting data, and comparing the two that comprises the "guts" of any TQM system.

However, if you don't establish quantifiable, measurable standards in the bidding and budgeting process, you can neither direct nor control your jobs or your company. You can't effectively job cost a job bid by means of material-times-two or one whose price is calculated by the Market-Driven Unit Pricing method. You have nothing to which you can compare actual performance data. This is why a good estimating system provides you with not only an accurate *Price* but also with a *Plan* by which to run your job (and your company) and a *Process* by which to self-adjust the whole system.

Crosby hits the nail on the head when he states, "In business, ... requirements must be clearly stated so that they cannot be misunderstood. Measurements are then taken continually to determine conformance to those requirements. The nonconformance detected is the absence of quality. Quality problems become nonconformance problems and quality becomes definable."[18] Throughout his book, whenever you see the word 'quality,' it means 'conformance to requirements' or standards.

SIX SIGMA

Six Sigma is the successor to the Total Quality Management movement and has evolved directly from it. Both have foundations based on the scientific method. Six Sigma constantly attempts to integrate managerial effectiveness with operational efficiency as it focuses on the customer, the process, and the employee. "Effectiveness is meeting and exceeding the needs and requirements of the customer. Efficiency is the time, cost, or value of the activities that lead to customer satisfaction."[19]

Peter Drucker said it best when he stated in his book, *The Effective Executive*, that managers make sure things get done right and leaders make sure the right things get done. Six Sigma integrates the strategic issues dealing with managerial efficiency with the tactical issues concerning operational efficiency.

Eckes goes on to describe Six Sigma, "At the most basic, Six Sigma is a way of measuring the variation in a process. It can enable you to determine how close you are to being world class in terms of performance."[20] "Another definition of Six Sigma is cultural—having everyone in the organization develop and refine the never-ending pursuit of perfection."[21]

Some in the Green Industry would appear to prefer that small business (businesses under 100 employees and $10 million in annual sales) be an intuitive maze of mysterious processes. TQM and Six Sigma both fly in the face of this model. Measurement of key data is at the heart of science and management improvement processes. "If you have no data, you are just another person with an opinion."

There's also this quote attributed to Lord Kelvin: "I often say that when you can measure what you are speaking about and express it in numbers, you know something about it, but when you cannot measure it, when you cannot express it in numbers, your knowledge is of a meager and unsatisfactory kind."[22]

W. Edwards Deming, like Tom Peters, wholeheartedly approves of this paradigm when he emphatically states, "What gets measured, gets done."[23]

Six Sigma and TQM are based upon facts. Decisions are based on facts, not some seat-of-your-pants subjective feeling. Too often, business decisions in the Green Industry are made on whims and by-gosh-and-by-golly methods. This may be fine for the beginning entrepreneur. However, if the business is going to grow, a sounder approach is necessary.

I must warn you that Six Sigma does get technical. If you're easily bored with charts, graphs, statistics, and data, Six Sigma can overload you very quickly. However, some understanding of Six Sigma is essential in order to appreciate its value. Eckes explains that, "The symbol for the standard deviation is the lowercase Greek letter, *sigma*. As simply put as possible, the technical concept of Six Sigma is to measure current performance and to determine how many sigmas exist that can be measured from the current average until customer dissatisfaction occurs. When customer dissatisfaction occurs a defect results. A defect is any event that does not meet the requirements of a customer. Six Sigma is a process that produces no more than 3.4 defects per million opportunities."[24]

The long and short of it is that Six Sigma is a very sophisticated management improvement process you're going to be hearing much about in the near future. Frankly as it currently exists, it's far too sophisticated for most small businesses. However, as information management technology for the small business improves, you'll see Six Sigma methods applied at that level.

SUMMARY

Total Quality Management and Six Sigma methods can significantly improve your operation. However, in order to use these processes effectively, you have to analyze and measure things against predetermined standards (budgets, goals, bids, and so on). This book, in essence, shows you how to establish the standards on which to build an effective TQM program.

Don't be tricked into thinking that only budgeting and bidding fall under the TQM realm. Chapter 40 covers the Bid Board and the M.A.D. report, which help you monitor the nebulous process of bringing business into the company. They help you "grab the handle," so to speak, by measuring the process of selling jobs and comparing targeted standards to actual performance.

Just about anything can be measured and brought under the TQM umbrella. It's simply not necessary to measure everything, but only what's important. Analysis can lead to paralysis if not properly monitored and when information is simply collected and never used. One of the key roles of the owner/manager is to collect and focus on the right data at the right time and to understand the process in doing so.

As I mentioned earlier in this chapter, Peter Drucker said it best when he stated that managers make sure things get done right while leaders make sure the right things get done.

TQM can improve the whole company and the systems/processes in it if it's understood and used properly. Otherwise, magic wand management and **management by mysticism** prevail, as owners and/or managers employ **rain-dance methods** in their attempts to control and direct their companies and make them more profitable.

Managers make sure things get done right. Leaders make sure the right things get done.

ACTION POINT

Read Peter Drucker's classic book, *The Effective Executive.* It's a quick read and well worth the time spent.

Corparate Vital Signs
(The TQM Process)

CHAPTER 48

Bonuses and Incentives

TERMS

Bonuses
Incentives
Micro Bonuses
Non-Monetary Incentives

PURPOSE

To explain the difference between the "traditional" bonus and an incentive

To explain numerous forms of bonus and incentive methods

Introduction

What happens in your business when you're not there? If you left for six months, would you return and still have a financially viable company or does everything depend on you?

Not too many years ago, one of the nation's largest retailers was exposed for its faulty incentive program in its automobile repair department. Managers were rewarded for "up selling" customers. Unfortunately, this practice got out of control; customers were sold many repairs they simply didn't need. The national news media got wind of the problem, did an exposé of the retailer, and customer loyalty still suffers.

How It Works

One of my clients was very interested in changing the culture within his company. He wanted his managers to "buy into" the company and take ownership for key divisions of the organization. He had heard rave reviews about a company that specialized in helping businesses like his accomplish this goal. My client ended up spending over $50,000 and investing hundreds of man-hours with this company, hoping to change the culture within his organization. Unfortunately, he never did achieve the cultural change he desired and, to this day, he considers the time and money he spent as being wasted.

BONUSES AND INCENTIVES

Quite often we use the terms bonus and incentive interchangeably. However, some confusion exists concerning the two terms that we should address. Let's start our discussion with some basic definitions.

According to the dictionary, a **bonus** is "something given or paid in addition to the usual." An **incentive**, on the other hand, is "something inciting one to action or effort; stimulus." While the two definitions may not appear to vary much, there is a subtle difference.

A bonus is "something given or paid in addition to the usual."

An incentive is "something inciting one to action or effort; stimulus."

A bonus—the traditional Christmas bonus is a good example—is generally paid with little or no input from the recipient. The person receiving the bonus usually has very little knowledge as to how it's calculated or determined. It somehow appears from above cloaked in mystery.

The whole purpose of an incentive, on the other hand, is to get the participant involved in the business processes, to help improve those processes, and to share in the monetary rewards of doing so. Owners are encouraged to open up their "books," and share vital company information with employees. You want them to think like entrepreneurs, who are concerned about the company as an entity. You basically want to create a culture within the organization where everyone works to build a great company.

The following axioms may seem simplistic but I think they clearly communicate two very important principles you want to echo throughout your organization:

We have to take care of the goose that lays the golden eggs.

We don't get to take cookies out of the cookie jar unless we first put them in.

It really boils down to just that. If we can create a culture in our company that fosters its long-term financial health and viability, and if everyone participates in the rewards for doing so, we'll have implemented the key components of an effective incentive system.

There are numerous versions of bonuses and incentives being used today. Some are very simple; others are quite elaborate. Whole industries have sprung up whose primary focus is to teach other businesses how to implement an incentive program. I've seen particular methods be extremely effective in one company but not in another. What works for one business doesn't necessarily work for the other. However, there are some principles that prevail.

- Keep it simple—the simpler the better.
- Design the incentive method to fit the culture of the company.
- If the incentive method fails, it isn't the fault of the company using it.
- Employees need to buy into the process, not just contribute the money.
- Incentive methods should be self-funding.
- Entrepreneurial thinking is the goal of an incentive plan.
- Think scoreboards. Remember, what gets measured, gets done!
- Think simple charts and graphs.

We're going to review three basic incentive system methods, plus a number of "micro" or mini-methods. First, let's talk about non-monetary incentives.

Non-Monetary Incentives

Studies have repeatedly shown that money is not the primary force that motivates people to come to work, buy into the company, and do a good job. In their book, *Built to Last*, the authors construct an excellent case for **non-monetary incentives** and the principles and core values that make a great company endure. Companies with the right culture not only endure, they thrive. They're also the most profitable companies. However, profits and making money are of secondary or tertiary importance at best.

One of the enduring principles of the great companies is that they put their people and the development of their people first. They invest heavily and constantly in the people who make the organization work. Do employees respond to this type of culture? Absolutely!

The dictionary defines mercenary as "serving merely for pay or sordid advantage; venal; also: greedy." Companies and employees focusing just on "making money" usually don't, over the long haul. They may end up "rich" in monetary terms but in little else. Companies, whose primary concern is to create the right culture and to focus upon core values and enduring principles, create and sustain corporate greatness. They're also the most profitable companies. However, money and profits are by-products of the culture, not the primary objectives of the organization.

If money and profits are your primary objectives, you'll create a culture filled with mercenaries. And mercenaries don't build great companies.

Who Gets an Incentive?

Preferably everyone will participate in the incentive program. However, this isn't always possible. Many of my clients like to assign a point value to all the various positions within their companies. Or they might have two separate incentive programs: one for managers and one for field staff. The plan might look like this.

Position	Number of People	Points	Total Points
Division managers	1	5	5
Assistant managers	1	4	4
Office manager	1	4	4
Foremen/Crew leaders	3	3	9
Leadmen	3	2	6
Laborers/Administrative clerks	5	1	5
Totals	14		33

How Much Will Each Person Get?

Once the values are assigned, the points are calculated and totaled. The total of the incentive to be paid is divided by the point total. This provides a per-point value. An individual's incentive amount is determined by multiplying his or her point total by the value for one point.

When Should You Pay the Incentive?

The timing for paying the incentive is important. Many of my seasonal clients pay their incentives twice a year. One payment is made in early July, and the second at year's end. Other clients choose to pay field crews twice a year, but key management personnel at the end of either the calendar or fiscal year.

Companies that aren't seasonal in nature often prefer to pay out quarterly incentives. Doing so requires a little more paperwork, but it helps keep the incentive system uppermost in the minds of staff.

A Penny Saved

The timeless adage, "A penny saved is a penny earned," certainly applies to incentive programs. To put this maxim in perspective, ask yourself some questions.

Question 1: If you increase sales by $1.00, how much pre-tax net profit goes to the bottom line (assuming a 10% net profit)?

Answer: $0.10

Question 2: If you save $1.00 in cost by being more efficient, how much pre-tax net profit goes to the bottom line (assuming a 10% net profit)?

Answer: $1.00

Question 3: Would you rather have $1.00 or $0.10 in extra net profit?

Answer: You see where this is going.

My point is that an incentive program shouldn't just reward additional sales. It should also focus on operational efficiency. Both are important and necessary.

What About Total Quality Management (TQM)?

TQM and an incentive system should work hand in hand. Remember what Philip Crosby said in his book, *Quality is Free*: "... quality is precisely measurable by the oldest and most respected of measurements—cold hard cash."[25] Improvements in quality will go to your bottom line. If your incentive method reflects the bottom line, the two will reinforce one another.

Do Incentive Systems Have Anything to Do with Exit Strategies?

Let me answer this question with a resounding, "Yes!" A properly designed incentive system rewards everyone for taking ownership of the company and for thinking like an entrepreneur. It empowers people throughout the organization, and it encourages and allows the person experiencing the problem to solve it.

As people are properly trained, most problems are identified and solved at the lowest levels within the organization. This is not only the most cost-effective solution but it also allows for and promotes absentee ownership. As everyone is allowed to solve problems and implement creative solutions, the company depends on top leadership less and less for tactical or production decision making. Top management is then able to focus its primary attention on strategic issues, rather than on daily tactical ones. It's this very process which creates and optimizes exit strategy options.

An exit strategy is a well-planned process by which you transfer ownership of the company to employees, relatives, another company, etc. The possibilities are numerous. The objective of this process is to transfer legal ownership in a manner that optimizes your return for the business and the continued success of the company. A properly designed incentive system will normally greatly enhance the exit strategy process.

THE GROSS PROFIT MARGIN (GPM) INCENTIVE MODEL

The gross profit model focuses on achieving a predetermined amount of gross profit dollars. Note that the focus is on *dollars*, not *percentages*. A gross profit percentage is not an absolute. If your goal was 35% gross profit and you paid incentives on anything above it, you could actually be paying incentives while you're losing money.

I like to identify a dollar amount of gross profit for the company or division to attain during the fiscal year. Once it's achieved, the incentive kicks in. Normally the incentive is a percentage of the amount of gross profit above the targeted goal. Many of my clients pay out 25% of the dollars above the targeted amount as an incentive. However, first we need to determine who gets paid and how much to pay them. Let's use a specific example shown in Figure 48-1 on page 386.

Key managers and staff from ABC Landscape Company have formulated a budget with a sales revenue goal of $1,000,000 for the upcoming year. Direct costs are budgeted at $650,000. General and administrative (G&A) overhead is budgeted at $250,000 and net profit before tax is budgeted to be $100,000. For the purposes of simplicity, we'll assume we have four quarters of equal revenue and costs. Our breakdown looks as follows:

TABLE 48-1 Budget Breakdown

	Annual Budget		Quarterly Budget	
Sales revenue	$1,000,000	100%	$250,000	100%
Direct costs	650,000	65%	162,500	65%
Gross profit target	$ 350,000	35%	$ 87,500	35%
G&A overhead	250,000	25%	62,500	25%
Net profit	$ 100,000	10%	$ 25,000	10%

We'll pay the incentives on a quarterly basis. However, we'll pay 25%, 50%, 75%, and 100% of the accumulated incentives after the first, second, third, and fourth quarters, respectively. This should compensate for a bad quarter.

At the end of the first quarter, sales were $225,000 and the gross profit was $90,000, or 40%. The incentive paid works out as follows:

Sales revenue	$225,000	100.0%
Gross profit actual	90,000	40.0%
Gross profit target	– 87,500	35.0%
Over/under	$ 2,500	1.1%
Incentive percent (25%)	× .25	
Incentive earned	$ 625	0.3%
Incentive paid % (1st Qtr. 25%)	× .25	
Incentive paid $ amount	**$ 156**	**0.075%**

At the end of the second quarter, cumulative sales were $525,000 and the cumulative gross profit was $194,000, or 37%. The incentive paid works out as follows:

Sales revenue	$525,000	100.0%
Gross profit actual	194,000	35.0%
Gross profit target	–175,000	37.0%
Over/under	$ 19,000	3.6%
Incentive percent (25%)	× .25	
Incentive earned	$ 4,750	0.9%
Incentive paid % (2nd Qtr. 50%)	× .50	
Incentive paid $ amount	**$ 2,375**	**0.5%**

Date bonus to be paid on:	____/____/20___		<-----*Enter incentive pay date*
1. Cash received (sales):	$ 1,025,000	100.0%	<-----*Enter sales for the period*
2. Direct cost expenses:	$ 646,000	63.0%	
Materials	290,000.00	28.3%	<-----*Enter direct costs for the period*
Labor	200,000.00	19.5%	
Labor burden	50,000.00	4.9%	
Equipment	100,000.00	9.8%	
Equipment rentals	5,000.00	0.5%	
Subcontractors	-	0.0%	
Misc.	1,000.00	0.1%	
Misc.	-	0.0%	
	-	0.0%	
	-	0.0%	
	-	0.0%	
	-	0.0%	
3. GPM actual:	$ 379,000	37.0%	
4. GPM minimum hurdle:	$ 350,000	34.1%	<-----*Enter GPM hurdle*
5. GPM above hurdle:	$ 29,000	2.8%	
6. Incentive as a percent of line # 5:	$ 7,250	0.7%	25% <-----*Enter incentive percent paid on amount above GPM hurdle*
7. Total amount of incentive to be paid:	$ 7,250	0.7%	100% <-----*Enter percent of incentive to be paid this quarter (Suggested: 25, 50, 75 & 100% in quarters 1 through 4 respectively)*

8. Distribution calculation(s):
A. Enter quantity of individuals in each category in column A
B. Enter participant's payroll for incentive period minus vacation, holiday, sick pay, etc. in column B (Set to 1 if not based on payroll)
C. Enter participant's "multiplier" in column C, if applicable.
D. Total incentive amount is calculated in column D
E. Incentive to be paid to each member in category in column E

	A	B	C			D	E	
Totals--->	14	$ 6		33	100.0%	$ 7,250		
Division manager	1	$ 1	5	5	15%	$ 1,098	$ 1,098	<-----*Incentive paid each member*
Assistant manager	1	$ 1	4	4	12%	$ 879	$ 879	
Office manager	1	$ 1	4	4	12%	$ 879	$ 879	
Foremen / crew leaders	3	$ 1	3	9	27%	$ 1,977	$ 659	
Leadmen	3	$ 1	2	6	18%	$ 1,318	$ 439	
Laborers, admin clerks	5	$ 1	1	5	15%	$ 1,098	$ 220	
		$ -	-	-	0%	$ -	#DIV/0!	
		$ -	-	-	0%	$ -	#DIV/0!	
		$ -	-	-	0%	$ -	#DIV/0!	
		$ -	-	-	0%	$ -	#DIV/0!	
		$ -	-	-	0%	$ -	#DIV/0!	
		$ -	-	-	0%	$ -	#DIV/0!	
		$ -	-	-	0%	$ -	#DIV/0!	

FIGURE 48-1 The GPM Incentive Model

At the end of the third quarter, cumulative sales were $725,000 and the cumulative gross profit was $276,000, or 38%. The incentive paid works out as follows:

Sales revenue	$725,000	100.0%
Gross profit actual	276,000	38.0%
Gross profit target	–262,500	36.2%
Over/under	$ 13,500	1.9%
Incentive percent (25%)	× .25	
Incentive earned	$ 3,375	0.5%
Incentive paid % (3rd Qtr. 75%)	× .75	
Incentive paid $ amount	**$ 2,531**	**0.4%**

At the end of the fourth quarter, cumulative sales were $1,025,000 and the cumulative gross profit was $379,000, or 37%. The incentive paid works out as follows:

Sales revenue	$1,025,000	100.0%
Gross profit actual	379,000	37.0%
Gross profit target	– 350,000	34.2%
Over/under	$ 29,000	2.8%
Incentive percent (25%)	× .25	
Incentive earned	$ 7,250	0.7%
Incentive paid % (4th Qtr. 100%)	× 1.0	
Incentive paid $ amount	**$ 7,250**	**0.7%**

You'll notice that in the third quarter the cumulative incentive earned of $3,375 was actually less than the $4,750 earned in the second quarter. However, the sliding payout percentage still allowed us to pay an incentive. Otherwise, the employees would owe the company money if the full $4,750 was paid out at the end of the second quarter.

The value for one point in this scenario would be calculated as follows:

Total incentive amount $7,250 ÷ 33 total points = $220

Each category of staff member would be paid the following amounts:

Position	Points		$/Point		Incentive Amount
Division manager	5	×	$220	=	$1,100
Assistant manager	4	×	$220	=	$ 880
Office manager	4	×	$220	=	$ 880
Foremen/Crew leader	3	×	$220	=	$ 660 each
Leadmen	2	×	$220	=	$ 440 each
Laborers/Administrative clerks	1	×	$220	=	$ 220 each

Benefits The benefits of such a method are as follows:

- They are objective and quantifiable.
- The incentive is "self-funding" in that it is gross profit above what was anticipated.

- Owners can always pay more if they so choose.
- They reward both increased sales and production efficiency.
- They are well-thought-out and planned.
- They reward everyone.
- They focus on the company or division as a whole.

Cautions When using such a method, remember that

- It's somewhat complex.
- It requires accurate financial statements.

THE NET PROFIT (NPM) INCENTIVE MODEL

A mid-sized installation company on the East Coast uses a similar approach as the gross profit model for providing an incentive to its top four people. The owner's objective is to provide these four individuals with an incentive for taking care of the company. However, this company calculates its incentive from net profit instead of gross profit. Ten percent of pre-tax net profit is split evenly among the four people who basically run the company. The bonus is paid at the end of the fiscal year. If sales are $4 million and net profit is 13%, the total incentive for all four individuals is $52,000. This amount is then divided evenly among the four. See Figure 48-2.

A separate but similar method is used to provide an incentive to all other staff. This approach has been effective for this company. The four top management people really do "run" the company and feel they're an integral part of the operation. They have the best interest of the company at heart.

Benefits The benefits of such a method are as follows:

- They are objective and quantifiable.
- Owners can always pay more if they so choose.
- They reward both increased sales and production efficiency.
- They are well-thought-out and planned.
- They reward key individuals who are an integral part of the operation.
- They focus on the company or division as a whole.
- They are extremely simple to calculate.
- This method can greatly facilitate "absentee" ownership, as it rewards key individuals for effectively running the company.

Cautions When using such a method, remember that

- It's somewhat complex.
- It requires accurate financial statements.
- The incentive is not "self-funding."
- Net profit must be well defined and its calculation agreed to by all, as the owner can "play" with net profit by means of perks and other personal expenses.
- Adjustments must be made to net profit to ensure that it reflects true net profit.
- It works best when key individuals have free access to company financial information.

Date bonus to be paid on:	______________		*<-----Enter incentive pay date*
1. Cash received (sales):	**$ 4,000,000**	100.0%	*<-----Enter sales for the period*
2. Direct cost expenses:	**$ 2,680,000**	67.0%	
Materials	1,200,000.00	30.0%	*<-----Enter direct costs for the period*
Labor	700,000.00	17.5%	
Labor burden	175,000.00	4.4%	
Equipment	480,000.00	12.0%	
Equipment rentals	50,000.00	1.3%	
Subcontractors	50,000.00	1.3%	
Misc.	25,000.00	0.6%	
Misc.	-	0.0%	
	-	0.0%	
	-	0.0%	
	-	0.0%	
	-	0.0%	
3. GPM actual:	**$ 1,320,000**	33.0%	
4. G&A overhead:	**$ 800,000**	20.0%	*<-----Enter G&A overhead*
5. Net profit margin actual:	**$ 520,000**	13.0%	
6. Incentive as a percent of line # 5:	**$ 52,000**	1.3%	10% ***<-----Enter incentive percent paid on Net Profit Margin***
7. Total amount of incentive to be paid:	**$ 52,000**	1.3%	100% ***<-----Enter percent of incentive to be paid this quarter/period*** *(Suggested: 25, 50, 75 & 100% in quarters 1 through 4 respectively)*

8. Distribution calculation(s):

A. Enter quantity of individuals in each category in column A
B. Enter participant's payroll for incentive period minus vacation, holiday, sick pay, etc. in column B (Set to 1 if not based on payroll)
C. Enter participant's "multiplier" in column C, if applicable.
D. Total incentive amount is calculated in column D
E. Incentive to be paid to each member in category in column E

	A		B	C			D	E	
Totals--->	**4**	**$**	**4**		**4**	**100.0%**	**$ 52,000**		
Operations manager	1	$	1	1	1	25%	$ 13,000	$ 13,000	***<-----Incentive paid each member***
Construction manager/estimator	1	$	1	1	1	25%	$ 13,000	$ 13,000	
Residential manager/estimator	1	$	1	1	1	25%	$ 13,000	$ 13,000	
Office manager	1	$	1	1	1	25%	$ 13,000	$ 13,000	
		$		# ##	-	0%	$ -	#DIV/0!	
		$		# ##	-	0%	$ -	#DIV/0!	
		$		# ##	-	0%	$ -	#DIV/0!	
		$		# ##	-	0%	$ -	#DIV/0!	
		$		# ##	-	0%	$ -	#DIV/0!	
		$		# ##	-	0%	$ -	#DIV/0!	
		$		# ##	-	0%	$ -	#DIV/0!	
		$		# ##	-	0%	$ -	#DIV/0!	
		$		# ##	-	0%	$ -	#DIV/0!	

FIGURE 48-2 The NPM Incentive Model

INCENTIVES BASED ON INDIVIDUAL JOBS AND/OR FIELD PRODUCTION

There are a number of methods that attempt to reward field labor for bringing jobs in on or under budget. I tend to disagree with this individual job approach because it doesn't focus on the entire company, just on field operations.

Please don't misunderstand. Getting field staff involved in an incentive program is essential, but it must be tied to productivity and efficiency. However, this approach only deals with field efficiency and not with managerial effectiveness. It doesn't take into account the larger strategic issues owners and managers have to deal with, which the gross profit and net profit models address.

Beating the Budget

Many contractors provide an incentive or bonus based on "beating the budget," which usually means bringing the job in below budget for field-labor hours. A predetermined amount per labor hour saved is identified, for instance $25. For every labor hour below budget, the crew gets $25 to divide among its members.

While this approach has its merits, managers must monitor quality control and safety issues very closely. Corners can be cut in order to shave extra hours. Field crews can also work against one another: they are focused on their *individual* jobs and not the company as a whole.

If the crews consistently beat the labor hour budget, shouldn't the estimators adjust their methods to accurately reflect these improved production rates? What happens if management invests in a new piece of equipment, a mini-skid steer for instance, that saves crews many labor hours? How do you reflect this change in both your estimated production rates and your incentive system?

Commissions for Field Crews

This approach doesn't work in all situations, but it can be effective in some. An arborist in the Northwest paid his crews a percentage of what's billed for a job. He calculated crew labor at approximately 30% of the price he charged. Crews were paid 30% of whatever they billed. If a $2,000 job was performed in one day, the crew would get $600, or 30%. If it took them two days, they'd still get the $600. All callbacks had to be handled by the crew without any remuneration.

This method worked well for the field crew. However, it was very narrow in its focus, and didn't take into account overall company managerial effectiveness. Accurate estimating was essential, using this model. Management had to ensure that crew safety, as well as quality control, didn't suffer, as crews might rush to get jobs done.

The Foreman's Bonus Checklist

While it doesn't just focus on one particular job, the bonus checklist outlined in Figure 48-3 can be effective. It's straightforward and self-explanatory. Management reviews and identifies the items on the checklist on a month-to-month basis. Changes are made to these items as management deems necessary. Management also determines the amount each item is worth. Regular pay for foremen before the bonus is at fair market value. The bonus provides an excellent incentive for foremen to ensure that jobs are run efficiently.

The downside of the bonus checklist method is that it only addresses field efficiency and at only the foreman or crew leader level. It doesn't address strategic company effectiveness or incentives for field labor. The bonus checklist is also somewhat subjective and time-consuming in that someone, usually the field supervisor or owner, has to monitor all the items on the list for every crew leader. Disagreements can ensue if all items aren't documented properly and thoroughly.

To: **Dusty Lane** **Date:** ____/____/200____

Subject: **Field crew leader's monthly bonus checklist**

I. The items listed below will be reviewed every month and you will be paid $40.00 for every item that you successfully complete. If you miss the same item two months in a row, you will forfeit the entire month's bonus. If you miss three items in the same month, you will forfeit the entire month's bonus.

Item

1. No water problems:
   a. Keep clocks wired into power.
   b. Take care of weekend water.
   c. Water plants properly on job, not too wet or dry.
   d. Make berms properly.
2. Keep our schedule:
   a. Discuss schedules with operations manager daily.
   b. Review and maintain schedules on all jobs.
3. Keep trucks and equipment in order:
   a. Remove trash from trucks daily.
   b. PM (preventative maintenance) all equipment daily.
4. Turn in all paperwork to office daily (receipts, delivery tickets, hours, extras).
5. Use up parts and plant inventory.
6. Inform operations manager of problems immediately.
7. Run a safe job (no accidents):
   a. Immediately inform operations manager and office of all accidents.
   b. Conduct and document weekly safety meetings.
8. Get crews out of shop on time.

II. Items may be added to or deleted from this list as requirements change.

______________________________ _____/_____/20___
Signature Date

FIGURE 48-3 The Bonus Checklist Model

Unit or Piece Work

As a young boy in Pennsylvania, I'd often pick apples in the fall. We were all paid by the bushel basket. I believe the going rate was $.35 per bushel. If you picked 20 bushels of apples, you were paid $7.00 by the field supervisor at the end of the day. Remember, this was back in the 1950s and early 1960s. The supervisor would mark you down for a bushel of apples in his book every time you brought a bushel to the field truck. Everything was pretty clear and objective. If you didn't like the rate or the conditions, you'd simply go to another orchard to work. Fortunately, I quickly found other forms of work.

The piecework approach may be fine for factories and situations where there are well defined and controlled working conditions. However, it breaks down for the construction and service industries. It also tends to make crews too focused on themselves and individual productivity, as compared to promoting a team atmosphere within the whole company. While the piecework approach may work in some limited areas of the Green Industry, it's normally not practical as an incentive approach on a large-scale basis.

MICRO BONUSES

The following are a number of approaches for providing an incentive to your employees that you might find insightful and helpful. Quite often management will provide these **micro** (or mini) **bonuses** as a supplement to a more all-inclusive approach.

Funny Money

One contractor makes copies of $20 bills. If he "catches" a field or office staff person doing something worthy of a reward, he signs and gives the individual one of them. At the end of the month, the employee can exchange the copy for cash.

Safety and Attendance Reward

A number of my clients provide employees with a $25 per month incentive to show up on time and to work safely. If they're on time all month, they get an extra $25 at the end of the month. The same goes for safety. If they're safe all month and have no accidents, they get an extra $25 at the end of the month.

The $.25 Per Man-Hour Bank

A contractor in the Northeast banks $.25 per labor hour for all of his field staff. Staff members who stay to the end of the season receive an extra $.25 for every hour worked throughout the season. Someone working 1,600 hours would receive an extra $400 at season's end.

The Gross Profit Margin Hurdle Method

An arborist in the Northeast provided his field crew with a monthly gross profit incentive. Gross profit was calculated at the end of each month. Ten percent of the dollar amount over $10,000 GPM was paid out as an incentive. Individuals received a percentage of the total bonus pool.

This percentage was calculated by dividing the individual's pay for the month by the total eligible payroll for all staff. For instance, if the total eligible monthly payroll was $20,000 and an individual's pay was $2,000, that person would get 10% of the bonus pool ($2,000 ÷ $20,000 = .1, or 10%). If the pool was $2,500, the individual would be paid $250 at the end of the month.

The Split Hourly Pay Method

An irrigation contractor decided to pay his irrigation service technician at two different pay rates. He paid him $25 per hour for every billable hour he produced. However, non-billable hours were paid at $12 per hour. Billable hours for the technician went from five or six per day to eight or nine per day.

Percentage of Materials Sold

Another irrigation service contractor paid his service technicians a bonus based on the marked-up price charged to customers for materials. Technicians were paid 5% of the retail price for all materials sold. However, replacement of large ticket items such as controllers had to be approved by the office prior to installation.

SUMMARY

Businesses are primarily comprised of two types of issues. One set of issues has to do with line production or service. I like to refer to these as tactical issues. They're readily visible and easily quantifiable. The other set of issues deals with strategic concerns in the form of managerial effectiveness. You can set them apart as tactical versus strategic, production versus management, or efficiency versus effectiveness.

As mentioned previously, Peter Drucker, in his book *The Effective Executive*, summarized it well by stating that managers make sure that things get done right and leaders make sure that the right things get done.

An incentive program that rewards company personnel for simply increasing sales can be disastrous. Operational efficiency needs to be addressed in the incentive formula as well.

An effective bonus or incentive system has to address both ends of the management spectrum. Top management has to have a vested interest in steering the ship in the right direction, while production people must have a vested interest in pulling the oars, without which the ship would be dead in the water.

To effectively address both areas, a twofold incentive method approach is normally best. Incentive programs tend to be dynamic. There's no one-size-fits-all approach, and no method that works best all the time. Owners and managers need to study their corporate culture and determine what will work best for their particular company. Often you just have to experiment to see what works best.

Quite often the terms "bonus" and/or "incentive system" are used interchangeably. This is understandable because the term "bonus" is so ingrained into today's business jargon. However, there's an important difference. The recipient of a bonus usually has little input into the process that creates the bonus. It somehow mysteriously appears. Incentives, on the other hand, are designed to involve the recipient in the very processes and methods of the organization. The incentive is a by-product of the processes and methods in which the individual participates.

Non-monetary incentives are more powerful motivators than mere monetary ones. Great companies primarily focus upon creating a corporate culture based on core values and enduring principles—the by-product of which is money and profits. Companies and individuals whose primary motivation is making money are called mercenaries. You don't build a great company with mercenaries.

ACTION POINT

Evaluate the culture within your company. Ask yourself what would happen if you were out of the picture for 6 or 12 months. Review the incentive and bonus benchmarks discussed in Chapter 46 and Appendix E.

CHAPTER

49 Computer Estimating

TERMS

Garbage In, Garbage Out (GIGO)

Making Mistakes at the Speed of Light

Purpose

To outline the pros, cons, and pitfalls of computer estimating

Introduction

Estimating with a personal computer (PC) holds great potential for you and your company, *if* it's approached wisely and done correctly. PCs can "move" (calculate and reformat) huge quantities of numbers, letters, and symbols in a very short time. PCs can do to data what backhoes do to dirt.

How It Works

A client in New England paid almost $20,000 for an industry-specific estimating program. He spent hundreds of hours building and loading databases into the software so that he could start estimating his work with it. The program was so complex and the support so limited that he never completed one bid with the program. Unfortunately, I have heard this story all too often.

POTENTIAL BENEFITS OF PC ESTIMATING

The following list will help you understand what PC estimating can do for your business. With a moderate expenditure of money, time, and energy PC estimating

- Increases accuracy and consistency.
- Increases your ability to control the bidding process.
- Increases confidence (yours and your client's).
- Increases bid volume per bidding labor hour (up to a 100% increase).
- Decreases general and administrative overhead per field-labor hour (up to 20 to 30%).

- Increases your ability to plan and run jobs.
- Provides data for job costing.
- Can be used as a sales tool.
- Provides a packaged system for teaching other employees how to bid.
- Eliminates errors in arithmetic.
- Thoroughly analyzes job prices.
- Produces unit and lump sum prices simultaneously.
- Familiarizes your employees with computers (and their other applications within your company).
- Clearly defines quality standards.
- Produces tools for quick analysis and review of bids.
- Permits large amounts of data to be manipulated accurately by means of task data libraries.
- Excites and motivates your people by improving their professional skill level.
- Increases bidding flexibility and versatility.

DRAWBACKS OF PC ESTIMATING

Some people become entranced by these little boxes called computers, thinking they're a panacea for their corporate ills. But, you must combine the right hardware and software. Your estimating software must reflect the correct business philosophies, methodologies, systems, and strategies. If not, all you're doing is **making mistakes at the speed of light**.

LESSONS LEARNED

I've computerized the estimating of hundreds of construction and maintenance service contractors throughout North America. Here are some of the lessons I've learned.

1. You must have a stable staff in place, who have the aptitude and time to get your estimating software (or any software) up and running.
2. Implementation should take 30 days, as long as you work with the system two to three hours per day producing bids. In other words, you should feel comfortable producing bids after about a month if you've consistently used the system. I tell my clients their goal is to re-bid six or seven small jobs with the software within the next couple of weeks. I like to have them re-bid completed jobs because this gives them a benchmark, a point of reference. The prices coming from the estimating program should be fairly close to prices for their previous bids. Once they re-bid these six or seven jobs, they're off and running.
3. During the implementation period, *qualified support* and *training* for your staff is crucial.
4. You should plan to have a qualified estimating trainer return to your office every six months in order to review your bidding system (tune it up) and provide additional training.

Making Mistakes at the Speed of Light

TOOLS PROVIDED BY COMPUTER ESTIMATING

Estimating software should provide the following tools and items that will help you run your company, and run those jobs that were bid (see Exhibits 10, 12 and 13):

- Unit and lump-sum prices
- Material lists for ordering material

- Capacity to produce proposals
- G&A overhead costs per field-labor hour (OPH)
- Sales or revenue per field-labor hour (SPH or RPH)
- Net profit as a margin
- Gross profit as a margin
- Net profit per field-labor hour (PPH)
- Unit pricing by the square foot, square yard, cubic yard, irrigation head, etc.
- Equipment-to-labor ratio analysis
- Material-to-labor ratio analysis
- Equipment costs analysis
- Labor tables by type of labor and type of crew
- Prevailing wage tables
- Equipment tables for specific equipment rates
- G&A overhead recovery
- Field-labor hours per job per function
- Detailed analysis of the bid
- Ability to identify general conditions and spread them over other bid items
- Numerous reports
- A direct link with your accounting program for job costing
- Much more

What Backhoes Do To Dirt...

THE BIG MISTAKE

A good estimating system should provide you with a tool that does one more very important thing for you. It should help prevent you from getting jobs you'd be wise not to take. I know numerous contractors who've taken jobs they shouldn't have—jobs they wouldn't have taken if they'd had the right information in front of them when bids were being prepared.

Eliminating big mistakes by eliminating little ones that add up to big ones is one of the advantages of a computerized estimating system. It should help you recap and review a bid quickly once the bid is finalized.

Remember **GIGO: Garbage In, Garbage Out!** Ensure that you have good take-off techniques and bidding procedures in place. And bid in the same sequence that you will build or perform the project in the field.

The proper reviewing of a bid can identify production rate errors, erroneous units, mathematical formula errors, inaccurate costs, wrong labor rates, burdens, average wage, and so on. When reviewing bids, it's not uncommon for me to find mistakes that total 2 to 10% of the total bid price. That's a lot of percentage points to come out of the net profit margin (where else is it to come from?), especially when you're only bidding 10% (+/–) net profit to begin with.

Certainly you want your computer estimating system to get you work by bidding it more accurately and quickly. However, in so doing you also want it to provide a tool that will help you review bids and accurately calculate *all* costs associated with a particular job. This is your break-even point (BEP). You then know with confidence how low you can go on a bid before you start cutting into meat and bone. Identifying this number properly (the BEP) can save you a lot of lost dollars because it will help prevent you from getting into the mud with "low-ballers" and winning bids and getting jobs you don't want. It can help prevent you from making that big mistake.

SUMMARY

Computerized estimating provides significant potential to improve your bottom line. By developing the right philosophies, methodologies, systems, and strategies (PMSS), you can learn to bid with confidence and develop tools to help you better understand your bidding and the bidding of your competitors.

If your estimating software doesn't reflect the correct methods, all you'll be doing is making mistakes at the speed of light.

Computerized estimating offers many ways to improve profits (by providing the tools to recap and review bids easily and accurately) and to prevent big mistakes that can take years from which to recover. But you have to be careful. If your estimating software doesn't reflect the correct methods, all you'll be doing is making mistakes at the speed of light.

ACTION POINTS

Review the following:

1. Exhibits 10, 14 and 15. Take note of how they display many of the numerous estimating methods previously discussed, as well as other key data, ratios, and standards.
2. The estimating section in Chapter 50.
3. Chapter 41 on job costing.

CHAPTER 50

Marketing Strategies

TERM

Due Diligence

Purpose

- To explain why the estimating budget is the primary tool for measuring a company's marketing effectiveness
- To explain why the primary purpose of marketing is to ensure that the sales goals in the estimating budget are achieved
- To explain why the secondary goal of marketing is to negotiate as much work as possible, and to maximize repeat business and referrals
- To explain the marriage between the analytical science of cost estimating and the intuitive art of marketing

Introduction

Marketing for the Green Industry is both unique and dynamic. I say unique because the traditional advertising and marketing approaches to which we've become so accustomed don't work very well. The Madison Avenue and mass media approaches that bombard us from all quarters are relatively ineffective when it comes to selling landscapes, irrigation systems, and the services to maintain them. Residential and commercial clients alike are much more sophisticated and market-aware than they were just 10 or 15 years ago. Unfortunately, it's the contractor who's not.

The Green Industry is dynamic primarily because it's a relatively new one. Twenty-five years is not a long time; 25 years ago this industry was in its infancy. It still is. The Green Industry is an emerging, youthful market that's just beginning to take advantage of capital financing from the public markets and stock exchanges.

The marketing methods and techniques necessary to fuel such an industry are in a state of research and development. The Internet is slowly but profoundly changing the way we all do business. One residential irrigation client told me that while he was preparing a quote for a potential customer in his truck the homeowner checked out the controller he suggested from the manufacturer's Web site. When he returned to the house, my client found out the homeowner had verified everything he'd told him. This made for an easy sale.

MARKETING IS BUILDING RELATIONSHIPS

Doing business within the Green Industry is extremely personal. Relationships are paramount. I don't mean your price isn't important. However, professional relationships, combined with solid performance and savvy pricing, are the key to increasing and maintaining a client base. Today's consumer has a lot of disposable income for at least a couple of reasons.

One is the consumer's primary vocation. High-paying jobs have been plentiful in much of our economy. A second is rarely spoken about. The largest wealth transfer in history is taking place as the baby-boomer generation inherits trillions of dollars from its parents' generation. (I don't know about you, but I didn't get my share.)

Green Industry clients today are also well informed, educated, and extremely busy. Many have growing families, developing careers, demanding schedules, and little tolerance for contractors who are non-performing "flakes." Your preferred client today, both residential and commercial, isn't going to pick up the telephone directory, call AAA Landscape, AAB Landscape, and AAC Landscape; obtain three quotes; and go with the low bid. Today's preferred clients choose Green Industry professionals much as they do a family dentist. They network with their associates and friends to find them. They don't find them from a billboard advertisement on the side of the road.

Marketing is that part of the business where most contractors can realize the greatest return in relation to energy invested. In an off-economy, marketing is also where you need to expend most of your energy. You have to work twice as hard to bring in the same amount of work because there are twice as many other contractors pursuing the available jobs.

How It Works

Not long ago I received a call from a contractor in New England, where the economy has been through some very bleak times in recent years. We talked for almost an hour about marketing and how he could bring more work into his company. He told me he usually faces 10 or more other contractors when bidding on a project.

I know this man, his company, and his people. I've tracked his company (virtually monthly) for several years. Our primary discussion revolved around marketing because I know he has good systems in place (estimating, accounting, budgets, etc.), a lean operation, and crews that can produce the work as well and as quickly as anyone. If he gets the work, he'll get the most out of it. He just needs to get more work. If he'd had serious leaks in his estimating system or his production, I'd have started to plug them.

Marketing is no substitute for a well-run company. Four companies in four different markets—all doing over three million dollars in sales—come to mind. All four are in serious trouble; not because they can't get the business, but because they can't effectively produce it. Don't pour water into a bucket with a hole in the bottom. Fix the bucket!

Marketing is the combination of the systems and effort needed to bring enough work into the business. Marketing encompasses salespeople, estimating, contract administration, and the like. In a quarter-of-a-million dollar company, it may be just a desk and one person—the owner. Larger companies have more people and more systems.

However, once you establish a budget and determine the amount of sales you need to make the budget work, it's all the same—you go to work to bring in the sales. It's rather simple, but there are some tools that can focus your energies and maximize the results you achieve for your efforts. These tools not only provide focus, but also can deliver continuous feedback on your progress toward your goals. They show where you need to put more effort to get maximum results.

Marketing is actually a cause-and-effect series of events leading to signed contracts. Some would say it's a numbers game, which is true to a certain extent. However, it sometimes needs to be more sophisticated. Let me illustrate with an example of a contractor from the Midwest.

How It Works

Robert did mostly residential landscape construction and carpentry. He had an office manager/contract administrator who was very good at tracking information by computer. The owner did the selling, and the administrator did the estimating. Sales were at $750,000 the previous season. The budget for sales for the upcoming year was $1 million. We computerized the estimating system and the contract administrator took over.

I visited their office in February, a month or two before the season started. We all wanted to know if they were going to meet their sales goal. We didn't have adequate information, but indications looked positive. We reviewed budget figures, production rates and a few other items. I left, and everyone pressed on.

Four months later, I returned, and the contract administrator had more ammunition for us. He'd spent 600 hours estimating $1.8 million of work. Of the $1.8 million bid, $600,000 in contracts was signed. In other words, he could bid $3,000/hour on the computer, and 33 percent of the $3,000 ($1,000) was sales. At 15 percent net profit, each hour he spent on the computer produced $150 in net profit to the company.

Before my visit, there was some conflict as to where the contract administrator should spend his time. Should he be estimating all the time, or catching up on other paperwork? Once we sifted through this data, the answer jumped up and smacked us all in the face: all bids *had* to go through the computer. Each hour of computer time produced $1,000 in sales and $150 in net profit. Conclusion: Chain this boy to the computer for another 400 hours. This should produce the $1 million in sales needed to make the budget work.

During economic slowdowns the first inclination for many contractors is to adjust their pricing down. Rather, you should ratchet your marketing up.

Marketing becomes even more critical in times of economic slowdowns or recessions. The primary purpose of marketing, at any time but especially during a recession, is to ensure that the sales goals outlined in the estimating budget are met. If not, adjustments need to be made to the expense portion of the budget, primarily in the area of G&A overhead.

The estimating budget and budget-to-actual performance are the primary tools used to measure marketing effectiveness. Individual jobs can be performed and installed at or above their budgeted gross profit margins. However, if you don't have enough jobs to meet your annual budget, it's all for naught because G&A overhead and other fixed costs will eat you alive. During economic slowdowns the first inclination for many contractors is to adjust their pricing down. Rather, you should ratchet your marketing up.

Individual contractors' marketing aggression far outpaced the economic recession. The result was an increase in sales during extremely trying times.

During the recessions of the early 1980s, 1990s, and the year 2000, many contractors experienced a slowdown in sales, while others experienced an increase. This increase in sales was especially true for young, aggressive contractors just entering the market. Individual contractors' marketing aggression far outpaced the economic recession. The result was an increase in sales during extremely trying times.

To have an effective, lasting business, the hard analytical science of cost estimating has to be married to the intuitive art of marketing. This juncture is where the logic of the left side is joined to the creative right side of the brain. You need both to run an effective contracting business. I've seen contractors who could sell snow

To have an effective, lasting business, the hard analytical science of cost estimating has to be married to the intuitive art of marketing.

to Eskimos but had no clue as to their costs and margins. Their businesses grow but their costs are out of control.

I know other contractors who haven't underbid a job in years, yet they can't grow their businesses. It's essential that a contractor understand both cost estimating and marketing as they relate to the business.

When estimating, marketing, and field operations are successfully combined, the secondary objective of marketing is met; that is, to negotiate as much work as possible and to maximize repeat business and referrals for the company.

MARKETING STRATEGY AND SYSTEMS

Your marketing strategy and systems can be analyzed and broken down into the four traditional marketing categories: (1) the product or service you provide; (2) the place—or facilities and location—of your business; (3) the promotion of your products/services; and (4) the price, which we'll cover in the estimating portion of this chapter. To these four I'm going to add a fifth: the process.

Product

In order to maximize revenues and profits, start asking questions and researching your various options concerning your product or service line.

1. **Expand the existing volume/diversify the existing base.**
   Can you increase your sales by simply becoming more aggressive, by just bidding more of your current type of work? We tend to get lazy when times are good. Often, if we just get off the dime and pursue more work, the rewards are well worth the effort.

   A subcontractor we know did all the landscape and irrigation work for a large homebuilder in Southern California. He did little work for other developers and was lulled into a false sense of security. We tried to get him to diversify his base but he thought it was unnecessary. All went well until the bottom fell out of the new-home market. He was never able to adjust his marketing plan and went out of business a year later.

   Be aggressive. Smash old habits. Don't be lulled into a false sense of security.
2. **Decrease volume and concentrate on quality.**
   Big is not always better, or more profitable. Growth in sales without growth in control spells disaster. If you sense you're out of control because of a lot of "slop" in the operation, cut general and administrative (G&A) overhead, lay off some people, and get small again. Once you regain control and are running a tight operation, then consider pursuing increased sales. Too often contractors burn out during "good" times and lose their grip on the business. Getting small can often significantly improve quality control throughout the company, improve the bottom line, provide a needed rest, and make the business fun again.
3. **Start a new division.**
   The name of the game at all times—once you have the proper control and systems in place—is getting the right amount of profitable sales volume. To get the sales you need to develop the attitude of doing whatever it takes to get the job done. A good question to ask yourself is whether you can start a new division. Start small, do your homework, and expand your existing line of products or services, if possible.

Landscape (or even janitorial) maintenance can be a natural division to add to a construction operation. Be warned, however, that a maintenance operation has some significant differences from a construction division. The equipment, organizational structure, G&A overhead recovery, and the personalities of the crews are different, to name but a few.

Irrigation repair and service can be a good way to add revenue. One irrigation construction and maintenance client, located in an area experiencing a drought and subsequent water restrictions, decided to market water management. He gained a municipal client by demonstrating how by spending $25,000 the client could cut his water bill by $50,000 to $75,000.

I know landscape and irrigation contractors who plow snow, chop wood, sweep and paint parking lots, seal coat driveways, trim trees, etc. Many in seasonal parts of North America offer full-service maintenance to property managers. These services include the above, plus interiorscaping, window cleaning, and janitorial services. Others expand into light site-prep and grading, nursery operations, and pools, decks and patios.

It's amazing how we limit our options because of laziness and old habits. I know two contractors who are experiencing a serious decrease in revenues in the commercial landscape and irrigation market. They refuse to consider entering a fairly healthy public works market because the paperwork is "too hard." Some of us need to get off our "buts" (*but* it's too hard ... *but* I don't know how ... *but* this, *but* that), forget the excuses, and charge ahead.

Do some R&D (Research and Development) on new types of operations. Talk to those who have experience in the new business; talk to them *before* you jump in with both feet.

4. **Eliminate unprofitable divisions.**
While getting small is one way to improve the bottom line, identifying and eliminating unprofitable product lines and services is another. To do so usually requires having your accounting system set up to provide separate profit and loss statements for your respective divisions. Otherwise, it's very difficult to identify where you're bleeding red ink.

A client comes to mind who thought his maintenance division was losing money. He was seriously considering eliminating it. Upon further analysis, we concluded it was breaking even and—with a little restructuring and some more sales—on the verge of being a moneymaker.

Be prepared to cut unprofitable divisions, but *be sure* you've correctly analyzed the problem before you cut.

5. **Increase/decrease the size of the largest/smallest job you'll take.**
A $1 million-plus residential landscape design-build contractor completed close to five hundred jobs one year. The majority of them were under $1,000 in size, and many were under $500. He was beating himself to death. Can you imagine one man dealing with 500 different residential owners in a year's time? So, he all but eliminated the jobs under $1,000 and concentrated on doing fewer but larger ones. His bottom line improved, and his life became less stressful.

Not long ago a large commercial landscape and irrigation contractor, primarily in the new-home market, refused to pursue jobs much under $250,000. At the time, he could afford that luxury. Today he can't, and that figure has come down considerably.

Both of the above contractors improved their bottom line by shifting the size of the jobs they pursued, in order to better suit their companies and/or markets.

6. **Improve product/service quality.**
   Clients want products and services to be consistently delivered per the agreed upon standards, schedule, and price. This is a theme that rings true in virtually every market. Consistency and dependability breed repeat customers and referrals. This is what builds companies.

   A contractor and president of a national trade association emphasized a great principle to me. He said that if you're not building your business on repeat business and referrals, you're building it wrong. I wholeheartedly agree.

   He also said he's seldom the low bidder for the commercial projects he bids and wins. Satisfied clients will pay a little more and spread the good word. Clearly identified and consistently met quality standards make for satisfied clients. If you have to be low bidder to get a job, you probably have a quality control problem. Be smart. Clearly identify to your customer the quality standard they can expect, and then be absolutely certain you and your people meet (or exceed) that standard every time. "Under-promise and over-deliver" should be your motto.

Place (Location/Facilities)

This category deals with the geographical location of your business and the condition of the facilities.

1. **Expand the geographical radius (arena of operations) of your business.**
   During normal economic times, contractors usually operate within a 50 to 60 mile radius of their office (about one hour in travel time in any one direction); however, when economic factors dictate, this radius should be increased as necessary. I have clients in New England who used to operate within an hour's drive time from their yard. This radius has subsequently doubled and is up to 120 miles. Today these companies routinely work within this increased "arena of operations." Their goal is to know as much as possible about this expanded arena, to focus on it, and to pursue as much work as possible within it.
2. **Pursue long-distance jobs.**
   Another option worth considering for commercial companies is to travel beyond their arena of operations in the pursuit of specific jobs and/or markets. Contractors often travel up to a thousand miles from home to pursue specific jobs. Many times they do work for general contractors or developers for whom they've worked in the past—contractors and developers who like their work and who "piggyback" them into long-distance markets.

   Another option is to scan the various construction reports and look for and bid jobs that are similar to ones you've done in the past, ones with which you and your crews feel comfortable. Also, keep your eyes open for "hot" markets where the demand for your type of work is still strong.

   For example, at one time in the early 1990s, the Southern California new homebuilding market was off 27%. The *Los Angeles Times* reported that 80% of the drop was accounted for by only five counties in Southern California. The article said other parts of the state were still strong, and that some parts were very strong.

   I know of large and small construction and services companies that have adjusted and gone to where the action is. The majority, however, just discuss it as a possibility—only a few ever actually pursue it.

   Remember, the best and safest way to enter a long-distance market is to piggyback with an existing client into that market. Otherwise, do your homework. Research potential general contractors and developers. If possible, talk to subcontractors already on jobs and ask questions about receiving payments, obtaining payment for extras, processing paperwork and other special considerations.

Talk to bankers and/or lenders, if possible, to confirm that funding is available for the project. Consider joint venturing a long-distance job with another contractor who's already established in the targeted market, one who needs your expertise or is too small to do the job alone. This company can act somewhat as a "host," and often can provide insight into the market that would otherwise take you years to learn.

Long-distance jobs can be a source of new work for your company, but remember to do your homework. This can reduce your risks substantially.

3. **Start a satellite division.**
Once you do some long-distance jobs in a target market and feel established in it, you should consider forming a satellite division. Some contractors have field superintendents who leave the home office and operate independently five hundred to a thousand miles away. Usually all that's needed is a small office, a fax machine, and a phone line. Plans can be express-mailed overnight to the home office to be bid. Augmenting the field office with a personal computer and a modem can allow you to transfer bids and vital information over the phone line.

   Field equipment, as needed, is usually trucked (often overnight) from the home office location to the job sites. Daily field reports, job-costing, and payroll can be faxed, sent via the Internet, or express mailed to and from the satellite operation. The on-site field superintendent often receives a supplemental monthly living allowance. The superintendent also normally hires the remainder of the field crew from the local community.

4. **Consider joint ventures.**
The joint venture can provide needed sales and jobs in an otherwise tight market. Many people think joint ventures are just for the "big boys." That's not so. A number of our smaller clients have done them. Usually, two contractors who know each other and each other's capabilities rather well combine forces to tackle jobs they wouldn't feel comfortable tackling alone. By combining forces they not only reduce risk, but also often bring a competitive edge to the bid table.

   A couple of very important points, however, should be kept in mind. First, the joint venture has legal and insurance implications you need to fully understand within the context of the state in which you're doing business. Second, spell everything out—in writing—for the parties involved. Leave nothing to chance and poor memory. It's usually best that separate companies bid and perform separate portions of the total job. Combine and submit the separate bids as one bid to the general contractor, but spell out all the details in writing.

   A joint venture contract is available from the American Institute of Architects. Call or write the AIA to obtain a copy of its "Joint Venture Agreement" form C801. You can also visit its Web site. The address is:

   The American Institute of Architects Bookstore
   1735 New York Avenue N.W.
   Washington, DC 20006
   800-242-3837, option #4 or 202-626-7475
   E-mail: www.bookstore@aia.org
   Web site: www.aia.org

Your surety and/or insurance company should also be able to provide you with joint venture and partnership agreements.

5. **Relocate or reorganize the home office to better serve your market.** The importance of the location of your business and yard (and its layout) is often overlooked. A high-end residential landscape contractor in California, who works primarily in the Beverly Hills and Hollywood areas, recently moved his office and yard closer to his market. His competitors didn't understand why he was so far ahead of them and so strong in the marketplace.

   Part of it, of course, was due to this contractor's drive, pursuit of excellence, creative talent, and experience level. However, much of it was due to this strategic relocating of the yard and office to better serve the client base. The previous location was good, but the new one was much better. Everything was more convenient for the clients who came to his office, for the field superintendents who were in and out of the office during the day, and for the field crews.

   This contractor, his field superintendents, and his crews spent upward to an hour less per day per man mobilizing to and from job sites. This translates into increased productivity and higher sales per field-labor hour. Office and yard locations are extremely important to your operation.

   There are three more items you should consider concerning facilities.

   A. If you work in your home, plan to move out and get an office as soon as possible. Once you do, virtually everything in your operation becomes more objective and businesslike. I've encouraged and seen dozens of contractors make this move, and I always ask them after the move how they (and their spouse, if they have one) feel about it. No one yet has moved back home.

      Unless you have a completely separate office in your home and an iron will, working there gives you the worst of both worlds: you can never get away from home and concentrate on the business, and you can never really relax and enjoy your home. I know you won't believe me until two months after you move, but trust me. In 95% of the cases your own and your company's productivity will increase dramatically, your spouse (if you have one) will be much happier, and your home life will improve.

   B. Nepotism is almost always negative and partnerships rarely work. Although these two are not directly a facility issue, we'll cover them here. I've yet to see a "family" business, where one or more relatives are employed, that excites me. Nepotism—even husband and wife teams (as American as apple pie as they may sound)—will eventually impose serious limitations on a business and send negative signals throughout the organization.

      As for partnerships, nine out of ten I work with would operate better without shared ownership. I'm not saying they *can't* work, but that they *rarely* work. I realize family businesses and partnerships are here to stay but, wherever there's a multiplicity of relatives and/or owners, there's an increased number of problems. If you can avoid nepotism and/or partnerships, do so. Enough said!

   C. Communication is vital for your organization. Two-way radios and cell phones can, in many cases, dramatically decrease response time to a client's needs, increase productivity by cutting communication lag time, and increase teamwork and cooperation throughout the organization. Pagers and/or beepers can provide similar results. Construction and services contracting thrives on effective communication and teamwork. All new technology may not be applicable or cost-effective for you, but do your homework and explore some of these possibilities.

6. **Merge with or buy a company.**
Another option worth considering is the possibility of merging with or buying another company. Mergers and acquisitions are becoming increasingly popular. They can help you attain desired advantages (new locations, increased capabilities, lower G&A overhead due to economies of scale, market advantages, etc.) virtually overnight. Mergers can also create a fresh, new enthusiasm and sense of mission for the companies involved—if they're handled properly and if all concerned have well-thought-out goals and incentives to shoot for. Without these goals and incentives, though, there'll still be plenty of shooting. Unfortunately, the targets of choice are usually other employees.

   You should develop a **due diligence** list with your attorney and accountant and follow it! Look for latent and tail liabilities and be sure to discuss these issues thoroughly with qualified legal and financial counsel.

   A. Guidelines to follow when considering a merger:

      (1) *Identify the pros and cons before* any *discussions with anybody.* Put down on paper the potential benefits (with a brief "best case" scenario) and the possible liabilities (and a brief "worst case" scenario). Simply ask yourself, "What's the best/worst thing that could result from this?" Then, in the strictest confidence, "feel out" your lawyer, CPA, and—if possible—one or two other close advisors (especially your spouse, if applicable). Take notes and listen intently. If you talk to two or three of these people, you may not get the best analytical advice, but you will get some good gut-level input, which may prove more valuable than the analytical feedback.

      (2) *Feel out possible mergers.* Once you know what your goals are, then and only then, approach—in confidence—a potential partner. If that individual (or group) is open to the possibility of a merger, set up a meeting (preferably within 48 to 72 hours) to discuss the matter more fully. Again, keep all discussions about the possible merger confidential.

      (3) *Set a target date.* If all parties are receptive at this meeting to a merger, set up a target date for the final decision. This date should be no longer than 30 to 60 days from the first meeting, and provides an "engagement" period of sorts prior to the "wedding." Before the wedding anyone can bow out of the process for any reason.

      (4) *Set an agenda (with due dates) of items to complete before the target date.* Establish and verify inventory and equipment lists. Review financial statements and signed contracts. Verify work-in-progress and percentage of completion. Meet with lawyers and CPAs. The agenda, due dates, and target dates provide goals and deadlines that will help you evaluate your prospective partner(s) ability to perform. You may decide you simply can't work with your prospective partner, or you may adjust your expectations and/or your approach. Discuss with your attorney the possible need to have all parties involved sign confidentiality statements prior to in-depth sharing of corporate information.

      (5) *Decide.* Once you've done your homework and talked to adequate legal and personal counsel, make a decision. This decision should be

made (at a minimum) two to three days prior to the target date. Up to now, any party can bow out gracefully for any reason. If both parties are agreeable to merge at the target date, have all legal documents drawn up and ready to be signed within 48 to 72 hours, or as soon as possible. Drawing up these documents prior to the target date may incur unnecessary legal expense. On the target date, you may consider having the prospective parties involved place an earnest deposit or fee (which is non-refundable) into an escrow account. If a party bows out prior to signing the legal documents for the merger, the deposit is forfeited.

(6) *Implement the merger quickly and unequivocally.* I recommend that you tell no one, except those absolutely necessary, about the possible merger until it's a "done deal." This can prevent a lot of unnecessary questions, anxiety, and lost momentum from employees becoming distracted from their jobs. However, once the merger is completed and legal, implement it quickly and forcefully within all companies concerned. The key is to maintain and gain as much momentum as possible by using clearly defined goals for everyone. Explain to your staff: (a) why the merger was made, (b) what anticipated changes will take place, and (c) that everyone needs to pitch in and accomplish the transition with a positive attitude—especially during the initial four to six months.

(7) *Plan personnel and paperwork changes* before *implementation, after the decision to merge,* and *before the announcement is made to all your staff.* Top management should decide what, if any, personnel changes will take place. Job descriptions should be written for all partners involved in order to identify each one's duties and responsibilities. Paperwork changes (forms, reports, etc.) should be addressed and clearly spelled out. This will eliminate confusion and speed up the merger process. It will help employees focus on getting the job done instead of on the aggravation of change.

(8) *Anticipate conflict.* It's inevitable, especially after the honeymoon period between new partners. Identify (in writing) who's boss, who makes the final decision about what, and what decisions are to be delegated. Salaries, bonuses, and other remuneration should be clearly spelled out (in writing) as well. The more clearly that problems are anticipated and spelled out, the better the chances of a successful merger. Consider taking and typing up the minutes of your meetings prior to the merger. This can eliminate misunderstandings due to lapses in memory.

(9) *Maintain accountability.* Unless you're going to form a whole new entity from the ground up or simply absorb one company into another, it's recommended that you maintain accountability in the new organization by forming separate divisions out of the merging companies. You can do this for accounting purposes and for field crews.

The idea is to keep partners and your staff focused on and accountable to goals by maintaining the individual identities of the companies before the merger. This will help to eliminate finger pointing and a passing-the-buck atmosphere. Accurate, timely job-costing is probably the best way to keep field crews focused on the task at hand, instead of "jaw-hacking" about corporate politics. Four to six months down the road, when all the dust has cleared and everyone has settled into the new organization, would be a good time to mix crews and personnel. The idea is to maintain productivity and focus during the transition period, which may (and often does) last 12 to 18 months. Clear goals and accountability tend to foster productivity and eliminate dissension. Otherwise, you can lose much needed momentum and dollars due to decreased productivity.

B. Buying another company. The considerations concerning this option are very similar to those of a merger, and you should seek legal advice early in the process. In addition, you should stress the following:

(1) *Act quickly.* Once all partners decide they're seriously interested in buying or selling a company, don't get bogged down in negotiations. Do your homework, decide upon the terms, do all the necessary paperwork, and finish the deal. The longer the negotiations drag out, the more distracting the process becomes. Momentum is often lost as tempers and subjectivity take over, and the less likely your chances for a successful purchase or sale.

(2) *Evaluate the business to be bought.* There are basically three elements involved in purchasing a business: (a) assets, which include (but are not limited to) inventory, equipment, real property, accounts receivable, and signed contracts; (b) liabilities, which include (but are not limited to) accounts payable, warranty work/guarantees, and debts; (c) "blue sky" or goodwill.

Subtracting total liabilities from total assets is rather easy, but blue sky or goodwill is a somewhat nebulous term, which basically describes what you're willing to pay over and above the figure you get when subtracting total liabilities from total assets.

This isn't an easy figure to calculate. Often it depends on how badly one party wants out, or how much the other party wants in. Blue sky is what you're willing to pay for future cash flow into the business. It's somewhat based on the type of business, past performance and profitability, the economic outlook, systems and trained personnel in place, and other factors.

The fundamental reason that some franchise fees (which is essentially blue sky) are so expensive is that you're buying proven, almost guaranteed, cash flow in the future. Their "system" has proven itself. Generally, the more proven the system, the more expensive the blue sky. Consult with your lawyer, CPA, and/or possibly with a construction and services contracting company evaluator to arrive at a reasonable price for the business to be purchased.

(3) *Earnest money deposit.* If I were selling a business, once a party expressed serious interest I'd get some earnest money from the potential buyer. The money would go into an escrow account or trust fund until the deal was completed. If the buyer backs out of the deal for non-specified reasons, the money goes to the seller. Making someone pull out a checkbook and write a check cuts through all the smoke and determines right away who's serious and who isn't. Conversely, if I were the buyer, I wouldn't volunteer writing such a check.

(4) *Maintain accountability after the deal.* Accountability and momentum are crucial. Follow the advice given in the previous section on mergers.

A merger or acquisition can provide a quick foothold in a new market or help you expand quickly into one in which you're already located. But remember: do your homework, seek out appropriate legal and personal counsel, and maintain momentum (through effective accountability) to clearly spelled-out goals and objectives.

7. **Co-locate with another company.**
Another possibility that can improve your "place" of operations is to co-locate with a company (which may or may not be of a similar trade to yours). It's not uncommon for three or four *different types* of construction and services companies to lease or buy the same building and even share G&A overhead personnel and equipment. This can cut G&A overhead cost per field-labor hour and provide referrals from the other businesses. You may also benefit from the invaluable feedback and support that can come from other construction and services company owners.

Price

For a detailed discussion of pricing, see the section on estimating in this chapter.

Promotion

These are the means and methodologies you use to become known and recognized in your arena of operations. It may be direct or passive (or both) in nature. The goal is to have prospective clients think about you whenever they desire to have work performed for them in your trade/specialty.

When you reevaluate your promotional efforts (which should happen every three or four months), you should review the following:

1. **Advertising.**
   A. Company Brochure. This can be an effective tool for reaching the residential market. Look at it as the company business card. It can set you apart from your competition and build confidence and trust in prospective clients. A nicely done brochure with color pictures may cost you $6,000 to $12,000 (for approximately a three-year supply), but the results can be well worth it. Remember though: you must show discrimination in its use, and the rest of your presentation and company performance must back up the image portrayed on the brochure.
   B. Company Résumé. Similar to a résumé for an individual seeking a job, a company résumé is a typed, one- to three-page document listing your company's capabilities, references, and perhaps corporate philosophy. It's used primarily when pursuing commercial work. Stored in your computer, it can be very effective when printed on company letterhead and tailored to a specific client.
   C. Door Knockers. A very effective tool, doorknockers are low in cost to produce and distribute; and they allow you to target a specific market.
   D. Yellow Pages. This is perhaps the costliest and most commonly used advertising medium for construction and services companies, and tends not to get the results the cost would lead you to expect. The salesperson usually tries to sell you on the proposition that you need to: (1) stand out—have a large, more costly ad; (2) be included in other directories for multiple geographical locations; (3) be seen under numerous construction and services and non-contracting subheadings; and (4) be in the forefront of the alphabet within the various sections. This sounds great, but it's not uncommon to see 10 to 20 pages of listings under a particular trade. As the number of companies advertising in the yellow pages grows, this flawed logic tells you that you have to invest in larger and larger ads in more and more directories.

Consider these three observations. One, the salesperson and the company producing the various yellow-page directories have a vested interest in promoting this logic. Two, if you're properly building your company on referrals and repeat business, you don't need a large, expensive ad to reach your prospective clients. Three, historically, when you analyze their impact, Yellow-Page ads just don't produce the desired results—primarily because of the unique nature of the construction and service contracting business.

Dozens of construction and service company owners I know have come to a similar conclusion. They (and I) recommend that you have your company's name—and perhaps a small display ad (primarily if you're in the residential market)—in the directory. Beyond that, unless you can specifically justify it, you're probably wasting your money. One client, after doing a little analysis, cut his Yellow-Page ad bill by $24,000 one year. Because of more effective marketing in other directions, he saw his business grow beyond his previous projections, which were based on using the more expensive ads.

E. Miscellaneous Advertising. Newspaper ads can be effective for residential contractors, as can radio (especially National Public Radio) and even television spots. However, log the leads and the results of those leads, and analyze the results. This simple procedure can open your eyes and help you invest your advertising dollars where they'll get you the best results.

One final note: Combined advertising that exceeds one percent of your gross annual sales is usually excessive and unnecessary.

2. **Bid/plan rooms and construction service bureaus.**
Commercial leads can be obtained by subscribing to various published and computer-generated construction reports (e.g., *Dodge Reports*, green sheets, construction daily reports, etc.). Bid/plan rooms are specifically set up to bring developers, general contractors, and subcontractors together. Fees are usually charged for these services, but they can be a good source of commercial jobs to bid in your area. Look in the various Yellow Pages under "Construction Reports" or "Contractor Plan Rooms."

3. **Computer database clearing houses and Internet plan services.**
Many of the service bureaus referred to above offer their services via computer data links and the Internet. Whole sets of plans for both private and public work can be downloaded in minutes. I know of one company that's in the process of establishing a network containing all the various commercial jobs for all trades in a geographical area. Subscribers pay an access fee to obtain information tailored to their trade, location, and type of job desired. These clearing houses can be found in your local Yellow Pages under headings similar to those mentioned in the previous section.

4. **Bid lists.**
General contractors, developers, government offices (city, county, state, federal, Department of Defense, Department of Transportation, etc.) are usually very receptive to placing your company on their bid lists. Whenever a job comes up to bid, they'll usually notify you. Identify the specific individual within that agency's office who's in charge of bid list notifications. Send that individual a copy of your company's résumé with a cover letter on letterhead. Place this agency, the name of the person in charge, and the telephone number on your Bid Board, which was discussed in Chapter 40, and contact them on a regular basis concerning work to bid.

5. **Architectural/engineering firms.**
   This is an often overlooked source of repeat commercial and residential work. You should identify 8 to 10 architectural/engineering firms whose work you want to pursue. It's not uncommon for clients to make it a marketing goal to do the majority of a specified firm's work. Architects/engineers who are pleased with your work, your ability to keep your schedules, and the professional caliber of your company can provide many jobs to bid, as well as leads. They can also be ready references to developers and general contractors. Professional, dependable contractors who communicate well and who strive to prevent problems while looking out for an architect/engineer (as well as an owner, general contractor, developer, etc.), will make lasting friends. These friends will often market your company for you by providing well-qualified referrals.
6. **Owners and developers/general contractors.**
   The same holds true for this category as for architects/engineers. Professionals look for other professionals whose goal it is to simplify their lives while helping them achieve their goals. Dependability, good planning, effective and timely communication, consistency, preventing problems—all these add up to satisfied clients who provide repeat business and referrals. These people usually don't want to be "wined and dined" (forget the ones who do). They want performance. Perform, and you'll get these people on your side. They'll promote your company by word of mouth.
7. **Repeat business.**
   The prime purpose of promotion is to obtain repeat business with commercial clients and referrals from residential clients. The only way to get these is to price your work reasonably, communicate with your clients, and consistently meet quality standards and schedules. These are themes you can never stop pushing throughout your company. As soon as you let up, you're open to disaster.

How It Works

A once-thriving contractor had done millions of dollars worth of work over a 12-year period for a large, quality homebuilder in his area. The business grew beyond his ability to manage and control it. Relatives were brought in, and things worsened as favoritism was noticed by other employees. A son was put in charge of a crew, but he disliked the work and performed poorly. Dad wouldn't make changes. Junior didn't keep promises made to the builder, and much of his work had to be redone.

The builder repeatedly told the father about the problem, but Dad refused to correct it. Calls from the developer weren't returned, and Dad didn't listen to the rather clear signals given by the developer's purchasing agent. Because the father refused to deal with his son, quality control suffered tremendously, and the company lost a $250,000 contract that was all but signed. For over 10 years that company had done all the concrete, landscape, masonry, and irrigation work for the homebuilder, and was the envy of other contractors in the area. Unfortunately, he lost that client, and eventually his business because he didn't pay attention to quality control and effective communication.

8. **Residential referrals.**
   What holds true for repeat business with commercial work holds true for residential work. The only difference is that with residential clients you get referrals more often than repeat business. If you perform well, customers will gladly provide you with referrals and word-of-mouth promotion. It's not uncommon to see a swimming pool, masonry, room-addition, or landscape

and irrigation contractor do four or five jobs on a block due to using referrals and company signs on projects, and by producing an excellent product for the customer. Happy, satisfied clients mean money in the bank. Remember what the president of the contracting association said, "If you're not building your business on referrals and repeat business, you're building it wrong." He's right!

But you have to *ask* for the referrals and letters of appreciation and/or introduction. Put referrals on a mailing list and send them a flyer every six months.

9. **Surveys.**
   One easy way to promote your company (while obtaining invaluable feedback from clients) is to survey them after the job is done. They may never return the survey form, but you've at least provided the opportunity—and their impression of you will be greatly enhanced because you'll have shown you're concerned about their input.

10. **Video use.**
    One picture is worth a thousand words, and one video is comprised (literally) of thousands of pictures. The impact can be tremendous as a communication tool for prospective residential clients. Photos taken before, during, and after various jobs get the attention of prospective clients, while involving them in the process. You can (and should) include a small segment with the satisfied customer at the end of the video—be sure to include yourself in the shot, as well.

11. **Timely communication.**
    It's unfathomable how sloppily we sometimes handle our prospective clients. I heard the following joke on television recently: "Did you hear about the man who was going to build himself a home and be his own general contractor? First thing he did was not show up for a week." It's true. Contractors have a bad reputation for missing appointments, not returning phone calls, and generally not following through and keeping the concerned parties informed.

    Implement a callback log that indicates the date, time, and nature of each complaint. Then enter when (and how) the problems were resolved. Monitor it constantly. Residential contractors should log and number all contacts and leads for new business. Log (at a minimum) who is given the lead, when the design and/or bid were presented, and the results obtained. Use a separate column for each item.

    Have your receptionist fill out qualifying information fact sheets about prospective clients, including how they found out about your company (Yellow Pages, referral, saw office, etc.). Track these items in a computer database.

    The above items will help you monitor and control what's happening in your company and will promote an image of professionalism as you build a reputation for truly effective communication.

12. **Awards and articles.**
    An excellent way to promote your business (and to build confidence and trust with a client) is to feature awards your company has won and magazine/newspaper articles written about your company. One client of ours used a photograph, on the front of his company brochure, of an award-winning home that had been featured in an architectural magazine. His company had done the landscaping for the home, and he built additional credibility for his business by showing prospective clients copies of the magazine. Others have used similar means to convey to prospective clients that they and their company are worthy of their clients' trust.

There are some contractors who belittle this approach. Certainly it can be over-used; however, you need to see things through the eyes of your clients and prospects. You have to build credibility and warrant their business. Awards and newspaper articles can be effective tools for accomplishing this.

Process (The Power of the Process)

You and I are in a problem-solving business. Our clients pay us (too often too little) to solve their problems, simplify their lives, and help them achieve their goals. To accomplish these objectives for our clients, we build a business entity that has a "culture." This entity is comprised of people, computers, systems, equipment, and all the other components that go into making our businesses. Too often, we get so involved in the process of "doing" business that we fail to step back and work on the processes that make the business what it is in the first place.

First-rate businesses have processes that are both effective and efficient. They create an atmosphere or aura of its own. This ambiance, so to speak, can create a distinct marketing advantage for the company that understands its market and customer base.

How It Works

Two clients come to mind whose offices are but a few miles apart. Both specialize in residential landscape construction. Both have excellent reputations. The average job for one company is in the $10,000 range. The other won't look at a job unless it's at least $80,000. I refer to the first company as a "bread and butter" landscape company. I refer to the second as "truly snooty landscaping." The first owner caters to a middle-class market. He'd love to get more of the larger, prestigious jobs, but they seem to elude him. The other owner specifically designed his company and its "culture" to attract and cater to the ultra high-end client.

Don't get me wrong here. I'm not saying one's better or worse than the other. They're simply different. Both companies are great companies. However, the owner of the second company not only designs excellent landscapes, he designed a great company with his target client in mind. The first did not. The second company now has a reputation, built over many years with excellent service and production, that precedes it. If you want an ultra high-end landscape experience, you call the latter company. Otherwise, the former will do.

A client in New England is in the process of creating a new residential design-build installation division in an area with an emerging upper-middle-class market comprised mainly of white-collar professionals. This company has an excellent reputation for commercial and public landscape installation work. The owner is as hard charging as anyone in the business. He loves the challenge of the commercial and public installation market. However, I think it fair to say he dislikes landscape maintenance and residential installation work. Maintenance jobs bore him, and homeowners drive him nuts.

Fortunately, this owner has allowed one of his key managers to step into and develop this division. The manager, a designer himself, has two full-time designers who design and sell jobs. The manager primarily estimates and directs the field operation, while the designers interact with clients. The culture created by the manager and designers runs totally counter to the historic culture of the company. This culture is very creative and intuitive, yet very professional. One of its primary objectives is to provide this upscale client base with an exceptional "studio" type of experience offered by no one else in its market.

This company has had to recreate itself to pursue this new facet of its market. It has done so in similar fashion as did Toyota when it introduced its Lexus line of automobiles several years ago. Both have had to evolve from their past culture and client base and create totally new processes in order to adapt to and meet the expectations of a new market opportunity. I don't buy into the "image is everything" approach. However, presentation backed by solid performance is much more than just image.

The old culture and processes created an atmosphere that fits well with the commercial and public markets. However, this straightforward yet effective approach simply wouldn't work in an upscale market where presentation is so important. This "bulldog," fast-food approach wouldn't fly with customers seeking an elegant restaurant experience. When the rule, "Presentation is everything" prevails, eating is secondary to the desire for an experience; whereas eating is the primary concern for the fast-food customer.

You have to adapt your processes to meet client expectations. To do so, you have to be aware of process management. If you're in the commercial market, shape your processes to meet the expectations of the customer. If you're in a blue collar, "Joe Six-Pack" market, design and deliver your products and services accordingly. However, if you're pursuing an upscale market, you may have to recreate yourself and rethink your processes and the manner in which you deliver them to your clients.

If it's meat and potatoes that the customers want, give them meat and potatoes and a "meat and potatoes" approach. If it's presentation they want, don't offer them a New England dinner of boiled cabbage and corned beef. Give them what they want, wrapped up in the ambiance of presentation. The three criteria of appealing to the upscale market are: "Presentation, Presentation, Presentation."

Strive to become the "Price Leader" in your market. Many of my clients are known for producing consistently good prices. I once worked in a company where everyone knew our prices were accurate and consistent. We'd get calls from companies who wanted us to bid their work. After bidding a number of jobs with them and getting no work, we finally figured out that these companies never intended to give us any work. They simply wanted to use us to double-check their landscapers and keep them honest.

Negotiate as much work as you possibly can. Negotiated work is your most profitable work, and it is the least risky. The net profit margin on negotiated work is normally 5 to 10% higher than competitive bid work. It's the least risky because it's repeat work. You and your client know each other. You've worked together in the past. Because it's more predictable, it contains less risk.

Don't seek to be low bidder. This goes hand in hand with negotiating work. My clients are rarely the lowest bidders. They can be if they need to be, but they are usually in the middle to high end of the pricing range. They often tell prospects right up front, during the initial telephone call, that they will not be the lowest priced. They tell them that if they're looking for a low price, they should call someone else. Often, they'll provide names and numbers of other contractors to call.

Sometimes, I hear people tell me they're glad they have and use my methods and can produce good prices, but they don't want their competition to have them. I disagree. You want three to four other contractors in your market who have great reputations and good pricing. The four or five of you become the industry and price leaders in your area. You all reinforce professionalism and good pricing in your market. This makes you and your market more resistant to "low ballers." Work in your local association and strive to set the bar high for both yourself and other contractors in your market.

How It Works

The contractor in New England once told me he didn't want his competition to use my software and related hardware. I disagreed. He went on to tell me his estimating system was so efficient that he could "sneeze" and produce a good bid. Estimating for his competition, on the other hand, was a grueling and tedious process marked by inaccuracy and inconsistency. Competitors would beat themselves to death trying to produce as many bids as he did. The process was powerful. He set me straight.

The franchise approach to business has become very popular in the last 50 years. And deservedly so. This "turnkey" approach has many merits. The success rate for many franchises is very high. Systems, processes, and marketing are all tried and proven. Some consulting companies have tried to implement this approach in the Green Industry. However, the results have been mixed. A cookie-cutter, one-size-fits-all approach to contracting just doesn't work—yet. As methods and software are adapted and consultants gain a better understanding of the dynamic of a contracting business, you'll soon see a much more planned "womb-to-tomb" or "cradle-to-grave" approach to this industry. Just you wait! Some exciting things are in the business management pipeline.

How It Works

A large commercial contractor in Southern California once complained to me that if he wasn't low bidder, he didn't get any work. After trying to work with him, I understood why. Remember the kid who had to tie a pork chop around his neck to get his dog to play with him? This guy was so disorganized and chaotic that no one in his or her right mind would want to repeat a business experience and negotiate work with him.

ESTIMATING STRATEGY AND COMPUTER SOFTWARE

Review Figure 2-1 as we discuss estimating. The main goal of this aspect of marketing is to ensure that you bid enough work as cost-effectively and as accurately as possible while maintaining profitability. Computers, software, and other tools need to be evaluated and used, if feasible. Keep these definitions in mind as you read on.

Estimating: The science of determining what a job costs.

Bidding: Arriving at a reasonable price for a job by adding the appropriate markups and margins to the estimated costs.

During the remaining discussion on estimating, keep two guiding principles in the back of your mind. First, because they've been bid into specific jobs, you should be able to place any and every expense you incur in your business into a specific bid and be able to see where every check you write is coming back to you. If you can't trace every check you write to a bid (income source), then you have a leak in your company.

Second, we're primarily concerned about identifying two numbers during the bidding process. One is the total cost for the job, including sales tax, labor burden, and G&A overhead, but minus net profit and any contingency factor. This is your break-even point. The other is the price the market will bear.

The difference between the two is your gross profit margin (GPM). You can't identify your gross profit margin unless you can identify your total costs (including G&A overhead, sales tax, and labor burden) and the pricing your market will bear. Our goal is to identify these two numbers, as much as possible, for every job you bid. Unfortunately, the vast majority of estimating systems used by contractors cannot consistently calculate these two numbers.

Estimating System Review

See Chapter 2 for a more thorough discussion of an estimating system, as I'm only going to cover a few highlights in this section.

1. **The finished product or service.**
   This stage of the bidding process includes costs for items physically included in the finished product and/or service. Material is included at a re-wholesale cost. Labor is calculated in field-labor hours, multiplied by either an average wage or specific wage rate for differing classes of labor. Equipment is included by multiplying hours by cost per hour for each piece of equipment. Subcontractors are included at cost.
2. **General conditions.**
   Included are costs for those items required by the finished product or service (material, labor, equipment, and subcontractor costs as above), but which are not part of it after the job is complete. These include but are not limited to crew trucks, supervision time, drive time, load and unload time, mobilization of equipment, material hauling time, portable toilets, fences, permits, fees, and so on.
3. **Margins and markups.**
   A. Sales Tax. Appropriate sales tax markups are applied to materials and other items as required by state and local laws.

   B. Labor Burden. Labor is marked up by a predetermined percentage in order to recover FICA, FUTA, SUTA, liability insurance, field-crew vacations, holidays, sick days, etc.

   C. G&A Overhead. Here we multiply the labor hours in both Phases I and II of the bid by the company or division G&A overhead per hour (OPH) amount. This process is explained in further detail in the next section.

   D. Net Profit. The items identified up to now, when added together, produce your break-even point (BEP). Net profit is then added to your BEP, assuming you've identified it accurately. See the net profit margin section in Chapter 46 for a discussion on industry benchmarks for net profit. Your choice of a specific percentage to use on a particular job is usually determined by how badly you need the job, its size, the risk involved, and what the market will bear.

   E. Contingency Factor. Contractors will sometimes add a fifth markup category that's often referred to as the "aggravation factor." Basically, this is additional money tacked onto the price of a job that will make it worth it to you to incur additional risk or to put up with certain situations or individuals (architects, owners, developers, homeowners, and so forth).

   Remember though, that despite aggravation and risk, you're constantly attempting to determine and work with *true* costs and the price the market will bear.

We can now equate estimating to determining those costs involved with Phases I and II in the bid. The bidding process is completed when we add margins and markups in Phase III to the first two phases, and arrive at our sales price for a particular job.

One last note: Direct costs consist of all costs in Phases I and II plus sales tax on material and labor burden on labor. Indirect costs, or General & Administrative overhead costs (also called G&A overhead), are all other costs that can't be directly identified to a particular job.

General and Administrative (G&A) Overhead Recovery

There are a number of ways of attempting to identify G&A overhead and to recover it. The goal is to recover a predetermined amount of G&A overhead (or indirect costs as opposed to direct costs) that will cover your G&A overhead expenses throughout the year. The challenge is determining just how much G&A overhead you should add to a job above the other costs. See Chapters 8, 38, and 39 for a more thorough discussion of general and administrative overhead costs and applying them to jobs.

I use the G&A overhead costs per field-labor hour (OPH) method for allocating indirect costs to bids. This approach simplifies the concept of G&A overhead recovery, as compared to percentage-based methods for doing so. You simply determine the amount of G&A overhead to be recovered for the year (for example: $200,000) and divide it by the projected field-labor hours (for example: 20,000). You then determine the G&A overhead recovered on a job by multiplying the field-labor hours included in Phases I and II by the OPH ($200,000 ÷ 20,000 = $10 OPH). A job requiring 3,500 field-labor hours would be charged $35,000 (3,500 × $10 = $35,000) for G&A overhead recovery.

The OPH method is very easy to use. It's also easy to adjust and trace throughout the year. It will provide you with the minimum, safe amount of G&A overhead to recover on a job, as long as your budgeted field-labor hours for the year are in line with your actual field-labor hours used.

The one area where you need to be cautious using the OPH method is when you have an inordinately high ratio of material, equipment, or subcontractors, as compared to labor. In these instances you may be charging too little for G&A overhead, when you could realistically charge more and still get the job. I always compare the amount of G&A overhead recovered on a job, using the OPH method, to other methods. If the results are dramatically different, I know the OPH amount is a safe, minimum amount to use.

The following exceptions should be included in your bidding strategy:

1. **Bidding a large job.**
   If you bid a large job that would increase your actual field-labor hours for the year, while your G&A overhead remains the same, revise your OPH by dividing your G&A overhead ($200,000) by the new projected field hours (25,000). Your OPH to recover on that job drops from $10 per field-labor hour to $8 ($200,000 ÷ 25,000 = $8) per labor hour. This could make you more competitive on your bids or increase your net profit margin.

   Caution: Until you win that particular job and are confident your field-labor hours will increase for the year, bid all other work at the previous OPH figure (in this case, $10 per labor hour).

2. **If you've reached your break-even point.**
   If you meet your BEP prior to the end of the fiscal year (in this case, your BEP is reached when your gross profit margin equates to your G&A overhead budget for the year), any dollar amounts on bids above Phases I and II costs, plus sales tax and labor burden, will be net profit for that year *if* the work is completed prior to the end of the fiscal year. An example may help:

   Your G&A overhead budget is $200,000 for the fiscal year ending December 31. At the end of October your P&L Statement shows you have a gross profit margin of $200,000. Therefore, for all practical purposes, your G&A overhead is covered and paid for the year. All amounts billed above direct costs after October 31 now go to net profit since G&A overhead has already been covered.

   Work bid after the BEP is met, which will be completed and billed before the fiscal year end, can be bid with the realization that any amount above direct costs in the bid goes to net profit. If your net profit margin is 10%, and your G&A overhead is another 15%, your net profit margin is really 25%, since your G&A overhead is already covered for the year.

Some contractors who understand this concept bid end-of-the-year work cheaper than they normally would, without hurting themselves or cutting into profits.

3. **Seasonal business.**
   If you're a seasonal business that does landscape and irrigation work 9 or 10 months of the year, you may consider bidding work differently as the season draws to a close. For instance, if you're bidding a job late in the season that you could complete before the end of it and if there are slim to no other real possibilities for getting additional work, you might want to cut G&A overhead recovery and net profit to improve your chances of getting that work. Here's why.

   Since there's little hope for getting any more work this season, any additional work you complete and bill above direct costs goes directly to gross profit for the year. Your G&A overhead costs won't change (or will change very little) due to this job, so G&A overhead costs are fixed regardless of what happens. Therefore, any gross profit from this job will improve the bottom line.

   Your choice is essentially whether you want a larger percentage (for G&A overhead and net profit) of nothing, or a smaller percentage of something. If you can get the job using your normal margins, by all means do it. However, you may have to become more flexible and creative as economic factors and the season dictate.

4. **G&A overhead-cutting strategies.**
   The following ideas may help you cut G&A overhead, and thereby increase your net profit margin or allow you to lower your prices and become more competitive. Space doesn't allow us to exhaust the list of possibilities, but this should give you a place to start.

   A. Co-Locate with Another Company. By sharing facilities, G&A overhead personnel, office equipment (copiers, computers, etc.), and other related business needs you can cut not only operating costs for G&A overhead but also have another company owner to talk to, obtain leads from, and bounce ideas off. The company may or may not be doing your type of business. If it is, preferably it won't be in the same market (e.g., one could be in commercial work and the other in residential, etc.). Otherwise, problems will probably arise somewhere down the road because you'll inevitably be competing against each other for work.

   B. Increase Field-Labor Hours for Existing Types of Work. By expanding your volume in your present line of work, you'll increase your field-labor hours, and (in all likelihood) your G&A overhead will remain the same or increase at less of a percentage than your volume. The result will be that your OPH goes down. Actual G&A overhead may increase slightly but, for bidding purposes, you're realistically reducing your OPH.

   C. Increase Field-Labor Hours with New Types of Work. Field-labor hours are field-labor hours. If you increase them, your OPH goes down. It makes no difference whether you're plowing snow, cleaning windows, chopping wood, doing janitorial work, etc. Any increase in field-labor hours (and thus in sales) where you can bill above direct costs while holding your G&A overhead relatively steady, decreases your OPH—and that's beneficial for your company.

   D. Use Personal Computers Wisely. Personal computers are like any other piece of equipment. They need to be "tuned" regularly and "driven" properly. Ninety-nine percent of the construction and services companies today could improve their "bureaucracy" and streamline their procedures by improving their use of PCs. I've yet to see a company that couldn't decrease its OPH with a little extra homework in this area.

Spreadsheet, accounting, estimating, and word processing software can increase your administrative staff's productivity, accuracy, and even their motivation—if they're using the correct philosophies, methodologies, systems and strategies. Otherwise, you're just making mistakes at the speed of light. Garbage in, garbage out (GIGO).

E. Monitor OPH. I like the phrase, "What gets measured, gets done." If you measure the OPH figure you use for bidding on a graph, you'll find realistic ways to make it come down. I've seen this figure range from \$1.68 to over \$22. In all likelihood, you'll fall somewhere in between. The important thing is to graph it and note the change on the graph *every* time the figure fluctuates.

F. Reach the Maximum Size Your G&A Overhead Will Support. While direct costs increase in proportion to increased sales, G&A overhead will plateau or increase in steps (see Figures 39-1 and 39-2). The key is to determine the amount of maximum sales your G&A overhead can support. This will make you as profitable as possible. Points of greatest profitability vary somewhat, but for a typical construction and services company, they usually fall close to the points indicated in the figure.

By obtaining and maintaining your point of greatest profitability as quickly as possible, while minimizing the length of your points of least profitability, you recover your G&A overhead sooner. This allows you to reduce your OPH by growing to the next step or by increasing sales, while keeping G&A overhead constant.

G. Consider Working Overtime. One option worth considering is to work overtime—as long as productivity isn't affected. This is possible because G&A overhead won't increase (or will increase very little), while work completed and installed will. Consider our example of 20,000 labor hours and \$200,000 for G&A overhead. If your construction field crew of approximately 10 full-time people worked five 10-hour days per week, as compared to five 8-hour days per week, field-labor hours for the year would increase from about 2,000 hours per person to about 2,500. Total field-labor hours would increase to about 25,000, but G&A overhead costs would remain the same. Hence, your G&A overhead per hour (OPH) would drop from \$10 per labor hour to \$8. This would decrease your bidding OPH by \$2 per field-labor hour.

There are, however, other factors here that must be dealt with. First, you must consider the overtime tradeoff. If your average wage was \$10 per field-labor hour and your labor burden was 30%, the normal total field-labor hour cost would be \$13 (without overtime). With overtime, the cost would increase to \$14.30 per field-labor hour. The result is that you'd save \$2 per field-labor hour in G&A overhead cost, but \$1.30 of it would be eaten up by increased labor costs.

Secondly, you must monitor productivity. If you're not careful, the remaining 70 cents could well be eaten up by lost productivity. The best way to monitor this is through job costing, if it's detailed enough. Another quick method is by monitoring your increase in billables by means of your sales per field-labor hour (SPH).

For instance, by dividing your projected annual sales budget by your projected field-labor hours you arrive at your average SPH. This usually ranges between \$45 to \$65 per field-labor hour (throughout North America for landscape and irrigation construction work—maintenance crews not included). We'll use a \$50 average for our purposes.

If you have 10 people in the field full-time, who consistently work five 8-hour days per week, your monthly billables should be almost \$87,000 per month, or about \$870,000 per year (10 men × 40 hours per week × 4.33 weeks per month × \$50 SPH = \$86,600). If you then change to five 10-hour days per week, and if your productivity doesn't drop, you should be able to bill roughly \$108,000 per month versus \$87,000, without overtime. The formula is as follows:

Monthly Revenue without Overtime:

10 people × 40 hrs/wk × 4.33 wks/mo × \$50 SPH = \$86,600

Monthly Revenue with Overtime:

10 people × 50 hrs/wk × 4.33 wks/mo × \$50 SPH = \$108,250

Keep in mind that these formulas will give you a quick method for monitoring overtime productivity on a monthly average basis. You should use specific SPH figures for individual jobs, as they'll vary from the average. Accurate, detailed job-costing is the best way to monitor overtime productivity, but the above method will provide a quick, fairly accurate alternative if you don't have it in place.

5. **Good and bad G&A overhead.**
   G&A overhead that doesn't improve the support provided to field operations is always suspect. If G&A overhead increases, field-labor hours should increase and/or productivity should increase. Your OPH should gradually fall as your sales volume increases. If it doesn't, something's probably wrong. Good G&A overhead ultimately supports the people in the trenches, and these people are the ones who justify the existence of the whole company. Bad G&A overhead merely makes life more comfortable for the bureaucrats without benefiting field crews.

Field Equipment Use

Estimating equipment costs to include in a bid can be a source of much confusion to contractors. Here are a few points to keep in mind.

1. **Bidding.**
   Other than G&A overhead vehicles used by G&A overhead bureaucrats (people who are not in the trenches producing the product), all field equipment is bid into jobs at Phases I and II in the bid. Pickup trucks (one-ton and under, and used in the field) are bid into the job at eight hours per day whether the truck's running or not. Total hours are multiplied by a cost-per-hour for the whole time the truck's on the job. Trucks above one-ton, tractors, trenchers, mowers, bucket trucks, chippers, etc., are bid into the job using actual meter hours. As a general rule, I like to bid the larger trucks into jobs for a minimum of four hours per day. Actual running time, or four hours per day, is a good goal to shoot for.
2. **Using.**
   Unless a piece of equipment is a specialty piece you can't rent, or is paid for, thus incurring no monthly payment, it should be used on jobs approximately 50% of the time and reflected in your bids accordingly.

3. **Budgeting.**
   Field equipment should be bid into jobs as hours budgeted for use on a job multiplied by a predetermined cost per hour figure. It should *not* be factored into bids as a percentage markup or as a factor added to labor costs.

Average Wage

A company or division average wage is determined by dividing the total field payroll budget (minus holiday, vacation, and sick leave pay) by the total field-labor hours in the budget (minus holiday, vacation, and sick leave hours). Many contractors, however, use a more precise crew average wage for bidding purposes because one crew may be more expensive than another due to the type of work performed (e.g., masonry, concrete, irrigation, maintenance crews, etc.) or due to the size of the crew (e.g., a three-person crew being more expensive per average crew hour than a five-person crew). Overtime and risk factors are then added to the crew average wage.

Net Profit

Net profit is what's left after all costs, both direct and indirect, are deducted from the sales price for a job.

1. **Checking for leaks.**
   If you're consistently bidding a 10 to 15% net profit margin on your jobs, you should see very close to that amount as net profit on your financial statements. Otherwise, you have a "leak" in your company. What you're bidding isn't reflecting your actual costs. Dollars are somehow leaking out of your company that are not being recaptured in your bids. You should strive to have a watertight, leakproof operation.

   Leaks occur when productivity rates aren't being accurately reflected in bids; when drive time, warranty work, equipment costs, or G&A overhead isn't being accurately included in bids; or due to general conditions missed, theft, ad infinitum. One of your top jobs as an owner is to persistently look for leaks within your operation and to train others in the organization to do the same.

   A quick check for maintenance crew operation leaks is to divide your monthly maintenance route billable dollar amount (minus extras) by field payroll labor hours (minus hours spent on extras). The resulting figure should be within a few cents of your average estimated sales per field-labor hour rate. In other words, if you're consistently bidding your work at $30 per hour, your monthly billables divided by payroll hours had better be pretty close to $30. Otherwise, you have a leak.
2. **Net profit markups.**
   The traditional method for determining a net profit markup is to predetermine a net profit range (i.e., 10 to 25%) for your company. A net profit percentage is chosen for each of four categories: need, risk, size, and what the market will bear. The four are averaged and the resulting percentage is used as the net profit markup. However, just as the single and multiple G&A overhead recovery systems (SORS and MORS) have flaws (because they're based on a percentage markup), so does the traditional method have flaws for calculating net profit.

   A. Net Profit per Field-Labor Hour (PPH). We always compare the percent and the dollar amount arrived at by the traditional method to a net profit per field-labor hour (PPH) figure for the job and the company average

PPH on the yearly budget. This allows us to adjust our net profit in the event a material- or labor-intensive job distorts it. Let's build on our previous example.

The budgeted 20,000 field hours is projected to install $1 million worth of construction work for the year. This calculates out to be a $50 SPH figure ($1,000,000 ÷ 20,000 hours = $50). Net profit is projected to be 10% of sales, or $100,000. That equates to $5 net profit for every field-labor hour ($100,000 ÷ 20,000 = $5). If we bid a material-intensive job and our SPH for the job climbs to $75, at 10% net profit our PPH is now $7.50 per hour ($75.00 × .1 = $7.50).

I know some contractors who refuse to bid jobs with less than 10% net profit on them. That's fine. However, I'm not very concerned about a 10% figure. I'm concerned about achieving a targeted dollar amount of net profit for every labor hour running around out there in the field.

In this case, I could lower my net profit on the material-intensive job to 7% ($5.25 PPH) and still be ahead of my average budgeted amount of $5 PPH. This might give me a better chance to get the job. Of course, if I can get $7.50 (or more) PPH, I'll certainly do it. Using a PPH figure gives you greater flexibility than the traditional method.

The PPH is equally insightful when you're bidding a labor-intensive job (perhaps something that might require a lot of demolition). For instance, if your SPH goes down to $40, 10% net profit is only $4 per labor hour. Perhaps you should raise your net profit to 12 to 13% to pick up the additional $1 net profit, or maybe you should look for more profitable jobs to bid and avoid doing the less profitable work if you can.

B. Gross Profit Margin. One other method that helps to evaluate your net profit markup is to combine your G&A overhead recovery percentage and your net profit percentage. This gives you your gross profit margin (GPM). Many contractors keep a target GPM figure in mind as they bid work, especially highly competitive commercial work.

During the recession of the early 1990s, a residential landscape and irrigation contractor in the Southern California market told me that if his GPM on a bid was above 18%, he could count on not getting the job. Eighteen percent was very tight, but at least he had the tools and the know-how to analyze his bids and his market.

Monitoring Estimating

At the beginning of this chapter, I mentioned a contractor from the Midwest and some of the analysis work done by his office manager. The following are some of the tools the office manager used to gather his information:

1. **The Bid Board.**
   The purpose of the Bid Board is to provide a tool that displays and tracks the entire process of bringing business into the company. This will help you gain more control over the bidding process and, in many cases, accelerate it. This, in turn, motivates individuals by providing effective feedback and vital, continuous information. See Chapter 39 for a thorough discussion of the Bid Board.
2. **The Bid Status Report.**
   The purpose of the Bid Status Report is to provide a computerized version of key elements of the Bid Board. You should also see Chapter 39 for a thorough discussion of the Bid Status Report. You can obtain a computerized version of this report by contacting our offices.

3. **The Bid Recap Report.**
   The purpose of the Bid Recap Report is to provide a weekly, systematic means of collecting data and tracking the process of bringing sales into your business.

   This report, shown in Figure 50-1 can be useful in identifying key trends over a long period of time (6 to 18 months). It can be particularly useful if you're in a seasonal location, as it allows you to compare sales, backlog, bids outstanding compared to sales, etc. Many of our clients have appreciated its value more as they entered an economic slowdown, because it provided solid statistics (versus anxious feelings) on which to base business decisions.

   The Bid Recap Report eventually evolved into the Monthly Audit Data Report.
4. **The Monthly Audit Data Report.**
   The purpose of the Monthly Audit Data (M.A.D.) Report is to provide a simple yet thorough monthly report that collects critical sales, financial, and production information in one place. It also provides a place for identifying the strategic problems and challenges facing the company.

   This report (see Chapter 40) can also be very useful in identifying key trends over a long period of time (6 to 18 months).

React Quickly to Market Changes

It's frightening to realize just how quickly a market can slow down. As the pipeline of work dries up, a slowdown often happens almost overnight. New home starts and commercial work can suddenly become drastically reduced and catch some otherwise savvy people by surprise. Of course, everyone will say later that they saw it coming.

Always be prepared to cut your G&A overhead and expenses—and cut them quickly. Too often, contractors wait too long to bite the bullet and make necessary cuts. If you can't get sales to where they need to be, you may have to reduce office working hours, implement pay cuts, get rid of G&A overhead vehicles, and make difficult decisions. Tell your employees what you (as a company) are facing, and allow them to feel the urgency of the situation. Quite often, they'll come up with creative ideas to increase revenues and sales, cut G&A overhead, or both. But do it, and do it quickly.

Study/Know Your Competition

You can develop some competitive advantages by understanding your competition. The best way to gain that understanding is through the bidding process. By monitoring the many facets of estimating (sales per hour, G&A overhead per hour, net profit per hour, gross profit margins, etc.), you can develop a very accurate standard by which to judge and monitor those who bid against you. It's not uncommon for contractors who understand the bidding process, their production rates, and their market to set the standard for pricing in their area because general contractors and developers have come to trust the accuracy of their bidding process. This would be impossible without many of the tools we've discussed.

Avoid Becoming a "Captive" Sub

There's a tendency for subcontractors to want to work for only one client. The problem is that you'll rise and fall with that one client. If subcontractors do this, they tend to become lazy, lose their competitive edge, and lose touch with the market and with their competition. I call this contracting "incest," or inbreeding. The question isn't *if* you're going to lose your sugar daddy, but *when*.

From: Bill **Date:** July 1, 20___

To: John

Subject: **Bid Board Recap Report for month ending June 20___ (Const. Div. Only)**

1. Bid Board Recap:

A. FY 20___ sales goal		$ 1,000,000
B. Contracts signed Y-T-D		$ 729,144
C. Additional contracts needed to sign (1A -1B)		$ 270,856
D. Work installed and billed Y-T-D		$ 344,185
E. Work installed and not billed Y-T-D		$ 35,000
F. Additional work needed to install and bill (1A - 1D - 1 E)		$ 620,815

2. Jobs bid and awaiting award:

A. Bids pending previous month thru bid #	156	$ 1,549,216
B. Bids submitted this month thru bid #	171	$ 268,982
C. Total bids pending today		$ 1,560,483
D. Net increase or decrease (2C - 2A)		$ 11,267
E. Number of bids pending today		$ 63
F. Average size of bid pending (2C ÷ 2E)		$ 24,770

3. Jobs to bid:

A. Number of sets of plans or designs to complete and bid	$ 18
B. Projected dollar amount to bid (2F x 3A)	$ 445,852

4. Goals for next month:

A. Key jobs to bid / design	B. Plans to pick up
Green Mountain Park	Costa Vista College
Saddleback Middle School	Valley Central Mall
Davis project	

5. Notes and/or additional remarks:

FIGURE 50-1 The Bid Board Recap Report

In addition, quite often the client begins to control you, as though they owned your company (and, in fact, they virtually do). Soon they subtly begin to manipulate you to your disadvantage. They know they have you over a barrel.

Always strive to diversify. Don't allow any one client to account consistently for more than 15 to 25% of your sales volume.

Salespeople

If their remuneration is handled properly, good salespeople can be worth their weight in gold. Whether they're paid on a straight commission, draw against commission, or on a salary basis, it doesn't matter. The main issues are: what is their preference and is the remuneration reasonable for both the salesperson and the company. A few guiding principles may help.

1. Commissioned salespeople should not bid the work they sell unless it's reviewed. The temptation is ever present to lower prices to unrealistic levels in order to sell jobs.
2. Provide a minimum sales price to the salespeople for each job, but allow them to raise it if they can sell it. Of course, they're entitled to a portion of the added revenue.
3. The salesperson should be the one responsible for keeping the customer happy while the job is being performed—and for picking up the final payment for the project.
4. If necessary, consider using a draw against commissions as a method of remuneration, but always tie salespeople's salaries to sales, either directly (as a commission) or indirectly (as a salary). Let them all know that if they don't produce a certain amount of sales, they don't have a job. Every salesperson is working for a commission. It's the method of payment that differs. See Chapter 4 for a more thorough discussion of salespeople and commissions.

Marketing Personnel

Some companies hire a marketing person who has responsibilities different from that of sales personnel. This position is usually reserved for larger companies. Such a person oversees the development of a marketing strategy for the company. Some key areas of responsibility might be as follows:

- The development and production of marketing materials
- Press releases
- Company newsletters
- Client relations
- Advertising and advertising campaigns
- Company résumé
- Company brochures

A Price, A Plan, and A Process

Most estimating systems only produce a questionable price and little else. A good estimating system produces not only an accurate *Price* for your jobs, but it also produces a *Plan* and a *Process* (the tools) for implementing that bid in the field.

It's not uncommon for contractors to pore over plans and go through sheets and sheets of yellow pads and reels of adding machine tape, searching for the "right" number. Once they have that figure, everything used to get it is either illegible, indecipherable, or thrown out. All that work goes to waste when, in fact, the entire process should be used to plan and run jobs in the field. Unfortunately, this is rarely the case.

I repeat, good estimating systems produce accurate prices—and a plan and a process.

Personal Computer (PC) Estimating Considerations

Estimating with a PC holds great potential for you and your company, if it's approached wisely and done correctly. See Chapter 49 for a more thorough discussion of computer estimating.

Section Summary

In order to maximize your sales revenues and profit margins, estimating provides significant potential to increase your sales and improve your bottom line. By developing the right philosophies, methodologies, systems, and strategies, you can learn to bid with confidence and to develop tools that will help you understand your bidding and your competition's bidding.

Computer estimating offers even more ways to improve profits by providing the tools to recap and review bids easily and accurately. But you have to be careful. If your estimating software doesn't reflect the correct methods, all you'll be doing is making mistakes at the speed of light.

SUMMARY

In order to maximize sales revenues and profit margins *and* to meet your sales goals, marketing is where you need to exert the majority of your energies. We aren't talking about taking on fancy Madison Avenue marketing strategies here. Rather, we're reviewing and analyzing our product line, promotional efforts, place (location and facilities), and pricing in order to ensure that we get enough work to meet budget projections.

We're also reviewing the processes and culture within our organization to ensure that they match the expectations of the client. This doesn't mean that operations aren't important. They're extremely important. However, unless there are serious problems in operations that need your immediate attention, you need to focus your efforts on securing the revenues required to meet your budget targets and to keep the company moving forward.

We've recommended that computer estimating and systems offer some of the greatest potential in your marketing efforts. Effectively computerizing your organization will boost your revenues, hold down general and administrative overhead costs, and provide numerous tools that will make your company easier to run, more profitable, more successful, and more fun.

The estimating budget and budget-to-actual performance are the primary tools used to measure marketing effectiveness. Meeting budgeted sales goals is the primary objective of marketing. When estimating, marketing, and field operations are successfully combined, the secondary objective of marketing is met. That is, to negotiate as much work as possible and to maximize repeat business and referrals for the company.

To have an effective, lasting business, the hard analytical science of cost estimating has to be married to the intuitive art of marketing. This juncture is where the logic of the left side is joined to the creative right side of the brain. You need both to run an effective contracting business.

ACTION POINT

Review your marketing strategy according to the five Ps (Product, Place, Price, Promotion, and Process) outlined in this chapter. Involve your staff and brainstorm how you might implement some of the ideas discussed here.

CHAPTER

51

Company Structure and Growth Patterns

Purpose

To explain and outline the typical growth patterns for construction and service companies with sales revenues up to $5 million and the organizational structure that accompanies such growth patterns

Introduction

Let's face it. The contracting business is still a male-dominated industry. Fortunately, the influence of women in leadership positions is slowly trickling into the industry and shaping the philosophies, processes, methods, systems, and strategies within it. Unfortunately, this influence is slow in coming.

I've observed that male contractors are more confident but less competent. It's the "bull in the china shop" syndrome. Women contractors, on the other hand, tend to be more competent but less confident.

Because of the current male dominance in this industry, you have to understand the male psyche in order to understand company growth patterns and the related structure. This will change, but for now it's what we have to deal with. This "psyche" within this industry will continue to evolve as women gain more prominence in it. This, I think, is good.

Fortunately (I hope fortunate is the right word) for me, I relate well to this male-dominated psyche. I played all sorts of sports as a young boy (still would if I could). I fished, camped, hunted, and trapped; ran track, played baseball and football in high school; was a gymnast both in high school and college; served as a captain in the U.S. Marine Corps; was a single dad to my three sons for 10 years; and I work with numerous men's ministries today. I may be self-deceived, but I think I understand guys. Otherwise, I couldn't write this chapter. In 10 or 20 years, I may be disqualified from rewriting it.

You don't go into business, you grow into business. At least that's how it should be.

It's also fortunate (probably much more so) that I've had the opportunity to talk with, observe, and listen to many women who have helped shape my perspective on people, business, and life. Many would say they "straightened me out," or at least tried to. I'm forever grateful to my mother, grandmothers, sisters, aunts, female business associates, and friends, with whom I've spent thousands of hours.

You don't *go* into business, you *grow* into business. At least that's how it should be. I've observed that corporate growth parallels one's personal managerial growth. You hear the phrase in sports, "play within your game," or "play within yourself." In other words, you need to concentrate on who you are and what your capabilities are, and play within that framework. Understanding yourself and your personal assets and liabilities is essential if you're going to develop to your maximum potential.

Individuals who attempt to play "someone else's game" often become frustrated and disengaged. This doesn't mean you don't try to emulate others and incorporate some of their elements into your "game." It just means that you focus on developing yourself and not on trying to be someone else.

In other industries, the modern franchise movement has changed the dynamic I'm about to describe. However, its influence on the Green Industry has been minimal up to now.

A few definitions are in order before we begin our discussion:

- *Entrepreneur:* One who launches or manages a business venture, often assuming risks.
- *Leader:* One who ensures that the right things are done (according to Peter Drucker).
- *Manager:* One who ensures that things are done right (according to Peter Drucker).
- *Coach:* One who may or may not be part of the organization, who guides, encourages, and supports another through the business development process.
- *Team Builder:* One directly responsible for the development of a group of individuals comprised of diverse skill levels.
- *Technician:* A person highly skilled in a certain field or process.
- *Crew Leader or Foreman:* One with technical skills, but who can also effectively direct the work of two to five technicians.
- *Supervisor:* One with technical skills, but who can also effectively direct the work of two to five crew leaders/foremen.

We're going to discuss business development up to the $5 million mark. This will comprise 99% of all Green Industry businesses. Companies over this mark are unique and need to customize management systems and processes.

Please keep in mind that the patterns we're going to discuss are typical or common ones I've observed in the industry. Use these patterns as a point of reference only. Your company will, in all likelihood, vary from what's described here, and that's fine. Adapt my models to your specific company.

COMPANY GROWTH PATTERNS AND STRUCTURE

Construction Companies

Annual revenue generated per full-time field employee is approximately $100,000. This includes materials, equipment, labor and burden, general and administrative (G&A) overhead, and net profit. The average crew size is three people.

1. **The first plateau**
   - A. *Field crew:* Owner works with two full-time people in the field, making a total of three
   - B. *Annual sales:* $300,000 (without any subcontractor revenue included)
   - C. *Office staff:* A part-time bookkeeper and/or office person
   - D. *Other staff:* None

E. *Owner:* Owner runs jobs, runs the company, and designs and sells jobs. He or she is working 65 to 75 hours per week doing two full-time jobs. The owner is trying to learn how to delegate and become a manager.

2. **The second plateau**
   A. *Field crew:* Owner works with two three-person crews. Each crew has a foreman and two laborers.
   B. *Annual sales:* $600,000 (without any subcontractor revenue included)
   C. *Office staff:* A full-time bookkeeper or office manager
   D. *Other staff:* Either a working field supervisor or an estimator/salesperson
   E. *Owner:* Owner still runs jobs and the company and designs and sells jobs. He or she is working 65 to 75 hours per week doing three full-time jobs and still trying to figure out how to delegate work to others and build a team.
3. **The third plateau**
   A. *Field crew:* Supervisor works with three three-person crews. Each crew has a foreman and two laborers
   B. *Annual sales:* $900,000 (without any subcontractor revenue included)
   C. *Office staff:* A full-time bookkeeper or office manager with part-time help
   D. *Other staff:* A working field supervisor and an estimator/salesperson
   E. *Owner:* If the owner is still trying to run jobs and the company and designs and sells jobs, he or she is becoming sterile or insane, or both. He or she is working 60 to 70 hours per week doing two or three full-time jobs and still trying to figure out how to delegate work to others and build a team. The primary focus of the owner should be to build the team and the systems to run the company. It's at this stage that the owner(s) must begin to transition from being a manager of the company to being a coach to the company.
4. **The fourth plateau**
   A. *Field crew:* Supervisor works with four to six three-person crews. Each crew has a foreman and two laborers. Often multiple crews will work on one job or form "super" crews.
   B. *Annual sales:* Up to $1,800,000 (without any subcontractor revenue included)
   C. *Office staff:* A full-time bookkeeper or office manager with full-time help of one or two people
   D. *Other staff:* A working field supervisor and one or two estimator/salespersons
   E. *Owner:* He/she is working 55 to 65 hours per week, hopefully with a team in place that can do the bookkeeping, run the jobs, and sell the work. The primary focus of the owner should still be to build and solidify the team and the systems to run the company. Future growth should not occur until this team is in place with effective systems to run the company.

Because it takes very little additional general and administrative cost to go from revenues of $1 million to $2 million, you should attempt that growth as quickly as possible. This will maximize your profitability.

5. **The fifth plateau**
   - A. *Field crew:* Supervisor works with crews proportionately with the amount of sales. Each crew has a foreman and two laborers. Often, multiple crews will work on one job or form "super" crews.
   - B. *Annual sales:* $2 to $5 million (without any subcontractor revenue included)
   - C. *Office staff:* A comptroller or general manager/office manager with full-time help of two or three people
   - D. *Other staff:* A working field supervisor and one or two estimator/salespersons
   - E. *Owner:* He or she is working 50 to 60 hours per week. It's at this level that owner(s) have successfully transitioned from manager to coach.

Service or Maintenance Companies

Annual revenue generated per full-time field employee is approximately $50,000. This includes materials, equipment, labor and burden, G&A overhead, and net profit. The average crew size is two for residential and four for commercial work.

1. **The first plateau**
   - A. *Field crew:* Owner works on jobs with five full-time people in the field, making a total of six
   - B. *Annual sales:* $300,000 (without any subcontractor revenue included). Extras run about 10% of contract revenue.
   - C. *Office staff:* A part-time bookkeeper and/or office person
   - D. *Other staff:* None
   - E. *Owner:* Owner runs jobs, runs the company, and sells jobs. He or she is working 65 to 75 hours per week doing two full-time jobs. The owner is trying to learn how to delegate and become a manager.
2. **The second plateau**
   - A. *Field crew:* Owner has 12 full-time people in the field, making a total of 12. Three or four strong crew leaders must emerge at this time to help run the crews with minimal supervision from the owner.
   - B. *Annual sales:* $600,000 (without any subcontractor revenue included). Extras run about 10% of contract revenue.
   - C. *Office staff:* A full-time bookkeeper and/or office person
   - D. *Other staff:* None
   - E. *Owner:* Owner still oversees jobs, runs the company, and sells jobs. He or she is still working 65 to 75 hours per week and doing two or three full-time jobs. The owner is trying to learn how to delegate and become a manager.
3. **The third and fourth plateaus**
   For residential maintenance companies, which see revenues reach $1 million and $2 million, respectively, the third and fourth plateaus follow no particular pattern. Usually these companies are branching out into separate divisions at this point (i.e., irrigation installation and service, landscape installations, outdoor lighting, outdoor ponds, extras, etc.).

   These companies tend to grow in all sorts of directions. As they reach $2 million in revenue, it's essential that a strong detail-oriented office manager is in place, with one or two full-time assistants. Managers of the respective divisions normally assume operational responsibility for field crews, and often for sales as well.

At the $2 million mark an owner has to have a solid management team in place if the company's going to grow sales revenue. At the $3 to $4 million mark, a comptroller or very strong general manager is usually brought on board to run the administrative side of the business, while an operations manager is hired to coordinate field operations. Division managers or account managers will typically take charge of their respective divisions.

Commercial maintenance companies usually build around the three- to five-man crew, with roughly $200,000 of revenue per crew. Owners will normally get the company to $1 million in annual sales with minimal help (one office person or office manager/bookkeeper with part-time help).

This gets them to the third level, or plateau. At this point, the owner usually brings in (or has been grooming) a strong field supervisor who runs the crews, while the owner attempts to market the company, implement systems, develop a management team, and grow the business.

To get to the fourth level, or approximately $2 million in revenues, owners will often begin to bring in account managers who manage $500,000 to $750,000 of annual work each. This translates into the account manager managing three to four crews. An "enhancement" account manager is often put in place to handle construction enhancements and to maximize extras. An operations manager who coordinates field operations is normally in place no later than midway through the fourth level.

This foundational structure is sufficient to handle revenues up to and through $3 million. It's typically at the $3 to $4 million mark that the general manager and/or comptroller position is created for the company.

4. **The fifth plateau**
   At the $4 to $5 million mark, it's almost essential to hire a comptroller (or controller) to handle and concentrate on the financial part of the business. Responsibilities of a comptroller include overseeing accounting, negotiating and overseeing loans, negotiating leases for equipment, negotiating and monitoring lines of credit, monitoring and evaluating company insurance policies, conducting cost-benefit analyses for such things as professional employment organizations (PEOs), software and its implementation, service contracts, acquisitions, etc. Comptrollers have very strong financial and information management backgrounds. Many of them are CPAs.

EQUIPMENT MECHANICS

Question: When should you hire and have a full-time mechanic?

Answer: As late in the game as possible.

Contractors love equipment. They also tend to love the people who fix and repair it. However, equipment and the associated people needed to keep it running are a two-edged sword.

How It Works

I've seen contractors keep equipment until it rusts to death and has to be buried (with much grieving, I might add). At one time, I monitored the financial statements of three separate maintenance companies, each doing just over $1 million is sales.

Two of the companies kept their trucks and field equipment until they had to be buried. These companies also had a full-time mechanic. The cost of the mechanics (payroll and labor burden), plus repair parts, was roughly $75,000 at each of these companies. The third company replaced its large mowers, walk-behinds, and riders every three years, or 1,500 hours. Crew trucks were also regularly traded in about every five years. The cost for a part-time mechanic and repair parts at this company was about $12,000 annually.

A fourth company was only doing $800,000 in annual sales, but had just about every piece of equipment imaginable and two full-time mechanics. During the recession of the early 1990s this company had gone from sales of $1.5 million to $800,000. Prior to the recession, management bought a lot of equipment. Fortunately, most of it was paid for. Unfortunately, it was just sitting in the yard rusting and not being used. This company could have kept four full-time mechanics busy working on unused equipment.

It gets to the point where you're maintaining a junkyard.

It gets to the point where you're maintaining a junkyard. The older and more dilapidated your equipment gets, the more money you have to spend on repair parts and mechanics. Unless you've tracked your costs and can prove otherwise, I recommend that you strongly consider buying new equipment and keep turning it over.

Point of Diminishing Returns

I encourage my clients not to have a full-time mechanic if their sales are under $1 million. Many of my clients are doing $2 million-plus in sales, and still don't have a full-time mechanic. You need to evaluate your operation, your access to dealer and independent repair shops and act accordingly. Table 51-1 shows approximate lifespans of some major landscaping equipment.

TABLE 51-1 Equipment Lifespan

Item	Hours or Years
Walk-behind mowers	1,200 to 1,500 hours or 3 years
Ride-on mowers	1,500 to 2,000 hours or 3 years
Skid steers	3,000 to 4,000 hours
Tractors, small ¼ CY bucket	2,000 to 3,000 hours
Tractors, small ½ CY bucket	2,500 to 3,500 hours
Tractors, small 1+ CY bucket	3,000 to 4,000 hours
Trenchers and pullers, small ride-on	2,000 to 3,000 hours
Trenchers and pullers, mid-size ride-on	2,500 to 3,500 hours
Trenchers and pullers, large ride-on	3,000 to 4,000 hours
Chippers, small tow-behind units	2,000 to 3,000 hours
Chippers, mid-size tow-behind units	2,500 to 3,500 hours
Chippers, large tow-behind units	3,000 to 4,000 hours

You quickly reach a point of diminishing returns with equipment. Unless there's a compelling reason to do so or if you have costing data that shows otherwise, it's normally cost-effective to regularly turn over your smaller trucks (one-ton and under), and your larger mowers, skid steers, trenchers, pullers, chippers, and the like.

SUMMARY

There's simply no "one-size-fits-all" structure that works for all companies all the time. You have to base your company structure around the people and talent you have. It's easy to design a "perfect" company organizational chart. However, if you can't find the right people with the correct skill base to fill it, you're out of luck.

Company structure is dynamic and it changes dramatically as company revenues increase from $100,000 to $5 million. The primary issue is not what structure is best for the company. It's whether owners can transition from being technicians to being managers, from being managers to being team builders, and beyond.

If owners have the capacity to recreate their companies at the various plateaus or levels through which they'll grow, the structure will generally follow.

ACTION POINT

Read or listen to the audio book, *Built to Last*, by James C. Collins and Jerry I. Porras.

CHAPTER
52

Ordering and Controlling Materials

Purpose

To explain the process of ordering and controlling materials and the tools used to do so

Introduction

The ability to produce accurate bids means little if you can't control your material inventory, resources, and tools. The following information is offered to help you maintain accountability of some of the "nuts and bolts" of your operation.

PURCHASE ORDERS

Purchase orders can cut material order processing time while increasing your ability to job cost quickly and accurately.

Further ordering time can be saved, and you'll have greater control over the amount of material you order if you have computerized estimating that produces a materials list for the job. This list of items and quantities can then be annotated onto purchase orders and subsequently faxed or e-mailed to vendors.

Benefits of Using Purchase Orders

Job Costing Accuracy Increases

All orders can be identified as belonging to a particular job and generated by a specific individual ordering the material.

Reduced Labor is Required to Job Cost

Providing purchase order numbers to vendors for specific deliveries to specific jobs speeds up the verifying and matching of purchase orders to delivery tickets and invoices.

Accountability, or an Audit Trail, Is Established

This allows you to

1. Verify how much of a particular material was ordered for a particular job.
2. Identify and stop potential theft.

Control Inventory

By putting "stock" in the supplier/vendor portion of the purchase order, it can help you track the use of inventory or stock on hand.

Verification of Bid Quotes

Purchase orders allow you to match and compare actual invoice prices to quotes provided when you were bidding the job. This allows you (or your bookkeeper) to request credit for overcharges.

Simplifies Work for Foremen

Purchase orders can help your foremen organize themselves by providing a simple, yet effective tool that clearly identifies the material ordering process.

Procedure for Using Purchase Orders

The individual using and/or installing the materials should be the person ordering them. This eliminates finger pointing and excuses. Your foremen should realize that part of the job is the scheduling and ordering of materials and the processing of necessary paperwork.

Specific individuals allowed to order materials should be identified, in writing, to vendors. Only these individuals should be allowed to order materials, and *only* if they provide a purchase order number when ordering. No purchase order should be used to order materials for more than one job. This will greatly simplify job costing.

Vendors should be asked to enter your purchase order numbers on all delivery tickets and invoices. It's not uncommon for contractors to fax copies of their purchase orders to vendors, thus eliminating the need to dictate items ordered over the phone. Some contractors use a different size purchase order (e.g., 5″ × 8″ vs. 8″ × 11″) to help identify and document change orders.

Sources for Purchase Orders

Purchase orders can be printed with your company name and address on them. Buy blank two-part NCR paper and make your own purchase orders on your computer printer. Buy generic purchase orders (available from an office supply store, 50 to the pad, in two-part NCR format). See Figure 52-1 for a sample purchase order form.

Format

Each purchase order should have a different purchase order number, and have a place for the following:

- Vendor's name and salesperson's name
- Job name
- Date materials required
- Date ordered
- Unit

PURCHASE ORDER

ORDER NO.
0496

TO		**SHIP TO**	
ADDRESS		**ADDRESS**	
CITY		**CITY**	

REQ. NO.	FOR	DATE REQUIRED	TERMS	HOW SHIP	DATE

	QUANTITY ORDERED	QUANTITY RECEIVED	PLEASE SUPPLY ITEMS LISTED BELOW	PRICE		UNIT
1						
2						
3						
4						
5						
6						
7						
8						
9						
10						
11						
12						
13						
14						
15						
16						
17						
18						
19						
20						
21						
22						

IMPORTANT

OUR ORDER NUMBER MUST APPEAR ON ALL INVOICES, PACKAGES, ETC.

PLEASE NOTIFY US IMMEDIATELY IF YOU ARE UNABLE TO SHIP COMPLETE ORDER BY DATE SPECIFIED.

PLEASE SEND COPIES OF YOUR INVOICE WITH THE ORIGINAL BILL OF LADING

PURCHASING AGENT

1H 146 REDIFORM

ORIGINAL

FIGURE 52-1 Sample Purchase Order Form

- Quantity
- Item description
- Signature of person ordering material

INVENTORY CONTROL OF STOCK AND MATERIAL UPON RECEIPT

There are several tasks that must be done to ensure accuracy and accountability for inventory.

1. Make it a rule to take a personnel inventory or a count at delivery before signing for it. Make no exceptions. This may take a little more time, but can be well worth it.
2. Use purchase orders when items are taken out of company stock (put "stock" or "inventory" in the vendor section of the purchase order). Use fair market value for these items when you job cost them.
3. Inventory stock on a regular basis. Conduct an in-depth inventory at least every six months. Do a random spot check on 5 to 10% of your line items during the months between inventories. If you discover a discrepancy, investigate more fully.
4. Provide secure inventory locations. *Remember,* "A lock isn't meant to keep a thief out; it's meant to keep an honest man honest." Don't provide temptation or opportunity for your people to steal. Without locked and secure facilities, it's not a question of *if* people will steal, but *when.* If you allow for the opportunity, *it will happen.*
5. Job cost quickly. One of your best methods of preventing unnecessary loss or theft is to job cost invoices quickly. Identify overages ASAP. Show everyone there's a system in place to hold people accountable.

TOOLS

Keeping track of tools and ordering new ones requires a process similar to keeping an accurate inventory.

1. All tools should be ordered by purchase order. Again, make *no* exceptions.
2. Keeping your tools requires very little effort and saves time and money.
   A. Paint hand tools an obnoxious color. They'll stick out like a sore thumb, and fewer people will want to take them home.
   B. Assign specific tools, or a basic issue of tools, to each individual.
      (1) Provide a specific place where people can store their tools (e.g., a locker or bin with the employee's name on it).
      (2) Foremen should inventory these tools at the end of each day.
      (3) If legal in your locality, hold individuals responsible for replacing "lost" tools.
   C. Subtract dollars spent on "lost" tools, or tools broken due to negligence, from the bonus pool. Be certain to identify to everyone involved in the pool the amount deducted for tools.
   D. Buy high quality. Good tools last longer. The question is whether your company or a thief is going to be the benefactor of this extended life.

GASOLINE AND FUEL

Checks and balances prevent theft. Without them, theft is going to happen. The key to controlling gasoline and fuel purchases and preventing abuse is twofold. The following two items are essential to preventing abuse:

1. Have a system that tracks purchases to specific individuals and/or vehicles.
   Whether you use commercial credit cards or a bulk fuel outlet, be certain to review your monthly statements and/or receipts. Ensure that you're able to identify who made the purchase. Have individuals put the vehicle mileage on all receipts and turn in fuel receipts to the office on a daily basis.
2. As you review statements and receipts, look for excess quantities or the fueling of non-company vehicles.
   Let people know you're monitoring fuel purchases by asking questions. It subtly lets people know someone's monitoring this area; and that fact alone may reduce the temptation, and possibly prevent a theft.

PAYING INVOICES/BILLS

The method by which you process and pay your invoices can help save thousands of dollars by identifying overcharges, missed credits, and possible misappropriation. Here are some tips:

Processing Invoices

1. Process invoices quickly.
2. Job cost invoices within two to three days of receiving them.
   Memories tend to fade the longer invoices sit around unprocessed. It then becomes more difficult to solve any problems or to answer with accuracy those questions that may arise.
3. Match purchase orders to delivery tickets and invoices.
   Again, this matching is done as soon as the invoice arrives, not when you're ready to submit it to the owner and/or field superintendent for final approval before payment.

Paying Invoices

1. Only one person (possibly two) should be authorized to sign checks.
   Bookkeeping and accounting personnel should *not* be allowed to sign checks.
2. Checks should not be signed unless all supporting data (i.e., purchase orders, delivery tickets, invoices) are attached to them prior to signing.
   Since you have (hopefully) already pre-approved these items, the whole process should be very simple and completed very quickly.
3. Staple a copy of the check to the company's copy of the invoice, or annotate the check number on the invoice copy.
4. Attach the purchase order and delivery tickets to the copy of the check and/or invoice.
5. File this supporting documentation in a vendor file for future reference.

Safeguarding Bank Statements and Canceled Checks

The owner or CEO should be the *only* person authorized to open bank statements that contain canceled checks. This is done to prevent someone from doctoring checks or removing fraudulent payments.

SUMMARY

Accurate and insightful bidding won't mean a thing if *leaks*, misappropriations, or thefts drain your business. Good people do bad things when checks and balances are not in place.

This may seem mean and harsh, but I've seen case after case of theft by people I've known and trusted. I've testified at courts-martial and have seen military officers lose their careers and their futures over a couple of thousand dollars worth of merchandise.

How It Works

Not long ago, a contractor I know well told me that three of his employees embezzled over $40,000 from his company. This shocked me, as I knew all three of them.

I've seen large companies that were out of control lose $20,000 a month in inventory. It just disappeared.

You may have a family business and think you're exempt. I know of an individual who was embezzling thousands of dollars from his own brothers by running invoices for "side jobs" through the company. I know of a man and wife who were doing the same thing in a business owned by the man's father.

Believe me, if you provide the opportunity, theft is going to happen.

Believe me, *if you provide the opportunity, theft is going to happen*. The key to ordering and processing materials is to implement a system of checks and balances that will remove the possibility of theft or misappropriation.

ACTION POINT

Review your procedures and policies for ordering and controlling materials, and establish sound checks and balances where needed.

CHAPTER

53

A Word to Your CPA or Accountant

TERMS

Information Management System (IMS)
Line of Credit (LOC)

Purpose

To explain my role as a consultant to the CPA/outside accountant and how *we* can best work together as a team for the benefit of the contractor

Introduction

The pace of operations both in the field and in the office of a landscape or irrigation company make it essential that outside professionals associated with the company work together and are all "pulling" in the same direction. Otherwise, the contractor receives conflicting information and is often confused.

When I begin to work with a new client, I like to meet or at least talk with his or her CPA and/or outside accountant as early as possible in the process. I want to be more than just a name or a face (who in some cases may be perceived as a threat) to these key individuals who impact decision making and who help implement systems in the organization. To this end, I encourage clients to bring their CPAs or outside accountants (at no charge) to my one- and two-day estimating workshops.

The better we understand what the other is attempting to accomplish, the more we can supplement each other and implement information management systems that allow clients to direct and control their operations more effectively and more profitably. It's almost axiomatic that good business results from good relationships. As a member of a cohesive team, I can better meet the expectations of the client, implement sound business systems, and improve the directing and controlling of the company.

MY CONSULTING OBJECTIVES FOR THE CONTRACTOR

There is *no magic wand* to wave and no "pixie dust" to throw around that can implement the systems, methodologies, and strategies we desire overnight. It takes two to three seasons to collect and refine the data and to thoroughly train everyone on how to use the systems necessary to run a company.

There is *no magic wand* to wave and no "pixie dust" to throw around that can implement the systems, methodologies, and strategies we desire overnight.

Even when good systems are already in place, it takes this long for two reasons. First, the fast pace and operational necessity simply don't allow you to stop everything to fix what's broken. It's like changing a flat tire on a car that's still moving down the road—pretty difficult.

Implementing change in a contracting company requires a marathon approach, not a 100-yard dash one.

Second, it requires two seasons of data collection and analysis to diagnose all (or most) of what's happening within a company. Therefore, it's not until the third year that the fine details can be effectively addressed. Consequently, my desire is to develop a long-term relationship with a client and to bring about change in this manner. Implementing change in a contracting company requires a marathon approach, not a 100-yard dash one.

It will take a contractor four to five years to master and implement all the products and services I have to offer, whether it be budgeting and estimating, strategic planning, computer systems, etc. Meanwhile, I'm busy adding new products and services my clients will need in the years ahead. Lifetime clients, repeat business, and referrals are at the very center of my business plan.

My long-term objective for my clients is to not only implement sound information management systems as quickly as possible, but also to provide them and their related staffs with an MBA (Masters Degree in Business Administration) type of education concerning their business. Therefore, the team approach becomes even more critical when viewed over the entire life cycle of the business.

MY CONSULTING STYLE

I build a consulting relationship on the following foundational principles:

1. Business is a *process*. You don't *go* into business, you *grow* into business. The "quick-fix" approach simply isn't effective. It doesn't work.
2. All the systems, methods, and strategies I employ in a business are based, as much as possible, on *objective historical data*. This approach provides a logical audit trail that others can understand and relate to. This is not management by "mysticism."
3. *Lifetime clients*, repeat business, referrals, and *"partnering"* (where clients aid in the development and refinement of products and services) are at the center of my business plan. Customers are in a position to best critique all my services. Therefore, I continually attempt to qualify customers; and my customers, as part of a partnering relationship, continually qualify and improve me, the consultant, as well.
4. Business often appears *paradoxical*. Consequently, my style of consulting is
   - A. Immediate-results-driven, but over a long period.
   - B. Market/big-picture-oriented, while focused on the minute details of the business.
   - C. Market/big-picture-oriented, while focused on the personal development of individuals within the context of a business, by means of "mentoring."
   - D. Seriously humorous (or is it humorously serious?) in an attempt to break through the tension, mental blocks, anxiety, and tunnel vision that develop in the heat of operational battles.
   - E. Revenue- and bottom-line-driven, within the constraints of budgets, quality standards, safety, and schedules.
   - F. Entrepreneurial, yet socially responsible.
   - G. Analytical, yet intuitive. Analysis must lead to action; otherwise, it results in paralysis. Decisions must be made at the "gut" level but be based on, not contrary to, sound analysis. Otherwise, decision making becomes arbitrary and incomprehensible to other members of the organization.

MISCONCEPTIONS CLIENTS HAVE ABOUT A CPA

Landscape and irrigation contractors quite often don't understand the area of expertise of a CPA/accountant and the limitations of the profession. I often hear contractors complain that their CPA doesn't understand their business and fails to provide needed business advice. On further questioning, I usually discover that the contractor is expecting operational guidance, which really isn't part of the CPA's field of expertise.

I tell the contractor to look at the situation a little differently. Actually, asking your CPA or accountant for detailed operational guidance is placing an unfair expectation on them. It's like an NFL football coach asking the team's sports medicine doctor for strategy as to how to play the next game. The doctor can tell him all about a specialized area (e.g., training regimens, injury prevention, nutrition, etc.) concerning the players, but that doesn't include "field operations" (playing the game).

How It Works

A client in California had a CPA who for many years had done his taxes and tax planning. The CPA had an excellent reputation with many clients in the construction industry. However, his practice grew so quickly that he was unable to service his client base with the personal attention and thoroughness that had gained him his excellent reputation. My client decided to go elsewhere with his accounting needs so that he could once again obtain the personal attention that he desired.

I hear two other common complaints from contractors. The first is that the accountant's business has grown to the point that personal attention is no longer available. The second is that tax planning occurs too late in the fiscal year. Consequently, actions can't be taken to reduce the tax liability at year end. This often costs a contractor thousands of dollars, and an accountant loses a client.

HOW THE CPA AND I CAN BEST HELP A CONTRACTOR

I believe the best way for both of us to help a contractor is to understand each other's discipline and field of expertise, and where the two overlap. However, we both need to understand some important differences between our disciplines. In this manner, we can complement each other, without duplicating each other's work. I see the key areas of overlap, or "juncture points," as follows:

Budgeting

Three types of budgets were discussed in the Introduction to this book. They're the tax planning budget, the cash flow budget, and the estimating budget. The first falls within the expertise of an accountant. The third is in my domain, while the second could be either. It's important for us to realize that, although the three types of budgets do overlap, there are important differences, which are spelled out in the Introduction. It's extremely helpful to a contractor to have all three types of budgets in place, and that they be in similar formats. This will help the contractor better relate to the budgeting process, and it will eliminate confusion.

Formatting the Profit and Loss Statement

The P&L statement should have a format similar to that of the budgets above. Identifying direct versus indirect costs and the resulting gross profit margin (GPM) are very important in order for a contractor to properly identify job-related costs compared to administrative ones. Splitting and allocating general and administrative overhead item costs to divisions is not nearly as important as correctly identifying the GPM for that division. A sample format of a P&L statement is contained in Figure II-1 and is discussed in Section II and Chapter 3.

Job Costing

Timely, accurate feedback on a job-by-job basis is the number one need of any contractor. Whether job-cost reports are produced manually or by an accounting software program, getting this information in front of owners, division managers, crew foremen, etc., is the primary job for any **information management system (IMS)**. Accurately identifying actual field performance gross profit margins (GPMs) for each job (to include equipment costs) can improve not only the corporate bottom line, it can also focus management attention on the right problems at the right time.

It's important for both the CPA and me to strive to help the contractor implement an information management system that provides this type of information easily, accurately, and regularly. This leads to my next point.

Accounting Software

If job costing is the number one need of a contractor, a timely, accurate P&L statement is a close second. Identifying the GPM by division on a monthly basis is a very important management tool for a contractor. While job cost reports provide a focused job-by-job scoreboard, the monthly division P&L statement looks at the big picture. These two, used on a consistent basis and in the hands of the right people, can empower key decision makers and improve production dramatically.

It doesn't matter if monthly statements are produced in-house or by an outside accountant. The important thing is that they're accurate, and produced and used on a timely, regular basis. Producing these reports within the company is usually best if qualified personnel are available to do so. This allows the contractor to run reports as they're required. It also empowers the contractor and educates his or her team about essential components of the business.

Because job costing is so critical to the directing and controlling of a contracting operation, it should be one of the primary considerations when purchasing accounting software. Chapter 41 identifies the key information a job-cost program should be able to provide.

Because an accounting software program touches two critical yet different disciplines (accounting/tax planning, and operations in the form of job costing and the P&L statement), it's imperative that both the CPA and I work in harmony concerning this crucial information management system for the company.

Audited Statements for Bonding

It's important that both the accountant and I are on the same information management systems if we're to maximize our assistance in helping a client obtain bonding.

Line of Credit (LOC)

A contractor with timely, accurate financial statements, thorough budgets (all three types), and a strategic business plan (backed by two professional consultants just a telephone call away and who are reinforcing each other's position and backing the client), presents a formidable force when meeting with a banker to negotiate a **line of credit (LOC)**, or obtain other financing.

SUMMARY

It's essential that CPAs, accountants, and I understand where our disciplines overlap and where they don't. In order to meet the needs of our mutual clients, it's necessary that we work together, complement, and reinforce one another. It's also important that we share certain foundational consulting principles if we're to effectively service the needs of our clients.

Let's talk. Other items could be added to this list. The important thing is that you (the accountant) and I develop the list together in support of "our" client. We prosper only when the client prospers.

Please don't hesitate to call my 24-hour toll-free telephone number to discuss matters of mutual interest, or to provide feedback about what I've written in these pages. The more closely we work together, the better it is for our clients, and thus the better it is for us. As one of my favorite sayings goes, "The right hand washes the left, the left hand washes the right, and both hands wash the face."

ACTION POINT

Encourage your CPA or accountant to read this chapter and contact me if they have questions.

CHAPTER

54

Maximizing the Value of Your Business and the Business Life Cycle

TERM

Business Life Cycle

Purpose

To explain the process of maximizing the growth of business owners and staff and, consequently, the value of the business

Introduction

I love to talk with college students who are just starting out in their careers. I tell them that if they apply the principles in my estimating workshop and book, it will put an extra million dollars in their pockets throughout their careers.

Write down your answer to the following questions.

1. How many (more) years do you plan to be in business? __________
2. Enter what you expect your average revenue per year to be during this period. $__________
3. Multiply #1 by #2 (this is your total [remaining] revenue). $__________
4. Enter your expected annual net profit % before taxes for #3. __________%
5. Multiply #3 by #4 (this is your total [remaining] earnings). $__________
6. If you could implement the methods and systems described in this book, how much would #4 increase (i.e., 2 to 3%, 5 to 10%)? __________%
7. Multiply #6 by #3 (this is your improved earnings). $__________

LEARNING TO THINK LIKE AN ENTREPRENEUR

The vast majority of contractors (I'm talking primarily about the men here) wouldn't think twice about purchasing a new $10,000 mower. A new $20,000 to $30,000 skid steer, tractor, trencher, or chipper might cause a guy to kick the tires a second time. If it's a new $30,000 to $40,000 truck, fully loaded with gun rack and ornamental steer horns on the hood, we're back to not thinking twice.

However, try to get this guy (ladies, there's a reason I'm picking on the men here) to invest a few thousand dollars in systems (computers, business management software, consulting, etc.) and training for the office, and you have a major battle on your hands.

Starting a business in the Green Industry is almost too easy. It's staying in business that's the hard part. The vast majority of Green Industry start-up entrepreneurs are technicians. They understand the product or service, but they don't understand the business. But this is America, and this is how we pursue the American Dream in most cases.

I like to say that there are three great myths regarding business:

1. We should all be in business for ourselves.
2. It's great to work in and have your business in your home.
3. It's great to have and work in a family business.

In Chapter 51 on company structure, I stated that corporate sales and financial growth should follow the personal growth of the owners. That same principle applies regarding maximizing the value of your company. However, we'll take a slightly different path in this chapter.

A problem well defined is a problem half solved.

Whoever said, "A problem well defined is a problem half solved," hit the nail on the head. I'd add that a well-defined business (understood and laid out) is on its way to being successful. Figuring out a puzzle or riddle the second, third, or fourth time is easy. It's figuring it out the first time that kills you. By the time you figure out accounting, estimating, financing, management, administration, and leadership, in addition to the technical side of the business, you're probably ready to retire.

Understanding the life cycle of your business is essential if you're going to maximize its value.

Understanding the life cycle of your business is essential if you're going to maximize its value. You might think of it as a "cradle-to-grave" or "womb-to-tomb" approach. Or you might think of your **business life cycle** as the puzzle "box top."

A friend of mine was given a very large jigsaw puzzle with hundreds (perhaps thousands) of pieces to it. He spent hours one night attempting to put the puzzle together, but nothing seemed to fit in its proper place. Finally, he realized he was the victim of the gift giver's practical joke. The puzzle box top had been switched with one from a different puzzle.

Most contractors are operating their businesses without ever seeing the puzzle box top. Worse yet, they don't even know one exists.

THE CORPORATE "BOXTOP"

How It Works

A contractor in his midthirties started his business before he became a teenager. He had a plan and he worked it persistently. Years of 70- to 80-hour weeks were common. Perhaps he became a little too focused on all of the details of his business and he missed some of the more strategic employee issues impacting it. In any event, some of his staff had become too content. They were not pulling their load, nor were they behaving like managers. This was primarily because the owner did not cloud up, rain all over them, and make them do their jobs. They took advantage of the owner's blind side. Some of the managers even chided my client about all of the hours that he worked and his occasional dour disposition. They told him that he needed to lighten up and enjoy life. Where was all of this hard work getting him, anyway? They had a pretty good deal, mostly at my client's expense.

Frankly, all of this began to irk me. I felt that my client was overpaying his managers who were consistently under-delivering. I also knew that my client was a very shrewd businessman even if he did have some areas that needed some work. As he and I discussed this situation at the end of a very long week over a couple of beers, I asked him, "After working your business for the last 20 plus years and putting up with all of the headaches that accompany it, what do you think is your total net worth?"

We calculated that his net worth was close to $2 million.

Sure, my client had some blind spots and some management issues but he had an end-game strategy. He was also building equity. He understood the big picture and how to make money. His managers had no idea how much this man was worth.

THE PREDICAMENT

You must learn to think like an entrepreneur, not like a technician, when it comes to your business. If you are a technician, you need to know how to think like a technician. However, if you're a business owner, you'd better be able to think like a business owner. The same rule applies if you're a manager. Remember what Peter Drucker said: "Managers make sure things get done right. Leaders make sure that the right things get done."

Most people look at market chaos and see problems, obstacles, and deadends. Entrepreneurs look at this same chaos and see opportunity. They think investment and value. They don't stop at the obstacles; they see beyond them. They've learned to thrive on chaos. Tom Peters picked up on this theme when he entitled one of his classics, *Thriving on Chaos*. As entrepreneurs, that's what you and I need to do. We shouldn't be intimidated by it, as most people are. Rather, we should learn to thrive on it.

Most contractors don't see beyond their immediate chaos (or crisis), much of which they've probably created. To get beyond this quagmire, so to speak, one has to learn to think outside the box. To do so, you need a puzzle box top. Otherwise, you have no direction.

THE PROCESS

Get help!

Leaders are made, not born. We men like to think we're self-made. I assume women fall prey to this thinking too. As a single parent, I once jokingly bragged to my sons that I was a self-made man. They retorted that it was great that I would take such responsibility, because they then knew who to blame for all my mistakes.

See the big picture. Study your business and the people in and around it. Call in and/or visit the experts. Do your homework. Explore all the options. Never stop networking. Study and master the processes that make businesses successful. But do so within the context of the puzzle box top—the business life cycle.

A contractor who doesn't have a panoramic view, the puzzle box top, of his or her company is like a coach who doesn't understand the totality of the game. How can you expect to win if you don't understand the basics of the game you're playing?

THE PAYOFF

Whenever I do a seminar, I ask the attendees who among them has an exit strategy. Usually, only one or two hands go up.

I'm convinced that most contractors have an exit strategy that's something like this. They hope they die on a job site, preferably one where the crew is planting large trees that require a backhoe. They're gonna die right there. The crew is going to dig a big hole and bury them under a huge red maple. That's it! That's their exit strategy.

Unfortunately, even this plan contains more forethought than most contractors have put into their exit strategy.

If you had a McDonald's Restaurant® and you retired, would you chain up the doors and let weeds grow all over the parking lot? Of course not! You'd sell it. And you'd sell it for more than you paid for it. In fact, you probably knew the day you bought the restaurant that this was how you were going to exit from it. Why don't landscape and irrigation contractors and arborists think this way? It's because they're thinking like technicians and not business professionals.

Learn to think like a business professional, an entrepreneur. The payoff will be huge, not just 30 years from now when you sell your business. It will be "huge" today as well, as you learn to "think big."

Study Figures 54-1 and 54-2. They can help you understand how we attempt to maximize the value of a business. Figure 54-3 on page 452 will help you see where you need to focus your management attention in order to begin the business maximization process.

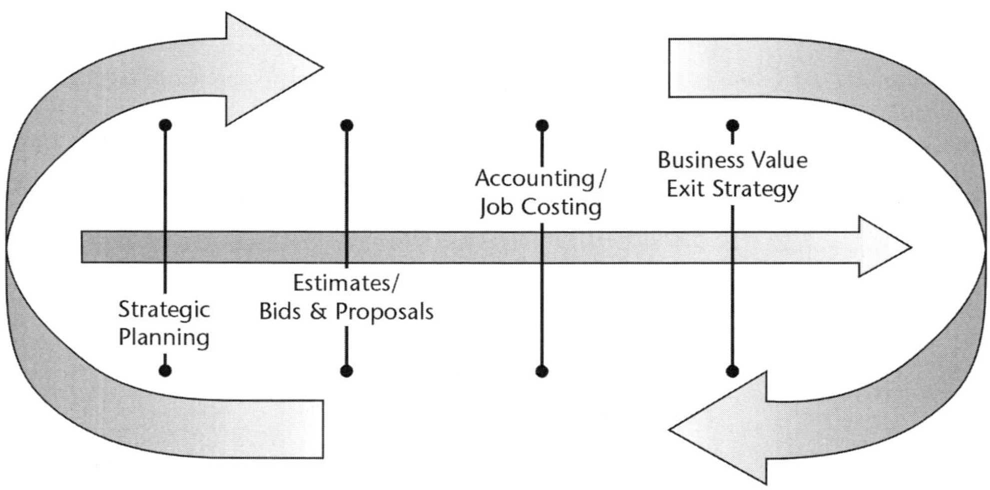

FIGURE 54-1 The Business Life Cycle

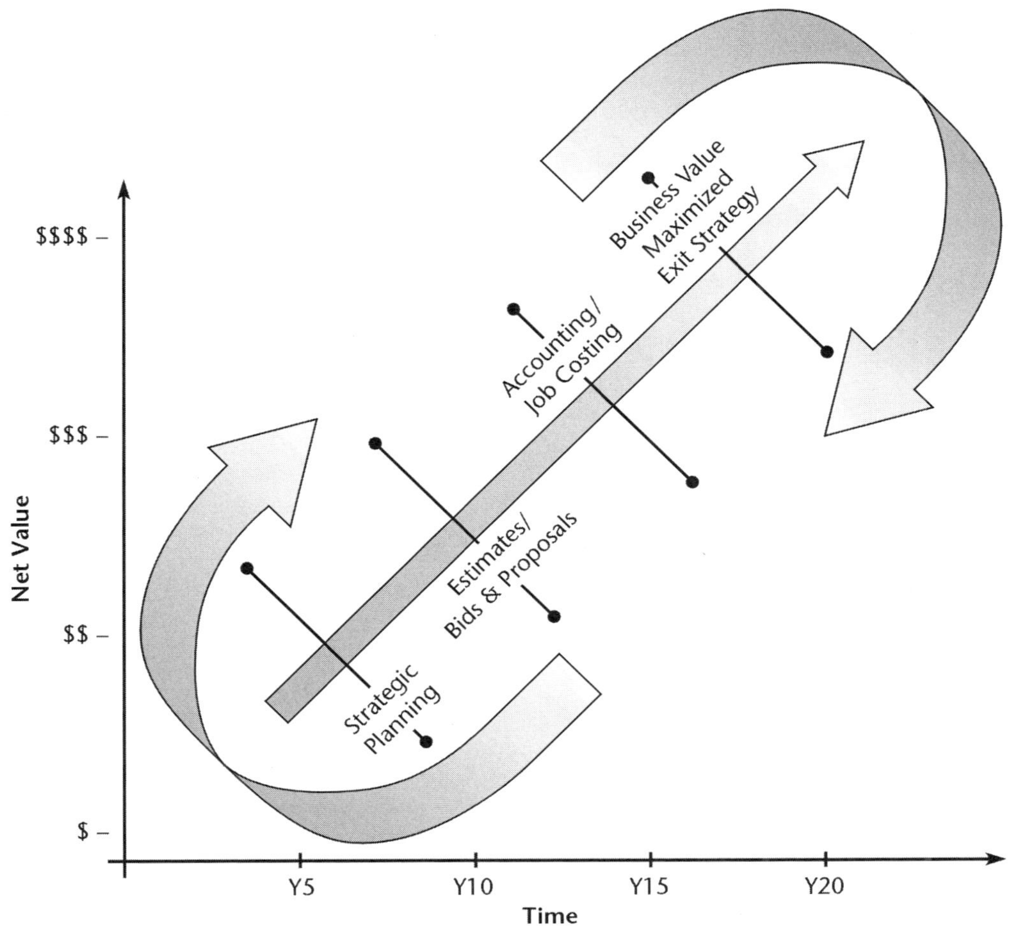

FIGURE 54-2 The Business Life Cycle Maximized

SUMMARY

There's a natural life cycle for any business. Maximizing the value of this business should be a primary objective for a contractor. Implementing the philosophies, methodologies, systems, and strategies outlined in this book will not only help you understand the life cycle of your business, it will also help you optimize its value.

ACTION POINT

Fill in your answers to the exercise at the beginning of this chapter. Then ask yourself what you should do next. Once you decide what your next step should be, take decisive action and begin to implement it.

Tactical issues prevail

Sales: $100K to 1.0M

___-Accurate estimating in place
___-GPM concept understood
___-Accounting & job costing in place
___-Incentives understood
___-Budgeting in place
___-General business plan
___-Basic marketing understood
___-Market predisposition understood
___-Basic finances understood
___-Coaches / mentors in place for owner
___-Basic systems understood
___-Legal, contract basics understood
___-Key crew leaders in place
___-Office manager in place
___-Build company infrastructure
___-______________________
___-______________________

Strategic issues prevail

Sales: $1.0M to 5M+

___-Standardizing operating procedures
___-Formalized training for all
___-Comptroller / general manager in place
___-Job costing for all divisions in place
___-Staff trained how to run divisions
___-Business & strategic plan in place
___-Sales training for managers
___-Managers understand marketing basics
___-Financial training for managers
___-Coaches / mentors in place for all
___-Information systems in place
___-Legal, contract basics, non-competes
___-Division manager(s) in place
___-Operations manager(s) in place
___-Exit strategy in place
___-______________________
___-______________________

JRHEI products / services that apply:

___-Business & personal coaching
___-Estimating book, audio & MSX CDs
___-Down economy book
___-Estimating workshop
___-Accounting workshop
___-Bidding with confidence on-site consult
___-Accounting w/confidence consult
___-Estimating budget software
___-Quick Bid software
___-Estimating starter kit software
___-Estimating Platform software
___-Job costing software
___-Bid Board software
___-Bid Board (manual)
___-M.A.D. Report
___-Maintenance consulting 1-2 x/year
___-Company structure / staffing coaching
___-______________________
___-______________________

___-Business & personal coaching
___-Strategic planning book & coaching
___-Standard operating procedures (SOPs)
___-Maintenance consulting 1-2 x/year
___-Strategic company retreats
___-Integrated accounting system
___-Buy / sell companies coaching
___-Market analysis for managers
___-Training for division managers
___-Incentive programs for all
___-Business evaluation training
___-Business value maximization coaching
___-Team building coaching
___-Systems implementation coaching
___-Exit strategy development coaching
___-Exit strategy execution training
___-______________________
___-______________________
___-______________________

Note: Check the categories that apply.

FIGURE 54-3 The Business Life Cycle Maximization "Point of Entry" Checklist)

CHAPTER

55

Evaluating, Buying, and Selling a Business (Business Exit Strategies)

TERM

Exit Strategy

Purpose

- To briefly explain the process of buying, selling, and evaluating a business
- To offer some examples and ideas concerning exiting your business

Introduction

Buying, selling, or merging with another business is a team event that can be quite challenging. Developing a viable **exit strategy** can be even more challenging. You don't want to do it alone. Assembling a good team to help you with the process is as important as the process itself. The quality of the team you put together will often determine the success of the deal. And by success we mean both short-term and long-term.

The primary team members you need are an attorney and a CPA who are familiar with the merger, acquisition, and divestiture process. Ask around, or call the Better Business Bureau for a referral to such specialists. Your personal CPA and/or attorney aren't always the right people for this team. However, they should be able to refer you to others who are.

It's also wise to talk to other business persons who've actually bought or sold businesses. Their "hindsight" wisdom can provide some invaluable insight into this process. Discussing this matter with a consultant can also be wise. I generally shy away from business brokers and some of the firms who specialize in selling businesses. Unless you're certain they can deliver, I'd especially shy away from brokers who charge a large up-front fee to help you package and sell your business.

How It Works

I had just gotten off the telephone with a client in the Midwest. Bob is in his mid-50s and has wanted to sell his business for some time in order to make a career change. His company is mostly construction, with some maintenance. The maximum sales for Bob's company were a little over $300,000. Last year sales were way down, less than half the maximum, because Bob had to take off a lot of time due to family issues. You wouldn't think his company was a good candidate to sell, but he just sold it for a little over $300,000. Both the buyer and he are very pleased with the deal.

Four years ago an irrigation client on the East Coast was approached (unsolicited) by the owners of two separate irrigation companies, neither of whom knew each other. Nor did they know the other had also approached my client. Both owners, one in his 30s and one in his late 50s, were doing sales in the $300,000 to $350,000 range and wanted to sell their companies to my client.

The potential buyer made a very good offer to each of the two target companies. However, both owners decided not to do the deal. My client and I were a little disappointed but felt the offer was a good one, which we didn't want to increase.

A year later, the owners of both companies came back to my client to ask if he was still interested in making a deal. My client said he was, and bought both companies for the same amount offered earlier.

An attendee at one of my seminars phoned one day. He had a million-dollar commercial maintenance company he wanted to sell. I told him it would probably sell for about $.60 to $.75 on the sales dollar, or in the $600,000 to $750,000 range. This would include assets and goodwill. I added that, depending on circumstances and the motivation of a buyer, he might get up to $850,000.

He said his CPA evaluated his business (using some elaborate business-school model) in the $1.7 to $2 million range, or about $1 million higher than my estimate. I told him that was great, but that he'd better get all his money up front, because he'd never see it if he carried a note for any of it. The numbers simply wouldn't work out. I never heard back from him.

Not too long ago, I spoke with a former client who sold his maintenance business to a private individual. A year or two later he went to work for one of the large consolidators. He was less than thrilled with what he saw. Management of the organization was chaotic and quality in the field was suffering tremendously.

He said to me, "Jim, you should tell your clients that if they want more work they should follow our trucks, find out who our clients are, and market to them." The insinuation was that quality control in the field was so bad that these accounts were ripe for the picking. My reply was, "Harry, they already are."

A few years ago the big story on the street, in the trade journals, and in the *Wall Street Journal*, was about all the acquisitions, roll-ups, and consolidations within the Green Industry. Most have turned out to be disasters. While not true in every case, you basically had a bunch of MBAs playing with Monopoly® money. Meanwhile, customer service, quality control in the field, and long-term financial stability went to hell.

TWO BASIC BUSINESS EVALUATION MODELS

I'm going to present two basic business models for evaluating your business and some considerations concerning the process of buying, selling, or merging with a business. The first of the two evaluation models is one I've used for many years. It's an empirical, rather than a theoretical model. It's an empirical process in that it has evolved over the years, as I've observed clients buying and selling companies. I call this model the Gross Profit Margin (GPM) model.

The second model is much more formal and of a theoretical nature. It's the basic model used for evaluating a business whose stock is listed and publicly traded. I call it the Wall Street model. Both models have their place. However, I'll primarily deal with the first one here.

Due diligence is a term with which you should become familiar. Basically, it's the legal term that means: do your homework. *Be prepared to do your homework.*

Due diligence is a term with which you should become familiar. Basically, it's the legal term that means: do your homework. *Be prepared to do your homework.*

Buying, selling, or merging with a business isn't just a numbers game. Many of the big consolidators have tried to turn this process into a Monopoly game of sorts. In some cases, I've seen heavy-handed tactics used, and that's one of the reasons for their failure. It was a "shotgun" wedding of sorts.

There's a definite psychology involved with merger, acquisition, and divestiture (MAD) transactions. Maybe that's why it's often referred to as going MAD. By psychology, I don't mean you're trying to "psych" out the other party. Rather, there's a psychological process you need to understand, especially from the seller's perspective.

If friends or family are involved, you particularly want them all to do their homework and to look out for their best interests. Encourage participants to obtain their own counsel or accountant to independently verify the numbers and the process. Go the extra mile to protect the relationships of all concerned.

Too often I hear "friends" encourage other business associates to violate or ignore good business practices because they're "friends." This often takes the form of borrowing or lending money without any written agreement about paying it back. My position is that, if you're truly friends, you want to have everything above board and in writing in order to protect the relationship.

I'm not going to discuss how you should structure the deal or value the assets. That's between you, your attorney, and your CPA. The buyer might even want to carry a life insurance policy on the seller, with the buyer named as beneficiary. You should also consider how you're going to pay the seller. Here are some options worth considering:

- After the sale, pay the seller a consulting fee for work done.
- After the sale, pay the seller a salary or a fee based on an hourly basis as an employee for work done.
- Pay the seller for a non-compete agreement.
- Pay the seller a signing bonus. This can sometimes be an incentive to do the deal.

How It Works

One day, I had lunch with three brothers who are clients of mine. One of their employees also joined us. I'd helped my clients buy the employee's company. I was a little anxious about the luncheon, as I hoped the employee was still happy with the deal. He was also a rather big, husky guy. I gambled that if he was unhappy and mad with me, I could outrun him. Fortunately, the former competitor and now employee was still happy with the deal, as were the three brothers.

MAD PSYCHOLOGY

I mention this story because one of my main goals in helping a client put together some sort of deal is that the deal has "legs," and no one suffers from buyer's or seller's remorse. The more we pay attention to certain key psychological factors in the due diligence phase of the process, the more successful it usually is.

Why Buy?

Someone who wants to buy a business is motivated for many reasons. Here are a few to consider. The buyer desires to

- Make a career change and buying a company is one way to do so.
- Gain market share and grow.
- Gain the assets (staff, systems, equipment, etc.) of the target company.
- Eliminate or reduce competition.

Why Sell?

Someone who wants to sell a business is also motivated for many reasons. Here are a few that are common. The seller desires to

- Retire.
- Make a career change and/or make a mid-life "adjustment."
- Simplify his or her life.
- Eliminate the headaches of ownership.
- Be part of a larger, better-financed team.
- Realize the value of the business that's been built.

Why Merge?

Reasons for merging with another company vary. They can even be a combination of the reasons for buying and selling. The following may satisfy the needs of both parties:

- Gain market share and grow
- Gain the assets (staff, systems, equipment, etc.) of the target company
- Eliminate or reduce competition
- Simplify one's life by sharing the responsibilities of ownership
- Eliminate some of the headaches of single ownership
- Be part of a larger better-financed team

Keep in mind that many contractors doing up to $400,000 in annual sales are often prime candidates for purchasing. It's not uncommon for an excellent technician to start a business and get sales up to the $300,000 to 400,000 range by providing great service and technical expertise. However, the strength of these types of contractors lies in providing great technical service, not in building a company with all sorts of conflicting personalities and the related bureaucracy. Their reputation for great work and service gets them plenty of work.

Unfortunately, they tend to focus on doing the work and not building the company. They'd much rather play the game than "sit on the bench" and coach it. These individuals are players, not managers. As a result, they create a monster for themselves. They don't develop the team to whom they can delegate administrative responsibilities, so it all falls back on them.

These individuals, their companies, and staffs are excellent candidates for acquiring. However, you have to understand how ego plays into this situation. It's an admission of failure for many men to consider selling their company. You have to pay attention to the psychology of this situation and explain why selling a business is not defeat. Rather, it's a very smart business decision if done for the right reasons and with the right people.

You should emphasize the following to the seller:

- You want to become part of an exciting team that's growing and going places.
- This will be good for you personally; you can focus on what you do best.
- This will be good for your family; it will give you more free time to be with them.
- This will relieve you of the bureaucracy.
- This will eliminate a lot of your headaches.
- You'll make a good salary (and bonus, if applicable).
- This will reward you and your family for what you've built over the years.
- This will allow you to make a mid-life adjustment of sorts.

EVALUATION MODELS

Both of our models are straightforward mathematically. Which method you use depends on who the buyer is. The large consolidators will use a method similar to the Wall Street model, while smaller private sales will often employ the GPM model to value a business.

What is the buyer actually buying? There are certainly hard assets and liabilities involved in the process. However, the buyer isn't just buying tractors, trenchers, and office equipment. The buyer is really buying the business as an entity that will generate future revenue streams. It's these future revenue streams and their profitability that the buyer's betting on. The likelihood of the future revenue streams and their profitability continuing is what risk is all about. Goodwill or blue-sky evaluation takes these items, which are not part of the hard assets or liabilities of the company, into account.

The Gross Profit Margin (GPM) Model

As its name suggests, the GPM model uses GPM to value the goodwill or blue-sky portion of the value for a service business. I've observed in the past 15 years that service companies normally sell for one year of gross profit margin for the blue-sky portion of the company. Assets (office equipment, field equipment, inventory, accounts receivable, etc.) and liabilities (loans, accounts payable, etc.) are handled separately from goodwill. Why the goodwill value for these companies calculates out to be one year of GPM is anybody's guess. It's simply the number that keeps reappearing in market transactions.

Based on Past Sales and Good Historical Documentation

The GPM model, based on past sales, is an excellent way to value a service business with good historical documentation. Three to five years of financial statements are available and complete. Analysis of the financial statements determines that the internal ratios and percentages within them are consistent and in line with industry benchmarks. Customer records and files are complete and in good order.

After the appropriate documents are signed and/or exchanged, I begin the evaluation of the company's goodwill by reformatting three years of the seller's profit and loss (P&L) statements. Basically, I put them in the format of our standard P&L, as outlined in Figure II-1.

The purpose of this exercise is twofold. First, we want to calculate the gross profit margin. Second, we want to calculate and verify the items in cost of goods sold, and general and administrative overhead costs. This will allow us to accurately determine the company's ratios and cost percentages, check them for internal consistency, and compare them to industry benchmarks.

The determination of the gross profit margin is extremely important for evaluating a service company. For whatever reason, buyers will pay approximately one year of gross profit margin for the goodwill of such a company. Benchmark GPM ranges for all Green Industry market segments in non-recessionary times are listed in Table 55-1 on page 458.

Determining the gross profit margin for smaller (up to $1 million in annual sales) target companies isn't always as easy as it sounds. Often the owner's salary is not a fair market value (FMV) salary. Also, it's usually not split accurately between the field and G&A overhead. As a result, the GPM is distorted.

The first thing we do in this case is determine the fair market value for the owner's time spent actually working in the field. Simply multiply the owner's hours working in the field by a FMV labor gross rate. This rate is normally the rate for a

Table 55-1 Green Industry Market Segments

Market Segment	GPM %
Residential installation (all types)	30 to 40%
Commercial installation (all types)	20 to 30%
Maintenance, commercial and residential	30 to 40%
Tree work	30 to 40%
Fertilizations and insecticides	40 to 50%
Irrigation service	40 to 50%s
Outdoor lighting	40 to 50%
Christmas decorations	40 to 50%

crew leader or a little higher. This is not the rate the client is charged. Rather, it's the amount the worker is paid per hour. Once the FMV labor pay is determined for the owner, you should then be able to calculate the GPM for the company.

In some cases, when you have a mixture of service work and construction work, you'll have to divisionalize the target company's P&L statement for sales and cost of goods sold. This makes the process a little more complex, but it's still the same.

You should then compare the GPM on the two to three years of P&L statements you calculated with the industry benchmarks. They should be within 5 to 10% of one another. If they're not, you should consider using the GPM method that's based on future sales for evaluation purposes.

Based on Future Sales

It's not uncommon that good historical documentation is unavailable for evaluating the goodwill value of companies with less than $1 million in annual sales. This doesn't preclude you from buying such a company. However, you have to protect yourself and manage the risk. To do so, you base the price to be paid for the goodwill portion of the company, not on the gross profit margin of past sales (because you either don't have or don't trust the documentation available), but on future sales. This method can and should protect both buyer and seller if it's set up properly. However, there are a couple of caveats when using this method.

Even if thorough documentation is available, many buyers prefer this method for new acquisitions—it provides the seller with an incentive for staying with the buyer and maximizing sales. This method also appeals to many buyers because it's "self-funding." This means a percentage of new sales is paid to the seller in addition to any salary or other compensation. If there are no new sales, there's no payment. However, if sales increase above historic levels, the seller has the opportunity to make more than if the goodwill were based entirely on historic sales. Assuming a 30 to 35% GPM on new sales, the buyer is willing to give up 5 to 15% of this amount to buy the company.

The other advantage of this method is that it can be applied to all types of sales. Construction work for companies with annual sales under $5 million generally have no historic goodwill value because the revenue stream is usually very dependent on the owner. When the owner leaves, the revenue stream tends to leave with him or her.

Construction company owners are typically much more directly involved with construction projects, their respective clients, and the relationships with them. Therefore, it's very difficult to remove and replace the owner. Service revenue, on the other hand, is much less dependent on ownership. Service customers tend to be more interested in the service than the relationship with the owner. Service companies are also normally more systems-oriented.

These factors make selling a service company much easier and more desirable than selling a construction company. However, one of the advantages of the GPM method based on future sales is that it can be applied to both.

When using this method, 99% of the time the owner of the purchased company becomes an employee of the buying company for at least two to four years. This is the normal length of the payout period for the goodwill dollar amount. The motivation for the seller to stay on as an employee is (1) to have a job, and (2) to maximize sales and thus increase his or her payment for the company sold. This can create a couple of areas of conflict that must be dealt with effectively.

- Future sales have to be priced correctly. Because the seller is being paid a percentage of all sales, you, the buyer, should check the prices on all bids to ensure that they cover costs accurately and that they have an appropriate GPM on them.
- You must clearly identify and define what "future sales" are and how you're going to track them. To do otherwise is to invite problems.

The Payout

The goodwill payout for such a deal is usually over three to four years. Payment for equipment and any other assets is usually paid upon the consummation of the deal. I've seen the payment percentage structure for goodwill vary. Some examples are 10/10/10, 5/10/10/5, 15/10/10, etc. where the first year is based on sales for the previous year. Payments for years two, three, and four are based on subsequent years' sales.

If sales remain the same as they were for the year before the sale (for all of the periods involved), you'll notice that the total of the percentages falls within our industry GPM benchmarks outlined earlier in this chapter. The incentive to the seller is to help the new owner sell as much as possible in order to maximize the goodwill payment, which is not a set amount.

The Wall Street Model

Since the late 1990s, consolidations within the Green Industry have gained much notoriety. Quality control in the field and customer attentiveness have suffered considerably. I believe this trend will improve as the large consolidators get their act together. In the short term, though, you have a lot of chiefs and laborers in the field, but too few middle managers to ensure that jobs get done and the expectations of the clients are met.

Roll-ups in the Green Industry were the craze when the consolidations seriously got underway. A roll-up is a form of consolidation. It's a stock market term describing a company that simultaneously consolidates $200 to 300 million in businesses and goes public at the same time. A roll-up is also referred to as a "puff" company—one that goes from zero sales to a minimum of $250 million overnight. Hence, the term "puff" company. Roll-ups fell out of favor on Wall Street prior to the Green Industry getting involved in them. Today, they are few and far between in the public markets.

Consolidations, both public and private, are the current trend. A consolidation is just what the name implies. A company or group of companies and/or investors gain market share by purchasing other companies. The acquisition of other companies is the easy part. However, these companies need to have "legs." In other words, they have to function efficiently and make money after all the acquiring's done.

This is where many consolidators within the Green Industry have had serious problems. They're just not run efficiently, primarily due to a lack of middle management and the appropriate systems to manage them. By systems, I mean a computer system that consolidates the entire operation and does the estimating, accounting, job costing, and so forth.

The Wall Street net earnings model is fairly straightforward. The formula is as follows:

([Annual sales – All costs + Add-ins] – taxes) × Industry multiple = Price

All costs includes cost of goods sold and general and administrative overhead. Add-ins are adjustments for the extra "perks" afforded a small privately held company that are not allowed in a publicly traded company. These add-ins essentially achieve fair market value as they adjust the financial statements of a privately held company and bring them in line with publicly traded company accounting standards. This formula brings us to EBIT, or earnings before interest and taxes.

Corporate taxes at the 40% rate are then normally deducted from EBIT. This is the tax rate the consolidator expects to pay the government. The result is projected net earnings for the target company. Net earnings are then multiplied by an industry multiplier agreed upon by the financial analysts of the consolidator. The industry multiplier is then applied to the net earnings. The product of these two numbers produces the price the consolidator is willing to pay for the target company. While some adjustments may be made, this price normally includes equipment and related inventories. Real estate is normally handled separately from these transactions.

Payment for the target company is typically made in cash and stock. Normally, the seller is paid one-third of the selling price in cash and two-thirds in the consolidator company's stock. The seller is also normally required to work for the new owner for three years. This is, theoretically, to ensure management and profitability continuity.

The Process

In order to avoid repetition, see the mergers, acquisitions, and divestitures section of Chapter 50 for a thorough discussion of this process.

How It Works

One recent winter, a client, an irrigation contractor in New England, was approached by a former employee who wanted to sell my client his company. My client and I worked for many hours on this deal as we tried to make it work for all parties. My client made the potential seller a very good offer, but it wasn't enough in the seller's eyes. Although disappointed, my client walked away from the deal, because he knew when to say "when."

A landscape contractor in the Midwest wanted to start a lawn maintenance division. A young man in his early 20s had a small maintenance business he'd started a few years earlier. He was a hard worker and his customers loved him. He had good values and was a good team player. More importantly, he was getting married, and was smart enough to set his entrepreneurial ego aside in order to be part of a larger team. This would also allow him to focus on his marriage at a crucial time.

Recently, I talked with one of my best clients in New England. Three years earlier, he'd bought a company. This client is one of the sharpest landscape business owners in the country. He did his homework and due diligence. He dotted all the "i"s and crossed all the "t"s. He'd talked to the seller numerous times, and knew his business very well. And still it didn't work.

Go figure!

SUMMARY

Evaluating a business is a rather straightforward process. We've covered two basic methods for doing so. However, buying or selling a business is quite different. There's a psychology that needs to be understood in order to have a successful experience.

Do your "due diligence." In other words, do your homework and call in the experts early in the process. Spend the time to find a good attorney and a CPA who have expertise in these areas. Not long ago, I talked with two of my clients who had just sold their companies. One sold to a large, privately held tree company on the East Coast. The other sold to a couple of private individuals in the Midwest. Both these individuals did their homework and both walked away with good deals. I should add—good deals for all concerned.

Set goals and deadlines when you're either buying, selling to, or merging with another company. And don't be afraid to walk away from the deal. This can be difficult, but it's often a critical tactic that can change the psychology of the process and ultimately help you get the deal done.

Remember, whether you're involved with a merger, acquisition, or divestiture, you want everyone to walk away from the process knowing they got a good deal. You do so through "risk management." You want everyone involved to feel good about the deal two years after it's done. Doing your homework, calling in the professionals, and doing the deal right will help ensure that both long- and short-term goals are met.

Doing your due diligence won't necessarily guarantee success, but it will usually significantly increase the odds.

Good luck!

ACTION POINTS

1. Review Chapter 50 for a thorough discussion of mergers, acquisitions, and divestitures.
2. Review the additional information in Chapter 51 on exit strategies.

CHAPTER

56 Concluding Remarks and Thoughts

DON'T PANIC!

This book covers a lot of material. The initial writing of *Estimating for Landscape and Irrigation Contractors* took me 888 hours. By the time I complete this rewrite of it, I will have over 1,700 hours into these two projects. Since 1987, I have spent approximately 45,000 hours working with and talking to clients; traveling to/from seminars, meetings and appointments; and researching and developing products for Green Industry professionals. This time spent in the "trenches" teaching hundreds of contractors and their staffs how to apply the material contained in these pages has been an enlightening experience. Believe me when I say that I understand if you feel somewhat overwhelmed right now. But don't panic. Numerous contractors have successfully implemented the methods and systems described in this book. There also is plenty of help available so you can do the same.

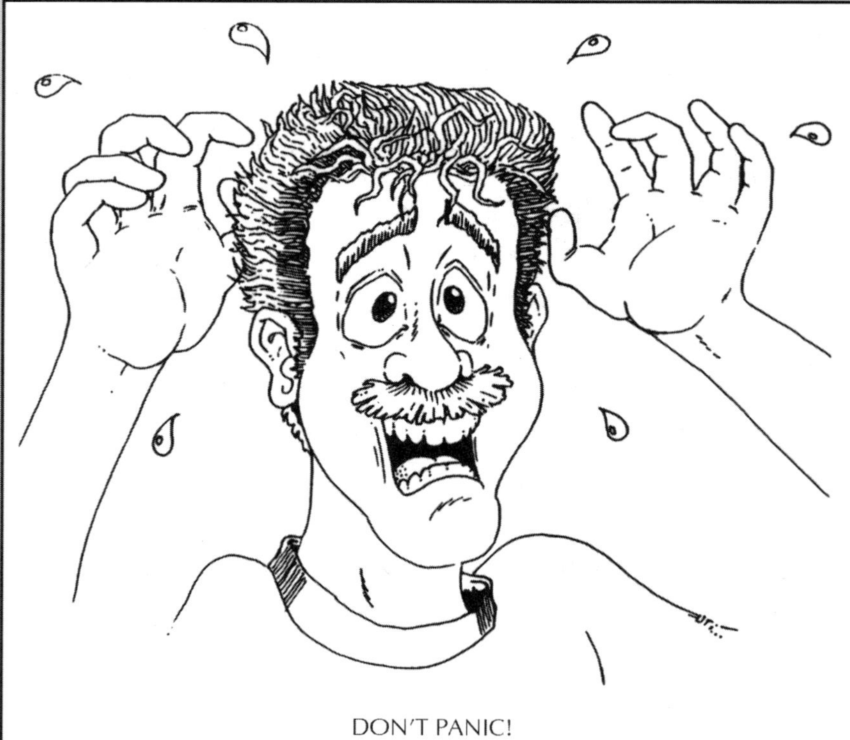

DON'T PANIC!

SEE THE BIG PICTURE (But Work the Details)

It is important that you see and understand the big picture (the puzzle box top) for your company. Once you do, the various pieces of it begin to fall into place almost automatically. You can then begin to properly plan success into your company using the methods of science to establish goals, targets, and budgets (standards) and to compare actual performance to them. It is this process of measuring actual performance against predetermined standards that produces a variance or deviation and allows you to gain control over the organization as you attempt to reduce the variances to zero. Remember, a good estimating system not only produces an accurate *price* but also a *plan* and a self-correcting *process* as well.

Peeling an Onion

Use this book as a reference tool in your company. Train estimators how to apply these principles at the bid table. Share the financial statement formats, definitions, and report formats with your accountant and CPA. However, keep in mind that you cannot expect to see significant results if you merely dabble with the methods described here. You must make a commitment and implement the whole system. Otherwise, you will not format and collect the data that you will need to adjust and refine the whole process. It is like having a race car with only three tires. You do not have a race car, just a pile of very expensive rubber, metal alloy, and plastic that is not going anywhere.

Compare the prices obtained from the OPPH (overhead and profit per hour) method to the prices produced by your present method of estimating. They should be reasonably close. If they are not, examine why and attempt to explain the difference. The OPPH method will produce a "safety net" price of sorts if you have done your homework. If you still have questions, call our offices to set up a telephone appointment to further examine your bid.

Keep in mind as you price a particular job that the key question is not how the GPM (gross profit margin) on that job compares to your annual budget. Rather, ask whether the job being bid at a certain price will help you realize your budgeted amounts of gross and net profit dollars (not percentages) for the year. Percentages are too misleading and mathematically incorrect when comparing yearly budgeted gross and net profit margins to individual jobs. It is dollars of gross and net profit that we desire, not percentages.

This leads to my next point: there is no right way to charge for or recover general and administrative (G&A) overhead. If there were, G&A overhead would be a direct cost. However, this does not mean that there are not wrong ways to recover G&A overhead. Consequently, the goal is not to determine the "right" way to charge for overhead but rather to effectively measure, allocate, recover, and control (MARC) G&A overhead costs throughout the company. The OPPH method facilitates this process better than any other.

UNDERSTAND AND INCORPORATE "PARADOXICAL" THINKING

Entrepreneurs think differently! They see something that ordinary individuals do not.

Entrepreneurs think differently! They see something that ordinary individuals do not. Within the context of business, we all need to think like entrepreneurs and understand the big picture. In order to build a great company, you have to learn to think like an entrepreneur. Sometimes you have to entertain concepts and thoughts that appear contradictory.

One definition for paradox is: "a statement that is seemingly contradictory as opposed to common sense and yet is perhaps true." There are many such concepts in business that appear paradoxical at first. They appear to force you into an "either/or" choice. However, upon further examination, that is not necessarily the case. Here are some that are worth considering.

Effectiveness as Compared to Efficiency Old school thinking often tells us that you cannot have both an effective organization and an efficient one. This simply is not the case. Effective organizations are often the best run ones. Certainly, there is some chaos as they respond to market changes. However, Peter Drucker in his classic book, *The Effective Executive*, reminds us of the roles of leaders and managers. Managers, he says, make sure that things get done right. Leaders, on the other hand, make sure the right things get done. One deals with that which is strategic, while the other is concerned about tactical issues.

Strategic as Compared to Tactical People going into business quite often come from a technical background. They understand one aspect of a given technology. However, they do not understand business. Worse yet, they often do not realize that technical skills and business skills are two very different and valid skill sets. You need both. You could call it "big picture" as compared to "little picture."

Big Picture as Compared to Little Picture When it comes to bidding and estimating, you have to keep two aspects of the business constantly in mind. First, you need to price your projects accurately. However, your job as an estimator does not stop there. Second, you have to bid and win enough work to meet your budget for the year. Otherwise, individual jobs may look great but you go broke because you do not have enough of them.

Analytical as Compared to Intuitive Cost estimating is an extremely analytical, scientific process. Bidding or adding margins and markups to estimated costs, on the other hand, is intuitive. How much net profit can you add onto a bid and still get the job? Bidding is more like playing poker than it is like accounting. You often have no idea how high or low the competitions' bids are going to be. Good estimators and entrepreneurs have to be somewhat schizophrenic to be effective.

Cost as Compared to Investment or Value Contractors often ask me how much one of my books, seminars, or consulting days costs. My response is always the same: "A fraction of what it is worth." They ask in terms of cost. I answer in terms of "value" and "investment." Entrepreneurs use terms like value-added and value-engineering. They do not just think hard, cold costs. They see activity and resources in terms of producing a greater good.

Startups as Compared to Exit or "End-Game" Strategies Why do we do what we do? Why go into or start a business in the first place? Great individuals, whether they be soldiers, leaders of countries, athletes, or small business owners have a "sense of destiny." They seem to have a keen awareness of what they want and where they are heading. They have an "end-game" strategy of sorts. Entrepreneurs have an uncanny ability to create and build wealth. And by wealth, I do not mean just money.

Cost-Up as Compared to Market-Down Analysis We estimators usually think about building a job in our minds much like we will build it in the field. We add cost upon cost. Finally, we get to a price for the project. Customers normally see things from a totally different perspective. Rarely do they share our cost analysis perspective. They see things from the perspective of the market. They could not care less about how much general and administrative overhead we have. They want to know what they are getting, when they will get it, and how much it will cost. "What are the specs? What is the budget?" and "What is the schedule?" are their main concerns. Entrepreneurs see things from their client's perspective as well as from a cost perspective.

Production as Compared to Marketing Lee Iacocca, former chairman of Chrysler Corporation, said that Chrysler trimmed the process of producing a new car model from five years to two. Chrysler did so by co-locating the designers, engineers, marketing personnel, and production people under one roof at the newly built Chrysler Tech Center. Ideas were shared, communication was enhanced, and creativity flourished. Entrepreneurs think about the "process." This book is all about the understanding the process of business and estimating.

THINK LONG-TERM

I used to say that it took 2 to 3 years to implement all of the systems and methods contained in this book. However, with the advent of business enterprise software and new technology and training methods, the timeframe has been cut in half. It now takes 12 to 18 months for a contractor on the fast-track to implement them. Once implemented, you still must constantly monitor and refine them. There are *no magic wands* to wave or pixie dust to throw at your business problems to make them go away. Study your business. Keep peeling (analyzing) its layers away like the proverbial onion, until there is nothing left to peel. Forget about the quick fix. We're talking about hard work, long hours, bulldog tenacity, and good old

There are *no magic wands* to wave or pixie dust to throw at your business problems to make them go away.

American ingenuity. You *will* see significant progress but it takes time because, as I said in the introduction, fixing your business is like fixing a tire on a car that is still moving down the road—extremely difficult.

STICK TO AND CONSTANTLY REVIEW THE BASICS

Since page one, we have discussed pricing (bidding) in conjunction with planning and within the context of the overall business process. They all must work together. You take care of the business (the systems) and the business (the systems) will take care of you. It is the responsibility of top management (officers, owners, and managers) to ensure that the correct systems are in place and used properly.

An estimating system, whether manual or computerized, must reflect the correct philosophies, methodologies, systems, and strategies. Otherwise it may contain serious and even fatal flaws. The primary function of an estimating system is to identify two numbers. The first is the BEP (break-even point) or *how low* can you go on a bid and still cover all of your costs. The second is the maximum price that the market will bear or *how high* you can go and still get the job. It is this bidding "envelope" that you are attempting to identify in the bidding process. Successful companies consistently price their jobs within this envelope. In this light, five of the six most common methods of pricing used in the market today contain serious shortcomings as they do not accurately or easily identify this bidding envelope.

The OPPH method of estimating compensates for the shortfalls of the other five methods better than any other. Use it, compare prices produced by it to your present pricing methods, and collect job-cost data to compare bid-to-actual performance. Make adjustments as necessary.

Fill out a blank bid analysis review worksheet for jobs that you have already bid using your present system and compare the ratios, percentages, and per hour standards to ones for the same jobs bid using the OPPH method. This exercise should give you some significant insight into your market as well as your present bidding methods.

GET HELP

Our books, computer estimating software, audio and video tapes, workshops, seminars, and personal consultations are all designed to help you implement sound business management systems as quickly and as efficiently as possible. However, in order to optimize this process as we attempt to drive, direct, change, and control the whole company toward increased profitability, let me offer some suggestions that many of our clients have used successfully.

Talk to other contractors about the systems and methods covered in this book.

Obtain a list of references either from us, a client, or a state or local association with whom we work.

Read our other books and attend our two-day estimating workshop or a brainstorming seminar and meet other contractors who use these methods.

Show this book to your CPA or accountant and discuss it with her or him.

Clients who take advantage of the full range of services and products that we offer realize the most improvement in their companies. Just like you, they were once skeptical. They were not about to waste valuable time and hard-earned dollars on unproven methods and overnight-wonder consultants. However, they did the smart thing. They obtained additional information, did their homework, and made an informed decision. Once that decision was made and the process begun, most found that the best way to get everybody trained (estimators, bookkeepers, owners, etc.) and marching in the same direction was to have one of our consultants come into their offices for a day every six months or so. This approach maximizes training while shortening the learning curve. Such 5 to 6 month increments of training allow individuals to use the information presented and to absorb it at their own pace. Questions between visits are usually easily handled by telephone.

I tell contractors to think of us in terms of that regular doctor's examination that we all should get. Have us come in and monitor the company's "vital" signs and train everyone how to get and stay healthy. It usually costs less than the amount that a contractor pays his accountant and lawyer each year. More often than not, the money saved (or the extra money made) on a couple of bids that we help you with throughout the season will cover our costs.

Do not fall into the trap that some contractors fall into. They like the systems and the methods taught in this book. However, they do not want their competition to discover them. This is myopic thinking. Think of it this way. If contractors in a given geographical area all had accurate estimating methods, they would reinforce one another's prices more often than not. You want 2 to 3 other contractors in your area reinforcing good pricing.

Costs are costs and, with few exceptions, everyone's costs are about the same. The problem occurs when low-ballers bid work and ruin the pricing in a market because they do not identify all of their costs. They keep grinding down and diluting prices until finally they go out of business. Unfortunately, it takes them five years to do so and for every one low-baller who goes under, two more spring up and take his or her place. It's like killing one fly and having 50 more come to the funeral.

Contractors with accurate estimating systems should and will reinforce one another's pricing. Therefore, the more contractors who use accurate estimating methods in a given market, the better. Encourage your local, state, and national associations to provide estimating training materials and workshops in your local market. It will help all concerned.

CONSTANTLY TRAIN YOUR PEOPLE (and Yourself)

Successful contractors consistently teach their staff good business skills. They coach and train their people by providing a "protected" environment of sorts. Call it a business greenhouse, if you will. Within this environment are all the ingredients necessary for success: systems, goals, budgets, methods, and more. It is within this protected environment that people are constantly pursuing goals while exchanging ideas and information. It is a beehive of networking activity.

Leaders are readers. They never stop learning. They teach their people to do the same. Leaders constantly take notes, ask questions, and seek out new technologies and ideas. Today's leading small business contractors see the benefits of the management and information revolution that personal computers are bringing to the industry, and they are constantly training their staffs to take advantage of them.

CONCLUSION

I trust that this book has helped you deal with the "numbers" side of your business more effectively. If you love numbers (like the Count on "Sesame Street"), great! If you do not, I hope that I have made using them more meaningful and a little less painful.

If you have it, listen to the six-part audio program that accompanies this book. I'd recommend that you listen to it in its entirety five times within the next thirty days. I would also recommend that you use the worksheets on the Microsoft Excel Worksheet CD that is available for this book.

I trust that the expanded portion of this book has been helpful. The sections on the business life cycle, market predisposition, industry benchmarks, Six Sigma, bonuses and incentives, company structure and growth patterns, evaluating your business, and others are designed to help you understand the context within which a contracting business operates. Call it a panoramic view.

And don't forget to work hard, to study hard, and to help people. If you help enough people get what they want, you'll get what you want!

I need to hear from you: the veteran contractor or estimator, the contractor or estimator just starting out, and the college student and/or professor using these methods in the classroom. Please make a copy of and fill out the survey form in the back of the book and tell me what you think of *How to Price Landscape and Irrigation Projects*. Better yet, get on board that train that is revolutionizing construction and service contracting management as it heads toward the year 2010. Come join me at a seminar. The trip won't be easy. Nor will it be a stroll through Hollywood. However, it should be fun, and it should help us to make a little money.

Come join the revolution!

Just another day in Hollywood

REFERENCES

Practical Exercises

INTRODUCTION

The following Practical Exercises assume normal site conditions. Unless otherwise provided, the following cost information applies.

Crew	3 crew members, 10 man-hours each per day
CAW	$12 per man-hour
OTF	10.0% (company average for the season)
RF	10.0%
CAW (w/OTF and RF)	$15.00 (rounded up for ease of math)
Labor burden	30.0%
Sales tax	6.0%
OPH	$10.00
Foreman/crew leader	$20 per man-hour (with OTF and RF)
Supervisor	$25 per man-hour (with OTF and RF)

Answers to Practical Exercises are found at the end of Appendix A. Some computer calculations on the computer worksheets differ from manual calculations due to rounding.

Exhibits 10, 14, and 15 provide additional computerized commercial maintenance, residential maintenance, and construction bid examples, respectively. They were bid using the J.R. Huston Enterprise, Inc. Estimating Program. The printout in Exhibit 15 is for the Henderson residence project outlined below. Review these bids to gain additional insight into the various ways of formatting your bids and the data contained in them.

Chapter 11 Phase I: Production Costs

1. Mr. Barkley wants two 2″ to 2.5″ caliper red maples and 10 assorted five-gallon shrubs planted in his front yard. He also wants 600 square feet of sod installed with the appropriate amount of soil preparation included. Mr. Barkley's home is approximately 45 minutes from the yard. The desired net profit margin for the job is 20%. Re-wholesale material costs, equipment costs, and production rates are as follows:

Amendments	$20.00 per cubic yard
Labor	1 cubic yard per man-hour to spread
Rototiller CPH	$10.00
Red maples	$175 each or $185 with a 5% loss factor
Labor	1 man-hour per tree
Stake kits	$10.00 each

Labor	2 stake kits per man-hour
Plant tabs	$0.10 each, 10 per tree
Five gallon shrubs	$14.00 each or $15 with a 5% loss factor
Labor	5 shrubs per man-hour
Plant tabs	$0.10 each, 2 per shrub
Sod	$0.32 per square foot
Labor	200 square feet per man-hour
Crew truck and trailer CPH	$8.00

A. Fill out the Recap Bid Worksheet for the project.

B. Fill out the Planting Bid Worksheet for the project.

C. Fill in the material and labor portions of the Planting Bid Worksheet

D. Fill in the rototiller portion of the Planting Bid Worksheet.

2. Prepare seven Bid Worksheets (the recap, soil prep, irrigation, planting, sod, maintenance, and general condition worksheets) and fill in all of the data for the Henderson project as outlined below. Do not fill in the General Conditions or Markup and Margins portions of the worksheets.

A. Materials list and production rates:

Item	Qty	Unit	Unit Cost	Qty/MHR
1. Point of connection	2	HR	CAW	N/A
2. Controller w/hardware	1	EA	370.00	.5
3. Wire UF #14	2,000	LF	.06	500
4. Backflow preventer	1	EA	347.00	.25
5. Quick coupler .75″	4	EA	40.00	1
6. ML schedule 40 1.25″	240	LF	.85	25
7. Sleeving schedule 40 2.5″	120	LF	2.25	25
8. Laterals class 200 1″	520	LF	.30	25
9. Laterals class 200 .5″	1,200	LF	.20	25
10. Valves w/box and fittings	14	EA	85.00	.5
11. Heads, 6″ pop-up	170	EA	9.00	5
12. Heads, 4″ pop-up	60	EA	9.00	5
13. Fine tune system labor	8	HR	CAW	N/A
14. Soil prep	6,300	SF	N/A	1,500
15. Trees 24″ box	6	EA	150.00	.5
16. Trees 15 gal	15	EA	45.00	1
17. Stake kits (2/tree)	21	EA	10.00	3
18. Palm (Wash.Rob.) 10′ BTF	3	EA	350.00	.25
19. Grade	6,300	SF	N/A	1,000
20. Shrubs 5 gal	215	EA	13.00	5

Item	Qty	Unit	Unit Cost	Qty/MHR
21. Shrubs 5 gal espalier	3	EA	25.00	4
22. Shrubs 1 gal	283	EA	4.00	12
23. Vine 1 gal	24	EA	5.00	12
24. Grnd cover (8″ OC 64/flt)	23	FLT	12.00	2
25. Grnd cover (12″ OC 64/flt)	36	FLT	12.00	2
26. Sod	3,345	SF	.32	225
27. Mulch (1″ deep 2,955 SF)	9	CY	20.00	1
28. Maint. 90 days w/1 fert.	3	MO	N/A	N/A

B. Miscellaneous notes:

Item	Qty	Unit	Unit Cost	Qty/MHR
1. Pipe fittings	25% of pipe cost			
2. Soil amendments (4CY/M)	25	CY	20.00	1
3. Fretilizer (125#/M)	16	BAG	15.00	15
4. Gypsum (120#/M)	10	BAG	9.00	15
5. As-builts	1	LS	100.00	N/A
6. Soil test	1	LS	100.00	N/A
7. Plant tabs	96	EA	.10	N/A

C. Equipment:

Item	CPH	Qty/HR
1. Tractor/skid steer with trailer	20.00	
2. Rototiller	10.00	1,500
3. Construction crew 1-ton truck with trailer	10.00	
4. Trencher, walk-behind	15.00	100
5. Supervisor's 3/4-ton pickup	7.00	
6. 21″ mower	3.00	5,000
7. Edger or trimmer	3.00	
8. Maintenance crew truck with trailer	8.00	
9. Materials/mobiliaztion truck	15.00	

Chapter 12 Phase II: General Condition Costs

1. Fill in the General Conditions Bid Worksheet for the Barkley project.
2. Fill in the General Conditions Bid Worksheet as outlined below for the Henderson project.

Foreman administrative time	1 man-hour per day
Crew truck	8 hours per day
Mobilization labor	2 man-hours at $15.00 CAW
Mobilization truck	2 hours at $15.00 CPH
Haul materials labor	6 man-hours at $15.00 CAW
Haul materials truck	6 hours at $15.00 CPH
Clean up at end of each day	15 minutes per man per day
Warranty labor	16 man-hours at $15.00 CAW
Warranty truck/equipment	8 hours at $8.00 CPH
Supervisor	1 man-hour per day
Supervisor's truck	1 hour per day at $7.00 CPH
Detail job at end of job	8 man-hours at $15.00 CAW
As-builts	$100.00
Soil test	$100.00
Crew drive time	1 man-hour per crew member per day
Load and unload time	1 man-hour per day

Chapter 13 Phase III: Completing the Bid

1. Calculate *your* company/division annual budget for:

   A. Total billable field-labor hours ________________

   B. Total estimating overhead budget $________________

   C. Annual budget SPH $________________

   D. Annual budget OPH $________________

   E. Annual budget PPH $________________

2. Complete the following exercise:
   Calculate a price for the Fuller's residence project using the data provided, the OPPH G&A overhead recovery method, and a Bid Analysis Review (B.A.R.) Worksheet found in Exhibit 9 in the back of the book.

Materials	$6,000
Field-labor CAW	$15.00 (with RF and OTF)
Labor burden	30.0%
Sales tax	6.0%
Equipment	10 days for a 1-ton truck and trailer at $10 CPH; 32 hours of tractor time at $20 CPH
Subcontractors	None
Job duration	10 crew-days at 10 hours per crew member per day of which 60 hours are general conditions

Warranty labor	16 man-hours for a 2-person crew with the crew truck
Crew	3 people
OPH	$12.00

3. Add the appropriate markups from your company and a net profit margin of 20% to the Barkley project.
4. Add the appropriate markups from your company and a net profit margin of 20% to the Henderson project.
   A. Include maintenance as a normal in-house crew.
   B. Include maintenance as an in-house subcontractor.
5. Fill out a B.A.R. Worksheet from Exhibit 9 in the back of the book for the Barkley project.
6. Fill out a B.A.R. Worksheet from Exhibit 9 in the back of the book for the Henderson project.
   A. Fill out a B.A.R. Worksheet with maintenance as a normal in-house crew.
   B. Fill out a B.A.R. Worksheet with maintenance as an in-house subcontractor.

Chapter 14 Unit Price Bids

1. Calculate the markup percent (or decimal) for the Henderson project using a 10-column accounting pad. Utilize an OPH of $10.00 and a net profit margin of 20%. Do not include maintenance in your unit price calculations.
2. Calculate the unit and lump sum prices for the irrigation items in the Henderson project.
3. Calculate the unit and lump sum prices for the landscaping and remaining items in the Henderson project.

Chapter 19 Time and Materials (T&M) Pricing

1. Use a B.A.R. Worksheet from Exhibit 9 in the back of the book to recalculate the curb-time and portal-to-portal crew rates, and GPM for the example in Figure 19-1 (shown at the end of Appendix A) after changing it as follows:
   A. Change the CAW from $11 to $12.
   B. Decrease the G&A OPH from $12 to $10.
   C. Decrease 10 man-hours per day per crew member to 9 man-hours, 5 days per week, and decrease the OTF from 10% to 5.6%.
   D. Decrease the daily production labor hours from 9 to 8 per crew member.
   E. Decrease the net profit margin from 20% to 10%.

Chapter 24 Irrigation Service Work

1. Use a B.A.R. Worksheet from Exhibit 9 in the back of the book to recalculate the curb-time and portal-to-portal crew rates, and the GPM for the example in Figure 24-1 (shown at the end of Appendix A) after changing it as follows:
   A. Change the CAW from $15 to $17.
   B. Increase the G&A OPH from $12 to $13.
   C. Increase the hours per week from 50 to 55 and re-calculate the OTF accordingly for time-and-a-half paid for hours worked over 40 hours per week.
   D. Decrease the labor burden from 35% to 30%.
   E. Decrease the crew truck CPH rate from $8 to $7.

Chapter 25 Lawn Maintenance Packages

1. Use a B.A.R. Worksheet from Exhibit 9 in the back of the book to recalculate the curb-time and portal-to-portal crew rates, and the GPM for the example in Figure 25-1 (shown at the end of Appendix A) after changing it as follows:

   A. Change the CAW from $10 to $11.

   B. Increase the G&A OPH from $8 to $10.

   C. Decrease the hours per week from 50 to 45 and re-calculate the OTF accordingly for time-and-a-half paid for hours worked over 40 hours per week.

   D. Decrease the labor burden from 30% to 25%.

Note: The above exercises were compiled utilizing numerous bidding scenarios found throughout North America. They may differ somewhat from the practices found in your specific geographical region. However, they are still valid for instructional purposes.

Remember: Estimating is often as much an art as it is a science. In many bidding situations, you may have less than complete information. In these cases you have to use your best judgment and make a "guesstimate" of sorts. Ultimately, you have to "sell" the prices that you calculate to your prospective clients (or instructor or classmates).

BID WORKSHEET

PROJECT: BARKLEY RES.

PAGE (1) OF (3)

LOCATION: 789 McKINLEY ST. LOS ANGELES

DATE PREPARED: 7 / 25 / 20__

P.O.C./G.C.: JOHN BARKLEY OTF = 10%

ESTIMATOR: I.M. DUNN

DUE: 8 / 1 / 20__ PH.: 714-726-2185 FAX: RF = 10%

CREW SIZE: 3 <16·10·10>

TYPE WORK: RECAP

HOURS/DAY: 10 CAW: $ 15.00

REMARKS:

DESCRIPTION	QTY	UNIT	U/C	MAT'L	LABOR	EQUIP	SUBS
- PLANTING							
- GENERAL CONDITIONS							

PRACTICAL EXERCISE 11-1 Bid Worksheet: Part A

BID WORKSHEET

PROJECT: BARKLEY RES. PAGE (2) OF (3)

LOCATION: ______ DATE PREPARED: ___/___/___

P.O.C./G.C.: ______ ESTIMATOR: ______

DUE: ___/___/___ PH.: ______ FAX: ______ CREW SIZE: 3

TYPE WORK: PLANTING HOURS/DAY: 10 CAW: $ 15.00

REMARKS:

DESCRIPTION	QTY	UNIT	U/C	MAT'L	LABOR	EQUIP	SUBS
-SOIL PREP <5CY/M>	3	CY	20-	60-			
-SPREAD AMEND <1CY/MHR>	3	HR	15-		45-		
-ROTOTILL LABOR <1 MHR>	1	HR	15-		15		
-ROTOTILLER <1HR MIN>	1	HR	10-			10-	
-RED MAPLES 2-2.5"	2	EA	185-	370-			
-LABOR <1/MHR>	2	HR	15-		30-		
-STAKE KITS	2	EA	10-	20-			
-LABOR <2/MHR>	1	HR	15-		15-		
-PLANT TABS <10/TREE>	20	EA	.10	2-			
-SHRUBS 5 GALLON	10	EA	15-	150-			
-LABOR <5/MHR>	2	HR	15-		30-		
-PLANT TABS <2/SHRUB>	20	EA	.10	2-			
-FINE GRADE	1	HR	15		15		
-SOD	600	SF	.32	192-			
-LABOR <200 SF/MHR>	3	HR	15-		45-		
-ROLL SOD	1	HR	15-		15-		
				796-	210-	10-	Ø

PRACTICAL EXERCISE 11-1 Bid Worksheet: Parts B, C, and D

Project:	Henderson Residence	Date:	5/20/20__
Location:	22 Berg St., Riverdale, CA	Estimator:	Ben Hadd
P.O.C./G.C.:	Bob & Sarah Henderson	Crew Size:	3
Phone / Fax:	909-248-4628	Hours/Day:	10
Due Date:	5/30/20__	CAW:	$ 12.00
Type Work:	Irrigation	Risk Factor	10%
		OT Factor	10%

CAW Loaded	$	14.40

Phase 1	Quantity	Unit
Total Labor Hrs	182	Hrs L

#	Description	Quantity	Unit	Unit Cost	Material	Labor	Equip	Subs
		Column Calcualtions			#VALUE!	#VALUE!	#VALUE!	#VALUE!
	TOTALS				5,357	2,621	293	-
	POC LABOR	2	Hrs L	14.40		28.80		
	BACKFLOW	1	EA	279.00	279.00			
	FITTINGS	1	LS	68.00	68.00			
	LABOR (2MHR/EA)	4	Hrs L	14.40		57.60		
	MAIN LINE 1.25" SCH 40	260	LF	0.85	221.00			
	FITTINGS 25%	260	LF	0.21	55.25			
	LABOR (4MHR/100')	10	Hrs L	14.40		144.00		
	TRENCHER (100'/HR)	2.5	HR	15.00			37.50	
	SLEEVES 2.5" SCH 40	140	LF	2.25	315.00			
	LABOR (4MHR/100')	5	Hrs L	14.40		72.00		
	VALVES	14	EA	66.00	924.00			
	BOX	14	EA	10.00	140.00			
	FITTINGS(7/VLV/$1EA)	14	EA	7.00	98.00			
	PENTITES(3/VLV/$.5EA)	14	EA	1.50	21.00			
	LABOR (2MHR/EA)	28	Hrs L	14.40		403.20		
	WIRE UF # 14	2000	LF	0.06	120.00			
	LABOR (500'/MHR)	4	Hrs L	14.40		57.60		
	QUICK COUPLERS .75"	4	EA	24.00	96.00			
	BOX	4	EA	12.00	48.00			
	FITTINGS	4	EA	4.00	16.00			
	LABOR (1MHR/EA)	4	Hrs L	14.40		57.60		
	CONTROLLER, WALL MOUNT	1	EA	370.00	370.00			
	LABOR (2MHR/EA)	2	Hrs L	14.40		28.80		
	LATERALS 1" CL 200	580	LF	0.30	174.00			
	FITTINGS 25%	580	LF	0.02	11.60			
	LABOR (4MHR/100')	21	Hrs L	14.40		302.40		
	TRENCHER (100'/HR)	5	HR	15.00			75.00	
	LATERALS 1/2" CL 315	1320	LF	0.20	264.00			
	FITTINGS 25%	1320	LF	0.050	66.00			
	LABOR (4MHR/100')	48	Hrs L	14.40		691.20		
	TRENCHER (100'/HR)	12	HR	15.00			180.00	
	HEADS, 6" POP-UP	170	EA	6.00	1,020.00			
	SWING JOINT	170	EA	3.00	510.00			
	LABOR (5/MHR)	34	Hrs L	14.40		489.60		
	HEADS, 4" POP-UP	60	EA	6.00	360.00			
	SWING JOINT	60	EA	3.00	180.00			
	LABOR (5/MHR)	12	Hrs L	14.40		172.80		
	FINE TUNE	8	Hrs L	14.40		115.20		

PRACTICAL EXERCISE 11-2 Henderson Residence Irrigation

Project:	Henderson Residence	Date:	5/20/20__		
Location:	22 Berg St., Riverdale, CA	Estimator:	Ben Hadd	CAW Loaded	$ 14.40
P.O.C./G.C.:	Bob & Sarah Henderson	Crew Size:	3		
Phone / Fax:	909-248-4628	Hours/Day:	10		
Due Date:	5/30/20___	CAW:	$ 12.00	Phase 1 / Total Labor Hr	Quantity 17 / Unit Hrs L
Type Work:	Sod	Risk Factor	10%		
		OT Factor	10%		

# Description	Quantity	Unit	Unit Cost	Material	Labor	Equip	Subs
	Column Calcualtions			#VALUE!	#VALUE!	#VALUE!	#VALUE!
TOTALS				1,070	245	-	-
SOD	3,345	SF	0.32	1,070.40			
LABOR (225/MHR)	15	Hrs L	14.40		216.00		
LABOR TO ROLL SOD	2	Hrs L	14.40		28.80		

PRACTICAL EXERCISE 11-2A Henderson Residence Sod

Project:	Henderson Residence	Date:	5/20/20__		
Location:	22 Berg St., Riverdale, CA	Estimator:	Ben Hadd	CAW Loaded	$ 14.40
P.O.C./G.C.:	Bob & Sarah Henderson	Crew Size:	3		
Phone / Fax:	909-248-4628	Hours/Day:	10		
Due Date:	5/30/20___	CAW:	$ 12.00	Phase 1 / Total Labor Hrs	Quantity 160 / Unit Hrs L
Type Work:	Planting	Risk Factor	10%		
		OT Factor	10%		

# Description	Quantity	Unit	Unit Cost	Material	Labor	Equip	Subs
	Column Calcualtions			#VALUE!	#VALUE!	#VALUE!	#VALUE!
TOTALS				8,309	2,304	90	-
TREES 24" BOX or 2" CAL	6	EA	165.00	990.00			
PLANT TABS (6/TREE)	36	EA	0.10	3.60			
LABOR (2MHR/EA)	12	Hrs L	14.40		172.80		
STAKE KITS (2/TREE)	6	KIT	10.00	60.00			
LABOR (3/MHR)	2	Hrs L	14.40		28.80		
TRACTOR (.25HR/EA)	1.5	HR	20.00			30.00	
OPERATOR	1.5	Hrs L	14.40		21.60		
TREES 15 GL or 1.5" CAL	15	EA	47.25	708.75			
PLANT TABS (4/TREE)	60	EA	0.10	6.00			
LABOR (1/MHR)	15	Hrs L	14.40		216.00		
STAKE KITS (2/TREE)	15	KIT	10.00	150.00			
LABOR (3/MHR)	5	Hrs L	14.40		72.00		
PALM TREE 10' BTF	3	EA	385.00	1,155.00			
LABOR (4MHR/EA)	12	Hrs L	14.40		172.80		
TRACTOR (.33HR/EA)	1	HR	20.00			20.00	
OPERATOR	1	Hrs L	14.40		14.40		
SHRUBS 5 GL	215	EA	13.65	2,934.75			
LABOR (5/MHR)	43	Hrs L	14.40		619.20		
SHRUBS 5 GL (ESPALIER)	3	EA	26.25	78.75			
LABOR (4/MHR)	1	Hrs L	14.40		14.40		
SHRUBS 1 GL	283	EA	4.20	1,188.60			
LABOR (12/HR)	24	Hrs L	14.40		345.60		
VINES 1 GL	24	EA	5.25	126.00			
LABOR (12/HR)	2	Hrs L	14.40		28.80		
GROUND COVER (8"OC)	655	SF					
MATERIALS (64 CNT/FLAT)	23	FLT	12.00	276.00			
LABOR (2/MHR)	11.5	Hrs L	14.40		165.60		
GROUND COVER (12"OC)	2,300	SF					
MATERIALS (64 CNT/FLAT)	36	FLT	12.00	432.00			
LABOR (2/MHR)	18	Hrs L	14.40		259.20		
MULCH (1" DEEP)	2,955	SF					
MULCH	10	CY	20.00	200.00			
LABOR (1CY/MHR)	10	Hrs L	14.40		144.00		
TRACTOR (5CY/HR)	2	HR	20.00			40.00	
OPERATOR	2	Hrs L	14.40		28.80		

PRACTICAL EXERCISE 11-2B Henderson Residence Planting

Project:	Henderson Residence	Date:	5/20/20__
Location:	22 Berg St., Riverdale, CA	Estimator:	Ben Hadd
P.O.C./G.C.:	Bob & Sarah Henderson	Crew Size:	3
Phone / Fax:	909-248-4628	Hours/Day:	10
Due Date:	5/30/20___	CAW:	$ 12.00
Type Work:	Soil prep	Risk Factor	10%
		OT Factor	10%

CAW Loaded	$ 14.40

Phase 1	Quantity	Unit
Total Labor Hrs	20	Hrs L

#	Description	Quantity	Unit	Unit Cost	Material	Labor	Equip	Subs
		Column Calcualtions			#VALUE!	#VALUE!	#VALUE!	#VALUE!
	TOTALS				830	288	140	-
	SOIL PREP	6300	SF					
	SOIL AMENDMENTS (4 CY/M)	25	CY	20.00	500.00			
	TRACTOR (5CY/HR)	5	HR	20.00			100.00	
	OPERATOR	5	Hrs L	14.40		72.00		
	GYPSUM (120#/M-80#/BAG)	10	BG	9.00	90.00			
	FERTILIZER (125#/M-50#)	16	BG	15.00	240.00			
	LABOR (1 MAN W/TRACTOR)	5	Hrs L	14.40		72.00		
	ROTOTILLER (1500/HR)	4	HR	10.00			40.00	
	OPERATOR	4	Hrs L	14.40		57.60		
	GRADE	6,300	SF					
	LABOR (1,000/MHR)	6	Hrs L	14.40		86.40		

PRACTICAL EXERCISE 11-2C Henderson Residence Soil Prep

Project:	Henderson Residence	Date:	5/20/20__
Location:	22 Berg St., Riverdale, CA	Estimator:	Ben Hadd
P.O.C./G.C.:	Bob & Sarah Henderson	Crew Size:	3
Phone / Fax:	909-248-4628	Hours/Day:	10
Due Date:	5/30/20___	CAW:	$ 12.00
Type Work:	Maintenance	Risk Factor	10%
		OT Factor	10%

CAW Loaded	$ 14.40

Phase 1	Quantity	Unit
Total Labor Hrs	38.97	Hrs L

#	Description	Quantity	Unit	Unit Cost	Material	Labor	Equip	Subs
		Column Calcualtions			#VALUE!	#VALUE!	#VALUE!	#VALUE!
	TOTALS				30	561	140	-
	LABOR (WEED, MOW, ETC.)	39	Hrs L	14.40		561.17		
	MOWING (3,345 SF/VISIT)	43,151	SF					
	21" MOWER (5000 SF/MHR)	8	HR	3.00			24.00	
	EDGE/TRIM	4	HR	3.00			12.00	
	FERTILIZE (10#/M)	2	BG	15.00	30.00			
	CREW TRUCK & TRAILER	13	HR	8.00			104.00	

PRACTICAL EXERCISE 11-2D Henderson Residence Maintenance

CREW DAYS = $\frac{23.0}{30.0}$ = .77

BID WORKSHEET

PAGE (3) OF (3)

PROJECT: BARKLEY RES.

LOCATION:

P.O.C./G.C.:

DUE: __/__/__ PH.: FAX:

TYPE WORK: GENERAL CONDITIONS

DATE PREPARED: __/__/__

ESTIMATOR:

CREW SIZE: 3

HOURS/DAY: 10 CAW: $ 15.00

REMARKS:

DESCRIPTION	QTY	UNIT	U/C	MAT'L	LABOR	EQUIP	SUBS
-FOREMAN ADMIN <1 MHR/DAY>	1	HR	20 -		20 -		
-LOAD/UNLOAD <.5 MHR/MAN/DAY>	1.5	HR	15 -		23 -		
-DRIVETIME <1.5 MHR/MAN/DAY>	4.5	HR	15 -		68 -		
-CREW TRUCK <8 HR/DAY>	8	HR	8 -			64 -	
-WATERIN PLANTS/CLEANUP	1	HR	15		15 -		
-WARRANTY LABOR	4	HR	15		60 -		
-WARRANTY TRUCK	4	HR	8			32 -	
-DETAIL JOB SITE	1	HR	15		15		
				Ø	201 -	96 -	Ø

PRACTICAL EXERCISE 12-1 Bid Worksheet

Project:	Henderson Residence	Date:	5/20/20__
Location:	22 Berg St., Riverdale, CA	Estimator:	Ben Hadd
P.O.C./G.C.:	Bob & Sarah Henderson	Crew Size:	3
Phone / Fax:	909-248-4628	Hours/Day:	10
Due Date:	5/30/20___	CAW:	$ 12.00
Type Work:	General conditions	Risk Factor	10%
		OT Factor	10%

CAW Loaded	$	14.40

Phase 2	Quantity	Unit
Total Labor Hrs	144	Hrs L

# Description	Quantity	Unit	Unit Cost	Material	Labor	Equip	Subs
Column Calcualtions				#VALUE!	#VALUE!	#VALUE!	#VALUE!
TOTALS				200.00	2,322.56	1,320.00	-
FOREMAN (1MHR/DAY)	16	Hrs L	19.36		309.76		
CREW TRUCK (8HR/DY)	128	HR	8.00			1,024.00	
MOBILIZATION (LABOR)	2	Hrs L	14.40		28.80		
MOBILIZATION (EQUIP)	2	HR	15.00			30.00	
HAUL MATERIALS (LABOR)	6	Hrs L	14.40		86.40		
HAUL MATERIALS (EQUIP)	6	HR	15.00			90.00	
CLEAN UP (.33 HR/MAN/DAY)	16	Hrs L	14.40		230.40		
WARANTY (LABOR)	16	Hrs L	14.40		230.40		
WARANTY (EQUIP)	8	HR	8.00			64.00	
SUPERVISOR (1HR/DAY)	16	Hrs L	25.00		400.00		
SUPERVISOR'S TRUCK	16	HR	7.00			112.00	
DETAIL JOB	8	Hrs L	14.40		115.20		
AS-BUILTS	1	LS	100.00	100.00			
SOIL TEST	1	LS	100.00	100.00			
CREW DRIVE TIME(1HR/M/DY)	48	Hrs L	14.40		691.20		
LOAD TIME(1 HR/DAY)	16	Hrs L	14.40		230.40		

PRACTICAL EXERCISE 12-2 Henderson Residence General Conditions

Scenario cost data	**$ or %**	**Remarks**
Crew size (# people)	3.0	Crew leader and 2 laborers
Crew average wage (CAW)	$ 12.50	
Overtime factor (OTF)	10.0%	50 hours per week
Risk factor (RF)	10.0%	
Crew average wage w/OTF & RF	$ 15.00	
Labor burden	30.0%	
Sales tax	6.0%	
G&A overhead per hour (OPH)	$ 12.00	
Net profit margin	20.0%	
Crew truck & trailer	$ 10.00	
Curb-time man-hours per day	240.0	
Number of units	1.0	LS

Scenario	**Materials**	**Labor**		**Equipment**	**CPH**	**Hours**	**Item**
I. Production (on-site or curb-time costs)							
	$ 6,000.00	240.0	Man-hours	$ 640.00	$ 20.00	32.0	Tractor
	$ -			$ -	$ -	0.0	
	$ -	$ 15.00		$ -	$ -	0.0	
	$ 6,000.00	$ 3,600.00		$ 640.00			
II. General conditions (off-site or non-curb-time) costs							
		60.0	Man-hours	$ 800.00	$ 10.00	80.0	Crew truck & trailer
		16.0	Warranty	$ 80.00	$ 10.00	8.0	Crew truck & trailer (Warranty)
	$ -	$ 15.00		$ -	$ -	0.0	
	$ -	$ 1,140.00		$ 880.00			
Subtotals	**$ 6,000**	**$ 4,740**		**$ 1,520**			
III. Margins & markups							
A. Sales tax	$ 360						
B. Labor burden		$ 1,422					
Subtotals	**$ 6,360**	**$ 6,162**		**$ 1,520**			
Total direct costs (TDC)						**$ 14,042**	**TDC**
C. G&A overhead costs 300 (Total number of man-hours x OPH)				$ 12.00	=	$ 3,600	
BEP (TDC + G&A overhead)						**$ 17,642**	**BEP**
D. Contingency factor (if desired)						$ -	
E. Net profit margin 20.00%						$ 4,411	
F. Total price						**$ 22,053**	**Total price**

IV. Scenario analysis

A. Curb-time rate (Total price ÷ Curb-time hours)

$ 22,053 divided by 240.0 = **$ 91.89** **Curb-time rate**

B. Portal-to-portal rate (Total price ÷ all hours)

$ 22,053 divided by 300.0 = **$ 73.51** **Portal-to-portal rate**

C. Gross profit margin ((G&A overhead + Net profit) ÷ Total price)

$ 8,011 ÷ $ 22,053 = **36.3%** **GPM**

PRACTICAL EXERCISE 13-2 Fuller Residence Recap

BID WORKSHEET

PROJECT: BARKLEY RES. PAGE (1) OF (3)

LOCATION: 789 McKINLEY ST. LOS ANGEES DATE PREPARED: 7 / 25 / 20__

P.O.C./G.C.: JOHN BARKLEY OTF = 10% ESTIMATOR: I. M. DUNN

DUE: 8 / 1 / 20__ PH.: 714-726-2185 FAX: RF = 10% CREW SIZE: 3 <16·10·10>

TYPE WORK: RECAP HOURS/DAY: 10 CAW: $ 15.00

REMARKS:

DESCRIPTION	QTY	UNIT	U/C	MAT'L	LABOR	EQUIP	SUBS
- PLANTING				796 -	210 -	10 -	—
- GENERAL CONDITIONS				Ø	201 -	96 -	—
				796 -	411 -	106 -	Ø -
- SALES TAX	6	%		48 -	—	—	—
- LABOR BURDEN	30	%		—	123 -	—	—
				844 -	534 -	106 -	Ø -
					844 -		
					106 -		
					Ø		
SUBTOTAL					1484 -	◁—— TDC	
- G&A OVERHEAD	27	HR	10 -		270 -		
SUBTOTAL					1754 -	◁—— BEP	
- CONTINGENCY FACTOR	0	%			Ø -		
SUBTOTAL					1754 -		
- NET PROFIT MARGIN	20	%			439 -		
- FINAL PRICE					2193 -		

TDC = $1,484 or 68%

BEP = $1,754 or 80%

G&A OVHD = $270 or 12%

NET PM = $439 or 20%

GPM = $709 or 32%

SPH or RPH: $2,193 ÷ 27 HRS = $81.22

PRACTICAL EXERCISE 13-3 Bid Worksheet

BID WORKSHEET

PROJECT: HENDERSON RES. PAGE (1) OF (7)

LOCATION: 22 BERG ST. RIVERDALE, CA DATE PREPARED: 5 / 20 / 20__

P.O.C/G.C.: BOB & SARAH HENDERSON OTF = 10% ESTIMATOR: BEN HADD

DUE: 5 / 30 / 20__ PH.: 909-248-4628 FAX: RF = 10% CREW SIZE: 3 <16·10·10>

TYPE WORK: RECAP HOURS/DAY: 10 CAW: $ 15.00

REMARKS:

DESCRIPTION	QTY	UNIT	U/C	MAT'L	LABOR	EQUIP	SUBS
-IRRIGATION				5357-	2621-	293-	—
-PLANTING				8309-	2304-	90-	—
-SOIL PREP				830-	288-	140-	—
-SOD				1070-	245-	—	—
-MAINTENANCE				30-	561-	140-	—
-GENERAL CONDITIONS				200-	2323-	1320-	—
SUBTOTAL				15796-	8342-	1983-	Ø
-SALES TAX	6	%		948-	—	—	—
-LABOR BURDEN	30	%		—	2503-	—	—
SUBTOTAL				16744-	10845-	1983-	Ø
					16744-		
					1983-		
					Ø		
					29572- (TDC)		
-G&A OVERHEAD	562	HR	10-		5620-		
					35192- (BEP)		
-CONTINGENCY FACTOR	Ø	%			Ø		
					35192-		
-NET PROFIT MARGIN	20	%			8798-		
-FINAL PRICE					43990-		

$35,192 ÷ <1-.2> = (→ FINAL PRICE)

PRACTICAL EXERCISE 13-4 Bid Worksheet: Part A

BID WORKSHEET

PROJECT: HENDERSON RES. PAGE (1) OF (7)
LOCATION: 22 BERG ST. RIVERDALE, CA DATE PREPARED: 5 / 20 / 20__
P.O.C./G.C.: BOB & SARAH HENDERSON OTF = 10% ESTIMATOR: BEN HADD
DUE: 5 / 30 / 20__ PH.: 909-248-4628 FAX: RF = 10% CREW SIZE: 3 <16·10·10>
TYPE WORK: RECAP <MAINT. AS SUBCONTRACTOR> HOURS/DAY: 10 CAW: $ 15.00
REMARKS:

DESCRIPTION	QTY	UNIT	U/C	MAT'L	LABOR	EQUIP	SUBS
- IRRIGATION				5357 -	2621 -	293 -	—
- PLANTING				8309 -	2309 -	90 -	—
- SOIL PREP				830 -	288 -	140 -	—
- SOD				1070 -	245 -	—	—
- MAINTENANCE				—	—	—	1300 -
- GENERAL CONDITIONS				200 -	2323 -	1320 -	—
SUBTOTAL				15766 -	7781 -	1843 -	1300 -
- SALES TAX	6	%		946 -			
- LABOR BURDEN	30	%			2334 -		
SUBTOTAL				16712 -	10115 -	1843 -	1300 -
				→	16712 -		
					1843 -	←	
					1300 -	←	
					29970 -	← TDC	
- G&A OVERHEAD	523	HR	10 -		5230 -		
					35200 -	← BEP	
- CONTINGENCY FACTOR	Ø	%			Ø -		
					35200 -		
- NET PROFIT MARGIN	20	%			8800 -		
- FINAL PRICE					44000 -		

$35,200 ÷ <1 − .2> =

PRACTICAL EXERCISE 13-4 Bid Worksheet: Part B

Scenario cost data	$ or %	Remarks
Crew size (# people)	3.0	Crew leader and 2 laborers
Crew average wage (CAW)	$ 12.00	
Man-hours per man per day	$ 10.00	
Overtime factor (OTF)	10.0%	50 hours per week
Risk factor (RF)	10.0%	
Crew average wage w/OTF & RF	$ 14.40	
Labor burden	30.0%	
Sales tax	6.0%	
G&A overhead per hour (OPH)	$ 10.00	
Net profit margin	20.0%	
Crew truck & trailer	$ 10.00	
Curb-time man-hours	NA	
Number of units	1	LS

Scenario	Materials	Labor	Equipment	Subcontractors	Subtotals
I. Production or "Curb" time costs					
	$ 796	$ 202	$ 10	$ -	
	$ 796	$ 202	$ 10	$ -	**$ 1,008.00**
II. General conditions (off-site or non-curb-time) costs					
	$ -	$ 192	$ 96	$ -	
	$ -	$ 192	$ 96	$ -	**$ 288**
Subtotals	**$ 796**	**$ 394**	**$ 106**	**$ -**	**$ 1,296**
III. Margins & markups					
A. Sales tax	$ 48				
B. Labor burden		$ 118			
Subtotals	**$ 844**	**$ 512**	**$ 106**	**$ -**	
Total direct costs (TDC)				**$ 1,462**	**TDC**
C. G&A overhead costs 27.0 (Number of man-hours x OPH)			$ 10.00 =	$ 270	
BEP (TDC + G&A overhead)				**$ 1,732**	**BEP**
D. Contingency factor (if desired)				$ -	
E. Net profit margin 20.00%				$ 433	
F. Total price				**$ 2,165**	

IV. Scenario analysis

A. Unit Price (Total price ÷ units)

$ 2,165 divided by 1.0 = **$ 2,165 Total price**

B. Sales or revenue per man-hour (Total price ÷ all man hours)

$ 2,165 divided by 27.0 = **$ 80.17 SPH or RPH**

C. Gross profit margin ((G&A overhead ÷ Net profit) ÷ Total price)

$ 703 ÷ $ 2,165 = **32.5% GPM**

PRACTICAL EXERCISE 13-5 Recap Worksheet for Barkley Residence

Scenario cost data	$ or %	Remarks
Crew size (# people)	3.0	Crew leader plus 2 laborers
Crew average wage (CAW)	$ 12.00	
Man-hours per man per day	10.0	
Overtime factor (OTF)	10.0%	50 hours per week
Risk factor (RF)	10.0%	
Crew average wage w/OTF & RF	$ 14.40	
Labor burden	30.0%	
Sales tax	6.0%	
G&A overhead per hour (OPH)	$ 10.00	
Net profit margin	20.0%	
One ton crew truck with trailer	$ 10.00	
Curb time man-hours	NA	
Number of units	1	LS

Scenario	Materials	Labor	Equipment	Subcontractors	Subtotals
I. Production or "Curb" time costs					
	$ 15,629	$ 6,019	$ 663	$ -	
	$ 15,629	$ 6,019	$ 663	$ -	$ 22,310
II. General conditions (off-site or non-curb-time costs)					
	$ 200	$ 2,323	$ 1,320	$ -	
	$ 200	$ 2,323	$ 1,320	$ -	$ 3,843
Subtotals	**$ 15,829**	**$ 8,341**	**$ 1,983**	**$ -**	**$ 26,152**
III. Margins & markups					
A.Sales ta	$ 950				
B.Labor burden		$ 2,502			
Subtotals	**$ 16,778**	**$ 10,844**	**$ 1,983**	**$ -**	
Total direct costs (TDC)				**$ 29,605**	**TDC**
C. G&A overhead costs					
562.0 (Number of man-hours x OPH)			$ 10.00 =	$ 5,620	
BEP (TDC + G&A overhead)				**$ 35,224**	**BEP**
D. Contingency factor (if desired)				$ -	
E. Net profit margin 20.00%				$ 8,806	
F. Total price				**$ 44,030**	

IV. Scenario analysis

A. Unit price (Total price ÷ units)

$ 44,030 divided by 1.0 = **$ 44,030 Total price**

B. Sales or revenue per man-hour (Total price ÷ all man-hours)

$ 44,030 divided by 562.0 = **$ 78.35 SPH or RPH**

C. Gross profit margin ((G&A overhead + Net profit) ÷ Total price)

$ 14,426 ÷ $ 44,030 = **32.8% GPM**

PRACTICAL EXERCISE 13-6A Recap Worksheet for Henderson Residence

Scenario cost data	$ or %	Remarks
Crew size (# people)	3.0	Crew leader plus 2 laborers
Crew average wage (CAW)	$ 12.00	
Man-hours per man per day	10.0	
Overtime factor (OTF)	10.0%	50 hours per week
Risk factor (RF)	10.0%	
Crew average wage w/OTF & RF	$ 14.40	
Labor burden	30.0%	
Sales tax	6.0%	
G&A overhead per hour (OPH)	$ 10.00	
Net profit margin	20.0%	
One ton crew truck with trailer	$ 10.00	
Curb time man-hours	NA	
Number of units	1	LS

Scenario	Materials	Labor	Equipment	Subcontractors	Subtotals
I. Production or "Curb" time costs					
	$ 15,599	$ 5,458	$ 523	$ 1,300	
	$ 15,599	$ 5,458	$ 523	$ 1,300	**$ 22,879**
II. General conditions (off-site or non-curb-time costs)					
	$ 200	$ 2,323	$ 1,320	$ -	
	$ 200	$ 2,323	$ 1,320	$ -	**$ 3,843**
Subtotals	**$ 15,799**	**$ 7,780**	**$ 1,843**	**$ 1,300**	**$ 26,721**
III. Margins & markups					
A.Sales ta	$ 948				
B.Labor burden		$ 2,334			
Subtotals	**$ 16,747**	**$ 10,114**	**$ 1,843**	**$ 1,300**	
Total direct costs (TDC)				**$ 30,003**	**TDC**
C. G&A overhead costs 523.0 (Number of man-hours x OPH)			$ 10.00 =	$ 5,230	
BEP (TDC + G&A overhead)				**$ 35,233**	**BEP**
D. Contingency factor (if desired)				$ -	
E. Net profit margin 20.00%				$ 8,808	
F. Total price				**$ 44,042**	

IV. Scenario analysis

A. Unit price (Total price ÷ units)

$ 44,042 divided by 1.0 = **$ 44,042 Total price**

B. Sales or revenue per man-hour (Total price ÷ all man-hours)

$ 44,042 divided by 523.0 = **$ 84.21 SPH or RPH**

C. Gross profit margin ((G&A overhead + Net profit) ÷ Total price)

$ 14,038 ÷ $ 44,042 = **31.9% GPM**

PRACTICAL EXERCISE 13-6B Recap Worksheet for Henderson Residence (Maintenance as Sub)

HENDERSON RESIDENCE

UNIT PRICE BID

(1) 2130 ÷ .57 = 3737

(2) 3737 ÷ 14 <# units in Col #1> = 266.93

(3) Round to 275

(4) multiply 275 by # units

UNIT PRICE WORKSHEET SMITH HUSTON, INC.-16-A

ITEM NO.	DESCRIPTION	QUANTITY (1)	UNIT (2)	MATERIALS + SALES TAX (3)	LABOR + BURDEN (5)	EQUIPMENT (7)	TOTALS (8)	MARKUP .57 (9)	UNIT PRICE (10)	UNIT PRICE ROUNDED (11)	TOTAL PRICES (12)
1	MOBILIZATION	1	LS								
2	BACKFLOW PREVENTER	1	EA	368	112	—	480	842	842	845	845
3	VALVES <W/FINE TUNE + WIRE>	14	EA	1381	749	—	2130	3737	266 93	275	3850 (4)
4	QUICK COUPLERS	4	EA	170	75	—	245	430	107 50	110	440
5	MAIN LINE 1.25"	240	LF	293	187	38	518	909	379	395	948
6	SLEEVES 2.5"	120	LF	334	94	—	428	751	626	650	780
7	CONTROLLER	1	EA	392	37	—	429	753	753	755	755
8	LATERAL LINE 1"	520	LF	197	393	75	665	1167	224	225	1170
9	LATERAL LINE .5"	1200	LF	350	899	180	1429	2507	209	215	2580
10	SPRAY HEADS 6"	170	EA	1622	636	—	2258	3961	2230	25	4250
11	SPRAY HEADS 4"	60	EA	572	225	—	797	1398	2325	25	1500
12	SOIL PREP	6300	SF	880	374	140	1394	2446	.39	.40	2520
13	TREES 24" BOX on 2" CAL.	6	EA	1117	290	30	1437	2521	42017	425	2550
14	TREES 15 GAL.	15	EA	917	374	—	1291	2265	151	155	2325
15	PALMS <WASH. ROB. 10' BTF>	3	EA	1224	243	20	1487	2609	86967	875	2625
16	SHRUBS 5 GAL.	215	EA	3111	805	—	3916	6870	3195	32	6880
17	SHRUBS 5 GAL. ESP.	3	EA	83	19	—	102	179	5967	60	180
18	SHRUBS 1 GAL.	283	EA	1260	449	—	1709	2998	1059	11	3113
19	VINES 1 GAL.	24	EA	134	37	—	171	300	1250	13	312
20	GROUND COVER	59	FLT	750	552	—	1302	2284	3871	40	2360
21	SOD <W/GRADING>	3345	SF	1135	319	—	1454	2551	.76	.80	2676
22	MULCH 1" DEPTH	2955	SF	212	225	40	477	837	.28	.30	887
	SUBTOTAL <#1>			16502	7094	523	24119	<DOUBLE CHECK #1>			43546
	GENERAL CONDITIONS			212	3020	1320	4552				
	SUBTOTAL <#2>			16714	10114	1843	28671	<DOUBLE CHECK #2>			
	G&A OVERHEAD <OPH = $10.00>	523	HR				5230	<DOUBLE CHECK #3>			
	SUBTOTAL <#3>						33701				
	CONTINGENCY FACTOR						0				
							33701				
	NET PROFIT MARGIN	20	%				8475				
							42376				# 1170
1	$42,376 − 24,119 = $18,257										DIFFERENCE DUE TO ROUNDING
2	$18,257 ÷ 42,376 = .43083										
3	.43083 ≈ .43										
4	1.0 − .43 = .57						ADD SUBCONTRACTORS <WITH ALL MARKUPS> HERE				1300
											# 44896

SALES TAX:	6.0%	**PRICE:**	$43,624	**G&A OVHD:**	12.33%
CAW:	$12.00	**SPH:**	$83.41	**NET PROFIT:**	20.00%
OTF:	10.0%			**GPM:**	32.33%
RF:	10.0%				
CAW (w/OTF & RF):	$14.40				
OPH:	$10.00	**HRS:**	523.0	**PPH:**	$16.22
DESIRED MINIMUM PPH:	$5.00	**CREW:**	4	**GPM:**	32.33%
LABOR BURDEN:	30.00%	**HRS/DAY:**	8	**GC:**	10.73%
NET PROFIT AS A %	20.00%				

#	DESCRIPTION	QTY	UNIT	MATL+TAX	LABOR+LB	EQUIP	TOTALS	U/C	+ G.C.	+OH (BEP)	+ Net Profit	U/P	ROUNDED	TOTAL BID	VARIANCE
									15.86%	15.41%	20.00%				
								SET----->	15.86%	15.41%	20.00%				
		1	2	3	5	7	8	CALCS	15.86%	15.41%	20.00%	10	11	12	
1	MOBILIZATION	1	LS				0	0.00	0	0	0	0.00	0.00	0.00	0.00
2	BACKFLOW	1	EA	368	112		480	480.14	571	675	843	843.25	845.00	845.00	1.75
3	VALVES(F.TUNE & WIRE)	14	EA	1,381	749		2,130	152.14	2,531	2,993	3,741	267.20	275.00	3,850.00	109.19
4	QUICK COUPLERS	4	EA	170	75		244	61.12	291	343	429	107.34	110.00	440.00	10.63
5	MAIN LINE 1.25"	240	LF	293	187	37.50	518	2.16	615	727	909	3.79	3.95	948.00	39.09
6	SLEEVES 2.5"	120	LF	334	94		428	3.56	508	601	751	6.26	6.50	780.00	29.20
7	CONTROLLER	1	EA	392	37		430	429.64	511	604	755	754.56	755.00	755.00	0.44
8	LATERAL PIPE 1"	520	LF	231	393	75.00	699	1.34	830	982	1,227	2.36	2.40	1,248.00	20.95
9	LATERAL PIPE 1/2"	1200	LF	350	899	180.00	1,428	1.19	1,698	2,007	2,509	2.09	2.15	2,580.00	71.42
10	RB 1806 SAM HEADS	170	EA	1,622	636		2,258	13.28	2,684	3,173	3,966	23.33	25.00	4,250.00	283.86
11	RB 1804 SAM HEADS	60	EA	572	225		797	13.28	947	1,120	1,400	23.33	25.00	1,500.00	100.19
12	SOIL PREP	6300	SF	880	374	140.00	1,394	0.22	1,657	1,959	2,449	0.39	0.40	2,520.00	71.42
13	TREES 24" box or 2" CAL	6	EA	1,117	290	30.00	1,437	239.50	1,708	2,019	2,524	420.62	425.00	2,550.00	26.29
14	TREES 15 GL	15	EA	917	374		1,291	86.07	1,534	1,814	2,267	151.16	155.00	2,325.00	57.60
15	PALMS (WASH ROB) 10'	3	EA	1,224	243	20.00	1,488	495.89	1,768	2,090	2,613	870.91	875.00	2,625.00	12.28
16	SHRUBS 5 GL	215	EA	3,111	805		3,916	18.21	4,654	5,502	6,877	31.99	32.00	6,880.00	2.83
17	SHRUBS 5 GL ESPALIER	3	EA	83	19		102	34.07	121	144	179	59.83	60.00	180.00	0.52
18	SHRUBS 1 GL	283	EA	1,260	449		1,709	6.04	2,031	2,401	3,002	10.61	11.00	3,113.00	111.20
19	VINES 1 GL	24	EA	134	37		171	7.13	203	240	300	12.51	13.00	312.00	11.68
20	GROUND COVER	59	FLT	750	552		1,303	22.08	1,548	1,830	2,288	38.78	40.00	2,360.00	72.08
21	SOD (+GRADE)	3345	SF	1,135	319		1,453	0.43	1,727	2,042	2,552	0.76	0.80	2,676.00	123.93
22	MULCH 1" DEEP	2955	SF	212	225	40.00	477	0.16	566	670	837	0.28	0.30	886.50	49.39
	SUBTOTAL:			16,535	7,095	523	24,152	56.9%	28,704	33,934	42,418	XXXXXX	XXXXXX	**43,624**	
	General conditions			212	3,020	1,320	4,552	15.86%	V						
	SUBTOTALS:			16,747	10,115	1,843	28,704	67.67%	$0.00 0.00%						
	G&A overhead	523.0					5,230	15.41%	**(DBL CK-1)**	V					
	SUBTOTALS:						33,934	------->	------->	$0.00					
	Net protig margin	20.00%					8,484	20.00%		0.00% **(DBL CK-2)**	V			V VARIANCE	
							42,418	100.00%	------->	------->	$0.00 0.00% **(DBL CK-3)**	------->	------->	$1,205.93 2.84% **(DBL CK-4)**	

Scenario cost data	**$ or %**	**Remarks**
Crew size (# people)	3.0	Crew leader, leadman and laborer
Crew average wage (CAW)	$ 12.00	
Overtime factor (OTF)	5.6%	45 hours per week
Risk factor (RF)	10.0%	
Crew average wage w/OTF & RF	$ 13.87	
Labor burden	30.0%	
Sales tax	6.0%	
G&A overhead per hour (OPH)	$ 10.00	
Net profit margin	10.0%	
Crew truck	$ 8.00	
Curb-time man-hours per day	24.0	
Number of units	24.0	Curb-time man-hours

Scenario	**Materials**	**Labor**		**Equipment**	**CPH**	**Hours**	**Item**
I. Production (on-site or curb-time costs)							
	$ -	24.0	Man-hours	$ -	$ -	0.0	
	$ -			$ -	$ -	0.0	
	$ -	$ 13.87		$ -	$ -	0.0	
	$ -	$ 332.80		$ -			
II. General conditions (off-site or non-curb-time costs)							
		3.0	Man-hours	$ 64.00	$ 8.00	8.0	Crew truck
		0.0		$ -	$ -	0.0	
	$ -	$ 13.87		$ -	$ -	0.0	
	$ -	$ 41.60		$ 64.00			
Subtotals	**$ -**	**$ 374**		**$ 64**			
III. Margins & markups							
A.Sales tax	$ -						
B.Labor burden		$ 112					
Subtotals	**$ -**	**$ 487**		**$ 64**			

Total direct costs (TDC)			**$ 551**	**TDC**
C. G&A overhead costs				
27.0 (Number of man-hours x OPH)	$ 10.00	=	$ 270	
BEP (subtotal of TDC + G&A overhead)			**$ 821**	**BEP**
D. Contingency factor (if desired)			$ -	
E. Net profit margin				
10.00%			$ 91	
F. Total price			**$ 912**	**Total price**

IV. Scenario analysis

A. Curb-time rate (total price ÷ curb-time hours)

$ 912 divided by	24.0 =		**$ 38.00**	**Curb-time rate**

B. Portal-to-portal rate (total price ÷ all man-hours)

$ 912 divided by	27.0 =		**$ 33.77**	**Portal-to-portal rate**

C. Gross profit margin ((G&A overhead + Net profit) ÷ Total price)

$ 361	÷	$ 912 =	**39.6%**	**GPM**

PRACTICAL EXERCISE 19-1 Crew Time and Materials Rate: Parts A–E

Scenario cost data	$ or %	Remarks
Crew size (# people)	1.0	Irrigation technician
Crew average wage (CAW)	$ 17.00	
Overtime factor (OTF)	13.6%	55 hours and 5.5 days per week
Risk factor (RF)	10.0%	
Crew average wage w/OTF & RF	$ 21.02	
Labor burden	30.0%	
Sales tax	6.0%	
G&A overhead per hour (OPH)	$ 13.00	
Net profit margin	20.0%	
Crew truck	$ 7.00	
Curb-time man-hours per day	8.0	
Number of units	8.0	Curb-time man-hours

Scenario	Materials	Labor		Equipment	CPH	Hours	Item
I. Production (on-site or curb-time costs)							
	$ -	8.0	Man-hours	$ -	$ -	0.0	
	$ -			$ -	$ -	0.0	
	$ -	$ 21.02		$ -	$ -	0.0	
	$ -	$ 168.15		$ -			
II. General conditions (off-site or non-curb-time costs)							
		2.0	Man-hours	$ 56.00	$ 7.00	8.0	Crew truck
		0.0		$ -	$ -	0.0	Warantee truck
	$ -	$ 21.02		$ -	$ -	0.0	
	$ -	$ 42.04		$ 56.00			
Subtotals	**$ -**	**$ 210**		**$ 56**			
III. Margins & markups							
A. Sales tax	$ -						
B. Labor burden		$ 63					
Subtotals	**$ -**	**$ 273**		**$ 56**			

Total direct costs (TDC)		**$ 329**	**TDC**
C. G&A overhead costs 10 (Number of man-hours x OPH)	$ 13.00 =	$ 130	
BEP (TDC + G&A overhead)		**$ 459**	**BEP**
D. Contingency factor (if desired)		$ -	
E. Net profit margin 20.00%		$ 115	
F. Total price		**$ 574**	**Total price**

IV. Scenario analysis

A. Curb-time rate (Total price ÷ curb-time man-hours)

$ 574 divided by 8.0 =		**$ 71.76**	**Curb-time rate**

B. Portal-to-portal rate (Total price ÷ all hours)

$ 574 divided by 10.0 =		**$ 57.40**	**Portal-to-portal rate**

C. Gross profit margin ((G&A overhead + Net profit) ÷ Total price)

$ 245 ÷ $ 574 =		**42.6%**	**GPM**

PRACTICAL EXERCISE 24-1 Irrigation Service Work: Parts A–E

Scenario cost data	$ or %	Remarks
Crew size (# people)	2.0	Crew leader with a laborer
Crew average wage (CAW)	$ 11.00	
Overtime factor (OTF)	5.6%	45 hours per week
Risk factor (RF)	10.0%	
Crew average wage w/OTF & RF	$ 12.71	
Labor burden	25.0%	
Sales tax	6.0%	
G&A overhead per hour (OPH)	$ 10.00	
Net profit margin	10.0%	
Crew truck & trailer	$ 8.00	
Curb-time man-hours per day	14.0	
Number of units	14.0	Curb-time man-hours

Scenario	Materials	Labor		Equipment	CPH	Hours	Item
I. Production (on-site or curb-time costs)							
	$ -	14.0	Man-hours	$ 30.00	$ 5.00	6.0	36" WB mower
	$ -	0.0		$ 6.00	$ 3.00	2.0	21" mower
	$ -	$ 12.71		$ 12.00	$ 3.00	4.0	Edger, blower & stick trimmer
	$ -	$ 177.96		$ 48.00			
II. General conditions (off-site or non-curb-time costs)							
		4.0	Man-hours	$ 64.00	$ 8.00	8.0	Crew truck & trailer
		0.0		$ -	$ -	0.0	
	$ -	$ 12.71		$ -	$ -	0.0	
	$ -	$ 50.84		$ 64.00			
Subtotals	**$ -**	**$ 229**		**$ 112**			
III. Margins & markups							
A.Sales tax	$ -						
B.Labor burden		$ 57					
Subtotals	**$ -**	**$ 286**		**$ 112**			

Total direct costs (TDC)			**$ 398**	**TDC**
C. G&A overhead costs 18 (Number of man-hours x OPH)	$ 10.00	=	$ 180	
BEP (TDC + G&A overhead)			**$ 578**	**BEP**
D. Contingency factor (if desired)			$ -	
E. Net profit margin 10.00%			$ 64	
F. Total price			**$ 642**	**Total price**

IV. Scenario analysis

A. Curb-time man-hour rate (Total price ÷ curb-time man-hours)

$ 642 divided by 14.0 = **$ 45.87** **Curb-time rate**

B. Portal-to-portal rate (Total price ÷ all man-hours)

$ 642 divided by 18.0 = **$ 35.68** **Portal-to-portal rate**

C. Gross profit margin ((G&A overhead + Net profit) ÷ Total price)

$ 244 ÷ $ 642 = **38.0%** **GPM**

PRACTICAL EXERCISE 25-1 Lawn Maintenance Package with 14 Hours of Curb Time: Parts A–D

Labor Production Rates

Item	Unit	Qty/Mhr	Time/Unit	Remarks
I. Irrigation				
1. Point of connection (POC)	LS	.25–.5	2–4 Hrs	
2. Automatic controllers	EA	.5–1.0	1–2 Hrs	
3. Trench/clean/fittings/backfill (6″ × 12–18″)*	LF	20–30	2.4 Min	walk-behind trencher
4. Trench/clean/fittings/backfill (6″ × 12–18″)*	LF	25–35	2.0 Min	ride-on trencher
5. Trench/clean/fittings/backfill (6″ × 24″)*	LF	20–30	2.4 Min	ride-on trencher
6. Pull/fittings/backfill 10-16″ depth*	LF	20–30	2.4 Min	
7. Trench only	LF	65–100	.9–.6 Min	walk-behind
8. Trench only	LF	100–150	.6–.4 Min	ride-on trencher
9. Install pipe (only)	LF	100–125	.5–.6 Min	
10. Backfill (only)	LF	100–125	.5–.6 Min	w/tractor
11. Backflow preventers	EA	.5–1.0	1–2 Hrs	
12. Remote control valves	EA	2–3.0	15–20 Min	
13. Quick coupler valves	EA	2–4.0	15–30 Min	
14. Ball/gate valves	EA	2–3.0	20–30 Min	
15. Wire	LF	500–600	6–7.2 Sec	
16. Shrub heads	EA	5–6	10–12 Min	
17. Turf spray heads	EA	4–5	12–15 Min	
18. Turf rotor heads	EA	2–3	20–30 Min	
19. Drip emitters	EA	20–30	2–3 Min	
20. Drip pipe tubing	LF	100–125	.5–.6 Min	
21. Sleeving	LF	20–30	2.5 Min	

II. Soil Prep

1. Rough grade to +/–.1 ft	SF	4,000–6,000	10–15 Min/M**	w/tractor
2. Rototill (4″ depth)	SF	1,500–2,500	30 Min/M	w/walk behind rototiller
3. Rototill (6″ depth)	SF	1,000–2,000	40 Min/M	w/walk behind rototiller
4. Rototill (4″ depth)	SF	3,500–4,500	15 Min/M	w/tractor tiller
5. Rototill (6″ depth)	SF	2,500–3,500	20 Min/M	w/tractor tiller
6. Finish/fine grade	SF	1,000	60 Min/M	
7. Finish/fine grade	SF	2,500	24 Min/M	w/tractor

III. Planting

Rates include spotting, digging the hole, amending, cutting container, planting, and basin preparation.

1. Trees (box)				
72″ box	EA	.125	8 Hrs	1 Hr for backhoe
60″ box	EA	.167	6 Hrs	.8 Hr for backhoe
48″ box	EA	.25	4 Hrs	.5 Hr for backhoe
36″ box	EA	.33	3 Hrs	.3 Hr for backhoe
24″ box	EA	.5	2 Hrs	.25 Hr for backhoe
15 gallon	EA	1.0	1 Hr	
5 gallon	EA	5.0	12 Min	
2 gallon	EA	7–10	6–8 Min	
1 gallon	EA	12–15	4–5 Min	
2. Trees (B&B)				
5″ cal/60″ B&B	EA	.167	6 Hrs	.8 Hr for backhoe
4″ cal/48″ B&B	EA	.25	4 Hrs	.5 Hr for backhoe
3″ cal/36″ B&B	EA	.33	3 Hrs	.3 Hr for backhoe
2.5″ cal/30″ B&B	EA	.4	2.5 Hrs	.3 Hr for backhoe
2″ cal/24″ B&B	EA	.5	2 Hrs	.25 Hr for backhoe
1.5″ cal/18″ B&B	EA	.75	1.5 Hrs	
1″ cal/12″ B&B	EA	1	1 Hr	
Stake kit (1 stk/tree)	KIT	4	15 Min	
Stake kit (2 stk/tree)	KIT	3	20 Min	
Stake kit (3 stk/tree)	KIT	2	30 Min	
Guying kit (3 pt guy)	KIT	2	20 Min	
3. Shrubs				
3.0′	EA	.75	1.3 Hrs	
2.5′	EA	1.0	1.0 Hrs	
24″	EA	1.2	.8 Hrs	
18″	EA	2–2.5	.33–.5 Hrs	

12″	EA	3–4.0	15–20 Min
15 gallon	EA	1.0	1.0 Hrs
5 gallon	EA	4–5.0	12–15 Min
2 gallon	EA	7–10	6–8 Min
1 gallon	EA	12–15	4–5 Min
4. Ground cover			
1 gallon	FL	12–15	4–5 Min
Flat (2 ¼″ pots)	FL	1.5–2	30–45 Min
Flat (4″ pots)	FL	2–2.5	24–30 Min
Flat (64 cnt)	FL	2–2.5	24–30 Min
Flat (81 cnt)	FL	1.5–2	30–45 Min
Flat (100 cnt)	FL	1–1.5	45–60 Min
5. Miscellaneous			
Mulch	CY	1.5–2	30–45 Min
Sod	SF	200–300	20–30 Min/100

IV. Maintenance

1. Mowing		
18–21″ rotary	SF	5,000–7,500
36″ rotary	SF	20,000–30,000
48″ rotary	SF	30,000–40,000
60″ rotary	SF	50,000–65,000
72″ rotary	SF	65,000–80,000
72″ reel	SF	50,000–60,000
12′ reel	SF	100,000–120,000
____________	___	________
____________	___	________
____________	___	________
2. Power edging	LF	3,000–4,000
3. Stick edgers	LF	3,000–5,000
4. Trim around objects	EA	100–150

*Trenching and pulling includes all functions (e.g., trenching, cleaning, installing fittings, and backfilling trench).

**M = 1,000

Note: The above rates are approximations and based on normal/flat site conditions. They are provided for purposes of comparisons only. Your production rates will vary depending upon site conditions, experience of labor force, types of equipment used, etc.

Equipment Cost Per Hour (CPH) Rates

	Cost/Hour	Cost/Day (8 hrs)	Cost/Week (40 hrs)	Cost/Month (175 hrs)	Remarks
I. Trucks					
Mini-pickup	$ 4	$ 32	$ 160	$ 688	All hours for one ton and smaller trucks and automobiles are based on 8 hours per day, not engine run time.
1/2-ton pickup	$ 6	$ 48	$ 240	$1,032	
3/4-ton pickup	$ 7	$ 56	$ 280	$1,204	
1-ton pickup	$ 8	$ 64	$ 320	$1,376	
1-ton with dump body	$10	$ 80	$ 400	$1,720	
5 CY Dump	$15	$120	$ 600	$2,580	Hours for trucks larger than one ton are based on actual engine run time.
8 CY Dump	$20	$160	$ 800	$3,440	
10 CY Dump	$25	$200	$1,000	$4,300	
Semi with trailer	$25	$200	$1,000	$4,300	Adjust your hours/costs accordingly.
Bucket or boom truck	$30	$240	$1,200	$5,160	
Tank truck (500 GL)	$15	$120	$ 600	$2,580	
Tank truck (1,000 GL)	$20	$160	$ 800	$3,440	
Hydroseeder (500 GL)	$25	$200	$1,000	$4,300	
Hydroseeder (1000 GL)	$30	$240	$1,200	$5,160	
Explorer or comparable vehicle	$ 6	$ 48	$ 240	$1,032	
Expedition or comparable SUV	$ 8	$ 64	$ 320	$1,376	
Isuzu NPR or NPQ or equivalent	$12	$ 96	$ 480	$2,064	
________	___.__	___.__	___.__	___.__	
________	___.__	___.__	___.__	___.__	
________	___.__	___.__	___.__	___.__	

	Cost/Hour	Cost/Day (8 hrs)	Cost/Week (40 hrs)	Cost/Month (175 hrs)	Remarks
II. Automobiles/Overhead Vehicles					
Sub-compact	$ 4	$ 32	$ 160	$ 688	
Compact	$ 5	$ 40	$ 200	$ 860	
Mid-size	$ 6	$ 48	$ 240	$1,032	
Full-size	$ 7	$ 56	$ 280	$1,204	
Suburban Utility Vehicle	$ 8	$ 64	$ 320	$1,376	
____________	___.___	___.___	___.___	___.___	
____________	___.___	___.___	___.___	___.___	
____________	___.___	___.___	___.___	___.___	
____________	___.___	___.___	___.___	___.___	
____________	___.___	___.___	___.___	___.___	
III. Tractors					
1/8 CY, 12–15 HP	$12	$ 96	$ 480	$2,064	Remarks: All hours are actual engine running hours. Adjust your hours/costs accordingly.
¼ CY, 15–20 HP	$15	$120	$ 600	$2,580	
½ CY, 25–35 HP	$18	$144	$ 720	$3,096	
1 CY, 45–55 HP	$22	$176	$ 880	$3,784	
3 CY, 55–75 HP	$26	$208	$1,040	$4,472	
Wheel/Uni-loader	$30	$240	$1,200	$5,160	
Backhoe, small	$25	$200	$1,000	$4,300	
Backhoe, large	$30	$240	$1,200	$5,160	
Dozer, small	$30	$240	$1,200	$5,160	
Dozer, mid-size	$35	$280	$1,400	$6,020	
Mini-skid steer (Dingo or equivalent)	$15	$120	$ 600	$2,580	With bucket only
Mini-skid steer with auger	$22	$176	$ 880	$3,784	
Mini-skid steer with trencher	$25	$200	$1,000	$4,300	
____________	___.___	___.___	___.___	___.___	
____________	___.___	___.___	___.___	___.___	
____________	___.___	___.___	___.___	___.___	
____________	___.___	___.___	___.___	___.___	
____________	___.___	___.___	___.___	___.___	

IV. Trenchers/Vibratory Plows

	Cost/Hour	Cost/Day (8 hrs)	Cost/Week (40 hrs)	Cost/Month (175 hrs)	Remarks
Trencher, walk-behind	$10	$ 80	$ 400	$1,720	
Trencher, small ride-on	$17	$136	$ 680	$2,924	
Trencher, mid-size ride-on	$24	$192	$ 960	$4,128	
Trencher, large ride-on	$35	$280	$1,400	$6,020	
Puller, small	$15	$120	$ 600	$2,580	
Puller, medium	$20	$160	$ 800	$3,440	
Puller, large	$23	$184	$ 920	$3,956	
______________	___.___	___.___	___.___	___.___	
______________	___.___	___.___	___.___	___.___	
______________	___.___	___.___	___.___	___.___	
______________	___.___	___.___	___.___	___.___	
______________	___.___	___.___	___.___	___.___	

V. Mowers

	Cost/Hour	Cost/Day (8 hrs)	Cost/Week (40 hrs)	Cost/Month (175 hrs)	Remarks
21″ Push	$ 3	$ 20	$ 100	$ 430	
21″ Self-propelled	$ 3	$ 24	$ 120	$ 516	
36″ Rotary	$ 4	$ 32	$ 160	$ 688	
48″ Rotary	$ 5	$ 40	$ 200	$ 860	
51″ Rotary	$ 6	$ 48	$ 240	$1,032	
60″ Rotary	$ 7	$ 56	$ 280	$1,204	
72″ Rotary	$ 8	$ 64	$ 320	$1,376	
15′ Rotary (bat-wing)	$20	$160	$ 800	$3,440	
15′ Reel	$20	$160	$ 800	$3,440	
Maint. Package (2 men)*	$ 6	$ 48	$ 240	$1,032	
Maint. Package (3 men)**	$ 8	$ 64	$ 320	$1,376	
______________	___.___	___.___	___.___	___.___	
______________	___.___	___.___	___.___	___.___	
______________	___.___	___.___	___.___	___.___	
______________	___.___	___.___	___.___	___.___	
______________	___.___	___.___	___.___	___.___	

	Cost/Hour	Cost/Day (8 hrs)	Cost/Week (40 hrs)	Cost/Month (175 hrs)	Remarks
VI. Miscellaneous Construction Equipment					
Jackhammer (electric)	$ 4	$ 32	$ 160	$ 688	
Chain saw	$ 5	$ 40	$ 200	$ 860	
Auger, 2-man	$ 5	$ 40	$ 200	$ 860	
Sod cutter	$ 8	$ 64	$ 320	$1,376	
Aerator	$ 8	$ 64	$ 320	$1,376	
Tamper/compactor	$ 6	$ 48	$ 240	$1,032	
Rototiller, small	$ 6	$ 48	$ 240	$1,032	
Rototiller, large	$10	$ 80	$ 400	$1,720	
Chop saw	$ 5	$ 40	$ 200	$ 860	
Chop saw with diamond blade	$15	$120	$ 600	$2,580	
______________	___.__	___.__	___.__	___.__	
______________	___.__	___.__	___.__	___.__	
______________	___.__	___.__	___.__	___.__	
VII. Miscellaneous Maintenance Equipment					
Trimmer, hedge	$ 3	$ 24	$ 120	$ 516	
Weed-eater	$ 3	$ 24	$ 120	$ 516	
Edger	$ 3	$ 24	$ 120	$ 516	
Trailer (1 axle)	$ 1	$ 8	$ 40	$ 172	
Trailer (2 axle)	$ 2	$ 12	$ 60	$ 258	
Trailer, lowboy	$ 3	$ 20	$ 100	$ 430	
Hydroseeder (500 gl)***	$ 6	$ 48	$ 240	$1,032	
Hydroseeder (1000 gl)***	$ 8	$ 64	$ 320	$1,376	
Hydroseeder (1500 gl)***	$10	$ 80	$ 400	$1,720	
Brick saw (w/o blades)	$ 3	$ 24	$ 120	$ 516	
Concrete mixer	$ 4	$ 32	$ 160	$ 688	
______________	___.__	___.__	___.__	___.__	
______________	___.__	___.__	___.__	___.__	
______________	___.__	___.__	___.__	___.__	
______________	___.__	___.__	___.__	___.__	

	Cost/Hour	Cost/Day (8 hrs)	Cost/Week (40 hrs)	Cost/Month (175 hrs)	Remarks
VIII. Miscellaneous Arborist Equipment					
Chipper, small	$10	$ 80	$ 400	$1,720	
Chipper, tow-behind mid-size	$20	$160	$ 800	$3,440	
Chipper, tow-behind large	$25	$200	$1,000	$4,300	
Stump grinder, small	$15	$120	$ 600	$2,580	
Stump grinder, large	$20	$160	$ 800	$3,440	
________	___.___	___.___	___.___	___.___	
________	___.___	___.___	___.___	___.___	
________	___.___	___.___	___.___	___.___	
________	___.___	___.___	___.___	___.___	
________	___.___	___.___	___.___	___.___	
IX. Miscellaneous Attachments					
York rake	$10	$ 80	$ 400	$1,720	
Rotadairon	$15	$120	$ 600	$2,580	
Harley rake	$16	$128	$ 640	$2,752	
________	___.___	___.___	___.___	___.___	
________	___.___	___.___	___.___	___.___	
________	___.___	___.___	___.___	___.___	
________	___.___	___.___	___.___	___.___	
________	___.___	___.___	___.___	___.___	

*Crew with push mower, edgers, trimmers, blowers, and 36″ or 48″ walk-behind mower.

**Crew with push mower, edgers, trimmers, blowers, and 36″ or 48″ walk-behind mower and possibly a riding mower.

***Mounted on a trailer. Does not include truck.

Abbreviations and Acronyms

ACT	actual
AIMS	advanced information management system
ASAP	as soon as possible/practical
AW	average wage
B&B	balled & burlapped
BAR	bid analysis review worksheet
BEP	break-even point
BF	board foot
BL	bale
BUD LITE	unrealistically low budget
BUD	budget
C	hundred
CAD	computer aided design
CAL	caliper
CAW	crew average wage
CF	cubic foot
CF	contingency factor
CI	cubic inch
CIP	constant improvement process
CO/DIV	company/division
CO	company
COB	close of business
COGS	cost of goods sold (same as COS)
CON or CONST	construction
COPH	corporate overhead per hour
COS	cost of sales (same as COGS)
CPA	certified public accountant
CPH	cost per hour
CY	calendar year
CY	cubic yard

DCPH	direct costs per hour
DOPH	division overhead per hour
DORS	dual overhead recovery system
EA	each
EQ/L RATIO	equipment-to-labor ratio
EQ or EQUIP	equipment
EQPH	equipment per hour
FDR	field daily report
FF	fudge factor
FICA/F.I.C.A.	Federal Insurance Contributions Act
FLH	field-labor hour
FMV	fair market value
FT	foot
FUTA/F.U.T.A.	Federal Unemployment Tax Act
FY	fiscal year
FYTD	fiscal year-to-date
G&A	general and administrative
GA	gauge
GAS	gross annual sales
GC	general conditions
GCH/TH	general condition hours divided by total hours
GCPH	general conditions per hour
GL	gallon
GLI	general liability insurance
GPM	gross profit margin
GPM	gallons per minute
GPMH or GPMPH	gross profit margin per hour
GVW	gross vehicular weight
HD	head
HP	horsepower
HR(S)	hour(s)
IMS	information management system
IRR or IRRIG	irrigation
K or M	thousand
KT	kit
LB, #	pound
LB	labor burden
LF	linear foot

LLC	limited liability corporation
LOC	line of credit
LS	lump sum
LSC	landscape
M/L/E/S or MLES	material, labor, equipment, subcontractors
M/L RATIO	material-to-labor ratio
M or K	thousand
MAT/LAB RATIO	material-to-labor ratio
MAT'L	material
MDAY	man day
MDUP	market-driven unit pricing
MHR or MH	man-hour
MMT	meaningful management term(s)
MO	month
MORS	multiple overhead recovery system
MOY	monthly
MPH	material per hour
MSF	thousand square feet
MTBF	mean-time between failures
NO, #, NR	number
NPH or NPMPH	net profit margin per hour, same as PPH
NPM	net profit margin
NWC	net working capital
OC	on center
OH or OVHD	overhead
OPH	overhead per hour
OPPH	overhead & profit per hour
OT	overtime
OTF	overtime factor
P&L	profit & loss
PATT	place, activity, time, tools
PC	personal computer
PKG	package
PMSS	philosophies, methodologies, systems, and strategies
POC	point of connection
POC	point (person) of contact
POL	petroleum, oil, lubricants
PPH	profit per hour, same as NPH
PSI	pounds per square inch
PVC	polyvinyl chloride

PW	prevailing wage
QA	quality assurance
QCP	quality control process
QTR	quarter
QTRLY	quarterly
QTY	quantity
RF	risk factor
RL	roll
RPH	revenue per hour
SDI	state disability insurance
SF	square foot
SI	square inch
SORS	single overhead recovery system
SPH	sales per hour
SUB(S)	subcontractors
SUTA/S.U.T.A.	State Unemployment Tax Act
SY	square yard
T/O	takeoff
T&M	time and materials
TAF	timely, accurate feedback
TAT	turn around time
TDC	total direct costs
TN	ton
TOPH	total overhead per hour
TQM	total quality management
U/P or UP	unit price
U/C or UC	unit cost
W/S or WS	worksheet
WCI	workers' compensation insurance
Y-T-D or YTD	year-to-date
YR	year

Industry Benchmarks

The industry benchmarks contained in this Appendix are averages that are commonly realized in Green Industry construction and/or maintenance/service companies throughout North America. Figures for your company will, of course, vary somewhat from those outlined here.

1. The Profit and Loss Statement (or Income Statement)

> "A statement of revenues and expenses is called a profit and loss statement or an income statement. Expenses are deducted from revenue. If revenue exceeds expenses, the difference is called net income. If expenses exceed revenue, the difference is called net loss. The income statement shows the net changes in owners' equity that result from operating at profit or at a loss. The income statement is used to measure revenue and expenses for a given accounting period or a fiscal period." (Moore, Jaedicke, and Anderson 1984)

See Figure II-1 in Section II for a sample Profit and Loss Statement.

A. **Sales or revenue per hour (SPH or RPH)** Sales revenue including all costs divided by the respective billable field-labor hours.

	Market Segment	SPH or RPH
a.	Residential installation (all types)	$50 to $75
b.	Commercial installation (all types)	$40 to $65
c.	Maintenance, commercial and residential	$20 to $40
d.	Tree work	$50 to $65
e.	Fertilizations and insecticides (all types)	$100 to $150
f.	Irrigation service	$40 to $65
g.	Bark blowing	$80 to $160
h.	Hydroseeding	$100 to $200
i.	Interior landscaping, installation	$50 to $75
j.	Interior landscaping, maintenance	$20 to $40
k.	Outdoor lighting	$60 to $85
l.	Outdoor ponds	$50 to $75
m.	Pavers	$80 to $120

	Market Segment	SPH or RPH
n.	Snow plowing	$55 to $150*
o.	Sanding and salting	$200 to $300
p.	Christmas decorations	$60 to $85

*Varies dramatically

B. **Man-hours per man-year**

	Market Segment	Man-Hours per Man-Year
a.	Residential installation (all types)	1,700 to 2,100
b.	Commercial installation (all types)	1,700 to 2,100
c.	Maintenance, commercial and residential	1,700 to 2,000
d.	Tree work	1,800 to 2,000
e.	Fertilizations and insecticides (all types)	1,500 to 2,000
f.	Irrigation service	1,500 to 2,000
g.	Bark blowing	200 to 400*, **
h.	Hydroseeding	1,300 to 2,000*, **
i.	Interior landscaping	2,000
j.	Outdoor lighting	1,700 to 2,000
k.	Outdoor ponds	1,700 to 2,000
l.	Pavers	1,700 to 2,000
m.	Snow plowing	50 to 200*, **
n.	Sanding and salting	25 to 100*, **
o.	Christmas decorations	250 to 350*, **

*Varies dramatically

**Seasonal

C. **Sales or revenue per man-year (SPY or RPY)** Sales revenue including all costs divided by the related labor man-years.

	Market Segment	SPY or RPY
a.	Residential installation (all types)	$100,000 to $125,000
b.	Commercial installation (all types)	$90,000 to $110,000
c.	Maintenance, commercial and residential	$40,000 to $65,000

	Market Segment	SPY or RPY
d.	Tree work	$90,000 to $110,000
e.	Fertilizations and insecticides (all types)	$125,000 to $175,000
f.	Irrigation service	$110,000 to $125,000
g.	Bark blowing	$10,000 to $40,000
h.	Hydroseeding	$130,000 to $350,000*, **
i.	Interior landscaping, installation	$100,000 to $125,000
j.	Interior landscaping, maintenance	$40,000 to $65,000
k.	Outdoor lighting	$110,000 to $125,000
l.	Outdoor ponds	$100,000 to $125,000
m.	Pavers	$110,000 to $130,000
n.	Snow plowing	**, ***
o.	Sanding and salting	**, ***
p.	Christmas decorations	$15,000 to $25,000

*Varies dramatically

**Seasonal

***Varies too much to benchmark

D. **Cost of goods sold (COGS) as a percent of sales**

	Market Segment	COGS as a % of Sales
a.	Residential installation (all types)	60% to 70%
b.	Commercial installation (all types)	65% to 75%
c.	Maintenance, commercial and residential	60% to 70%
d.	Tree work	60% to 70%
e.	Fertilizations and insecticides (all types)	50% to 65%
f.	Irrigation service	50% to 65%
g.	Bark blowing	55% to 65%
h.	Hydroseeding	55% to 65%
i.	Interior landscaping, installation	60% to 70%
j.	Interior landscaping, maintenance	60% to 70%
k.	Outdoor lighting	55% to 65%
l.	Outdoor ponds	60% to 70%
m.	Pavers	60% to 70%

	Market Segment	COGS as a % of Sales
n.	Snow plowing	50% to 60%
o.	Sanding and salting	40% to 55%
p.	Christmas decorations	55% to 65%

E. **Materials cost (including sales tax) as a percent of sales**

	Market Segment	Materials as a % of Sales
a.	Residential installation (all types)	27% to 33%
b.	Commercial installation (all types)	30% to 40%
c.	Maintenance, commercial and residential	5% to 10%
d.	Tree work	2% to 5%
e.	Fertilizations and insecticides (all types)	15% to 20%
f.	Irrigation service	15% to 25%
g.	Bark blowing	25% to 35%
h.	Hydroseeding	25% to 35%
i.	Interior landscaping, installation	25% to 35%
j.	Interior landscaping, maintenance	5% to 15%
k.	Outdoor lighting	20% to 30%
l.	Outdoor ponds	25% to 35%
m.	Pavers	25% to 35%
n.	Snow plowing	None
o.	Sanding and salting	20% to 30%
p.	Christmas decorations	20% to 30%

F. **Material to labor (M/L) ratios** Material costs are divided by the related labor (without labor burden) to install them. The abbreviation CAW is for crew average wage and MPH is for materials per man-hour. The CAW of $10.00 is used to show you what the corresponding MPH would calculate to be. Adjust your rates accordingly.

	Type Work	M/L Ratio	CAW	MPH (in $)
a.	Planting	3.0–5.0:1	$10.00	$30 to $50
b.	Hardscape (all types)	1.0–1.5:1	$10.00	$10 to $15
c.	Planting with hardscape	1.5–2.5:1	$10.00	$15 to $25
d.	Irrigation installation	1.0–2.5:1	$10.00	$10 to $15

Type Work		M/L Ratio	CAW	MPH (in $)
e.	Irrigation service	0.15–0.2:1	$10.00	$1.50 to $2.00
f.	Planting, hardscape and irrigation	1.25–2.0:1	$10.00	$12 to $20
g.	Maintenance	0.05–0.1:1	$10.00	$0.50 to $1.00

G. **Direct field-labor costs (excluding labor burden) as a percent of sales**

Market Segment		Labor as a % of Sales
a.	Residential installation (all types)	18% to 22%
b.	Commercial installation (all types)	17% to 21%
c.	Maintenance, commercial and residential	35% to 45%
d.	Tree work	35% to 45%
e.	Fertilizations and insecticides (all types)	20% to 25%
f.	Irrigation service	20% to 30%
g.	Bark blowing	15% to 25%
h.	Hydroseeding	15% to 25%
i.	Interior landscaping, installation	17% to 21%
j.	Interior landscaping, maintenance	35% to 45%
k.	Outdoor lighting	20% to 30%
l.	Outdoor ponds	17% to 21%
m.	Pavers	17% to 21%
n.	Snow plowing	20% to 25%
o.	Sanding and salting	15% to 20%
p.	Christmas decorations	20% to 25%

H. **Direct field-labor burden as a percent of direct field labor cost**

Market Segment		Labor Burden as a % of Labor
a.	Residential installation (all types)	20% to 45%
b.	Commercial installation (all types)	20% to 35%
c.	Maintenance, commercial and residential	20% to 35%
d.	Tree work	30% to 50%
e.	Fertilizations and insecticides (all types)	20% to 35%
f.	Irrigation service	20% to 35%

	Market Segment	Labor Burden as a % of Labor
g.	Bark blowing	20% to 35%
h.	Hydroseeding	20% to 35%
i.	Interior landscaping, installation	20% to 35%
j.	Interior landscaping, maintenance	20% to 35%
k.	Outdoor lighting	20% to 30%
l.	Outdoor ponds	20% to 35%
m.	Pavers	20% to 35%
n.	Snow plowing	20% to 35%
o.	Sanding and salting	20% to 35%
p.	Christmas decorations	20% to 35%
q.	Canada (all divisions)	20% to 25%

I. **Direct field equipment costs (including rentals) as a percent of sales**

	Market Segment	Field Equipment as a % of Sales
a.	Residential installation (all types)	8% to 12%
b.	Commercial installation (all types)	8% to 12%
c.	Maintenance, commercial and residential	6% to 15%
d.	Tree work	10% to 20%
e.	Fertilizations and insecticides (all types)	6% to 10%
f.	Irrigation service	6% to 10%
g.	Bark blowing	10% to 15%
h.	Hydroseeding	10% to 20%
i.	Interior landscaping, installation	6% to 10%
j.	Interior landscaping, maintenance	6% to 10%
k.	Outdoor lighting	6% to 10%
l.	Outdoor ponds	8% to 12%
m.	Pavers	8% to 12%
n.	Snow plowing	10% to 20%
o.	Sanding and salting	8% to 12%
p.	Christmas decorations	6% to 10%

J. **Direct maintenance equipment cost per field man-hour** The abbreviation CAW is for crew average wage and EQPH is for equipment per man-hour. The CAW of $10.00 is used to show you what the corresponding EQPH would calculate to be. Adjust your rates accordingly.

Equipment Intensity	Equipment Cost as a % of Labor Cost	CAW	Company Average EQPH (in $)
Light	25% to 35%	$10.00	$2.50 to $3.50
Moderate	35% to 45%	$10.00	$3.50 to $4.50
Heavy	45% to 65%	$10.00	$4.50 to $6.50

K. **Direct construction equipment cost per field man-hour** The abbreviation CAW is for crew average wage and EQPH is for equipment per man-hour. The CAW of $10.00 is used to show you what the corresponding EQPH would calculate to be. Adjust your rates accordingly.

Equipment Intensity	Equipment Cost as a % of Labor Cost	CAW	Company Average EQPH (in $)
Light	15% to 25%	$10.00	$1.50 to $2.50
Moderate	25% to 35%	$10.00	$2.50 to $3.50
Heavy	35% to 50%	$10.00	$3.50 to $5.00
Extra Heavy	50% to 100%	$10.00	$5.00 to $10.00

L. **Subcontractor costs as a percent of sales**

Market Segment	Subcontractor Cost as a % of Sales
a. Residential installation (all types)	5% to 25%
b. Commercial installation (all types)	2% to 10%
c. Maintenance, commercial and residential	2% to 5%
d. Tree work	1% to 2%
e. Fertilizations and insecticides (all types)	0% to 2%
f. Irrigation service	0% to 2%
g. Bark blowing	N/A
h. Hydroseeding	N/A
i. Interior landscaping, installation	2% to 10%
j. Interior landscaping, maintenance	2% to 5%
k. Outdoor lighting	0% to 2%
l. Outdoor ponds	0% to 5%
m. Pavers	0% to 5%

n.	Snow plowing	***
o.	Sanding and salting	***
p.	Christmas decorations	0% to 2%

***Varies too much to benchmark

M. **Gross profit margin (GPM) as a percent of sales** Also as a gross profit margin per man-hour dollar amount (GPMPH) in a normal to very good economy.

	Market Segment	GPM %	GPMPH
a.	Residential installation (all types)	30 to 40%	$18 to $30
b.	Commercial installation (all types)	20 to 30%	$10 to $15
c.	Maintenance, commercial and residential	30 to 40%	$6 to $10
d.	Tree work	30 to 40%	$18 to $30
e.	Fertilizations and insecticides (all types)	40 to 50%	$18 to $24
f.	Irrigation service	40 to 50%	$24 to $30
g.	Bark blowing	30 to 40%	$36 to $48
h.	Hydroseeding	30 to 40%	$45 to $60
i.	Interior landscaping, installation	25 to 35%	$16 to $22
j.	Interior landscaping, maintenance	30 to 40%	$9 to $12
k.	Outdoor lighting	40 to 50%	$30 to $35
l.	Outdoor ponds	30 to 40%	$20 to $25
m.	Pavers	25 to 35%	$25 to $35
n.	Snow plowing	40 to 60%	$40 to $60
o.	Sanding and salting	50 to 70%	$125 to $175
p.	Christmas decorations	40 to 50%	$30 to $37

N. **Gross profit margin (GPM) as a percent of sales** Also as a gross profit margin per man-hour dollar amount (GPMPH) in a recession.

	Market Segment	GPM %	GPMPH
a.	Residential installation (all types)	20 to 30%	$12 to $20
b.	Commercial installation (all types)	15 to 25%	$8 to $13
c.	Maintenance, commercial and residential	25 to 35%	$8 to $14
d.	Tree work	25 to 35%	$14 to $20
e.	Fertilizations and insecticides (all types)	40 to 50%	$50 to $65

	Market Segment	GPM %	GPMPH
f.	Irrigation service	40 to 50%	$21 to $27
g.	Bark blowing	25 to 35%	$30 to $42
h.	Hydroseeding	25 to 35%	$35 to $55
i.	Interior landscaping, installation	15 to 25%	$9 to $17
j.	Interior landscaping, maintenance	25 to 35%	$7 to $10
k.	Outdoor lighting	35 to 45%	$25 to $35
l.	Outdoor ponds	25 to 35%	$15 to $22
m.	Pavers	25 to 35%	$25 to $35
n.	Snow plowing	40 to 60%	$40 to $60
o.	Sanding and salting	50 to 70%	$125 to $175
p.	Christmas decorations	35 to 45%	$25 to $35

O. General & administrative overhead costs as a percent of sales

	Market Segment	G&A as a % of Sales
a.	Residential installation (all types)	20% to 28%
b.	Commercial installation (all types)	15% to 25%
c.	Maintenance, commercial and residential	15% to 25%
d.	Tree work	20% to 28%
e.	Fertilizations and insecticides (all types)	15% to 25%
f.	Irrigation service	20% to 25%
g.	Bark blowing	20% to 25%
h.	Hydroseeding	20% to 25%
i.	Interior landscaping, installation	20% to 25%
j.	Interior landscaping, maintenance	20% to 25%
k.	Outdoor lighting	20% to 25%
l.	Outdoor ponds	20% to 25%
m.	Pavers	20% to 25%
n.	Snow plowing	10% to 20%
o.	Sanding and salting	10% to 20%
p.	Christmas decorations	20% to 25%
q.	Companies/divisions (all) over $10M in sales	8% to 12%

P. **General & administrative overhead cost per man-hour (OPH)**

	Market Segment	8- to 10-Month Season	12-Month Season
a.	Residential installation (all types)	$10 to $16	$8 to $12
b.	Commercial installation (all types)	$10 to $14	$7 to $10
c.	Maintenance, commercial and residential	$7 to $12	$5 to $10
d.	Tree work	$10 to $16	$8 to $12
e.	Fertilizations and insecticides (all types)	$10 to $16	$8 to $12
f.	Irrigation service	$10 to $13	$8 to $10
g.	Bark blowing	$15 to $25	$11 to $21
h.	Hydroseeding	$15 to $25	$11 to $21
i.	Interior landscaping, installation	$10 to $14	$7 to $10
j.	Interior landscaping, maintenance	$7 to $12	$5 to $10
k.	Outdoor lighting	$10 to $16	$8 to $10
l.	Outdoor ponds	$10 to $16	$8 to $10
m.	Pavers	$10 to $16	$8 to $10
n.	Snow plowing	$15 to $25	N/A
o.	Sanding and salting	$15 to $25	N/A
p.	Christmas decorations	$10 to $16	$8 to $10
q.	Companies/divisions over $10M in sales	$6 to $9	$4 to $7
r.	Maintenance over $10M in sales	$5 to $8	$3 to $6

Q. **General & administrative overhead salary costs (owner's at a fair market value salary) as a percent of sales**

	Annual Company Sales	Salaries as a % of Sales
a.	Up to $5,000,000	8% to 12%
b.	$5,000,000 to $10,000,000	6% to 8%
c.	Over $10,000,000	Under 7%

R. **General & administrative overhead salary labor burden cost (owner's at a fair market value salary) as a percent of overhead salary cost**

Annual Company Sales	Labor Burden as a % of Salaries
All	10% to 15%

S. **Commission costs as a percent of sales** Commissions include all benefits such as medical insurance, automobile expenses, etc. Commission remuneration does not include payment for design time, work performed as field labor, and administration time other than that directly involved in sales. Commission remuneration covers time for selling the job, coordinating with the field supervisor and client to ensure that the job is done correctly, and the final walk-through with the client.

	Market Segment	Commissions as a % of Sales
a.	Residential installation (all types)	8% to 12%
b.	Commercial installation (all types)	0% usually in G&A overhead
c.	Maintenance, commercial and residential	8% to 12%
d.	Maintenance extras (both)	8% to 12%
e.	Tree work	8% to 12%
f.	Fertilizations and insecticides (all types)	8% to 12%
g.	Irrigation service	0% usually in G&A overhead
h.	Bark blowing	0% usually in G&A overhead
i.	Hydroseeding	0% usually in G&A overhead
j.	Interior landscaping, installation	0% usually in G&A overhead
k.	Interior landscaping, maintenance	8% to 12%
l.	Outdoor lighting	8% to 12%
m.	Outdoor ponds	8% to 12%
n.	Pavers	8% to 12%
o.	Snow plowing	0% usually in G&A overhead
p.	Sanding and salting	0% usually in G&A overhead
q.	Christmas decorations	8% to 12%

T. **Owner's salary (at fair market value) for G&A overhead responsibilities performed** Pay for work performed in the field, other than light supervision, is in addition to G&A overhead salary. G&A overhead pay is before any bonuses are paid to owners.

	Annual Company Sales	FMV G&A Salary	Total Pay w/Bonuses & Perks
a.	Up to $300,000	$15,000 to $30,000	$50,000 to $65,000
b.	$300,000 to $600,000	$25,000 to $45,000	$65,000 to $85,000
c.	$600,000 to $1,000,000	$45,000 to $60,000	$75,000 to $100,000
d.	$1,000,000 to $2,500,000	$55,000 to $100,000	$95,000 to $250,000
e.	$2,500,000 to $5,000,000	$100,000 to $150,000	$150,000 to $350,000
f.	Over $5,000,000	Owner's prerogative	Owner's prerogative

U. **Net profit margins (before interest, taxes and bonuses) as a percent of sales** Owner(s) salary is at fair market value.

	Market Segment	NPM %	NPMPH $
a.	Residential installation (all types)	12% to 17%	$8 to $15
b.	Commercial installation (all types)	10% to 15%	$5 to $8
c.	Maintenance, commercial and residential	10% to 15%	$2 to $5
d.	Tree work	10% to 15%	$6 to $12
e.	Fertilizations and insecticides (all types)	15% to 25%	$15 to $30
f.	Irrigation service	15% to 25%	$9 to $15
g.	Bark blowing	15% to 25%	$15 to $30
h.	Hydroseeding	15% to 25%	$22 to $38
i.	Interior landscaping, installation	10% to 15%	$5 to $8
j.	Interior landscaping, maintenance	10% to 15%	$2 to $5
k.	Outdoor lighting	15% to 25%	$9 to $15
l.	Outdoor ponds	15% to 20%	$10 to $13
m.	Pavers	10% to 15%	$10 to $15
n.	Snow plowing	15% to 25%	$15 to $25*
o.	Sanding and salting	25% to 50%	$60 to $125*
p.	Christmas decorations	15% to 25%	$9 to $15
q.	Companies/divisions (all) over $10M in sales	8% to 12%	$4 to $8

*Varies dramatically

V. **Bonuses as a percent of net profit (before interest, taxes and owner's bonus) and sales** Owner(s) bonus is not included.

	Company Staff	Total Bonus %
a.	Division managers and/or key staff	Up to 10% of net profit
b.	Division managers and/or key staff	.5% to 2% of total sales
c.	Foremen and crew leaders	Up to 5% of net profit
d.	Foremen and crew leaders	.25% to 1% of total sales
e.	Field laborers	Owner's prerogative
f.	Administrative staff	Owner's prerogative

2. The Balance Sheet

The balance sheet is a snapshot of the business at a particular point in time. It can be very useful to the contractor who understands how to apply it to his or her business. Refer to Figure 46-1, which displays a sample Balance Sheet format.

> For purposes of exploring the interrelationship of uses and sources of funds and the allocation of risk for business enterprises, it is very helpful to refer to the balance sheet. The balance sheet is a summary or report that shows the assets and the sources of financing of a business at a particular point in time. It reveals two broad categories of information: the properties owned by a business, referred to as assets; and the creditors' claims and the owners' equity in the business assets. The creditors' claim, which are the financial obligations of the business, are referred to as liabilities.
>
> The balance sheet is in the nature of a snapshot, revealing the condition of a business as of a given date. Like a cutaway section of an automobile motor, however, the balance sheet also reveals much of the dynamic quality of the structure. The various classes of assets indicate at once the result of recent business operations and the capacity for future operations. The creditors' claims and the owners' equity in the assets reveal the sources from which the assets of the business were derived. The term "balance sheet" itself conveys a relationship of equality between the assets of the business and the sources of funds for their acquisition that may be expressed as follows: Assets = Liabilities + Owners' Equity. (Welshans and Melicher 1984)

There are a number of other ratios that you might want to explore. A list of references for doing so is included in the For Further Reading/Reference Material section on page 585. I have only included the most common ratios here.

Balance Sheet Ratio Analysis

Liquidity Ratios

A. **Current ratio** Current Assets ÷ Current Liabilities
The current ratio measures the ability of the company to pay its bills. A current ratio above 2.0 is desired.

B. **Quick ratio or "acid test"** (Cash + Accounts Receivable) ÷ Current Liabilities
The quick ratio excludes inventory and receivables other than current ones. It is a more stringent "acid test" measurement of the ability of the company to pay its bills. A quick ratio above 1.0 is desirable.

C. **Working capital** Total Current Assets – Total Current Liabilities
Working capital is a measure of cash flow. You want this calculation to be a positive number. The higher the current ratio, quick ratio, and working capital, the better. This is of particular importance to banks.

D. **Leverage ratio or Debt/Worth ratio** Total Liabilities ÷ Net Worth
The leverage ratio indicates how reliant the company is on creditor money as compared to owner's equity. A ratio of 1:1 is preferred.

Management or Productivity Ratios

A. **Inventory turnover** Materials Cost ÷ Average Inventory at Cost
This ratio is very seldom tracked in construction or service companies on a regular basis, but it is worthy of note. A ratio of 6 to 8:1 is not uncommon for such companies.

B. **Return on assets ratio** Net Profit After Tax ÷ Total Assets
The return on assets (ROA) ratio measures how efficiently profits are being produced from the assets being used in the business. A ratio of .25 to .5:1 is acceptable.

C. **Return on investment ratio** Net Profit After Tax ÷ Net Worth (Total Owner's Equity)
The return on investment (ROI) ratio measures the return the business is generating compared to the investment that the owners have in the company. Basically, it tells owners if they are obtaining an acceptable return on their investment in the company or whether they should consider liquidating the company and investing in something that provides a better rate of return (i.e., put your money in a bank savings account). A ratio of .1 to .15 is acceptable.

3. Bidding Benchmarks

You will see many of the benchmarks explained in the profit and loss statement on individual bids. We will not repeat them. However, there are some additional benchmarks that we need to cover regarding your bids.

A. **Percent won rate** The percent won rate is the percentage of bids that you win. Industry benchmarks are as follows:

	Market Segment	NPM as a % of Sales	Remarks
a.	Residential installation (all types)	30% to 40%	Open bid work
b.	Residential installation (all types)	60% to 90%	Designed by you
c.	Commercial installation (all types)	10% to 15%	Open bid work
d.	Commercial installation (all types)	Up to 100%	Negotiated work
e.	Maintenance, commercial	10% to 15%	
f.	Maintenance, residential	30% to 50%	
g.	Tree work	30% to 50%	
h.	Fertilizations and insecticides (all types)	30% to 50%	
i.	Irrigation service	25% to 45%	
j.	Bark blowing	30% to 50%	
k.	Hydroseeding	30% to 50%	
l.	Interior landscaping, installation	10% to 20%	
m.	Interior landscaping, maintenance	10% to 20%	
n.	Outdoor lighting	30% to 60%	
o.	Outdoor ponds	30% to 50%	
p.	Pavers	30% to 50%	
q.	Snow plowing	30% to 50%	
r.	Sanding and salting	30% to 50%	
s.	Christmas decorations	30% to 60%	

B. **Risk factor** The risk factor is a factor that is applied to your direct field-labor cost in a bid. For instance, a 10% risk factor applied to a $10 crew average wage would increase the labor rate in the bid to $11.

	Type Work	Risk Factor %	
a.	Construction projects	10% to 15%	Work is familiar to your crew
b.	Construction projects	15% to 20%	Work is unfamiliar to your crew
c.	Maintenance projects	First-time bid	
d.	Maintenance projects	Re-bidding of current work	

C. **Overtime factor (OTF)** The overtime factor is a multiplier that is also applied to your direct field- labor cost in a bid in order to adjust the labor rate for overtime hours worked. It is calculated by dividing the overtime hours paid by the total hours actually worked in a given week. For instance, you would add 10% to the crew average wage for a crew working a 50-hour week that gets time-and-a-half pay after working 40 hours in a week. You calculate the overtime factor by dividing the 5 hours of overtime paid by the 50 hours actually worked (5 ÷ 50 = .1 or 10%). The 10% overtime factor applied to a $10 crew average wage would increase the labor rate in the bid to $11.

Hours Worked per Week	Overtime Factor (Time-and-a-half after 40 hours)		
40	.000	or	00.0%
45	.056	or	05.6%
50	.100	or	10.0%
55	.136	or	13.6%
60	.167	or	16.7%
65	.192	or	19.2%
70	.214	or	21.4%

The overtime factor for the various industry market segments for companies in a 12-month work season as compared to an 8- to 10-month work season.

	Market Segment (12-Month Season)	Average Work Week Hours	OTF %
a.	Residential installation (all types)	40 to 45	0% to 5%
b.	Commercial installation (all types)	40 to 45	0% to 5%
c.	Maintenance, commercial	40 to 45	0% to 5%
d.	Maintenance, residential	40 to 45	0% to 5%
e.	Tree work	40 to 45	0% to 5%
f.	Fertilizations and insecticides (all types)	40 to 45	0% to 5%
g.	Irrigation service	40 to 45	0% to 5%

	Market Segment (12-Month Season)	Average Work Week Hours	OTF %
h.	Bark blowing	40 to 50	0% to 10%
i.	Hydroseeding	40 to 50	0% to 10%
j.	Interior landscaping, installation	40 to 50	0% to 10%
k.	Interior landscaping, maintenance	40 to 45	0% to 5%
l.	Outdoor lighting	40 to 50	0% to 10%
m.	Outdoor ponds	40 to 45	0% to 5%
n.	Pavers	40 to 45	0% to 5%
o.	Snow plowing	N/A	N/A
p.	Sanding and salting	N/A	N/A
q.	Christmas decorations	45 to 55	5% to 15%

N/A = Not applicable

	Market Segment (12-Month Season)	Average Work Week Hours	OTF %
a.	Residential installation (all types)	45 to 55	5% to 15%
b.	Commercial installation (all types)	45 to 60	5% to 17%
c.	Maintenance, commercial	40 to 50	0% to 10%
d.	Maintenance, residential	42 to 55	2% to 15%
e.	Tree work	40 to 50	0% to 10%
f.	Fertilizations and insecticides (all types)	40 to 50	0% to 10%
g.	Irrigation service	45 to 60	5% to 17%
h.	Bark blowing	45 to 60	5% to 17%
i.	Hydroseeding	45 to 60	5% to 17%
j.	Interior landscaping, installation	40 to 50	0% to 10%
k.	Interior landscaping, maintenance	40 to 50	0% to 10%
l.	Outdoor lighting	40 to 50	5% to 10%
m.	Outdoor ponds	40 to 50	0% to 10%
n.	Pavers	40 to 50	0% to 10%
o.	Snow plowing	N/A	N/A
p.	Sanding and salting	N/A	N/A
q.	Christmas decorations	45 to 60	5% to 20%

N/A = Not applicable

D. **Field labor rates and crew average wage (CAW)** The labor rates are for the various market industry segments and have no risk or overtime factor applied. It is assumed that the skill level of the crew leaders used in our illustrations is such that they require *minimal supervision.*

	Market Segment (12-Month Season)	Supervisor	Crew Leader*	CAW
a.	Residential installation (all types)	$15 to $20	$12 to $18	$11 to $13
b.	Commercial installation (all types)	$15 to $20	$12 to $18	$10 to $12
c.	Maintenance, commercial	$14 to $18	$10 to $14	$9 to $11
d.	Maintenance, residential	$14 to $18	$10 to $14	$9 to $11
e.	Tree work	$15 to $20	$14 to $20	$12 to $15
f.	Fertilizations and insecticides (all types)	$15 to $20	$11 to $16	$11 to $16
g.	Irrigation service	$15 to $20	$12 to $16	$12 to $16
h.	Bark blowing	$15 to $20	$12 to $16	$12 to $16
i.	Hydroseeding	$15 to $20	$12 to $16	$12 to $16
j.	Interior landscaping, installation	$15 to $20	$12 to $18	$10 to $12
k.	Interior landscaping, maintenance	$14 to $18	$10 to $14	$9 to $11
l.	Outdoor lighting	$15 to $20	$12 to $18	$12 to $14
m.	Outdoor ponds	$15 to $20	$12 to $18	$10 to $12
n.	Pavers	$15 to $20	$12 to $18	$10 to $12
o.	Snow plowing	N/A	N/A	N/A
p.	Sanding and salting	N/A	N/A	N/A
q.	Christmas decorations	$15 to $20	$12 to $18	$11 to $13

*Requires minimal supervision

	Market Segment (8- to 10-Month Season)	Supervisor	Crew Leader*	CAW
a.	Residential installation (all types)	$17 to $25	$14 to $24	$12 to $14
b.	Commercial installation (all types)	$17 to $25	$14 to $24	$11 to $13
c.	Maintenance, commercial	$15 to $20	$12 to $16	$10 to $12
d.	Maintenance, residential	$15 to $20	$12 to $16	$10 to $12
e.	Tree work	$18 to $25	$14 to $23	$13 to $16
f.	Fertilizations and insecticides (all types)	$18 to $25	$12 to $16	$12 to $16
g.	Irrigation service	$18 to $25	$12 to $18	$12 to $18
h.	Bark blowing	$18 to $25	$12 to $18	$12 to $18
i.	Hydroseeding	$18 to $25	$12 to $18	$12 to $18
j.	Interior landscaping, installation	$17 to $25	$14 to $24	$11 to $13

k.	Interior landscaping, maintenance	$15 to $20	$12 to $16	$10 to $12
l.	Outdoor lighting	$17 to $25	$14 to $24	$12 to $14
m.	Outdoor ponds	$17 to $25	$14 to $24	$12 to $14
n.	Pavers	$17 to $25	$14 to $24	$12 to $14
o.	Snow plowing	$17 to $25	$14 to $24	$12 to $14
p.	Sanding and salting	$17 to $25	$14 to $24	$12 to $14
q.	Christmas decorations	$17 to $25	$14 to $24	$12 to $14

*Requires minimal supervision

E. **General conditions** General condition costs as a percentage of the price of the bid and general condition man-hours as a percentage of all of the total man-hours in a bid.

	Market Segment	GC Cost/Price	GC Hours to Total Hours
a.	All installation work	5% to 10%	15% to 25%
b.	All maintenance/service work	10% to 15%	15% to 30%
c.	On-site maintenance/service work	5% to 10%	10% to 20%

F. **Net profit margin** Net profit as a percentage of the price for a job and net profit margin per field-labor hour in a bid.

	Market Segment	NPM %	NPM per Man-Hour
a.	Residential installation (all types)	12% to 17%	$8 to $15
b.	Commercial installation (all types)	10% to 15%	$5 to $8
c.	Maintenance, commercial and residential	10% to 15%	$2 to $5
d.	Tree work	10% to 15%	$6 to $12
e.	Fertilizations and insecticides (all types)	15% to 25%	$15 to $30
f.	Irrigation service	15% to 25%	$9 to $15
g.	Bark blowing	15% to 25%	$15 to $30
h.	Hydroseeding	15% to 25%	$22 to $38
i.	Interior landscaping, installation	10% to 15%	$5 to $8
j.	Interior landscaping, maintenance	10% to 15%	$2 to $5
k.	Outdoor lighting	15% to 25%	$9 to $15
l.	Outdoor ponds	15% to 20%	$10 to $13
m.	Pavers	10% to 15%	$10 to $15

n.	Snow plowing	15% to 25%	$15 to $25
o.	Sanding and salting	25% to 50%	$60 to $125
p.	Christmas decorations	15% to 25%	$9 to $15
q.	Companies/divisions (all) over $10M in sales	8% to 12%	$4 to $8

G. **Commissions on bids** Commissions, if they are paid at all, normally run 8 to 12% of the price of the job. Commission costs as a percentage of the bid price include all benefits such as medical insurance, automobile expenses, etc. Commission remuneration does not include payment for design time, work performed as field labor, and administration time other than directly involved in sales. Commission remuneration covers time for selling the job, coordinating with the field supervisor and client to ensure that the job is done correctly, and the final walk-through with the client.

Commissions are normally not paid on commercial installation and irrigation service work. Occasionally, a 2 to 3% commission is paid on commercial installation work.

4. General Industry Benchmarks

General industry benchmarks are not as specific as the ones already covered. However, they are important.

A. **Good will or blue sky** Good will or blue sky is the value of a business separate from any of its "hard" assets. In other words, it is the value of the business as a business. There are two main components for evaluating a business. The first is the assets of the business. Assets normally include inventory field equipment and office equipment. Real estate assets are normally handled separately from the evaluation of the hard assets of a business. Hard assets are normally evaluated at fair market value. Good will or blue sky, on the other hand, is not as easy to evaluate. There are as many theories as there are people evaluating businesses. The following blue sky and good will benchmarks are taken from actual situations involving Green Industry business either being bought or sold. Chapter 55 covers this subject in greater detail.

We will use two evaluation methods for evaluating a business. The first is the gross profit margin (GPM) model, which is based on past or historic sales. The second is the gross profit margin model, which is based on future sales taking place after the sale is completed.

	Market Segment	GPM % (past)	GPM % (future)
a.	Residential installation (all types)	not used	25% to 35%
b.	Commercial installation (all types)	not used	25% to 35%
c.	Maintenance, commercial	25% to 35%	25% to 35%
d.	Maintenance, residential	30% to 35%	30% to 35%
e.	Tree work	not used	25% to 35%
f.	Fertilizations and insecticides (all types)	35% to 55%	35% to 55%
g.	Irrigation service	35% to 55%	35% to 55%
h.	Bark blowing	not used	25% to 35%
i.	Hydroseeding	not used	25% to 35%
j.	Interior landscaping, installation	not used	25% to 35%
k.	Interior landscaping, maintenance	25% to 35%	25% to 35%
l.	Outdoor lighting	not used	25% to 35%

m.	Outdoor ponds	not used	25% to 35%
n.	Pavers	not used	25% to 35%
o.	Snow plowing	not used	25% to 35%
p.	Sanding and salting	not used	25% to 35%
q.	Christmas decorations	35% to 55%	35% to 55%

B. **Material pricing** We will utilize a sample item that retails for $10.00. The re-wholesale price is normally discounted 30 to 40% off of the retail or list price. The wholesale price is normally discounted 40 to 60% off of the retail or list price.

a. Retail price	$10.00	The price paid by a residential customer
b. List price	$10.00	The manufacturer's suggested retail price
c. Re-wholesale price	$ 7.00	The price paid to a supplier by a contractor
d. Wholesale	$ 5.00	The price a supplier pays a grower or manufacturer

C. **Rental equipment pricing** Rental equipment rates are normally 40 to 60% higher than the actual cost to own and operate a piece of equipment for a given period of time (day, week, or month). For instance, a mid-size skid steer with just a bucket that costs $30,000 new would cost approximately $18 per hour to own and operate. Remember, rental rates do not include fuel. The rental rate would calculate as follows:

Equipment CPH	$18.00
Daily Rental Rate	$18.00 × 1.5 = $27.00
	$27.00 × 8 hours per day = $216 per day

Endnotes

[1]Phillip B. Crosby, *Quality Is Free* (New York: Mentor, 1979) 66.

[2]James R. Huston, *Strategic Planning for Landscape & Irrigation Contractors* (Oceanside, CA: Smith Huston, Inc., 1990) 73.

[3]Crosby, *Quality Is Free* 66.

[4]*Yard & Garden Remodeling*, The Garden Council, Plant a Little Paradise™ brochure (Chicago, 1991).

[5]Tom Peters, *Thriving on Chaos* (New York: Knopf, 1987) 490.

[6]Peters 91.

[7]Peters 490.

[8]Peters 484–5.

[9]*Construction Industry Institute* (1989) 1.

[10]*Ernst & Young's Contractor Briefing*, vol. XI, no.2, March/April 1992 (Washington) 1.

[11]Robert H. Schaeffer and Harvey A. Thomson, "Successful Change Programs Begin with Results," *Harvard Business Review*, (Jan/Feb 1992) 80–81.

[12]Tracy E. Benson, "Quality Is Not What You Think It Is," *Industry Week* (October 5, 1992) 22.

[13]Benson, "A Business Strategy Comes of Age" (May 3, 1993) 40.

[14]Crosby, *Quality Is Free* 14–15.

[15]Crosby 14–15.

[16]Peters, *Thriving on Chaos* 481.

[17]Peters 490.

[18]Crosby, *Quality Is Free* 15.

[19]George Eckes, *The Six Sigma Revolution* (New York: John Wiley & Sons, Inc., 2001) 28.

[20]Eckes 37.

[21]Eckes 39.

[22]Eckes 70–71.

[23]Eckes 70.

[24]Eckes 94–95.

[25]Crosby, *Quality Is Free* 15.

[26]Carl L. Moore, Robert K. Jaedicke, and Lane K. Anderson, *Managerial Accounting* (Cincinnati: South-Western Publishing Co., 1984) 608.

[27]Merle T. Welshans and Ronald W. Melicher, "Finance," *Introduction to Markets, Institutions and Management* (Cincinnati: South-Western Publishing Co., 1984) 116–117.

EXHIBIT		PAGE REFERENCES
1.	Company Budget Worksheet	20, 53, 65
2.	Field-Labor Hours, Average Wage, and Payroll Worksheet	26, 27
3.	Crew Average Wage (CAW) Worksheet	32
4.	Labor Burden Worksheet (USA)	37
5.	Labor Burden Worksheet (Canada)	37, 41
6.	Budget Definitions	53
7.	Equipment CPH Worksheet	61, 65
8.	Bid Worksheet	75
9.	Bid Analysis Review (BAR) Worksheet	113
10.	Large Commercial Maintenance Bid Example	202, 396, 471
11.	The M.A.D. (Monthly Audit Data) Report	337
12.	Construction Field Daily Report	352
13.	Maintenance Field Daily Report	352
14.	Small Maintenance/Residential Bid Example	396, 471
15.	Henderson Construction Bid Example	396, 471

	Landscape	Irrigation	Maintenance	Total
I. Sales (Revenue)	$______	$______	$______	$______
II . Cost of Goods Sold (COGS) or Direct Costs				
1. Material and Supplies				
2. Direct Labor				
3. Direct Labor Burden				
4. Subcontractors				
5. Equipment				
6. Rental Equipment				
7. Misc.				
Total COGS				
III. Gross Profit Margin (GPM)				
IV. G&A Overhead or Indirect Costs				
1. Advertising				
2. Bad Debts				
3. Computers & Digitizers				
4. Donations				
5. Downtime Labor (_________Hrs)				
6. Downtime Labor Burden (_____%)				
7. Dues / Subscriptions				
8. Insurance: Office, Med., Keyman				
9. Interest and Bank Charges				
10. Licenses and Surety Bonds				
11. Office Equipment				
12. Office Supplies				
13. Professional Fees				
14. Radios / Beepers / Car Phones				
15. Rent (Office & Yard)				
16. Salaries: Office Staff (_______%)				
17. Salaries: Officer (s) (_______%)				
18. Salaries: Labor Burden (_______%)				
19. Small Tools and Supplies				
20. Taxes: Business / Asset Tax				
21. Telephone				
22. Training and Education				
23. Travel and Entertainment				
24. Uniforms and Safety Equipment				
25. Utilities				
26. Vehicles, Overhead				
27. Yard Expense / Leasehold Improv.				
28. Miscellaneous				
29. ______________________				
Total G&A Overhead				
V. Net Profit: Gain / (Loss)	$______	$______	$______	$______
VI. Overhead Per Hour by Division	$_____.____	$_____.____	$_____.____	$_____.____
VII. Sales Per Hour by Division	$_____.____	$_____.____	$_____.____	$_____.____
VIII. Filed-labor hours by Division				

EXHIBIT 1 Company Budget Worksheet—Projected Company/Division Budget for the Next Twelve Months

1. Average wage (AW) calculation:

A. Landscape **Division**:

	(a) Qty	(b) Hrs/Mo	(c) Mos/Yr	(d) Total Hours	(e) Hourly Rate	(f) Total Payroll
(1) Foremen	_______	__________	__________	__________	\$_____.___	\$____________
(2) Foremen	_______	__________	__________	__________	\$_____.___	\$____________
(3) Leadmen	_______	__________	__________	__________	\$_____.___	\$____________
(4) Leadmen	_______	__________	__________	__________	\$_____.___	\$____________
(5) Laborers	_______	__________	__________	__________	\$_____.___	\$____________
(6) Laborers	_______	__________	__________	__________	\$_____.___	\$____________
(7) Totals:				* __________		** \$____________

(8) AW = Total Payroll / Total Hours = ____________________ = \$________.____

(9) AW Multiplied by (1+OTF) = \$_________._____ x (1.____) = \$________.____

B. Irrigation Division:

(1) Foremen	_______	__________	__________	__________	\$_____.___	\$____________
(2) Foremen	_______	__________	__________	__________	\$_____.___	\$____________
(3) Leadmen	_______	__________	__________	__________	\$_____.___	\$____________
(4) Leadmen	_______	__________	__________	__________	\$_____.___	\$____________
(5) Laborers	_______	__________	__________	__________	\$_____.___	\$____________
(6) Laborers	_______	__________	__________	__________	\$_____.___	\$____________
(7) Totals:				* __________		** \$____________

(8) AW = Total Payroll / Total Hours = ____________________ = \$________.____

(9) AW Multiplied by (1+OTF) = \$_________._____ x (1.____) = \$________.____

EXHIBIT 2 Field-Labor Hours, Average Wage, and Payroll Worksheet

C. Maintenance / Service Division:

	(a) Qty	(b) Hrs/Mo	(c) Mos/Yr	(d) Total Hours	(e) Hourly Rate	(f) Total Payroll
(1) Foremen	______	______	______	______	\$____.__	\$______
(2) Foremen	______	______	______	______	\$____.__	\$______
(3) Leadmen	______	______	______	______	\$____.__	\$______
(4) Leadmen	______	______	______	______	\$____.__	\$______
(5) Laborers	______	______	______	______	\$____.__	\$______
(6) Laborers	______	______	______	______	\$____.__	\$______
(7) Totals:				*______		** \$______

(8) AW = Total Payroll / Total Hours = ____________ = \$______.___

(9) AW Multiplied by (1+OTF) = \$______.____ x (1.___) = \$______.___

2. Overtime Factor (OTF):

	Sample	Your Co.
A. Average number hours worked per man per week	50	______
B. Average number overtime hours worked per man per week	10	______
C. Average number overtime hours paid per man per week	15	______

D. OTF = $\frac{C - B}{A}$ = $\frac{15-10}{50}$ = $\frac{5}{50}$ = .1 or 10%

E. Landscape division OTF = ______-______ = ______ = .______

F. Irrigation division OTF = ______-______ = ______ = .______

G. Maintenance division OTF = ______-______ = ______ = .______

3. **Risk Factor (RF):** (Used on specific jobs. Do not use in the field-labor hour budget)

4. **Total Hours and Payroll for the Year:**

	Landscape	Irrigation	Maintenance
A. Total labor hours (see * above):	______	______	______
B. Total payroll (see ** above):	\$______	\$______	______
C. Last year's field payroll if available:	\$______	\$______	______
D. Last year's field-labor hours if available:	______	______	______

EXHIBIT 2 Field-Labor Hours, Average Wage, and Payroll Worksheet (*continued*)

Date: ______/______/______ Prepared by: ________________________

Job: ____________________________ Crew size: ________

Type crew: ______________________ Hours per person per day: _______

Type of labor	Name (if applicable)	Labor Rate(s)
		$_______._____
		$_______._____
		$_______._____
		$_______._____
		$_______._____
		$_______._____
		$_______._____
		$_______._____
		$_______._____
		$_______._____
		$_______._____
		$_______._____

Total number in crew ______ Labor total $_______._____

1. Divide labor total $__________ by # in crew ______ = $_______._____

2. Add OTF % (_____%) $_______._____

   Subtotal $_______._____

3. Add RF % (10-20%) $_______._____

   Subtotal $_______._____

4. Round up as appropriate to obtain CAW $_______._____

EXHIBIT 3 Crew Average Wage (CAW) Worksheet

	Landscape	Irrigation	Maintenance	Office
F.I.C.A. (company portion) rate	.________	.________	.________	.________
F.U.T.A. (federal unemp.) rate	.________	.________	.________	.________
S.U.T.A. (state unemp.) rate	.________	.________	.________	.________
Workers' compensation rate	.________	.________	.________	.________
General liability insurance rate (1)	.________	.________	.________	N/A
Vacations (2)	.________	.________	.________	N/A
Holidays (3)	.________	.________	.________	N/A
Sick days (4)	.________	.________	.________	N/A
Medical/health insurance (5)	.________	.________	.________	N/A
________________	.________	.________	.________	.________
Totals------------------→	.________	.________	.________	.________

Calculations for above:

1. **General liability insurance:**
   Use policy rate for hundred dollars of field payroll or divide annual premium $__________ by projected annual field payroll $____________ = .________.

2. **Field-labor vacations:**
   Divide total field crew vacation weeks paid in the year____________ by the total field work force weeks in the year______________ = .______________.

3. **Field-labor holidays:**
   Divide total field crew holidays paid in the year______________ by the total field work force man days in the year ______________ = .______________.

4. **Field-labor sick days:**
   Divide total field crew sick days earned in the year ____________ by the total field work force man days in the year ______________ = .______________.

5. **Field-labor health/medical insurance:**
   Divide total annual health/medical insurance payment (for field personnel only) $__________ by projected annual field payroll $____________ = .________.

EXHIBIT 4 Labor Burden Worksheet (USA)

	Construction	Maintenance	Irrigation	Office
Canada pension plan (CPT)	.________	.________	.________	.________
Employment insurance (EI)	.________	.________	.________	.________
Workers' compensation board	.________	.________	.________	.________
________________	.________	.________	.________	.________
General liability insurance rate (1)	.________	.________	.________	N/A
Vacations (2)	.________	.________	.________	N/A
Holidays (3)	.________	.________	.________	N/A
Sick days (4)	.________	.________	.________	N/A
Medical/health insurance (5)	.________	.________	.________	N/A
________________	.________	.________	.________	.________
Totals---------------------------→	.________	.________	.________	.________

Calculations for above:

1. **General liability insurance:**
   Use policy rate for hundred dollars of field payroll or divide annual premium $________ by projected annual field payroll $________ = .________.

2. **Field-labor vacations:**
   Divide total field crew vacation weeks paid in the year________ by the total field work force weeks in the year________ = .________.

3. **Field-labor holidays:**
   Divide total field crew holidays paid in the year________ by the total field work force man days in the year ________ = .________.

4. **Field-labor sick days:**
   Divide total field crew sick days earned in the year ________ by the total field work force man days in the year ________ = .________.

5. **Field-labor health/medical insurance:**
   Divide total annual health/medical insurance payment (for field personnel only) $________ by projected annual field payroll $________ = .________.

EXHIBIT 5 Labor Burden Worksheet (Canada)

1. ADVERTISING:

A. Yellow pages. $________
B. Newspaper ads/help wanted ads. ________
C. Magazines, bill boards, door hangers, bulk mail. ________
D. Web page (depreciate over 3 years) and monthly fee. ________
E. Company brochures (pro rate over # of years). ________
F. Garden, trade and home shows. ________
G. Company resume. ________
H. Web site development (spread over 3 years). ________
I. Web site maintenance fees. ________
$________

Note: Does not include business cards, which are put in office supplies.

2. BAD DEBTS:

A. Usually .5 to 1% of gross sales.
B. Percent of Accounts Receivables which are written off.
$________

3. COMPUTERS and SOFTWARE:

A. Computer, software, and digitizers are included in this category (Depreciate over a three-to-five year period). $________
B. Include costs to have consultants train your staff (in-house). ________
C. Maintenance contracts and repairs. ________
$________

4. **DONATIONS:** Do not include donations from profits made to reduce taxes.

A. Cash or time (hours _______ x ________ CAW) = $________
B. Only a donation that will put you in a good light in the public eye. ________
C. Team uniforms (i.e., Little League teams). ________
$________

5. **DOWNTIME LABOR:** Time field crews are still paid but are not working in the field and producing billable hours. Time spent working on/repairing equipment is not included. Is usually one hour per week for field employee.

A. Rain/weather - can include non-productive winter crew time. ________ Hrs
B. Equipment breakdown (i.e., to and from jobs). ________ Hrs
C. Busy work - fixing shovels, cleaning/fixing yard, watering nursery plants. ________ Hrs

EXHIBIT 6 Budget Definitions

D. Safety meetings, crew seminars and miscellaneous crew meeting time. ________ Hrs
E. Watering nursery material (only if nursery is not separate division). ________ Hrs
F. ____ ________ Hrs
Total ________ Hrs

6. **DOWNTIME LABOR BURDEN:** A percent markup on down time labor to cover FICA, FUTA, SUTA, WCI, etc.

7. **DUES and SUBSCRIPTIONS:**

A. Dues to national, state and local organizations. $__________
B. Chamber of Commerce, Better Business Bureau, etc. __________
C. Professional magazines. __________
D. Dodge reports, Plan rooms, Green sheets, etc. __________
E. Any type of business-related publications. __________
F. Discount warehouse dues. __________
G. ____ __________
$__________

8. **INSURANCE:**

A. Office contents insurance (usually $100 to 250 per year). $__________
B. Health insurance for G&A overhead people (i.e., owner(s), secretary, accountant, bookkeeper, estimator, sales/field supervisors). __________
C. Life and keyman insurance is included as long as the company is the beneficiary. __________
$__________

9. **INTEREST and BANK CHARGES:**

A. Interest on line of credit. $__________
B. Lost interest on company's retained earnings used for working capital (interest on 4-5 weeks of payroll). __________
C. Supplier interest on past due payables. __________
D. Credit card interest. __________
E. Bank bounced check fees and service fees.
F. Credit card processing fees. __________
$__________

Note: Does not include:
(1). Past due receivables owed to you.

EXHIBIT 6 Budget Definitions (*continued*)

(2). Interest on equipment or mortgage payments.

10. LICENSES and SURETY BONDS: City licenses are usually not included here and are put in general conditions on bids.

A. State contractor's license, city and county business license. $__________
B. Surety bond on contractor's license. __________
$__________

11. OFFICE EQUIPMENT DEPRECIATION, REPAIRS and SERVICE CONTRACTS: Divide total cost for each category by its years of useful life. Does not include field equipment, overhead vehicles, computers, telephones, radios and digitizers.

A. Office equipment (general office equipment). $__________
B. Office furniture, desks (10 years). __________
C. File cabinets (10 years). __________
D. Coffee machine, copy machine, blue print machine. __________
E. Calculators, typewriters. __________
F. Plan rack. __________
G. Drafting table (10 years). __________
H. Plants, pictures, art. __________
I. Repairs/maintenance contracts. __________
J. ______________________________ __________
$__________

12. OFFICE SUPPLIES:

A. Pens, pencils, paper, paper clips, toner, etc. $__________
B. Stationery, invoices, printing of forms, etc. __________
C. Business cards. __________
D. Postage. __________
E. ______________________________ __________
$__________

13. PROFESSIONAL FEES:

A. Outside CPA or bookkeeper. $__________
B. Legal fees (not to include cost of law suits). __________
C. Consultants (other than computer consultants). __________
D. Outside payroll services. __________
E. Cost of Corporate Tax preparation at end of year. __________
F. Incorporation cost spread over five years. __________

EXHIBIT 6 Budget Definitions (*continued*)

G. ______________________________________ ________
$________

14. RADIO SYSTEM and CAR PHONE:

A. 2-way radio system (depreciate over 5-10 years of useful lifetime). $________
B. Beepers, pagers. ________
C. Cellular phones (depreciate over 2-3 years). ________
D. Maintenance of above items (to include anticipated repairs). ________
E. Repeater charge. ________
F. Monthly line charges and monthly long distance charges. ________
G. ______________________________________ ________
$________

15. RENT (OFFICE and YARD):

A. Office space (fair market value). $________
B. Storage facilities and yard. ________
$________

16. **SALARIES - OFFICE:** Bookkeeper, office manager, secretary, estimator, designer, field supervisor (pro-rate if a "working" supervisor). $________

17. **SALARIES - OFFICER (S):** Corporate officers' salaries at fair market value. Total of 16 and 17 should total between 8% to 12% of gross sales. $________

18. **SALARIES - LABOR BURDEN (OFFICE):** A percent markup on 16 and 17 to cover FICA, FUTA, SUTA, WCI, etc. $________

19. SMALL TOOLS and NON-OFFICE SUPPLIES:

A. Wheelbarrows and non-motorized items. $________
B. Hand tools to repair equipment, rakes, shovels, hoes, etc. ________
C. Tarps, nails, paint and miscellaneous hardware for office use. ________
$________

20. TAXES (ASSET or MILL TAX)

A. Business privilege tax/Mill tax. $________
B. G&A office (not field equipment) portion of asset tax. ________
$________

EXHIBIT 6 Budget Definitions (*continued*)

21. TELEPHONE:

A. Line charges. $__________
B. Long distance charges. __________
C. Rental (if any). __________
D. Depreciate system over 5-10 years. __________
E. Answering service/machine, fax machine. __________
F. Repairs and maintenance contracts. __________
G. DSL lines or internet cable fees. __________

$__________

22. TRAINING and EDUCATION: See # 23 for travel and entertainment costs.

A. Books, videos, tapes, VCR, digital camera, etc. $__________
B. Workshops and seminar entrance fees. __________
C. Community college/continuing education classes. __________
D. Convention entrance fees/registration fees. __________

$__________

23. TRAVEL and ENTERTAINMENT:

A. Travel cost(s) to go to seminars, workshops or conventions. $__________
B. Hotel bills associated with seminars, workshops and conventions. __________
C. Lunches/dinners for clients. __________
D. Christmas party for employees/gifts at Thanksgiving, etc. __________
E. Employee parties/meals if company pays for them. __________
F. ______________________________ __________

$__________

24. UNIFORMS and SAFETY EQUIPMENT:

A. T-shirts and ball caps. $__________
B. Uniform rental and/or cleaning services. __________
C. Cold weather gear. __________
D. Safety equipment (i.e., goggles, gloves, ear protectors and hard hats if not included in small tools/supplies). __________

$__________

25. UTILITIES:

A. Water, sewer and electricity for office/yard. $__________
B. Gas and oil for heating office/yard spaces. __________

EXHIBIT 6 Budget Definitions (*continued*)

C. Trash service, non-job related dumpster, yard dumpster fees. __________
D. Office and/or yard security services. __________
E. Office cleaning services. __________

$__________

26. VEHICLES, OVERHEAD:

A. Vehicles used by overhead personnel for overhead purposes (e.g., trucks that do not go out on the job). $__________
B. Office staff mileage reimbursement for personal vehicle use. __________

$__________

27. YARD EXPENSE/LEASEHOLD IMPROVEMENTS:

A. Cost associated with maintaining a storage yard. $__________
B. Leasehold improvements to your office depreciated over the life of improvements (carpet, painting, tenant improvements, etc.). __________

$__________

28. MISCELLANEOUS: A catch-all category. Keep under $500. $__________

EXHIBIT 6 Budget Definitions (*continued*)

Equipment Cost Per Hour (CPH) Calculations

Item & Use	Purchase Price (Incl. Interest & Deduct Salvage Value)	÷	Life Expectancy (In Hours)	=	(1) Acquisition CPH	Anticipated Lifetime Maint., Insur., & License Costs		÷	Life Expectancy (In Hours)	=	(2) Maintenance CPH	(3) Fuel & Oil CPH	(1 + 2 + 3) TOTAL CPH
Pickup, Mini Owner/office	14,000		8,320		$1.68	$9,000			8,320		$1.08	$1.20	$3.96
______ Item ______ Use	$______		______		$____.__	Total Insurance License / registrations Oil changes Tires Tire repairs Brakes Hydraulic system Blades / sharpening Transmissions / clutches Teeth, pins, etc. Hoses & belts Washing vehicles Preventitive maint. Misc. ______ ______	$______ ______ ______ ______ ______ ______ ______ ______ ______ ______ ______ ______ ______ ______ ______ ______ ______	÷	______	=	$____.__	$____.__ A. GL/HR × $/GL = CPH ____ × $____.__ = $____.__ B. (1) Lifetime miles/Miles per GL = Lifetime GLs ______ = ______ (2) Lifetime GLS × $/GL = Lifetime $ ____ × $____.__ = $____.__ (3) Lifetime $/Life Expectancy = CPH $______ = $______.__	$____.__
______ Item ______ Use	$______	÷	______	=	$____.__	Total Insurance License / registrations Oil changes Tires Tire repairs Brakes Hydraulic system Blades / sharpening Transmissions / clutches Teeth, pins, etc. Hoses & belts Washing vehicles Preventitive maint. Misc. ______ ______	$______ ______ ______ ______ ______ ______ ______ ______ ______ ______ ______ ______ ______ ______ ______ ______ ______	÷	______	=	$____.__	$____.__ A. GL/HR × $/GL = CPH ____ × $____.__ = $____.__ B. (1) Lifetime miles/Miles per GL = Lifetime GLs ______ = ______ (2) Lifetime GLS × $/GL = Lifetime $ ____ × $____.__ = $____.__ (3) Lifetime $/Life Expectancy = CPH $______ = $______.__	$____.__

EXHIBIT 7 Equipment CPH Worksheet

BID WORKSHEET

PROJECT: ______________________ PAGE ( ) OF ( )

LOCATION: ______________________ DATE PREPARED: ____/____/____

P.O.C./G.C.: ______________________ ESTIMATOR: ______________________

DUE: ____/____/____ PH.: ____________ FAX: ____________ CREW SIZE: ______________________

TYPE WORK: ______________________ HOURS/DAY: ____________ CAW: $______.___

REMARKS:

DESCRIPTION	QTY	UNIT	U/C	MAT'L	LABOR	EQUIP	SUBS

EXHIBIT 8 Bid Worksheet

Date: ____/____/____ **Job:** ______________________

I. PRODUCTION OF FINISHED PRODUCT / SERVICE:

Materials	Labor	Equipment	Subcontractors
(A) $________	(B) $________	(C) $________	(D) $________

II. GENERAL CONDITIONS:

	Materials	Labor	Equipment	Subcontractors
	(A) $________	(B) $________	(C) $________	(D) $________
(Subtotal 1)	$________	$________	$________	$________

III. MARGINS and MARKUPS:

A. $________ (Sales tax ______% on materials)

B. (Labor burden ______%) $________

(Subtotal 2) $________ $________ $________ $________

(Subtotal 3) Total direct costs or **TDC** (Sum of all items in subtotal 2 above) $________

C. G&A overhead recovery (Total hours in I & II multiplied by OPH) $________

D. **BEP**: (Total direct costs plus G&A overhead) $________

E. Contingency factor if applicable $________

F. Net profit margin $________

G. Total price for the job (D+E+F) $________

IV. RATIO / PER HOUR ANALYSIS:

A. SPH / RPH:	$_____.___		J. MAT/LAB:	_____: 1
B. DCPH:	$_____.___		K. MPH:	$_____.___
C. OPH:	$_____.___		L. EQ/LAB:	_____: 1
D. PPH:	$_____.___		M. EQPH:	$_____.___
E. BEP:	$_____.___	_____.___%	N. GC:	$_____.___
F. G&A ovhd.:	$_____.___	_____.___%	O. GCPH:	$_____.___
G. NPM:	$_____.___	_____.___%	P. GCH/TH:	_____.___%
H. GPM:	$_____.___	_____.___%	Q. FACTOR:	_____.___
I. GPMPH:	$_____.___	_____.___%	R. UNIT PRICE:	$_____.___

EXHIBIT 9 Bid Analysis/Review (BAR) Worksheet

J. R. Huston Enterprises, Inc.

Bid Worksheet Recap

JCN: Mowing-2 **Job Description: Large Commercial Maintenance Job**

	Material	Labor	Equipment		Subcontract	% of Total
I. Production Costs	$10,170.00	$173,576.11	$77,072.91		$0.00	59.05%
II. General Conditions	$0.00	$0.00	$0.00		$0.00	0.00%
Subtotal	$10,170.00	$173,576.11	$77,072.91		$0.00	59.05%
III. Margins & Markups						
A. Sales Tax (mat. cost)	$788.18					0.18%
B. Labor Burden		$52,072.83				11.79%
Subtotal	$10,958.18	$225,648.94	$77,072.91		$0.00	
Total Direct Costs					**$313,680.10**	71.02%
C. G & A Overhead Recovery	13,969.20	labor hours times	$6.00	OPH	$83,815.20	18.98%
BEP Subtotal (Direct Costs + Overhead)					**$397,495.30**	90.00%
D. Net Profit						
Net Profit Margin:	10.00%		$44,166.18*			
Profit per Hour:	13,969.20 hours X PPH	$1.00	$13,969.20			
Price Override:	0.00%		$0.00			
* 0.34 difference due to rounding.					$44,166.52*	10.00%
E. Job Price Subtotal:					$441,661.82	100.00%
F. Sales Tax (if on whole job):					$0.00	0.00%
G: Job Price Total:					**$441,661.82**	100.00%

EXHIBIT 10 Large Commercial Maintenance Bid Example

J. R. Huston Enterprises, Inc.

Ratio Analysis

JCN: Mowing-2 **Job Description:** Large Commercial Maintenance Job

Market Comparison Analysis Report (using estimating methods):

1. Factor (price divided by materials) 40.30

2. Unit Price (job total price divided by units) $441,661.82 per LS

3. Gross Profit:

Net Profit Margin	Overhead	Gross Profit Margin
44,166.52	83,815.20	$127,981.72
10.00%	18.98%	28.98%

4. Material Overhead Recovery System (MORS) method:

	Factor	Overhead Allocation
A. Materials	10.0%	$1,095.82
B. Equipment	25.0%	$19,268.23
C. Subcontractors	5.0%	$0.00
D. Labor (with labor burden)	28.12%	$63,451.15
Total G & A overhead allocation		$83,815.20

5. G & A Overhead and Profit per Field-Labor Hour method:

A. Total field labor hours in bid	13,969.20
B. Overhead per Hour (OPH)	$6.00
C. Net Profit per Hour (PPH)	$3.16
D. Gross profit per Hour (GPPH)	$9.16
E. Sales per Hour (SPH)	$31.62

Ratio & Per Hour Analysis Report:

1. Sales per Hour (SPH)	$31.62
2. Materials:	
A. Materials to Labor ratio (w/o tax or LB)	0.06 : 1
B. Materials per Hour (w/o tax)	$0.73
C. Materials Factor (price divided by materials w/o tax)	43.43
3. Labor:	
A. Total field-labor hours in bid	13,969.20
B. Job Average Wage (including OTF & RF)	$12.43
4. Equipment:	
A. Equipment to Labor ratio (w/o LB)	0.44 : 1
B. Equipment to Labor percent (w/o LB)	44.40%
C. Equipment per Hour	$5.52
5. Subcontractors:	
A. Total subcontractor costs in bid	$0.00
B. Total subcontractor cost as a percent of price	0.00%
6. General Conditions:	
A. General Conditions as percent of price	0.00%
B. General Conditions per Hour (GCPH)	$0.00
C. General Conditions hours to Total hours (GCHTH)	0.00%
7. Direct Costs:	
Total Direct Costs in bid	$313,680.10
Total Direct Costs as percent of Price	71.02%

EXHIBIT 10 Large Commercial Maintenance Bid Example (*continued*)

J. R. Huston Enterprises, Inc.
Unit Price Lite

JCN: Mowing-2 **Job Description: Large Commercial Maintenance Job**

Bid #	Bid Description	Type Code	Qty	Unit	Unit Price	Set	Total Price	Labor Hrs	Labor	Equipment	Material	Subcontract	Total Cost
1	Spring Cleanup	Cleanup	1.0	LS	$6,312.90		$6,312.90	170.0	$2,862.86	$1,260.00	$538.75	$0.00	$4,661.61
2	Mowing, 72"	Mow	40.0	Each	$2,466.93		$98,677.33	3,520.0	$55,369.60	$12,320.00	$0.00	$0.00	$67,689.60
3	Mowing, 72"	Mow	2,080.0	AC	$36.34		$75,580.27	2,288.0	$35,990.24	$18,304.00	$0.00	$0.00	$54,294.24
4	Mowing, 48"	Mow	40.0	Each	$380.36		$15,214.22	502.9	$7,909.94	$2,765.71	$0.00	$0.00	$10,675.66
5	Mowing, 21" Push Mower	Mow	40.0	Each	$1,143.08		$45,723.02	1,664.0	$26,174.72	$4,992.00	$0.00	$0.00	$31,166.72
6	Mowing, 21" Push Mower	Mow	189.0	AC	$241.80		$45,701.04	1,663.2	$26,162.14	$4,989.60	$0.00	$0.00	$31,151.74
7	Edging	Maint	40.0	Each	$142.88		$5,715.38	208.0	$3,271.84	$624.00	$0.00	$0.00	$3,895.84
8	Back-Pack Blower	Maint	40.0	Each	$549.56		$21,982.22	800.0	$12,584.00	$2,400.00	$0.00	$0.00	$14,984.00
9	Weeding	Maint	40.0	Each	$1,255.51		$50,220.44	2,080.0	$32,718.40	$0.00	$0.00	$0.00	$32,718.40
10	General Cleanup	Maint	40.0	Each	$24.14		$965.78	40.0	$629.20	$0.00	$0.00	$0.00	$629.20
11	Redwood Mulch	Mulch	300.0	CY	$53.39		$16,018.43	360.0	$5,238.09	$1,200.00	$5,818.50	$0.00	$12,256.59
12	Fertilizer	Fertilizer	17,600.0	LB	$0.32		$5,623.08	35.2	$775.10	$281.60	$3,792.80	$0.00	$4,849.57
13	Fall Cleanup	Cleanup	1.0	LS	$8,644.59		$8,644.59	238.0	$4,008.00	$1,536.00	$808.13	$0.00	$6,352.13
14	General Conditions	GC	1.0	LS	$45,283.11		$45,283.11	400.0	$11,954.80	$26,400.00	$0.00	$0.00	$38,354.80
							$441,661.82	**13,969.3**	**$225,648.94**	**$77,072.91**	**$10,958.18**	**$0.00**	**$313,680.10**

EXHIBIT 10 Large Commercial Maintenance Bid Example *(continued)*

J. R. Huston Enterprises, Inc.

Bid Worksheet Detail

JCN: Mowing-2 **Job Description: Large Commercial Maintenance Job**

Assembly	MLESN Code	Detail Description	Qty Unit	PLES Code	Remarks	Unit Cost	Warr %	Qty 1 /MHr	MHRS	Cost ($)
Bid Item:	**Spring Cleanup**		**1.0000 LS**		**Type: Cleanup**		**Phase:**			
CLEANUP, SPRING, COMMERCIAL	L	LABOR, 4 MEN	140.0000 HR	MM	MAINT CREW (4 MEN)	$10.00		1.000	140.00	$2,202.20
	E	CREW TRUCK	40.0000 HR	103	TRUCK, PICKUP-1 TON	$10.00		1.000	40.00	$400.00
	M	DUMP FEES	1.0000 LS			$500.00				$538.75
	E	STREET CLEANING	12.0000 HR	129	STREET SWEEPER	$35.00		1.000	12.00	$420.00
	E	DUMPTRUCK	20.0000 HR	106	DUMPTRUCK, 5 CY	$20.00		1.000	20.00	$400.00
	L	LOAD/UNLOAD TIME	10.0000 HR	MM	MAINT CREW (4 MEN)	$10.00		1.000	10.00	$157.30
	L	DRIVE TIME	10.0000 HR	MM	MAINT CREW (4 MEN)	$10.00		1.000	10.00	$157.30
	L	SUPERVISOR'S TIME	10.0000 HR	S	SUPERVISOR STEP #1	$22.00		1.000	10.00	$346.06
	E	SUPERVISOR'S TRUCK	10.0000 HR	100	TRUCK, MINI PICKUP	$4.00		1.000	10.00	$40.00
								Bid Item Subtotal:	252.00	$4,661.61
								Bid Item Unit Price:		$6,312.90
Bid Item:	**Mowing, 72"**		**40.0000 Each**		**Type: Mow**		**Phase:**			
MOWING, 36"	E	MOW SITE	1,760,000.0000 HR	141	MOWER 36"	$3.50		20,000.000	88.00	$308.00
	L	OPERATOR	1,760,000.0000 SF	MM	MAINT CREW (4 MEN)	$10.00		20,000.000	88.00	$1,384.24
								Bid Item Subtotal:	176.00	$1,692.24
								Bid Item Unit Price:		$2,466.93
Bid Item:	**Mowing, 72"**		**2,080.0000 AC**		**Type: Mow**		**Phase:**			
MOWING, 60" - PER ACRE	E	MOW SITE	44,000.0000 SF	143	MOWER 60"	$8.00		40,000.000	1.10	$8.80
	L	OPERATOR	44,000.0000 SF	MM	MAINT CREW (4 MEN)	$10.00		40,000.000	1.10	$17.30
								Bid Item Subtotal:	2.20	$26.10
								Bid Item Unit Price:		$36.34

EXHIBIT 10 Large Commercial Maintenance Bid Example (*continued*)

J. R. Huston Enterprises, Inc.
Bid Worksheet Detail

JCN: Mowing-2 **Job Description: Large Commercial Maintenance Job**

Assembly	MLESN Code	Detail Description	Qty Unit	PLES Code	Remarks	Unit Cost	Warr %	Qty 1 /MHr	MHRS	Cost ($)
Bid Item:	**Mowing, 48"**		**40.0000 Each**		**Type: Mow**		**Phase:**			
MOWING, 48"	E	MOW SITE	440,000.0000 SF	142	MOWER 48"	$5.50		35,000.000	12.57	$69.14
	L	OPERATOR	440,000.0000 SF	MM	MAINT CREW (4 MEN)	$10.00		35,000.000	12.57	$197.75
								Bid Item Subtotal:	25.14	$266.89
								Bid Item Unit Price:		$380.36
Bid Item:	**Mowing, 21" Push Mower**		**40.0000 Each**		**Type: Mow**		**Phase:**			
MOWING, 21" - PUSH MOWER	E	MOW SITE	208,000.0000 SF	140	MOWER 18-21"	$3.00		5,000.000	41.60	$124.80
	L	OPERATOR	208,000.0000 SF	MM	MAINT CREW (4 MEN)	$10.00		5,000.000	41.60	$654.37
								Bid Item Subtotal:	83.20	$779.17
								Bid Item Unit Price:		$1,143.08
Bid Item:	**Mowing, 21" Push Mower**		**189.0000 AC**		**Type: Mow**		**Phase:**			
MOWING, 21" - PER ACRE	E	MOW SITE	44,000.0000 SF	140	MOWER 18-21"	$3.00		5,000.000	8.80	$26.40
	L	OPERATOR	44,000.0000 SF	MM	MAINT CREW (4 MEN)	$10.00		5,000.000	8.80	$138.42
								Bid Item Subtotal:	17.60	$164.82
								Bid Item Unit Price:		$241.80
Bid Item:	**Edging**		**40.0000 Each**		**Type: Maint**		**Phase:**			
EDGING, 500 LF/HR	E	EDGE	2,600.0000 SF	149	EDGER	$3.00		500.000	0.52	$15.60
	L	OPERATOR	2,600.0000 SF	MM	MAINT CREW (4 MEN)	$10.00		500.000	5.20	$81.80
								Bid Item Subtotal:	5.72	$97.40
								Bid Item Unit Price:		$142.88
Bid Item:	**Back-Pack Blower**		**40.0000 Each**		**Type: Maint**		**Phase:**			
BACK-PACK BLOWER, HOURS	E	BACK-PACK BLOWER	20.0000 HR	150	BACKPACK BLOWER	$3.00		1.000	0.04	$60.00
	L	OPERATOR	20.0000 HR	MM	MAINT CREW (4 MEN)	$10.00		1.000	20.00	$314.60
								Bid Item Subtotal:	20.04	$374.60
								Bid Item Unit Price:		$549.56

EXHIBIT 10 Large Commercial Maintenance Bid Example *(continued)*

J. R. Huston Enterprises, Inc.
Bid Worksheet Detail

JCN: Mowing-2 **Job Description: Large Commercial Maintenance Job**

Assembly	MLESN Code	Detail Description	Qty Unit	PLES Code	Remarks	Unit Cost	Warr %	Qty 1 /MHr	MHRS	Cost ($)
Bid Item: Weeding			**40.0000 Each**		**Type: Maint**		**Phase:**			
WEEDING, HAND LABOR	L	WEED HAND LABOR	52.0000 HR	MM	MAINT CREW (4 MEN)	$10.00		1.000	52.00	$817.96
							Bid Item Subtotal:		52.00	$817.96
							Bid Item Unit Price:			$1,255.51
Bid Item: General Cleanup			**40.0000 Each**		**Type: Maint**		**Phase:**			
CLEANUP, HAND LABOR	L	HAND LABOR	1.0000 HR	MM	MAINT CREW (4 MEN)	$10.00		1.000	1.00	$15.73
							Bid Item Subtotal:		1.00	$15.73
							Bid Item Unit Price:			$24.14
Bid Item: Redwood Mulch			**300.0000 CY**		**Type: Mulch**		**Phase:**			
MULCH, RW BARK 1"	M	REDWOOD BARK MULCH	1.0000 CY			$18.00				$19.40
	L	INSTALL MULCH	1.0000 CY	LL	LANDSCAPE CREW (4 MEN)	$9.25		1.000	1.00	$14.55
	E	TRACTOR	1.0000 CY	116	TRACTOR, 1/2 CY BUCK	$20.00		5.000	0.20	$4.00
	L	OPERATOR	1.0000 CY	LL	LANDSCAPE CREW (4 MEN)	$9.25		5.000	0.20	$2.91
							Bid Item Subtotal:		1.40	$40.86
							Bid Item Unit Price:			$53.39
Bid Item: Fertilizer			**17,600.0000 LB**		**Type: Fertilizer**		**Phase:**			
FERTILIZER, TRACTOR & LABOR	M	FERTILIZER	1.0000 LB			$0.20				$0.22
	E	TRACTOR	1.0000 LB	115	TRACTOR, 1/4 CY BUCK	$16.00		1,000.000	0.00	$0.02
	L	OPERATOR	1.0000 LB	O	OPERATOR STEP #1	$18.00		1,000.000	0.00	$0.03
	L	HAND LABOR	1.0000 LB	MM	MAINT CREW (4 MEN)	$10.00		1,000.000	0.00	$0.02
							Bid Item Subtotal:		0.00	$0.28
							Bid Item Unit Price:			$0.32

EXHIBIT 10 Large Commercial Maintenance Bid Example (*continued*)

J. R. Huston Enterprises, Inc.

Labor Master Table

Labor Code	Description/Remarks	Crew Si	CAW
<None>	Not Defined	0	$0.00
A	AVERAGE WAGE (GROSS PAY)	1	$10.00
B	BASIC ENTRY LEVEL LABOR	1	$9.00
C	L/S CREW (3 MEN)	3	$12.00
CC	L/S CREW (4 MEN)	4	$11.00
D	DRIVER	1	$12.00
E	ESTIMATOR	1	$18.00
F	FOREMAN	1	$16.00
FF	FOREMAN	1	$18.00
I	IRR CREW (4 MEN)	4	$12.00
II	IRR TECH	1	$18.00
M	MAINT CREW (2 MEN)	2	$11.00
MM	MAINT CREW (4 MEN)	4	$10.00
O	OPERATOR STEP #1	1	$18.00
OO	OPERATOR STEP #1	1	$20.00
P	PREVAILING WAGE	1	$26.00
S	SUPERVISOR	1	$20.00
SS	SUPERVISOR	1	$25.00
DD	DESIGNER	1	$20.00
L	LEADMAN	1	$12.00

EXHIBIT 10 Large Commercial Maintenance Bid Example (*continued*)

J. R. Huston Enterprises, Inc.

Equipment Master Table

Equipment Code	Description	Unit	Unit Cost
100	TRUCK, MINI PICKUP	HR	$5.0000
101	TRUCK, PICKUP-1/2 TON	HR	$6.0000
102	TRUCK, 3/4 TON W/TRAILER	HR	$7.0000
103	TRUCK, 1 TON & TRAILER	HR	$8.0000
105	TRUCK, 2 TON	HR	$15.0000
106	DUMP TRUCK, 6 CY	HR	$20.0000
107	TRUCK W/500 GL WATER TANK	HR	$25.0000
114	BOBCAT 753 & TRAILER	HR	$20.0000
115	TRACTOR, 1/4 CY & TRAILER	HR	$16.0000
116	TRACTOR, 1/2 CY & TRAILER	HR	$20.0000
117	TRACTOR, 1 CY & TRAILER	HR	$25.0000
118	BACKHOE & TRAILER	HR	$30.0000
119	DOZER, SMALL	HR	$35.0000
120	TRENCHER, WB	HR	$15.0000
121	TRENCHER, SMALL RIDER	HR	$18.0000
122	TRENCHER, MEDIUM RIDER	HR	$20.0000
123	TRENCHER, LARGE RIDER	HR	$25.0000
125	PIPE PULLER, SMALL	HR	$15.0000
126	PIPE PULLER, MEDIUM	HR	$17.0000
127	PIPE PULLER, LARGE	HR	$20.0000
129	STREET SWEEPER	HR	$35.0000
130	ROTOTILLER, SMALL	HR	$8.0000
131	ROTOTILLER, LARGE	HR	$12.0000
134	COMPACTOR	HR	$8.0000
135	SOD CUTTER	HR	$10.0000
137	CHAIN SAW	HR	$5.0000
138	CHOP SAW W/DIAMOND BLADE	HR	$15.0000
139	GOLF CART	HR	$6.0000
140	MOWER 18-21"	HR	$3.0000
141	MOWER 36"	HR	$3.7500
108	TRUCK W/VACUUM	HR	$20.0000
146	CART W/SPREADER	HR	$10.0000
145	MOWER 72"	HR	$9.0000
142	MOWER 42"	HR	$5.5000
143	MOWER 48"	HR	$7.5000
144	MOWER 60"	HR	$8.5000
147	STICK EDGER	HR	$3.0000
148	WEEDEATER	HR	$3.0000
149	TRIMMER	HR	$3.0000
150	BACKPACK BLOWER	HR	$3.0000

EXHIBIT 10 Large Commercial Maintenance Bid Example (*continued*)

From: ______________________________ Date: _____/_____/20___

Subject: M.A.D. Report for the month of: __________________, 20___

1. Financial information:

		(Month)	(Y-T-D)
A. Sales:	Construction	$ ________	$ ________
	Maintenance	$ ________	$ ________
	Irrigation	$ ________	$ ________
	Trees	$ ________	$ ________
	________	$ ________	$ ________

B. Payables:	$ ________	$ ________	$ ________	$ ________	$ ________
C. Receivables:	$ ________	$ ________	$ ________	$ ________	$ ________
	(Current)	(30)	(60)	(90)	(Total)

D. Financial ratios:

(1). Total receivables ÷ total payables	$ ________	÷ $ ________	=	___.___
(2). Current receivables ÷ total payables	$ ________	÷ $ ________	=	___.___
(3). Quick ratio: Cash + total receivables / Current liabilities	$ ________ / $	+ $ ________	=	___.___

2. Production (Cost of Goods Sold):

A. Labor:	**Month $**	**Month Hours**	**Y-T-D $**	**Y-T-D Hours**
(1). Construction	$ ________	________	$ ________	________
(2). Maintenance	$ ________	________	$ ________	________
(3). Irrigation	$ ________	________	$ ________	________
(4). Trees	$ ________	________	$ ________	________

B. Materials:	**Month $**	**Y-T-D $**
(1). Construction	$ ________	$ ________
(2). Maintenance	$ ________	$ ________
(3). Irrigation	$ ________	$ ________
(4). Trees	$ ________	$ ________

C. Production ratios:	**Month SPH**	**Month CAW**	**Y-T-D SPH**	**Y-T-D CAW**
(1). Construction	$ ________	$ ________	$ ________	$ ________
(2). Maintenance	$ ________	$ ________	$ ________	$ ________
(3). Irrigation	$ ________	$ ________	$ ________	$ ________
(4). Trees	$ ________	$ ________	$ ________	$ ________

D. Material / Labor ratios:	**Month**	**Y-T-D**
(1). Construction	________ : 1	________ : 1
(2). Maintenance	________ : 1	________ : 1
(3). Irrigation	________ : 1	________ : 1
(4). Trees	________ : 1	________ : 1

EXHIBIT 11 The M.A.D. (Monthly Audit Data) Report

E. GPM per hour:

	Budget	Actual	Variance
(1). Construction	\$ ______.____	\$ ______.____	\$ ______.____
(2). Maintenance	\$ ______.____	\$ ______.____	\$ ______.____
(3). Irrigation	\$ ______.____	\$ ______.____	\$ ______.____
(4). Trees	\$ ______.____	\$ ______.____	\$ ______.____

F. G&A overhead per hour (OPH):

	Budget	Actual	Variance
(1). Construction	\$ ______.____	\$ ______.____	\$ ______.____
(2). Maintenance	\$ ______.____	\$ ______.____	\$ ______.____
(3). Irrigation	\$ ______.____	\$ ______.____	\$ ______.____
(4). Trees	\$ ______.____	\$ ______.____	\$ ______.____

3. Estimating:

A. Sales:

	Construction	Maintenance	Irrigation	Trees
(1). Budget for the year	\$ ________	\$ ________	\$ ________	\$ ________
(2). Contracts signed Y-T-D	\$ ________	\$ ________	\$ ________	\$ ________
(3). Additional work needed	\$ ________	\$ ________	\$ ________	\$ ________
(4). Work installed and billed	\$ ________	\$ ________	\$ ________	\$ ________
(5). Work installed & to be billed	\$ ________	\$ ________	\$ ________	\$ ________
(6). Additional work to install & bill	\$ ________	\$ ________	\$ ________	\$ ________

B. Field-labor hours (Billable):

(1). Budget for the year	________	________	________	________
(2). Actual Y-T-D	________	________	________	________
(3). Variance Y-T-D	________	________	________	________

C. Bidding (all categories as of the last day of the month):

(1). # sets of plans in office to bid	________
(2). # projects in office to be designed	________
(3). # projects in office in process of being designed	________
(4). # jobs bid (pending) but not awarded yet	________
(5). \$ amount of jobs bid (pending) but not awarded yet	\$ ________
(6). Average \$ amount of pending bids (5 ÷ 4)	\$ ________

4. Management issues:

A. 5 Main challenges to be faced next month:

(1). ____
(2). ____
(3). ____
(4). ____
(5). ____

B. 5 Main goals for next month:

(1). ____
(2). ____
(3). ____
(4). ____
(5). ____

EXHIBIT 11 The M.A.D. (Monthly Audit Data) Report (*continued*)

DAILY JOB SITE LOG

TEMP. ________
WEATHER: CLEAR SNOW WINDY
RAIN OVERCAST

JOB SITE: ________ DATE: ________

SUPERVISOR: ________ JOB SUPERVISOR: ________

1. LABOR/EQUIPMENT: WORK NAME

START TIME: ________
QUIT TIME: ________

WORKMEN							TOTAL	INITIALS
TOTALS								

EQUIPMENT ON JOB

ITEM	HOURS
TOTALS	

2. WORK ACCOMPLISHED: ________

3. SUB-CONTRACTORS:

	TIME-IN	TIME-OUT	TIME-IN	TIME-OUT	TOTAL

4. CHANGES: ________

5. EXTRAS: ________

6. COMMENTS: ________

7. JOB SITE SUPERVISOR SIGNATURE: X ________

EXHIBIT 12 Construction Field Daily Report

DATE: ____/____/20__

WEATHER CONDITIONS: ____________________

CREW NO: ________

CREW MEMBERS: ____________________

JOB-SITE	START TIME (I.E. 7:30 TO 8:00 AM)		FINISH TIME	MORNING LOAD MAN-HRS	DRIVETIME LABOR MAN-HRS	LOAD/UN-LOAD MAN-HRS	21" MOW LABOR& EQ HRS	36" MOW LABOR& EQ HRS	52" MOW LABOR& EQ HRS	BLOWER LABOR& EQ HRS	TRIMMER LABOR& EQ HRS	WEED & CLN-UP MAN-HRS	____ LABOR MAN-HRS	____ LABOR MAN-HRS	SUPVSR. ON-SITE MAN-HRS	TOTALS MAN-HRS
TIME PRIOR TO FIRST JOB	__:__	TO	__:__	__:__	__:__	__:__	__:__	__:__	__:__	__:__	__:__	__:__	__:__	__:__	__:__	__:__
	__:__	TO	__:__	__:__	__:__	__:__	__:__	__:__	__:__	__:__	__:__	__:__	__:__	__:__	__:__	__:__
	__:__	TO	__:__	__:__	__:__	__:__	__:__	__:__	__:__	__:__	__:__	__:__	__:__	__:__	__:__	__:__
	__:__	TO	__:__	__:__	__:__	__:__	__:__	__:__	__:__	__:__	__:__	__:__	__:__	__:__	__:__	__:__
	__:__	TO	__:__	__:__	__:__	__:__	__:__	__:__	__:__	__:__	__:__	__:__	__:__	__:__	__:__	__:__
	__:__	TO	__:__	__:__	__:__	__:__	__:__	__:__	__:__	__:__	__:__	__:__	__:__	__:__	__:__	__:__
	__:__	TO	__:__	__:__	__:__	__:__	__:__	__:__	__:__	__:__	__:__	__:__	__:__	__:__	__:__	__:__
	__:__	TO	__:__	__:__	__:__	__:__	__:__	__:__	__:__	__:__	__:__	__:__	__:__	__:__	__:__	__:__
	__:__	TO	__:__	__:__	__:__	__:__	__:__	__:__	__:__	__:__	__:__	__:__	__:__	__:__	__:__	__:__
	__:__	TO	__:__	__:__	__:__	__:__	__:__	__:__	__:__	__:__	__:__	__:__	__:__	__:__	__:__	__:__
	__:__	TO	__:__	__:__	__:__	__:__	__:__	__:__	__:__	__:__	__:__	__:__	__:__	__:__	__:__	__:__
	__:__	TO	__:__	__:__	__:__	__:__	__:__	__:__	__:__	__:__	__:__	__:__	__:__	__:__	__:__	__:__
	__:__	TO	__:__	__:__	__:__	__:__	__:__	__:__	__:__	__:__	__:__	__:__	__:__	__:__	__:__	__:__
	__:__	TO	__:__	__:__	__:__	__:__	__:__	__:__	__:__	__:__	__:__	__:__	__:__	__:__	__:__	__:__
	__:__	TO	__:__	__:__	__:__	__:__	__:__	__:__	__:__	__:__	__:__	__:__	__:__	__:__	__:__	__:__
	__:__	TO	__:__	__:__	__:__	__:__	__:__	__:__	__:__	__:__	__:__	__:__	__:__	__:__	__:__	__:__
	__:__	TO	__:__	__:__	__:__	__:__	__:__	__:__	__:__	__:__	__:__	__:__	__:__	__:__	__:__	__:__
	__:__	TO	__:__	__:__	__:__	__:__	__:__	__:__	__:__	__:__	__:__	__:__	__:__	__:__	__:__	__:__
	__:__	TO	__:__	__:__	__:__	__:__	__:__	__:__	__:__	__:__	__:__	__:__	__:__	__:__	__:__	__:__
	__:__	TO	__:__	__:__	__:__	__:__	__:__	__:__	__:__	__:__	__:__	__:__	__:__	__:__	__:__	__:__
	__:__	TO	__:__	__:__	__:__	__:__	__:__	__:__	__:__	__:__	__:__	__:__	__:__	__:__	__:__	__:__
	__:__	TO	__:__	__:__	__:__	__:__	__:__	__:__	__:__	__:__	__:__	__:__	__:__	__:__	__:__	__:__

REMARKS / MATERIALS / SPECIAL NOTES: ____________________

EXHIBIT 13 Maintenance Field Daily Report

J. R. Huston Enterprises, Inc.

Bid Worksheet Recap

JCN: Mowing-1 **Job Description: Small Commercial / Residential Maintenance Job**

	Material	Labor	Equipment	Subcontract	% of Total
I. Production Costs	$250.00	$2,224.95	$961.90	$0.00	57.30%
II. General Conditions	$0.00	$0.00	$0.00	$0.00	0.00%
Subtotal	$250.00	$2,224.95	$961.90	$0.00	57.30%
III. Margins & Markups					
A. Sales Tax (mat. cost)	$15.00				0.25%
B. Labor Burden		$667.48			11.13%
Subtotal	$265.00	$2,892.43	$961.90	$0.00	
Total Direct Costs				**$4,119.33**	68.68%
C. G & A Overhead Recovery	159.80	labor hours times	$8.00 OPH	$1,278.40	21.32%
BEP Subtotal (Direct Costs + Overhead)				**$5,397.73**	90.00%
D. Net Profit					
Net Profit Margin:	10.00%		$599.74		
Profit per Hour:	159.80hours X PPH	$1.00	$159.80		
Price Override:	0.00%		$0.00		
				$599.75	10.00%
E. Job Price Subtotal:				$5,997.48	100.00%
F. Sales Tax (if on whole job):				$0.00	0.00%
G: Job Price Total:				**$5,997.48**	100.00%

EXHIBIT 14 Small Maintenance/Residential Bid Example

J. R. Huston Enterprises, Inc.

Ratio Analysis

JCN: Mowing-1 **Job Description:** Small Commercial / Residential Maintenance Job

Market Comparison Analysis Report (using estimating methods):

1. Factor (price divided by materials) 22.63

2. Unit Price (job total price divided by units) $5,997.48 per LS

3. Gross Profit:

Net Profit Margin	Overhead	Gross Profit Margin
599.75	1,278.40	$1,878.15
10.00%	21.32%	31.32%

4. Material Overhead Recovery System (MORS) method:

	Factor	Overhead Allocation
A. Materials	10.0%	$26.50
B. Equipment	25.0%	$240.48
C. Subcontractors	5.0%	$0.00
D. Labor (with labor burden)	34.97%	$1,011.43
Total G & A overhead allocation		$1,278.40

5. G & A Overhead and Profit per Field-Labor Hour method:

A. Total field labor hours in bid	159.80
B. Overhead per Hour (OPH)	$8.00
C. Net Profit per Hour (PPH)	$3.75
D. Gross profit per Hour (GPPH)	$11.75
E. Sales per Hour (SPH)	$37.53

Ratio & Per Hour Analysis Report:

1. Sales per Hour (SPH)	$37.53	
2. Materials:		
A. Materials to Labor ratio (w/o tax or LB)	0.11	: 1
B. Materials per Hour (w/o tax)	$1.56	
C. Materials Factor (price divided by materials w/o tax)	23.99	
3. Labor:		
A. Total field-labor hours in bid	159.80	
B. Job Average Wage (including OTF & RF)	$13.92	
4. Equipment:		
A. Equipment to Labor ratio (w/o LB)	0.43	: 1
B. Equipment to Labor percent (w/o LB)	43.23%	
C. Equipment per Hour	$6.02	
5. Subcontractors:		
A. Total subcontractor costs in bid	$0.00	
B. Total subcontractor cost as a percent of price	0.00%	
6. General Conditions:		
A. General Conditions as percent of price	0.00%	
B. General Conditions per Hour (GCPH)	$0.00	
C. General Conditions hours to Total hours (GCHTH)	0.00%	
7. Direct Costs:		
Total Direct Costs in bid	$4,119.33	
Total Direct Costs as percent of Price	68.68%	

EXHIBIT 14 Small Maintenance/Residential Bid Example (*continued*)

J. R. Huston Enterprises, Inc.
Unit Price Lite

JCN: Mowing-1 **Job Description:** Small Commercial / Residential Maintenance Job

Bid #	Bid Description	Type Code	Qty	Unit	Unit Price	Set	Total Price	Labor Hrs	Labor	Equipment	Material	Subcontract	Total Cost
1	Spring Clean-up	Cleanup	1.0	LS	$716.23		$716.23	18.0	$325.61	$69.00	$106.00	$0.00	$500.61
2	Maintenance	Maint	28.0	Each	$158.51		$4,438.23	121.8	$2,206.60	$813.40	$0.00	$0.00	$3,020.00
3	Fall Cleanup	Cleanup	1.0	LS	$843.02		$843.02	20.0	$360.22	$79.50	$159.00	$0.00	$598.72
							$5,997.48	**159.8**	**$2,892.43**	**$961.90**	**$265.00**	**$0.00**	**$4,119.33**

EXHIBIT 14 Small Maintenance/Residential Bid Example (*continued*)

J. R. Huston Enterprises, Inc.

Bid Worksheet Detail

JCN: Mowing-1 **Job Description: Small Commercial / Residential Maintenance Job**

Assembly	MLESN Code	Detail Description	Qty Unit	PLES Code	Remarks	Unit Cost	Warr %	Qty 1 /MHr	MHRS	Cost ($)
Bid Item:	**Spring Clean-up**		**1.0000 LS**		**Type: Cleanup**		**Phase:**			
CLEANUP, SPRING, SMALL RESID	L	LOAD/UNLOAD TIME	2.0000 HR	M	MAINT CREW (2 MEN)	$11.00		1.000	2.00	$34.61
	L	LABOR, 2 MEN	14.0000 HR	M	MAINT CREW (2 MEN)	$11.00		1.000	14.00	$242.24
	E	CREW TRUCK	8.0000 HR	103	TRUCK, 1 TON & TRAILER	$8.00		1.000	8.00	$64.00
	L	DRIVE TIME	1.0000 HR	M	MAINT CREW (2 MEN)	$11.00		1.000	1.00	$17.30
	M	DUMP FEES	1.0000 LS			$100.00				$106.00
	L	SUPERVISOR'S TIME	1.0000 HR	S	SUPERVISOR	$20.00		1.000	1.00	$31.46
	E	SUPERVISOR'S TRUCK	1.0000 HR	100	TRUCK, MINI PICKUP	$5.00		1.000	1.00	$5.00
							Bid Item Subtotal:		27.00	$500.61
							Bid Item Unit Price:			$716.23

EXHIBIT 14 Small Maintenance/Residential Bid Example (*continued*)

J. R. Huston Enterprises, Inc.

Bid Worksheet Detail

JCN: **Mowing-1** **Job Description:** **Small Commercial / Residential Maintenance Job**

Assembly	MLESN Code	Detail Description	Qty Unit	PLES Code	Remarks	Unit Cost	Warr %	Qty 1 /MHr	MHRS	Cost ($)
Bid Item:	**Maintenance**		**28.0000 Each**		**Type: Maint**		**Phase:**			
MOW PKG, 2 MEN W/EQUIP	E	36" MOWER	20,000.0000 HR	141	MOWER 36"	$3.75		20,000.000	1.00	$3.75
	L	36" MOWER LABOR	20,000.0000 SF	M	MAINT CREW (2 MEN)	$11.00		20,000.000	1.00	$17.30
	E	21" PUSH MOWER	8,000.0000 SF	140	MOWER 18-21"	$3.00		5,000.000	1.60	$4.80
	L	21" MOWER LABOR	8,000.0000 SF	M	MAINT CREW (2 MEN)	$11.00		5,000.000	1.60	$27.68
	E	BACKPACK BLOWER	0.2500 HR	150	BACKPACK BLOWER	$3.00		1.000	0.25	$0.75
	L	BP BLOWER LABOR	0.2500 HR	M	MAINT CREW (2 MEN)	$11.00		1.000	0.25	$4.33
	E	STRING TRIMMER	175.0000 LF	147	STRING TRIMMER	$3.00		350.000	0.50	$1.50
	L	STRING TRIM. LABOR	175.0000 LF	M	MAINT CREW (2 MEN)	$11.00		350.000	0.50	$8.65
	L	WEED & CLEAN UP	0.5000 HR	M	MAINT CREW (2 MEN)	$11.00		1.000	0.50	$8.65
	E	DRIVE TIME, TRUCK	0.1250 HR	103	TRUCK, 1 TON & TRAILER	$8.00		1.000	0.13	$1.00
	L	DRIVE TIME	0.2500 HR	M	MAINT CREW (2 MEN)	$11.00		1.000	0.25	$4.33
	E	CREW TRUCK ON-SITE	2.0000 HR	103	TRUCK, 1 TON & TRAILER	$8.00		1.000	2.00	$16.00
	L	SUPERVISOR INSPECT	0.2500 HR	S	SUPERVISOR	$20.00		1.000	0.25	$7.87
	E	SUPERVISOR'S TRUCK	0.2500 HR	100	TRUCK, MINI PICKUP	$5.00		1.000	0.25	$1.25
								Bid Item Subtotal:	10.08	$107.86
								Bid Item Unit Price:		$158.51

EXHIBIT 14 Small Maintenance/Residential Bid Example (*continued*)

J. R. Huston Enterprises, Inc.

Bid Worksheet Detail

JCN: Mowing-1 **Job Description: Small Commercial / Residential Maintenance Job**

Assembly	MLESN Code	Detail Description	Qty Unit	PLES Code	Remarks	Unit Cost	Warr %	Qty 1 /MHr	MHRS	Cost ($)
Bid Item:	**Fall Cleanup**		**1.0000 LS**		**Type: Cleanup**		**Phase:**			
CLEANUP, FALL-SMALL RESID	E	36" MOWER	2.0000 HR	141	MOWER 36"	$3.75		1.000	2.00	$7.50
	E	21" MOWER	1.0000 HR	140	MOWER 18-21"	$3.00		1.000	1.00	$3.00
	L	LABOR, 2 MEN	14.0000 HR	M	MAINT CREW (2 MEN)	$11.00		1.000	14.00	$242.24
	L	DRIVE TIME	1.0000 HR	M	MAINT CREW (2 MEN)	$11.00		1.000	1.00	$17.30
	L	LOAD/UNLOAD TIME	4.0000 HR	M	MAINT CREW (2 MEN)	$11.00		1.000	4.00	$69.21
	M	DUMP FEES	1.0000 LS			$150.00				$159.00
	E	CREW TRUCK	8.0000 HR	103	TRUCK, 1 TON & TRAILER	$8.00		1.000	8.00	$64.00
	L	SUPERVISOR'S TIME	1.0000 HR	S	SUPERVISOR	$20.00		1.000	1.00	$31.46
	E	SUPERVISOR'S TRUCK	1.0000 HR	100	TRUCK, MINI PICKUP	$5.00		1.000	1.00	$5.00
							Bid Item Subtotal:		32.00	$598.72
							Bid Item Unit Price:			$843.02

EXHIBIT 14 Small Maintenance/Residential Bid Example (*continued*)

J. R. Huston Enterprises, Inc.

Bid Worksheet Recap

JCN: Henderson **Job Description: Henderson Residence**

	Material	Labor	Equipment	Subcontract	% of Total
I. Production Costs	$15,717.14	$5,607.22	$545.40	$1,291.00	51.79%
II. General Conditions	$212.00	$2,420.00	$1,320.00	$0.00	8.84%
Subtotal	$15,929.14	$8,027.22	$1,865.40	$1,291.00	60.62%
III. Margins & Markups					
A. Sales Tax (mat. cost)	$955.75				2.14%
B. Labor Burden		$2,408.17			5.38%
Subtotal	$16,884.89	$10,435.39	$1,865.40	$1,291.00	
Total Direct Costs				**$30,476.67**	68.15%
C. G & A Overhead Recovery	530.17	labor hours times	$10.00 OPH	$5,301.70	11.85%
BEP Subtotal (Direct Costs + Overhead)				**$35,778.37**	80.00%
D. Net Profit					
Net Profit Margin:	20.00%		$8,944.59		
Profit per Hour:	530.17hours X PPH	$1.00	$530.17		
Price Override:	0.00%		$0.00		
				$8,944.58	20.00%
E. Job Price Subtotal:				$44,722.95	100.00%
F. Sales Tax (if on whole job):				$0.00	0.00%
G: Job Price Total:				**$44,722.95**	100.00%

EXHIBIT 15 Henderson Construction Bid Example

J. R. Huston Enterprises, Inc.

Ratio Analysis

JCN: Henderson **Job Description:** Henderson Residence

Market Comparison Analysis Report (using estimating methods):

1. Factor (price divided by materials) 2.65

2. Unit Price (job total price divided by units) $44,722.95 per LS

3. Gross Profit:

Net Profit Margin	Overhead	Gross Profit Margin
8,944.58	5,301.70	$14,246.28
20.00%	11.85%	31.85%

4. Material Overhead Recovery System (MORS) method:

	Factor	Overhead Allocation
A. Materials	10.0%	$1,688.49
B. Equipment	25.0%	$466.35
C. Subcontractors	5.0%	$64.55
D. Labor (with labor burden)	29.54%	$3,082.31
Total G & A overhead allocation		$5,301.70

5. G & A Overhead and Profit per Field-Labor Hour method:

A. Total field labor hours in bid	530.17
B. Overhead per Hour (OPH)	$10.00
C. Net Profit per Hour (PPH)	$16.87
D. Gross profit per Hour (GPPH)	$26.87
E. Sales per Hour (SPH)	$84.36

Ratio & Per Hour Analysis Report:

1. Sales per Hour (SPH)	$84.36
2. Materials:	
A. Materials to Labor ratio (w/o tax or LB)	1.98 : 1
B. Materials per Hour (w/o tax)	$30.05
C. Materials Factor (price divided by materials w/o tax)	2.81
3. Labor:	
A. Total field-labor hours in bid	530.17
B. Job Average Wage (including OTF & RF)	$15.14
4. Equipment:	
A. Equipment to Labor ratio (w/o LB)	0.23 : 1
B. Equipment to Labor percent (w/o LB)	23.24%
C. Equipment per Hour	$3.52
5. Subcontractors:	
A. Total subcontractor costs in bid	$1,291.00
B. Total subcontractor cost as a percent of price	2.89%
6. General Conditions:	
A. General Conditions as percent of price	10.46%
B. General Conditions per Hour (GCPH)	$8.82
C. General Conditions hours to Total hours (GCHTH)	27.16%
7. Direct Costs:	
Total Direct Costs in bid	$30,476.67
Total Direct Costs as percent of Price	68.15%

EXHIBIT 15 Henderson Construction Bid Example (*continued*)

J. R. Huston Enterprises, Inc.
Unit Price Lite

JCN: Henderson **Job Description: Henderson Residence**

Bid #	Bid Description	Type Code	Qty	Unit	Unit Price	Set	Total Price	Labor Hrs	Labor	Equipment	Material	Subcontract	Total Cost
1	Point of connection	IRR	1.0	LS	$111.80		$111.80	2.0	$37.75	$0.00	$0.00	$0.00	$37.75
2	Controller	IRR	1.0	Each	$602.05		$602.05	2.0	$37.75	$0.00	$392.20	$0.00	$429.95
3	Wire, 14 Gauge	IRR	2,000.0	LF	$0.19		$382.59	4.0	$75.50	$0.00	$127.20	$0.00	$202.70
4	Backflow Preventer, Standard	IRR	1.0	Each	$683.37		$683.37	4.0	$75.50	$0.00	$367.82	$0.00	$443.32
5	Quick Coupler Valves, .75"	IRR	4.0	Each	$108.90		$435.59	4.0	$75.50	$0.00	$169.60	$0.00	$245.10
6	Mainline, Sch 40, 1.25"	IRR	260.0	LF	$3.75		$973.77	10.0	$188.76	$39.00	$292.83	$0.00	$520.59
7	Sleeve, Sch 40, 2.5"	IRR	140.0	LF	$5.72		$801.21	5.0	$94.38	$0.00	$417.38	$0.00	$511.76
8	Valves, 1"	IRR	14.0	Each	$223.76		$3,132.63	28.0	$528.53	$0.00	$1,253.98	$0.00	$1,782.51
9	Lateral Line, PVC Class 200, 1"	IRR	580.0	LF	$2.72		$1,575.89	21.1	$398.11	$87.00	$230.55	$0.00	$715.66
10	Lateral Line, Mainline, PVC Class 315, .5"	IRR	1,320.0	LF	$2.48		$3,277.54	48.0	$906.05	$178.20	$297.33	$0.00	$1,381.58
11	Heads, 6"	IRR	170.0	Each	$23.10		$3,927.80	34.0	$641.78	$0.00	$1,621.80	$0.00	$2,263.58
12	Heads, 4"	IRR	60.0	Each	$23.10		$1,386.28	12.0	$226.51	$0.00	$572.40	$0.00	$798.91
13	Flush & Fine Tune Irrigation System	IRR	1.0	LS	$447.19		$447.19	8.0	$151.01	$0.00	$0.00	$0.00	$151.01
14	Soil Prep	Site	6,300.0	SF	$0.33		$2,098.55	14.2	$268.82	$151.20	$890.82	$0.00	$1,310.84
15	Trees, 24" Box	Trees	6.0	Each	$387.98		$2,327.90	16.0	$302.02	$30.00	$1,116.82	$0.00	$1,448.83
16	Trees, 15 Gallon	Trees	15.0	Each	$155.58		$2,333.64	21.3	$401.12	$0.00	$916.64	$0.00	$1,317.75
17	Trees, Palm, Wash.Robusta 10 BTF	Trees	3.0	Each	$760.69		$2,282.06	13.0	$245.39	$20.00	$1,224.30	$0.00	$1,489.69
18	Fine Grade, Hand Labor	Site	6,300.0	SF	$0.06		$352.16	6.3	$118.94	$0.00	$0.00	$0.00	$118.92
19	Shrubs, 5 Gal Plants	Plants	215.0	Each	$30.46		$6,549.46	46.6	$879.31	$0.00	$3,156.42	$0.00	$4,035.72
20	Shrubs, 5 Gallon Espalier	Plants	3.0	Each	$54.61		$163.83	1.1	$19.82	$0.00	$84.11	$0.00	$103.93
21	Shrubs, 1 Gallon	Plants	283.0	Each	$10.67		$3,018.55	25.2	$474.84	$0.00	$1,289.91	$0.00	$1,764.75
22	Vines, 1 Gallon	Plants	24.0	Each	$12.06		$289.38	2.1	$40.27	$0.00	$136.10	$0.00	$176.37
23	Ground Cover, 8" OC, 64 Count	Plants	23.0	Flat	$43.98		$1,011.58	11.5	$217.07	$0.00	$295.00	$0.00	$512.07
24	Ground Cover, 12" OC, 64 Count	Plants	36.0	Flat	$43.98		$1,583.34	18.0	$339.77	$0.00	$461.74	$0.00	$801.50
25	Sod	Plants	3,345.0	SF	$0.71		$2,375.28	16.9	$318.38	$0.00	$1,145.96	$0.00	$1,464.35
26	Mulch, 1" Depth. RW Bark	Site	10.0	CY	$98.58		$985.78	12.0	$226.51	$40.00	$212.00	$0.00	$478.51
27	Maintenance, 90 Day	Maint	3.0	MO	$537.92		$1,613.75	0.0	$0.00	$0.00	$0.00	$1,291.00	$1,291.00
28	General Conditions	GC	1.0	LS	$0.00		$0.00	144.0	$3,146.00	$1,320.00	$212.00	$0.00	$4,678.00
							$44,722.95	**530.2**	**$10,435.39**	**$1,865.40**	**$16,884.89**	**$1,291.00**	**$30,476.67**

EXHIBIT 15 Henderson Construction Bid Example (*continued*)

J. R. Huston Enterprises, Inc.

Labor Job Recap

JCN: Henderson **Description: Henderson Residence**

Labor Code	Labor Task Description	Hours	Cost
C	L/S CREW (3 MEN)	308.08	$5,815.30
D	DRIVER	8.00	$151.01
F	FOREMAN	16.00	$402.69
I	IRR CREW (4 MEN)	182.09	$3,437.15
SS	SUPERVISOR	16.00	$629.20
	Job Totals	530.17	$10,435.34

J. R. Huston Enterprises, Inc.

Equipment Job Recap

JCN: Henderson **Description: Henderson Residence**

Equipment Code	Equipment Description	$/Hr	Hours	Cost
102	TRUCK, 3/4 TON W/TRAILER	$7.00	16.00	$112.00
103	TRUCK, 1 TON & TRAILER	$8.00	136.00	$1,088.00
105	TRUCK, 2 TON	$15.00	8.00	$120.00
116	TRACTOR, 1/2 CY & TRAILER	$20.00	9.54	$190.80
120	TRENCHER, WB	$15.00	20.28	$304.20
131	ROTOTILLER, LARGE	$12.00	4.20	$50.40
	Job Total			$1,865.40

EXHIBIT 15 Henderson Construction Bid Example (*continued*)

J. R. Huston Enterprises, Inc.
Bid Worksheet Detail

JCN: Henderson **Job Description: Henderson Residence**

Assembly	MLESN Code	Detail Description	Qty	Unit	PLES Code	Remarks	Unit Cost	Warr %	Qty 1 /MHr	MHRS	Cost ($)
Bid Item:	**Point of connection**		**1.0000**	**LS**		**Type: IRR**	**Phase:1**				
POC, POC	L	Labor to install POC	1.0000	LS	I	IRR CREW (4 MEN)	$12.00		0.500	2.00	$37.75
									Bid Item Subtotal:	2.00	$37.75
									Bid Item Unit Price:		$111.80
Bid Item:	**Controller**		**1.0000**	**Each**		**Type: IRR**	**Phase:2**				
	M	Controller	1.0000	EA	n/d		$370.00				$392.20
	L	Labor	1.0000	EA	I	IRR CREW (4 MEN)	$12.00		0.500	2.00	$37.75
									Bid Item Subtotal:	2.00	$429.95
									Bid Item Unit Price:		$602.05
Bid Item:	**Wire, 14 Gauge**		**2,000.0000**	**LF**		**Type: IRR**	**Phase:3**				
	M	Wire, 14 gauge	1.0000	LF	n/d		$0.06				$0.06
	L	Install Wire	1.0000	LF	I	IRR CREW (4 MEN)	$12.00		500.000	0.00	$0.04
									Bid Item Subtotal:	0.00	$0.10
									Bid Item Unit Price:		$0.19
Bid Item:	**Backflow Preventer, Standard**		**1.0000**	**Each**		**Type: IRR**	**Phase:4**				
	M	Backflow Preventer	1.0000	EA	n/d		$347.00				$367.82
	L	Labor	1.0000	EA	I	IRR CREW (4 MEN)	$12.00		0.250	4.00	$75.50
									Bid Item Subtotal:	4.00	$443.32
									Bid Item Unit Price:		$683.37
Bid Item:	**Quick Coupler Valves, .75"**		**4.0000**	**Each**		**Type: IRR**	**Phase:5**				
	M	QCV .75"	1.0000	EA	n/d		$24.00				$25.44
	L	Labor	1.0000	EA	I	IRR CREW (4 MEN)	$12.00		1.000	1.00	$18.88
	M	Box	1.0000	EA	n/d		$12.00				$12.72
	M	Fittings	1.0000	EA	n/d		$4.00				$4.24
									Bid Item Subtotal:	1.00	$61.28
									Bid Item Unit Price:		$108.90
Bid Item:	**Mainline, Sch 40, 1.25"**		**260.0000**	**LF**		**Type: IRR**	**Phase:6**				
	M	PVC SCH 40, 1.25"	1.0000	LF	n/d		$0.85				$0.90
	M	Fittings 25% of PVC	0.2500	LF	n/d		$0.85				$0.23
	E	Trencher	1.0000	LF	120	TRENCHER, WB	$15.00		100.000		$0.15
	L	Install Mainline	1.0000	LF	I	IRR CREW (4 MEN)	$12.00		26.000	0.04	$0.73
									Bid Item Subtotal:	0.04	$2.00
									Bid Item Unit Price:		$3.75

EXHIBIT 15 Henderson Construction Bid Example (*continued*)

J. R. Huston Enterprises, Inc.

Bid Worksheet Detail

JCN: Henderson **Job Description: Henderson Residence**

Assembly	MLESN Code	Detail Description	Qty	Unit	PLES Code	Remarks	Unit Cost	Warr %	Qty 1 /MHr	MHRS	Cost ($)
Bid Item:	**Sleeve, Sch 40, 2.5"**		**140.0000**	**LF**		**Type: IRR**	**Phase:7**				
	M	PVC SCH 40, 2.5"	1.0000	LF	n/d		$2.25				$2.39
	M	Fittings, 25% of PVC	0.2500	LF	n/d		$2.25				$0.60
	L	Install Sleeves	1.0000	LF	I	IRR CREW (4 MEN)	$12.00		28.000	0.04	$0.67
									Bid Item Subtotal:	0.04	$3.66
									Bid Item Unit Price:		$5.72
Bid Item:	**Valves, 1"**		**14.0000**	**Each**		**Type: IRR**	**Phase:8**				
	M	Valve 1"	1.0000	EA	n/d		$66.00				$69.96
	M	Box	1.0000	EA	n/d		$10.00				$10.60
	M	Hardware	1.0000	EA	n/d		$8.50				$9.01
	L	Install Valve	1.0000	HR	I	IRR CREW (4 MEN)	$12.00		0.500	2.00	$37.75
									Bid Item Subtotal:	2.00	$127.32
									Bid Item Unit Price:		$223.76
Bid Item:	**Lateral Line, PVC Class 200, 1"**		**580.0000**	**LF**		**Type: IRR**	**Phase:9**				
	M	PVC Class 200, 1"	1.0000	LF	n/d		$0.30				$0.32
	M	Fittings 25% of PVC	0.2500	LF	n/d		$0.30				$0.08
	L	Install Mainline	1.0000	LF	I	IRR CREW (4 MEN)	$12.00		27.500	0.04	$0.69
	E	Trencher	1.0000	LF	120	TRENCHER, WB	$15.00		100.000	2.00	$0.15
									Bid Item Subtotal:	2.04	$1.23
									Bid Item Unit Price:		$2.72
Bid Item:	**Lateral Line, Mainline, PVC Class 315, .5"**		**1,320.0000**	**LF**		**Type: IRR**	**Phase:10**				
	M	PVC Class 315, .5"	1.0000	LF	n/d		$0.20				$0.21
	M	Fittings 25% of PVC	0.2500	LF	n/d		$0.05				$0.01
	E	Trencher	0.9000	LF	120	TRENCHER, WB	$15.00		100.000		$0.14
	L	Install Mainline	1.0000	LF	I	IRR CREW (4 MEN)	$12.00		27.500	0.04	$0.69
									Bid Item Subtotal:	0.04	$1.05
									Bid Item Unit Price:		$2.48
Bid Item:	**Heads, 6"**		**170.0000**	**Each**		**Type: IRR**	**Phase:11**				
	M	Heads, 6"	1.0000	EA	n/d		$9.00				$9.54
	L	Install Head	1.0000	EA	I	IRR CREW (4 MEN)	$12.00		5.000	0.20	$3.78
									Bid Item Subtotal:	0.20	$13.32
									Bid Item Unit Price:		$23.10

EXHIBIT 15 Henderson Construction Bid Example (*continued*)

J. R. Huston Enterprises, Inc.
Bid Worksheet Detail

JCN: Henderson **Job Description: Henderson Residence**

Assembly	MLESN Code	Detail Description	Qty	Unit	PLES Code	Remarks	Unit Cost	Warr %	Qty 1 /MHr	MHRS	Cost ($)
Bid Item:	**Heads, 4"**		**60.0000**	**Each**		**Type: IRR**	**Phase: 12**				
	M	Heads, 4"	1.0000	EA	n/d		$9.00				$9.54
	L	Install Head	1.0000	EA	I	IRR CREW (4 MEN)	$12.00		5.000	0.20	$3.78
								Bid Item Subtotal:		0.20	$13.32
								Bid Item Unit Price:			$23.10
Bid Item:	**Flush & Fine Tune Irrigation System**		**1.0000**	**LS**		**Type: IRR**	**Phase: 13**				
	L	Labor to install POC	8.0000	Hr	I	IRR CREW (4 MEN)	$12.00		1.000	8.00	$151.01
								Bid Item Subtotal:		8.00	$151.01
								Bid Item Unit Price:			$447.19
Bid Item:	**Soil Prep**		**6,300.0000**	**SF**		**Type: Site**	**Phase: 14**				
	M	Fertilizer	0.0026	BAG	n/d		$15.00				$0.04
	M	Amendments (4CY/M)	0.0040	CY	n/d		$20.00				$0.08
	M	Gypsum	0.0016	BAG	n/d		$9.00				$0.02
	E	Rototill 6" Depth	1.0000	SF	131	ROTOTILLER, LARGE	$12.00		1,500.000		$0.01
	E	Tractor	0.0040	SF	116	TRACTOR, 1/2 CY & TRAILER	$20.00		5.000		$0.02
	L	Hand Labor	1.0000	SF	C	L/S CREW (3 MEN)	$12.00		1,260.000	0.00	$0.01
	L	Operator	0.0040	SF	C	L/S CREW (3 MEN)	$12.00		5.000	0.00	$0.02
	L	Labor	1.0000	SF	C	L/S CREW (3 MEN)	$12.00		1,500.000	0.00	$0.01
								Bid Item Subtotal:		0.00	$0.21
								Bid Item Unit Price:			$0.33
Bid Item:	**Trees, 24" Box**		**6.0000**	**Each**		**Type: Trees**	**Phase: 15**				
	M	Trees, 24" Box	1.0000	EA	n/d		$150.00	10.000			$174.90
	M	Plant Tabs	6.0000	EA	n/d		$0.10				$0.64
	L	Spot / Dig / Plant	1.0000	EA	C	L/S CREW (3 MEN)	$12.00		0.500	2.00	$37.75
	E	Spot/Dig/Plant	1.0000	EA	116	TRACTOR, 1/2 CY & TRAILER	$20.00		4.000		$5.00
	L	Operator	1.0000	EA	C	L/S CREW (3 MEN)	$12.00		4.000	0.25	$4.72
	M	Stake Kits (2 Stakes)	1.0000	KIT	n/d		$10.00				$10.60
	L	Stake Trees	1.0000	KIT	C	L/S CREW (3 MEN)	$12.00		3.000	0.33	$6.29
	L	Water In	1.0000	EA	C	L/S CREW (3 MEN)	$12.00		12.000	0.08	$1.57
								Bid Item Subtotal:		2.67	$241.47
								Bid Item Unit Price:			$387.98

EXHIBIT 15 Henderson Construction Bid Example (*continued*)

J. R. Huston Enterprises, Inc.

Bid Worksheet Detail

JCN: Henderson | **Job Description: Henderson Residence**

Assembly		MLESN Code	Detail Description	Qty	Unit	PLES Code	Remarks	Unit Cost	Warr %	Qty 1 /MHr	MHRS	Cost ($)
Bid Item:	**Trees, 15 Gallon**			**15.0000**	**Each**		**Type: Trees**	**Phase:16**				
		M	Trees, 15 Gal	1.0000	EA	n/d		$45.00	5.000			$50.09
		M	Plant Tabs	4.0000	EA	n/d		$0.10				$0.42
		L	Spot/Dig/Plant	1.0000	EA	C	L/S CREW (3 MEN)	$12.00		1.000	1.00	$18.88
		M	Stake Kits (2 Stakes)	1.0000	KIT	n/d		$10.00				$10.60
		L	Stake Trees	1.0000	KIT	C	L/S CREW (3 MEN)	$12.00		3.000	0.33	$6.29
		L	Water In	1.0000	EA	C	L/S CREW (3 MEN)	$12.00		12.000	0.08	$1.57
										Bid Item Subtotal:	1.42	$87.85
										Bid Item Unit Price:		$155.58
Bid Item:	**Trees, Palm, Wash.Robusta 10 BTF**			**3.0000**	**Each**		**Type: Trees**	**Phase:17**				
		M	Palm, Wash. Rob. 10 BTF	1.0000	EA	n/d		$350.00	10.000			$408.10
		E	Spot/Dig/ Plant	1.0000	EA	116	TRACTOR, 1/2 CY & TRAILER	$20.00		3.000		$6.67
		L	Operator	1.0000	EA	C	L/S CREW (3 MEN)	$12.00		3.000	0.33	$6.29
		L	Spot/Dig/Plant	1.0000	EA	C	L/S CREW (3 MEN)	$12.00		0.267	3.75	$70.79
		L	Water In	1.0000	EA	C	L/S CREW (3 MEN)	$12.00		4.000	0.25	$4.72
										Bid Item Subtotal:	4.33	$496.56
										Bid Item Unit Price:		$760.69
Bid Item:	**Fine Grade, Hand Labor**			**6,300.0000**	**SF**		**Type: Site**	**Phase:18**				
		L	Fine Grade Labor	1.0000	SF	C	L/S CREW (3 MEN)	$12.00		1,000.000	0.00	$0.02
										Bid Item Subtotal:	0.00	$0.02
										Bid Item Unit Price:		$0.06
Bid Item:	**Shrubs, 5 Gal Plants**			**215.0000**	**Each**		**Type: Plants**	**Phase:19**				
		M	Shrub, 5 gallon	1.0000	EA	n/d		$13.00	5.000			$14.47
		M	Plant Tabs	2.0000	EA	n/d		$0.10				$0.21
		L	Spot/Dig/Plant	1.0000	EA	C	L/S CREW (3 MEN)	$12.00		5.000	0.20	$3.78
		L	Water In	1.0000	EA	C	L/S CREW (3 MEN)	$12.00		60.000	0.02	$0.31
										Bid Item Subtotal:	0.22	$18.77
										Bid Item Unit Price:		$30.46

EXHIBIT 15 Henderson Construction Bid Example (*continued*)

J. R. Huston Enterprises, Inc.
Bid Worksheet Detail

JCN: Henderson **Job Description: Henderson Residence**

Assembly	MLESN Code	Detail Description	Qty	Unit	PLES Code	Remarks	Unit Cost	Warr %	Qty 1 /MHr	MHRS	Cost ($)
Bid Item:	**Shrubs, 5 Gallon Espalier**		**3.0000**	**Each**		**Type: Plants**	**Phase:20**				
	M	Shrub, 5 gal. ESP.	1.0000	EA	n/d		$25.00	5.000			$27.83
	M	Plant Tabs	2.0000	EA	n/d		$0.10				$0.21
	L	Spot/Dig/Plant	1.0000	EA	C	L/S CREW (3 MEN)	$12.00		3.000	0.33	$6.29
	L	Water In	1.0000	EA	C	L/S CREW (3 MEN)	$12.00		60.000	0.02	$0.31
								Bid Item Subtotal:		0.35	$34.64
								Bid Item Unit Price:			$54.61
Bid Item:	**Shrubs, 1 Gallon**		**283.0000**	**Each**		**Type: Plants**	**Phase:21**				
	M	Shrub, 1 gallon	1.0000	EA	n/d		$4.00	5.000			$4.45
	M	Plant Tabs	1.0000	EA	n/d		$0.10				$0.11
	L	Spot/Dig/Plant	1.0000	EA	C	L/S CREW (3 MEN)	$12.00		12.000	0.08	$1.57
	L	Water In	1.0000	EA	C	L/S CREW (3 MEN)	$12.00		180.000	0.01	$0.10
								Bid Item Subtotal:		0.09	$6.24
								Bid Item Unit Price:			$10.67
Bid Item:	**Vines, 1 Gallon**		**24.0000**	**Each**		**Type: Plants**	**Phase:22**				
	M	Shrub, 1 gallon	1.0000	EA	n/d		$5.00	5.000			$5.57
	M	Plant Tabs	1.0000	EA	n/d		$0.10				$0.11
	L	Spot/Dig/Plant	1.0000	EA	C	L/S CREW (3 MEN)	$12.00		12.000	0.08	$1.57
	L	Water In	1.0000	EA	C	L/S CREW (3 MEN)	$12.00		180.000	0.01	$0.10
								Bid Item Subtotal:		0.09	$7.35
								Bid Item Unit Price:			$12.06
Bid Item:	**Ground Cover, 8" OC, 64 Count**		**23.0000**	**Flat**		**Type: Plants**	**Phase:23**				
	M	Flat, 64 Count	1.0000	FLAT	n/d		$11.00	10.000			$12.83
	L	Spot/Dig/Plant	1.0000	FLAT	C	L/S CREW (3 MEN)	$12.00		2.000	0.50	$9.44
								Bid Item Subtotal:		0.50	$22.26
								Bid Item Unit Price:			$43.98
Bid Item:	**Ground Cover, 12" OC, 64 Count**		**36.0000**	**Flat**		**Type: Plants**	**Phase:24**				
	M	Flat, 64 count	1.0000	FLAT	n/d		$11.00	10.000			$12.83
	L	Spot/Dig/Plant	1.0000	FLAT	C	L/S CREW (3 MEN)	$12.00		2.000	0.50	$9.44
								Bid Item Subtotal:		0.50	$22.26
								Bid Item Unit Price:			$43.98

EXHIBIT 15 Henderson Construction Bid Example (*continued*)

J. R. Huston Enterprises, Inc.

Bid Worksheet Detail

JCN: Henderson **Job Description: Henderson Residence**

Assembly		MLESN Code	Detail Description	Qty	Unit	PLES Code	Remarks	Unit Cost	Warr %	Qty 1 /MHr	MHRS	Cost ($)
Bid Item:	**Sod**			**3,345.0000**	**SF**		**Type: Plants**	**Phase:25**				
		M	Sod	1.0000	SF	n/d		$0.32	1.000			$0.34
		L	Lay Sod	1.0000	SF	C	L/S CREW (3 MEN)	$12.00		225.000	0.00	$0.08
		L	Roll sod	1.0000	SF	C	L/S CREW (3 MEN)	$12.00		1,672.500	0.00	$0.01
									Bid Item Subtotal:		0.01	$0.44
									Bid Item Unit Price:			$0.71
Bid Item:	**Mulch, 1" Depth. RW Bark**			**10.0000**	**CY**		**Type: Site**	**Phase:26**				
		M	Redwood Bark Mulch	1.0000	CY	n/d		$20.00				$21.20
		E	Tractor	1.0000	CY	116	TRACTOR, 1/2 CY & TRAILER	$20.00		5.000		$4.00
		L	Install Mulch	1.0000	CY	C	L/S CREW (3 MEN)	$12.00		1.000	1.00	$18.88
		L	Operator	1.0000	CY	C	L/S CREW (3 MEN)	$12.00		5.000	0.20	$3.78
									Bid Item Subtotal:		1.20	$47.85
									Bid Item Unit Price:			$98.58
Bid Item:	**Maintenance, 90 Day**			**3.0000**	**MO**		**Type: Maint**	**Phase:27**				
		S	Subcontractor	1.0000	MO	n/d		$430.33				$430.33
									Bid Item Subtotal:		0.00	$430.33
									Bid Item Unit Price:			$537.92

EXHIBIT 15 Henderson Construction Bid Example (*continued*)

J. R. Huston Enterprises, Inc.

Bid Worksheet Detail

JCN: Henderson **Job Description: Henderson Residence**

Assembly	MLESN Code	Detail Description	Qty	Unit	PLES Code	Remarks	Unit Cost	Warr %	Qty 1 /MHr	MHRS	Cost ($)
Bid Item:	**General Conditions**		**1.0000**	**LS**		**Type: GC**	**Phase:28**				
	L	Supervisor, 1 Hr/Day	16.0000	HR	SS	SUPERVISOR	$25.00		1.000	16.00	$629.20
	L	Foreman, 1 Hr/Day	16.0000	HR	F	FOREMAN	$16.00		1.000	16.00	$402.69
	E	Supervisors Truck	16.0000	HR	102	TRUCK, 3/4 TON W/TRAILER	$7.00		1.000		$112.00
	L	Mobilize Equipment	2.0000	HR	D	DRIVER	$12.00		1.000	2.00	$37.75
	E	Mobilize Equipment (Truck)	2.0000	HR	105	TRUCK, 2 TON	$15.00		1.000		$30.00
	L	Haul Materials (Lab)	6.0000	HR	D	DRIVER	$12.00		1.000	6.00	$113.26
	E	Haul Materials (EQ)	6.0000	HR	105	TRUCK, 2 TON	$15.00		1.000		$90.00
	L	Load/Unload	16.0000	HR	C	L/S CREW (3 MEN)	$12.00		1.000	16.00	$302.02
	E	Crew Truck	128.0000	HR	103	TRUCK, 1 TON & TRAILER	$8.00		1.000		$1,024.00
	L	Crew Drive Time	48.0000	HR	C	L/S CREW (3 MEN)	$12.00		1.000	48.00	$906.05
	L	Warranty-Labor	16.0000	HR	C	L/S CREW (3 MEN)	$12.00		1.000	16.00	$302.02
	E	Warranty-Truck	8.0000	HR	103	TRUCK, 1 TON & TRAILER	$8.00		1.000		$64.00
	L	Crew Clean-Up	16.0000	HR	C	L/S CREW (3 MEN)	$12.00		1.000	16.00	$302.02
	S	Commissions	1.0000	LS	n/d		$0.00				$0.00
	L	Crew Detail Job	8.0000	HR	C	L/S CREW (3 MEN)	$12.00		1.000	8.00	$151.01
	M	Soil test	1.0000	LS	n/d		$100.00				$106.00
	M	As-builts	1.0000	LS	n/d		$100.00				$106.00
								Bid Item Subtotal:		144.00	$4,678.00
								Bid Item Unit Price:			$0.00

EXHIBIT 15 Henderson Construction Bid Example (*continued*)

Glossary

Acquisition cost per hour The capitalization cost for a piece of equipment divided by its lifetime hours.

Add value The process of improving a project according to the client's perspective.

Aggravation factor *See* **contingency factor.**

Asset tax A property tax usually levied against office equipment and assets, and field equipment.

Average wage (AW) The average gross compensation paid to field personnel. It can be calculated for a crew, division, or company.

Balance sheet A financial statement that gives an accounting picture of property owned by a company and of claims against the property on a specific date. The left (debit) side of a balance sheet states assets; the right (credit) side shows liabilities and owners' equity. The two sides must be equal (balance). The balance sheet is like a snapshot of the position of an individual or business at one point in time.

Benchmark *See* **Industry benchmark.**

Bidding The process of adding Phase III G&A overhead, net profit, and a contingency factor, if used, to the first two phases of a bid (which include sales tax and labor burden) and arriving at the final price for a particular job.

Bidding overview The outline of an estimating system, which includes all of its major components.

Bidding template A pre-formatted estimating worksheet onto which bidding data is entered. Normally a paper form or computer spreadsheet.

Billable field-labor hours Direct labor hours that are either included in a bid or charged to the client directly in the form of cost plus time and materials billing.

Bonus Something given or paid in addition to the usual.

Break-even point (BEP) The sales dollar amount at which all costs (both G&A overhead and direct costs) are covered in either a specific bid or by company/division.

Budget The projected revenues and expenses for a project, company, or division.

Budget-to-actual A comparison of budgeted costs to actual costs for a project.

Budget, cash flow A budget designed to project cash flow into and out of a company. It is basically determined by the amount of cash available in your checkbook.

Budget, estimating A budget designed to project fair market value amounts for sales goals, direct costs, general and administrative (G&A) overhead costs, gross and net profit margins, average wage rates, office and field-labor burden, field-labor hours, and the various ratios and per-hour standards included in the same.

Budget, tax accounting A budget designed to help you plan for and meet the tax requirements, both state and federal, established by law.

Budget periods The time interval for a budget (month, quarter, year, etc.).

Business context The environment and market within which your business operates is often referred to as the business context. It is comprised of all of the external forces and market conditions that shape the environment surrounding your business.

Business strategies The strategies or plans by which you desire to grow or develop your business. It may be written in the form of a strategic business plan. However, it is often intuitive and not committed to written documentation.

Calendar year (CY) The continuous period beginning January 1 and ending December 31.

Cash flow budget *See* **budget, cash flow.**

Company/division average wage (AW) The cost of direct labor for a company or division divided by its respective field-labor hours.

Consolidation A reorganization in which two or more corporations are combined into a new corporation.

Contingency factor (CF) Additional net profit added to a job in Phase III of the bidding process that is designed to offset risk.

Corporate Overhead Per Hour (COPH) For companies with both division and corporate general and administrative overhead costs, it is the corporate portion of general and administrative costs divided by the total company billable field-labor hours.

Corporation A legal entity, chartered by a state or the federal government, and separate and distinct from the persons who own it, giving rise to a jurist's remark that it has "neither a soul to damn nor a body to kick." Nonetheless, it is regarded by the courts as an artificial person; it may own property, incur debts, sue, or be sued. It has four chief distinguishing features: (1) limited liability (owners can lose only what they invest); (2) easy transfer of ownership through the sale of shares of stock; (3) continuity of existence; and (4) centralized management. Other factors helping to explain the popularity of the corporate form of organization are its ability to obtain capital through expanded ownership, and the shareholders' ability to profit from the growth of the business.

Cost of goods sold (COGS) Direct costs normally comprised of materials, sales tax, direct labor and labor burden, field equipment, rental equipment, subcontractors' commissions, and any miscellaneous costs that can be directly attributed to a specific job.

Cost plus A contract under which the contractor receives payment for total costs plus a stated percentage or amount of profit. A cost-plus-percentage contract gives the contractor no incentive to economize; on the contrary, a contractor would be better off to spend more. A cost-plus fixed-fee contract is a more reasonable contract.

Crew average wage (CAW) The average gross compensation paid to either a specific or general field crew.

Crew average wage loaded The crew average wage plus the risk and overtime factor costs.

Crew days The number of days that an entire crew will be on a project.

Curb time Direct field-labor hours calculated from the time that an individual or crew shows up at a job (the "curb") until he/it leaves the job.

Daily billable goals The revenue that an individual or crew is required to generate on a daily basis.

Direct costs *See* **cost of goods sold (COGS).**

Direct costs per hour (DCPH) Total direct costs in a bid (including sales tax and labor burden) divided by the total field-labor hours in the bid.

Division Overhead Per Hour (DOPH) The individual division portion of general and administrative overhead divided by the respective division's billable field-labor hours.

Divisions Individual profit centers or revenue centers within a company for which a minimum of sales revenue and cost of goods sold are monitored by means of a profit and loss statement.

Double dipping Charging twice for the same cost in a bid.

Down time The man-hours field crews are being paid but are not working in the field or producing billable man-hours.

Draw against commissions Unlike a straight commission, with a draw salespeople are paid prior to collecting the final check for the project. Commissions are still a percentage of sales, but they are paid prior to all moneys being collected.

Dual overhead recovery system (DORS) A bidding system that utilizes two separate predetermined markup percentages for materials and field labor in order to allocate general and administrative costs into the bid.

Due diligence Making a reasonable effort to perform under a contract; making a reasonable effort to provide accurate, complete information.

Economies of scale In our discussions, the decrease in either general and administrative overhead costs expressed as a percentage of sales or as a per billable labor-hour amount, due to an increase in annual corporate revenues.

Enhancements Work performed in addition to that which is contained in a maintenance contract.

Equipment meter time The hours that the engine on a piece of equipment is actually running.

Equipment mobilization The moving of equipment on to or off of a project.

Equipment per hour (EQPH) Direct equipment costs divided by the billable field-labor hours in either a bid or a company/division.

Equipment to labor (EQ/LAB) ratio Direct equipment costs divided by direct labor costs in either a bid or a company/division.

Estimating The science of determining those bid costs involved with Phases I and II to include sales tax and labor burden.

Estimating budget *See* **budget, estimating.**

Exit strategy A plan (often written) by which an owner or stockholder intends to depart a company or liquidate their interest in it.

Factor The price for a bid divided by the re-wholesale cost of the materials in a bid. A factor is also one component in a mathematical multiplication formula where one factor is multiplied by another to produce the product (e.g., $2 \times 3 = 6$; 2 and 3 are factors of 6, which is the product).

Factoring A common bidding method where material costs are multiplied by a factor (2.0, 2.5, 3.0, etc.) in order to determine a final price for the bid.

Fair market value (FMV) A price at which an asset or service passes from a willing seller to a willing buyer. It is assumed that both buyer and seller are rational and have a reasonable knowledge of relevant facts.

Fair market value budget A budget that is based upon fair market value amounts as compared to real revenue and expense amounts.

Fatal flaw For our discussions, a systemic error in calculating costs in a company's estimating system that, if uncorrected, could lead to insolvency.

Federal Insurance Contributions Act (FICA) The federal law that provides for the imposition of the Social Security tax.

Federal Unemployment Tax Act (FUTA) The federal law that provides for federal unemployment insurance and is paid by employers.

Field daily report (FDR) A job (or group of jobs) report that is filled out on a daily basis and which reflects job costing and site data.

Final price The final price for a project or job that includes all costs, both direct and indirect, a contingency factor, if desired, and a net profit margin.

Fiscal year (FY) Any continuous 12-month period used by a business or government as its accounting period.

Fixed/variable contract A contract with a set price for a set amount of work. It transitions into a time and materials contract once the set or fixed amount of work is exceeded.

Flat rate pricing A form of pricing that attempts to simplify the pricing process by charging an all-inclusive flat rate for a particular product or service. The flat rate includes labor, materials, and any equipment needed to perform the task.

Flex contract *See* **fixed/variable contract.**

Fudge factor *See* **risk factor.**

Fuel cost per hour The cost of fuel to operate a piece of equipment for one hour.

General and administrative (G&A) overhead budget The projected costs for general and administrative costs for a company or division for either a calendar or fiscal year.

General and administrative (G&A) overhead costs Indirect costs (rent, advertising, office staff salaries, etc.) that cannot be directly tied to a specific job.

General conditions (Phase II of a bid) Those costs required in a bid that are not necessarily part of the end product. They include material, labor, labor burden, equipment, and subcontractor costs such as portable toilets, temporary fencing, drive time, load and unload time, job supervision, crew trucks, delivery trucks, traffic control, and job site security.

General condition hours to total hours The general condition hours in a bid divided by the total hours in the bid (usually 15 to 25%).

General conditions per hour (GCPH) The general conditions in a bid divided by the field-labor hours in the bid.

General liability insurance (GLI) Insurance for business firms that provide liability coverage for an insured who is sued because of negligent acts or omissions of an independent contractor or subcontractor resulting in bodily injury and/or property damage to a third party.

Generic day For our discussions, a typical or average-day scenario for a given type of work.

Gross annual sales (GAS) The total revenues for a company or division for a calendar or fiscal year.

Gross profit margin (GPM) G&A overhead costs plus net profit. Formatted either as a percent or in whole dollars.

Gross profit margin per hour (GPMPH) The gross profit margin for a bid or budget divided by the respective billable field-labor hours in the bid or budget.

Historical data Financial or other data that has been consistently calculated, formatted, and reported.

Hurdle amount A predetermined financial objective that must be met in order to enact (or trigger) an incentive, bonus, or waiving of a trip charge. *See* **trip charge** and **show-up fee**.

Hysterical data Financial or other data that has not been consistently calculated, formatted, and reported.

Incentive Something inciting one to action or effort.

Indirect costs General and administrative (G&A) overhead costs incurred by a business.

Industry benchmark A standard, common to a specific industry, used for comparison purposes.

Job costing The process of collecting, formatting, and comparing specific job budget costs to those costs actually incurred while performing the job.

Labor burden Those items (FICA, FUTA, SUTA, workers' compensation insurance, general liability insurance, etc.) that can be directly correlated to office and field payroll, and that vary in direct proportion to it.

Lawn maintenance package A combination of labor and equipment, the composition of which does not vary from job to job or site to site.

Leaks Costs that are not included in a bid but which should be.

Lifetime guarantee A method of offering clients "risk control" for products and/or services. It normally extends a lifetime guarantee (except for "acts of God" and vandalism) on materials installed and services provided as long as the company providing the initial product and/or service maintains the same.

Lifetime hours The number of hours that a piece of equipment will operate before the engine for it needs a complete overhaul.

Limited Liability Corporation (LLC) An organization form in some states that may be treated as a partnership for federal tax purposes and has limited liability protection for the owners at the state level.

Loaded crew average wage The crew average wage plus the risk and overtime factor costs.

Lump sum bid A price for a project. It is presented in a proposal as a single line item and is not broken down into subelements or units.

Magic wand management Management method based entirely on intuition as compared to objective analytical or historical data.

Maintenance cost per hour The total lifetime cost to maintain a piece of equipment divided by its lifetime hours.

Manage expectations For our purposes, the process of clearly identifying, communicating, and modifying the budget, standards, and schedule for a project with the client on a timely basis.

Management by mysticism Management method based entirely on intuition as compared to objective analytical or historical data.

Margin The difference between revenue and costs as in gross profit and net profit margin.

Market-driven unit pricing A bidding method where unit prices are estimated intuitively or without thorough scientific analysis and applied to the number of units in a bid. The estimator basically "guesstimates" what the going rate is for a particular unit and then applies that rate to the number of units in the project.

Market predisposition The "leaning" of prices for a product or service in a certain direction in the market. These prices are shaped by market influences and/or the forces that influence them.

Markups Commonly used in a bidding situation as a factor in the form of a percent or decimal and multiplied by a direct cost or combination of direct costs.

Material factor The quotient (or result) calculated by dividing the price for a project by its material costs.

Material per hour (MPH) Direct material costs divided by the billable field-labor hours in either a bid or a company/division.

Material-to-labor (M/L) ratio The ratio achieved by dividing the material costs by the direct labor costs in a bid or budget.

Meaningful managerial terms Terms that, even if not specifically quantifiable, are able to be communicated and interpreted clearly and consistently by all parties.

Meter time The time that an engine is actually operating or running.

Micro bonuses Bonuses normally under $100 and tied to specific acts or behavior.

Mileage rates Rates for vehicles calculated by dividing anticipated lifetime costs by lifetime miles.

Mill tax One tenth of a cent. The term is used in expressing tax rates on a per-dollar basis. For example, a tax rate of 60 mills means that taxes are 6 cents per dollar of assessed valuation.

Mobilization costs Direct costs related to mobilizing equipment on to and off of a project.

Multiple overhead recovery system (MORS) A bidding method that applies markup percentages to all four elements of direct costs (material, labor, equipment, and subcontractor costs) for the purposes of calculating the amount of G&A overhead to allocate to a job. The common markup percentages used are as follows: materials 10%, labor and labor burden 25% to 85%, equipment 25%, and subcontractors 5%.

Multiplier method An estimating system based on factoring where materials are commonly multiplied by a factor (2.0, 2.5, 3.0, etc.) in order to calculate the final price for a project.

Net profit or net profit margin (NPM) Earnings before interest and taxes (EBIT) that are calculated by subtracting both direct and indirect costs from sales revenues.

Non-monetary incentives Incentives that are not tied to remuneration.

Objective reference points Cost or production standards that are based upon accurate historical data, not just on intuition.

October surprise A company usually reaches its annual break-even point (BEP) in the ninth or tenth month of their fiscal year—normally September or October for companies on a calendar-year cycle for their accounting. Rather than a planned event, the achieving of the BEP is normally a surprise event. Hence the term "October Surprise."

On-site maintenance Maintenance or service work where a designated crew of either one or more individuals is on a single site full time throughout the year or season.

Over/under billing Adjustments made to financial reports that are designed to compensate for contracts that were either over or under billed in relation to the work actually performed.

Overhead and profit per hour (OPPH) A method of estimating where a company/division's total budgeted general and administrative (G&A) overhead costs for the year are divided by the projected billable field-labor hours for the year in order to calculate a G&A overhead cost per hour amount. Net profit, at the estimator's option, can also be calculated and allocated to a bid based on a budgeted average profit per labor-hour amount. Both are applied to individual bids by multiplying the G&A overhead and profit-per-hour amounts by the total number of labor hours included in the bid.

Overhead per hour (OPH) A company/division's total budgeted G&A overhead costs for the year divided by the projected billable field-labor hours for the year.

Overtime factor (OTF) The average number of hours qualifying for overtime per man per week throughout the entire year.

Overtime hours Labor hours worked for a given period that are in excess of a predetermined limit and for which an increased hourly amount is paid. Typically in the United States, hours worked in excess of 40 hours in one week are paid at one-and-a-half times the normal pay amount.

Per diem costs A cost reimbursement amount normally covering lodging and meals, based on a fixed amount, and paid on a per day basis.

Per-push contract A snow plowing contract that is billed only when work is actually performed.

Per hour analysis Analysis based on dividing any number of items (sales, materials, equipment, G&A overhead, etc.) by the related direct labor hours and comparing the same to industry benchmarks.

Phase I of a bid (produce the product or provide the service phase) Included here are costs for materials physically included in the finished product or service provided, plus the labor, labor burden, equipment, and subcontractor costs associated with it. It is part of the finished product or service provided; the cost is included in Phase I.

Phase II of a bid (general conditions) Included here are costs for those items required to produce the finished product or provide the service (material, labor, labor burden, equipment, and subcontractors), but that are not directly required to produce the end product or service. *See* **general conditions**.

Phase III of a bid (the margin and markup phase) This is the margin and markup phase of the bidding process where taxes are added to material costs (if appropriate), labor burden is applied to labor, G&A overhead is added into the bid, a contingency factor is added (if desired), and a net profit margin is added to the bid.

Portal-to-portal Compensation for all expenses incurred related to a particular project and while traveling to and from the project.

Prevailing wage (PW) A wage rate that is required to be paid on a project, normally a government one.

Produce the product or provide the service (Phase I of a bid) Included here are costs for materials physically included in the finished product or service provided, plus the labor, labor burden, equipment, and subcontractor costs associated with it. It is part of the finished product or service provided; the cost is included in Phase I.

Product The numeric result calculated by multiplying two or more numbers together.

Profit and loss (P&L) financial statement A summary of the revenues, costs, and expenses of a company during an accounting period.

Profit per hour (PPH) A company/division's projected net profit for the year divided by the projected billable field-labor hours for the year; or, the net profit margin on a specific bid divided by the total field-labor hours in the bid.

Quotient The result of division; the number of times one quantity is contained in another.

Rate card A brief form that contains company rates for services and/or materials.

Ratio analysis Analysis based on dividing two items and comparing the result to industry benchmarks. Examples would be the equipment-to-labor and material-to-labor ratios.

Residual capacity Work that a company is capable of performing but which it is not achieving.

Revenue per hour or sales per hour (RPH or SPH) Sales or revenue for a given period divided by the respective billable field-labor hours.

Re-wholesale price The price that a contractor pays a supplier or vendor for materials.

Risk factor (RF) Also referred to as the fudge factor, it is normally a 10 to 20% markup applied to an average wage in order to compensate for risk on a given project.

Risk management A procedure to minimize the adverse effect of a possible financial loss by (1) identifying potential sources of loss, (2) measuring the financial consequences of a loss occurring, and (3) using controls to minimize actual losses or their financial consequences.

Roll up A merger, acquisition, and divestiture term whereby a number of companies simultaneously consolidate and go public with a stock offering on a major stock exchange.

Single overhead recovery system (SORS) A bidding method in which all direct costs are combined and then multiplied by a common multiplier in order to calculate the final price for a project. It is also called the gross profit margin (GPM) method.

Sales per hour or revenue per hour (SPH or RPH) The price for a bid divided by the total field-labor hours included in the bid.

Scientific method A method of research in which a problem is identified, relevant data are gathered, a hypothesis is formulated from these data, and the hypothesis is empirically tested. When applying this definition to the Green Industry business process, the project to be bid would be the "problem." The "relevant data gathered" would be the plans and specifications for the project (or job). The estimate or budget for the job (containing objective measurable standards for materials, labor, labor burden, equipment, etc.) would be the "hypothesis." The "empirical testing of the hypothesis" would be accomplished by job costing, where you would "test" or compare your budget to actual performance in the field as you performed the project.

Show-up fee A set trip charge or fee billed to the client upon arrival at a job site by the technician and designed to cover non-site travel and administrative time. The show-up fee often covers a limited amount of time, normally one-half hour, spent on site by the technician. *See* **hurdle amount** and **trip charge**.

Sick days Paid time off for employees when they are sick.

Six Sigma A very sophisticated quantitative approach that fuels improved effectiveness and efficiency in an organization.

Sole proprietorship A business or financial venture that is carried on by a single person and is not a trust or corporation. A sole proprietor (sole owner) has unlimited liability.

Standards Industry or company benchmarks that are used to calculate the costs in a project. Production rates, labor burden, average wage rates, etc. are considered to be such standards.

Start-up company A company that is in the initial stages of its life cycle.

State Unemployment Tax Act (SUTA) The state law that provides for the imposition of a state unemployment tax.

Straight commission Payment basis whereby a salesperson does not get paid until he or she sells a job and collects the final check when that job is completed.

Strategic business plan A written plan for a business that takes into account market trends, risks and opportunities, and product and service offerings. It is designed to lend direction and control of the company.

Tax budget *See* **budget, tax accounting**.

Time and materials (T&M) pricing A pricing method whereby the client pays for work as it is performed and based upon predetermined rates for labor and company-owned equipment. Material, subcontractor, and rental equipment invoices are normally passed on to the client with a predetermined margin or markup added to them to cover the contractor's G&A overhead costs and a net profit margin.

Total direct costs (TDC) The total of all direct costs in a bid, including sales tax and labor burden.

Total OPH (TOPH) The total of corporate overhead per hour (COPH) plus the division overhead per hour (DOPH) for a specific division.

Total quality management (TQM) A scientifically-based method for improving the processes within a business.

Trip charge A set trip charge or fee billed to the client upon arrival at a job site by the technician and designed to cover non-site travel and administrative time. The show-up fee often covers a limited amount of time, normally one-half hour, spent on site by the technician. *See* **hurdle amount** and **show-up fee**.

Turnkey approach A business approach in which all the necessary components to operate a business successfully are present and operational on the day that the business opens or commences to operate. This is also referred to as a franchise approach.

Unit price (UP) The total price of a bid (or section thereof) divided by the respective unit quantity (i.e., square feet, square yards, cubic yards, man-hours, per plant, linear feet, heads, zones, etc.).

Unit price bid A proposal for a project that is presented as a list of line items included in the project with the respective price(s) for each of the line items.

Useful life The life expectancy for a piece of equipment that normally equals the average life expectancy of the engine for that respective item.

Value engineering The process of improving a project from the client's perspective.

Warranty A guarantee, given by a seller to a buyer, that the goods or services purchased will perform as promised, or a refund will be given, an exchange made, or a repair done at no charge.

Warranty costs The estimated costs in a bid for replacing a product or service that does not meet contract specifications.

Warranty of materials A markup normally applied to material re-wholesale costs designed to cover replacement costs for the subject material.

Well days Accumulated paid time off that an employee accrues based upon the amount of time actually worked.

Wholesale price The price paid for materials bought by a nursery for resale to a landscape contractor. The wholesale price is usually marked up 30 to 60% above cost when sold to the contractor.

Workers' compensation insurance (WCI) An insurance policy where an insurance company agrees to pay wage and benefit amounts to an injured employee for injuries incurred while the employee is working.

Reference List

Title	Author(s)	Publisher
AGC's Partnering: A Concept for Success (video)	AGC (1)	
Built to Last	Collins & Porras (2)	Harper Business
Dictionary of Business Terms	Jack P. Friedman	Barron's
The Effective Executive	Drucker (2)	Harper Business
The Eternally Successful Organization	Crosby	Plume
The "E" Myth	Gerber	Ballinger
Contractor's Equipment Cost Guide	Equipment Watch (3)	
Finance	Welshans & Melicher	South-Western
Finding a Job You Can Love	Mattson & Miller	Nelson
Further Up the Organization	Townsend	Harper & Row
The Gardening of America	Cetron & Davies	Chilton (4)
Good to Great	Collins (2)	Harper Business
Hand Me Another Brick	Swindoll	Nelson
In Search of Excellence	Peters & Waterman	Warner Books
Kerr's Cost Data Manual for Landscape Contractors	Dietrich (5)	Van Nostrand Reinhold
Landscape Data Manual	Griffin	CLCA, Inc. (6)
Legal Practices Manual for Subcontractors	Sklar (7)	American Subcontractors Association
Managerial Accounting	Moore, Jaedicke, & Anderson	South-Western
Means Site Work & Landscape Cost Data Manual	Hollman Fee (8)	R.S. Means Co., Inc.
Operating Cost Study	HRI, Inc.	HRI, Inc. (9)
Preparing for & Responding to a Down Economy	Huston	J.R. Huston Enterprises, Inc.
Quality and the Landscape Contractor	Crystal Ball Committee	ALCA, Inc. (10)
Quality Is Free	Crosby	Mentor

Road Construction Ahead (video)	Focus Video (11)	
The Six Sigma Revolution	Eckes (12)	John Wiley & Sons, Inc.
Strategic Planning for L&I Contractors	Huston	J. R. Huston Enterprises, Inc.
Thriving on Chaos	Peters	Knopf
Winning Management Strategies for the Real World (audio)	Peters & Townsend (13)	Nightingale-Conant

➤ **NOTE** Numbers in parentheses, (10), in the author or publisher column correspond to the list of contact information below.

(1)	Associated General Contractors of America, 1957 E. Street, NW, Washington DC 20006	202 393-2040
(2)	Harper Business, 10 E 53rd Street, New York NY 10022 www.harpercollins.com	212 207-7999
(3)	Equipment Watch (a Division of PRIMEDIA Business Magazines & Media, Inc.) www.ironmax.com	800 669-3282
(4)	Dickson Felix, Inc., 1441 Que Street, NW, Washington DC 20009	202 328-1540
(5)	Van Nostrand Reinhold, 115 Fifth Avenue, New York NY 10003	800 842-3636
(6)	California Landscape Contractor's Association, 1491 River Park Drive, Suite 100, Sacramento CA 95815	916 448-2522
(7)	American Subcontractors Association, 1004 Duke Street, Alexandria VA 22314-3512	703 684-3450
(8)	Construction Consultants & Publishers, 100 Construction Plaza, P.O. Box 800, Kingston MA 02364-0800	617 747-1270
(9)	Horticultural Research Institute, Inc., 1250 I Street, NW, Suite 500, Washington DC 20005	202 789-2900
(10)	Associated Landscape Contractors of America, 12200 Sunrise Valley Dr., Suite 150, Reston VA 22091	703 620-6363
(11)	Focus Video Productions, RD #5, Box 2108, Montpelier, VT 05602	800 843-3686
(12)	John Wiley & Sons, Inc., 111 River Street, Hoboken NJ 07030 www.wiley.com	201 748-6000
(13)	Nightingale-Conant Corp., 6245 W Howard Street, Niles IL 60714	800 323-5552

Major Green Industry Associations

For a comprehensive list of Green Industry Associations, go to http://www.greenmediaonline.com.

American Nursery and Landscape Association (ANLA)
1000 Vermont Avenue NW, Suite 300, Washington, DC 20005-4914
202-789-2900/202-789-1893 FAX
www.ANLA.org

American Society of Irrigation Consultants (ASIC)
111 E Wacker Drive, Chicago, IL 60601
312-372-7090/312-372-6160 FAX
www.ASIC.org

American Society of Landscape Architects (ASLA)
636 Eye Street NW, Washington, DC 20001-3736
202-898-2444/202-898-1185 FAX
www.ASLA.org

American Society of Professional Estimators (ASPE)
11141 Georgia Avenue, Suite 412, Wheaton, MD 20902
301-929-8848/301-929-0231 FAX
www.ASPEnational.com

American Subcontractors Association
1004 Duke Street, Alexandria, VA 22314-3512
703-684-3450/703-836-3482 FAX
www.ASAonline.com

Associated Builders and Contractors (ABC)
1300 North 17th Street, Rosslyn, VA 22209
703-812-2000/703-812-8235 FAX
www.ABC.org

Associated General Contractors of America (AGC)
333 John Carlyle Street, Suite 200, Alexandria, VA 22314
703-548-3118/703-548-3119 FAX
www.AGC.org

Associated Landscape Contractors of America (ALCA)
150 Elden Street, Suite 270, Herndon, VA 20170
800-395-2522/703-736-9668 FAX
www.ALCA.org

California Landscape Contractors Association (CLCA)
1491 River Park Drive, Suite 100, Sacramento, CA 95815
800-448-2522/916-830-2788 FAX
www.CLCA.org

Canadian Nursery Landscape Association
7856 Fifth Line South, RR#4, Station Main, Milton, ON L9T 2X8 Canada
905-875-1399/905-875-1840 FAX, 888-446-3499
www.canadanursery.com

The Garden Centers of America (GCA)
147 SE 102nd Avenue, Portland, OR 97216
503-261-0500/503-253-9172 FAX, 888-648-6463
www.gardencentersofamerica.org

Golf Course Superintendents Association of America
1421 Research Park Drive, Lawrence, KS 66049
785-841-2240/785-832-3643 FAX, 800-472-7878
www.GCSAA.org

International Society of Arboriculture
PO Box 3129, Champagne, IL 61826
217-355-9411/217-355-9516 FAX, 888-ISA-TREE
www.ISA-arbor.com

Irrigation Association
6540 Arlington Boulevard, Falls Church, VA 22042
703-536-7080/703-536-7019 FAX
www.irrigation.org

Landscape Materials Information Service
PO Box 216, Callicoon, NY 12723
845-887-4401/FAX Same
www.lmisonline.com

Landscape Ontario Horticultural Trade Association
7856 5th Line South, RR #4, Station Main, Milton, ON L9T 2X8 Canada
905-875-1805/905-875-3942 FAX, 800-265-5656
www.horttrades.com

The Lawn Institute
1855-A Hicks Road, Rolling Meadow, IL 60008
847-705-9898/847-705-8347 FAX, 800-405-8873
www.turfgrasssod.org/lawninstitute

National Arborist Association
3 Perimeter Road, Unit #1, Manchester, NH 03103
603-314-5380/603-314-5386 FAX, 800-733-2622
www.natlarb.com

National Association of Plumbing-Heating-Cooling Contractors
PO Box 6808, Falls Church, VA 22040
703-237-8100/703-237-7442 FAX, 800-533-7694
www.PHCCWEB.org

National Golf Foundation
1150 South US Highway One, Suite 401
Jupiter, FL 33477, 561-744-6006/561-744-6107 FAX
www.NGF.org

National Lighting Bureau
8811 Colesville Road, Suite G106, Silver Spring, MD 20910
301-587-9572/301-589-2017 FAX
www.NLB.org

Professional Lawn Care Association of America (PLCAA)
1000 Johnson Ferry Road, Suite C135, Marietta, GA 30068-2112
770-977-5222/770-578-6071 FAX, 800-458-3466
www.PLCAA.org

Professional Grounds Management Society (PGMS)
720 Light Street, Baltimore, MD 21230-3816
800-609-PGMS/410-752-8295 FAX
www.PGMS.org

Responsible Industry for a Sound Environment (RISE)
1156 15th Street NW, Suite 400, Washington, DC 20005
202-872-3860/202-463-0474 FAX
www.pestfacts.org

Sports Turf Managers Association
1027 South 3rd Street, Council Bluffs, IA 51503
712-322-7862/712-322-7838 FAX, 800-323-3875
www.sportsturfmanager.com

Snow and Ice Management Association (SIMA)
1903 West 8th Street, PMB 150, Erie, PA 16505-4998
814-835-3577/814-835-0527 FAX
www.SIMA.org

Texas A&M Department of Soil and Crop Sciences, Heep Center
370 Olsen Boulevard, Texas A&M University, 2474 TAMU, College Station, TX 77843
979-845-3041/979-845-0456 FAX
Http://soilcrop.tamu.edu

INDEX

Answers

"HOW IT WORKS"

P. 22 How can you compensate for skewed ratios and figures when preparing a budget with a lot of subcontractor costs in it?

For budget purposes, I would establish a separate division for subcontractor revenue and expenses if subcontractor revenues account for more than 10% of the revenue for the whole company.

P. 28 What "safety check" do we use in the bidding process to safeguard against allocating too little or too much G&A overhead to jobs being bid?

Gross profit margin (GPM) benchmarks provide a safety check of sorts when pricing our work. Even if our general and administrative overhead cost per hour (OPH) amount is inaccurate or in question, the GPM benchmark will allow us to compare our pricing to historical standards. These historical standards may be in the form of industry benchmarks or ones monitored in our own company. This will help to ensure that our pricing is within acceptable parameters even if our OPH is in question.

P. 43 If you have three divisions with equal sales and a $12,000 annual expense budgeted for telephone costs, you can put $4,000 into each division's annual budget for these costs. However, what do you do if one division has budgeted sales of $1.2 million and the other two divisions have budgeted sales of $300,000 each?

I would probably use a percentage of the $12,000 annual cost for each division, proportionate to each division's sales, as a percentage of the total budgeted sales for the entire company. In this case, I would budget $2,000 for each of the smaller divisions because their sales budget is 16.67% of the entire budgeted sales for the year.

$$\$300,000 \div \$1,800,000 = .1667 \text{ or } 16.67\%$$

$$\$12,000 \times .1667 = \$2,000$$

P. 58 How would you have corrected this flaw in this contractor's estimating system? Do you have similar flaws in your estimating system?

This contractor should have identified the specific pieces of equipment and the amount of time that they would be operating on each job. He then should have multiplied the respective operating hours by the cost per hour for each piece of equipment. This amount should be entered into the bid calculations and the appropriate net profit margin added to them.

P. 69 What should this contractor have done to catch and correct this problem earlier in the year?

This contractor should have monitored two things throughout the year that would have helped him to identify and compensate for this problem. First, he should have been monitoring his profit and loss (P&L) statement on a monthly basis. This would have identified his thin margins and the disproportionate amount of subcontractor revenue and expenses. Second, he should have been monitoring the number of field-labor hours that he had sold. He would have noticed that, while his sales were on track, his sold field-labor hours were not. This would have helped to alert him to the problem in question.

P. 107 How would you handle the situation with the retired engineer?

Surprisingly, my client negotiated with this "homeowner from hell," met his requirements, and got the job. I probably would have told the engineer that I simply did not do business this way and would have walked away from the job. Had I known the intentions of the engineer upon making the initial contact with him, I would have politely excused myself from this situation.

There is no right or wrong response to this question. If I needed the work and thought that I had a good chance of getting this project, I might be a little more flexible.

SHOULD I BUY THIS BOOK?

You should answer "false" or "no" to all of the following:

1. **Q** Estimating a job is the same as bidding a job.

   A Estimating is the scientific process of determining the costs for a project. Bidding is the process of adding margins and markups to project costs.

2. **Q** Different companies should have the same price for the same job.

   A Costs, both direct and indirect, can vary dramatically from company to company. Larger companies will normally experience an economy of scale in such areas as material purchases, direct labor crew average wage rates, equipment and fuel purchases, insurance costs, and general and administrative overhead costs, to name a few.

3. **Q** Field equipment costs should be included in general and administrative (G&A) overhead.

   A Field equipment, including trucks, should be included in a bid as a direct cost based upon how much a particular piece of equipment is used on a specific job.

4. **Q** You should always strive to have the same gross profit margin (GPM) on your bids.

   A The percentage of GPM in a bid can very dramatically from bid to bid. it will fluctuate due to the variances in the ratio of material, labor, equipment, and subcontractor costs on a job. It will also vary as the duration of the job for a given price changes.

5. **Q** If your desired company/division end-of-year GPM is 30% of sales, you should consistently add 30% GPM to your bids to achieve it at the end of the year.

   A For the reasons outlined above, there is no direct correlation between the amount of GPM that you desire to achieve at the end of your year and the amount of GPM that you put on individual bids throughout that year.

6. **Q** Larger companies have more G&A overhead than smaller ones, so they have to charge more G&A overhead to jobs.

   A While larger companies may have more G&A overhead in total dollar costs, they normally have less G&A overhead costs when measured as a percentage of sales. As a company grows in sales volume, its percentage of G&A overhead costs decline. This is referred to as "economies of scale."

7. **Q** If you do not competitively bid your work, you do not need to understand the estimating process described in this book.

   A Pricing is pricing, whether it is done in a competitive or non-competitive environment. The process of arriving at a sound price does not vary just because market forces change.

8. **Q** You will not be competitive if you include all of your costs for a job in the bid.

   A You will not be in business if you do not include all of your costs for a job in the bidding process.

9. **Q** A contractor's salary is what is left over after all the bills have been paid.

   A Who wants to work for leftovers? A contractor's fair-market-value salary should be built into estimates as a legitimate cost, either as a direct or an indirect cost.

10. **Q** I do not know—on a daily basis—if I am making money on each individual job.

    A Even though it is difficult, you should strive to know the profit and loss status of each of your jobs on a daily basis.

11. **Q** I do not know how to calculate equipment costs for a job and put them in a bid.

    A It is very important that contractors estimate their equipment operating costs accurately and effectively.

12. **Q** It is easier to negotiate an increase in the price of a job than it is to negotiate a decrease.

    A Without the aid of threats and bribes, it is always more difficult to negotiate up than it is to negotiate down.

13. **Q** Landscapers are so creative that they can figure out a way to go broke even in a great economy.

    A Get help! Have a qualified individual look over your operation from an independent, outside perspective.

14. **Q** If your geographical or industry market is going through a recession, you have little choice but to participate in it.

    A There simply is no direct correlation between the status of the global, national, or a regional economy and the economic status of a small business operating within them. Small business entrepreneurs drive our economy. They are the last to go into a recession and the first to come out of one. Due to their resiliency, creativity, flexibility, and perseverance, they have more control over their destiny (and their business) than just about any other group. Even though they are impacted by an economic downturn or recession, the impact is usually less for them than for the general economy.

SURVEY

Name: ______________________ Position: ______________________

Company: ____

Address: ____

City: ______________________ State: ______________ Zip: ____________

Phone: ______________ Fax: ______________ Email: ______________

We at J.R. Huston Enterprises, Inc. greatly appreciate your providing us your feedback regarding our book, *How to Price Landscape and Irrigation Projects* (*HTPLIP*). Your comments about our products and services are indispensable and are an integral part of the never-ending process to improve and to add to these products and services.

Please circle the number that corresponds to your answer. The numbers represent the following: 1 = no, not at all, or unsatisfactory; 2 = poor; 3 = fair; 4 = good; 5 = yes, very much, or excellent.

	NO/ UNSAT	POOR	FAIR	GOOD	YES/ EXCEL
BOOK					
1. Are the cover and format of the book pleasing to the eye?	1	2	3	4	5
2. Is the Table of Contents laid out well and does it facilitate locating key topics?	1	2	3	4	5
3. Is the book easy to read and understand?	1	2	3	4	5
4. Will you recommend to other contractors that they read *HTPLIP* ?	1	2	3	4	5
AUDIO CDs					
1. Do the audio CDs complement the book?	1	2	3	4	5
2. Do you like the flexibility of being able to study the book while in your car?	1	2	3	4	5
3. Are the CDs convenient to use?	1	2	3	4	5
4. Will you recommend the audio CDs to other contractors?	1	2	3	4	5
MS EXCEL CD					
1. Does the MS Excel CD complement the book?	1	2	3	4	5
2. Is it user friendly?	1	2	3	4	5
3. Will you recommend the MS Excel CD to other contractors?	1	2	3	4	5

Thank you for taking the time to answer the following questions.

- What did you find most helpful in the book, audio CDs, and/or MS Excel CD?

____

____

____

____

- What could have been added to or improved in *HTPLIP* book, audio CDs, or MS Excel CD?

____

____

____

____

- What immediate changes will you make in your company as a result of reading the *HTPLIP* book, listening to the audio CDs and/or using the MS Excel CD?

____

____

____

____

- What are any additional comments that you would like to make or that you think would be helpful?

____

____

____

____

- Have you read our other books or visited our Web site?

Strategic Planning for L&I Contractors	Yes ______	No ______
Preparing for & Responding to a Down Economy	Yes ______	No ______
Estimating for Landscape & Irrigation Contractors	Yes ______	No ______
Visited our Web site	Yes ______	No ______

Thank you for your participation in this survey. Please mail it to:

GreenBack Enterprises, LLC
P.O. Box 1244
Englewood, CO 80150
800-451-5588
Fax: 800-451-5494
E-mail: jrhei@jrhuston.biz
Web site: www.jrhuston.biz

PRODUCTS AND SERVICES

Following is a partial list of products and services offered by J.R. Huston Enterprises, Inc.
For a complete list of products and services, and for information and pricing visit our Web site at www.jrhuston.biz or call our office at 800-451-5588 or e-mail us at jrhei@jrhuston.biz.

Products:

Books

- *How to Price Landscape & Irrigation Projects*
- *Estimating for Landscape & Irrigation Contractors*
- *Preparing for & Responding to a Down Economy*
- *Strategic Planning for Landscape & Irrigation Contractors*

Audio CDs

- *How to Price Landscape & Irrigation Projects* (set of 6 CDs)

Software

- *How to Price Landscape & Irrigation Projects* MS Excel CD
- The Estimating Platform
- The Estimating Budget
- Quick Bid
- The Bid Board/Lead Tracker

Services

Workshops

- Estimating Workshop
- Strategic Planning Workshop

Seminars and Dinner Talks

- Estimating System Overview
- Preparing for & Responding to a Down Economy
- Strategic Planning for Landscape & Irrigation Contractors

On-Site Consulting

- Bid with Confidence
- Strategic Planning
- Software Training
- Establishing Bonus & Incentive Programs
- Formatting your Company's Financial Statement
- Coaching Contractors to Be Successful
- Exit Strategies
- Company Structure
- Evaluating Businesses
- Buying and Selling Businesses
- And more ...